MIDDLE ENGLISH LITERATURE

Garland Reference Library of the Humanities (Vol. 1330)

Library of Congress Cataloging-in-Publication Data

Middle English literature / edited and revised by
Charles W. Dunn and Edward T. Byrnes.
p. cm. —(Garland reference library of the humanities ; vol. 1330)
ISBN 8240-5298-6 (alk. paper); ISBN 0-8240-5297-8 (pbk. alk. paper)
1. English literature—Middle English, 1100-1500. I. Dunn, Charles W. (Charles
William), 1915-   . II. Byrnes, Edward T. III. Series.
PR1120.M525 1990
820.8'001—dc20 89-78116

Cover design by
Renata Gomes

Printed on acid-free, 250-year-life paper
Manufactured in the United States of America

MIDDLE ENGLISH LITERATURE

edited and revised by
Charles W. Dunn

and

Edward T. Byrnes

Garland Publishing, Inc. • New York & London
1990

PREFACE
TO THE REVISED EDITION

The purpose of this anthology is to present some of the outstanding works of literature that were produced in England, Scotland, and Ireland during approximately four hundred years that span what is now referred to as the period of "Middle English." This long period of time reaches from the Norman Conquest of 1066 down to the era that begins in 1476 with William Caxton's introduction of printing into England.

Despite the linguistic implications of our anthology's title, however, we are here concerned not with the history of our language but with the efflorescence of our literature. For that purpose we have selected either complete works or self-sufficient extracts from works that have, over the years, gained respect for their literary merit; and in the process we have taken for granted the sometimes overlooked fact that medieval authors assumed—quite justifiably—that the English of their day was "Modern English."

In order to facilitate an appreciation of the living voice of the various authors represented here, we have glossed all selections fully on the side of the page; we have introduced modern punctuation and capitalization; and we have normalized the vagaries of medieval spelling, so that we have distinguished between such words as *the* and *thee*, and *of* and *off*, and have, for instance, preferred to choose the manuscript spelling *quene* for modern *queen* rather than the scribe's confusing alternative spelling *whene*.

For those who may wish to learn more about the linguistic, literary, and cultural background of these authors, we have also provided full bibliographical guidance. And in order to cope with the extensive linguistic and literary scholarship that has been produced since the first publication of this anthology in 1973, we have also included an extensive Bibliographical Supplement.

Because of the wide scope of our survey, we have—albeit reluctantly—omitted from the anthology any of the works of Chaucer, and of the medieval dramatists, and of Malory, since excellent editions of these are readily available. In the other difficult matter of selection, we are still very much obliged to the advice of the commentators that we acknowledged in our original 1973 preface. They generously sat in judgment, though by no means unanimously, on our choice of authors, and their literary taste is reflected in this anthology.

In many cases we have based our texts on early scholarly editions that are no longer covered by international copyright, and we are thus eternally indebted to the pioneering editors of the Early English Text Society, the

Scottish Text Society, and similar enterprises. Whenever possible we have consulted facsimiles (listed in our head-notes) of original manuscripts, and we have occasionally introduced our own emendations or interpretations or have incorporated the suggestions of recent editors to whom it has not been possible to give specific acknowledgment.

We gratefully acknowledge the kind permission of the trustees of the British Museum and of the National Library of Scotland for permission to reprint the photographs of their original Middle English manuscripts shown in Plates 1 to 6. Without such libraries, to quote Chaucer, "Y-loren were of remembraunce the keye"—the key of memory would be lost.

Charles W. Dunn
Edward T. Byrnes

CONTENTS

Contents

<h1 style="text-align:center">*Contents*</h1>

LIST OF SELECTIONS
BY AUDIENCE, CENTURY, AND GENRE

Audience	Century	Genre	
		Lyric	*Verse Narrative*
Religious	Twelfth	Poema Morale	
	Thirteenth	A Love Rune	Judas
	Fourteenth	The Five Joys of Mary	
	Fifteenth	Christ and His Mother On the Resurrection of Christ	St. Stephen and Herod The Dance of the Seven Deadly Sins
Learned	Twelfth		The Owl and the Nightingale
	Fourteenth		The Bruce
	Fifteenth	The Golden Targe	The Tale of Beryn The Siege of Thebes
Courtly	Twelfth		The Brut
	Fourteenth	Now Springs the Spray Alysoun Spring April Love in Paris	Sir Orfeo Morte Arthure Sir Gawain and the Green Knight The Lover's Confession
	Fifteenth		The Testament of Cresseid
Popular	Thirteenth		King Horn The Fox and the Wolf Dame Sirith
	Fourteenth		Halidon Hill Thomas of Erceldoun
	Fifteenth	The Blacksmiths	Robyn and Gandeleyn

	Genre	
Prose Narrative	*Verse Instruction*	*Prose Instruction*
William the Conqueror The Anarchy of King Stephen	The Proverbs of Alfred	Holy Maidenhood
	The Bestiary The Sayings of St. Bernard The Land of Cokayne	The Anchoresses' Rule
	Handling Sin The Parliament of the Three Ages Piers Plowman The Pearl	The Form of Living The Wyclyfite Bible A Defense of Translation
		The Properties of Things
	The Regiment of Princes	

MIDDLE
ENGLISH
LITERATURE

BRITAIN AND IRELAND

Showing approximate distribution of English dialects
and Celtic languages in the fourteenth century

SCALE IN MILES

0   20   40   60   80   100

NORTH SEA

SCOTTISH GAELIC

Aberdeen

Arbroath

Perth

Bannockburn   Edinburgh

Berwick

ATLANTIC OCEAN

NORTHERN

Carlisle

IRISH SEA

York

IRISH GAELIC

WEST MIDLAND

Dublin

Mersey

Lincoln

Kildare

Flint

EAST MIDLAND

ANGLO-IRISH

Peterborough

WELSH   Worcester

Northampton

ST. GEORGES CHANNEL

Hereford

Cambridge

Shannon

Monmouth   Gloucester

Severn   Oxford   London

Thames

Pembroke

Bath

Canterbury

Salisbury

Glastonbury   Winchester   SOUTHEASTERN

SOUTHWESTERN

CORNISH

ENGLISH CHANNEL

Introduction

Middle English Literature

> Yf that olde bokes were aweye,
> Y-loren were of remembraunce the keye.
>
> Chaucer, *Legend of Good Women*

This anthology contains an abundant representation of the finest literature produced during the Middle English period. The term *Middle English* is awkward but convenient, for it identifies one distinct phase in the development of the English language (discussed below in the linguistic introduction) and also applies to a distinct epoch in the history of English culture that began with the Norman invasion of 1066 and ended at about the time that Caxton introduced printing in England, in 1476.

Old English literature, the predecessor of Middle English literature, differs greatly from what followed, emanating as it did from the pagan Germanic tribes who began to sweep into Britain in A.D. 449 and to subjugate the native Celtic-speaking British peoples. These Anglo-Saxon invaders maintained an interest in the traditions and legends of their continental fatherland and, even after they were Christianized, they composed works, such as the great epic *Beowulf,* that were cast in the conventional Germanic alliterative verse form and that reflected their ancient myths and legends. The arrival of the Normans in 1066 opened up new channels of cultural communications, and Britain subsequently shared with all the other countries of western Europe in the profound awakening of the renaissance of the twelfth century and became a productive and cosmopolitan center of letters.

During the long and eventful period from the Norman conquest to the end of the fifteenth century, Middle English was only one of several languages spoken and written within Great Britain and Ireland. The marvel is, indeed, that English succeeded in surviving as the primary language of the polyglot peoples who coexisted in the two small islands. The Normans brought with them their own dialect of French; the Cornish, the Welsh, the Irish, the Manx, and the Scottish Gaels continued to use their individual Celtic languages; Viking settlers used various Scandinavian dialects; Jewish scholars wrote in Hebrew; and other immigrants, such as the Bretons and the Flemings, retained their own languages, though their literary activities are unrecorded. Many men of letters were multilingual, and some of those who spoke and wrote Latin have left behind them outstanding works in that language.

RELIGIOUS LITERATURE

By far the largest proportion of surviving Middle English literature—and, for that matter, of medieval European literature in general—is devoted to some aspect of religion. Literacy was not widespread, but those men and women who were literate tended to be in some way connected with the church, whose influence pervaded town and country—manors, villages, guilds, municipalities, schools, universities, and the royal court. Every parish had a priest subordinate to the bishop of the diocese, who was in turn subordinate to the hierarchy of archbishops and pope, so that even the remotest parish was linked potentially with the culture of the outside world. Furthermore, monks and nuns who were dedicated to the contemplative life settled in rural retreats, where they accumulated their own libraries. The Benedictines (Black Monks) had been established in England since 597; the Cistercians (White Monks) arrived in 1128; and other orders of monks and of regular canons (Augustinians, Premonstratensians, and Gilbertines) also founded their own houses. Members of the mendicant orders, who in their pursuit of the active life went out on preaching missions and were often interested in literary matters, arrived somewhat later—the Dominicans (Black Friars) in 1221, the Franciscans (Grey Friars) in 1224, the Carmelites (White Friars) in 1240, and the Austin Friars in 1248. Understandably, the literary works produced by the better-educated members of these various branches of the church tended to reflect their authors' personal piety and religious zeal.

Much of the most distinguished literature composed in Middle English, as in the other languages of Britain and Ireland, was thus basically religious in focus; and though the modern reader may find a purely literary pleasure in the survivals of a now submerged culture, he cannot appreciate such literature historically unless he recognizes its fundamental purpose. As the following brief analysis of the contents of this anthology will suggest, almost half of the items selected for inclusion on literary merit are the products of church or cloister.

The annals kept by the two Peterborough chroniclers were recorded for the sake of preserving a summary of events affecting their Benedictine monastery, and their selection and interpretation of these events reflect a thoroughly monastic, theocentric view of history. *The Proverbs of Alfred* contains popular, everyday sayings as well as religious advice, but the overall intention of the poem is religious. As the title suggests, the *Poema Morale* is likewise religious in intent. In *The Owl and the Nightingale*, the nightingale is notably sympathetic toward worldly lovers and the singers of amatory lays, but the churchly owl constantly draws the argument into the realms of religion. And, of all the early works selected here, the most centrally religious are the two tracts *Holy Maidenhood* and *The Anchoresses' Rule*, which both deal with the justification and observance of the recluse's way of life.

In the latter part of the thirteenth century the range of Middle English literature began to grow more diverse, but the emphasis on religion remained paramount. *The Bestiary* presents a vernacular popularization of the medieval theologian's interpretation of the works of God. *Judas*, which has been called one of the earliest of English ballads and is derived from popular international oral tradition, is essentially more didactic than dramatic in intention and more religious than secular in function. *A Love Rune*, which is directed by a Franciscan friar toward those girls who might wish to become brides of Christ, deals with spiritual rather than fleshly love. *The Sayings of St. Bernard*, which emanated from the Cistercian tradition, serves to warn mankind against the world, the flesh, and the devil; and *The Land of*

Cokayne is a satire composed by a Franciscan friar and aimed at the worldliness of monks such as the Cistercians.

In the early fourteenth century Mannyng dedicated his gift as a storyteller to the edifying task of composing *Handling Sin;* and Richard Rolle wrote *The Form of Living* for a female reader who had adopted a hermit's mode of life. This century also produced many fine religious lyrics, such as *The Five Joys of Mary.*

The latter part of the fourteenth century—the worldly age of Chaucer— produced even more important religious works. *The Parliament of the Three Ages,* which presents an allegory of the life of man, is amply illustrated with descriptions of the contemporary world and with allusions to secular history, but its intention is just as otherworldly as that of the early *Poema Morale* and its artistry much more distinguished. Langland's monumental *Piers Plowman* deals with the vast problems of the salvation of man and society. The brilliant *Pearl* raises a complex range of questions concerning the human soul. This period also produced the pioneering work of the Wyclifite translators of the Bible and Trevisa's enterprising translation of Bartholomew's Latin encyclopedia, the central purpose of which, like that of all the other works already mentioned, is specifically religious.

In the fourteenth century the members of the Lollard movement had already begun to attack corruption within the church and to flout ecclesiastical authority, just as the Wyclifite translators had done when they provided laymen with a vernacular translation of the very work on which that authority rested its claim, namely the Bible. Early in the fifteenth century a complete cleavage between the Catholic church and the new Protestant sects that emerged from the Reformation took place. Yet even the comparatively barren culture of the fifteenth century produced such religious gems as the artistic lyric *Christ and His Mother,* the popular ballad *St. Stephen and Herod,* and two impassioned poems of the Scottish priest William Dunbar, *The Dance of the Seven Deadly Sins* and *On the Resurrection.*

LEARNED, COURTLY, AND POPULAR LITERATURE

Despite the ubiquity of religion in medieval culture, some of the outstanding works surviving from the Middle English period were not primarily designed for purposes of religious instruction. The source of these works was not Biblical, and their purpose was not doctrinal; their authors were not necessarily churchmen, and their audiences were not immediately intent on salvation. Some were learned works, written by authors who had gained an education in school or college; these were characteristically artistic in form, carefully wrought, adorned with figures of speech and scholarly allusions, and frequently allegoric in significance. Some were courtly works, aimed at an aristocratic audience familiar with the concepts of courtly love and with the ideals of knighthood; these were frequently as artistic in their own way as learned works but were primarily imaginative and fantastic. Some were popular works, emanating from the simple residents of farms and towns, drawn from the endless resources of international folklore, fashioned orally and transmitted orally with no fixed text; these were as imaginative and fantastic as courtly works though they were artistically limited by the fact that they were molded by the unpretentious taste of an insatiable popular audience. Learned literature might be said to depend on the scribe, courtly literature on the harpist, and popular literature on the ballad-singer; and as a consequence, learned literature is the most fully preserved, while much of the graceful but ephemeral courtly literature and the robust popular literature have vanished without a trace.

The classification of particular literary works, however, is complicated by the fact that medieval culture was less stratified than medieval society. To be sure, the aristocrat enjoyed almost unbounded feudal privileges, while the villager enjoyed hardly any, yet upward social mobility was possible for those culture-carriers who had gained sufficient education to become teachers or clerks. In the following summary of the nonreligious works contained in this anthology, the fluidity of feudal society and the corresponding diffusion of culture are constantly evident.

To turn first to verse narrative, Lawman's *Brut* illustrates the impossibility of following any rigid system in classifying Middle English literature. Lawman was a secular priest; his work was a translation of an Anglo-Norman courtly poem, and his audience was presumably made up of his rural neighbors in the West Country. Furthermore, his Anglo-Norman source was itself an adaptation of Geoffrey of Monmouth's pseudohistorical *History of the Kings of Britain*, written in ornate Latin prose and aimed at a learned audience of clerics and courtiers. *The Brut* is thus not so much a folk epic as a popularization.

King Horn belongs to the genre of romance, and again the classification is not entirely unambiguous. A romance can be described as a narrative poem dealing with the trials of a hero in the service of his ladylove, his overlord, and God. Some romances are highly sophisticated, while others are popular and have often been reworked as simple ballads. *King Horn* belongs to the latter category, and the narrative, in fact, survived in oral ballad tradition until a very recent date, long after the romance had dropped from circulation.

Romances, however, were not necessarily restricted to the popular level. *Sir Orfeo* is derived from the classical myth of Orpheus, and its romantic emphasis on the power of love seems to address the work particularly to a courtly audience, although its basic narrative also circulated as a simple ballad. *Sir Gawain and the Green Knight* is even more clearly a sophisticated courtly romance. It assumes an understanding of Geoffrey of Monmouth's pseudohistorical concept of Arthur's destiny; it emphasizes the ethical challenges involved in knighthood; it subtly assesses the artificial code of courtly love, according to which a knight sought self-improvement through service to his ladylove; psychological realism overrides the fantastic elements within the plot; and allegoric implications enrich the entire romance. So far as is known, it was never reduced to ballad form; and if it was, the loss of force would have been lamentable.

At a simpler level, *Thomas of Erceldoun*, which also circulated as a ballad, is essentially a popular romance, describing a miraculous encounter between a knight and a supernatural ladylove, but in its extant form it has been specially adapted to support a political prophecy. *Robyn and Gandelyn* is a pure and simple ballad of outlawry, antiaristocratic in theme and attitude, which could hardly have been expanded into a courtly romance.

Romances, which are the counterpart of modern novels, and ballads, which are the counterpart of short stories, are thus difficult to characterize by any one criterion other than preoccupation with the obligations of heroism. There are, however, other medieval verse narratives that differ from the romance and the ballad and are generally called, for lack of a better term, tales. One of these, *The Fox and the Wolf*, contains a single anecdote of universal appeal, derived from the popular French cycle of tales dealing with the exploits of Reynard, the wily fox. Another is *Dame Sirith*, which is a popular *fabliau*, or comic story pertaining to bourgeois life, the plot of which also turns up in Middle English in a short bourgeois drama entitled *The Interlude of a Cleric and a Girl*. Similarly, *The Tale of Beryn* may be classified as a bourgeois tale, since it centers more on the hero's success as a merchant and lawyer than as a lover.

Some medieval verse narratives, it may be added, altogether elude even the relatively imprecise classifications presented here. *Morte Arthure* is frequently referred to as a romance because it deals with knightly deeds, but it is more learned than courtly in its treatment of the subject of King Arthur's conquest of Rome and his final downfall. It is colored by the historiographic vision of Geoffrey of Monmouth's *History of the Kings of Britain* and presents Arthur as a victim of the wheel of fortune—a philosophical concept dominant in the Middle Ages because of Boethius's highly influential work *The Consolation of Philosophy*. For lack of any better term, it might indeed be called a tragedy, in keeping with the groping definition of that medieval genre offered by Chaucer's Monk:

> Tragedie is . . . a certeyn storie . . .
> Of hym that stood in greet prosperitee
> And is y-fallen out of heigh degree
> Into myserie, and endeth wrecchedly.

A similar analysis can also be made of Henryson's *Testament of Cressid*, which deals with the tragic downfall of the heroine.

The same range of popular, courtly, and learned backgrounds appears in the medieval tradition of the lyric. *Now Springs the Spray* and the Harley lyrics *Alysoun, Spring, April*, and *Love in Paris* reflect the life of the wandering scholars of western Europe and carry with them the flavor of courtly love. Minot's violent political lyric *Halidon Hill* seems to be clerical in origin, but its tone is more bourgeois than courtly. *The Blacksmiths*, dealing as it does with noise pollution, is certainly the composition of a villager or townsman. Dunbar's *Golden Targe* is the work of a scholarly ecclesiastic who could express himself with equal facility in the realms of courtly love, as here, and religious devotion and morality, as in his other poems already cited.

The remaining four major works have in common one characteristic, the dependence on the learned tradition. Barbour's *Bruce*, which recounts the national history of Scotland, is the work of an erudite churchman. His learning is every-where apparent, but the primary materials of his verse chronicle were drawn largely from oral tradition, and the style of the work is more like that of a simple romance than of the classical epics whose orderly pattern he attempted vainly to imitate. Gower's *Lover's Confession* draws upon that encyclopedia of love, the Old French *Romance of the Rose*, both for its presentation of courtly love and for its analysis of the role of love in human life and in God's plan.

Hoccleve's *Regiment of Princes* is an ecclesiastical adaptation of earlier writings on statesmanship. Lydgate's *Siege of Thebes* is an epic adapted from a French prose romance whose author had reworked the familiar materials of classical legend to suit a medieval audience.

THE SCOPE OF MIDDLE ENGLISH LITERATURE

The works included in this anthology, then, represent both the religious and the secular aspects of medieval life and reflect the various educational and social levels of medieval audiences. From the surviving literature of the Middle English period the religious culture could be much more fully exemplified by the inclusion of saints' lives, miracle plays, sermons, and the like, since such materials were reverently recorded and preserved. The courtly tradition could be further illustrated, for instance, by romances of Charlemagne and of Alexander the Great; the learned tradition by treatises on such matters as medicine, dreams, and hunting; and the popular tradition by bawdy songs and tales, which, though seldom recorded, undoubtedly circulated vigorously. Yet, a wider survey would not reveal a portrait of medieval man any different from that already discernible in those works that have been selected here on the basis of their literary appeal.

What then, one may ask, are the characteristics that differentiate medieval man, as revealed in his literature, from modern man? Though the answers to this question lie far beyond the scope of this brief introduction, the question is one that every reader of medieval literature would do well to ask himself. Here it may be appropriate to stress the obvious by pointing to the dominance of the universal concepts of Christianity in the Middle Ages. God was thought in a very literal sense to be the controller of the universe; past, present, and future for him were one, and all events were affected by his providence; earthly rulers of church and state were responsible to him, and they exercised authority over lesser mortals only to the extent that they were God's regents.

In this sense, all literature was potentially religious. Thus, even the most fantastic medieval romances tended to deal with the hero's duties rather than, as is the case in modern fiction, with the hero's personal development and self-discovery. Similarly, in medieval works of social criticism, such as Langland's *Piers Plowman*, the author is concerned with man's obedience to the divine plan, whereas a contemporary author, such as Sartre, maintains that man is responsible to himself alone and must choose his own values.

As a result of their religious point of view, medieval writers constantly tended to enrich the significance of their works by means of allegory. The church fathers had shown that everything in the Bible could be interpreted allegorically. Each narrative item could be shown to have a concealed spiritual meaning, and the events recorded in the Old Testament could be shown to prefigure events in the New Testament and even events in secular history. So, for example, St. Augustine of Hippo, in his *City of God*, declared not only that Noah's Ark prefigured Christ's Church but also that Cain and Abel prefigured Romulus and Remus. Biblical commentators developed a system for the interpretation of texts at four different levels—the literal (based on the written word), the mystical (based on faith), the moral (based on charity), and the anagogical (based on hope):

> *Littera gesta docet, quid credas allegoria,*
> *Moralis quid agas, quo tendas anagogia.*

> The literal teaches the facts, the allegorical teaches what you should believe,
> The moral what you should do, the anagogical what you should aim for.

(Augustine of Dacia)

This system was used not only by Biblical exegetes, as in the preface to the Wyclifite Bible, but also by men of letters, such as Langland in *Piers Plowman* and Gower in *The Lover's Confession*, and must have been familiar to every medieval layman who had listened to a sermon or had been taught the significance of the art that exemplified God's word in every Gothic cathedral. Authors also introduced morality into their writings by means of personification—a by-product of allegory—as in the lively characterizations of the Seven Deadly Sins in *Piers Plowman*, and by exemplification, as in the account of the Nine Worthies in *The Parliament of the Three Ages*. Even when the purpose was not explicitly religious, instruction was potentially present in much medieval literature.

Allegory is, of course, a difficult device. Sometimes it was employed very naively, as in *The Bestiary*, sometimes very subtly and even enigmatically, as in *The Owl and the Nightingale*, sometimes brilliantly, as in *The Pearl*. Sometimes, it should be added, allegory was certainly not intended, as in a simple romance such as *King Horn*, though any able exegete could no doubt have produced an edifying sermon even on this subject. Generally speaking, however, for medieval man the whole world was a symbol, and in this respect the medieval audience differs considerably from the modern. The modern reader does, to be sure, look for symbolic significance in a figure such as Moby Dick; but the medieval reader was prepared to discover in a whale four levels of allegory, for in a broad sense he had been trained, like Shakespeare's hero, to find "books in the running brooks, sermons in stone, and good in everything."

The other somewhat unfamiliar aspect of medieval culture that the modern reader should recognize is the general tendency of authors to approach the art of literature as apprentices who must serve a long course before they can become masters. At the popular level, for instance, minstrels were evidently expected to memorize traditional romances and lays before they could hope to compose anything new, and even as masters they consistently strove to rework traditional narratives rather than create completely original, imaginative topics. For them, as for other medieval artists and artisans, originality was irrelevant; what really counted was craftsmanship. The particular skill of the romancer lay in his ability to cater to popular taste, and much of the charm of a romance such as *King Horn* arises from the attempts of a long succession of minstrels to perfect their performance of it in the presence of responsive, living audiences. The ultimate source of *King Horn* was an Anglo-Norman romance aimed at a courtly audience; the final native English product was a popular poem that was unoriginal and yet new.

At the level of courtly literature the scope is more complex, but the principle remains the same. Here also, craftsmanship outweighs originality. Thus, *Sir Gawain and the Green Knight*, for instance, is a supremely great work, but not because its plot is original. In fact, the plot was at least six hundred years old when the Middle English romancer was inspired to reinterpret it for his own courtly audience. Rather, *Sir Gawain* is great because of the author's combination of human perceptivity and artistic skill. His perceptivity may have been born within him, but his skill was surely not just instinctive. It must have been nurtured by wide reading, by the laborious study of rhetoric, by long practice in the arts of composition, and by the patient study of such kindred arts as music and architecture. He was the kind of poet who, like Chaucer, would feelingly exclaim: "The lyf so short, the craft so long to lerne!"

The craftsmanship of medieval culture has appropriately received much attention from recent literary critics, including some who reject the study of sources and backgrounds as irrelevant. Here, fortunately, the modern reader can join with them in an appreciation of the structure, texture, and architectonics of the Middle English masterpiece even if he has not himself absorbed any of the established literary-historical lore; for works such as *The Owl and the Nightingale*, *Sir Gawain and the Green Knight*, *The Pearl*, and *Piers Plowman* share in the general triumph attained by apprentices and masters during the flowering of Romanesque and Gothic art.

Their language, style, and concepts are medieval, but they deal with the universal experience of human life.

The Middle English Language

> Ye knowe ek that in forme of speche is chaunge
> Withinne a thousand yeer; and wordes tho
> That hadden pris now wonder nyce and straunge
> Us thinketh hem; and yet thei spake hem so.
>
> Chaucer, *Troilus and Criseyde*

Every language is liable to continual historical change and to local dialectal variation. The Old English language brought by the Anglo-Saxons from the Continent differentiated itself from the other Germanic languages spoken by the peoples who remained behind, even though all the Germanic languages belong to the same Indo-European family; and the Anglo-Saxons themselves spoke different dialects of Old English. Middle English similarly followed the inevitable · processes of change and variation, so that it is not possible to present a single succinct description of the language that can apply equally to the Peterborough monk writing in Northamptonshire in 1121 and to William Dunbar writing in Southeastern Scotland in 1500.

The difficulty of describing Middle English is increased by the fact that language is a human oral behavior that is inadequately represented by even the most precise phonetic transcription and is only sketchily recorded by the usual haphazard processes of writing. Language is a signaling device dependent on an interconnected system of six different kinds of contrasts: phonemic contrasts between discrete sounds, both vowels (*bat/but*) and consonants (*bat/cat*); morphemic contrasts between forms (*cat/cats*); syntactic contrasts between constructions (*This is a cat/Is this a cat?*); semantic contrasts between words (*cat/dog*); stress contrasts between syllables (I'll *per-mít* you/I'll give you a *pér-mit*); and intonational contrasts between sentences (*This is a cat./This is a cat?*). English uses no contrasts other than these six (pitch provides intonational contrast but does not, as in Chinese, provide semantic tone contrast).

Despite the apparent simplicity of this signaling system, subtle historical changes and dialectal variations have differentiated our own Modern English from Middle English, so that we cannot be absolutely certain what a Middle English speaker sounded like or what he meant by what he said. Lacking native informants, we must therefore turn to the educated guesses of the philologists, which are briefly summarized below.

SOUNDS

For those readers who wish only the simplest possible advice, the following three rules provide the approximate sound contrasts intended by Middle English writers. The qualities of certain long stressed vowels, in particular, have changed considerably between the Middle English period and the present, even though the spelling of many of the words in which they occur has not changed at all.

(1) *Pronounce all written consonants as we do those in Modern English.* Also, pronounce the sound (now foreign to English) represented by *gh* in *night* as we pronounce the *h* sound in *how* but with a stronger breathing. (It is like the *ch* in the Scottish pronunciation of *loch*—not *lock*—or in the German pronunciation of *Bach*.)

(2) *Pronounce all final syllables,* even those represented by a final *-e,* no longer pronounced in Modern English. Middle English final *-e* has been marked *-è* in the following discussion. Thus, pronounce *damè* with two syllables as *dah-meh,* and *damès* as *dah-mess.* (The sound of the final *-è* is the same as that in the unstressed final syllable of the Modern English word *crooked.*)

(3) *Give all written vowels, both short and long, their so-called Continental sounds,* such as they would receive, for instance, in Modern French or Italian or in our modern pronunciation of Latin.

Therefore, pronounce the long vowel spelled *a* in Middle English *damè* as the *ah* sound of Modern French *dame* or Modern English *father.* Similarly, all of the following were pronounced with a stressed *ah* sound (and a final unstressed syllable, Rule 2): *barè, carè, famè, gamè, hatè, lamè, makè, namè, pagè, ragè, savè, takè, wakè.*

11

Pronounce the long vowel spelled *e* or *ee* in Middle English *regioun* as the *ay* sound of Modern French *région* or Modern English *rage*. Other instances are Middle English *be, he, me, she, thee*. For simplicity's sake, readers may ignore the set of words in which the *e* or *ee* as in Middle English *heeth* (modern *heath*) represents a distinctive vowel sound like that in Modern English *ebb*, but lengthened in duration.

Pronounce the long vowel spelled *i* or *y* in Middle English *finė* as the *ee* sound in Modern French *fine* or Modern English *machine*. Similarly: *bitė, glidė, kyndė, minė, primė, ridė, strivė, thinė, wyn* (modern *wine*).

Pronounce the long vowel *u* spelled *ou* or *ow* in Middle English *doutė* as the *ou* sound in Modern French *doute* or Modern English *rouge*. Similarly: *bour* (modern *bower*), *flour* (modern *flower*), *foul, hous, licour, mous, out, tour* (modern *tower*).

The other long vowels and diphthongs and all the short vowels have passed down into Modern English with less notable change, and the nonspecialist may therefore rely on his instinct for their pronunciation.

For a more detailed analysis of the Middle English sound system, see *Appendix I: Pronunciation of Middle English* (pp. 548–51).

FORMS

All obscure forms in the selections in this anthology have been interpreted in the marginal glosses, but a recognition of frequently recurring forms and constructions will facilitate the reading of Middle English.

Pronouns are the same as in Modern English, with the chief exception of two ambiguities that have now disappeared. The word variously spelled *her, here, hir, hire* is the Middle English equivalent not only of the modern *her* but also of the modern *their*, and the Middle English *his* is the equivalent not only of modern *his* but also of *its*.

In Old English the definite article, the adjective, and the noun were fully declined according to number, case, and gender. Early Middle English retained many of the inherited contrasting forms, which are interpreted in the glosses when necessary, but by the time of Chaucer, Middle English had reduced the number of contrasting forms so completely that it differed in usage only slightly from Modern English. Thus, in Old English the contrasting forms for the nominative singular, genitive singular, and nominative plural of the masculine article, adjective, and noun were respectively *sē gōda stān, thaes gōdan stānes, thā gōdan stānas;* in Chaucerian Middle English these became *the goodė ston, the goodė stonės, the goodė stonės;* and in Modern English, *the good stone, the good stone's* (or *of the good stone*), *the good stones.* The typical Old English feminine declension showed the following contrasting forms: *sēo gōdė caru, thaerė gōdan carė, thā gōdan cara;* the Chaucerian forms were *the goodė carė, the goodė carės, the goodė carės;* and the Modern English, *the good care, the good care's. the good cares.*

Verb forms generally resemble their modern counterparts, but the following peculiarities should be noted. The Middle English third person singular of the present usually appears as *he loveth*, rather than *he loves*. Verbs with roots ending

12

in -*d* or -*t*, however, regularly contracted the ending -*eth*, thus appearing as *he bit* (for *biddeth*), *fint* (*findeth*), *holt* (*holdeth*), *rit* (*rideth*), *stant* (*standeth*). Also, the commonly occurring *him lest* (or *list* or *lüst*) 'it pleases him,' is contracted from *lesteth* and has a past tense *him leste*, 'it pleased him.'

Many verb endings had a final -*n*, which by the fourteenth century was often dropped. Thus, the older form (*we, ye, they*) *lovèn* could optionally be replaced by *lovè* (the forerunner of the modern form *love*); (*we*) *lovedèn* by *lovedè* (modern *loved*); and *to lovèn* by *to lovè* (modern *to love*). Also the old prefix *y*- could optionally be dropped, so that *I have y-lovèd* could be replaced by *I have lovèd* (modern *I have loved*) and *I havè y-dronkè(n)* by *I have dronkè(n)* (modern *I have drunk*).

There were two alternative signs of the negative. One was the still familiar *not* (or its older variants *nought* and *naught*). The other was the now archaic *ne* (or *n'* before vowels). *Ne* combined with the following verb in certain frequently occurring collocations: *nadde* (*ne hadde*, modern *hadn't*), *nere* (modern *weren't*), *nolde* (modern *wouldn't*), *noot* (*ne woot*, modern *know not*), *nyl* (modern *will not*), *nyste* (*ne wiste*, modern *knew not*). *Ne* was often accompanied by other negative words, so that Chaucer's sentence *He nevere yet no vileynye ne sayde in al his lyf unto no maner wight* (literally, 'He never yet no villainy didn't say to no kind of person') was a perfectly grammatical expression of the statement *He never yet spoke any villainy to any kind of person*.

A frequent variant of the conjugated form of the past tense was provided by the verb *gan* (meaning literally 'began' followed by the infinitive, so that *he gan ridè(n)* could be used to mean either 'he began to ride' or 'he did ride' or simply 'he rode.'

For a more detailed account of the Middle English conjugational system, see *Appendix II: The Middle English Verb* (pp. 552–53).

SYNTAX

There are many subtle differences in syntax between Middle English and Modern English, but few will present any real difficulty to the reader. We occasionally may be surprised by the casual disregard for sentence structure and logic shown by such writers as Robert Mannyng and, ironically, the author of the preface to the Wyclifite translation of the Bible (notice his confusing attempt to coordinate ideas in the long sentence beginning "And these thre goostly understondingis," p. 486).

Many writers of Middle English, however, were masters of rhetorical control. In this respect, the highly literate author of *The Pearl* and *Sir Gawain and the Green Knight* particularly repays study. The poet knows instinctively how, for instance, to modulate *if*-clauses in Shakespearean style by means of inversion: *But wolde ye, lady lovely, then leve me grante* ("But, if you would, lovely lady, then grant me leave," p. 415). He develops long and intricate sentences with complete clarity, as in *Sir Gawain and the Green Knight*, page 425, lines 1508–1524, where he confidently inserts an eight-line, parenthetical sentence within a main sentence that, despite its extraordinary length, is not only completely comprehensible but also artistically effective. And these random examples of his virtuosity represent a norm and not an exception.

SEMANTICS

Readers should be constantly alert to the fact that words change their meanings through the ages. In a sense, a word conveys its meaning not so much by itself as by the contrast it implies between itself and other related words within the same semantic field; but words tend to shift unpredictably out of one field into another. The word *nice*, aptly used by Chaucer in the passage quoted above (p. 10), provides a good example. Borrowed through French from Latin *nescius* 'ignorant,' it used to mean 'ignorant,' in contrast to 'knowing.' But in the sense 'not knowing more than is immediately relevant,' it came to mean 'precise.' And in the sense 'not wishing to know too much,' it came variously to mean 'silly' or 'saintly' or 'pleasant,' according to the viewpoint of those who judged the "nice" person. We can, therefore, know what Chaucer intended by his use of the word only by examining his context and the available range of meanings recorded in the Middle English written during this period. Here dictionaries are more reliable than intuition, but the glosses in this anthology at least provide due warning of semantic traps.

STRESS AND INTONATION

In Middle English, syllabic stress tended to fall on the first syllable of words inherited from Old English, such as *lá-dy* (modern *lady*, unchanged in stress), and on the last syllable (not counting an unstressed final *-e*) of words borrowed from French, such as *li-cóur* and *cor-áge* (modern *líqu-or* and *cóur-age*, with stress now shifted to the first syllable). Thus, a rhyme between *rágè* and *corágè* was not artificial. Here again a dictionary is requisite.

Little can now be discovered about Middle English sentence intonation, but it probably did not differ considerably from that of Modern English.

WRITING

Writing is a device by which one records what one has said (or wishes one had said). As a device for communication between contemporaries who speak the same dialect, writing works well. But as a device for notifying readers who speak a later form of the language, it fails, for various technical reasons, to represent the living interplay of sounds, forms, arrangements, meanings, stresses, and intonations that constitutes an author's spoken utterance.

Furthermore, Middle English works seldom survive in manuscripts written by the author himself but have generally been copied or recopied from lost originals by scribes living in a later age and speaking some dialect other than the author's. Indeed, even under the author's supervision, scribes—like modern secretaries—could be fallible, as Chaucer attests in his *Words unto Adam His Own Scriven*:

Under thy long lokkes thou most° have the scalle°	may scale
But° after my makyng thou wryte more trewe,	Unless
So ofte a-daye I mot° thy werk renewe,	must
It to correcte and eek to rubbe and scrape,	
And al is thorough thy negligence and rape.°	haste

So that readers may have some idea of the nature of the manuscript tradition on which our knowledge of Middle English literature depends, we have reproduced, on pages 16–27, six pages (or columns of pages), all of which contain portions of the texts published in this anthology. (The manuscript sources of several other selections, as the headnotes indicate, are available in modern reproductions.) As will be clear from the literal transcriptions of the first few lines of these manuscript pages, Middle English scribes did not represent each contrasting sound by a contrasting letter, any more than Modern English writers do, nor did they indicate syllabic stress or sentence intonation. They sometimes used punctuation to indicate midpoints and end of poetic lines, but they seldom used it to indicate syntactic units; and their use of capitalization was individualistic rather than systematic.

of sele kineriche. And dune
forð wuned: mid wal þere bue-
de. fiftene leh afde. seoðliche
wunden. đon mihte þere lac-
re. tua gloune þurste. þa nas
þer na mare. Ipan felde tolæ-
ne: of tua hundred þusend
monnen. þa þer leien to haulse:
Buten arður þe king ene. 7 of
his cnihtes þreien. Ar þur ke
for wunded: wunder ane switðe.
þer to him com a cnitue: þe we
of his cunne. he wes Caðores
sune: þe eorles of Cornwaile.
Constantin beh te þe tune he
wes þan kinge deore. Ar þur
him lokede on: þer he lai on
folden. And þas word seide:
mid sorhfulle heorte. Costan-
tin þu art wilcume: þu weore
Caðores sone. Ich þe bitache
here: mine kineriche. And were mine brittes: a to þines lifes. And held heom alle þe la-
zen: þa habbeoð istonden a
mine dazen. And alle þe la-
zen gode: þa bi uðeres dazen
stode. And ich wulle uaren
to aualun: to neuwest alre mai
dene. To Argante þere quie-
ne: Aluen swiðe scoone. 7
heo scal mine wunden: ma-
kien alle isunde. Al hal me

makien: Mid haleweie dre-
chen. And soððich cume a zein
to mine kineriche. And wunien mid britten: mid muche
lere wunne. æfne þan worden:
þer comot se wenden. þat we
an sæort þat lið uni seorten
mid uðen. And þa þurine
þer inne. wunderliche idih-
te: And heo nomen arður ana
And ta ieourste hine uereden.
And sofere hiure adun leiden:
7 forð gunnen hine liðen. þa
wes hit iwurðen: þat arðin
seide wilulen. þer weore unmete cure: of arðures forð sil-
re. Brittes ileueð zete. þette
bon on liue. And wunnien
in auelun: and fuzest alre
aluen. And lokeð euere bri-
tes zete. When arður cume
liðe. Nis næuer þe mon iboren
of næuer nane burde icoren
þe cunne of þan soð. of arður suzen mare. Bute whi-
le wes an witeze er iotum
wette. he wes imid worde.
his quiðer wæren soð. þet
an arður sculde zete: cum
anglen to sulste. Costan
tin þus leouede on londe 7
Brittes hine lusede. And wi-
đe deore beomithe she s̄. s. ↄ

PLATE 1   British Museum Manuscript (ca. 1225), Cotton Caligula A ix, folio 171 verso. The corresponding passage of Lawman's *Brut* (ca. 1200), printed on page 52, begins in the first column at the middle of line 10 (opposite the cropped marginal note [*Ar*]*ður*) and ends in the second column, four lines from the bottom. Lines 10–14 can be transliterated as follows:

> his cnihtes tweien. Arður wes
> forwunded, wunder ane swiðe.
> þer to him com a cnaue, þe wes
> of his cunne. he wes Cadores
> sune, the eorles of Corwaile.

The graphemes (contrasting letter forms) used by the scribe are for the most part still familiar, though *i* is also used without contrast for *j*, *r* in its familiar form alternates with a now extinct variant shaped like the number *2*, *s* alternates with a long *s* variant still used by eighteenth-century printers (∫, not *f*), and *u* is also used without contrast for *v*. Additionally, the scribe uses three graphemes that were inherited from Old English writing but have gradually dropped out of use: ȝ (Old English yogh, here equivalent to two different sounds, *y* and *gh*), ð (Old English eth, equivalent to the modern grapheme *th*), and þ (Old English thorn, also equivalent to *th*).

The scribe often uses contractions for letters, such as an abbreviated *s* above the vowel it follows, and a long mark over a vowel to indicate a following *n* (which, however, he forgets to insert over the *o* in *Cor*[*n*]*waile* 'Cornwall'). He also uses contrasting capital letters, but not in the same consistent way that they are used in Modern English writing. His punctuation is intended to mark metrical lines and half-lines, but not, as in Modern English, syntactic divisions. A period marks the end of each full line; a kind of inverted semicolon marks the end of a half-line.

þ is a wel fair abbei
of white monkes & of grei
þ bey bowris & halles
al of pasteis bey þe walles
of fleis of fisse & a rich met
þe likfullist þ man mai et
Fluren cakes bey þe schingles alle
of chirch cloister bowr & halle
þe pinnes bey fat podinges
rich met to princez & kinges
man mai þer of et inoȝ
Al wiþ riȝt & noȝt wiþ woȝ
al is commune to ȝung & old
to stoute & sterne mek & bold
þ is a cloister fair & liȝt
brod & lang of sembli siȝt
þe pilers of þ cloister alle
bey itned of cristale
wiþ har las & capitale
of grene jaspe & rede corale
In þe praer is a tre
Swiþe likful forto se
þe rote is gingeiur & galingale
þe siouns bey al sedwale
te maces bey þe flure
þe rind canel of swet odur

PLATE 2   British Museum Manuscript (ca.1308–18), Harley 913, folio 4 recto. The corresponding passage of *The Land of Cokayne* (ca. 1275–1300) is printed on pages 189–90, lines 51–76. The first six lines can be transliterated as follows:

> þer is a wel fair abbei.
> of white monkes & of grei.
> þer beþ bowris & halles.
> al of pasteiis beþ þe walles.
> of fleis of fisse & [*second* & *deleted*] rich met.
> þe likfullist that man mai et.

The shapes of letters and the forms of contractions in both this plate and in Plates 3 and 4 differ somewhat from those in Plate 1, but the graphemic system is the same. Poetic lines are written separately, and the end of each line is marked with a nonsyntactic period.

þ	...thoz wiþ outen hade ·
	sum non armes nade ·
	sum þurth þe bodi hadde wounde ·
	sum lay wode y bounde ·
	sum armed on hors sete ·
	sum astrangled as þai ete ·
	sum were in water adreynt ·
	sum wiþ fire al forschreynt ·
	wiues þer lay onchild bedde ·
	sum ded & sum awedde ·
	wonder fele þer lay bisides ·
	riʒt as þai slepe her vndertides ·
	eche was þus in þis warld y nome ·
	wiþ fairi þider y come ·
	þer he seiʒe his owhen wiif ·
	dame heurodis his lef liif ·
	slepe vnder an ympe tre ·
	bi her cloþes he knewe þat it was she ·

When he hadde bihold þis meruails alle
& went in to þe kinges halle
þan seiʒe he þer a semly siʒt
A tabernacle blisseful & briʒt
þer in her maister king sete
& her quen fair & swete
her crounes her cloþes schine so briʒt
þat vnneþe bihold he hem miʒt
when he hadde biholden alþat þing
& kneled adoun bifor þe king
lord he seyd ʒif it þi wille were
mi menstraci þou schust y here
& þe king answerd what man artow
þat art hider y comen now
ich no non þat is wiþ me
no sent neuer after þe
Seþþen þat ich here regni gan
y no fond neuer so fole hardi man
þat hider to ous durst wende
bot þat ich him wald of sende
Ac quaþ he trowe ful wel
nam bot a pouer menstrel
sir it is þe maner of ous
to seche mani a lordes hous
& we nouʒt welcom nouʒe
ʒete we mot profery forþ our gle

B	...for þe king he sat adoun ·
	& toke his harp so miri of soun ·
	& tempreþ his harp as he wele can ·
	blissful notes he þer gan ·
	þat al þat in þe palays were ·
	com to him forto here ·
	& liggeþ adoun to his fete ·
	hem þenkeþ his melodi so swete ·
	þe king herkneþ & sitt ful stille ·
	to here his gle he haþ gode wille ·
	Gode wille he hadde of his gle ·
	þe riche quen al so hadde he ·
	When he hadde stint his harping ·
	þan seyd to him þe king ·
	menstrel me likeþ wele þi gle ·
	now aske of me what it be ·
	largelich ichil þe pay ·
	now speke & tow miʒt asay ·
	Sir he seyd ich biseche þe ·
	þatow woldest ʒiue me ·
	þat ich leuedi briʒt on ble ·
	þat slepeþ vnder þe ympe tre ·
	Nay quaþ þe king þat nouʒt nere ·
	A sori couple of ʒou it were ·
	for þou art lene rowe & blac ·
	& sche is louesum wiþ outen lac ·
	A loþlich þing it were forþi ·
	to sen hir in þi compaini ·

o sir he seyd gentil king
ʒete were it a wele fouler þing
to here a lesing of þi mouþe
So sir as ʒe seyd nouþe
what ich wald aski haue y schold
& nedes þou most þi word hold
þe king seyd seþþen it is so
take hir bi þe hond & go
& þi ich wil þatow be bliþe
he kneled adoun & þonked hi swiþe
his wiif he tok bi þe hond
& dede him swiþe out of þat lond
& went him out of þat þede
riʒt as he come þe way he ʒede
So long he haþ þe way y nome
To winchester he is y come ·

PLATE 3   National Library of Scotland Manuscript (London?, ca. 1330–40), Auchinleck, Advocates 19.2.1, folio 302 recto. The corresponding passage from *Sir Orfeo* (ca. 1330) is printed on pages 225–27, lines 391–478. The first six lines of the second column can be transliterated as follows:

> Bifor þe king he sat adoun.
> & tok his harp so miri of soun.
> & tempreþ his harp as he wele can.
> & blisseful notes he þer gan.
> þat al þat in þe palays were.
> com to him forto here.

Skottes out of berwik and of abirdene

at þe bannok burn war ȝe to kene

þare slogh ȝe many sakles als it was sene

and now has king Edward wroken it I wene

It es wroken I wene wele wurth þe while

war ȝit with þe skottes for þai er full of gile

Whare er ȝe skottes of saint Johnes toune

þe boste of ȝoure baner es beten all doune

when ȝe bostyng will bede sir Edward es boune

forto kindel ȝow care and crak ȝoure croune

he has crakked ȝoure croune wele werth þe while

schame bryd þe skottes for þai er full of gile

Skottes of striflin war steren and stout

of god ne of gude men had þai no dout

now haue þai þe peters pruked obout

bot at þe last sir Edward rifild þaire rout

he has rifild þaire rout wele wurth þe while

bot euer er þai under bot gaudes and gile

Ye nughtiute riueling now kindels þi care

bere bag with þi boste þi bigging es bare

fals wrecche and forsworn whider wilton fare

busk þe vnto brig and abide þare

þare wrecche saltou won and werp þe while

þi dwelling in donde es done for þi gile

Ye skottes gase in burghes and betes þe stretes

all þise inglis men harmes he hetes

fast makes he his mone to men þat he metes

bot fone frendes he findes þat his bale betes

fune betes his bale wele wurth þe while

he vses all threting with gaudes and gile

Bot many man thretes and spekes full ill

þat sum tyme war better to be stane still

þe skot in his wordes has wind forto spill

for at þe last Edward sall haue al his will

he had his will at berwik wele wurth þe while

skottes brogt him þe kayes bot get for þaire gile

PLATE 4 British Museum Manuscript (ca. 1400–25), Cotton Galba E ix, folio 52 verso, left-hand column. The corresponding version of Laurence Minot's *Halidon Hill* (ca. 1333) is printed in its entirety on pages 231–32. The first six lines can be transliterated as follows:

> Skottes out of berwik and of abirdene
> at þe bannok burn war ȝe to kene
> þare slogh ȝe many sakles als it was sene
> and now has king Edward wroken it I wene
> It es wrokin I wene wele wurth þe while
> war ȝit with þe skottes for þai er ful of gile

The grapheme *th* is now used alternately with the older form þ (thorn), and no punctuation is used at all. In line 2 ān represents *ann*.

Howe he þat deuout was mayden marie
And say his loue floure and fructifie

Al þogh his lyfe be queynt þe resemblaunce
Of him hath in me so fressh lyflynesse
Þat to putte othir men in remembraunce
Of his persone I haue heere his lyknesse
Do make to þis ende in soothfastnesse
Þat þei þat haue of him lest þought & mynde
By þis peynture may ageyn him fynde

The ymages þat in þe chirche been
Maken folk þenke on god & on his seyntes
Whan þe ymages þei beholden & seen
Were oft vnsyte of hem causith restreyntes
Of þoughtes gode whan a þing depeynt is
Or entayled if men take of it heede
Thoght of þe lyknesse it wil in hym brede

Yit somme holden oppynyoun and sey
Þat none ymages schuld maked be
Þei erren foule & goon out of þe wey
Of trouth haue þei scant sensibilite
Passe ovir þat now blessid trinite
Vpon my maistres soule mercy haue
Ffor him lady eke þi mercy I craue

Moore othir þing wolde I fayne speke & touche
Heere in þis booke but such is my dulnesse
Ffor þat al voyde and empty is my pouche
Þat al my lust is queynt wt heuynesse
And heuy spirit comaundeth stilnesse

PLATE 5 British Museum Manuscript (ca. 1412), Harley 4866, folio 88 recto. The corresponding passage from Thomas Hoccleve's *Regiment of Princes* (ca. 1412) is printed on page 508, lines 13–40. The second stanza on the page begins as follows:

> Al þogh his lyfe be queynt þe resemblaunce
> Of him haþ in me so fressh lyflynesse
> þat to putte othir men in remembraunce
> Of his persone I haue heere his lyknesse

Thorn is still used optionally as a grapheme for *th*, along with the more modern *th*, but yogh has been replaced by *gh*. No punctuation is used.

The British Museum MS. Arundel 38 may once have contained what would have been a slightly earlier version of this portrait, but the page is missing now. The earliest portrait of Chaucer appears in the Ellesmere MS. of *The Canterbury Tales* (ca. 1400). See Margaret Rickert, *Painting in Britain: The Middle Ages* (Harmondsworth, 1954), p. 185; Jerome Mitchell, *Thomas Hoccleve* (Urbana, 1968), pp. 110–15.

And ned not so mich thir heby boke
tel vs some thinge that draweth of to speke
Onely of goye and make no lengere lette
And when I sangste it wolde be no bette
I obered vnto his byddynge
And as the sawe me bonnde in alle thynge
As I koude with a ful pale chere
My tale I ganne anone as ye shal here

❧ Expliett prologus ❧

❧ Prima Pars ❧
Here begynneth the Segge of Thebes ful
lamentably tolde by John lidgate Monke of
Bury annexynge it to ye tales of Canbury

Sirs quod I sith of youre Curtesye
I entred am in to youre Companye
And admytted a tale for to tele
By hym that hath power to compele
I mene oure hoste governere and gyde
Of youre estbeone rydynge here by syde
Thogh my wit bareyne be and dulle
I wolle reherce a story wonderfulle
Touchynge the segge and destruccion
Of worthy Thebes the myghty royale Ton
Bilt and bygonne of olde auntquite
Vpon the tyme of worthy Josue
By diligence of kynge Amphion
Cheeff cause first of this foundacion

PLATE 6   British Museum Manuscript (prepared either in 1455–56 or 1461–62), Royal 18 D ii, folio 148 recto, lower right-hand column. The corresponding passage from John Lydgate's *Siege of Thebes* (ca. 1421) is found on pages 510–12, lines 38–125.

The rubric beneath the miniature and the following three lines of poetry can be transliterated as follows:

PRIMA PARS

Here begynneth the Segge of Thebes ful
lamentably tolde by John Lidgate Monke of
Bury anneyynge it to þe tallys of Canterbury

Sirs quod I. sith of youre Curtesye
I enterde am. in to youre Companye
And admytted. a tale for to tele

As in Plate 5, thorn is still used optionally for *th*, and yogh has been displaced by *gh*. A period is used to mark each half-line, and no other punctuation appears.

This handsome manuscript was commissioned by Sir William Herbert (later Earl of Pembroke) as a gift for either Henry VI or Edward IV. The miniature of the Canterbury pilgrims, painted around 1509–19 by an artist of the Flemish school, was added in a space that had been reserved for it by the scribe.

The pictorial and symbolic details in the miniature deserve attention. The third figure from the left is certainly John Lydgate, dressed in the ascetic clothing mentioned in his prologue. The other characters are drawn from Chaucer's Prologue to *The Canterbury Tales*. The fourth figure from the left is probably Chaucer's worldly monk, with sleeves trimmed in fur, who is thought to have been, like Lydgate, a Benedictine, though certainly not a strict member of the order. (The artist has perhaps deliberately provided the Monk's horse with donkey's ears.) The second figure from the left is probably Chaucer; both rider and horse, in fact, closely resemble their early counterparts in the Ellesmere Manuscript (ca. 1400–10) of *The Canterbury Tales*.

The other pilgrims are ambiguous. The first figure on the left might be Chaucer's Yeoman, but according to *The Canterbury Tales*, he should bear a mighty bow rather than a spear. The young rider, fifth from the left, could be the Squire, for his sleeves are appropriately long and wide, even though he is not "embroidered like a meadow." The bearded rider on the extreme right might be the Merchant, with his Flemish beaver hat.

The miniature, as is to be expected in this period, does not render the setting in true perspective or in precise detail, but it is at least schematically accurate, and its pattern may have a symbolic intention. The pilgrims on their return journey to Southwark have appropriately left the walled town of Canterbury by the West Gate (still standing). The massive cathedral within the walls can be readily identified, although it is not accurately oriented.

The nearer of the two buildings outside the walls, at the upper left of the miniature, may correspond to the actual inn where pilgrims used to stay when the city gates were shut at night. The building behind the inn may be St. Dunstan's Church, though the proportions are exaggerated and its position is incorrect. Its inclusion in the miniature could well be intended as a tribute to St. Dunstan, who was renowned not only as an archbishop of Canterbury but also as a monastic reformer who introduced a new standard of piety and asceticism to the English branch of the Benedictine order, of which Lydgate himself was such an outstanding representative.

For the standard description of this manuscript, see Sir George F. Warner and Julius P. Gilson, *Catalogue of Western Manuscripts in the Old Royal and King's Collections* (London, 1921), II, 308–10.

VERSIFICATION

Middle English versification reflects a wide range of traditions and innovations. Alliterative verse, inherited from the native tradition, is represented, for instance, by the uncomplicated lines of Lawman's *Brut*, which do not fully meet the strict Old English requirements, and also by the alliterative stanzas of *Sir Gawain and the Green Knight*, which, because of their patterning, exceed these requirements. Similarly, rhyming verse, originally adopted from French usage, is represented not only by the erratic couplets of *King Horn* but also by the intricate concatenations of *The Pearl*.

The various types represented in this anthology are enumerated below. Terminology has been standardized and simplified as far as possible, but some of the alternate terms often used in descriptions of metrics have been included. The term *beat* has been used in preference to the term *stress*, which is best reserved for grammatical descriptions. The beat (marked with an acute accent in the examples quoted below) can be thought of as the segment of a poetic measure where the listener may expect to find a recurrence of the emphasis that is implicit within the poet's metrical pattern. Usually, the beat coincides with a syllable carrying emphatic syllabic stress and also the pitch stress of intonation; but poets in the Middle English period, just as in other eras, felt free to invert stresses, to elide unstressed finals, and to syncopate or expand their syllabic count in order to avoid metrical imprisonment.

In describing forms of versification, *A* signifies a stressed initial sound alliterating with another identical initial sound *A*, *X* signifies a nonalliterating stressed sound in the same line. In rhyming verse, *a* signifies an ending rhyming with an identical ending *a* in another line, and *x* signifies an ending that does not rhyme with an ending in any other line. A superscript with the rhyming letter indicates the number of beats per line (thus, a^3 indicates a three-beat line).

ALLITERATIVE VERSE

1. Conventional alliterative verse

Middle English alliterative verse, sometimes referred to as long-line alliteration, was inherited from Old English. Each long line is divided by a break, or caesura, into two half-lines. Each half-line carries two beats and an unrestricted number of unstressed syllables. The half-lines are linked by alliteration, designated as *A*, between at least one of the stressed syllables in the first half and at least one stressed syllable in the second half. Alliterating consonants must be phonetically identical, no matter how they are represented in spelling; a vowel may alliterate either with itself repeated or with any other vowel.

As in Old English, the nonalliterating stressed syllables, designated as *X*, provide a melodic contrast. Schematically, *AA* or *AX* or *XA* in the first half-line must alliterate with either *AA* or *AX* or *XA*; there were thus nine different possible combinations. In Old English the historically dominant pattern was *AA AX*, while full alliteration *AA AA* was apparently not felt to be essentially desirable. But in Middle English verse, every possible pattern occurs, including an optional tenth combination *AA BB*, in which each half-line alliterates only within itself.

The most artistic alliterative verse appears in the West Country in the latter half of the fourteenth century, during the period known as the Alliterative Revival (which should perhaps be called the Alliterative Survival, since the tradition was unbroken). Alliterative verse apparently seemed provincial and even rustic to London audiences, accustomed as they were to rhyming verse. Chaucer's Parson patronizingly remarks that, being a southern man, he cannot "rum, ram, ruf by letter." Many poets of the western counties, however, used the device with great ability and subtlety. The author of *Sir Gawain and the Green Knight* appraises more sympathetically than the Parson its characteristic distinction. He intends, he says in a memorable phrase, to recite his romance "as it is stad [recorded] and stoken [set down] in story stif [brave] and strong with lel [loyal] lettres loken [linked], as in lond so [as] has ben longe." A typical example of alliterative verse can be found in *The Parliament of the Three Ages*:

> In the monethe of Mayè · when mirthès bene felè
>
> (l. 1, AA AX)
>
> With auntlers one aytherè sydè · éghelichè longè
>
> (l. 28, vowel alliteration, AA AX)
>
> And I slittè hym at the assayè · to see how me semydè
>
> (l. 70, full alliteration, AA AA)

Other selections using this type are *Morte Arthure*, *Piers Plowman*, and *Blacksmiths*.

2. Alliterative stanzas

Sir Gawain and the Green Knight is an unusual poem that contains stanzas of twelve to thirty-eight alliterative lines, each terminated by five rhyming lines—a one-beat "bob" of two syllables and a heavily alliterated four-line "wheel" of either three-beat lines or alternating four-beat and three-beat lines (a^1 $b^{3/4}$ a^3 $b^{3/4}$ a^3).

Sithen the *s*ege and the as*s*aut · was *s*esed at *T*royė,

(l. 1, alliterating AA AX)

wyth *w*ynnė,	a^1
Where *w*erre and *w*rake and *w*onder	b^3
Bi *s*ythės has *w*ont ther-innė,	a^3
And óft bothe *b*lysse and *b*lunder	b^3
Ful *s*kete has *s*kyfted *s*ynnė.	a^3

(ll. 15–19, rhyming)

3. Semi-alliterative, semi-rhyming verse

An early and generally crude transitional form of Middle English verse, still depending basically on the inherited patterns of Old English alliteration, introduced lines of rhyming couplets as an optional variation in place of alliterating lines. The model for this variation was probably the Old French and Anglo-Norman eight-syllable (octosyllabic) rhyming couplet, such as that used by Wace (the source of Lawman's *Brut*). This example is drawn from *The Proverbs of Alfred*:

And ėk Eálvred, · Énglenė hürdė

(I, 5, alliterating AA AX)

Byhüd hit on thirė heortė · that thee ėft ne smeortė

(XIII, 10, rhyming a a)

Other examples of this type of meter are *The Brut* and *The Bestiary*.

RHYMING VERSE

4. Three-beat couplets, a^3a^3

In *King Horn* alliteration within half-lines is frequent, and linking alliteration sometimes connects one line with the next, but the consistent rhyme scheme is the central device of versification. (Syllabic stress is often irregular.)

Rymenild ros of benchė
The beėr for tė shenchė.

(ll. 1107–08, alliterating and rhyming)

5. Four-beat couplets, a^4a^4

The French and Anglo-Norman eight-syllable couplet was only incompletely adapted by the first Middle English alliterative poets (see type 3), but the four-beat couplet (short couplet) became the favorite form among Middle English rhyming poets and dominated verse until Chaucer turned from it to the five-beat couplet. The selections that use the short couplet are *The Owl and the Nightingale*, *The Fox and the Wolf*, *The Land of Cokayne*, *Handling Sin*, *Sir Orfeo*, *The Bruce*, and *The Lover's Confession*.

6. Five-beat couplets, a^5a^5

This iambic-pentameter couplet (heroic couplet) was introduced into English narrative poetry by Chaucer at some time shortly before 1386. The only example here is *The Siege of Thebes*.

7. Seven-beat couplets, $x^4a^3x^4a^3$

This measure is known variously as common meter, septenary, heptameter, fourteener, and ballad meter. It is often printed as a four-line tail-rhyme stanza, and there is always a break (caesura) between the x^4 and the a^3. (Compare type 11.) Examples are *Poema Morale*, *Judas*, where in some stanzas, the first half-line has only three beats, not four, *The Tale of Beryn*, which was intended as a supplement to *The Canterbury Tales*, though Chaucer never used this meter, *St. Stephen and Herod*, and *Robyn and Gandelyn*.

8. Four-line stanzas, $a^2b^2a^2b^2$

The first and the last stanzas of *Christ and His Mother* are $a^2b^2x^2b^2$. The three symmetrical stanzas between these are linked by an a-rhyme: abab, acac, adad. Perhaps the poem is intended as an adaptation of the French *virelai*.

9. Four-line stanzas, $a^4b^4a^4b^4$

Thomas of Erceldoun is fundamentally built on four-line units but frequently has longer runs, such as ababababab (ll. 41–48) or ababacac (ll. 11–16).

10. Four-line stanzas, $a^6a^6a^6a^6$

In *Love in Paris* the lines of the macaronic stanzas, though irregular, can be scanned as six-beat, except for the last stanza, which apparently has $a^5a^6a^5a^6$.

11. Eight-line, tail-rhyme stanzas, $a^4b^3a^4b^3a^4b^3a^4b^3$

April is written in the manuscript in long-line, seven-beat couplets, but it has been printed here in eight-line stanzas, since every stanza except the third contains rhymes linking the first and following four-beat lines. The concluding stanza varies the rhyme scheme but reinforces the eight-line structure ($a^4b^3a^4b^3a^4b^3c^4c^3$).

12. Six-line stanzas, $a^4a^4a^4a^4b^4b^4$

In *Halidon Hill* the meter is irregular but, as in conventional alliterative poetry, primarily four-beat. Alliteration sometimes does not appear (l. 1), sometimes links two stressed words (l. 4), sometimes three (l. 3), and sometimes all four (l. 10).

13. Six-line, tail-rhyme stanzas, $a^4a^4a^4b^3a^4b^3$

This stanza is used in *The Five Joys of Mary*.

14. Six-line, tail-rhyme stanzas, $a^4a^4b^3c^4c^4b^3$

The pattern in *The Sayings of St. Bernard* resembles that of the so-called romance six ($a^4a^4b^3a^4a^4b^3$) parodied by Chaucer in "The Tale of Sir Thopas" (in *The Canterbury Tales*) but is not dominated by the insistent a-rhyme. *Dame Sirith* is also of this type, though some a-lines have only three beats, some b-lines have only two beats, and some passages are four-beat couplets (type 5).

15. Seven-line, tail-rhyme stanzas, $a^4b^2a^4b^2b^2b^4a^2$

The only example here is *Now Springs the Spray*, which is introduced by a three-line refrain, rhyming $a^2c^4a^2$ with the first stanza.

16. Seven-line, tail-rhyme stanzas, $a^4b^{3/4}a^4b^{3/4}b^{3/4}b^{3/4}c^3$

Alysoun is of this type, with a four-line refrain, $d^4d^4d^4c^3$, whose final c-line rhymes with each of the final lines in all four stanzas.

17. Seven-line stanzas, $a^5b^5a^5b^5b^5c^5c^5$

This stanza was introduced into English by Chaucer at some time shortly before 1372 and was made famous by his use of it in *Troilus and Criseyde*. It was subsequently called rhyme royal because of its later use in *The King's Quair*, attributed to James I of Scotland. The two examples here are *The Regiment of Princes* and *The Testament of Cressid*.

18. Eight-line stanzas, $a^4b^4a^4b^4a^4b^4a^4b^4$

A Love Rune exhibits this type of versification, an extension of the four-line, $a^4b^4a^4b^4$ stanza (type 9).

19. Eight-line stanzas, $a^5b^5a^5b^5b^5c^5b^5c^5$

On the Resurrection of Christ is the only example here of this type.

20. Nine-line stanzas, $a^5a^5b^5a^5a^5b^5b^5c^5c^5$

The Golden Targe is the only example here of this type.

21. Twelve-line, tail-rhyme stanzas, $a^4a^4b^3c^4c^4b^3d^4d^4b^3e^4e^4b^3$

This stanza is an extension of the six-line, tail-rhyme stanza (type 13). It appears in *Spring*, in which every line also contains alliteration, either within itself or with the following line. *The Dance of the Seven Deadly Sins* uses the same stanza.

22. Twelve-line stanzas, $a^4b^4a^4b^4a^4b^4a^4b^4c^4b^4c^4$

This stanza appears here only in *The Pearl*, in which more than two-thirds of the lines also have internal alliteration. For a discussion of concatenation of the stanzas, see below, page 339.

THE
TWELFTH
CENTURY

William the Conqueror

(ca. 1121, East Midland)

In the Benedictine monastery at Peterborough an anonymous scribe acquired a version of the *Old English Annals* and brought the compilation up to date as far as the year 1121. In summarizing the reign of King William I (1066–87) he presents a memorable prose account of the Conqueror, presumably drawn from his own observations. His extensive entry for the year 1087 (erroneously recorded as 1086) well illustrates the presence of a conscious literary style even at a time when Late Old English was about to become Early Middle English. The author writes critically, shows a real sense of history, understands the relation between cause and effect, and appreciates the significance of individual personality. He delights in rhetorical balance and, particularly in the passage quoted here, heightens his effects by the use of rhyme and alliteration. For the symbols ċ and ġ, see Appendix 1, page 548.

The best complete edition of all the *Old English Annals* is still Charles Plummer, *Two of the Saxon Chronicles Parallel* (Oxford, 1892), 2 vols. The best edition of *The Peterborough Chronicle* is edited by Cecily Clark (2nd ed., Oxford, 1970) and contains an important discussion of the development of prose style. The most convenient modernization is G. N. Garmonsway, *The Anglo-Saxon Chronicle* (London and New York, 1953). For the manuscript see *The Peterborough Chronicle*, in *Early English Manuscripts in Facsimile*, IV (Copenhagen and Baltimore, 1954). For bibliography see Wells, ch. 3.1; *CBEL*, 1.88–89, 5.84–86.

Witodliċe on his timan haefdon men myċel ġeswinc and swithe maniġe teonan. Castelas he let wyrċean and earme men swithe swenċean. Se cyng waes swa swithe stearc and benam of his undertheoddan man maniġ marc goldes and ma hundred punda seolfres, thet he nam be wihte and mid myċelan unrihte of his land-leode for
5 littelre neode. He waes on ġitsunge befeallan, and graedinaesse he lufode mid ealle.

He saette myċel deor-frith, and he laeġde laga thaerwith thet swa hwa-swa sloġe heort oththe hinde, thet hine man sċeolde blendian. He forbead tha heortas swylċe eac tha baras. Swa swithe he lufode tha hea-deor swilċe he waere heora faeder. Eac he saette be tham haran thet hi mosten freo faran. His rice men hit maendon,
10 and tha earme men hit beċeorodan. Ac he waes swa stith thet he ne rohte heora eallra nith. Ac hi moston mid ealle thes cynges wille folġian gif hi woldon libban oththe land habban—land, oththe eahta, oththe wel his sehta.

Wala-wa thet aeniġ man sċeolde modiġan swa, hine sylf upp ahebban, and ofer ealle men tellan! Se aelmihtiġa God cythae his saule mildheortnisse and do him
15 his synna forgifenesse!

36

[MODERNIZATION]

Truly in his time men had much toil and many, many troubles. He ordered castles to be built and poor men to toil exceedingly. The king was indeed most severe and seized from his subjects many a mark of gold and many more hundreds of pounds of silver. This he took by weight and with great injustice from the people of his land, with little need. He had fallen into avarice, and he was completely devoted to greed.

He established a great game preserve, and he laid down laws at the same time that, if anyone at all should slay a hart or a hind, he should be blinded. He closed the hunting of harts and also of boars. He loved the stags as much as if he were their father. As for the hares, also, he decreed that they were to travel free. His magnates complained about it, and the poor men grumbled about it. But he was so stubborn that he thought nothing of their unanimous hostility. They, however, had to follow the king's will completely if they wanted to survive or to have land—land, or possessions, or, indeed, his favors.

Alas that any man should be so proud, should exalt himself so high, and count himself above all men! May the Almighty God show mercy to his soul and grant him forgiveness for his sins!

The Anarchy of King Stephen

(ca. 1154, East Midland)

The final section of the Peterborough version of the *Old English Annals* was written by
another anonymous scribe at the end of Stephen's reign (1135–54), a generation later than
the entry concerning William the Conqueror.

A brief but dramatic portion of the entry for the year 1137 is presented here. In comparison
with the earlier chronicler, the last chronicler relies less on rhyme and alliteration and more
on parallelism and sentence structure to express his agitated emotions.

I ne can, ne I ne mai, tellen alle the wunder ne alle the pines that hi diden wrecce
men on this land, and that lastede tha nientiene wintre wile Stephne was king, and
aevre it was werse and werse.

Hi laeiden ġaeildes on the tunes aevre umwile and clepeden it "tenserie." Tha
5 the wrecce men ne hadden nan more to ġyven, tha raeveden hi and brendon alle
the tunes, that wel thu myhtes faren al a daeis fare, sculdest thu nevre finden man
in tune sittende ne land tiled. Tha was corn daere, and flesc and caese and butere,
for nan ne waes o the land. Wrecce men sturven of hungaer. Sume ieden on
aelmes the waren sumwile ricemen; sume fluġen ut of lande.

10 Wes naevre ġaet mare wrecched on land, ne naevre hethen men werse ne
diden than hi diden, for ofer sithon ne forbaren hi nouther circe ne cyrce-iaerd oc
namen al the god that tharinne was, and brenden sythen the cyrce and al tegaedere.
Ne hi ne forbaren biscopes land ne abbotes ne preostes ac raeveden munekes and
clerekes, and aevric man other the overmyhte.

15 Ġif two men other thrie coman ridend to an tun, al the tunscipe fluġaen for
heom, wenden that hi waeron raeveres. The biscopes and leredmen heom cursede
aevre, oc was heom naht tharof, for hi weron al forcursaed and forsworen and
forloren.

War-sae me tilede, the erthe ne bar nan corn, for the land was al fordon mid
20 swilce daedes, and hi saeden openlice that Christ slep and his halechen.

Swilc, and mare thanne we cunnen saein, we tholeden nientiene wintre for ure
sinnes.

[MODERNIZATION]

I neither know how, nor am able, to tell of all the horrors and all the tortures that they imposed upon the wretched men in this land, and this lasted for the nineteen winters while Stephen was king, and it was ever worse and worse.

They laid taxes upon the villages time after time and called it "protection." When the wretched men had no more to give, then they raided and burned all the villages, so that you could travel for a whole day's journey, yet would never find a man settled in a village, or land tilled. Then grain was dear, and meat and cheese and butter, for there was none in the land. Wretched men died of hunger. Some turned to alms who had once been rich men; some fled out of the country.

Never yet has there been a greater misery in any land, and heathen men never did worse than they did, for contrary to custom they spared neither church nor churchyard but took all the valuables that were within and then burned the church and all the rest together. They spared the land of neither bishop nor abbot nor priest but raided monks and clerics, and each one who could raided the other.

If two or three men came riding to a village, the entire community fled because of them, assumed that they were raiders. The bishops and clergymen anathematized them repeatedly, but that was nothing to them, for they were all utterly damned, forsworn, and abandoned.

Wheresoever one tilled, the earth bore no corn, for the land was all destroyed by such deeds, and they said openly that Christ and His saints were sleeping.

Such, and more than we are able to tell, we suffered for nineteen winters for our sins.

The Proverbs of Alfred

(ca. 1150–75, Southwestern)

The work known as *The Proverbs of Alfred* survives in four manuscripts, all of which were copied at dates considerably later than that of the lost original. They differ from each other in language, arrangement, and meter; but all agree in attributing the collection to Alfred. Alfred the Great, who became king of Wessex in 871 and died in 899, was a patron of letters and himself an author. Yet it seems unlikely that he prepared the original version of this poem in Old English. The contents are timeless, being derived partly from written sources, such as the Old Testament, and partly from universal oral tradition, but the linguistic and metrical evidence suggests that *The Proverbs* was composed in Sussex around 1150 or a little later. The poem, though conventional in content, is lively in style and was apparently popular enough to impress both Lawman and the author of *The Owl and the Nightingale*.

The selection is based on the Jesus College (Oxford) Manuscript (ca. 1280), which contains an early revision (ca. 1200?, Southwestern) divided into twenty-two sections, totaling 458 short lines. Approximately one-third of this version is printed here. The lines, usually printed as half-lines, have been expanded as long lines, as have the comparable lines of Lawman's *Brut* (pp. 49–53). The meter is semi-alliterative, semi-rhyming; see Introduction, type 3, page 30.

The best edition and commentary is O. S. Arngart, *The Proverbs of Alfred* (Lund, 1942, 1955), 2 vols. (The stanza numbers given here are not those of the conflated texts but of the separately edited Jesus College MS.) For bibliography see Wells, ch. 7.5; *CBEL*, 1.180, 5.121.

I

At Sevorde sete theynes monye,
Fele biscopes, and feole boc-ilered,
Eorles prute, knyhtes egleche.
Thar wes the eorl Alvrich, of thare lawe swithe wis,
5   And ek Ealvred, Englene hürde,
Englene dürlyng; on Englelonde he wes kyng.
    Heom he bigon lere, so ye mawe i-hüre,
Hu hi heore lif lede scholden.
Alvred, he wes in Englelond an king wel swithe strong.
10   He wes king, and he wes clerk; wel he luvede Godes werk.
He wes wis on his word and war on his werke;
He wes the wysüste mon that wes Englelonde on.

40

[MODERNIZATION]

At Seaford[1] many thanes met, many bishops, and many scholars, proud earls, and warlike knights. There was Earl Aelfric,[2] most wise in the law, and Alfred also, the shepherd of the English, the darling of the English; in England he was king.

He began to teach them, as you may hear, how they should conduct their lives. Alfred was in England a king most strong indeed. He was king, and he was cleric; well he loved the work of God. He was wise of word and wary in action; he was the wisest man that there was in England.

[1] In Sussex.
[2] Unidentified.

XIII

Thus queth Alvred:
"If thu havest seorewe, ne seye thu hit than arewe.
Seye hit thine sadelbowe, and ryd thee singinde forth.
Thenne wile wene thet thine wise ne con
5   That thee thine wise wel thee lyke.
Serewe if thu havest, and the erewe hit wot,
Byfore, he thee meneth; byhynde, he thee teleth.
Thu hit myht segge swych mon that hit thee ful wel on;
Wythute echere ore he on thee muchele more.
10   Byhüd hit on thire heorte, that thee eft ne smeorte;
Ne let thu hyne wite al that thin heorte bywite."

XIV

Thus queth Alvred:
"Ne schaltu nevere thi wif by hire wlyte cheose,
For never none thinge that heo to thee bryngeth.
Ac leorne hire cüste—heo cutheth hi wel sone!
5   For mony mon for ayhte üvele i-auhteth,
And ofte mon of fayre, frakele i-cheoseth.
Wo is him that üvel wif bryngeth to his cotlif;
So him is alyve that üvele y-wyveth,
For he schal uppon eorthe dreori i-würthe.
10   Mony mon singeth that wif hom bryngeth;
Wiste he hwat he brouhte, wepen he myhte."

XV

Thus queth Alvred:
"Ne würth thu never so wod ne so wyn-drunke
That evere segge thine wife alle thine wille.
For if heo i-seye thee bivore thine i-vo alle,
5   And thu hi myd worde i-wreththed hevedest,
Ne schulde heo hit lete, for thing lyvyinde,
That heo ne scholde thee forth upbreyde of thine baleu-sythes.
  "Wymmon is word-wod and haveth tunge too swift.
Theyh heo wel wolde, ne may heo hi nowiht welde."

[MODERNIZATION]

Thus said Alfred: "If you have a sorrow, do not tell it to one who is a betrayer. Tell it to your saddlebow, and ride forth singing. Then anyone who does not know your state of affairs will suppose that your state pleases you well. If you have a sorrow and the betrayer knows about it, in your presence he will commiserate with you; behind your back he will mock you. You might tell your sorrow to the very person who would heartily wish it on you; without any pity he will wish so much more on you. Conceal it in your heart, so that it may not bring you pain again; and do not let him know all that your heart may care about."

[MODERNIZATION]

Thus said Alfred: "You must never choose your wife by her looks, and never for anything that she brings to you. But learn to know her behavior—she will show that very quickly! For many a man because of wealth calculates amiss, and often a man chooses as one who is beautiful one who is vile. Woeful is he who brings an evil wife to his dwelling; so too is it for him in his life who marries badly, for he shall be miserable on the earth. Many a man sings who brings home a wife; if he knew what he brought, he might well weep."

[MODERNIZATION]

Thus said Alfred: "Never be so foolish or so drunk with wine that you ever tell all your counsel to your wife. For if she were to see all your enemies in front of you, and you had angered her with some word, she wouldn't be able to stop herself, for any living thing, from scolding you right then for your misfortunes.

"Woman is word-crazy and has too swift a tongue. Even though she might well wish to, she can't control it at all."

XVI

Thus queth Alvred:
"Idelschipe and overprute, that lereth yong wif üvele thewes,
And ofte that heo wolde do that heo ne scholde.
Thene unthew lihte leten heo myhte
5   If heo ofte a swote forswunke were.
Theyh hit is üvel to buwe that beo nüle treowe,
For ofte museth the kat after hire moder.
    "The mon that let wymmon his mayster i-würthe
Ne schal he never beon i-hürd his wordes loverd,
10   Ac heo hine schal steorne totrayen and toteone,
And selde würth he blythe and gled, the mon that is his wives qued.
    "Mony appel is bryht withute and bitter withinne;
So is mony wymmon on hyre fader bure
Schene under schete, and theyh heo is schendful.
15   So is mony gedelyng godlyche on horse
And is, theyh, lütel wurth—
Wlonk bi the glede and üvel at thare neode."

XVII

Thus queth Alvred:
"Nevre thu, bi thine lyve, the word of thine wyve
Too swithe thu ne arede.
If heo beo i-wreththed myd worde other myd dede,
5   Wymmon wepeth for mod oftere than for eny god,
And ofte, lude and stille, for to vordrye hire wille.
Heo wepeth otherwhile for to do thee gyle.
    "Salomon hit haveth i-sed that wymmon can wel üvelne red.
The hire red foleweth, heo bryngeth hine to seorewe,
10   For hit seyth in the Leoth as cuenes forteoth.
Hit is ifürn i-seyd that cold red is quene red;
Hu he is unlede that foleweth hire rede.
    "Ich hit ne segge nouht forthan that god thing nys god wymmon
The mon the hi may i-cheose and i-covere over othre."

[MODERNIZATION]

Thus said Alfred: "Idleness and conceit teach a young wife evil habits and often make her want to do what she should not. Vice she might easily avoid if often she were exhausted in sweat. Yet it is hard to bend that which does not wish to be straight, for often the kitten will chase mice in the same way as her mother.

"The man that lets a woman become his master will never be listened to as the lord of his own word, but she will severely torment and harass him, and seldom will he be contented and happy, the man who is his wife's victim.

"Many an apple is outwardly shiny and bitter within; so too many a woman in her father's bower is fair under the sheet and yet is disgraceful. So too, many a companion is handsome on horse and is yet worth little—brave at the fireside and useless at need."

[MODERNIZATION]

Thus said Alfred: "Never in your life accept the word of your wife too soon. If she is enraged by word or by deed, a woman will weep for anger more often than for any good reason, and often, loud or soft, to get her own way. At other times she will weep to cheat you.

"Solomon has said that woman well knows evil counsel. He who follows her counsel, she will bring him to sorrow, for it says in the Song[3] that women deceive. It is said of old that woman's counsel is cold counsel, that he is wretched who follows her counsel.

"I do not therefore say that a good woman is not a good thing for the man who can choose her and select her from among the others."

---

[3] Presumably in reference to Proverbs (attributed to Solomon) 7:5: ". . . keep thee from the strange woman, / from the stranger which flattereth with her words."

Poema Morale

(ca. 1175, Southwestern–West Midland)

ॐ

Poema Morale provides a fine example of the homiletic tradition of the twelfth century. Like the last Peterborough chronicler (pp. 38–39), the preacher is concerned with the collective sins of the people, but he is also aware of personal sin. He begins his poem dramatically by confessing his own frailty and then goes on to lecture his listeners on how to behave toward God and their fellow man. The Last Judgment, he warns them, will condemn the unrighteous to hell and will admit to heaven only those who have loved both God and man.

The poem evidently retained its popularity for a long time after it was composed and was imitated in other lyrics as late as the fourteenth century. It is preserved in seven different manuscript versions, varying in length and in wording, that represent revisions made by adapters who admired the spirit of the now vanished original. The selection is based on the earliest extant version (contained in the Lambeth Manuscript), which contains only 270 long lines as compared to others that run to some 400 lines. The section printed here is the beginning of the poem.

The meter is as remarkable as the spirit and contents. It is the first known English adaptation of the Latin septenary; see Introduction, type 7, page 31. The long seven-beat lines have here been printed, as is customary, in alternate four-beat and three-beat lines.

A useful sketch of the background of the poem and a reconstruction of its text will be found in the edition by Hans Marcus, *Das frühmittelenglische Poema Morale*, Palaestra 194 (Leipzig, 1934). For bibliography see Wells ch. 7.25; *CBEL*, 1.180, 5.121.

[Lines 1–48]

	Ich em nu alder° thene Ich wes	older
	A wintre and a lare.°	A ... In winters and in learning
	Ich welde mare thene Ich dede;°	
	Mi wit ahte bön° mare.	wit ... sense ought to be
5	Wel longe Ich habbe child i-bön°	been
	A worde and a dede;	

---

3. I possess more (experience now) than I had

46

	Poem	Gloss
	Thah° Ich bö° a wintre ald	Though am
	Too yung Ich em on rede.°	judgment
	Unnet° lif Ich habbe i-led°	Useless led
10	And yet,° me thingth, i-lede.°	still am leading
	Thenne° Ich me bithenche° wel,	When consider
	Ful sare° Ich me adrede;°	sorely dread
	Mest al thet Ich habbe i-don	
	Bifealt° to childhade.	Pertains
15	Wel° late Ich habbe me bithocht,°	Too considered
	Bute° God me nu rede.°	Unless advise
	Föle° idel word Ich habbe i-quethen°	Many spoken
	Söththen° Ich speke kuthe;°	Since could
	Föle yunge dede i-don	
20	The me ofthincheth nuthe.°	**The** . . . Which I regret now
	Mest al thet me likede er°	**me** . . . pleased me before
	Nu hit me misliketh.	
	Tha müchel fülieth° his wil,	**Tha** . . . He who (too) much follows
	Hine-sölf he biswiketh.°	**Hine-sölf** . . . Himself deceives
25	Ich mihte habbe bet° i-don,	better
	Hefde Ich the i-selthe.°	**Hefde** . . . If I'd had the fortune
	Nu Ich walde,° ah° Ich ne mei°	would but can't
	For elde° and for unhelthe.	**For elde** Because of age
	Elde is me bistolen on°	**is** . . . has stolen on me
30	Er° Ich hit wiste;°	Before knew
	Ne michte° Ich seon bifore me	**Ne michte** . . . Nor could
	For smike° ne for miste.	smoke
	Erghe° we beoth to done god,	Unwilling
	And to üfele° al too thriste.°	evil bold
35	Mare eie stondeth men of monne	
	Thanne höm do of Criste.°	
	The wel ne doth the hwile hö müghen,°	Very rue
	Wel° oft hit schal rowen°	
	Thenne hö mawen sculen and repen°	
40	Thet° hö er sowen.°	That which **er sowen** sowed before
	Do he to Gode thet he müghe°	can
	The hwile he bö° alive.	is
	Ne lipnie na mon° too müchel	**Ne** . . . Let no man trust
	To childe ne to wive;	

35–36. Men stand more in awe of man than they do of Christ.
37. Those who do not do well while they can
39. When they shall mow and reap

45   The him-sölve forget°
    For wive ne for childe,
    He scal° cumen in üvel stüde°
    Bute° him God bö° milde.

The ... He who forgets himself

shall   **üvel stüde** evil stead
Unless   is

LAWMAN

The Brut

(ca. 1200, Southwestern–West Midland)

☙

Lawman was a priest at Areley Church near Redstone (north of Worcester) on the River Severn. His name, which is often modernized as Layamon (in the manuscript of *The Brut* it is spelled Laʒamon, Laweman, Loweman), means "man of law." His father's name was Leovenath. Otherwise, we know nothing of him. His *Brut* is, however, a distinguished achievement reflecting the strength of the native English tradition in the West Country, which was later to produce other great poets, such as Langland. Lawman's *Brut* is derived from Wace's Anglo-Norman poem the *Roman de Brut*, which Wace had dedicated to Queen Eleanor in 1155. The *Roman de Brut* was itself a translation of Geoffrey of Monmouth's prose *History of the Kings of Britain*, composed in Latin (ca. 1138–39). Geoffrey's pseudohistory was written primarily for learned clerics; Wace addressed his poem to the members of the court of King Henry II; Lawman aimed at his rural English audience, whose culture evidently still remained relatively unaffected by the Norman Conquest.

Lawman's materials were ultimately determined by Geoffrey's original inventions, which Wace had followed closely. The first 9,000 lines of *The Brut* tell how Brutus (hence the title), a legendary descendant of Aeneas of Troy, founded a royal line in Britain; the next 5,000 recount the rise and fall of Arthur; and the last 2,000 lines complete the enumeration of the British kings to A.D. 689, when the descendants of the Anglo-Saxon invaders took over.

The two passages printed below represent Lawman at his most original, but even these are expansions of his source rather than completely new inventions. The legend of the Round Table is not mentioned at all by Geoffrey but is briefly alluded to by Wace (*Roman de Brut*, ll. 9747–60). Arthur's departure to Avalon is described perfunctorily by Geoffrey in his *History* (XI, iii) and by Wace (ll. 13,275–81). The details of Arthur's reception by Morgen la Fée in the Island of Apples are recounted by Geoffrey in his Latin poem *The Life of Merlin* (ll. 908–40), and Lawman had evidently learned something of this tradition second-hand, though he or his scribe mistakenly refers to the otherworld queen Morgen as Argante.

Stylistically, Lawman's verse is more primitive than Wace's, and its effect more rousing, for it echoes the tone of Old English heroic poetry, particularly in battle scenes. Lawman resolutely avoids the adoption of foreign words, even when he is translating directly from Anglo-Norman. Indeed, his resulting lines, both in imagery and meter, frequently sound as if they had been composed in Old English.

> For heore múchele móde · mórth-ǧomenn wrohten.
> (Because of their great spirit they wrought games of slaughter.)

The meter is semi-alliterative, semi-rhyming verse; see Introduction, type 3, page 30.

The only edition is *Laʒamons Brut*, edited and translated by Sir Frederick Madden (London, 1847), 3 vols. G. L. Brook has published *Selections from Laʒamon's Brut* (Oxford, 1963) and is publishing a definitive edition, *Laʒamon: Brut*, EETS 250– (London, 1963–). For manuscript see Plate 1, p. 16. For bibliography see Wells, ch. 3.3; *CBEL*, 1.163–65, 5.117. Also see: J. S. P. Tatlock, *The Legendary History of Britain* (Berkeley, 1950), pp. 483–531, and R. S. Loomis, "Layamon's *Brut*," in *Arthurian Literature in the Middle Ages*, ed. R. S. Loomis (Oxford, 1959), pp. 104–11.

The Round Table

Seoththen hit seith in there tale, the king ferde to Cornwale.
Ther him com to anan that waes a crafti weorcman,
And thene king i-mette, and feiere hine graette.
    "Hail seo thu, Arthur, athelest kinge.
Ich aem thin aghe mon. Moni lond Ich habbe thurh-gan.
Ich con of treo-werkes wunder feole craftes.
Ich i-herde süggen biyeonde sae neowe tidende
That thine cnihtes at thine borde gunnen fihte
A midewinteres daei; moni ther feollen;
For heore müchele mode morth-gomenn wrohten;
And for heore hehghe cünne aelc wolde beon withinne.
    "Ah Ich thee wülle wurche a bord swithe hende
That ther maghen setten to sixtene hundred and ma,
Al turn abuten, that nan ne beon withuten,
Withuten and withinne, mon to-yaeines monne.
Whenne thu wült riden, with thee thu miht hit leden,
And setten hit whar thu wülle after thine i-wille;
And ne dert thu navere adrede, to there worlde longen,
That aevere aeine modi cniht at thine borde makie fiht,
For ther scal the hehghe beon aefne than loghe.
Timber me lete biwinnen and that beord biginne."
    To feouwer wikene virste that werc wes i-vorthed.
To ane heghe daeie that hired wes i-somned,
And Arthur himseolf beh sone to than borde,
And hehte alle his cnihtes to than borde forthrihtes.
Tho alle weoren i-seten cnihtes to heore mete,
Tha spaec aelc with other alse hit weore his brother.
Alle heo seten abuten; nes ther nan withuten.
Aevere aelches cünnes cniht there wes swithe wel i-diht.
Alle heo weoren bi ane, the hehghe and tha laghe;
Ne mihten ther nan yelpen for othere künnes scenchen,
Other his i-veren the at than beorde weoren.
    This wes that ilke bord that Brüttes of yelpeth
And sügeth feole cünne lesinge bi Arthure than kinge.
Swa deth aver alc mon the other luvien con;
Yif he is him too leof, thenne wüle he lighen,
And süggen on him wurthscipe mare thenne he beon wurthe;
Ne beo he no swa lüther mon that his freond him wel ne on.
Aeft, yif on volke feondscipe arereth
An aever aei time betweone twon monnen,
Me con by than laethe lasinge süggen.

50

The Brut

Afterward, it says in the tale, the king went to Cornwall. There came to him then one who was a skillful carpenter and met the king and greeted him graciously.

"Hail to you, Arthur, noblest king. I am your own man. Many a land have I traveled through. In woodwork I am master of wondrous many skills. I have heard tell over the seas new tidings, that your knights at your table began to fight on a midwinter's day. Many fell there; out of their high pride they wrought deadly sport, and because of their high lineage each wished to be innermost.

"But I will construct for you a most convenient table, at which sixteen hundred men and more may sit down, all in turn around, so that none will be outermost—outer and inner, man opposite man. When you wish to ride forth, you can take it with you and set it up where you will according to your wish; and you need never fear, to the length of the world, that any proud knight will ever make strife at your table, for there the high shall be equal with the low. Allow me to gather the lumber and begin the table."

By the end of four weeks the work was completed. On a festival day the people were summoned, and Arthur himself came at once to the table and ordered all his knights to the table forthwith. When the knights were all seated for their meal, then each spoke to the next as if it were to his brother. They were all seated around; there was no one outermost. Every rank of knight was very well treated. They were all as one, the high and the low; nor could any there boast of a special serving of drinks different from that given his companions who were at the table.

This was the same table that the Bretons boast of and tell many kinds of lies about Arthur the king. Thus everyone does who loves someone else; if he is too dear to him, then he will lie and attribute more honor to him than he is worth; nor is there any man so base that his own friend will not wish him well. Again, if, among people, at any time enmity arises between two men, they will tell lies about the one who is loathed.

Theh he weore the bezste mon the aevere aet at borde,
The mon the him weore lath, him cuthe last finden.
Ne al soh ne al les that leod-scopes singeth;
45 Ah this is that soththe bi Arthure than kinge;
Nes naever ar swülc king, swa duhti thurh alle thing.
For that sothe stond a than writen hu hit is i-wurthen,
Ord from than aenden, of Arthure than kinge,
No mare no lasse buten alse his laghen weoren.

[Lines 28,589–651]

The Passing of Arthur

Arthur wes forwunded, wunder ane swithe.
Ther to him com a cnave the wes of his cünne.
He wes Cadores sune, the eorles of Cornwaile.
Constantin hehte the cnave; he wes than kinge deore.
5 Arthur him lokede on, ther he lai on folden,
And thas word seide mid sorhfulle heorte:
"Constantin, thu art wilcume. Thu weore Cadores sone.
Ich thee bitache here mine kineriche.
And wite mine Brüttes a to thines lifes;
10 And hald heom alle tha laghen tha habbeoth i-stonden a mine daghen,
And alle tha laghen gode tha bi Utheres daghen stode.
"And Ich wülle varen to Avalun to vairest alre maidene,
To Argante, there quene, alven swithe sceone;
And heo scal mine wunden makien alle i-sunde,
15 Al hal me makien mid haleweighe drenchen.
And seothe Ich cumen wülle to mine kineriche
And wunien mid Brütten mid müchelere wünne."
Aefne than worden ther com of se wenden
That wes an sceort bat lithen, sceoven mid üthen;
20 And two wimmen therinne, wunderliche i-dihte;
And heo nomen Arthur anan and a-neouste hine vereden
And softe hine a-dun leiden, and forth gunnen hine lithen.
Tha wes hit i-wurthen that Merlin seide whilen,
That weore unimete care of Arthures forthfare.
25 Brüttes i-leveth yete that he bön on live
And wunnien in Avalun mid fairest alre alven,
And lokieth evere Brüttes yete whan Arthur cumen lithe.
Nis naver the mon i-boren of naver nane bürde i-coren
The cunne of than sothe of Arthure sügen mare.
30 But while wes an witeghe, Merlin i-hate;
He bodede mid worde—his quithes weoren sothe—
That an Arthur sculde yete cum Anglen to fülste.

[MODERNIZATION]

Though he were the best man that ever ate at table, they could find objection to the man who is loath to them. What the people's poets sing is neither all truth nor all lies. But this is the truth about Arthur the king: never before was there such a king, in all things so doughty. For the truth has been set down in writing how the deeds of Arthur the king came to pass, from beginning to end, neither more nor less, but just as his way of life was.

[MODERNIZATION]

Arthur was mortally wounded, grievously and severely. To him there came a youth who was of his kin. He was the son of Cador, the earl of Cornwall. Constantine the youth was called; he was dear to the king. From where he lay on the ground, Arthur looked upon him and spoke these words with sorrowful heart:

"You are welcome, Constantine. You were Cador's son. I here entrust my kingdom to you. And guard my Britons ever in your lifetime; and on their behalf keep all the laws that existed in my days and all the good laws that in Uther's days existed.

"And I will go to Avalon to the fairest of all maidens, to Argant the queen, an elf most beautiful; and she will make my wounds all sound, make me all whole with healing potions. And then I shall come back to my kingdom and dwell with the Britons in great bliss."

Even at these words, there came traveling from the sea a short boat, moving, driven by the waves, and two women in it, wondrously clad; and they took Arthur into it and went in beside him and laid him down gently, and they journeyed away.

Then was fulfilled what Merlin had previously said, that there would be unbounded sorrow at the departure of Arthur. The Britons still believe that he is alive and dwells in Avalon with the fairest of all elves, and the Britons ever look for the time, even yet, when Arthur will come back. Never has the man been born of any chosen woman that can tell more of the truth concerning Arthur. But once there was a wizard called Merlin; he announced by word—his sayings were true—that an Arthur was still to come as an aid to the Angles.

The Owl and the Nightingale

(ca. 1198–1216, Southwestern)

❦

The Owl and the Nightingale is a typical product of the intellectual renaissance of the twelfth century. The two argumentative birds in the poem sound remarkably like the London schoolboys of that era, who, according to William FitzStephen (d. 1190), delighted in debating:

> Some engage in disputation for display . . . , others for truth. . . . In epigrams, rimes, and verses . . . they pull their comrades to pieces without mentioning names; they fling at them scoffs and sarcasms; they touch the failings of their schoolmates or even of greater people with Socratic salt.

The genre of the poetic debate was understandably popular in the scholarly world of the twelfth century, and extant Latin examples, such as *The Debate Between Wine and Water*, parallel *The Owl and the Nightingale* in several respects. Even the title *Altercacio inter Filomenam et Bubonem*, given to the Middle English poem by the scribe, reflects its academic tone; and the author's language and his use of all the techniques of disputation similarly reflect the rhetorical tradition of the period.

In one respect, however, *The Owl and the Nightingale* is unique, for it is the only extant debate composed in English during the twelfth century. If for no other reason than this, the identity of the author has excited scholarly inquiry. Possibly he was the "Maister Nichole of Guldeforde" (ll. 191 and 1,746) whom the birds chose as their umpire. If so, we may surmise that he had been reared in Guildford, Surrey, that he knew the intellectual excitement of the nearby London area, was a scholar (hence called Master) equally at home in English, French, and Latin, served as a cleric in the remote village of Portisham (l. 1,752), in Dorset, and elected to compose his poem in English rather than in the more fashionable French or Latin because he hoped to gain the attention of a simple, rural audience. Like the poor but brilliant curate in many an English novel, he may have hoped to make the best of his unpromising situation.

The meaning of the poem has also aroused extensive discussion. The medieval encyclopedists had accumulated much strange lore concerning such birds as the owl (see *The Properties of Things*, p. 490), but the author relies on his own observations of nature. He treats the nightingale as what it is, namely, a sweet songster who comes to England only as a fair-weather visitor and seldom ventures farther north; he also appropriately portrays the owl as the faithful, if unappreciated, companion of man. The nightingale favors the foreign fashion of amorous lyrics and courtly love; the owl instinctively clings to the traditional music of the church and upholds the contemplative life of the monasteries. But why does the author not tell us which bird deserves to win the argument? Probably the answer lies in the twelfth-century attitude toward the definition of truth. Scholars allowed that two arguments, even if mutually incompatable, could both be true provided that each was self-consistent. The author may have felt that the logical position of the nightingale was philosophically true while the religious position of the owl was theologically true.

The Owl and the Nightingale

The meter is rhyming, four-beat couplets; see Introduction, type 5, page 31.
The best edition of the poem is *The Owl and the Nightingale*, ed. E. G. Stanley (London, 1960). For a modernization see the edition by J. W. H. Atkins (Cambridge, 1922). For the two extant manuscripts see *The Owl and the Nightingale Reproduced in Facsimile*, ed. N. R. Ker, EETS 251 (London, 1963). For bibliography see Severs, ch. 7.45.

[handwritten: Once upon / It was one summer day]

Ich was in one sumere° dale;   *[handwritten: In one ... very hidden corner]*   **one sumere** a summer
In one swithe dighele hale°   **swithe** ... very hidden corner
I-herde Ich° holde grete tale   *[handwritten: I heard the matter of his great cattle]*   **I-herde Ich** I heard
An ule and one nightingale.
5   That plait° was stif and starc° and strong,   **debate**   **firm**
Sum hwile softe, and lud among;°   between
And either aghen° other swal°   against   swelled
And let that üvele mod° ut al;   **üvele mod** bad temper
And either seide of otheres cüste°   manners
10   That alre-wörste° that hö wüste;°   **That alre-wörste** Worst of all   **hö wüste** she knew
And, hure and hure, °of otheres songe   *[handwritten: a pleading / plaintiff]*   **hure** ... certainly
Hi holde plaiding swithe° stronge.   **Hi** ... They held a debate very
     The nightingale bigon the speche
In one hurne° of one breche,°   **one hurne** a corner   field
15   And sat upone vaire boghe,°   **vaire boghe** fair bough
Thar° were abute blosme inoghe,°   Where   enough
In ore vaste,° thicke hegge°   **ore vaste** a tight   hedge
I-meind mid spire° and grene segge.°   **I-meind** ... Mixed with grass   sedge
Hö° was the gladur for the rise°   She   branch
20   And song a vele cünne wise.°
Bet thughte° the dreim° that he° were   **Bet thughte** Rather seemed   sound   it
Of harpe and pipe, than he nere;°   **than** ... than that it were not
Bet thughte that he were i-shote°   cast
Of harpe and pipe than of throte.
25   Tho° stod an old stoc° thar biside   Then   stump
Thar° the ule song hire tide,°   Where   **song** ... sang her hours
And was mid° ivi al bigrowe;°   with   overgrown
Hit was thare ule earding-stowe.°   **thare** ... the owl's dwelling-place
The nightingale hi i-segh°   **hi i-segh** ... looked at her
30   And hi bihold and oversegh,°   looked her over
And thughte wel vul of thare ule,°   **thughte** ... considered the owl most foul
For me hi halt lodlich and fule.°

20. And sang in many a kind of manner.
32. For people think her loathly and foul.

NIGHTINGALE

    "Unwight," hö° sede, "awei thu flö!°
    Me is° the würs that Ich thee sö.°
35 I-wis,° for thine vule lete°
    Wel° oft Ich mine song forlete.°
    Min hörte atflith, and falt° mi tonge,
    Hwönne thu art to me i-thrunge,°
    Me lüste bet speten° thane singe
40 Of° thine fule yoghelinge."°
      Thös ule abod forth° hit was eve.
    Hö ne mighte no leng bileve,°
    Vor hire hörte was so gret
    That wel negh° hire fnast atschet,°
45 And warp° a word tharafter longe:

Unwight, hö Monster, she	flee
Me is I am	see
Indeed **vule lete** foul behavior	
Very	abandon
atflith . . . flies off and fails	
art . . . have pressed upon me	
Me . . . I'd sooner spit	
Because of **fule yoghelinge** foul hooting	
abod forth waited till	
Hö . . . She could no longer refrain	
wel negh very nearly **fnast atschet** breath exploded	
uttered	

OWL

    "Hu thincthe° nu bi mine songe?
    Wenst° thu that Ich ne cunne singe
    Thegh° Ich ne cünne of writelinge?°
    Ilome° thu dest° me grame°
50 And seist me° bothe töne° and schame.
    Yif Ich thee hölde° on mine vote°—
    So hit bitide° that Ich mote!°—
    And thu were ut of thine rise,°
    Thu sholdest singe an other wise."°
55   The nightingale yaf° answare:

Hu thincthe How do you think	
Suppose	
Though **ne . . .** don't know about chirping	
Often	cause grief
seist me utter against me	injury
held	foot
hit bitide might it happen	might
branch	
tune	
gave	

NIGHTINGALE

    "Yif Ich me loki with the bare°
    And me schilde with the blete,°
    Ne reche° Ich noght of thine threte.
    Yif Ich me holde in mine hegge,°
60 Ne reche Ich never what thu segge.°
    Ich wot° that thu art unmilde
    With höm that ne mughe° from thee schilde,
    And thu tukest wrothe and üvele,°
    Whar thu might, over° smale fughele.°
65 Vorthi° thu art loth° al fuel-künne,°
    And alle hö° thee driveth hönne°
    And thee bischricheth and bigredeth°
    And wel narewe° thee biledeth;°
    And ek, forthe,° the sülve möse,°
70 Hire-thonkes,° wolde thee totöse.°
      "Thu art lodlich° to biholde,
    And thu art loth in monie volde.°

loki . . . guard against the open	
schilde . . . hide against exposure	
care	
hedge	
say	
know	
ne mughe cannot	
tukest . . . pick angrily and maliciously	
on birds	
Therefore loathsome to bird-kind	
alle hö they all hence	
bischricheth . . . shriek at and scold	
wel narewe very closely chase	
therefore **sülve möse** very titmouse	
Gladly tear to pieces	
loathly	
loth . . . loathsome in many ways	

Thi bodi is short; thi swöre° is smal; neck
Grettere is thin heved° than thu al; head

75 Thin eyene böth° col-blake and brode **eyene böth** eyes are
Right swo hö° weren i-peint mid wode.° **Right**...Just as if they **mid wode** with
 woad
Thu starest so° thu wille abiten° as if bite up
Al that thu mighst mid clivres° smiten. talons
Thi bile is stif and scharp and hoked

80 Right so° an owel° that is croked; **Right so** Just like awl
Tharmid° thu clackest° oft and longe, With it chatter
And that is on° of thine songe!° one songs
Ac thu thretest to° mine fleshe; **Ac**...But you threaten
Mid thine clivres woldest me meshe.° **clivres**...talons you'd like to mash me

85 Thee were i-cündur to° one frogge **Thee**...You'd be better suited for
That sit at mülne° under cogge!° **sit**...sits at a mill cog-wheel
Snailes, müs, and fule wighte° **müs**...mice, and foul creatures
Böth° thine cünde° and thine righte. Are kind
 "Thu sittest a-dai and flight a-night;

90 Thu cüthest° that thu art on unwight.° show **on unwight** a monster
Thu art lodlich° and unclene— loathly
Bi° thine neste Ich hit mene Regarding
And ek bi thine fule° brode; foul
Thu fedest on höm a wel ful fode.° **wel**...very foul progeny

95 Wel wostu that° hi döth tharinne: **wostu that** do you know what
Hi fuleth° hit up to the chinne. dirty
Hö sitteth thar so hi bö bisne.° **so**...as if they were blind
Tharbi men seggeth° a vorbisne:° say proverb
'Dahet habbe that ilke best° **Dahet**...A curse on every beast

100 That fuleth his owe° nest.' own
 "That° other yer a faukun bredde;° The **faukun bredde** falcon was breeding
His nest noght wel he ne bihedde.° guarded
Tharto thu stele° in o day stole
And leidest tharon thi fule ey.° **fule ey** foul egg

105 Tho° hit bicom° that he haghte,° When happened **he haghte** it hatched
And of his eyre briddes wraghte,°
He broghte his briddes mete,
Bihold his nest, i-segh hi° ete. **i-segh hi** saw them
He i-segh bi one halve

110 His nest i-fuled uthalve.° **i-fuled uthalve** befouled outside
The faucun° was wroth with his bridde° falcon chicks
And lude yal and sterne chidde:
'Seggeth° me, hwo haveth this i-do? Tell
Öw nas never i-cünde° tharto. **Öw**...You were never accustomed

115 Hit was i-don öw a lothe cüste.° **öw**...to you in a loathsome way
Segge me yif ye hit wiste.'° knew of

106. And from his eggs chicks were born

57

Tho quath that on° and quad that other,   **that on** the one
'I-wis,° it was ure ower° brother,   Indeed   own
The yond° that haveth that grete heved.°   **The yond** That one there   head
120   Wai° that he nis° tharof bireved!   Alas   is not
Worp° hit ut mid° the alre-würste,°   Throw   with   worst of all
That his necke him toberste!'°   may burst
The faucun i-lefde° his bridde°   **faucun i-lefde** falcon believed   chicks
And nom° that fule brid amidde°   took   by the middle
125   And warp° hit of than° wilde bowe,   threw   **of than** off the
Thar pie° and crowe hit todrowe.°   **Thar pie** Where magpie   tore apart
    "Herbi men seggeth° a bispel,°   tell   parable
Thegh° hit ne bö fulliche spel.°   Though   **ne** ... isn't completely a fable
Al so° hit is bi than ungode°   **Al so** Just as   **than ungode** the worthless person
130   That is i-cumen of fule brode
And is meind° with frö° mönne;   **is meind** has mingled   well-born
Ever he cüth° that he com thönne,°   shows   **com thönne** came thence
That he com of than adel eye,°   **than** ... the addled egg
Thegh° he a° frö nest leie.°   Though   in a   might lie
135   Thegh appel trendli° from thon tröwe°   may roll   **thon tröwe** the tree
Thar° he and other mid° gröwe,   Where   together
Thegh he bö tharfrom bicume,°   **he** ... it may have moved away
He cüth° wel whönene° he is i-cume."   **He cüth** It shows   whence
    Thös word ayaf° the nightingale,   uttered
140   And after thare° longe tale   that
Hö song so° lude and so scharpe   as
Right so me grülde schille° harpe.   **Right** ... As if one plucked a shrill
Thös ule lüste thiderward°   **lüste thiderward** listened to it
And hold hire eye nötherward°   downward
145   And sat toswolle and i-bolwe°   **toswolle** ... swollen and bursting
Al so° hö hadde one frogge i-swolwe,   **Al so** As if
For hö wel wiste° and was i-war   knew
That hö song hire a bisemar:°   **hire** ... to her in mockery
And, notheles, hö yaf° andsware: gave

       OWL

150   "Whi neltu flön° into the bare°   **neltu flön** won't you fly   open
And schewi hwether unker bö°   **hwether** ... which of us is
Of brighter höwe,° of vairur blö?"°   hue   **vairur blö** fairer color

      NIGHTINGALE

    "No. Thu havest wel scharpe clawe,°   claws
Ne kepich noght° that thu me clawe.   **Ne** ... And I don't wish
155   Thu havest clivres swithe° stronge;   **clivres swithe** talons very
Thu twengst tharmid so° döth a tonge.°   **twengst** ... pinch with them as   pair of tongs
Thu thoghtest, so doth thine i-like,°   **thoghtest** ... thought, as those like you do

Mid° faire worde me biswike.° — With **me biswike** to betray me
Ich nolde don that° thu me raddest;° — **nolde** . . . wouldn't do what / advised
160 Ich wiste° wel that thu me misraddest.° — knew / misadvised
Schamie thee° for thin unrede!° — **Schamie thee** Shame on you / bad advice
Unwroghen° is thi swikelhede.° — Exposed / treachery
Schild° thine swikeldom° vram the lighte, — Hide / villainy
And hüd that woghe° among the righte. — **hüd** . . . hide the crooked
165 Hwane thu wilt thin unright spene,° — expend
Loke that hit ne bö° i-sene; — is
Vor swikeldom haveth schome and hete° — hate
Yif hit is ope and underyete.° — **ope** . . . open and perceived
   "Ne speddestu noght mid° thine unwrenche,° — **Ne** . . . Nor did you succeed with / guile
170 For Ich am war° and can wel blenche.° — wary / dodge
Ne helpth noght that thu bö too thriste.° — bold
Ich wolde vighte bet° mid liste° — better / cunning
Than thu mid al thine strengthe.
Ich habbe on brede° and ek° on lengthe — in breadth / also
175 Castel god on mine rise.° — branch
'Wel fight that wel flighth,'° seith the wise. — **Wel fight** . . . He fights well who flees well
   "Ac° lete we awei thös cheste,° — But / strife
Vor swiche wordes böth unwreste;° — **böth unwreste** are useless
And fo we on° mid righte dome,° — **fo** . . . let's begin / judgment
180 Mid faire worde,° and mid y-some.° — words / agreeable words
Thegh° we ne bö at one acorde, — Though
We mughe bet° mid fayre worde, — **mughe bet** can better
Withute cheste,° and bute° fighte, — strife / without
Plaidi mid foghe° and mid righte; — **Plaidi** . . . Plead with relevance
185 And mai ure either hwat hö wile
Mid righte segge and mid skile."°
Tho quath the ule:

OWL

        "Hwo schal us seme° — reconcile
That kunne° and wille right us deme?"° — may know how / **right** . . . allot us justice

        NIGHTINGALE
   "Ich wot° wel," quath the nightingale. — know
190 "Ne tharf° tharof bö no tale. — **Ne tharf** There need not
Maister Nichole of Guldeforde°— — Guildford
He is wis and war° of worde, — wary
He is of dome swithe glew,° — **dome** . . . judgment very wise
And him is loth evrich unthew.° — **him** . . . he hates every vice
195 He wot insight in° eche songe— — **wot** . . . has knowledge of
Hwo singeth wel, hwo singeth wronge;

185–86. And may each of us say whatever she will with right and with competence.

59

And he can schede° vrom the righte — distinguish
That woghe, that thüster° from the lighte." — **That woghe . . .** The wrong, the darkness
The ule one hwile hi° bithoghte — herself
200 And after than° this word upbroghte: — that

OWL

"Ich granti wel that he us deme,° — should judge
Vor, thegh° he were hwile breme,° — though **hwile breme** for a while wild
And löf him° were nightingale — **löf him** dear to him
And other wighte gente and smale,° — **wighte . . .** creatures gentle and slim
205 Ich wot° he is nu swithe acoled.° — know **swithe acoled** very much cooled down
Nis he vor thee noght afoled,° — **vor . . .** not deluded on your account
That° he for thine olde luve° — So that **thine . . .** former love of you
Me adun legge° and thee buve;° — **adun legge** may set down up
Ne schaltu nevre° so him queme° — **Ne . . .** Nor shall you ever please
210 That he, for thee, fals dom deme.° — **dom deme** judgment may utter
"He is him ripe and fast-rede,° — **him . . .** within himself mature and firm of counsel
Ne lüst him nu to none unrede.° —
Nu him ne lüst na more pleie.° — to play
He wile gon a° righte weie." — in the
215 The nightingale was al yare;° — ready
Hö hadde i-lörned wel aihware.° — everywhere

NIGHTINGALE

"Ule," hö sede, "seie me soth,° — truly
Hwi dostu that unwightis° doth? — **that unwightis** what monsters
Thu singist a-night and noght a-dai, —
220 And al thi song is 'Waila-wai!'° — Alas
Thu might mid thine songe afere° — frighten
Alle that i-hereth° thine i-bere.° — hear carrying-on
Thu scrichest and yollest to thine fere° — companion
That hit is grislich° to i-here; — horrible
225 Hit thincheth bothe° wise and snepe° — **thincheth bothe** seems to both foolish
Noght° that thu singe ac° that thu wepe. — Not but
Thu flighst a-night and noght a-dai! —
Tharof Ich wundri, and wel mai, —
Vor evrich thing that schunieth° right, — shuns
230 Hit luveth thüster° and hatieth light; — darkness
And evrich thing that° is löf° misdede, — to whom dear
Hit luveth thüster to his° dede. — **to his** for its
A wis word, thegh° hit bö unclene, — though
Is fele manne a muthe imene,° — **fele . . .** current in many men's mouths
235 For Alfred King¹ hit seide and wrot: —

212. Nor does he now delight in any folly.
¹ King Alfred (referred to on twelve occasions in *The Owl and the Nightingale* as an authority on proverbial lore); see the headnote to *The Proverbs of Alfred* (p. 40).

'He schuneth° that hine vul wot.'°   shrinks back   **hine** . . . knows himself to be foul
Ich wene° that thu dost also,   Suppose
Vor thu flighst nightes ever mo.°   **nightes** . . . at night constantly
  "Another thing me is a-wene:°   **me** . . . I suppose
240 Thu havest a-night wel brighte sene;°   **wel** . . . very clear vision
Bi daie thu art stare° blind,   completely
That thu ne sichst ne bow ne rind.°   **ne sichst** . . . see neither bough nor bark
A-day thu art blind other bisne.°   **other bisne** or purblind
Thar-bi men seggeth a vorbisne:°   **seggeth** . . . utter a proverb
245 'Right° so hit farth° bi than ungode°   Just   fares   **than ungode** the evil one
That noght ne süth° to none gode   sees
And is so ful of üvele wrenche°   tricks
That him ne mai° no man atprenche°   **ne mai** cannot   outwit
And can° wel than thüstre° wai   knows   **than thüstre** the dark
250 And thane brighte lat awai.'°   **brighte** . . . bright way leaves aside
So doth that böth° of thine cünde;°   **that böth** those that are   kind
Of lighte nabbeth hi none imünde."°   **none imünde** no concern
  Thös hule lüste swithe° longe   **lüste swithe** listened very
And was oftöned° swithe stronge.   offended
255 Hö quath:

OWL

  "Thu hattest° nightingale.   are called
Thu mightest bet hoten galegale,°   **bet** . . . better be called tattletale
Vor thu havest too monie° tale.   many a
Lat thine tunge habbe spale!°   time-out *tongue of a time-out*
Thu wenest that thes dai bö thin oghe.°   own *her own*
260 Lat me nu habbe mine throghe.°   turn *turn*
Bö nu stille and lat me speke.
Ich wille bön of° thee awreke;°   on   avenged
And lüst° hu Ich con me bitelle°   listen   defend
Mid righte sothe° withute spelle.°   **righte sothe** real truth   story *real truth without any story*
265 "Thu seist that Ich me hüde° a-dai.   hide
Tharto ne segge Ich 'nich' ne 'nai,'°
And lüst° Ich telle thee warevore,   listen
Al wi hit is and warevore.
  "Ich habbe bile stif and stronge
270 And gode clivres° scharp and longe   talons
So° hit bicumeth to havekes cünne.°   As   **havekes cünne** hawk's kin
Hit is min highte,° hit is mi wünne,°   joy   delight
That Ich me draghe° to mine cünde,°   draw   kind
Ne mai me no man tharevore schende.°   scold
275 On me hit is wel i-sene,°   **wel i-sene** very clear
Vor righte cünde° Ich am so kene.°   **Vor** . . . By very nature   aggressive

266. To that I say neither 'not I' nor 'nay'

Vorthi° Ich am loth° smale foghle° — Therefore loathsome to birds
That flöth° bi grunde and bi thüvele.° — fly thicket
Hi me bichermeth and bigredeth° — bichermeth ... scream at and cry at
280 And höre flockes to me ledeth.
Me is löf° to habbe reste — Me ... I like
And sitte stille in mine neste;
Vor nere Ich never no° the betere — nere ... I'd never be any
Yif Ich mid chavling° and mid chatere — squabbling
285 Höm schende° and mid fule worde, — should scold
So herdes° doth, other mid schit-worde.° — shepherds other ... or with dirty words
Ne lüst me with the screwen chide;°
Forthi° Ich wende from höm wide. — Therefore
Hit is a wise monne dome°— — wise ... judgment of wise men
290 And hi° hit seggeth wel ilome°— — they frequently
That me° ne chide with the gidie° — one foolish
Ne with than ofne me ne yonie.°
"At sume sithe,° herde I telle — time
Hu Alvred sede on his spelle,° — utterance
295 'Loke that thu ne bö thare
Thar chavling böth and cheste yare.°
Lat sottes chide,° and vorth thu go.' — sottes chide fools debate
And Ich am wis and do also.° — so
And yet Alvred seide, an other side,° — an ... on the other hand
300 A word that is i-sprunge wide:
'That° with the fule° haveth imene° — (He) that foul contact
Ne cumeth he never from him° cleine.' — it
Wenestu° that haveck° bö the worse — Do you suppose hawk
Thogh crowe bigrede° him bi the mershe — crowe bigrede crows cry at
305 And göth to him mid höre chirme° — höre chirme their screaming
Right so° hi wille with him schirme?° — Right so As if fight
The havek folgheth° gode rede° — follows advice
And flighth his wei and lat him grede.° — lat ... lets them cry
"Yet thu me seist° of other thinge° — me seist speak against me things
310 And telst° that Ich ne can noght singe, — complain
Ac° al mi rörde° is woning° — But that voice lamentation
And to i-hire grislich° thing. — i-hire grislich hear a horrible
That nis noght soth.° Ich singe efne° — true evenly
Mid fulle dreme° and lude stefne.° — sound voice
315 Thu wenist that ech song bö grislich
That thine pipinge nis ilich.° — nis ilich is not like
Mi stefne is bold and noght unorne;° — humble
Hö° is ilich one grete horne, — It

287. I don't like to debate with the shrews
292. Nor gape open in competition with the oven.
296. Where squabbling and strife are ready.

And thin is ilich one pipe
320 Of one smale wöde° unripe.   one . . . a narrow reed
Ich singe bet° than thu dest.   better
Thu chaterest so döth on Irish pröst.
Ich singe an eve a° righte time,   an . . . in evening (vespers) at the
And söththe wön° hit is bed-time,   söththe wön then when (compline)
325 The thridde sithe° ad middel-nighte,   thridde sithe third time (matins)
And so Ich mine song adighte°   prepare
Wöne Ich i-sö° arise vörre°   see   far off
Other dai-rim other° dai-sterre.   Other . . . Either daybreak (lauds) or
   "Ich do god mid mine throte
330 And warni men to höre note;°   höre note their profit
Ac° thu singest alle longe night   But
From eve forth° hit is dai-light,   until
And evre seist° thin o° song   utter   one
So longe so° the night is long,   So . . . As long as
335 And evre croweth thi wrecche crei°   craw
That he ne swiketh° night ne dai.   he . . . doesn't stop
Mid thine pipinge thu adünest°   deafen
Thas monnes earen thar° thu wunest°   Thas . . . The ears of man where   dwell
And makest thine song so unwürth°   worthless
340 That me ne telth of thar noght würth.°   me . . . one counts no value in it
Evrich mürghthe° mai so longe i-leste   pleasure
That hö shal liki wel unwreste,°   hö . . . it will satisfy very poorly
Vor harpe, and pipe, and fugheles° song   birds'
Misliketh° yif hit is too long.   Displeases
345 Ne bö the song never so mürie
That he ne shal thinche wel unmürie
Yef he i-lesteth over unwille;°
So thu might thine song aspille.°   waste
Vor hit is soth°—Alvred hit seidde—   true
350 And me° hit mai ine boke rede: one
'Evrich thing mai losen his godhede°   goodness
Mid unmethe° and mid overdede.'°   excess   superfluity
Mid este° thu thee might overquatie,°   pleasure   thee . . . can glut yourself
And overfulle maketh wlatie,°   overfulle . . . surfeit causes disgust
355 And evrich müreghthe mai a-gon°   mureghthe . . . pleasure can pass
Yif me hit halt evre-forth in on°
Bute° one, that° is Godes riche°   Except   which   kingdom
That evre is swete and evre iliche.°   the same
Thegh° thu nime° evere of than lepe,°   Though   take   of . . . from that basket
360 Hit is evre ful bi hepe.°   ful . . . heaping full

345–47. The song is (literally, 'Be the song') never so pleasant that it will not seem very unpleasant if it lasts beyond the point of displeasure
356. If one persists in it evermore continually

Wunder° hit is of Godes riche   A marvel
That evre spenth° and ever is iliche.   expends
  "Yüt thu me seist° another shome   **me seist** utter against me
That Ich am on mine eghen lome°   **eghen lome** eyes feeble
365 And seist, for that Ich flö° bi nighte,   fly
That Ich ne mai i-sö° bi lighte.   **ne** ... can't see
Thu liest! On me hit is i-sene
That Ich habbe gode sene,°   sight
Vor nis non so dim thüsternesse°   darkness
370 That Ich ever i-sö° the lasse.   see
Thu wenest that Ich ne mighte i-sö,
Vor Ich bi daie noght ne flö.°   **noght** ... don't fly at all
The hare luteth° al dai,   hides
Ac notheles i-sö he mai.
375 Yif hundes ürneth° to him-ward,   run
He gength wel swithe° awai-ward   **gength** ... goes very fast
And hoketh° pathes swithe narewe   winds along
And haveth mid him his blenches yarewe°   **blenches yarewe** tricks prepared
And hupth and stard° swithe cove°   **hupth** ... hops and starts   fast
380 And secheth pathes to the grove;
Ne sholde he, vor bothe his eghe,°   eyes
So don yif he the bet ni-seghe.°   **yif** ... unless he saw better
Ich mai i-sön so wel so on° hare,   **i-sön** ... see as well as a
Thegh Ich bi daie sitte and dare.°   hide
385 Thar aghte° men böth in worre   **Thar aghte** Where bold
And fareth bothe ner and förre°   far
And overfareth fele thöde°   **overfareth** ... overrun many nations
And doth bi nighte gode nöde,°   service
Ich folghi than° aghte manne°   **folghi than** follow those   men
390 And flö° bi nighte in höre banne."°   fly   **höre banne** their troop
  The nightingale in hire thoghte
Athold° al this and longe thoghte   Retained
Wat hö tharafter mighte segge,
Vor hö ne mighte noght alegge°   refute
395 That° the hule hadde hire i-sed,   What
Vor hö spac bothe right and red;°   reason
And hire ofthughte° that hö hadde   **hire ofthughte** it annoyed her
The speche so för vorth i-ladde°   **för** ... far forward led
And was oferd° that hire answare   afraid
400 Ne wurthe noght° aright i-fare.   **Ne** ... Would not
Ac notheles hö spac boldeliche—
Vor he is wis that hardeliche°   boldly
With his vo° berth grete ilete,°   foe   **grete ilete** a bold front
That he vor areghthe hit ne forlete;°   **areghthe** ... cowardice should not give up
405 Vor swich worth° bold yif thu flighst°   **swich worth** such a foe becomes   flee

That wile flö° yif thu vicst;°   flee   fight
Yif he i-sith that thu nart aregh,°   **nart aregh** aren't afraid
He wile of bore würchen baregh.°   **of** . . . from boar became a piglet
And forthi,° thegh the nightingale   therefore
410   Were a-ferd, hö spac bolde tale.

NIGHTINGALE

"Ule," hö seide, "wi dostu so?
Thu singest a-winter 'wo-la-wo.'°   alas
Thu singest so° döth hen a-snowe;   as
Al that hö singeth hit is for wowe.
415   A-wintere thu singest wrothe and yomere,°   **wrothe** . . . angrily and mournfully
And evre thu art dumb a-sumere.
Hit is for thine fule nithe°   malice
That thu ne might° mid us bö blithe,   **ne might** cannot
Vor thu forbernest wel negh for onde°   **forbernest** . . . very nearly burn up because of envy
420   Wane ure blisse cumeth to londe.
Thu farest so döth the ille:°   malicious man
Evrich blisse him° is unwille;°   for him   displeasing
Grucching and luring him böth rade°
Yif he i-söth° that men böth° glade.   sees   are
425   He wolde that he i-seghe°   saw
Teres in evrich monnes eghe;°   eye
Ne roghte he thegh flockes were
I-meind bi toppes and bi here.°
Al° so thu dost on thire° side,   Just   your
430   Vor wanne snow lith° thicke and wide,   lies
And alle wightes° habbeth sorghe,°   creatures   care
Thu singest from eve fort a-morghe.°   **fort a-morghe** till morning
    "Ac Ich alle blisse mid me bringe.
Ech wight is glad for mine thinge°   **for** . . . because of me
435   And blisseth hit° wanne Ich cume   **blisseth hit** rejoices
And highteth aghen° mine kume.°   **highteth aghen** looks forward to   coming
The blostme ginneth° springe and sprede   **blostme ginneth** blossoms begin to
Bothe ine trö and ek on mede.
The lilie mid hire faire wlite°   face
440   Wolcumeth me, that thu hit wite;°   **that** . . . I'll have you know
Bit° me mid hire faire blö°   Bids   countenance
That Ich shulle to hire flö.
The rose also mid hire rude°   radiance
That cumeth ut of the thorne-wode
445   Bit me that Ich schulle singe

423. Grumbling and scowling come quickly to him
427–28. Nor would he care though wool refuse were mixed in with choice wool and hair, *or* though flocks (of sheep or people?) were entangled by top-knots and by hair. (Both interpretations are possible.)

Vor hire luve° one skentinge,° **hire luve** love of her ditty
And Ich so do thurgh night and dai—
The more Ich singe, the more I mai°— can
And skente hi° mid mine songe, **skente hi** delight her
450 Ac notheles noght overlonge.
Wane Ich i-sö that men böth glade,
Ich nelle that hi bön too sade.° **nelle ...** don't want them to be oversated
Wan is i-do vor wan Ich com,°
Ich fare aghen° and do wisdom. **fare aghen** go away
455 Wane mon hogheth of° his sheve,° **hogheth of** thinks about sheaves
And falewi° cumeth on grene leve, fall coloring
Ich fare hom and nime° leve, take
Ne recche° Ich noght of winteres reve.° **Ne recche** Nor care spoil
Wan Ich i-sö that cumeth that harde,° hard time
460 Ich fare° hom to min erde° go abode
And habbe° bothe luve and thonc° receive gratitude
That Ich her com and hider swonk.° **hider swonk** labored here
Wan min erende is i-do,° done
Sholde Ich bileve?° Nai, warto?° linger what for
465 Vor he nis nother yep° ne wis **nis ...** is neither smart
That longe abid thar him nöd nis."° **thar ...** where he's not needed
 Thös hule lüste° and leide an hord° listened **an hord** in store
Al this mot,° word after word, argument
And after thoghte hu heo mighte
470 Answere vinde° best mid righte, find
Vor he mot hine ful wel bithenche°
That is aferd° of plaites wrenche.° afraid **plaites wrenche** tricks of pleading

OWL

"Thu aishest° me," the hule sede, ask
"Wi Ich a-winter singe and grede.° cry
475 Hit is gode monne i-wone°— **gode ...** for good men customary
And was from the worlde frome°— **worlde frome** world's beginning
That ech god man his frönd i-cnowe° recognize
And blisse° mid höm sume throwe° rejoice **sume throwe** at some time
In his huse at his borde° table
480 Mid faire speche and faire worde;
And hure and hure to° Cristesmasse, **hure ...** especially at
Wane riche and poure, more and lasse,
Singeth cundut° night and dai, carols
Ich höm helpe what Ich mai.° can
485 And ek° Ich thenche° of other thinge also think
Thane to pleien other° to singe. or

453. When what I came for is done
471. For one must full well bethink himself

"Ich habbe herto gode answare
Anon i-redi and al yare.°   prepared
Vor sumeres-tide is al too wlonc°   **al . . .** far too wanton
490 And doth misreken monnes thonk,°
Vor he ne recth noght of clennesse;°   **ne . . .** cares naught for purity
Al his thoght is of golnesse.°   lechery
Vor none dör no leng nabideth,°   **none . . .** no animal waits any longer
Ac evrich° upon other rideth.   each
495 The sülve stottes° ine the stode°   **sülve stottes** very horses   stud
Böth bothe° wilde and mere-wode.°   both   mare-crazy
And thu sülf art thar-among,
For of golnesse° is al thi song;   lechery
And aghen° thet thu wilt teme,°   toward the time   breed
500 Thu art wel modi° and wel breme.°   bold   wild
Sone so° thu havest i-trede,°   **Sone so** As soon as   coupled
Ne mightu leng° a word i-quethe°   **Ne . . .** You can no longer   say
Ac pipest al so° döth a mose°   as   titmouse
Mid chokeringe° mid stevne hose.°   choking   **stevne hose** hoarse voice
505 Yet thu singst worse thon the heï-sugge°   hedge-sparrow
That flighth bi grunde among the stübbe.°   stumps
Wane thi lust is a-go,°   gone
Thonne° is thi song a-go also.   Then
A-sumere, chorles awedeth°   **chorles awedeth** churls go mad
510 And vorcrempeth° and vorbredeth.°   cramp up   contort themselves
Hit nis° for luve, notheles,   is not
Ac is the chorles wode res;°   **wode res** crazy impulse
Vor wane he haveth i-do° his dede,   done
I-fallen is al his boldhede.°   boldness
515 Habbe he i-stunge° under gore,°   **Habbe . . .** When once he has thrust clothing
Ne last° his luve no leng° more.   lasts   longer
Al° so hit is on thine mode;°   Just   mood
So sone so° thu sittest a-brode,°   **So . . .** As soon as   on a brood
Thu forlöst° al thine wise.°   lose   song
520 Al so thu farest° on thine rise;°   behave   branch
Wane thu havest i-do° thi gome,°   finished   game
Thi stevne° goth anon to shome.°   voice   ruin
"Ac wane nightes cumeth longe
And bringeth forstes° stark and stronge,   frosts
525 Thanne erest° hit is i-sene   for the first time
War° is the snelle,° war is the kene.°   Where   swift one   bold one
At than harde me° mai avinde°   **At . . .** In bad times one   find out
Wo geth forth,° wo lith° bihinde.   **Wo . . .** Who advances   lies
Me mai i-sön at thare nöde°   **thare nöde** the time of need
530 Wan° me shal harde wike böde.°   From whom   **wike böde** service demand

490. And causes man's thought to go astray

Thanne Ich am snel° and pleie and singe   swift
And highte me° mid mi skentinge.°   **highte me** rejoice   singing
On none° wintere Ich ne recche,°   **On none** For any   **ne recche** care not
Vor Ich nam non aswunde° wrecche.   **nam** ... am no feeble
535 And ek° Ich frouri vele wighte°   also   **frouri** ... comfort many creatures
That mid höm nabbeth none mightte;°   **mid** ... in themselves have no power
Hi böth hoghfule° and wel arme°   anxious   miserable
And secheth yörne to the warme.°   **secheth** ... seek eagerly for warmth
Oft Ich singe vor höm the more
540 For lütli° sum of höre° sore.   **For lütli** To lessen   their
Hu thincth thee?° Artu yüt i-nume?°   **thincth thee** seems it to you   caught
Artu mid righte° overcume?"   **mid righte** properly

NIGHTINGALE

"Nay, nay," sede the nightingale.
Thu shalt i-here another tale.
545 Yet nis thös speche i-broght to dome.°   verdict
Ac bö wel stille, and lüst° nu to me.   listen
Ich shal mid one bare worde
Do that° thi speche wurth forworthe."°   **Do that** Cause   **wurth forworthe** to become worthless

OWL

"That nere noht° right," the hule sede.   **nere noht** would not be
550 "Thu havest bicloped al so° thu bede,°   **bicloped** ... laid charge just as   asked to do
And Ich thee habbe i-yive answare.
Ac, ar° we to unker dome° fare,   before   **unker dome** the verdict on us
Ich wille speke toward thee
Al so thu speke° toward me,   spoke
555 And thu me answare, yif thu might.
Seie me nu, thu wrecche wight,°   creature
Is in thee eni other note°   use
Bute° thu havest schille° throte?   Except that   a shrill
Thu nart noght to non° other thinge   **nart** ... are useless for any
560 Bute thu canst of° chateringe,   **canst of** know about
Vor thu art lütel and unstrong,
And nis thi reghel° nothing long.   garment
Wat dostu godes° among monne   **dostu godes** good do you do
Na mo the° deth a wrecche wrann!°   **Na** ... Any more than   wren
565 Of thee ne cumeth non other god°   benefit
Bute° thu gredest swich° thu bö wod,°   Except that   **gredest swich** cry out as if   **bö wod** were wild
And, bö thi piping overgo,
Ne böth on thee craftes namo.°
"Alvred sede, that was wis—
570 He mighte wel, for soth° hit is: true

567–68. And when your piping has passed, there aren't any other skills in you.

'Nis° no man for his bare songe   There is
Löf ne wurth° noght swithe longe,   **Löf** . . . Loved or honored
Vor that is a forworthe° man   useless
That bute singe noght ne can.'°   **bute** . . . knows nothing except how to sing
575 Thu nart bute on° forworthe thing;   **nart** . . . are but a
On thee nis bute chatering.
Thu art dim and of fule höwe°   hue
And thinchest° a lütel soti clöwe.°   seem like   **soti clöwe** sooty ball
Thu nart fair, no° thu nart strong,   nor
580 Ne thu nart thicke, ne thu nart long.
Thu havest i-mist al of fairhede,°   **i-mist** . . . fallen entirely short of beauty
And lütel is al thi godede.°   virtue
    "Another thing of thee Ich mene:°   complain
Thu nart vair ne thu nart clene.
585 Wane thu cumest to manne haghe°   **manne haghe** men's dwellings
Thar° thornes böth and ris i-draghe°   Where   **ris i-draghe** branches drawn together
Bi hegge° and bi thicke wöde°   hedge   weeds
Thar men göth oft to höre nöde,°   **to** . . . for their need
Tharto thu draghst,° tharto thu wunest,°   draw   dwell
590 And other clene stede° thu schunest.   places
Wan Ich flö nightes after müse,°   mice
I mai thee vinde° ate rum-huse.°   find   privy
Among the wöde,° among the netle,   weeds
Thu sittest and singst bihinde the setle.
595 Thar me° mai thee ilomest° finde   one   most often
Thar° men worpeth° höre bihinde!   Where   set down
    "Yet thu atwitest me° mine mete   **atwitest me** reproach me about
And seist that Ich fule wightes ete.
Ac wat etestu—that thu ne lighe°—   **ne lighe** may not lie
600 Bute atter-coppe° and fule vlighe°   **Bute atter-coppe** But spiders   flies
And wormes, yif thu might hi° finde   them
Among the volde° of harde rinde?°   folds   bark
Yet Ich can do wel gode wike,°   services
Vor Ich can loki manne wike;°   **loki** . . . guard men's dwellings
605 And mine wike böth wel gode,
Vor Ich helpe to° manne vode.°   with   food
Ich can nimen müs° at berne°   **nimen müs** catch mice   barn
And ek° at chirche in the derne,°   also   dark
Vor me is löf, to° Cristes huse,   **me** . . . I love, in
610 To clansi° hit with° fule müse,°   cleanse   of   mice
Ne schal thar nevre come to
Ful° wight, yif Ich hit mai i-vo.°   Any foul   catch
And, yif me lüst° on mi skentinge°   **me lüst** it pleases me   singing
To wernen° other wunienge,°   refuse   dwellings
615 Ich habbe at wude trön° wel grete   **at** . . . in the woods a tree

Mit thicke boghe nothing blete° **nothing blete** in no way bare
Mid ivi grene al bigrowe° grown over
That evre stont iliche i-blowe° **evre . . .** stands unchangingly in leaf
And his höw° never ne vorlöst° **his höw** its hue loses
620 Wan hit sniuth° ne wan hit fröst.° snows freezes
Tharin Ich habbe god ihold,° **god ihold** a good stronghold
A-winter warm, a-sumere cold.
Wane min hus stont° bright and grene, stands
Of thine nis nothing i-sene.
625 "Yet thu me telst° of other thinge; reproach
Of mine briddes seist gabbinge° lies
That höre nest nis noght clene.
Hit is fale° other wighte imene,° of many common
Vor hors a-stable and oxe a-stalle
630 Doth° al that höm wüle° thar falle, Let **höm wüle** they wish
And lütle children in the cradele,
Bothe chörles and ek athele,° **chörles . . .** low-born and also noble
Doth al° that in höre yoethe° **Doth al** All do youth
That° hi vorleteth° in höre dughethe.° Which abandon maturity
635 Wat! Can that yongling hit bihede?° **yongling . . .** youngster prevent it
Yif hit misdeth,° hit mod nede.° misbehaves **mod nede** must necessarily
A vorbisne° is of olde ivürne° proverb **olde ivürne** long ago
That nöde° maketh old wif ürne.° need run
  "And yet Ich habbe another andsware.
640 Wiltu to mine neste vare° go
And loki° hu hit is i-dight?° look made
Yif thu art wis, lörni° thu mighst. learn
Mi nest is holgh and rum° amidde, **holgh . . .** hollow and roomy
So hit is softest mine° bridde. for my
645 Hit is broiden° al abute woven
Vrom the neste vör withute.° **vör withute** far outward
Tharto hi goth to höre nöde;° necessity
Ac that thu menest,° Ich höm forböde.° complain of forbid
We nimeth yeme of manne bure,° **nimeth . . .** take example from men's bedrooms
650 And after than° we maketh ure;° **after than** like them ours
Men habbeth, among other iwende,° devices
A rum-hus° at höre bures ende privy
Vor that hi nelleth too vör go,° **nelleth . . .** don't want to go too far
And mine briddes doth al so.° **al so** the same
655 "Site nu stille, chaterestre!° chatterbox
Nere thu never i-bunde vastre.° **i-bunde vastre** bound more fast
Herto ne vindestu never andsware.
Hong up thin ax! Nu thu might fare!"° **might fare** can go
  The nightingale at thisse worde
660 Was wel negh ut of rede i-worthe° **negh . . .** nigh run out of ideas

And thoghte yörne° on hire mode°   eagerly   mind
Yif hö oght elles understode,°   **oght** . . . knew anything else
Yif hö kuthe° oght bute singe,°   understood   **bute singe** except how to sing
That mighte helpe to other thinge.°   **to** . . . for other purposes
665 Herto hö moste andswere vinde
Other mid alle bön° bihinde;   **Other** . . . Or completely be
And hit is swithe strong° to fighte   hard
Aghen soth° and aghen righte.   **Aghen soth** Against truth
He mot gon to° al mid ginne°   **mot** . . . must go at   ingenuity
670 Wan the hörte böth on winne;°   **böth** . . . is at strife
And the man mot on other segge°—   **on** . . . talk differently
He mot bihemmen and bilegge°—   **bihemmen** . . . decorate and gloze
Yif muth withute mai biwro,°
That me° the hörte noght ni-sö.°   **That me** So that one   **noght ni-sö** doesn't see
675 And sone° mai a word misreke°   quickly   miscarry
Thar° muth shal aghen° hörte speke;   Where   against
And sone mai a word misstörte°   misstart
Thar muth shal speken aghen hörte.
Ac notheles yüt, upe thon°   **upe thon** concerning that
680 Her is to red, wo hine kon;°
Vor never nis° wit so kene   is
So wane red him is a wene.°
Thanne erest° cumeth his yephede°   for the first time   **his yephede** its ingenuity
Wöne hit is alremest on drede;°   **alremest** . . . most of all in doubt
685 For Alvered seide of olde quide,°   a saying
And yüt hit nis of hörte i-slide:°   **of** . . . hasn't slipped from mind
'Wone the bale° is alre-hecst,°   trouble   highest of all
Thonne is the bote alre-necst.'°   **bote alre-necst** remedy nearest of all
Vor wit west among his sore,°   **west** . . . increases while on trial
690 And for his° sore hit is the more.   **for his** because of its
Vorthi nis nevere mon redles°   without a plan
Ar° his hörte bö witles.   Until
Ac, yif that he forlöst° his wit,   loses
Thonne is his red-purs° al to-slit;°   bag of schemes   split apart
695 Yif he ne kon° his wit atholde,°   **ne kon** can't   retain
Ne vint he red° in one volde.°   **Ne** . . . He won't find counsel   **one volde** a single fold
Vor Alvrid seide, that wel kuthe°—   knew how
Evre he spac mid sothe° muthe: truthful
'Wone the bale° is alre-hecst,°   trouble   highest of all
700 Thanne is the bote alre-nest.' "°   **bote alre-nest** remedy nearest of all
    The nightingale al hire hoghe°   mind
Mid rede° hadde wel bitoghe;°   counsel   exercised

673. If the mouth is to conceal outwardly
680. There is a remedy available for him who knows it (probable interpretation)
682. As when a plan of action (*red*, literally, 'counsel') is still in doubt for it (the debater's *wit*, 'mind').

71

Among the harde, among the toghte° — strained arguments
Ful wel mid rede hire bithoghte;° — had bethought herself
705 And hadde andswere gode i-funde
Among al hire harde stunde.° — moments

NIGHTINGALE

"Hule, thu axest me," hö seide,
"Yif Ich kon° eni other dede — can do
Bute singen in sumere tide° — **sumere tide** summertime
710 And bringe blisse för° and wide. — far
Wi axestu of craftes mine?
Betere is min on° than alle thine. — one craft
Betere is o° song of mine muthe — one
Than al that evre thi kün kuthe.° — **kün kuthe** kind could do
715 And lüst—Ich telle thee warevore.
Wostu to wan° man was i-bore?° — **Wostu** . . . Do you know for what born
To thare° blisse of hövene-riche° — the heaven's kingdom
Thar° ever is song and mürghthe iliche.° — Where **mürghthe iliche** pleasure consistently
Thider fundeth° evrich man — strives
720 That eni thing of gode kan.° — **gode kan** good knows
Vorthi me° singth in holi chirche, — **Vorthi me** For this reason one
And clerkes ginneth° songes wirche,° — undertake to compose
That man i-thenche° bi the songe — may ponder
Wider he shal° and thar bön longe, — is destined
725 That he the mürghthe ne voryete° — **mürghthe** . . . pleasure may not forget
Ac tharof thenche and biyete° — attain
And nime yeme of chirche stevene°
Hu mürie is the blisse of hövene.
Clerkes, munekes, and kanunes,°
730 Thar° böth thos gode wicke-tunes,° — Where communities
Ariseth up to midel-nighte
And singeth of the hövene lighte,° — **hövene lighte** heavenly light
And pröstes upe londe° singeth — **upe londe** in country parishes
Wane the light of daie springeth;
735 And Ich höm helpe wat I mai.
Ich singe mid höm night and dai,
And hö böth alle for° me the gladdere — because of
And to the songe böth the raddere.° — readier
"Ich warni° men to here° gode — warn **to here** for their
740 That hi bön° blithe on höre mode° — **hi bön** they should be spirit
And bidde° that hi moten i-seche° — urge **moten i-seche** must seek
Than ilke° song that ever is eche.° — **Than ilke** The same eternal
Nu thu might,° hule, sitte and clinge! — **thu might** may you

727. And take heed from the church's voice
729. Clerics, monks, and canons (living according to religious rule)

Her among nis° no chateringe.
745 Ich graunti° that we go to dome
Tofore the sülfe° Pope of Rome!
"Ac abid yete, notheles.
Thu shalt i-here another thes;°
Ne shaltu, for° Engelonde,
750 At thisse worde me atstonde.°
Wi atwitestu me mine unstrengthe°
And mine ungrete° and mine unlengthe°
And seist that Ich nam noght strong,
Vor° Ich nam nother° gret ne long?
755 Ac thu nost never wat° thu menst;°
Bute lese° wordes thu me lenst.°
For Ich kan° craft, and Ich kan liste,°
And tharevore Ich am thus thriste.°
Ich kan wit and song mani eine,°
760 Ne triste° Ich to° non other maine;°
Vor soth hit is that seide Alvred:
'Ne mai° no strengthe aghen red.'°
Oft spet° wel a lüte liste°
Thar° muche strengthe sholde miste;°
765 Mid lütle strengthe thurgh ginne°
Castel and burgh me° mai i-winne;
Mid liste me mai walles felle
And worpe of° horsse knightes snelle.°
Üvel° strengthe is lütel wurth,
770 Ac wisdom ne wurth° never unwurth;°
Thu myht i-seo° thurh alle thing
That wisdom naveth non evening.°
An hors is strengur than a mon,
Ac, for° hit non i-wit ne kon,°
775 Hit berth° on rügge° grete semes°
And draghth° bi sweore° grete temes°
And tholeth° bothe yerd° and spure
And stont° i-teid at mülne dure;°
And hit deth that° mon hit hot.°
780 And, for than that° hit no wit not,°
Ne mai his strenthe hit i-shilde
That hit nabughth the lütle childe.°
Mon deth° mid strengthe and mid witte
That other thing nis non his fitte.°
785 Thegh alle strengthe at one were,°
Monnes wit yet more were;°
Vorthe,° mon mid his crafte

Her ... In this there is
agree
very

thing about this
for all of
withstand
atwitestu ... do you twit me about my weakness
smallness shortness

Just because neither
nost ... don't know at all what say
Bute lese Nothing but false offer
know ingenuity
bold
mani eine many a one
trust in power

can prevail counsel
speeds **lüte liste** little ingenuity
Where fail
stratagem
burgh me stronghold one

worpe of throw off bold
Brute
becomes worthless
myht i-seo can see
naveth ... has no equal

because **non ...** has no understanding
carries its back loads
draws its neck plough-chains
suffers stick
stands **mülne dure** the mill door
deth that does what orders
for ... because **no ...** knows no understanding
standing

Mon deth Man brings it about
other ... no other thing is his equal
alle the strength of all things was united
would be
Therefore

781–82. Its strength cannot shield it from having to yield to the small child.

Overkumeth al örthliche shafte.° | **örthliche shafte** earthly creatures
Al so Ich do mid mine one songe
790 Bet° than thu al the yer longe. | Better
Vor mine crafte men me luvieth;° | love
Vor thine strenghte men thee shunieth.
Telstu bi me° the wurs for than° | **Telstu . . .** Do you count me **for than** because
That Ich bute anne° craft ne kan?° | **bute anne** only one know
795 "Yif tweie° men goth to wraslinge, | two
And either other faste thringe,
And the on can swenges swithe fele°
And kan his wrenches° wel forhele,° | tricks conceal
And the other ne can sweng but anne,° | **ne . . .** knows just one hold
800 And the° is god with° eche manne, | that against
And mid thon one leith° to grunde | **thon . . .** that one he lays
Anne after other a lütle stunde,° | **a . . .** in little time
Wat tharf° he recche of a mo° swenge | need **of . . .** for one more
Wone the on him° is swo genge?° | **the . . .** one for him **swo genge** so effective
805 "Thu seist that thu canst fele wike,° | **canst . . .** know how to do many services
Ac ever Ich am thin unilike.° | **thin unilike** unlike you
Do° thine craftes alle togadere, | Put
Yet is min on hörte° betere. | **on hörte** essentially
Oft wan hundes foxes driveth,
810 The kat ful wel himselve liveth° | survives
Thegh he ne kunne wrench bute anne.° | **ne . . .** may know just one trick
The fox so godne ne can nanne° | **so . . .** knows none so good
Thegh he kunne so vele° wrenche | many
That he wenth° eche hunde atprenche,° | expects to outwit
815 Vor he can° pathes righte and woghe,° | knows **righte . . .** straight and crooked
And he kan hongi bi the boghe,° | bough
And so forlöst° the hund his fore° | loses trail
And turnth aghen eft° to than more.° | **aghen eft** once more **than more** the moor
The vox kan cröpe° bi the heie° | **kan cröpe** knows how to creep hedge
820 And turne ut from his forme° weie | former
And eft sone° kume tharto. | **eft sone** again quickly
Thonne° is the hundes smel fordo;° | Then destroyed
He not,° thurgh the i-meinde smak,° | doesn't know **i-meinde smak** confused scent
Wether he shal avorth the abak.° | **avorth . . .** go forward or back
825 Yif the vox mist of° al this dwöle,° | **mist of** escapes by deception
At than ende he cröpth° to hole; | creeps
Ac natheles mid alle his wrenche
Ne kan he hine so bithenche,° | **Ne . . .** He can't so contrive
Thegh he bö yep° and swithe snel,° | smart quick
830 That he ne löst° his rede vel.° | **ne löst** doesn't lose **rede vel** red pelt
The cat ne kan wrench bute anne° | **ne . . .** knows no trick but one

796–97. And each presses the other hard, and one knows very many holds

Nother bi dune ne bi venne,°
Bute he kan climbe swithe wel;
Tharmid° he wereth° his greie vel.   By that   continues to wear
835 Al so Ich segge bi° mi sölve,   concerning
Betere is min on° than thine twelve.''   one

OWL

"Abid! Abid!'' the ule seide.
"Thu gest al to° mid swikelede.°   **gest** ... go at things entirely   treachery
Alle thine wordes thu bileist°   disguise
840 That hit thincth° soth al that thu seist.   **That** ... So that it seems
Alle thine wordes böth i-sliked°   smoothed over
And so bisemed and biliked°   **bisemed** ... plausible and likely
That alle tho° that hi avoth°   those   **hi avoth** hear them
Hi weneth° that thu segge soth.   suppose
845 Abid! Abid! Me shal thee yene.°   **Me** ... You are to be countered
Nu hit shal wurthe° wel i-sene   become
That thu havest müchel i-loghe°   **müchel i-loghe** greatly lied
Wone thi lesing° böth unwroghe.°   deception   revealed
   "Thu seist that thu singist mankünne°· for mankind
850 And techest höm that hi fundieth hönne° **fundieth hönne** strive to go hence
Up to the songe that evre i-lest;°   endures
Ac hit is alre wunder mest°   **alre** ... of all wonders most
That thu darst lighe so opeliche.°   openly
Wenest thu hi bringe° so lightliche° **hi bringe** to bring them easily
855 To Godes riche° al singinge?   kingdom
Nai, nai! Hi shulle wel avinde°   find
That hi mid longe wope mote°   **wope mote** weeping must
Of höre sünnen bidde bote°   **Of** ... For their sins ask relief
Ar° hi mote° ever kume thare.   Before may
860 Ich rede thi° that men bö yare°   **rede thi** advise so ready
And more wepe thane singe,
That fundeth° to than höven-kinge, strive
Vor nis no man withute sünne.
Vorthi he mot,° ar he wende hönne,° must hence
865 Mid teres and mid wope bete,°   **wope bete** weeping amend
That him bö sur that er was swete.°
Tharto Ich helpe, God hit wot,
Ne singe Ich höm no foliot;[2]
For al my song is of longinge,

832. Either by hill or by fen
866. So that, for him, that may be sour which previously was sweet.
[2] 'Nor do I sing them any folly.' The rare word *foliot* would inevitably convey to the poet's contemporaries an additional punning connotation, for Bishop Foliot (d. 1187) was widely known as a supporter of Henry II against Becket. The churchly owl instinctively scorns the king's party; the courtly nightingale predictably ignores the jibe and later (l. 1091) praises the king.

870 And i-meind sumdel° mid woninge,°
That mon bi° me hine bithenche°
That he groni° for his unwrenche.°
Mid mine songe Ich hine pülte,
That he groni for his gülte.

875 "Yif thu gest herof to disputinge,
Ich wepe bet° thane thu singe.
Yif right goth forth, and abak wrong,
Betere is mi wop° thane thi song.
Thegh sume men bö thurghut° gode

880 And thurghut clene on höre mode,°
Höm longeth hönne,° notheles.
That° böth her,° wo is höm thes,°
For, thegh hi bön hömsölve i-borwe,°
Hi ne söth her nowight° bote sorwe;

885 Vor other men hi wepeth sore
And for höm biddeth° Cristes ore.°
Ich helpe monne on either halve;
Mi muth haveth tweire künne salve:
Than gode° Ich fülste° to longinge,

890 Vor wan him longeth, Ich him singe;
And than sünfulle° Ich helpe alswo,
Vor Ich him teche ware° is wo.
"Yet Ich thee yene° in other wise,
For wane thu sittest on thine rise,

895 Thu draghst men to fleses lüste,°
That wülleth° thine songes lüste.°
Al° thu forlöst° the mürghthe° of hövene,
For tharto nevestu none stevene.°
Al that thu singst is of golnesse,°

900 For nis on thee non holinesse,
Ne weneth na man for° thi pipinge
That eni preost in chirche singe!
"Yet I thee wülle another° segge,
Yif thu hit const ariht bilegge:°

905 Wi nültu° singe an° other theode°
Thar hit is müchele° more neode?°
Thu neaver ne singst in Irlonde,
Ne thu ne cumest noght in Scotlonde.
Hwi nültu fare to Noreweie

910 And singen men° of Galeweie°?
Thar° beoth men that lütel kunne°
Of songe that is bineothe the sunne.
Wi nultu thare preoste° singe
And teche of thire writelinge,°

i-meind sumdel mixed somewhat lament
through **hine bithenche** bethink himself
may groan fault
hine pülte pelt him

better

weeping

throughout

spirit
Höm . . . They long to go hence
Those who here therefore

saved
ne . . . see here nothing

beseech mercy

tweire künne two kinds of
Than gode The good man help

than sünfulle the sinful
where
refute

fleses lüste flesh's lust
That wülleth Who will listen to
Completely lose bliss
nevestu stevene you have no voice
lust

Ne . . . Nor does any man suppose because of

another thing
construe
won't you among people
much need

singen men sing to men Galloway (Scotland)
There know

nultu . . . won't you there to priests
of . . . by your warbling

915 And wisi° höm mid thire° stevene — direct   your
Hu engeles singeth ine heovene?
Thu farest° so doth an ydel wel° — act   **ydel wel** useless spring
That springeth bi burne° that is snel° — **bi burne** beside a brook   swift
And let fordrüe the dune°
920 And flohth on idel° thar adune.° — **flohth** . . . flows uselessly   below
Ac Ich fare bothe north and south;
In everich londe Ich am cuth;° — known
East and west, fer and ner,
I do wel faire° mi mester° — **wel faire** very fairly   office
925 And warni men mid mine bere° — performance
That thi dweole° song heo ne forlere.° — deceiving   **heo** . . . mislead them not
Ich wisse° men mid mine songe — direct
That hi ne sünegi nowiht° longe. — **ne** . . . they sin not
I bidde° höm that hö i-swike° — beg   desist
930 That hömsölve ne biswike,° — **That** . . . From deceiving themselves
For betere is that hö wepen here
Than elleswhar to bön dövlene fere."° — **dövlene fere** devils' mates
The nightingale was i-gremet,° — enraged
And ek hö was sumdel ofschamed° — **sumdel ofschamed** somewhat ashamed
935 For the hule hire atwiten° hadde — twitted   insulted
In hwücche stüde° hö sat and gradde° — **In** . . . About the place in which   wept
Bihinde the bure° among the wede — bedroom
Wher men goth to here nöde;° — **to** . . . for their need
And sat sumdel,° and hö bithohte,° — a while   bethought herself
940 And wiste° wel on hire thohte — knew
That wraththe binimeth° monnes red.° — takes away   judgment
For hit seide the king Alfred,
"Selde° endeth wel the lothe,° — Seldom   loathsome person
And selde plaideth° wel the wrothe."° — pleads   angry
945 For wraththe meinth° the hörte° blod — disturbs   heart's
That° hit floweth so° wilde flod — So that   like a
And al the heorte overgeth,° — overwhelms
That hö naveth nothing bute breth°
And so forleost° al hire liht, — loses
950 That heo ne sith soth ne° riht. — **ne** . . . sees neither truth nor
The nightingale hi understod° — **hi understod** bethought herself
And overgan lette° hire mod. — **overgan lette** let pass by
Hö mihte bet speken a sele° — **a sele** in good spirits
Than mid wraththe° wordes deale. — **mid wraththe** in wrath

NIGHTINGALE

955 "Ule," heo seide, "lüst nu hider.
Thu schalt falle; the wei is slider.° — slippery

919. And lets the hill dry up
948. So that it has nothing but anger

77

Thu seist Ich fleo° bihinde bure.°   fly   the bedroom
Hit is riht; the bur is ure.°   ours
Thar laverd liggeth and lavedi,°   **Thar** . . . Where lord lies and lady
960   Ich schal heom° singe and sitte bi.   **schal heom** must for them
Wenstu° that wise men forlete,°   Do you think   would abandon
For° fule venne,° the righte strete;   Because of   mud
Ne sunne the later shine°
Thegh hit bö ful in neste thine?
965   Sholde Ich, for one hole brede,°   **one** . . . a plank with a hole
Forlete mine righte stede,°   place
That Ich ne singe° bi the bedde   **That** . . . So that I wouldn't sing
Thar loverd° haveth his löve i bedde?   **Thar loverd** Where lord
Hit is mi right, hit is mi laghe,°   law
970   That to the hexst° Ich me draghe.°   highest   **me draghe** draw myself
    "Ac yet thu yelpst° of thine songe   boast
That thu canst yolle wrothe° and stronge   angrily
And seist thu wisest° mankünne   direct
That hi biwepen höre sünne.°   **biwepen** . . . lament their sin
975   Solde euch° mon wonie° and grede°   **Solde euch** Should each weep wail
Right swich° hi weren unlede?°   **Right swich** Just as if accursed
Solde hi yollen also thu dest?°   **also** . . . as you do
Hi mighte oferen here pröst."°   **oferen** . . . frighten their priests
Man shal bö stille and noght grede.
980   He mot° biwepe his misdede;   must
Ac war° is Cristes heriynge°   where praise
Thar me° shal grede° and lude singe?   one wail
Nis nother° too lud° ne too long,   neither loud
At righte time, chirche-song.
985   Thu yolst and wonest,° and Ich singe;   weep
Thi stevene is wop,° and min, skentinge.°   weeping amusement
Ever mote° thu yolle and wepen   may
That° thu thi lif mote forleten,°   As if **mote forleten** must abandon
And yollen mote thu so heye
990   That ut berste bo° thin eye!   both
Wether° is betere of twere twom:°   Which **twere twom** the two
That mon bö blithe, other grom?°   **other grom** or gloomy
So bö hit ever in unker sithe°   **unker sithe** our situation
That thu bö sori and Ich blithe.
995   "Yüt thu aisheist wi Ich ne fare
Into other londe and singe thare?
No! Wat sholde Ich among höm do
Thar never blisse ne com to?
That lond nis god, ne hit nis este,°   pleasant

963. Or that the sun will shine any the later

1000	Ac wildernisse hit is and weste.	
	Knarres and cludes höven-tinge,°	**Knarres** . . . Crags and hills sky-high
	Snou and haghel höm° is genge.°	**haghel höm** hail for them usual
	That lond is grislich and unvele.°	**grislich** . . . horrible and unprosperous
	The men böth wilde and unisele;°	unpeaceful
1005	Hi nabbeth nother grith ne sibbe;°	**nother** . . . neither truce nor concord
	Hi ne reccheth hu hi libbe.°	live
	Hi eteth fish and flesh unsode°	uncooked
	Swich° wulves hit hadde tobrode;°	**As if** torn apart
	Hi drinketh milc and hwei tharto.	
1010	Hi nüte° elles wat hi do.°	don't know should do
	Hi nabbeth nother° win ne bör°	neither beer
	Ac libbeth also° wilde dör.°	like animals
	Hi goth bitight° mid rugh felle°	clad **rugh felle** rough skins
	Right swich° hi comen° ut of helle.	**Right swich** Just as if had come
1015	"Thegh eni god man to höm come,	
	So hwile düde sum from Rome,[3]	
	For höm to lere° gode thewes°	teach customs
	And for to leten° höre unthewes,°	halt vices
	He mighte bet sitte stille,	
1020	For al his wile° he sholde spille.°	time waste
	He mighte bet teche ane böre°	**ane böre** a bear
	To weghe° bothe sheld and spere	wield
	Thane that wilde folc i-bringe°	persuade
	That hi me wolde i-here° singe.	**wolde i-here** would wish to hear
1025	Wat soldich° thar mid mine songe,	should I do
	Ne sunge Ich höm never° so longe?	**Ne** . . . Even if I sang to them ever
	Mi song were i-spild ech del,°	**i-spild** . . . wasted every part
	For höm ne mai halter ne bridel	
	Bringe vrom höre wode wise°	**wode wise** crazy manner
1030	Ne mon° mid stele ne mid ire.°	**Ne mon** Nor a man iron
	"Ac war° lond is bothe este° and god,	where pleasant
	And war men habbeth milde mod,°	
	Ich noti mid° höm mine throte,°	**noti mid** use among
	Vor Ich mai do thar gode note°	service
1035	And bringe höm löve tithinge,°	**löve tithinge** welcome news
	Vor Ich of chirche-songe singe.	
	Hit was i-seid in olde laghe°—	tradition
	And yet i-last thilke soth-sagh°—	**yet** . . . still lasts that saw
	That man shal erien° and sowe	plow
1040	Thar he wenth after° sum god mowe,°	**wenth after** expects afterward to reap
	For he is wod° that soweth his sed	crazy

[3] 'As on one occasion a certain one did come from Rome.' Probably a reference to Cardinal Vivian's embassy (1176) to Scotland, Ireland, and Norway.

Thar never gras ne sprinth ne bled."°   **sprinth** . . . springs nor blade
    The hule was wroth, to cheste rad;°   **to** . . . ready for conflict
Mid thisse worde hire eyen abrad:°   **eyen abrad** eyes she widened

OWL

1045   "Thu seist thu witest manne bures,°   **witest** . . . guard men's bedrooms
    Thar leves böth and faire flores,
    Thar two i-löve° in one bedde   lovers
    Liggeth biclopt° and wel bihedde.°   **Liggeth biclopt** Lie clasped together   guarded
    Enes° thu sunge—Ic wod° wel ware°—   Once   know   where
1050   Bi° one bure and woldest lere°   At   instruct
    The lefdi° to an üvel luve   lady
    And sunge bothe loghe and buve°   **loghe** . . . low and high
    And lerdest hi° to don shome   **lerdest hi** taught her
    And unright of hire licome.°   body
1055   The loverd° that sone underyat;°   lord   perceived
    Liim and grine and wel eiwat°
    Sette° and leyde thee for to lacche.°   He set   catch
    Thu come sone to than hacche.°   casement
    Thu were i-nume° in one grine;   caught
1060   Al hit aboghte thine shine.°   **aboghte** . . . your shins paid for
    Thu naddest non° other dom ne laghe°   **naddest non** had no   **dom** . . . verdict or   law
    Bute mid wilde horse were todraghe.°   drawn
    Vonde° yif thu might eft misrede°   Try   **eft misrede** again misadvise
    Wather° thu wült, wif the° maide!   Whichever   or
1065   Thi song mai bö so longe genge°   effective
    That thu shalt wippen° on a sprenge."°   flutter   snare
    The nightingale at thisse worde
    Mid sworde and mid speres orde,°   point
    Yif hö mon° were, wolde fighte;   a man
1070   Ac, tho° hö bet do ne mighte,   since
    Hö vaght° mid hire wise tunge.   fought
    "Wel fight° that wel specth," seith° in the songe.   **Wel fight** He fights well   it says
    Of hire tunge hö nom red.°   **nom red** took counsel
    "Wel fight that wel specth," seide Alvred.

NIGHTINGALE

1075   "Wat! Seistu this for mine shome?
    The loverd° hadde herof grame.°   lord   **herof grame** harm from this
    He was so gelus of his wive
    That he ni mighte for his live
    I-sö that man with hire speke
1080   That his hörte nolde° breke.   wouldn't
    He hire bileck° in one bure°   locked up   bedroom
    That hire° was bothe stronge and sure.   for her

1056. Lime and snare and almost everything

Ich hadde of hire milse and ore° — milse . . . pity and compassion
And sori was for hire sore
1085 And skente hi° mid mine songe — skente hi entertained her
Al that Ich mighte rathe° and longe. — early
Vor than° the knight was with me wroth; — that
Vor righte nithe° Ich was him loth.° — righte nithe sheer malice   loathsome
He düde° me his oghene° shome, — put on   own
1090 Ac al him° turnde it to grome.° — on him   harm
That underyat° the king Henri⁴— — learned
Jesus his soule do merci!
He let forbonne thene knight° — let . . . had the knight outlawed
That hadde i-don so müchel° unright — much
1095 Ine so gode kinges° londe — a king's
Vor righte nithe° and fule onde° — righte nithe sheer malice   spite
Let thane lütle fughel nime
And him fordeme lif an lime.⁵
Hit was wurthsipe° al mine künne;° — an honor to   kin
1100 Forthon° the knight forles his wünne° — For this   happiness
And yaf° for me an hundred punde, — paid
And mine briddes seten i-sunde° — seten i-sunde sat safe
And hadde soththe blisse and highte° — joy
And were blithe, and wel mighte.
1105 Vorthon° Ich was so wel awreke,° — Thus   avenged
Ever eft° Ich dar° the bet° speke. — after   dare   more boldly
Vor° hit bitidde ene swo,° — Because   bitidde . . . happened once thus
Ich am the blithur ever mo.° — more
Nu Ich mai singe war Ich wülle,
1110 Ne dar me never eft mon agrülle.° — eft . . . again anyone annoy
"Ac thu, ereming!° Thu wrecche gost, — wretch
Thu ne canst finde, ne thu nost,° — ne . . . nor do you know
An holgh stok thar° thu thee might hüde — holgh . . . hollow stump where
That me ne twengeth° thine hüde.° — That . . . So that no one will pluck   skin
1115 Vor children, gromes, heme, and hine,° — gromes . . . boys, servants, and yokels
Hi thencheth alle of thire pine.° — thire pine tormenting you
Yif hi mughe° i-sö thee sitte, — hi mughe they can
Stones hi doth° in höre slitte° — put   pockets
And thee totorveth and toheneth° — thee . . . pelt and stone you
1120 And thine fule bon tosheneth.° — bon tosheneth bones smash
Yif thu art i-worpe other i-shote,° — i-worpe . . . hit or shot
Thanne thu might erest to note,° — might . . . can finally be useful
Vor me thee hoth in one rodde,° — me . . . people hang you on a stick
And thu, mid thine fule codde° — paunch

---

⁴ Henry II (d. 1189), here referred to as already dead. See page 75, footnote 2.
⁵ 'As to have the little bird taken and have it condemned illegally life and limb.' Under the laws of Henry II only the king could condemn a culprit to loss of life and limb, and the crime had to be a serious one.

1125 And mid thine ateliche swöre,°
    Biwerest manne corn vrom döre.°
    Nis nother noght,° thi lif ne° thi blod,
    Ac thu art shewles° swithe god.
    Thar nöwe° sedes böth i-sowe,°
1130 Pinnuc,° golfinc, rok,° ne crowe
    Ne dar° thar never cumen ihende°
    Yif thi buc° hongeth at than ende.°
    Thar trön° shulle a yere blowe,°
    And yunge sedes springe and growe,
1135 Ne dar no fughel° tharto vonge°
    Yif thu art tharover i-honge.°
    Thi lif is evre lüther and qued;°
    Thu nard noght bute° ded.
    "Nu, thu might wite sikerliche,°
1140 That thine leches° böth grisliche°
    The wile° thu art on lif-daghe,°
    Vor wane thu hongest i-slaghe,°
    Yüt° hi böth of thee ofdradde,°
    The fugheles that thee er bigradde.°
1145 Mid righte° men böth with thee wrothe,
    For thu singist ever of höre lothe;°
    Al that thu singst rathe° other late,
    Hit is ever of manne unwate.°
    Wane thu havest a-night i-grad,°
1150 Men böth of thee wel sore ofdrad.
    Thu singst thar sum man shal be ded;
    Ever thu bodest sumne qued.°
    Thu singst aghen eighte lüre°
    Other° of summe fröndes rüre,°
1155 Other thu bodest huses brüne°
    Other ferde° of manne other thöves rüne,°
    Other thu bodest cwalm° of oreve°
    Other that lond-folc wurth i-dorve°
    Other that wif löst° hire make,°
1160 Other thu bodest cheste and sake.°
    Ever thu singist of manne° harme;
    Thurgh thee hi böth sori and arme.°
    Thu ne singst never one sithe°
    That hit nis for sum unsithe.°
1165 Hervore hit is that me° thee shuneth
    And thee totorveth and tobuneth°
    Mid stave and stoone and turf and clute°
    That thu ne might nowar atrute.°
    Dahet° ever swich büdel° in tune

ateliche swöre horrid neck
Biwerest . . . Protect men's grain from animals
Nis . . . It's otherwise useless   or
a scarecrow
new sown
Sparrow   rook
dare   near
body   boundary
trees   **a** . . . in spring bloom

bird   molest
hung
lüther . . . useless and evil
nard . . . are useless unless
wite sikerliche know certainly
looks   horrible
The wile While   **on lif-daghe** alive
hongest i-slaghe hang slain
Still   afraid
thee . . . previously berated you
Mid righte Rightly
dislikes
early
manne unwate men's misfortunes
cried out

sumne qued some disaster
aghen . . . concerning loss of property
Or   **fröndes rüre** friend's ruin
burning
invasion   **thöves rüne** thief's pursuit
plague   cattle
lond-folc . . . people will be distressed
will lose   mate
cheste . . . quarrel and strife
man's
miserable
one sithe once
disaster
people
totorveth . . . pelt and thrash
clods
escape
A curse on   **swich büdel** such a herald

1170 That ever bodeth unwreste rune°   **bodeth** ... prophesies bad news
 And ever bringeth üvele tithinge°   tidings
 And that ever specth of üvele thinge!
 God Almighti wurthe him wroth°   **wurthe** ... be angry with him
 And al that werieth linnene cloth."[6]
1175 The hule ne abot noght° swithe longe   **ne** ... didn't wait
 Ah yef ondsware starke° and stronge: **Ah** ... But gave answer fierce

OWL

 "Wat?" quath hö. "Hartu i-hoded,°   **Hartu i-hoded** Are you ordained
 Other thu kursest al unihoded?[7]
 For prestes wike,° Ich wat,° thu dest.°   **prestes wike** the office of priest   **know** are performing
1180 Ich not° yef thu were yare° prest;   **don't know**   formerly
 Ich not yef thu canst masse singe.
 Inoh° thu canst° of mansinge,°   Enough   know   cursing
 Ah° hit is for thine alde nithe°   But   **alde nithe** ancient malice
 That thu me akursedest other sithe.°   **other sithe** a second time
1185 Ah tharto is lihtlich ondsware.°   **lihtlich ondsware** an easy answer
 'Drah to thee!'° cwath the cartare.°   **Drah** ... Slow up   carter
 "Wi attwitestu me° mine insihte°   **attwitestu me** do you twit me about   wisdom
 And min iwit° and mine mighte?°   insight   ability
 For Ich am witi, ful i-wis,°   **witi** ... wise, most certainly
1190 And wod° al that to kumen is.   know
 Ich wot of hunger, of her-gonge;°   invasion
 Ich wot yef men schule libbe° longe;   live
 Ich wat yef wif lüst° hire make;°   loses   mate
 Ich wat war° schal beo nith and wrake;°   where   **nith** ... malice and vengeance
1195 Ich wot hwo schal beon anhonge°   hung
 Other elles fulne° deth afonge.°   a foul   receive
 Yef men habbeth bataile i-nume,°   **bataile i-nume** undertaken judicial combat
 Ich wat hwather° schal beon overkume.   which one
 Ich wat yif cwalm° scal comen on orfe°   pestilence   cattle
1200 And yif dör° schul ligge astorve.°   animals   **ligge astorve** lie prostrate
 Ich wot yef treon° schule blowe;°   trees   blossom
 Ich wat yef cornes° schule growe;°   grains
 Ich wot yef huses schule berne;
 Ich wot yef men schule eorne other erne;°   **eorne** ... run or ride
1205 Ich wot yef sea schal schipes drenche;°   sink
 Ich wot yef smithes schal üvele clenche;°   **üvele clenche** rivet badly
 And yet Ich con müchel° more.   **con müchel** know much
 Ich con inoh° in bokes lore,   enough

[6] 'All that wear linen underclothing,' the upper classes and the clergy, but not the lower classes and monks.

[7] 'Or do you curse (excommunicate) even though you are not hooded (ordained)' (and therefore not entitled to do so). The owl refers to the nightingale's two curses (ll. 99 and 1169).

And eke° Ich can of the Goddspelle°   also   Gospel
1210 More than Ich nüle° thee telle,   will
For Ich at chirche come ilome°   frequently
And muche leorni of wisdome.
Ich wat al of the tacninge°   allegorical interpretation
And of other feole° thinge.   **other feole** many another
1215 Yef eni mon schal rem abide,°   **rem abide** be pursued by hue and cry
Al Ich hit wot ear° hit i-tide.°   before   happens
Ofte, for° mine müchele iwitte,°   because of   **müchele iwitte** great insight
Wel sori-mod and wroth° Ich sitte.   **sori-mod** . . . sorry-hearted and angry
Wan Ich i-seo that sum wrechede°   misery
1220 Is manne neh, innoh° Ich grede.°   **manne** . . . near to man, enough   wail
Ich bidde° that men beon iwarre°   pray   aware
And habbe gode reades yarre,°   **reades yarre** counsels ready
For Alfred seide a wis word—
Euch mon hit schulde legge° on hord:°   lay   store
1225 'Yef thu i-sihst er he° beo i-cume,   **i-sihst** . . . see ahead before it (misery)
His° strencthe is him wel neh binume.'°   Its   **him** . . . well nigh taken from it
And grete duntes° beoth the lasse°   blows   less
Yef me i-kepth° mid iwarnesse,°   **me i-kepth** one looks out   awareness
And flo° schal thee toward misyenge°   arrow   **thee** . . . miscarry toward you
1230 Yef thu i-sihst° hu fleo° of strenge,°   see   it flew   string
For thu might blenche° wel and fleo°   **might blenche** can dodge   flee
Yif thu i-sihst heo° to thee teo.°   it   coming
    "Thauh eni man beo falle in odwite,°   shame
Wi schal he me his sor atwite?°   **me** . . . blame me for his suffering
1235 Thah Ich i-seo° his harm bivore,   see
Ne cometh hit noght of me tharvore.
Thah thu i-seo that sum blind mon
That nanne rihtne wei ne con°   **nanne** . . . knows no straight way
To thare diche his dweole fulieth°   **his** . . . follows his wrong way
1240 And falleth and tharone sulieth,°   **tharone sulieth** is dirtied in it
Wenest° thu, thah Ich al i-seo,   Suppose
That hit for° me the rathere beo?°   because of   **the** . . . came to be any the sooner
    "Al swo hit fareth bi mine witte.
Hwanne Ich on mine bowe sitte,
1245 Ich wot and i-seo swithe brihte°   clearly
An summe men° kumeth harm tharrihte.°   **An** . . . To some man   directly
Schal he that tharof nothing not°   knows
Hit wite me for° Ich hit wot?   **Hit** . . . Blame it on me because
Schal he his mishap wite me
1250 For Ich am wisure thane he?
Hwanne Ich i-seo° that sum wrechede°   see   misery
Is manne neh, inoh° Ich grede°   **manne** . . . near to man, enough   wail
And bidde inoh that hi heom schilde,°   **heom schilde** shield themselves

For toward heom is harm unmilde.°   cruel
1255 Ah,° thah Ich grede° lude and stille,   But   cry out
     Al hit i-tid° thurh Godes wille.   happens
     Hwi wülleth men of me hi mene°   **hi mene** complain to themselves
     Thah Ich mid sothe heo awene?°   **heo awene** grieve them
     Thah Ich hi warni al that yer,°   **that yer** the year
1260 Nis heom tharfore harem no the ner.°
     Ah° Ich heom singe for Ich wolde°   But   wish
     That hi wel understonde schulde
     That sum unselthe heom is ihende°   **unselthe** ... disaster is near them
     Hwan Ich min huing° to heom sende.   hooting
1265 Naveth no man none sikerhede°   **Naveth** ... No one has any assurance
     That he ne mai wene and adrede°   **wene** ... expect and fear
     That sum unhwate neh him beo°   **unhwate** ... misfortune may be near him
     Thah he ne conne hit i-seo.
     Forthi seide Alfred swithe wel—
1270 And his worde was Goddspel°—   Gospel
     That evereuch° man, the bet him beo,°   every   **bet** ... better off he may be
     Eaver the bet he hine beseo;°   **hine beseo** should look out for himself
     Ne trüste° no mon to his weole°   **Ne trüst** Nor rely   wealth
     Too swithe° thah he habbe veole.°   much   much
1275 Nis nout° so hot that hit na coleth,°   nothing   **na coleth** doesn't cool
     Ne noght so hwit that hit ne soleth,°   doesn't soil
     Ne noght so leof° that hit ne alotheth,°   dear   doesn't grow loathsome
     Ne noght so glad that hit ne awrotheth;°   doesn't grow angry
     Ac eavereuch° thing that eche° nis   every   eternal
1280 Agon° schal, and al this worldes blis.   Pass away
     "Nu thu might wite readliche°   **might** ... can know readily
     That eavere thu spekest gideliche,°   giddily
     For al that thu me seist for schame
     Ever thee-seolve° hit turneth to grome.°   upon yourself   reproach
1285 Go so hit go, at eche fenge°   bout
     Thu fallest mid thine ahene swenge.°   **ahene swenge** own attack
     Al that thu seist for me to schende°   **me** ... to shame me
     Hit is mi wurschipe° at the ende.   **mi wurschipe** in my favor
     Bute° thu wille bet aginne,°   Unless   start out
1290 Ne shaltu bute schame i-winne."
     The nightingale sat and sighte°   sighed
     And hohful° was—and ful wel mighte—   anxious
     For the hule swo i-speke° hadde   **swo i-speke** so spoken
     And hire speche swo i-ladde.°   conducted
1295 Heo was hohful and erede°   uncertain
     Hwat heo tharafter hire sede,°   **hire sede** should say to her
     Ah° neotheles heo hire understod.°   But   **hire understod** bethought herself

1260. Harm is not for that reason any the nearer to them.

NIGHTINGALE

"Wat!" heo seide. "Hule, artu wod?° crazy

Thu yeolpest° of seolliche° wisdome; boast wondrous

1300 Thu nüstest wanene he° thee come **nüstest** ... didn't know whence it

Bute° hit of° wicchecrefte were. Unless from

Tharof thu, wrecche, moste thee skere° **moste** ... must keep yourself clear

Yif thu wült among manne beo,

Other thu most of londe fleo,° **most** ... must flee from the land

1305 For alle theo° that therof cuthe° those **therof cuthe** are expert at it

Heo were ifürn of° prestes muthe **ifürn of** previously by

Amanset.° Swüch° thu art yette!° Excommunicated So too now

Thu wiecchecrafte neaver ne lete.° **neaver** ... have never abandoned

Ich thee seide nu lütel ere,° **thee** ... told you so just a little while ago

1310 And thu askedest yef Ich were—

A bisemere°—to° prest i-hoded.° **A bisemere** Asked in scorn as ordained

Ah the mansing° is so i-broded,° **the mansing** excommunication widespread

Thah no preost a londe nere,° **a** ... were in the land

A wrecche° neotheles thu were,° outcast would be

1315 For eavereuch° child thee cleopeth fule,° every **thee** ... calls you foul

And evereuch man a wrecche hule.

Ich habbe i-herd—and soth hit is—

The mon mot beo wel större-wis

That wite inoh of wücch thing kume

1320 So thu seist thee is i-wune!°

Hwat canstu,° wrecche thing, of större° do you know stars

Bute° that thu bihaltest hi feorre?° Except **bihaltest** ... behold them from afar

Alswo deth mani dör° and man **Alswo** ... So does many an animal

Theo° of swücche nawiht ne con.° Who **swücche** ... such knows nothing

1325 On° ape mai a boc° bihalde, An book

And leves wenden and eft folde,° **wenden** ... turn and close again

Ac he ne con the bet° tharvore, **ne** ... doesn't know any the better

Of clerkes lore° top ne more.° learning **ne more** or bottom

Thah thu i-seo° the steorre alswa,° may see also

1330 Nartu the wisure° neaver the mo.° **Nartu** ... You aren't any the wiser more

"Ah yet thu, fule thing, me chist° chide

And wel grimliche me atwist° reproach

That Ich singe bi manne huse° **manne huse** men's houses

And teache wive breke spuse.° **wive** ... wives to break wedlock

1335 Thu liest, i-wis,° thu fule thing! indeed

Thurh me nas° neaver i-schend spusing.° was **i-schend spusing** marriage destroyed

Ah soth hit is, Ich singe and grede° cry

Thar lavedies beoth° and faire maide; **lavedies beoth** ladies are

1317–20. I have heard—and true it is—that the man must be very wise in stars (astrology) who could know enough of what may come as you say is customary with you!

And soth hit is, of luve Ich singe.

1340 For god wif mai i° spusing   within
Bet luvien° hire oghene were°   love   **oghene were** own man
Than awer° hire copenere;°   somewhere else   lover
And maide mai luve cheose
That hire wurthschipe ne forleose°   **wurthschipe** ... honor she won't forfeit
1345 And luvie mid rihte luve
Thane the° schal beon hire buve.°   **Thane the** Him who   above
Swiche luve Ich i-tache and lere;°   **i-tache** ... recommend and teach
Therof beoth al mine ibere.°   utterance
Thah sum wif beo of nesche mode°—   **nesche mode** yielding mood
1350 For wummon beoth of softe blode—
That heo,° thurh sume sottes lore°   **That heo** So that she   **sottes lore** fool's instruction
The yeorne bit and siketh° sore,   **The** ... Who eagerly begs and sighs
Misrempe and misdo sumne stunde,°
Schal Ich tharvore beon i-bunde?°   blamed
1355 Yif wimmen luvieth unrede,°   indiscretion
Witestu me° höre misdede?   **Witestu me** Do you blame me for
Yef wimmon thencheth luvie derne,°   **thencheth** ... decide to love in secret
Ne mai Ich° mine songes werne.°   **Ne** ... I cannot   abandon
Wummon mai pleie under clothe°   clothes
1360 Wether° heo wile, wel the wrothe,°   Whichever   **wel** ... virtuously or wickedly
And heo mai do bi mine songe
Hwather heo wüle, wel the wronge,°   or wrongly
For nis a worlde° thing so god   **a worlde** in the world
That ne mai do sum ungod°   evil
1365 Yif me° hit wüle turne amis.   someone
For gold and seolver, god hit is;°   **hit is** they are
And notheles tharmid° thu might°   with it   can
Spus-brüche büggen° and unright.   **Spus-brüche büggen** Procure adultery
Wepne° beoth gode, grith° to halde;   Weapons   peace
1370 Ah neotheles tharmide beoth men acwalde°   killed
Agheines riht an fale° londe   **Agheines** ... Against the law in many
Thar theoves hi bereth° an honde.   **hi bereth** bear them
Alswa° hit is bi mine songe: So
Thah he° beo god, me hine mai misfonge°   it   **me** ... one can misuse it
1375 And drahe hine° to sot-hede°   **drahe hine** apply it   folly
And to othre üvele dede.
    "Ah schaltu, wrecch, luve tele?°   blame
Bö wüch hö° bö, uich° luve is fele°   **Bö** ... Be whatever it   each   proper
Bitweone wepmon and wimmane;°   **wepmon** ... man and woman
1380 Ah yef heo° is atbroide,° thenne   it   extorted
Heo is unfele and forbrode.°   **unfele** ... improper and corrupt

1353. May go astray and misbehave sometime

Wroth wurthe heom the Holi Rode
The rihte ikunde swo forbreideth!°
Wunder hit is that heo na wedeth.°
1385 And swo heo doth,° for heo beoth wode°
The bute° nest goth to brode.
Wummon is of nesche° flesche,
And flesches lust is strong to cwesse;°
Nis wunder nan° thah heo abide.°
1390 For° flesches lustes hi° maketh slide,
Ne beoth heo nowt° alle forlore
That stumpeth at° the flesches more,°
For moni° wummon haveth misdo°
That arist op of° the slo.°
1395 "Ne beoth nowt ones° alle sünne,°
Forthan° hi beoth tweire künne.°
Sum arist° of the flesches lüste,°
And sum of the gostes cüste.°
Thar° flesch draheth° men to drunnesse°
1400 And to wrouehede° and to golnesse,°
The gost misdeth thurch nithe and onde°
And seoththe° mid mürhthe of monne shonde°
And yeoneth after° more and more
And lütel rehth of milce and ore°
1405 And stighth° on heh° thurh modinesse°
And overhoheth thanne lasse.°
  "Sei me soth, yef thu hit wost.°
Hwether° deth würse, flesch the° gost?
Thu might segge,° yef thu wült,°
1410 That lasse° is the flesches gült.
Moni° man is of his flesche clene
That is mid mode deovel imene;°
Ne schal non mon wumman bigrede°
And flesches lustes hire upbreide;°
1415 Swüch he may telen of golnesse
That sünegeth würse i modinesse.°
Hwet yif Ich schulde a luve° bringe
Wif other maide hwanne Ich singe?
Ich wolde with the maide holde.°
1420 Yif thu hit const ariht atholde,°
Lüst nu, Ich segge thee hwarvore
Up to the toppe from the more.°

Glosses:

heo ... they don't go crazy
do go mad
The bute Who without
yielding
suppress
Nis ... It's no wonder heo abide she persist
Even though them
Ne ... They aren't
stumpeth at trip on stumbling block
many a misbehaved
arist ... arises from mire
Ne ... Nor are alike sins
Since tweire künne of two kinds
arise lust
gostes cüste spirit's nature
Whereas draws drunkenness
irritability lechery
misdeth ... misbehaves through malice and spite
also mürhthe ... pleasure in a man's shame
yeoneth after yawns open for
rehth ... cares for mercy and compassion
climbs high pride
overhoheth ... scorns the lowlier
know
Which or
might segge can say will
less
Many a
mid ... in pride a match for the devil
berate
hire upbreide ... reproach her for

a luve to love

wolde ... would like to encourage the maid
const ... can properly understand

bottom

1382–83. May the Holy Cross show anger upon (literally, 'become angry with') those who thus pervert natural instincts!
1415–16. Such a woman he may reprove for lechery while he himself sins in a worse way through pride (literally, 'he may ... that sins ...').

Yef maide luveth dernliche,°   secretly

Heo stumpeth and falth icündeliche,°   **stumpeth** ... trips and falls by natural instinct

1425   For, thah° heo sum hwile° pleie,   even though   **sum hwile** for a while

Heo nis nout feor ut of the weie.°   **nis** ... isn't far astray

Heo mai hire güld atwende°   **güld atwende** guilt escape

A° rihte weie thurh chirche-bende°   In the   church rites

And mai eft° habbe to hire make°   then   **to** ... as her mate

1430   Hire leofmon° withute sake°   sweetheart   blame

And go to him bi daies lihte

That er stal to° bi theostre° nihte.   **That** ... Whom she previously stole to   dark

An yungling not° hwat swüch thing is;   **yungling not** young girl doesn't know

His° yunge blod hit drageth° amis,   Her   **hit drageth** draws her

1435   And sum sot° mon hit tihth° tharto   foolish   **hit tihth** leads her

Mid alle than that° he mai do.   **than that** that

He cometh and fareth and beod and bid°   **beod** ... demands and begs

And heo bistant and oversid°

And bisehth i-lome° and longe.   **bisehth i-lome** beseeches often

1440   Hwat mai that child thah hit misfonge?°

Hit nüste neaver° hwat hit was;   **Hit** ... She never knew

Forthi hit thohte fondi thas°   **Forthi** ... She thought to try it

And wite i-wis hwüch beo the gome°

That of so wilde° maketh tome.°   wild a creature   a tame one

1445   Ne mai Ich for reothe lete,

Wanne Ich i-seo the tohte ilete

The luve bring on the yunglinge,

That Ich of mürghthe him ne singe.°

Ich teache heom bi mine songe

1450   That swücch luve ne lest noght° longe,   **ne** ... lasts not

For mi song lütle° hwile i-lest,°   only a little   lasts

And luve ne deth noght bute rest°   **ne** ... does but alight

On swüch childre° and sone ageth,°   girls   goes away

And falth adun° the hote breth.°   **falth adun** subsides   passion

1455   Ich singe mid heom one throghe,°   **one throghe** a while

Biginne on heh, and endi laghe,°   **heh** ... high, and finish low

And lete mine songes falle

An lütle wile adun mid alle.°

That maide wot, hwanne Ich swike,°   cease

1460   That luve is mine songes iliche,°   like

For hit nis bute a lütel breth

That sone kumeth and sone geth.°   goes

1438. And urges her and sits over her
1440. How can that child (girl) help it though she (it) go wrong?
1443. And know for sure what is the sport
1445–48. Nor can I, when I see the drawn face that love brings on the young girl, resist out of pity singing (literally, 'that I sing') of pleasure to her.
1457–58. And let my songs subside in a little while completely.

That child bi° me hit understönd°
And his unred° to red i-wend,°
1465 And i-seghth° wel, bi mine songe
That düsi° luve ne last noght° longe.
    "Ah wel Ich wüle that thu hit wite,°
Loth° me beoth wives utschüte;°
Ah° wif mai of° me nime yeme:°
1470 Ich ne singe nawt hwan Ich teme.°
And wif ah lete sottes lore,°
Thah spusing-bendes thüncheth° sore.
Wundere me thüngth° wel starc and stor°
Hu eni mon so eavar for°
1475 That he his heorte mighte drive
To do hit to others° mannes wive.
For other° hit is of twam° thinge,
Ne mai that thridde° no man bringe:
Othar the laverd° is wel aht°
1480 Other aswunde and nis naht.°
Yef he is wurthful° and aht man,
Nele no man that wisdom can
Hure of his wive do him schame,°
For he mai him adrede grame°
1485 And that he forleose that° ther hongeth°
That him eft° tharto noght ne longeth.°
And thah he that noght ne adrede,°
Hit is unright and gret sothede°
To misdon° one gode manne
1490 And his ibedde° from him spanne.°
Yef hire laverd is forwurde°
And unorne° at bedde and at borde,
Hu mighte thar beo eni luve
Wanne a cheorles buc hire ley buve?°
1495 Hu mai thar eni luve beo
War swüch man gropeth° hire theo?°
Herbi thu might wel understonde,
That on° is harm, that other schonde,°
To stele to othres mannes bedde;
1500 For yif aht° man is hire ibedde,°
Thu might wene° that thee mistide°
Wanne thu list° bi hire side;
And yef the laverd is a wrecche,°
Hwüch este° mightistu thar vecche?°
1505 Yif thu bithenchest° hwo hire ofligge,°
Thu might° mid wlate° the este bügge.°

---

child bi girl through   understands
his unred her folly   **red i-wend** wisdom turns

she sees

giddy   ne . . . lasts not

know
Loathsome to   **wives utschüte** wives' excesses
And a   from   **nime yeme** take example
couple
ah . . . ought to ignore a fool's instruction
spusing-bendes thüncheth marriage-bonds seem
Wundere . . . A wonder it seems to me
great
behaved

another

either one   two
the third
lord   able
aswunde . . . feeble and is useless
an honorable

him . . . fear harm for himself
forleose that may lose what   pertains
That . . . So that he again   yearn
noght . . . doesn't fear
folly
betray
wife   entice
incapable
useless

cheorles . . . churl's belly lay upon her

feels   thighs

That on The one alternative   shame

an able   bedmate
might wene can expect   **thee mistide** you'll have trouble
lie
impotent
Hwüch este What satisfaction   get
think   **hire ofligge** may have lain on her
may   disgust   pay for

1482–83. No man who possesses wisdom will wish at all to do him (the lord) shame through his wife

90

Ich not° hu mai eni freo° man   don't know   well-bred
For hire sechen° after than.°   seek   that
Yef he bithencth bi hwan° he lai,   whom
1510   Al mai the luve gan awai."
      The hule was glad of swüche tale.
Heo thoghte that the nihtegale,
Thah heo wel speke° atte frume,°   spoke   first
Hadde at then ende misnume;°   miscarried
1515   And seide:

OWL

"Nu Ich habbe i-funde°   found
That maidenes beoth of thine imunde.°   **thine imunde** concern to you
Mid heom thu holdest and heom biwerest,°   defend
And overswithe° thu hi herest.°   excessively   praise
The lavedies° beoth to me i-wended;°   ladies   inclined
1520   To me heo hire mode° sendeth,   feelings
For hit i-tit° ofte and ilome°   happens   frequently
That wif and were° beoth unisome;°   husband   disunited
And therfore the were gülte°   is guilty
That leof is other wummon to pülte°
1525   And speneth on thare° al that he haveth   **speneth** . . . spends on her
And siweth thare° that no riht naveth°   **siweth thare** follows her   has
And haveth attom° his righte spuse,   at home
Wowes weste, and lere° huse,   **Wowes** . . . Waste walls, and empty
Wel thünne i-schrud, and i-ved wrothe°   **thünne** . . . thinly clad and badly fed
1530   And let heo bute° mete and clothe.   **let** . . . leaves her without
Wan he cometh ham° eft to his wive,   home
Ne dar° heo noght a word i-schire.°   dare   speak
He chid and gred swüch° he beo wod°   **chid** . . . chides and screams as if   crazy
And ne bringth hom non other god.°   good
1535   Al that heo° deth, him is unwile;°   she   **him** . . . he dislikes
Al that heo speketh, hit is him ille;
And oft hwan heo noght ne misdeth,°   **noght** . . . does nothing wrong
Heo haveth the füst° in hire teth.   fist
Ther is nan mon that ne mai i-bringe°   send
1540   His wif amis mid swücche thinge.
Me° hire mai so ofte misbeode°   One   maltreat
That heo do wüle° hire ahene neode.°   **heo** . . . she will fulfill   **ahene neode** own needs
La, Godd hit wot, heo nah i-weld°   **nah i-weld** can't help it
Thah heo hine makie kukeweld!°   **hine** . . . make him a cuckold
1545   For hit i-tit lome° and ofte   **i-tit lome** happens frequently
That his wif is wel nesche° and softe,   yielding
Of faire bleo° and wel i-diht;°   complexion   shaped

1524. Who likes to assail another woman

Thi° hit is the more unriht°   So   unjust

That he his luve spene° on thare°   spend   someone else

1550   That nis wurth one of hire heare,°   hairs

And swücche men beoth wel manifolde

That wif ne kunne noght aright holde.°   **wif** . . . can't adequately retain a wife

Ne mot non° mon with hire speke;   **Ne** . . . Nor can any

He weneth° heo wüle anon tobreke°   thinks   **anon tobreke** at once break

1555   Hire spusing° yef heo loketh°   marriage vow   looks

Other with manne faire° speketh.   nicely

He hire biluth° mid keie and loke.   locks up

Tharthurh° is spusing° ofte tobroke,°   Thereby   marriage   broken up

For yef heo is tharto i-broht,°   **tharto i-broht** brought to that point

1560   Heo deth that° heo nadde ear i-thoht.°   what   **nadde** . . . hadn't thought of before

Dahet° that too swüthe hit bispeke°   A curse on him   **too** . . . condemns it too much

Thah swücche wives heom awreke!°   **heom awreke** avenge themselves

Herof the lavedies° to me meneth°   ladies   complain

And wel sore me ahweneth;°   grieve

1565   Wel neh° min heorte wüle tochine°   nearly   break

Hwon Ich biholde hire pine.°   pain

Mid heom Ich wepe swithe sore

And for heom bidde° Cristis ore°   beg   mercy

That the lavedi° sone aredde°   lady   he may rescue

1570   And hire sende betere i-bedde.°   bedfellow

    "Another thing Ich mai thee telle

That thu ne schald,° for thine felle,°   **ne schald** won't   skin

Ondswere none° tharto finde.   **Ondswere none** Any answer

Al thi sputing° schal aswinde.°   disputation   fail

1575   Moni chapmon° and moni cniht   **Moni chapmon** Many a merchant

Luveth and hald° his wif ariht,   holds

And swa° deth moni bondeman.°   so   serf

That° gode wif deth after than°   The   **deth** . . . acts accordingly

And serveth him to bedde and to borde

1580   Mid faire dede and faire worde

And yeorne fondeth° hu heo muhe°   **yeorne fondeth** eagerly seeks out   can

Do thing that him beo i-dughe.°   **him** . . . may be useful for him

The laverd into thare theode°   country

Fareth ut on thare beire nede,°   **on** . . . for the needs of both

1585   And is that gode wif unblithe°   unhappy

For hire laverdes oudsithe,°   departure

And sit and sihth,° wel sore oflonged,°   sighs   **sore oflonged** sorely longing

And hire sore an hörte ongred,°

Al for hire loverdes sake

1590   Haveth daies° kare and nightes wake;°   by day   **nightes wake** by night sleeplessness

And swüthe longe hire° is the hwile,   for her

1588. And grieves herself sorely at heart

And ech steape hire thünth° a mile.   **hire thünth** seems to her
Hwanne othre slepeth hire abute,
Ich one° lüst thar withthute   alone
1595   And wot of hire sore mode°   **sore mode** sad spirits
And singe a-night for hire gode;
And mine gode song, for hire thinge,°   situation
Ich turne sumdel° to murninge.°   somewhat mourning
Of hüre seorhe° Ich bere sume;   sorrow
1600   Forthan° Ich am hire° wel welcume.   Thus to her
Ich hire helpe hwat I mai,
For hö geth thane° rehte wai.   **geth thane** goes the
    "Ah thu me havest sore i-gramed°   vexed
That° min heorte is wel neh alamed,°   So that paralyzed
1605   That Ich mai unneathe° speke.   hardly
Ah yet Ich wüle forthure reke.°   continue
Thu seist that Ich am manne ylath,°   **manne ylath** loathsome to man
And evereuch° man is with me wroth   every
And me mid stone and lugge threteth°   **lugge threteth** sticks threatens
1610   And me tobusteth and tobeteth,°   **tobusteth . . .** batters and beats to pieces
And hwanne heo habeth me ofslahe,°   slain
Heo hongeth me on heore hahe,°   hedge
Thar Ich aschewele pie° and crowe   **aschewele pie** scare away magpie
From than the° thar is i-sowe.°   **than the** that which sown
1615   Thah hit beo soth, Ich do heom god,
And for heom Ich schadde° mi blod.   shed
Ich do heom god mid mine deathe;
Warvore thee is wel unneathe,°
For, thah thu ligge dead and clinge,°   waste away
1620   Thi deth nis nawt° to none° thinge!   **nis nawt** is nothing any
Ich not neaver to hwan thu might,°
For thu nart bute° a wrecche wight.   **nart bute** are but
Ah thah mi life me beo atschote,°   **me . . .** be spent from me
The yet° Ich mai do gode note;°   **The yet** Still service
1625   Me° mai upone smale sticke   One
Me sette a° wude ine the thicke,°   in thicket
And swa mai mon tolli him to°   **tolli . . .** lure to himself
Lütle briddes and i-vo,°   catch them
And swa me° mai mid me biyete°   one obtain
1630   Wel gode brede° to his mete.   roasts
Ah thu nevre, mon to gode,°   **mon . . .** for man's good
Lives ne deathes stal ne stode.°   **Lives . . .** Alive or dead gave help
Ich not to hwan° thu breist° thi brod;   **not . . .** don't know for what breed

1618. Whence it is very troublesome for you (to argue on this matter, since you are useless whether alive or dead)
1621. I don't know ever what good you are (literally, 'for what you are capable')

Lives ne deathes ne deth hit god."°   **ne deth** . . . it does no good

1635   The nihtegale i-herde this

And hupte° uppon on blowe ris°   hopped   **blowe ris** a flowering branch

And herre° sat than heo düde ear.°   higher   previously

NIGHTINGALE

"Hule," heo seide, "beo nu wear.°   warned

Nülle Ich with thee plaidi° na more,   debate

1640   For her thee mist° thi rihte lore.°   fails   wisdom

Thu yeilpest° that thu art manne° loth   boast   to man

And evereuch° wiht is with thee wroth;   every

And mid yülinge° and mid igrede°   yelling   crying

Thu wanst° wel that thu art unlede.°   lament   miserable

1645   Thu seist that gromes° thee i-foth°   boys   catch

And heie on rodde° thee anhoth°   a stick   hang up

And thee totwichet and toschaketh,°   **totwichet** . . . pluck and shake to pieces

And summe of thee schawles° maketh.   a scarecrow

Me thüncth° that thu forleost that° game.   **Me thüncth** It seems to me   the

1650   Thu yülpest of thire oghe° schame.   **thire oghe** your own

Me thüncth that thu me gest an honde.°   **me** . . . fall into my hands

Thu yülpest of thire oghene° schomme."   own

Tho° heo hadde theos word i-cwede,°   When   uttered

Heo sat in one faire stüde°   place

1655   And tharafter hire stevene dihte°   **stevene dihte** voice prepared

And song° so schille° and so brihte   sang   clearly ·

That feor° and ner me° hit i-herde.   far   one

Tharvore anan° to hire cherde°   at once   came

Thrusche and throstle and wudewale°   **throstle** . . . mavis and oriole

1660   And fuheles bothe grete and smale,

Forthan heom thühte° that heo° hadde   **Forthan** . . . For it seemed to them   she

The houle overcome vorthan heo gradde,°   **vorthan** . . . because she cried out

And sungen alswa vale wise,°

And blisse was among the rise.°   branches

1665   Right swa me gred° the manne a° schame   **me gred** one calls out at   in

That taveleth° and forleost that gome.   gambles

OWL

Theos hule, tho° heo this i-herde,   when

"Havestu," heo seide, "i-banned ferde?°   **i-banned ferde** called up an army

And wültu, wreche, with me fighte?

1670   Nai, nai! Navestu none mighte.

Hwat gredeth theo° that hider come?   **gredeth theo** do those cry out

Me thüncth thu ledest ferde to me.

1663. And they sang also many songs

94

Ye schule wite, ar ye fleo heonne,°   hence

Hwuch° is the strenthe of mine kunne,   What kin

1675 For theo the° haveth bile i-hoked   **theo the** those that

And clivres° scharpe and wel i-croked,   talons

Alle heo beoth° of mine künrede   **Alle . . .** They all are

And walde° come yif Ich bede.°   would   should ask

The seolfe coc, that wel can fighte,   **seolfe coc** cock himself

1680 He mot° mid me holde mid° righte,   must   by

For bothe we habbeth stevene brighte

And sitteth under weolcne° by nighte.   the clouds

Schille Ich an utest uppen öw grede,°

Ich shal swo° stronge ferde° lede   such a   army

1685 That öwer prude° schal avalle°—   **öwer prude** your pride   collapse

A tort° ne give Ich for öw° alle!—   turd   you

Ne schal, ar hit beo fulliche° eve,   fully

A wreche° fether on öw bileave.°   wretched   leave

"Ah hit was unker voreward°   **unker voreward** our agreement

1690 Tho° we come° hiderward   When   came

That we tharto holde scholde

Thar riht dom us give wolde.°

Wültu nu breke foreward?

Ich wene,° dom thee thingth° too hard!   suppose   **thee thingth** seems to you

1695 For° thu ne darst domes abide,°   Because   **ne . . .** dare not wait for judgment

Thu wült nu, wreche, fighte and chide.

Yöt Ich öw° alle wolde rede°   you   advise

Ar Ich utheste° uppon öw grede°   hue and cry   call

That öwer fihtlac leteth beo°   **öwer . . .** your fight you let be

1700 And ginneth rathe° awei fleo.°   **ginneth rathe** begin quickly   to flee

For, by the clivres that Ich bere,

Yef ye abideth° mine here,°   wait for   army

Ye schule on other wise singe

And acursi° alle fightinge,   curse

1705 Vor nis of öw non so kene°   brave

That dürre° abide mine onsene."°   would dare   gaze

Theos hule spac wel baldeliche,°   boldly

For, thah° heo nadde swo hwatliche°   though   **nadde . . .** wouldn't have so quickly

I-fare° after hire here,°   Gone out   army

1710 Heo walde neotheles yeve° answere   **walde . . .** wanted nevertheless to give

The° nightegale mid swücche worde.   To the

For moni man mid speres orde°   point

Haveth lütle strencthe and mid his schelde,

Ah neotheles in one felde°   battlefield

1683. If I'm going to have to call out a hue and cry against you

1691–92. That we were to agree in accordance with whatever a legal judgment would award us.

1715   Thurh belde° worde and mid ilete°   bold   bearing
         Deth° his ivo° for arehthe swete.°   Causes   foe   **arehthe swete** cowardice to sweat
           The wranne,° for heo cuthe° singe,   wren   **heo cuthe** knew how to
           Thar com° in thare moregheninge   came
           To helpe thare° nightegale,   the
1720   For, thah° heo hadde stevene° smale,   though   voice
         Heo hadde gode throte and schille°   clear
         And fale manne song a wille.°
         The wranne was wel wis i-holde,°   **wel** . . . considered very wise
         Vor, thegh heo nere i-bred a wolde,°   **nere** . . . wasn't bred in the woods
1725   Hö was i-toghen° among mankenne°   raised   mankind
         And hire wisdom brohte thenne.°   thence (from man)
         Heo mighte speke hwar heo walde°—   would
         Tovore the king thah° heo scholde.°   though   should wish to

WREN

         "Lüsteth,"° heo cwath. "Lateth me speke.   Listen
1730   Hwat, wülle ye this pes tobreke°   **pes tobreke** peace break
         And do than kinge swüch schame?⁸
         Ye,° nis he nouther ded ne lame.   Yea
         Hünke° schal i-tide° harm and schonde°   On both of you   come   disgrace
         Yef ye doth grith-brüche° on his londe.   **doth grith-brüche** commit breach of peace
1735   Lateth beo, and beoth i-some,°   reconciled
         And fareth riht° to öwer° dome,   **fareth riht** go directly   your
         And lateth dom this plaid tobreke°   **this** . . . settle this dispute
         Alswo° hit was erur bispeke."°   As   **erur bispeke** previously agreed

NIGHTINGALE

         "Ich an wel,"° cwath the nightegale.   **an wel** agree willingly
1740   "Ah, wranne, nawt for thire° tale   **for thire** because of your
         Ah do° for mire lahfulnesse.°   do so   **mire lahfulnesse** my respect for law
         Ich nolde° that unrihtfulnesse°   wouldn't wish   illegality
         Me at then° ende overkome.   the
         Ich nam ofdrad° of none° dome.   **nam ofdrad** I am not afraid   any
1745   Bihote° Ich habbe—soth hit is—   Promised
         That Maister Nichole, that is wis,
         Bitwüxen us deme schülle.   judge
         And yet° Ich wene° that he wüle,   still   expect
         Ah war mihte we hine° finde?"   him
1750   The wranne sat in ore linde.°   **ore linde** a linden tree

---

1722. And sang for the delight of many men.
⁸ 'And cause such shame to the king.' The king referred to is apparently Richard I (reigned 1189–99). According to Anglo-Norman law, anyone creating a public disturbance could be charged before a royal court with breach of the king's peace.

WREN

"Hwat? Nüste ye,"° cwath heo, "his hom?   **Nüste ye** Didn't you know
He wuneth at Porteshom,°   Portesham
At one tune° ine Doresete°   village   Dorset
Bi thare° see in ore utlete.°   Near the   **ore utlete** an outlet
1755   Thar he demeth° manie righte dom   judges
And diht and writ° mani wisdom,   **diht** . . . composes and writes
And thurh his muthe and thurh his honde
Hit is the betere into° Scotlonde.   **the** . . . as far off as
To seche hine is lihtlich° thing;   an easy
1760   He naveth bute° one woning.°   **naveth bute** has only   dwelling
That is bischopen muchel° schame   **bischopen muchel** for the bishops a great
And alle than° that of his nome°   those   name
Habbeth i-hert° and of his dede!°   heard   deeds
Hwi nülleth° hi nimen heom to rede°   won't   **nimen** . . . adopt as their plan
1765   That he were mid heom ilome°   often
For° teche heom of his wisdome,   To
And give him rente a vale stüde°   **rente** . . . revenues in many places
That he mighte heom ilome be mide?"°   **heom** . . . often be with them

OWL

"Certes,"° cwath the hule, "that is soth.   Certainly
1770   Theos riche° men wel muche misdoth°   powerful   do wrong
That leteth thane° gode mon   **leteth thane** abandon the
That of so feole° thinge con°   many   knows
And giveth rente wel misliche°   **rente** . . . revenues very erratically
And of him leteth° wel lihtliche.°   **of** . . . esteem him   casually
1775   With heore cünne° heo beoth mildre°   kin   more kind
And yeveth rente° litle childre!   revenues to
Swo heore wit hi demth a dwole
That ever abid Maistre Nichole.°
"Ah ute we thah° to him fare,   **ute** . . . let us then
1780   For thar is unker° dom al yare."°   our   ready

NIGHTINGALE

"Do we," the nightegale seide.
"Ah wa° schal unker speche rede°   who   **unker** . . . present our pleas
And telle tovore unker deme?"°   **telle** . . . speak before our judge

OWL

"Tharof Ich schal thee wel i-cweme,"°   satisfy
1785   Cwath the houle, "for al, ende of orde,°   **ende** . . . from end to end
Telle Ich con word after worde.

1777–78. Thus their intelligence condemns them as being in error in that Master Nichole is still waiting (to receive additional ecclesiastical revenues).

And yef thee thincth° that Ich misrempe,°   **thee thincth** it seems to you   go wrong
Thu stond aghein and do me crempe."°   **Thu . . .** Protest and make me stop
   Mid thisse worde forth hi ferden°   went
Al bute here° and bute ferde°   **Al . . .** Without army   troops
To Portesham, ther° heo bicome.°   where   arrived
Ah hu heo spedde of heore dome°   judgment
Ne can Ich eu namore telle.
Her nis namore of this spelle.°   story

1790

Holy Maidenhood

(ca. 1200, Southwestern)

Hali Meidenhad (or *Hali Meiðhad*) was written by an unknown author to encourage girls to enter into religious life. His arguments are drawn from an ancient Christian tradition. In the early days of the hermitic movement in the fifth century, when Jovinian argued that the celibate's life was not necessarily better than that of a married person, Jerome directed against the heretic an angry tract that was still being quoted in the days of Chaucer's Wife of Bath. In a similarly violent tone the Middle English preacher attacks marriage in order to defend virginity.

Despite the vehemence of his argument, the preacher basically has much in common with the gentle author of *The Anchoresses' Rule* (pp. 106–13). He warns maidens against human marriage in order that he may recommend a more satisfying spiritual marriage with Christ, in which the recluse's soul may mystically conceive virtues rather than children as her offspring. He recognizes the danger of spiritual pride and warns his listeners that "a mild wife or a meek widow is better than a proud maiden." And he couples his rhetorical brilliance with the same perceptivity of everyday human affairs displayed by the author of the *Rule*.

The edition of *Hali Meidenhad*, ed. F. J. Furnivall, revised by Oswald Cockayne, EETS 18 (London, 1866, 1922), contains a modernization; the latest edition is *Hali Meiðhad*, ed. A. F. Colborn (Copenhagen, 1940). For the manuscript see *Facsimile of Ms. Bodley 34*, ed. N. R. Ker, EETS 247 (London, 1960). For bibliography see Wells, ch. 5.1; *CBEL*, 1.168, 5.118.

Ah schawi we yet witerlüker, as we ear biheten, hwet drehen the i-weddede
thet thu i-cnawe therbi hu mürie thu maht libben meiden i thi meithhad over
thet heo libbeth, to eche the mürhthe and the menske in Heovene thet muth ne
mei nümnen. . . .

5   Thus, wümmon, yif thu havest were after thi wil and wünne ba of weorldes
weole, thee schal nede i-tiden. And hwat yif ha beoth thee wone that thu nabbe
thi wil with him ne weole nowther, and schalt greni godles inwith wasti wahes,
and in breades wone bredes thi barn-team, and, t'eke this, liggen under lathest
mon that, thah thu hafdest alle weole, went hit thee to weane?

10   For beo hit nu that thee beo richedom rive, and thine wide wahes wlonke and
welefulle, and habbe monie under thee, hirdmen in halle, and thi were beo thee
wrath and i-wurthe thee lath swa that inker either heasci with other, hwat
worldlich weole mei beo thee wünne? Hwen he beoth ute, havest ayain his
ham-cume sar, care, and eie. Hwil he bith at hame, alle thine wide wanes thüncheth
15 thee too narewe. His lokinge on thee agasteth thee; his ladliche mürhth and his
untohe bere maketh thee to agrisen. Chit thee and cheoweth thee and schent thee
schomeliche; tuketh thee to bismere as huler his hore; beateth thee and busteth
thee as his i-bohte threl and his ethell theowe. Thine banes aketh thee, and thi
flesch smerteth; thin heorte inwith thee swelleth of sar grome, and thi neb utewith
20 tendreth ut of tene.

Hwüch schal beo the somnunge bituhhen öw i bedde? Me theo that best
luvieth ham tobeoreth ofte thrin, thah ha therof na semblaund ne makien inne
marhen; and ofte of moni nohtunge, ne luvien ha ham neaver swa, bitterliche
bi hamseolf teonith either. Ha schal his wil, müchel hire unwil, drehen, ne luve
25 ha him neaver swa wel, with muche weane ofte. Alle hise ful-itoheschipes and
hise unhende gomenes—ne beon ha neaver swa with fülthe bifunden, nomeliche i
bedde—ha schal, wülle ha nülle ha, tholien ham alle. Crist schilde euch meiden
to freinen other to wilnen for to wite hwücche heo beon! For theo that fondeth
ham meast i-findeth ham forcuthest and clepeth ham selie i-wis the nüten neaver
30 hwat hit is and hatieth that ha haunteth. Ah hwa-se lith i leiven deope bisunken,
thah him thünche üvel thrin, he ne schal nawt up acoveren hwen he walde. . . .

Ga we nu forthre! Loke we hwüch wünne ariseth therafter i burtherne of bearne
hwen that streon i thee awakeneth and waxeth. Hu moni earmthen anan awakeneth
therwith that würcheth thee wa inoh, fehteth o thi selve flesch, and weorreth with
35 fele weanen o thin ahne cünde. Thi rudie neb schal leanen and as gres grenen.
Thin ehnen schulen doskin and underthon wonnen, and of thi breines turnunge
thin heaved ake sare; inwith thi wombe swelin the bitte, that beoreth forth as a
water bulge. . . .

After al this, cumeth of that bearn i-boren thus wanunge and wepunge that
40 schal abute midniht makie thee to wakien, other theo that thi stede halt, that thu
most fore carien. . . .

Holy Maidenhood

But let us, as we promised earlier, show more clearly what those who are married suffer, so that you may thus perceive how happily you can live as a maiden in your virginity in comparison to the way they live, in addition to the bliss and honor in Heaven which mouth cannot describe. . . .

Thus, woman, if you do have a husband according to your desire and the pleasure also of worldly wealth, necessity will still befall you. And what if these are lacking to you, so that you have neither pleasure in him nor wealth either, and must groan penuriously within your waste walls, and in dearth of bread give birth to your brood, and, besides, must lie under a most hateful man who, even if you possessed every wealth, would turn it into misery for you?

For now, even if you abound in riches, and your wide walls are splendid and luxurious, and you have many people under you as servants in hall, and your husband should become enraged with you and loathsome to you so that each of you quarrels with the other, what worldly wealth can be a delight for you? When he is out, you have sorrow, care, and fear for his home-coming. While he is at home, all your wide dwellings seem too narrow for you. His looking at you terrifies you; his hateful merriment and his rude behavior make you shudder. He chides you and bickers with you and scolds you shamefully; he mocks you as a lecher does his whore; he beats you and mawls you as his purchased slave and his family servitor. Your bones ache, and your flesh smarts; your heart swells within you from sore mortification, and your face flushes outwardly from anger.

What sort of coupling will there be between you in bed? Even those that love one another best often disagree in that, even if they may show no semblance of it in the morning; and often over many a frustration, though they love each other ever so much, one or other suffers bitterly by himself. She must endure his will, much against her own, however well she love him, often with much misery. All his lasciviousness and his improper pranks—no matter with what impurity they be conceived, especially in bed—she must suffer them all, willy nilly. May Christ prevent every maiden from asking or from wishing to know what they may be! For those that try them out the most find them to be the most despicable and call those blessed indeed who have never known what this is and who hate what such ones practice. But whoever lies deep sunken in a bog, though it seems ill to him to be in it, is not going to recover when he would wish to. . . .

Let us continue further! Let us see what joy ensues afterward in the bearing of children when the seed awakens and grows within you. How many miseries from this at once ensue that cause you woe aplenty, contend with your own body, and with many tribulations war on your own nature. Your radiant face will grow lean and turn green as grass. Your eyes will cloud and fail at this time, and your head will sorely ache from the whirling of your brains; within your belly your womb will swell and bulge out like a water bag. . . .

After all this, from the child born thus will come lamentation and weeping that will force you to wake up at midnight, or the one who takes your place, so that you must tend to it. . . .

And hwat yif ich easki yet, thah hit thünche egede, hu that wif stonde that ihereth, hwen ha cumeth in, hire bearn screamen, seoth the cat at the flicke, and the hund at the huide? Hire cake bearneth o the stan, and hire calf suketh; the
45 croh eorneth i the für, and the cheorl chideth. Thah hit be egede sahe, hit ah, meiden, to eggi thee swithre therframward, for nawt ne thünche hit hire egede that hit fondeth!

Ne tharf that seli meiden that haveth al i-don hire ut of thüllich theowdom ase Godes fre dohter and his Sunes spuse drehe nawt swücches. Forthi, seli meiden,
50 forsac al thüllich sorhe for utnume mede, that thu ahes to don withuten euch hüire.

[MODERNIZATION]

And what if I ask still further, though it may seem silly, how the wife is placed who, when she comes in, hears her baby screaming, sees the cat at the bacon and the dog at the hide? Her cake is burning on the stone, and her calf is sucking up the milk; the pot is running over into the fire, and the servant is grumbling. Though it may be a silly story, it ought to urge you away from it all the more strongly, maiden, for it does not seem in the least silly to the one who tries it!

The blessed maiden who as God's free daughter and the spouse of his Son has excluded herself completely from such servitude need not endure anything like this. So, blessed maiden, forsake all such sorrow in exchange for an exceptional reward, as you ought to do without any payment.

THE
THIRTEENTH
CENTURY

The Anchoresses' Rule

(ca. 1200, Southwestern)

The Anchoresses' Rule was prepared by an unknown cleric for a group of three aristocratic ladies who had decided to retire from the world into a life of spiritual contemplation. Usually such candidates would have joined a nunnery. The Benedictines had established convents for women in England even before the Norman Conquest and admitted new orders of nuns after the conquest; by 1200, the Gilbertines had admitted nuns to their order; and the Augustinians and Premonstratensians had founded orders for canonesses. The three anchoresses, however, had evidently decided to live by themselves, and their adviser therefore undertook to warn them of their duties and of what might be called the psychological hazards of their profession. Within the eight brief and clearly organized divisions of his manual the author (1) advocates observance of the divine services, (2) shows how the five senses may be directed toward the worship of God, (3) explains allegorically how the inner self should be controlled, (4) enumerates the temptations of the Seven Deadly Sins and prescribes remedies, (5) advocates confession, (6) advocates penance, (7) extolls the love of Christ as the highest form of love, and (8) appends some practical suggestions concerning the recluse's everyday life.

His treatment follows the method to be expected from someone trained in the scholastic tradition of the twelfth century. His convenient subdivisions within each topic are often more arbitrary than logical, and his allegorical interpretations of the scriptures are not intended so much to explain the passages quoted as to support his own arguments. Despite his scholastic method, however, his tone and style are highly personal and intimate. The concept of divine love that illuminates the works of the two great Cistercians he so frequently quotes—Bernard of Clairvaux and Ailred of Rievaulx—provides a similar warmth in his own writing.

His rule is thus not a series of restrictions. In the first excerpt included here, from his Introduction, he minimizes the importance of the outer or external regulations compared to the basic principles of the inner rule. In the second excerpt, from Book 2, when he turns to the dangers associated with the five senses, he recognizes that a small, defenseless group of ladies may be exposed to the unscrupulous advances of seducers skilled in the deceptive dalliance of courtly love. In a contemporary treatise on *The Art of Courtly Love*, the author, a French chaplain known as Andreas Capellanus, admits that he himself had once been drawn into a love affair with a nun. His reasons for discontinuing provide a striking contrast with the advice the unknown cleric gives the anchoresses. Andreas claims that he desisted for fear of God's wrath, of punishment by the civil authorities, and of the loss of his reputation, while the idealistic English confessor upholds the love of Christ rather than fear as a sufficient reason for overcoming untimely passions. In the third excerpt, from Book 8, when he deals with the problems of daily living, he praises the example of Mary Magdalen, who, on the occasion of Christ's visit, showed her love toward him, while her sister Martha was "cumbered about much serving" (Luke x.40); characteristically, he applies this commonly maintained distinction in an eminently practical and positive manner.

The *Ancrene Riwle*, as it was called in Middle English, was a widely disseminated and influential work. (The alternate title *Ancrene Wisse* 'Anchoresses' Guide' is sometimes applied by scholars to the Corpus Manuscript version and sometimes to the work as a whole.) Amplifications were introduced in the text for the sake of larger conventual communities, both male and female, and translations were prepared in both Latin and Anglo-Norman.

The Nero Manuscript version has been excerpted here; the latest edition of this is EETS 225, ed. Mabel Day (London, 1946); a modernization was prepared by James Morton (Camden Society, 1853; later eds. 1905, 1926). The Corpus Manuscript, containing the author's own revisions, has been published under the title *Ancrene Wisse*, eds. J. R. R. Tolkien and N. R. Ker, EETS 249 (London, 1960), and in modernization as *The Ancrene Riwle*, ed. M. B. Salu (London, 1955). The best introduction to the anchoritic tradition is *Ancrene Wisse: Parts Six and Seven*, ed. Geoffrey Shepherd (London, 1959). For bibliography see Severs, ch. 6.1.

The Inner and the Outer Rule

[INTRODUCTION]

Nu, aski ye hwat riwle ye ancren schullen holden? Ye schullen alles weis, mid
alle mihte, and mid alle strencthe, wel witen the inre and the uttre vor hire sake.
The inre is evere iliche; the uttre is misliche, vor everich schal holden the uttre
efter thet the licome mei best mid hire servi the inre. . . .

5   The uttre riwle, thet Ich thuften cleopede and is monnes findles, nis for nothing
elles i-stald bute forto servie the inre. Thet maketh festen, wakien, kold, and here
werien, and swüche othre heardschipes thet moni flechs mai tholien and moni ne
mai nout.

   Vor-thi mot theos riwle chaungen hire misliche efter euch ones manere and
10 efter hire efne. Vor sum is strong; sum is unstrong and mei ful wel beo cwite and
paie God mid lesse. Sum is clergesse, and sum nis nout and mot the more wurchen
and an other wise siggen hire ures. Sum is old and atelich and is the lease dred of;
sum is yung and livelich and is neode the betere warde.

   Vor-thi schal efrich ancre habben the uttre riwle after schriftes read and, hwat
15 se he bit and hat hire, don in obedience, the cnoweth hire manere and hire strencthe.
He mai the uttre riwle chaungen efter wisdom alse he i-siht thet the inre mai beon
best i-holden.

   Non ancre bi mine read ne schal makien professiun, thet is, bihoten ase hest, bute
threo thinges, thet is, obedience, chastete, and stude-stathelvestnesse (thet heo ne
20 schal thene stude never more chaungen bute vor neod one, als strengthe, and
deathes dred, obedience of hire bischope other of hire herre). Vor hwoa-se nimeth
thing on hond and bihat hit God alse heste to donne, heo bint hire therto and
sünegeth deadliche ithe brüche yif heo hit breketh willes and woldes. Yif heo hit
ne bihat nout, heo hit mai don thauh and leten hwon heo wel wüle, alse of mete,
25 and of drünch, fleschs forgon other visch, and alle other swüche thinges of weriunge,
liggunge, of vres, of beoden. Sigge so monie and o hwüche wise so heo ever wüle.
Theo and swüche othre beoth alle ine freo wille to donne other to leten hwon me
ever wüle bute heo beon bihoten.

   Auh cherite (thet is, luve), and edmodnesse, and tholemodness, treoweschipe, and
30 holding of the Tene olde Hesten, schrift and penitence—theos and swüche othre
thet beoth summe of the Olde Lawe, summe of the Neowe, ne beoth nout monnes
fündles, ne riwle thet mon stolde, ah beoth Godes hesten. And for-thi, everiche mon
ham mot nede holden, and ye over alle thing!

[MODERNIZATION]

Now, you ask what rule you anchoresses are to follow? You must in all ways, with all your power and all your strength, know the inner rule well and the outer for its sake. The inner rule is always the same; the outer is varied, for each person must follow the outer in such a way that the body can best serve the inner rule by means of it. . . .

The outer rule, which I have called a handmaiden and which is the invention of man, is established for no other reason but to serve the inner. It requires fasting, keeping vigil, enduring cold, and wearing haircloth, and such other hardships that the flesh of many can endure and of many others cannot.

Therefore this rule must change variously according to the manner and nature of each. For some are strong; some are not and can be perfectly well acquitted and satisfy God with less. Some are scholarly, and some are not and must strive the more and in another way recite their hours. Some are old and ugly and are to be less feared for; some are young and lively and in need of better protection.

Therefore each anchoress ought to follow the outer rule according to the advice of a confessor, and whatever he, who knows her manner and strength, orders and commands her, she should perform in obedience. He can change the outer rule at discretion as he sees that the inner rule can best be observed.

No anchoress, by my advice, ought to make profession, that is, promise as an obligation, except for three matters, namely, obedience, chastity, and permanence of residence (that she will never change her place of residence unless because of absolute necessity, such as force, fear of death, and obedience to her bishop or to her superior). For whoever undertakes something and promises it to God under obligation to do it, commits herself to it and sins mortally in breaking it if she breaks it willingly and intentionally. If she does not promise, she can still perform it and cease to perform it whenever she wishes, as for instance with eating and drinking, abstaining from meat or fish, and all other such matters concerning clothing, resting, reciting hours, and prayers. Let her recite them as many and in such manner as she may wish. These and such other matters are all within free choice to be performed or not whenever one wishes, unless they have been promised.

But charity (that is, love), and humility, and long-suffering, fidelity, and the observation of the Ten Commandments of old, of confession, and of penitence— these and such other matters that are partly of the Old Law and partly of the New, are not the invention of man or a rule that man instituted but are the commands of God. And therefore everyone must observe them, and you in particular!

The Love of Man and of Christ

[BOOK 2]

Vor-thi, mine leove süstren, yif eni mon bit fort i-seon ou, asketh of him hwat
god therof muhte lihten, vor moni üvel Ich i-seo therinne and none biheve. And
yif he is methleas, i-leveth him the wurse. And yif eni wurtheth so wod and so
awed that he worpe his hond forth touward the thurl-cloth, swiftliche anonricht
5 schutteth al the thurl to and letteth hine i-wurden. And also sone ase eni mon
valleth into lüther speche thet falle touward fule live, tüneth thet thurl anonriht, and
ne answerie ye him nowiht, auh wendeth awei mit thisse vers thet he hit muwe
i-heren: "Narraverunt mihi iniqui fabulaciones sed non ut lex tua." And goth forth
bivoren ower weovede mit the *Miserere*.
10   Ne chastie ye never nenne swüchne mon bute o thisse wise, vor mit the chastie-
ment he muhte onswerien so and blowen so litheliche thet sum sperke muhte
acwiken. No wouhleche nis so culvert ase is o pleinte wis, ase hwo se thus seide:
"Ich nolde, vor to tholien deathe, thenche fülthe touward thee. Auh Ich hevede
i-sworen hit, luvien Ich mot thee. And nu me is wo thet thu hit wost. Auh foryif
15 hit me nu thet Ich hit habbe i-told thee, and, thauh Ich schulde i-wurthe wod, ne
schalt thu never more eft witen hu me stont."
   Ant heo hit foryiveth him, for he speketh thus feire, and speketh theonne of
otherwhat. Auh "ever is the eie to the wude leie; therinne is thet Ich luvie!" Ever
is the heorte in there vorme speche; and yet, hwon he is forthe, heo went in hire
20 thuhte ofte swüche wordes hwon heo schulde otherhwat yearneliche yemen. He
eft secheth his point vorte breke voreward and swereth thet he mot nede, and so
waxeth the wo se lengre se wurse. Vor no freondschipe nis so üvel ase is fals freondschipe; feond thet thüncheth freond is swike over alle swike.
   Vor-thi, mine leove süstren, ne yive ye to none swüche monne non inyong to
25 spekene, for ase Holi Writ seith, "Höre speche spret ase cauncre." Auh for alle
onsweres wendeth ou ant wrencheth frommard him. . . .
   This beoth nu two thinges thet beoth i-luved swüthe: swete speche and schene
hwite. Hwo-se ham haveth togederes, swüche cheoseth Jesu Crist to leofmon and
to spuse. Yif thu wilt beon swüch, ne scheau thu none monne thi hwite, ne ne lete
30 blitheliche i-heren thine speche. Auh turn bothe to Crist, to thi deorewurthe spus,
ase he bit theruppe, ase thu wilt thet thi speche thünche him swete, and thi hwite
schene, and habben him to leofmon thet is a thusentfold schenre then the sunne.

[MODERNIZATION]

If, then, my dear sisters, a man asks to see you, ask him what good might come of it, for here I forsee many evils and no advantage. And if he is importunate, consider him the worse for it. And if any man becomes so wild and so disturbed that he thrusts his hand forth toward the curtain, at once shut the window swiftly and let him be. And as soon as any man falls into seductive speech pertaining to an impure way of life, close the window at once and answer him nothing, but turn away with this verse so that he may overhear it: "The wicked have told me fables, but not as thy law." And go in before your altar with the psalm "Have mercy upon me."

Never reprove any such man in any other way than this, for upon the reproof he might answer and blow so subtly that some spark might be kindled. No seduction is so subtle as that which is in a plaintive manner, as if he were to say: "I would not, on pain of death, think of indecency directed toward you. But, even if I had sworn the contrary, I must love you. And now I regret that you know it. But forgive me now that I have told you, and even if I should turn mad, you will never again know how things stand with me."

And she forgives him, for he speaks so gracefully, and then she speaks of something else. But "ever is the eye toward the shelter of the woods; the one whom I love is there!" Ever is the heart on the previous speech; and when he is gone, still she often turns such words in her thoughts when she ought to attend diligently to other matters. Still he seeks his opportunity to break his promise and swears that he must needs do so, and thus the longer the worse the calamity grows. For no friendship is so evil as is false friendship; an enemy who seems a friend is a villain above all villains.

So, my dear sisters, give no admittance to any such man to speak, for as Holy Writ says, "Their speech spreadeth as a cancer." But in place of all answers, turn and draw away from him. . . .

Now these are two things that are much beloved: sweet speech and fair beauty. Whoever has both of these together, such a one Jesus Christ chooses as his beloved and his bride. If you wish to be such, do not show any man your beauty, and do not blithely let him hear your speech. But turn both to Christ, for your precious spouse, as he summons you thither, as you wish that your speech may seem sweet and your beauty seem fair to him, and choose as your beloved him who is a thousandfold more beauteous than the sun.

Domestic Life

[BOOK 8]

Ye, mine leove süstren, ne schulen habben no best bute kat one. Ancre thet
haveth eihte thüncheth bet husewif ase Marthe was then ancre, ne none wise ne
mei heo beon Marie mid grithfulnesse of heorte. Vor theonne mot heo thenchen
of the kues foddre and of heorde-monne huire, oluhnen thene heiward, warien
5 hwon me punt hire, and yelden thauh the hermes. Wat Crist, this is lodlich thing
hwon me maketh mone in tune of ancre eihte. Thauh, yif eni mot nede habben
ku, loke thet heo none monne ne eilie ne ne hermie, ne thet hire thouht ne beo
nout theron i-vestned.

Ancre ne ouh nout to habben no thing thet drawe utward hire heorte. None
10 cheffare ne drive ye. Ancre thet is cheapild, heo cheapeth hire soule the chepmon
of helle. Ne wite ye nout in oure huse of other monnes thinges, ne eihte, ne clothes;
ne nout ne undervo the chirche vestimenz ne thene caliz bute yif strencthe hit makie
other muchel eie, vor of swüche witunge is i-kumen muchel üvel oftesithen. . . .

Vor-thi thet no mon ne i-sihth ou, ne ye i-seoth nenne mon, wel mei don of
15 ower clothes, beon heo hwite, beon heo blake, bute thet heo beon unorne and
warme and wel i-wrouhte, velles wel i-tauwed; and habbeth ase monie ase ou to-
neodeth to bedde and eke to rügge.

The Author's Prayer

[EPILOGUE]

O thisse boc redeth everiche deie hwon ye beoth eise, everiche dei lesse other
more. Vor Ich hopie thet hit schal beon ou, yif ye redeth ofte, swüthe biheve thuruh
Godes grace—and elles ich hevede üvele bitowen muchel of mine hwüle! God hit
wot, me were leovere vorto don me touward Rome then vorto biginnen hit eft
5 forto donne.

And yif ye i-vindeth thet ye doth al so ase ye redeth, thonketh God yeorne; and
yif ye ne doth nout, biddeth Godes ore, and beoth umbe ther abuten thet ye hit
bet hol holden efter ower mihte.

Veder and Sune and Holi Gost, and on Almihti God, he wite ou in his warde.
10 He gledie ou, and froure ou, mine leove sustren. And for al thet ye vor him drieth
and suffreth, he ne yive ou never lesse huire then altogedere himsülven. He beo
ever i-heied from worlde to worlde, ever on ecchenesse. Amen.

[MODERNIZATION]

My dear sisters, you must not keep any animal except for a cat. An anchoress that has property seems more like a housewife such as Martha was than an anchoress, nor can she in any way be Mary in peacefulness of heart. For then she must think of the cow's fodder and the herdsman's hire, must flatter the heyward, guard against the impounding of her cattle, and furthermore pay damages. Christ knows, it is a sorry matter when complaint is made in town over the property of anchoresses. However, if any anchoress, absolutely must have a cow, see that it neither annoys nor harms anyone and that her concern is not attached to it.

An anchoress ought not to have anything that might draw her heart outward. Deal in no business. An anchoress who is a dealer sells her soul to the tradesman of hell. Do not store in your house other people's possessions or property or clothes; and do not accept the church vestments and chalice unless compulsion or some great alarm require it, for great harm has often come from such custody. . . .

Since no man sees you and since you see no man, you may well be satisfied with your clothes, whether they be white or black, provided that they be simple and warm and well made, and the leather-skins well prepared; and have as many as you need both for bed and for your back.

[MODERNIZATION]

Read in this book every day when you are free, either less or more each day. For I hope that, if you read it often, it will by the grace of God be very profitable for you—otherwise, I would have ill spent much of my time! God knows, I would sooner set out for Rome than begin to do it again.

And if you find that you are doing exactly what you read, thank God heartily; and if you are not doing so, pray for God's mercy, and attempt to follow it better according to your ability.

May the Father, Son, and Holy Ghost, the one Almighty God, keep you in his care. May he gladden you and comfort you, my dear sisters. And for all that you endure and suffer on his behalf, may he never grant you a recompense less than himself entirely. May he be ever exalted from generation to generation, ever in eternity. Amen.

King Horn

(ca. 1225, Southwestern)

King Horn is an outstanding example of what may be called a primitive romance. The composer is resolutely concerned with the basic and universal ingredients of romance—religion, love, and warfare (Dante's *salus*, *venus*, and *virtus*)—but he is not concerned with the attendant subtleties of pictorialization, characterization, and motivation. Here, as with the ballad, the listeners provided their own interpretations. The highly developed art of *Sir Gawain and the Green Knight* (p. 376) with all its ethical, courtly, and chivalric nuances was not to emerge in England until a century and a half later. Yet the very simplicity of *King Horn* gives it a universal appeal.

It is not only the earliest surviving English romance but also one of the most enduringly popular. The oldest recorded form of the tale is an Anglo-Norman poem composed around 1170–80 by a certain Master Thomas. The Middle English romance printed here is preserved in three closely similar manuscript versions. An alternate and inferior version known as *Horn Child* was composed around 1320; and this or some other later form entered the popular oral tradition of balladry with such vigor that the ballad of *Hind Horn* was still being sung in the nineteenth century.

The version that follows is based on the Harley Miscellany (2253), compiled in Hereford around 1330–39. Two lines, unnumbered, have been borrowed from the Laud Manuscript, and a few variants have been introduced from the other manuscripts when the Harley version seems inconsistent. The composer of *King Horn* may have had a clear sense of geography, but the minstrels who transmitted his romance and the scribes who recorded it were evidently indifferent. For clarification, his movements between Sudene (his home), Westnesse (his sweetheart's home), Ireland (his place of exile), and Reynis or Reme (the unwanted suitor's home) have therefore been supplied in the text. The reader will also note that Horn's father, Allof, is alternately called Murry in some passages.

The meter is rhyming, three-beat couplets; see Introduction, type 4, page 30.

The standard edition of the three manuscript versions (and of *Horn Child*) is *King Horn, A Middle English Romance*, ed. Joseph Hall (Oxford, 1901); for *Hind Horn* see F. J. Child, ed., *English and Scottish Popular Ballads* (Cambridge, Mass., 1882), No. 17 (cf. No. 252). The manuscript followed here is reproduced in *Facsimile of British Museum MS. Harley 2253*, ed. N. R. Ker, EETS 255 (Oxford, 1965), item 70. For bibliography see Severs, ch. 1.1.

Alle heo ben° blythe   **Alle** ... May they all be
That to my song y-lythe.°   listen
A song Ychülle ou° singe   **Ychülle ou** I will to you
Of Allof the gode kynge—

King Horn

[HORN IN SUDENE]

5 Kyng he wes by° weste,   *in the*
     The whiles hit y-leste°—   *lasted*
     Ant Godylt his gode quene—
     No feyrore myhte bene—
     Ant hüere° sone hihte° Horn—   *her   called*
10 Feyrore child ne myhte° be born;   **ne myhte** couldn't
     For reyn ne myhte byryne°   *touch on*
     Ne sonne myhte shyne°   *shine on*
     Feyrore child then he was,
     Bryht so° ever eny glas,   *as*
15 So whit so eny lylye flour,
     So rose red wes his colour.
     He wes feyr ant eke° bold   *also*
     Ant of fyftene wynter old.
     Nis non° his yliche°   **Nis non** There is none like
20 In none kinges ryche.°   *realm*
       Tweye feren° he hadde   **Tweye feren** Two companions
     That he with him ladde,
     Alle riche menne° sones,   **riche menne** powerful men's
     Ant alle swythe° feyre gomes,°   *very   lads*
25 Wyth him for te° pleye.   *to*
     Mest° he lovede tweye.   *Most*
     That on° wes hoten° Athulf Chyld, **That on** The one   called
     Ant that other Fykenyld.
     Athulf wes the beste,
30 Ant Fykenyld the werste.
       Hyt was upon a someres day,
     Also° Ich ou° telle may,   *As   you*
     Allof the gode kyng
     Rod upon ys pleyghyng°   **ys pleyghyng** his sport
35 Bi the see side,
     Ther° he was woned° to ryde.   *Where   accustomed*
     With him ne ryde bote° two.   **ne . . .** rode only
     Al too fewe hüe° were tho.°   *they   then*
     He fond by the stronde
40 Aryved on is° londe   *his*
     Shipes fyftene
     Of Sarazynes kene.°   *bold*
     He askede whet hüe sohten°   *sought*
     Other° on is lond brohten.   *Or*
45 A payen° hit y-herde   *pagan*
     Ant sone° him onswerede: *at once*
      "Thy lond-folk° we wölleth slon° *people* **wölleth slon** will slay
     That° ever Crist leveth on,°   *Who* **leveth on** believe in

Ant thee we wölleth° ryht anon.
 50 Shalt thou never henne gon."°
       Thy kyng lyhte of° his stede,
    For tho° he hevede nede,
    Ant his gode feren° two.
    Mid y-wis, hüem wes ful wo.°
 55 Swerd° hy gonne° gripe
    Ant togedere smyte.
    Hy smyten under shelde
    That hy somme y-felde.
    The kyng hade too fewe
 60 Agheyn° so monie schrewe.°
    So fele° myhten ethe°
    Bringe thre to dethe.
    The payns° come to londe
    Ant nomen° hit an° honde.
 65 The folk hy gonne quelle°
    Ant cherches for to felle.
    Ther ne myhte° libbe
    The fremede° ne the sibbe°
    Bote° he is° lawe forsoke
 70 Ant to hüere° toke.
       Of alle wymmanne
    Werst wes Godyld thanne.
    For Allof hy° wepeth sore
    Ant for Horn yet more.
 75 Godild hade so muche sore
    That habbe myhte hüe° na more.
    Hüe wente out of halle
    From hire maidnes alle
    Under a roche of stone,
 80 Ther° hüe wonede° alone.
    Ther hüe servede Gode
    Agheyn° the payenes forbode;°
    Ther hüe° servede Crist
    That° the payenes hit nüst;°
 85 Ant ever hüe bad° for Horn Child
    That Crist him wurthe° myld.
       Horn wes in payenes hond
    Mid is feren° of the lond.
    Muche wes the feyrhade°
 90 That Jhesu Crist him° made.
    Payenes° him wolde slo,°
    Ant summe him wolde flo.°

will slay
henne gon go hence
lyhte of alighted from
then
companions
Mid . . . Certainly, they were very woeful
Swords began to

Against villains
many easily

pagans
took in

gonne quelle began to kill

ne myhte couldn't
stranger relation
Unless his own
theirs

she

she

Where dwelt

Despite **payenes forbode** pagans' prohibition
she
So that didn't know
prayed
him wurthe to him might be

Mid . . . With his companions
attractiveness
in him
Pagans **wolde slo** wanted to slay
flay

Yyf Hornes feyrnesse nere,°   it hadn't been for
Y-slawe° this children were.°   Slain   would have been
95   Tho spec on admyrold°—   **Tho** . . . Then spoke an emir
Of wordes he wes swythe° bold: very
   "Horn, thou art swythe kene,°   bold
Bryht of hewe, ant shene;°   beautiful
Thou art fayr ant eke° strong   also
100   Ant eke eveneliche long.°   **eveneliche long** proportionately tall
Yef thou to-lyve mote° go   **to-lyve mote** alive may
Ant thyne feren° also,   companions
That Y may byfalle:°   suffer
That ye shule slen° us alle.   slay
105   Tharefore thou shalt to streme° go,   sea streams
Thou ant thy feren also;
To° shipe ye shule founde°   On a   go
Ant sinke to the grounde.°   bottom
The see thee shal adrenche,°   drown
110   Ne shal hit us ofthenche,°   distress
For, yef thou were alyve,
With swerd other° with knyve   **swerd other**   sword or
We shulden alle deye,
Thy fader° deth to beye."°   father's   atone for
115   The children ede° to the stronde,   went
Wryngynde hüere° honde,   their
Ant into shipes borde
At the fürste worde.°   words
Ofte hade Horn be wo°   **be wo** been woeful
120   Ah° never wors then him° wes tho.°   But   **then him** than he   then
   The see bygon to flowen
Ant Horn faste to rowen,
Ant that ship wel swythe° drof,   **wel swythe** very quickly
Ant Horn wes adred° therof.   afraid
125   Hüe wenden mid y-wisse°   **Hüe** . . . They expected certainly
Of hüere lyve to misse.°   **Of** . . . To lose their lives
Al the day ant al the nyht
Othat° sprong the day-lyht   Until
Flotterede° Horn by the stronde   Hovered
130   Er° he seye° eny londe.   Before   saw
   "Feren," quoth Horn the yynge,°   young
"Y telle ou° tydynge.   you
Ich here foules° singe   birds
Ant se the grases springe.
135   Blythe° be ye alyve;   Happy
Ur ship is come to ryve."°   shore

[HORN IN WESTNESSE]

	Of° shipe hy gonne founde°	By **gonne founde** did go
	Ant sette fot to grounde.	
	By the see syde	
140	Hüre° ship bigon to ryde.	Their
	Thenne spec him° Child Horn—	**spec him** spoke
	In Sudenne he was y-born:	
	"Nou, ship, by the flode	
	Have dayes gode.	
145	By the see brynke	
	No water thee adrynke.°	**No** ... May no water sink you
	Softe mote° thou sterye°	**Softe mote** Gently must steer
	That water thee ne derye.°	**ne derye** doesn't harm
	"Yef thou comest to Sudenne,	
150	Gret° hem that me kenne;°	Greet know
	Gret wel the gode	
	Quene Godild, mi moder,	
	Ant sey thene hethene° kyng,	**thene hethene** to the heathen
	Jhesu Cristes wytherlyng,°	adversary
155	That Ich hol ant fere°	**hol** ... whole and well
	In londe aryvede here,	
	Ant say that he shal fonde°	undergo
	Then deth of° myne honde."	**Then** ... Death from
	The ship bigon to fleoten°	sail
160	Ant Horn Child to weopen.	
	By dales ant by doune°	upland
	The chidren eoden° to toune.°	went town
	Metten hüe° Eylmer the kyng—	they
	Crist him yeve° god tymyng—	give
165	Kyng of Westnesse.	
	Crist him myhte blesse!	
	He spec° to Horn Child	spoke
	Wordes swythe° myld:	very
	"Whenne° be ye gomen°	From where lads
170	That büeth her a° londe y-comen,	**büeth** ... are here to
	Alle threttene°	thirteen
	Of bodye swythe kene?°	bold
	By God that me made,	
	So feyr a felaw-rade°	company
175	Ne seh° Y never stonde	saw
	In Westnesse londe.	
	Say me whet ye seche."°	seek
	Horn spec hüere° speche.	**spec hüere** spoke their
	Horn spac for hüem alle,	
180	For so hit moste byfalle;	

He wes the wyseste
Ant of wytte the beste.
   "We büeth° of Sudenne,   are
Y-come° of gode kenne°   Descended   kin
185 Of Cristene blode,
Of cünne swythe° gode.   **cünne swythe** kin very
Payenes° ther connen° aryve   Pagans   did
Ant Cristine brohten of lyve,°   **brohten . . .** killed
Slowen ant todrowe°   **Slowen . . .** Slaughtered and drew to pieces
190 Cristine men ynowe.°   enough
   "So Crist me mote rede,°   **mote rede** may counsel
Ous hy düden° lede   **Ous . . .** Us they did
Into a galeye
With the see to pleye.
195 Day is gon ant other°   **Day . . .** For a day and another
Withoute seyl ant rother°   rudder
Ure ship flet° forth y-lome,°   sailed   steadily
Ant her to londe hit ys y-come.
   "Now thou myht us slen° and bynde   strike
200 Oure honde us bihynde,
Ah,° yef hit is thi wille,   But
Help us that we ne spille."°   **ne spille** don't perish
   Tho spac° the gode kyng—   **Tho spac** Then spoke
He nes° never nythyng:°   was   a niggard
205 "Sey, Child, whet is thy name?
Shal thee tide bote game."°
   The child him onswerede
So sone° he hit y-herde: **So sone** As soon as
"Horn Ych am y-hote,°   called
210 Y-come out of this bote
From the see side.
Kyng, wel thee bitide."°   **wel . . .** may well befall you
   "Horn Child," quoth the kyng,
"Wel brouc° thou thy nome yyng.°   enjoy   **nome yyng** young name
215 Horn him° göth so stille°   **Horn him** A horn   quietly
Bi dales ant by hülles;
Horn hath loude soune°   sound
Thurhout üch-a toune.°   **üch-a toune** each town
So shal thi nome springe
220 From kynge to kynge
Ant thi feirnesse
Aboute Westnesse.
Horn, thou art so swete,
Ne shal Y thee forlete."°   desert

206. You shall receive nothing but kind treatment.

225   Hom rod Aylmer the kyng,
       Ant Horn with him, his fundlyng,°   *foundling*
       Ant alle his yfere°   *companions*
       That him were so düere.°   *dear*
         The kyng com into halle
230   Among his knyhtes alle.
       Forth he clepeth° Athelbrus,   *calls*
       His stiward, ant him seide thus:
         "Stiward, tac° thou here   *take*
         My fundlyng° for to lere°   *foundling   instruct*
235   Of thine mestere°   *profession*
       Of wode ant of ryvere°   *river*
       And toggen o° the harpe   **toggen o** *to play on*
       With is nayles sharpe,
       And tech him alle the listes°   *skills*
240   That thou ever wystest°   *knew*
       Byfore me to kerven°   *carve*
       Ant of my coupe to serven,
       Ant his feren° devyse   **his feren** *for his companions*
       With ous° other servise.   *us*
245   Horn Child—thou understond—
       Tech him of harpe ant of song."
         Athelbrus gon leren°   **gon leren** *instructed*
       Horn and hyse feren.
       Horn mid herte lahte°   **mid . . .** *took to heart*
250   Al that mon him tahte.
       Withinne court and withoute
       Ant overal aboute
       Lovede men Horn Child,
       Ant most him lovede Rymenyld,
255   The kynges oune dohter,
       For he wes in hire thohte.
       Hüe° lovede him in hire mod,°   *She   heart*
       For he wes feir and eke° god;   *also*
       Ant, thah° hüe ne dorste° at bord°   *though* **ne dorste** *dared not*   *table*
260   Mid° him speke ner a word   *With*
       Ne in the halle
       Among the knyhtes alle,
       Hyre sorewe ant hire pyne°   *pain*
       Nolde° never fyne°   *Would   cease*
265   Bi daye ne by nyhte
       For hüe° speke ne myhte°   **For hüe** *Because she* **ne myhte** *couldn't*
       With Horn that wes so feir ant fre°   *noble*
       Tho° hüe ne myhte with him be.   *When*
         In herte hüe hade care° ant wo,   *sorrow*

270	Ant thus hüe bithohte hire tho.°	**bithohte** . . . bethought herself then
	Hüe sende hyre sonde°	messenger
	Athelbrus to honde°	**Athelbrus** . . . To Athelbrus
	That he come hire to	
	Ant also shulde Horn do°	bring
275	Into hire boure,	
	For hüe° bigon to loure.°	she look ill
	Ant the sonde° sayde	messenger
	That seek° wes the mayde	sick
	Ant bed° him come swythe,°	bade quickly
280	For hüe nis nout° blythe.	**nis nout** isn't
	The stiward wes in hüerte wo,°	**hüerte wo** heart woeful
	For he nüste° whet he shulde do.	didn't know
	What Rymenild bysohte	
	Gret wonder him thohte°	seemed to him
285	Aboute Horn the yinge°	young
	To boure for te° bringe.	to
	He thohte on is mode°	**is mode** his mind
	Hit nes° for none gode.	was
	He tok° with him another,	took
290	Athulf, Hornes brother.	
	"Athulf," quoth he, "ryht anon	
	Thou shalt with me to boure gon°	go
	To speke with Rymenild stille°	secretly
	To wyte° hyre wille.	know
295	Thou art Hornes yliche;°	image
	Thou shalt hire byswyke.°	deceive
	Sore me adrede°	**me adrede** I fear
	That hüe° wole Horn mysrede."°	she lead astray
	Athelbrus ant Athulf bo°	both
300	To hire boure beth y-go.°	**beth y-go** have gone
	Upon Athulf Childe	
	Rymenild con waxe° wilde.	**con waxe** grew
	Hüe wende° Horn it were	supposed
	That hüe hade there.	
305	Hüe seten° adoun stille°	**Hüe seten** They sat quietly
	Ant seyden hüre wille.°	**hüre wille** what they wanted to
	In hire armes tweye°	two
	Athulf he con leye.°	**con leye** lay down
	"Horn," quoth heo, "wel longe	
310	Y have loved thee stronge.	
	Thou shalt thy treuthe plyhte°	pledge
	In myn hond with ryhte	
	Me to° spouse welde°	as to take
	Ant Ich thee loverd° to helde."°	as lord hold

315 So stille so° hit were,   **So** . . . As quietly as
Athulf seyde in hire eere,
"Ne tel thou no more speche,
May,° Y thee byseche.   Maiden
Thi tale gyn thou lynne,°   **Thi** . . . Cease from your talk
320 For Horn nis nout° herynne; **nis nout** isn't
Ne be we nout yliche,°   **Ne** . . . Nor are we alike
For Horn is fayr ant ryche,
Fayrore by one ribbe¹
Then ani mon that libbe.°   lives
325 Thah° Horn were under molde,° Though earth
Other ellewher° he sholde° **Other ellewher** Or elsewhere should be
Hennes° a thousent milen,° Hence miles
Y nülle° him bigilen."   won't
Rymenild hire bywente,°   **hire bywente** turned around
330 Ant Athelbrus thus heo shende:° scolded
"Athelbrus, thou foule thef,
Ne worthest thou me never lef!°
Went° out of my boure.   Go
Shame thee mote byshoure,° **Shame** . . . May shame shower on you
335 Ant evel hap° to underfonge,° fate suffer
Ant evele rode° on to honge.° cross hang
Ne speke Y nout° with Horne; **Ne** . . . I'm not speaking
Nis he nout° so unorne."° **Nis** . . . He isn't ugly
Tho Athelbrus a stounde° **a stounde** at once
340 Fel akneu° to grounde.   on his knees
"Ha, levedy° myn owe,°   lady own
Me lythe° a lütel throwe,° hear while
Ant list° werefore Ych wonde° listen hesitate
To bringen Horn to honde,
345 For Horn is fayr ant riche;
Nis° non his ylyche.°   There is **his ylyche** like him
Aylmer the gode kyng
Düde° him me in lokyng.° Put **me** . . . in my care
Yif Horn thee were aboute,
350 Sore Ich myhte doute°   fear
With him thou woldest pleye
Bitwene ou selven tweye.° **ou** . . . your two selves
Thenne shulde, withouten othe,° question
The kyng us make wrothe.° **us** . . . show anger on us
355 "Ah foryef° me thi teone,° **Ah foryef** But forgive **thi teone** for grieving you
My levedy° ant my quene. lady
Horn Y shal thee fecche,

¹ 'Fairer by a rib.' The rib is a measure of beauty, since fair Eve is made of Adam's rib.
332. You'll never be dear to me!

	Wham so Whomever may vex
Wham so° hit y-recche."°	could have
Rymenild, yef heo couthe,°	
360 Con lythe° with hyre mouthe.	**Con lythe** Listened
Heo loh ant made hire blythe,°	**loh** . . . laughed and rejoiced
For wel° wes hyre o lyve.°	happy **hyre** . . . she alive
"Go thou," quoth heo, "sone,°	at once
Ant send him after none°	noon
365 A skuyeres wyse°	**A** . . . In squire's clothing
When the king aryse.°	arises
He shal myd° me bileve°	with stay
That° hit be ner eve.	Till
Have Ich° of him mi wille,	**Have Ich** If I have
370 Ne recchi° whet men telle."	**Ne recchi** I don't care
Athulbrus goth with alle;	
Horn he fond in halle,	
Bifore the kyng o° benche	on
Wyn for te shenche.°	**for** . . . to pour out
375 "Horn," quoth he, "thou hende,°	noble one
To boure gyn thou wende°	**boure** . . . the bower go
To speke with Rymenild the yynge,°	young
Dohter oure° kynge.	of our
Wordes swythe° bolde	very
380 In hörte gyn thou holde.°	**In** . . . Hold in your heart
Horn, be thou me° trewe,	**be** . . . if you're to me
Shal thee nout arewe."°	**Shal** . . . You will not regret it
He eode° forth to ryhte°	went **to ryhte** directly
To Rymenild the bryhte.	
385 Aknewes° he him sette	On his knees
Ant swetliche hire grette.°	greeted
Of is fayre syhte°	
Al that bour gan lyhte.°	**gan lyhte** began to lighten
He spak faire is° speche,	his
390 Ne durth non° him teche.	**Ne** . . . And no one needed to
"Wel thou sitte° ant softe,	**thou sitte** may you sit
Rymenild, kinges dohter,	
Ant thy maydnes here	
That sitteth thyne yfere.°	**thyne yfere** as your companions
395 Kynges styward oure°	**Kynges** . . . Our king's steward
Sende° me to boure	Sent
For te y-here, levedy° myn,	**For** . . . To hear, lady
Whet be wille thyn."	
Rymenild up gon stonde°	**gon stonde** stood
400 Ant tok° him by the honde.	took
Heo made feyre chere	

387. From the fair sight of him

Ant tok him bi the swere.° — neck
Ofte heo him cüste° — kissed
So wel hyre lüste.° — **So . . .** As well as she wished
405 "Welcome, Horn," thus sayde
Rymenild that mayde,
"An° even ant a° morewe — On on
For thee Ich habbe sorewe
That Y have no reste
410 Ne slepe me ne lyste.° — **Ne slepe . . .** Nor want to sleep
     "Horn, thou shalt wel swythe° — **wel swythe** very quickly
Mi longe sorewe lythe.° — lessen
Thou shalt withoute strive° — opposition
Habbe me to wyve.
415 Horn, have of° me reuthe,° — on pity
Ant plyht° me thi treuthe." — pledge
     Horn tho hym bythohte
Whet he speken ohte.
     "Crist," quoth Horn, "thee wisse,° — direct
420 Ant yeve° thee hevene° blisse — give heaven's
Of thine hosebonde
Who° he be a° londe. — Whoever on
     "Ich am y-bore thral,° — **y-bore thral** born a thrall
Thy fader fundlyng° withal. — **fader fundlyng** father's foundling
425 Of künde me ne felde° — **to . . .** as spouse to have
Thee to spouse welde.° — would be
Hit nere° no fair weddyng
Bitwene a thral ant the kyng!"
     Tho gon° Rymenild mislyken,° — began to grieve
430 Ant sore bigon to syken,° — sigh
Armes bigon unbowe,° — to unclasp
Ant doun heo fel y swowe.° — **y swowe** in a swoon
Horn hire up hente° — took
Ant in is armes trente.° — folded
435 He gon° hire to cüsse° — began kiss
Ant feyre for te wisse.° — **te wisse** to direct
     "Rymenild," quoth he, "düere,° — dear
Help me that Ych were° — may be
Y-dobbed° to be knyhte, — Dubbed
440 Swete, bi al thi myhte° — power
To° mi loverd° the kyng — Over lord
That he me yeve° dobbyng. — give
Thenne is my thralhede° — thralldom
Al wend° into knyhthede. — turned
445 Y shal waxe more° — **waxe more** grow greater

425. By nature it wouldn't befit me

Ant do,° Rymenild, thi lore."°   perform   instruction
    Tho Rymenild the yynge°   young
Aros of hire swowenynge.°   swoon
    "Nou, Horn, to sothe,°   **to sothe** in truth
450   Y leve° thee by thyn othe.°   believe   oath
Thou shalt be maked knyht
Er then° this fourteniht.   **Er then** Before
Ber thou her thes° coppe   this
Ant thes ringe theruppe°   also
455   To Athelbrus the styward,
Ant say him he holde foreward.°   **holde foreward** should hold agreement
Sey Ich him biseche
With loveliche° speche   loving
That he for thee falle°   **for . . .** on your behalf should fall
460   To the kynges fet in halle
That he with is° worde   his
Thee knyhty° with sworde.   may knight
With selver ant with golde
Hit worth him° wel y-yolde.°   **worth him** will be to him   paid
465   Nou, Crist him lene° spede.   give
Thin erndyng° do bede."°   errand   declare
    Horn tok° is leve,   took
For hit wes neh° eve.   nearly
Athelbrus he sohte
470   Ant tok him that° he brohte,   what
Ant tolde him thare
Hou he hede y-fare.
He seide° him is nede   told
Ant him bihet° is mede.°   promised   reward
475   Athelbrus so blythe°   happy
Eode° into halle swythe°   Went   quickly
Ant seide, "Kyng, nou leste°   hear
O° tale mid° the beste.   A   among
Thou shalt bere coroune
480   Tomarewe in this toune.°   town
Tomarewe is thi feste;°   festivity
Thee bihoveth geste.°   **Thee . . .** You need an occasion
Ich thee rede mid° al my myht   **rede mid** advise with
That thou make Horn knyht.
485   Thin armes do him welde.°   **do . . .** let him have
God° knyht he shal thee yelde."°   A good   **thee yelde** make for you
    The kyng seide wel sone,°   promptly
"Hit is wel to done.°   do
Horn me wel quemeth.°   pleases
490   Knyht him° wel bysemeth.°   he   seems

He shal have mi dobbyng
Ant be myn other derlyng,°   favorite
Ant hise feren twelve
He shal dobbe himselve.
495 Alle Y shal hem knyhte
Byfore me to fyhte."
    Al that° the lyhte day sprong   **Al that** Till
Aylmere thohte long.
The day bigon to springe;
500 Horn com byfore the kynge
With his twelf fere.
Alle ther y-were.°   **ther y-were** were there
Horn knyht made he
With ful gret solempnité,°   pomp
505 Sette him on a stede
Red so° eny glede,°   as   glowing coal
Smot° him a lüte wiht,°   Tapped   **lüte wiht** little bit
Ant bed° him büen° a god knyht.   bade   be
Athulf vel akne° ther   **vel akne** fell on his knees
510 Ant thonkede kyng Aylmer.
    "Nou is knyht Sire Horn,
That in Sudenne wes y-born.
Lord he is of londe
Ant of us that by him stonde.
515 Thin armes he haveth ant thy sheld
For te fyhte in the feld.
Let him us alle knyhte
So° hit is his ryhte."   As
    Aylmer seide ful y-wis:°   **ful y-wis** very certainly
520 "Nou do that° thi wille ys."   what
    Horn adoun con lyhte°   **con lyhte** alighted
Ant made hem alle to knyhte,°   **alle . . .** all knights
For müchel° wes the geste,°   great   occasion
Ant more wes the feste.°   festivity
525   That Rymenild nes nout° there   **nes nout** wasn't
Hire thohte seve° yere.   **Hire . . .** Seemed to her like seven
Efter Horn hüe sende;°   **hüe sende** she sent
Horn into boure wende.°   went
He nolde gon is one;°   **nolde . . .** wouldn't go alone
530 Athulf wes hys ymone.°   companion
Rymenild welcometh Sire Horn
Ant Athulf knyht him biforn.°   **him biforn** before him
    "Knyht, nou is tyme
For to sitte by me.
535 Do nou that° we spake;°   what   spoke of

To thi wyf thou me take.
Nou° thou hast wille thyne,   Now that
Unbynd me of this pyne."°   pain
    "Rymenild, nou be stille.
540 Ichülle don° al thy wille.   **Ichülle don** I will do
Ah her° hit so bitide,   **Ah her** But before
Mid spere Ichülle ryde
Ant my knyhthod prove
Er then° Ich thee wowe.°   **Er then** Before   woo
545 We büeth° now knyhtes yonge   are
Alle today y-spronge,°   sprung forth
Ant of the mestere°   profession
Hit is the manere
With sum other knyhte
550 For his lemmon° to fyhte   sweetheart
Er ne° he eny wyf take   **Er ne** Before
Other° wyth wymmon forewart° make.   Or   agreement
Today—so° Crist me blesse°—   as   may bless
Y shal do pruesse°   prowess
555 For thi love mid° shelde   with
Amiddewart° the felde.   Amid
Yef Ich come to-lyve,°   alive
Ychül° thee take to wyve."   I will
    "Knyht, Y may y-leve° thee.   **may y-leve** can trust
560 Why, ant° thou trewe be,   if
Have her this gold ring.
Hit is ful god° to thi dobbyng.   **ful god** very appropriate
Y-graved is on the rynge:
'Rymenild thy lüef° the yynge.'°   sweetheart   young one
565 Nis° non betere under sonne   There is
That eny mon of conne.°   **of conne** knows of
For mi love thou hit were,°   wear
Ant on thy fynger thou hit bere.
The ston haveth suche grace°   power
570 Ne shalt thou° in none place   **Ne . . .** That you will
Deth underfonge°   suffer
Ne büen y-slaye° with wronge   **Ne . . .** Nor be slain
Yef thou lokest theran
Ant thenchest o° thi lemman;°   **thenchest o** think of   sweetheart
575 Ant Sire Athulf thi brother
He shal han° enother.   have
Horn, Crist° Y thee byteche°   to Christ   commend
Mid mourninde° speche.   anxious
Crist thee yeve° god endyng   give
580 Ant sound ayeyn thee brynge."°   **sound . . .** bring you back safe

The knyht hire gan° to cüsse,°   began   kiss
Ant Rymenild him to blesse.
Leve at° hyre he nom,°   **Leve at** Leave from   took
Ant into halle he com.
585   Knyhtes eode° to table,   went
Ant Horn eode to stable.
Ther he toc° his gode fole,°   took   foal
Blac so ever eny cole.
With armes he him sredde,°   **him sredde** clad himself
590   Ant is° fole he fedde.   his
The fole bigon to springe
Ant Horn mürie to synge.
    Horn rod one whyle
Wel more then a myle.
595   He seh° a shyp at grounde°   saw   **at grounde** at the shore
With hethene hounde.°   **hethene hounde** heathen hounds
He askede wet hüe° hadden   **wet hüe** what they
Other° to londe ladden.°   Or   brought
An hound him gan biholde°   **gan biholde** beheld
600   Ant spek wordes bolde:
    "This land we wölleth° wynne   will
Ant sle that° ther büeth° inne."   **sle that** slay those who   are
    Horn gan is swerd gripe°   **swerd gripe** sword to grip
Ant on is arm hit wype.
605   The Sarazyn he hitte so
That is hed fel to ys to.°   toes
Tho gonne° the houndes gone°   began   to go
Ayeynes° Horn ys one.°   Against   **ys one** alone
He lokede on is rynge
610   Ant thohte o° Rymenyld the yynge.   of
He sloh° therof the beste,°   slew   best
An houndred at the leste;
Ne mihte no mon telle°   **Ne ...** No man could count
Alle that he gon quelle.°   **gon quelle** killed
615   Of that° ther were oryve°   those who   ashore
He lafte lüt olyve.°   **lüt olyve** few alive
    Horn tok the maister heved°   **maister heved** great head
That he him hade byreved°   bereft of
Ant sette on is swerde°   sword
620   Aboven o then orde.°   **o ...** on the tip
He ferde° hom to halle   went
Among the knyhtes alle.
    "Kyng," quoth he, "well thou sitte°   **thou sitte** may you sit
Ant thine knyhtes mitte.°   with you
625   Today Ich rod o my pleyyng°   **rod ...** rode out in sport

After my dobbyng.
I fond a ship rowen°   rowing
In the sound byflowen°   afloat
Mid unlondisshe° menne foreign
630 Of Sarazynes kenne°   kin
To dethe for te pyne°   **To** . . . To put to the death
Thee ant alle thyne.
Hy gonne° me asayly.°   began to assail
Swerd° me nolde fayly.° Sword **nolde fayly** wouldn't fail
635 Y smot hem alle to grounde
In a lütel stounde.°   while
The heved° Ich thee bringe head
Of the maister kynge.
Nou have Ich thee yolde° repaid
640 That thou me knyhten woldest."° **knyhten woldest** were willing to knight
 The day bigon to springe;
The kyng rod on° hontynge **rod on** rode out
To the wode wyde
Ant Fykenyld bi is syde
645 That fals wes ant untrewe,
Who se° him wel y-knewe. **Who se** Whoever
 Horn ne thohte nout him on° **him on** about him
Ant to boure wes y-gon.
He fond Rymenild sittynde
650 Ant wel° sore wepynde very
So whyt so the sonne,
Mid terres° al byronne.° **Mid terres** With tears drenched
Horn seide, "Lüef,° thyn ore.° Sweetheart favor
Why wepest thou so sore?"
655 Hüe° seide, "Ich nout ne wepe, She
Ah° Y shal er° Y slepe. But before
Me thohte o° my metyng° **Me** . . . It seemed to me in dream
That Ich rod o° fysshyng **rod o** rode out
To see my net y-caste,
660 Ant wel fer° hit laste.° **wel fer** very far extended
A gret fyssh at the ferste
My net made berste.
That fyssh me so bycahte° overcame
That Y nout ne lahte.° **nout** . . . caught nothing
665 Y wene° Y shal forleose° suppose lose
The fyssh that Y wolde cheose."° prefer
 "Crist ant Seinte Stevene,"
Quoth Horn, "areche° thy swevene!° interpret dream
No shal Y thee byswyke° **No** . . . I won't deceive you
670 Ne do that° thee mislyke.° what may displease

	Ich take thee myn owe°	**myn owe** as my own
	To holde ant eke° to knowe	also
	For° everüch other wyhte.°	Before person
	Therto my trouthe Y plyhte."°	pledge
675	Wel° muche was the reuthe°	Very sorrow
	That wes at thilke treuthe.°	**thilke treuthe** that betrothal
	Rymenild wep° wel ylle,°	wept sadly
	Ant Horn let terres stille.°	**let . . .** stilled the tears
	"Lemmon,"° quoth he, "dere,°	Sweetheart dear
680	Thou shalt more y-here.	
	Thy sweven° shal wende.°	dream come about
	Summon° us wole shende.°	Someone **wole shende** wants to harm
	That fyssh that brac° thy net,	broke
	Y-wis,° it is sumwet°	Indeed something
685	That wol us do sum teone.°	injury
	Y-wys,° hit worth y-sene."°	Indeed **worth y-sene** will be seen
	Aylmer rod° by Stoure,°	rode the River Stour
	Ant Horn wes yne boure.	
	Fykenhild hade envye	
690	Ant seyde theose folye:°	**theose folye** this slander
	"Aylmer, Ich thee werne,°	warn
	Horn thee wole forberne.°	**wole forberne** wants to destroy
	Ich herde wher he seyde—	
	Ant his swerd he leyde°—	wagered
695	To brynge thee of lyve°	**of lyve** from life
	Ant take Rymenyld to wyve.	
	He lyht° nou in boure	lies
	Under covertoure°	bedclothes
	By Rymenyld thy dohter,	
700	Ant so he döth wel ofte.	
	Do° him out of londe	Put
	Er he do more shonde."°	harm
	Aylmer gon hom turne°	**gon . . .** turned home
	Wel mody° ant wel sturne.	angry
705	He fond Horn under arme°	her arm
	In Rymenyldes barme.°	bosom
	"Go out," quoth Aylmer the kyng,	
	"Horn, thou foule fundlyng,°	foundling
	Forth out of boures flore°	**boures flore** the bedroom floor
710	For° Rymenild thin hore.°	Because of whore
	Wend° out of londe sone.°	Go at once
	Her nast° thou nout to done.°	have **nout . . .** nothing to do
	Wel sone, bote° thou flette,°	unless flee
	Myd swert° Y shal thee sette."°	sword **thee sette** set on you
715	Horn eode° to stable	went

Wel modi° for that fable.° — angry   slander
He sette sadel on stede;
With armes he gon him shrede;° — gon ... dressed himself
His brünie° he con lace,° — coat of mail   **con lace** laced
720 So he shulde, into place;
His swerd he gon fonge,° — **gon fonge** took
Ne stod° he nout too longe. — tarried
To° is swerd he gon teon,° — For   **gon teon** reached
Ne durste non wel° him seon.° — **Ne** ... Nor would anyone dare willingly   see
725 He seide, "Lemmon,° derlyng, — Sweetheart
Nou thou havest thy swevenyng.° — dream
The fyssh that thyn net rende° — tore
From thee me he sende.° — has sent
The kyng with me gynneth° strive; — begins to
730 Awey he wole° me dryve. — wants to
Tharefore have nou godne-day.° — good day
Nou Y mot founde and fare° away — **mot** ... must set out and go
Into uncouthe° londe — unknown
Wel° more for te fonde.° — Much   **for** ... to attempt
735 Y shal wonie° there — live
Fulle seve° yere. — seven
At the seve yeres ende,
Yyf Y ne come ne sende,° — **ne come** ... don't come or send for you
Tac thou hosebonde;
740 For me that thou ne wonde.° — **that** ... don't hesitate about that
"In armes thou me fonge,° — take
Ant cüs° me swythe longe." — kiss
Hy cüsten hem° a stounde,° — **Hy** ... They kissed   while
And Rymenyld fel to grounde.
745 Horn toc his leve;
He myhte nout byleve.° — **myhte** ... couldn't stay
He toc° Athulf is fere — clasped
Aboute the swere° — neck
Ant seide, "Knyht so trewe,
750 Kep° wel my love newe. — Guard
Thou never ne forsoke° — **ne forsoke** failed
Rymenild to kepe ant loke."° — **kepe** ... guard and watch
His stede he bigan stryde,
Ant forth he con hym ryde.° — **con** ... rode
755 Athulf wep with eyyen,
Ant alle that hit y-seyyen.° — saw
Horn forth him ferde.° — **him ferde** went
A god ship he him herde° — **him herde** hired
That him shulde passe
760 Out of Westnesse.

The wynd bigon to stonde°   rise
Ant drof hem up o londe.°   **londe** on land (Ireland)

[HORN IN IRELAND]
     To° londe that hy fletten°   On the   reached
Fot out of ship hy setten.
765 He fond bi the weye
Kynges sones tweye.°   two
That on° wes hoten° Athyld,   **That on** The one   called
Ant that other Beryld.
Beryld hym con° preye   did
770 That he shulde seye
What he wolde° there   wanted
Ant what ys nome° were.   name
     "Godmod," he seid, "Ich hote,°   am called
Y-comen out of this bote
775 Wel fer° from by-weste°   far   the west
To seche° myne beste."°   seek   advantage
     Beryld con ner him ryde°   **con . . .** rode nearer to him
Ant toc him bi the bridel.
     "Wel be thou, knyht, y-founde.
780 With me thou lef° a stounde.°   stay   while
Also° Ich mote sterve,°   As sure as   **mote sterve** must die
The kyng thou shalt serve;
Ne seh° Y never alyve   **Ne seh** Nor saw
So feir knyht her aryve."
785   Godmod he ladde to halle,
Ant he adoun gan° falle   did
Ant sette him a-knelyng
Ant grette thene° gode kyng.   **grette thene** greeted the
Tho saide Beryld wel sone,°   **wel sone** at once
790   "Kyng, with him thou ast done.
Thi lond tac° him to werie,°   choose   guard
Ne° shal thee no mon derye,°   Nor   **no . . .** anyone harm
For he is the feyreste man
That ever in this londe cam."
795   Tho seide the kyng wel dere,
"Welcome be thou here.
Go, Beryld, wel swythe,°   quickly
Ant make hym wel blythe,°   happy
Ant when thou farest° to wowen,°   set out   woo
800 Tac him° thine gloven!°   for him   gloves as pledge
Ther° thou hast münt° to wyve   Where   intended
Awey he shal thee dryve.
For° Godmodes feyrhede°   Because of   attractiveness

Shalt thou nower spede."°   **nower spede** nowhere succeed
805   Hit wes at Cristesmasse,
Nouther° more ne lasse,   Neither
The kyng made feste°   festivities
Of° his knyhtes beste.   For
Ther com in at none
810 A geaunt swythe sone°   **geaunt** . . . giant very fast
Y-armed of paynyme°   **of paynyme** from pagandom
Ant seide thise ryme:
   "Site kyng bi° kynge,   beside
Ant herkne my tidynge.
815 Her° büeth paynes aryve.   Here
Wel more then fyve
Her beth upon honde,°   **beth** . . . are at hand
Kyng, in thine londe.
On° therof wol fyhte   One
820 Toyeynes° thre knyhtes.   Against
Yef eure° thre sleh oure on,°   your   **sleh** . . . slay one of ours
We shulen of° eure londe gon.°   from   go
Yef ure on° sleh eure thre,   **ure on** one of ours
Al this lond shal ure° be.   ours
825 Tomorewe shal be the fyhtynge
At the sonne upspringe."
   Tho seyde the kyng Thurston,
"Godmod shal be that on;°   **that on** the one
Beryld shal be that other;°   second
830 The thridde,° Athyld is brother;   third
For hüe büeth strongeste
Ant in armes the beste.
Ah° wat shal us to rede?°   But   **shal** . . . is our best plan
Y wene° we büeth dede."°   suppose   dead
835 Godmod set° at borde°   was sitting   the table
Ant seide theose wordes:
"Sire kyng, nis no ryhte°   **nis** . . . it's not right
On° with thre fyhte°—   One   to fight
Ayeynes° one hounde   Against
840 Thre Cristene to founde.°   strive
Ah, kyng, Y shal alone
Withoute more ymone°   companion
With my swerd ful ethe°   **ful ethe** very easily
Bringen hem alle to dethe."
845   The kyng aros a-morewe;
He hade muche sorewe.
Godmod ros of bedde;
With armes he him shredde;°   **him shredde** clad himself

His brünye° he on caste   coat of mail
850 Ant knütte° hit wel faste°   tied   firmly
Ant com him to the kynge
At his uprysynge.
   "Kyng," quoth he, "com to felde
Me for te byhelde
855 Hou we shule flyten°   contend
Ant togedere smiten."
   Riht at prime tide°   **prime tide** the first hour
Hy gonnen out to ryde.
Hy founden in a grene
860 A geaunt° swythe kene,°   giant   bold
His feren him biside,
That day for to abyde.°   endure
Godmod hem gon asaylen;°   **hem** ... began to attack them
Nolde he nout° faylen.   **Nolde** ... He didn't want to
865 He yef duntes ynowe;°   **yef** ... gave blows enough
The payen fel y swowe.°   **y swowe** into a faint
Ys feren gonnen° hem withdrawe,   began to
For hüere maister wes neh slawe.°   **neh slawe** nearly slain
   He° seide, "Knyht, thou reste   He (the giant)
870 A whyle yef thee leste.°   **thee leste** you wish
Y ne hevede ner° of monnes hond   **ne** ... never had
So harde duntes in non lond
Bote° of the kyng Murry,°   Except   Allof
That wes swithe sturdy.
875 He wes of Hornes kenne.°   kin
Y sloh° him in Sudenne."   slew
   Godmod him gon agryse,°   **gon agryse** began to shudder
Ant his blod aryse.°   began to rise
Byforen him he seh° stonde   saw
880 That drof° him out of londe   **That drof** The one who drove
Ant fader his aquelde.°   **fader** ... killed his father
He smot him under shelde;
He lokede on is rynge
Ant thohte o Rymenild the yynge;
885 Mid god swerd at the fürste°   **at** ... directly
He smot him thourh the hüerte.
   The payns bigonne to fleon°   flee
Ant to hüere shype teon.°   withdraw
To ship hüe° wolden erne;°   they   run
890 Godmod hem con werne.°   **con werne** prevented
The kynges sones tweyne°   two (Beryld and Athyld)
The paiens slowe beyne.°   **slowe beyne** slew both
Tho wes Godmod swythe wo,°   woeful

	Ant the payens he smot so	
895	That in a lütel stounde°	while
	The paiens hy felle to grounde.	
	Godmod ant is men	
	Slowe° the payenes everüchen.°	Slew each one
	His fader° deth ant ys lond	father's
900	Awrek° Godmod with his hond.	Avenged
	The kyng with reuthful° chere	sorrowful
	Lette leggen is sones° on bere°	Lette … Had his sons laid bier
	Ant bringen hom° to halle.	bringen hom had them brought home
	Muche sorewe hüe maden alle.	
905	In a chirche of lym ant ston	
	Me buriede hem° with ryche won.°	Me … They were buried display
	The kyng lette forth calle	
	Hise knyhtes alle	
	Ant seide, "Godmod, yef thou nere,°	thou nere it weren't for you
910	Alle ded we were.	
	Thou art bothe god ant feyr.	
	Her Y make thee myn heyr,	
	For my sones büeth y-flawe°	gone
	Ant y-broht° of lyfdawe.°	bereft life
915	Dohter Ich habbe one—	
	Nis° non so feyr of blod ant bone—	There is
	Ermenild that feyre may,°	maiden
	Bryht so eny someres day.	
	Hire wolle Ich yeve° thee,	give
920	Ant her kyng shalt thou be."	
	He seyde, "More Ichül° thee serve,	I will
	Kyng, er then° thou sterve.°	er then before die
	When Y thy dohter yerne,°	yearn for
	Heo ne shal me nothyng werne."°	refuse
925	Godmod wonede° there	lived
	Fulle six yere,	
	Ant, the sevethe yer bygon,°	being past
	To Rymynyld sonde° ne sende he non.	messenger
	Rymenyld wes in Westnesse	
930	With muchel sorewenesse.	
	A kyng ther wes aryve	
	Ant wolde hyre han° to wyve.	have
	At one° were the kynges	At one Agreed
	Of° that weddynge.	About
935	The dayes were so sherte,°	short
	Ant Rymenild ne derste°	ne derste dared not
	Latten° on none wyse.	Delay
	A wryt hüe düde devyse;°	düde devyse composed

Athulf hit düde wryte,
940 That Horn ne lovede nout lyte.°
Hüe sende hire sonde°   messenger
Into everüche° londe   each
To sechen° Horn knyhte   seek
Whe-so-er me myhte.°   **Whe-so-er** ... Wherever one could seek
945 Horn therof nout herde
Til o° day that he ferde°   one   went
To wode for te shete,°   shoot
A page he gan° mete.   did
    Horn seide, "Leve° fere,   Dear
950 Whet dest thou nou here?"
    "Sire, in lütel spelle°   space
Y may thee sone telle.
Ich seche° from Westnesse   seek
Horn knyht of Estnesse,
955 For Rymenild, that feyre may,°   maiden
Soreweth for him nyht ant day.
A kyng hire shal wedde
A Sonneday° to bedde—   **A Sonneday** On Sunday
Kyng Mody of Reynis,
960 That is Hornes enimis.°   enemy
    "Ich habbe walked wyde
By the see side,
Ne mihte Ich him never cleche°
With nones künnes° speche,   **nones künnes** any kind of
965 Ne may Ich of him here°   hear
In londe fer no nere.
Weylawey° the while!°   Alas   delay
Him may hente gyle."°   **hente gyle** treachery capture
    Horn hit herde with earen°   ears
970 Ant spec with wete tearen:
"So wel, grom,° thee bitide!°   page   may betide
Horn stond° by thi syde.   stands
Ayeyn° to Rymenild turne,   Back
Ant sey that hüe ne murne.°   **ne murne** shouldn't grieve
975 Y shal be ther bi° time   on
A Sonneday° er prime."°   **A Sonneday** On Sunday   the first hour
    The page wes wel blythe°   happy
Ant shipede° wel swythe.   embarked
The see him gon adrynke;°   **gon adrynke** drowned
980 That Rymenil may ofthinke!°   regret
The see him con ded throwe°   **con** ... threw dead

940. Who loved Horn not a little.
963. Nor could I ever catch him

Under hire chambre wowe.°   wall
Rymenild lokede wide
By the see syde
985 Yef heo seye° Horn come   might see
Other° tidynge of eny gome.°   Or   lad
Tho fond hüe° hire sonde°   **Tho** . . . Then she found   messenger
Adronque° by the stronde   Drowned
That shulde° Horn brynge.   **That shulde** Who was going to
990 Hire hondes gon hüe wrynge.
    Horn com to Thurston the kynge
Ant tolde him thes tidynge,
Ant tho° he was biknowe°   then   **was biknowe** revealed
That Rymenild wes ys owe°   own
995 Ant of his gode kenne°   **gode kenne** true kindred
The kyng of Sudenne
Ant hou he sloh a-felde°   **sloh a-felde** slew on the field
Him that is fader aquelde,°   killed
Ant seide, "Kyng so wyse,
1000 Yeld° me my service.   Repay
Rymenild help me to wynne
Swythe, that thou ne blynne,°   **ne blynne** may not fail
Ant Y shal do to house°   **do** . . . have at home
Thy dohter wel to spouse,°   **wel** . . . well married
1005 For hüe shal to spouse have
Athulf my gode felawe.°   companion
He is knyht mid the beste
Ant on of the treweste."
    The kyng seide so stille,°   quietly
1010 "Horn, do al thi wille."
He sende° tho by sonde°   sent   messenger
Yend° al is londe   Throughout
After knyhtes to fyhte
That were° men so lyhte.°   would be   agile
1015 To him come ynowe°   **come ynowe** came enough
That into shipe drowe.°   embarked
    Horn düde him in° the weye   **düde** . . . set out on
In a gret galeye.
The wynd bigon to blowe
1020 In a lütel throwe.°   while
The see bigan with ship to gon,°   go
To Westnesse hem brohte anon.°   soon

[HORN IN WESTNESSE]
Hüe striken° seyl of maste   lowered
Ant ancre gonnen caste.°   **ancre** . . . cast anchor
1025 Matynes° were y-ronge   Matins
Ant the masse y-songe
Of Rymenild the yynge°   young
Ant of Mody the kynge;
Ant Horn wes in watere,
1030 Ne mihte he come no latere.
He let° is ship stonde°   had   stand to
Ant com him up to londe.
His folk he made abyde°   wait
Under a wode syde.
1035   Horn eode forh al one°   **eode** . . . went forth alone
So° he sprong of the stone.   As if
On° palmer he y-mette   A
Ant with wordes hyne grette:°   **hyne grette** greeted him
"Palmere, thou shalt me telle,"
1040 He seyde, "of thine spelle.°   news
So brouke thou° thi croune,   **So** . . . So may you save
Why comest thou from toune?"°   town
Ant he seide on is tale,
"Y come from a brüdale,°   wedding
1045 From brüdale wylde
Of maide Remenylde,
Ne mihte hüe nout dreye
That hüe ne wep with eye.°
Hüe seide that hüe nolde°   didn't want to
1050 Be spoused° with golde.   married
Hüe hade hosebonde,°   a husband
Thah° he were out of londe.   Though
"Ich wes in the halle
Withinne the castel walle.
1055 Awey Y gon glide;°   **gon glide** stole
The dole° Y nolde abyde.°   sad event   **nolde abyde** didn't want to stand
Ther worth° a dole reuly.°   is happening   sorrowful
The brüde° wepeth bitterly."   bride
Quoth Horn, "So Crist me rede,°   counsel
1060 We wölleth° chaunge wede.°   will   clothes
Tac thou robe myne,
Ant Y sclaveyn° thyne.   cloak
Today Y shal ther drynke
That° summe hit shal ofthynke."°   Where   regret
1065 Sclaveyn he gon doun legge° —   **gon** . . . laid down

1047–48. Nor could she manage not to weep with her eyes.

Ant Horn hit düde on rügge°—   **düde** . . . put on his back
Ant toc Hornes clothes,
That nout him were lothe.°   **nout** . . . weren't unwelcome to him
Horn toc bordoun ant scrippe°   **bordoun** . . . staff and wallet
1070 Ant gan° to wrynge° is lippe;   began   twist
He made foule chere°   **foule chere** a foul appearance
Ant bicollede° is swere.°   blackened   neck
He com to the yateward,°   porter
That him onswerede froward.°   defiantly
1075 Horn bed undo° wel softe°   **bed und**o asked to open   gently
Moni tyme ant ofte;
Ne myhte he y-wynne°   **Ne** . . . But he couldn't manage
For to come therynne.
Horn the wyket puste°   **wyket puste** door pushed
1080 That° hit open fluste.°   So that   sprang
The porter shulde abügge;°   **shulde abügge** had to make atonement
He threw him adoun the brügge°   **adoun** . . . over the drawbridge
That thre ribbes crakede.
Horn to halle rakede°   went
1085 Ant sette him doun° wel lowe   **sette** . . . sat down
In the beggeres rowe.
He lokede aboute
Myd is collede snoute.°   **collede snoute** blackened nose
Ther seh he Rymenild sitte
1090 Ase° hüe were out of wytte,°   As if   her wits
Wepinde sore;
Ah he seh nower thore°   **seh** . . . saw nowhere there
Athulf is gode felawe
That trewe wes in üch plawe.°   **üch plawe** each engagement
1095 Athulf wes o tour° ful heh°   **o tour** in a tower   high
To loke fer ant eke neh°   **fer** . . . far and also near
After° Hornes comynge   For
Yef water him wolde brynge.
The see he seh flowe
1100 Ah Horn nower rowe.°   **nower rowe** nowhere sailing
He seyde on is songe,
"Horn, thou art too longe.
Rymenild thou me bitoke°   **me bitoke** entrusted to me
That Ich hire shulde loke.°   guard
1105 Ich have y-loked evere,
Ant thou ne comest nevere."
Rymenild ros of benche
The beer al for te shenche°   pour out
After mete in sale,°   hall
1110 Bothe wyn ant ale.

An horn° hüe ber an° honde,   drinking horn   **ber an** carried in her
For that wes lawe° of londe.   the custom
Hüe dronc of the beere
To knyht ant skyere.°   squire
1115   Horn set at grounde;
Him thohte° he wes y-bounde.°   **Him thohte** It seemed as if   overwhelmed
He seide, "Quene so hende,°   gracious
To me hyderward thou wende.°   come hither
Thou shenh us° with the vürste;° **Thou** . . . Pour for us   foremost
1120 The beggares büeth afurste."°   thirsty
Hyre horn hüe leyde adoune
Ant fülde him° of the broune°   **fülde him** filled for him   brown jug
A bolle of a galoun;°   **bolle** . . . gallon tankard
Hüe wende° he were° a glotoun. expected   must be
1125 Hüe seide, "Tac the coppe,
Ant drync this ber al uppe.
Ne seh Y° never, Y wene,°   **Ne** . . . I saw   suppose
Beggare so kene."°   bold
    Horn toc hit hise y-fere°   **toc** . . . gave it to his companion
1130 Ant seide, "Quene so dere,
No beer nüllich i-bite°   **nüllich i-bite** will I take
Bote° of coppe white.   Except
Thou wenest° Ich be a beggere.   suppose
Y-wis,° Ich am a fysshere   Indeed
1135 Wel fer° come by weste°   far   **by weste** westward
To seche° mine beste.°   seek   advantage
Min net lyht° her wel hende°   lies   convenient
Withinne a wel feyr pende.°   enclosure
Ich have leye there°   **leye there** placed the net there
1140 Nou is this the sevethe yere.
Ich am i-come to loke
Yef eny fyssh hit toke.
Yef eny fyssh is therinne,
Therof thou shalt wynne.°   gain
1145 For° Ich am come to fyssh,   Since
Drynke nüll° Y of dyssh.   won't
Drynke to Horn of horn.
Wel fer° Ich have y-orne."°   far   traveled
    Rymenild him gan bihelde;° **gan bihelde** beheld
1150 Hire herte fel to kelde.°   **fel** . . . ran cold
Ne kneu° hüe noht is° fysshyng **Ne kneu** Neither recognized **hüe** . . . his
                         reference to
Ne° himselve nothyng,°   Nor   in any way
Ah wonder hyre gan thynke°   **hyre** . . . it seemed to her
Why for Horn he bed° drynke.   bade
1155 Hüe fülde the horn of wyne,

140

Ant dronk to that pelryne.°   pilgrim
Hüe seide, "Drync thi felle,
Ant seththen° thou me telle   then
Yef thou Horn ever seye°   saw
1160 Under° wode leye."°   In grove
    Horn dronk of horn a stounde°   while
Ant threu is ryng to grounde,°   the bottom
Ant seide, "Quene, thou thench°   **thou thench** think about
What Y threu° in the drench."°   have thrown drink
1165 The quene eode to boure
Mid hire maidnes foure;
Hüe fond that° hüe wolde,°   what wanted
The ryng y-graved° of golde   engraved
That Horn of her hedde.
1170 Ful sore hyre adredde°   **hyre adredde** she feared
That Horn ded were,
For his ryng was there.
Tho sende° hüe a damoisele   sent
After thilke° palmere.   that
1175   "Palmere," quoth hüe, "so trewe,
The ryng that thou yn threwe,
Thou sey° wer thou hit nome°   **Thou sey** Say got
Ant hyder hou thou come."
He seyde, "By Seint Gyle,
1180 Ich eode mony a myle
Wel fer yent° by weste   away
To seche° myne beste,°   seek advantage
Mi mete for te bydde,°   **for . . .** to beg
For so me tho bitidde.°   it happened to
1185 Ich fond Horn knyht stonde°   heading
To shipeward° at stronde.   **To shipeward** For a ship
He seide he wolde gesse°   **wolde gesse** was planning
To aryve at Westnesse.
The ship nom into flode°   **nom . . .** took to the sea
1190 With me ant Horn the gode.
Horn bygan be sek° ant deye   **be sek** to sicken
Ant for his love me preye°   begged
To gon with the rynge
To Rymenild the yynge.
1195 Wel ofte he hyne keste,°   **hyne keste** kissed it
Crist yeve is soule reste!"
    Rymenild seide at the firste,
"Herte, nou toberste.°   break
Horn worth thee° no more   **worth thee** exists for you
1200 That haveth thee pyned° sore."   **That . . .** Who has tormented you

Hüe fel adoun a bedde
Ant after° knyves gredde° — for cried out
To slein mide hire kyng lothe° — **slein** . . . slay her loathed king with
Ant hireselve bothe° — too
1205 Withinne thilke° nyhte, — that very
Come yef Horn ne myhte.° — **Come** . . . If Horn couldn't come
To herte knyf hüe sette.° — would set
Horn in is armes hire kepte.° — took
His shürte-lappe° he gan take — shirt's edge
1210 Ant wypede awey the foule blake
That wes opon his swere° — neck
Ant seide, "Lüef° so dere, — Sweetheart
Ne const° thou me y-knowe?° — **Ne const** Don't recognize
Ne am Ich Horn thyn owe?° — own
1215 Ich, Horn of Westnesse,
In armes thou me kesse."
Y-clüpten° ant kyste — They embraced
So longe so hem lyste.° — **hem lyste** they wished
"Rymenild," quoth he, "Ich wende° — am going
1220 Doun to the wodes ende,
For ther büeth myne knyhte,
Worthi men ant lyhte,° — eager
Armed under clothe;° — their outer clothing
Hüe° shule make wrothe° — They angry
1225 The kyng and hise gestes
That büeth at thise festes;° — festivities
Today Ychülle° hüem cacche. — will
Nou Ichülle hüem vacche."° — fetch
Horn sprong out of halle;
1230 Ys sclavin° he let falle. — cloak
Rymenild eode of boure;
Athulf hüe fond loure.° — **fond loure** found hiding
"Athulf, be wel blythe,° — happy
Ant to Horn go swythe.
1235 He is under wode bowe° — boughs
With felawes ynowe."° — enough
Athulf gon froth° springe — forth
For that ilke° tydynge. — same
Efter Horn he ernde;° — ran
1240 Him thohte° is herte bernde. — **Him thohte** It seemed as if
He oftok° him, y-wisse,° — overtook indeed
Ant cüste° him with blysse. — kissed
Horn tok is preye° — band
Ant düde him° in the weye. — **düde him** set them
1245 Hüe comen° in wel sone— — came

The yates° weren undone—   gates
Y-armed swithe thicke°   heavily
From fote to the nycke.
Alle° that ther evere weren,   All those
1250 Withoute° is trewe feren   Except for
Ant the kyng Aylmare,
Y-wis° hüe hade muche care.   Indeed
Monie that ther sete,
Hüre lyf hy gonne lete.°   **gonne lete** lost
1255 Horn understondyng ne hede°   **understondyng** . . . had no idea
Of Fykeles falssede.
Hüe sworen alle ant seyde
That hüre non° him wreyede°   **hüre non** none of them   betrayed
Ant swore othes holde°   **othes holde** to maintain their oaths
1260 That hüere non ne sholde°   would
Horn never bytreye
Thah° he on dethe leye.   Though
   Ther hy ronge the belle
That wedlake° to fulfülle.   wedding
1265 Hüe wenden höm with eyse°   **Hüe** . . . They went at leisure
To the kynges paleyse.
Ther wes the brüdale° swete,   wedding feast
For riche° men ther ete.°   noble   ate
Telle ne mihte no tonge
1270 The gle° that ther was songe.   music
   Horn set in chayere
Ant bed° hem alle y-here.°   bade   to listen
He seyde, "Kyng of londe,
Mi tale thou understonde.
1275 Ich wes y-bore in Sudenne;
Kyng wes mi fader of kenne.°   **of kenne** by descent
Thou me to knyhte hove;°   raised
Of knyhthod habbe Y prove.
Thou dryve° me out of thi lond   drove
1280 Ant seydest Ich wes traytour strong.
Thou wendest° that Ich wrohte°   assumed   did
That° Y ner ne thohte,°   What   **ner** . . . never thought of
By Rymenild for te lygge.°   lie
Y-wys,° Ich hit withsügge,°   Indeed   deny
1285 Ne° shal Ich hit ner agynne°   Nor   **hit** . . . ever begin it
Er Ich Sudenne wynne.
   "Thou kep hyre me° a stounde,°   **Thou** . . . Guard her for me   while
The while that Ich founde°   attempt to go
Into myn heritage
1290 With this Yrisshe page.

That lond Ichülle thorhreche°   recover
Ant do mi fader wreche.°   **do ...** avenge my father
Ychül be kyng of toune°   the community
Ant lerne kynges roune.°   **kynges roune** a king's lore
1295 Thenne shal Rymenild the yynge
Ligge° by Horn the kynge."   Lie
    Horn gan to ship drawe°   come
With hyse Yrisshe felawe,°   companion
Athulf with him, his brother;
1300 He nolde habbe non other.
The ship bygan to croude;°   push forward
The wynd bleu wel loude.
Wythinne dawes° fyve   days
The ship began aryve.
1305 Under° Sudennes side°   At shore
Hüere ship bygon to ryde
Aboute the midnyhte.

    [HORN IN SUDENE]
    Horn eode wel rihte.°   **wel rihte** directly
He nom° Athulf by honde   took
1310 Ant ede° up to londe.   went
Hüe fonden° under shelde   found
A knyht liggynde° on felde.   lying
O° the shelde wes y-drawe°   On drawn
A croyz° of Jhesu Cristes lawe.°   cross religion
1315 The knyht him lay on slape,°   **on slape** asleep
In armes wel y-shape.°   provided
    Horn him gan y-take°   **gan y-take** seized
Ant seide, "Knyht, awake.
Thou sei° me whet thou kepest°   **Thou sei** Tell are guarding
1320 Ant here whi thou slepest.
Me thüncheth,° by crois liste,°   **Me thüncheth** It seems to me   **crois liste** the
    devices of the cross
That thou levest on° Criste.   **levest on** believe in
Bote° thou hit wolle shewe,°   Unless reveal
My swerd shal thee tohewe."°   hew to pieces
1325   The gode knyht up aros;
Of° Hornes wordes him agros.°   At **him agros** he shuddered
He seide, "Ich servy ille°   **servy ille** serve miserably
Paynes toyeynes° mi wille.   against
Ich was Cristene sumwhile.°   once
1330 Y come° into this yle;°   came isle
Sarazyns lothe° ant blake   loathsome
Me made Jhesu forsake.
[Bi God, on wam Y leve,°   believe

Tho° hüe makeden me reve°]²   Then   warden
To loke° this passage   guard
For° Horn that is° of age,°   Against   has come
1335 That woneth her by weste,°   **woneth** . . . lives west of here
God° knyht mid the beste.   A good
   "Hüe slowe° mid hüere honde   slew
The kyng of thisse londe
Ant with him mony honder.°   **mony honder** many hundred
1340 Therfore me thüncheth wonder°   **me** . . . it seems to me strange
That he° ne cometh to fyhte.   he (Horn)
God yeve him the myhte°   opportunity
That wynd him hider dryve°   may drive
To don° hem alle of° lyve!   put   out of
1345 Hüe slowen° kyng Mury,°   slew   Allof
Hornes cünesmon° hardy;   kinsman
Horn, of londe hüe senten;
Twelf children with him wenten.
With hem wes Athulf the gode,
1350 Mi child, myn oune fode.°   offspring
Yef Horn is hol° ant sounde,   whole
Athulf tit° no wounde.   suffers
He lovede Horn with mihte,
Ant he° him with ryhte.   he (Horn)
1355 Yef Y myhte se hem tweye,°   both
Thenne ne roht I for te deye."°   **ne** . . . I wouldn't care if I died
   "Knyht, be thenne blythe
Mest° of alle sythe.°   Most now   times
Athulf ant Horn is fere,
1360 Bothe we beth here."
   The knyht to Horn gan skippe
Ant in his armes clippe.°   embraced him
Muche joye hüe maden yfere°   together
Tho° hüe togedere y-come were.   When
1365 He saide with stevene° thare,   voice
"Yunge men, hou habbe ye yore y-fare?°   **yore y-fare** fared up to now
Wolle ye this lond wynne
Ant wonie° therynne?"   live
He seide, "Swete Horn child,
1370 Yet° lyveth thy moder Godyld.   Still
Of joie hüe ne miste°   **ne miste** wouldn't be lacking
Olyve° yef hüe thee wiste."°   Alive   knew to be
   Horn seide on is ryme,°   speech
"Y-blessed be the time!
1375 Ich am i-come into Sudenne

² These lines from another manuscript supply a necessary connection.

With fele° Yrisshemenne.   many
We shule the houndes kecche°   catch
Ant to the deghe vecche;°   **to** . . . bring to death
Ant so we shulen hem teche
1380 To speken oure speche."
    Horn gon is horn blowe.
Is folc hit con y-knowe;°   **con y-knowe** recognized
Hüe comen out of hürne°   hiding
To Horn swythe yürne.°   eagerly
1385 Hüe smiten° ant hüe fyhten°   struck   fought
The niht ant eke° the ohtoun.°   also   early dawn
The Sarazyns hüe slowe°   slew
Ant summe quike todrowe;°   **quike todrowe** alive tore to pieces
Mid speres ord° hüe stong°   point   pierced
1390 The olde and eke the yonge.
    Horn lette sone würche°   **lette** . . . had built
Bothe chapel and chyrche.
He made belle rynge°   **made** . . . ordered bells to be rung
Ant prestes masse synge.
1395 He sohte is moder° halle   mother's
In the roche° walle.   rock
He cüste° hire ant grette°   kissed   greeted
Ant into the castel fette.°   brought
Croune he gan werie°   **gan werie** began to wear
1400 Ant make feste° merye.   festivities
Mürie° he ther wrohte,°   Happiness   produced
Ah Rymenild hit abohte.°   **hit abohte** suffered for it
    The whiles Horn wes oute,
Fikenild ferde° aboute.   went
1405 The betere for te spede,°   succeed
The riche° he yef mede,°   **The riche** To the powerful **yef mede** gave bribes
Bothe yonge ant olde,
With him for te holde.°   retain
Ston he düde lade°   **düde lade** had delivered
1410 Ant lym therto° he made.   for it
Castel he made sette°   **made sette** caused to be placed
With water byflette,°   surrounded
That° theryn come ne myhte°   So that   **ne myhte** couldn't
Bote foul° with flyhte;   **Bote foul** Anything but a bird
1415 Bote when the see withdrowe,
Ther mihte come ynowe.°   enough
Thus Fykenild gon bywende°   **gon bywende** proceeded
Rymenild for te shende.°   **for** . . . to disgrace
To° wyve he gan hire yerne;°   As   **gan** . . . yearned for her
1420 The kyng ne durst° him werne°   dared   refuse

146

Ant habbeth set the day
Fykenild to wedde the may.°   maiden
Wo° was Rymenild of mode;° Woeful **of mode** in spirit
Terres° hüe wepte of blode.   Tears
1425 Thilke° nyht Horn swete That
Con wel harde mete°   **Con**... Dreamed very vividly
Of Rymenild his make°   mate
That into shipe wes take.
The ship gon overblenche;° **gon overblenche** began to overturn
1430 Is lemmon shulde adrenche;° **lemmon**...sweetheart was to drown
Rymenild mid hire honde
Swymme wolde° to londe;   was trying to
Fykenild ayeyn hire pylte° **ayeyn**...pushed her back
Mid his swerdes hylte.
1435 Horn awek in is bed;
Of° his lemmon he wes adred.° For afraid
"Athulf," he seide, "felawe,° my companion
To shipe nou we drawe.°   **we drawe** let us go
Fykenild me hath gon under° **gon under** betrayed
1440 Ant do° Rymenild sum wonder.° has done **sum wonder** something strange
Crist, for his wondes° fyve, wounds
Tonyht thider us dryve!"
Horn gon to shipe ride,
His knyhtes bi his side.
1445 The ship bigon to stüre° sail
With wynd god of cüre;°   choice
Ant Fykenild, her° the day-springe, before
Seide° to the kynge   Spoke
After° Rymenild the bryhte° For radiant
1450 Ant spousede° hyre by nyhte. married
He ladde hire by derke
Into is newe werke.°   castle
The feste° hüe bigonne   festivities
Er then aryse° the sonne.   **Er**... Before arose

   [HORN IN WESTNESSE]
1455 Hornes ship atstod° in Stoure stood to
Under Fykenildes boure.
Nüste° Horn alyve°   Didn't know at all
Wher he wes aryve.
Thene° castel hüe ne knewe, The
1460 For he° was so newe.   it
The see bigon to withdrawe;
Tho seh Horn his felawe°   companion
The feyre knyht Arnoldyn,

That wes Athulfes cosyn,
1465 That ther set° in that tyde   sat
Kyng Horn to abide.°   wait for
    He seide, "Kyng Horn, kynges sone,
Hider thou art welcome.
Today hath Sire Fykenild
1470 Y-wedded thi wif Rymenild.
White thee° nou this while,   **White thee** Guard yourself
He haveth do thee gyle.°   **do ...** deceived you
This tour he düde make
Al for Rymenildes sake;
1475 Ne may ther comen ynne
No mon with no gynne.°   **no gynne** any stratagem
    "Horn, nou Crist thee wisse°   direct
Rymenild that thou ne misse."
    Horn couthe° alle the listes°   knew   tricks
1480 That eni mon of wiste.°   **of wiste** knew of
Harpe he gon shewe
Ant toc him to felawe°   **him ...** to him as companions
Knyhtes of the beste
That he ever hede of weste.°   **of weste** from the west
1485 Oven o° the sherte   **Oven o** Over
Hüe gürden hüem° with swerde.   **gürden hüem** equipped themselves
Hüe eoden on the gravele
Towart the castele.
Hüe gonne mürie singe
1490 Ant makeden hüere gleynge°   music
That Fykenild mihte y-here.
    He axede who hit were.
Men seide hit were harpeirs,
Jogelers, ant fythelers.
1495 Hem me düde in lete.°   **Hem ...** They were allowed in
At halle dore hüe sete.°   sat down
Horn sette him a° benche;   **him a** himself on a
Is harpe he gan clenche.°   **gan clenche** began to pluck
He make Rymenild a lay,
1500 Ant hüe seide "Weylawey."°   Alas
Rymenild fel y swowe;°   **y swowe** in a swoon
Tho nes ther° non that lowe.°   **nes ther** there was   laughed
Hit smot Horn to herte;
Sore con him smerte.°   **con ...** he smarted
1505 He lokede on is rynge
Ant o Rymenild the yynge.
He eode up to borde.°   the table
Mid his gode sworde

	Fykenildes croune°	head
1510	He fel° ther adoune,	cut
	Ant alle is men a rowe°	**a rowe** in turn
	He düde adoun throwe,	
	Ant made Arnoldyn kyng there,	
	After kyng Aylmere	
1515	To be kyng of Westnesse,	
	For° his mildenesse;	Because of
	The kyng ant is baronage	
	Yeven° him truage.°	Gave tribute
	Horn toc Rymenild by honde	
1520	Ant ladde hire to stronde	
	Ant toc with him Athelbrus,	
	The gode stiward of hire fader° hous.	father's
	The see bigan to flowen,	
	Ant hy° faste to rowen.	they

[HORN IN REYNIS]

1525	Hüe aryveden under Reme°	**under Reme** at Reynis
	In a wel feyr streme.	
	Kyng Mody wes kyng in that lond,	
	That Horn sloh° with is hond.	slew
	Athelbrus he made ther kyng	
1530	For his gode techyng;	
	For Sire Hornes lore°	instruction
	He wes mad kyng thore.°	there

[HORN IN IRELAND]

	Horn eode to ryve;°	the shore
	The wynd him con wel dryve.	
1535	He aryvede in Yrlonde,	
	Ther Horn wo couthe er fonde.°	**wo . . .** previously found woe
	He made ther Athulf Chyld	
	Wedde mayden Ermenyld;	
	Ant Horn com to Sudenne,	
1540	To is oune kenne.°	kin

[HORN IN SUDENE]

	Rymenild he made ther is quene,	be
	So hit myhte bene.°	
	In trewe love hüe lyveden ay,	law
	Ant wel hüe loveden Godes lay.°	
1545	Nou hüe beoth bothe dede.	
	Crist to heovene us lede.	

Amen.

149

The Bestiary

(ca. 1225–50, East Midland)

The lore of beasts, birds, and fishes provided a rich and enduring popular source of Christian allegory throughout the Middle Ages. As early as the fifth century, a scholar now known only as Physiologus prepared an allegorical bestiary in Greek, and his work was subsequently imitated throughout the western world. The Old English bestiary contained in the *Exeter Book* (ca. 970–80), though fragmentary, is typical of the tradition; it demonstrates that the panther betokens Christ, the whale betokens the devil, and the partridge betokens God. For the Norman aristocracy Philipe de Thaun produced a much more extensive Anglo-Norman *Bestiaire* (ca. 1125), which was soon followed by other Anglo-Norman versions. The bestiary excerpted here is the only extant example of the genre recorded in Middle English. It is based on a Latin adaptation composed in the eleventh century by Theobald the Italian and contains 802 lines.

The Middle English author includes Theobald's lion, eagle, worm (serpent), ant, hart, fox, spider, whale, mermaid, elephant, turtledove, and panther; he omits Theobald's centaur and adds from another source the culver (dove). He matches the artistic variations of Theobald's Latin meters by moving between the older English alliterative patterns and the newer rhyming lines; see Introduction, type 3, p. 30.

Naive and derivative though it may be, this remnant of the Middle English period serves well to indicate the continuity of medieval allegory in the native English tradition. Chaucer's Nun's Priest blandly cites Physiologus as the authority for his assertion that mermaids sing. Even in the Elizabethan period the fashionable euphuistic style of John Lyly depended heavily, as Drayton complained, on the ancient topics:

> Talking of stones, stars, plants, of fishes, flies,
> Playing with words and idle similes.

And in seeking an appropriate epic simile for Satan, Milton resorted to the familiar figure of the deceptive whale, already expounded in the Old English and the Middle English bestiaries.

The best edition of the Middle English bestiary is in Joseph Hall, *Selections from Early Middle English* (Oxford, 1920), I, 176–96; II, 579–626. For background see Beatrice White, "Medieval Animal Lore," *Anglia*, 72 (1954), 21–30, and Francis Carmody, "Bestiary," *New Catholic Encyclopedia*, II (Washington, 1967), 367–69. For bibliography see Wells, ch. 2.24; *CBEL*, 1. 182–83, 5.122.

The Bestiary

[Lines 384–455]

Natura Wulpis[1]

A wilde der is°
That is ful of fele° wiles;
Fox is hire to name.
For hire quethsipe°
5 Husebondes° hire haten,
For hire harm-dedes.
The coc and the capun
Ge° feccheth ofte in the tun,°
And the gandre and the gos
10 Bi the necke and bi the nos°
Haleth is° to hire hole.
For-thi° man hire hatieth,
Hatien and hulen°
Bothe men and fules.°
15 Listneth° nu a wunder
That this der° doth for hunger:
Goth o felde° to a furgh°
And falleth tharinne,
In eried° lond er° in erth-chine,°
20 For to bilirten fugeles.°
Ne stereth ge noght of° the stede°
A god stund deies°
Oc dareth so° ge ded were;
Ne drageth° ge non onde.°
25 The raven is swithe° redi,
Weneth° that ge rotieth,°
And othre fules hire fallen bi°
For to winnen fode
Derflike° withuten dred.°
30 He° wenen that ge° ded beth.°
He wüllen on° this foxes fel,°
And ge° it wel feleth.°
Ligtlike° ge lepeth up
And letteth° hem sone;°
35 Gelt° hem here billing°
Rathe° with illing;°
Tetoggeth° and tetireth° hem
Mid hire teth sharpe;
Fret° hire fille
40 And goth than ther ge° wille.

[1] The nature of the fox.

der is creature there is
many
wickedness
Householders
She enclosure
beak
Haleth is She brings them
Therefore
howl at her
birds
Hear
this der this creature
Goth . . . She goes afield furrow
ploughed or gully
bilirten fugeles deceive birds
Ne . . . She doesn't stir from spot
stund deies part of a day
Oc . . . But lies still as if
draws breath
very
Assumes ge rotieth she (the fox) is decaying
hire . . . alight beside her
Boldly fear
They she is
wüllen on want to get onto skin
she perceives
Quickly
stops at once
She repays here billing for their jabbing
Swiftly malice
She rends rips
Devours
ther ge where she

151

Significacio prima[2]

	Twifold forbisne° in this der°	**Twifold forbisne** A twofold example creature
	To frame° we mugen° finden her,	**To frame** Of use may
	Warsipe° and wisedom	Prudence
	With° devel and with ivel man	Against
45	The devel dereth dernelike.°	**dereth dernelike** lies secretly
	He lat° he ne wile us nogt biswike.°	pretends **ne** . . . will not deceive us
	He lat he ne wile us don° non loth°	do harm
	And bringeth us in a sinne	
	And ther° he us sloth.°	there slays
50	He bit° us don ure bukes° wille,	bids **ure bukes** our belly's
	Eten and drinken with unskil,°	imprudence
	And in° ure skemting°	during amusement
	He doth rathe a foxing.°	**doth** . . . swiftly acts the fox's role
	He billeth one° the foxes fel°	**billeth one** jabs at skin
55	Wo-so° telleth idel spel,°	Whosoever **idel spel** a lying tale
	And he tireth on° his ket°	**tireth on** rips at carrion
	Wo-so him° with sinne fet,°	himself feeds
	And devel geld swilk billing°	**geld** . . . repays such jabbing
	With shame and with sending°	disgrace
60	And, for his sinfule werk,	
	Ledeth man to helle merk.°	**helle merk** hell's darkness

Significacio secunda[3]

	The devel is thus the fox ilik°	like
	Mid ivele breides° and with swik;°	**ivele breides** evil tricks deception
	And man° also the foxes name	men
65	Arn° wurthi to haven shame.°	Are in shame
	For wo-so seieth other god°	**wo-so** . . . whoever says good to another
	And thenketh ivel on his mod,°	mind
	Fox he is and fend i-wis.°	**fend i-wis** fiend indeed
	The Boc ne legeth nogt° of this.	**ne** . . . does not lie
70	So was Herodes fox and flerd°	deceiver
	Tho° Crist kam into this middel erd;°	When earth
	He seide he wulde him leven on°	**leven on** believe in
	And thogte he wulde him fordon.°	destroy

[2] First allegorical meaning.
[3] Second allegorical meaning.

Judas

(ca. 1250, Southwestern)

❦

Judas has been called the earliest recorded example of an English ballad, though strictly speaking, it belongs to the genre of religious carol. The narrative is drawn in part from the New Testament and in part from the medieval traditions associated with Judas. Here, in a unique development, it is the sister of Judas who is ultimately responsible for the betrayal of Christ—a thoroughly antifeminist invention in keeping with the medieval assumption that Eve was the origin of evil.

The meter is seven-beat couplets; see Introduction, type 7, page 31.

The ballad may be found in F. J. Child, ed., *English and Scottish Popular Ballads* (Cambridge, Mass., 1882), No. 23, and in Carleton Brown, ed., *English Lyrics of the Thirteenth Century* (Oxford, 1932), pp. 38–39. For bibliography see Wells, ch. 5.48; Chambers, OHEL, pp. 51–53.

	Hit wes upon a Scere° Thorsday	Maundy
	That ure Loverd° aros.	Lord
	Ful milde were the wordes	
	He spec° to Judas.	spoke
5	"Judas, thou most° to Jurselem	must go
	Oure mete for to bügge.°	buy
	Thritti platen° of selver	pieces
	Thou bere upo° thi rügge.°	**Thou** . . . Carry upon back
	"Thou comest fer i° the brode stret,	**fer i** far in
10	Fer i the brode strete.	
	Summe of thine tunesmen°	townspeople
	Ther thou meight i-mete."°	**meight i-mete** may meet
	I-mette° wid is söster,°	He met **is söster** his sister
	The swikele wimon.°	**swikele wimon** treacherous woman
15	"Judas, thou were würthe°	**were würthe** deserve that
	Me stende° thee wid ston.	**Me stende** People stone
	"Judas, thou were würthe	
	Me stende thee wid ston	

20	For the false prophete That thou bilevest upon."	

	"Be stille, leve söster.°
	   Thin herte thee tobreke!°
	Wiste min loverd Crist,°
	   Ful wel he wolde be wreke."°
		leve söster dear sister
		Thin . . . May your heart shatter
		Wiste . . . If my lord Christ knew
		avenged

25	"Judas, go thou on the roc,
	   Heie upon the ston.
	Lei thin heved i° my barm.°
	   Slep thou thee° anon."
		heved i head on bosom
		Slep . . . Sleep

30	Sone so° Judas
	   Of° slepe was awake,
	Thritti platen° of selver
	   From hym weren i-take.
		Sone so As soon as
		From
		pieces

35	He drou° hymselve bi the cop°
	   That° al it lavede a° blode.
	The Jewes out of Jurselem
	   Awenden° he were wode.°
		tore crown
		So that **lavede a** was bathed in
		
		Assumed crazy

40	Foreth hym com° the riche Jeu
	   That heighte° Pilatus.
	"Wolte sülle° thi Loverd°
	   That hette° Jesus?"
		Foreth . . . Forth came
		was called
		Wolte sülle Will you sell Lord
		is called

	"I nül° sülle my Loverd
	   For nones cünnes eighte°
	Bote° hit be for the thritti platen°
	   That he me bitaighte."°
		won't
		nones . . . any kind of property
		Unless pieces
		entrusted

45	"Wolte sülle° thi Lord Crist
	   For enes° cünnes golde?"
	"Nay, bote hit be for the platen
	   That he habben wolde."
		Wolte sülle Will you sell
		any

50	In him com ur Lord gon°
	   As is postles seten° at mete.°
	"Wou° sitte ye, postles,
	   Ant wi nüle° ye ete?
		In . . . In came our Lord
		is . . . his apostles sat their meal
		Why
		won't

"Wou sitte ye, postles,
    Ant wi nüle ye ete?
55   Ic am i-bought ant i-sold today
      For oure mete."

Up stod him Judas:
    "Lord, am I that?
I nas° never o° the stüde°   was   in   place
60   Ther me thee° evel spec."°   **Ther** ... Where people against you   spoke

Up him stod Peter
    Ant spec wid al is° mighte: his
"Thau° Pilatus him come   Though
    Wid ten hundred cnightes,

65   "Thau Pilatus him com
    Wid ten hundred cnightes,
Yet Ic wolde, Loverd,
    For thi love fighte."

"Still thou be, Peter.
70   Wel I thee i-cnowe.
Thou wolt fursake me thrien°   thrice
    Ar° the coc him crowe."   Before

THOMAS OF HAILES

A Love Rune

(ca. 1224–72, Southwestern)

Nothing is known about the author of this remarkable poem except that, according to the scribe of the only surviving manuscript, "Frater Thomas de Hales" belonged to the order of Fratres Minores (the Minorites, or Franciscans, who first came to England in 1224) and composed the work for a girl who had dedicated herself to God. Presumably Friar Thomas or his family originated in the village of Hailes (near Gloucester); the Southwestern dialect of the piece supports this likelihood.

The friar's transfer of the language of love to the language of religion is a standard medieval device; his argument that the girl should find contentment by becoming the bride of Christ is a familiar one, already fully developed in *The Anchoresses' Rule* (p. 106); and the various reminders of the vanity of the world are commonplace. Yet the poem has a striking individuality because of the rich allusiveness of its imagery. The *love rune* (l. 2), which the girl requests, according to medieval usage would normally be a love spell by which to bind an earthly lover to herself; but the friar redirects the incantation toward heavenly love. The heroes and lovers whom he mentions (ll. 65–70) are the favorite exemplars of medieval narrative: Hector and Caesar, two of the Nine Worthies; Paris and Helen, from the classical tradition; Amadas and Ydoine, from Anglo-Norman romance; and Tristram and Isolde, from Celtic legend. But the friar introduces these names only to epitomize all that is transitory. The precious stones (ll. 169–76) that he lists are such that, in a courtly lay, bedeck a heroine, but the friar subordinates all of these to the gemstone of virginity. His theme is *fyn amur* (l. 182), but the usual sense of 'refined courtly love' is here irrelevant, for the friar has exalted his poem to the higher level of spiritual love.

The meter is eight-line stanzas, with four beats to a line; see Introduction, type 18, page 32.

The best edition is found in Carleton Brown, ed., *English Lyrics of the Thirteenth Century* (Oxford, 1932), pp. 68–74. For bibliography see Wells, ch. 13.173; Legge, pp. 227–28.

A mayde Cristes me bit yörne°
  That Ich hire würche° a luve ron
For-whan heo° myhte best i-leorne
  To taken onother soth lefmon°
5 That treowest were° of alle berne°
  And best wyte cuthe° a freo° wymmon.
Ich hire nüle nowiht werne;°
  Ich hire wüle teche as Ic con:

bit yörne is asking eagerly
hire würche compose for her
For-whan heo So that she
soth lefmon true lover
treowest were most faithful would be men
wyte cuthe would know how to protect noble
nüle . . . will in no way refuse

"Mayde, her thu myht biholde°
10 This worldes luve nys bute o res°
And is byset° so fele-volde,°
Vikel and frakel and wok and les.°
Theos theines° that her weren bolde
Beoth aglyden so° wyndes bles;°
15 Under molde° hi liggeth° colde
And faleweth so° döth medewe gres.°

myht biholde can see that
nys . . . is only on the run
harassed variously

Theos theines The leaders
Beoth . . . Have glided away like gust
earth lie
faleweth so fade as grass

"Nis° no mon i-boren o lyve°
That her may beon stüdevest,°
For her he haveth seorewen ryve,°
20 Ne tyt° him never ro° ne rest.
Toward his ende he hyeth blyve,°
And lütle hwile he her i-lest.°
Pyne° and deth him wile ofdryve°
Hwenne° he weneth° to libben° best.

There is i-boren . . . born alive
may . . . can be steadfast
seorewen ryve sorrows rife
Ne tyt Nor befall never ro ever peace
hyeth blyve hastens fast
survives
Pain kill
Just when expects live

25 "Nis° non so riche ne non so freo°
That he ne schal heonne° sone away;
Ne may hit never his waraunt beo
Gold, ne seolver, vouh, ne gray.°
Ne beo he no the° swift, ne may he fleo°
30 Ne weren° his lif enne° day.
Thus is thes world, as thu mayht seo,°
Also° the schadewe that glyt° away.

There is noble
ne . . . shall not go hence

Ne . . . Be he ever so ne . . . he can't fly
Ne weren Or save for one
see
Just like glides

"This world fareth hwilynde;°
Hwenne on° cumeth, another göth;
35 That° wes bifore nu is bihynde;
That er° was leof,° nu hit is loth.°
Forthi° he doth as the blynde°
That in this world his luve döth.°
Ye mowen i-seo° the world aswynde.°
40 That wouh° göth forth,° abak that soth.°

fareth hwilynde passes in transition
one
What
once dear hated
Therefore blind man does
puts
mowen i-seo can see decay
That wouh Wrong forward abak . . .
backward truth

"The luve that ne may her abyde,°
Thu treowest hire° myd müchel wouh,°
Also° hwenne hit schal toglide,°
Hit is fals, and mereuh, and frouh,°
45 And fromward° in üych-on tide.°
Hwile hit lesteth is° seorewe inouh;°
An° ende, ne werie mon so syde,°
He schal todreosen so° lef on bouh.°

ne . . . can't last here
treowest hire trust it müchel wouh
much wrong
As schal toglide is to vanish
mereuh . . . weak, and brittle
perverse üych-on tide every occasion
lesteth is lasts there is enough
In the ne . . . even if a man guard ever so
widely
todreosen so decay like bough

12. Fickle and foul and weak and deceiving.
27–28. Nor can gold or silver or striped fur or gray ever be his guarantee.

"Monnes luve nys buten o stunde;°   **nys** . . . lasts but awhile
50   Nu he luveth, nu he is sad;°   sated
Nu he cumeth, nu wile he funde;°   go
Nu he is wroth,° nu he is gled.   angry
His luve is her and ek a lunde.°   **her** . . . here and also away (?)
Nu he luveth sum that he er bed.°   **er bed** previously challenged
55 Nis he never treowe i-funde;°
That° him tristeth,° he is amed.°   He who   trusts   mad

"Yf mon is riche of° worldes weole,°   in   wealth
Hit maketh his heorte smerte and ake.
If he dret° that me° him stele,°   dreads   people   rob
60   Thenne döth° him pyne° nyhtes wake.°   causes   torment   to lie awake
Him waxeth° thouhtes monye and fele°   **Him waxeth** In him rise   various
Hu he hit may witen° withuten sake.°   guard   strife
An° ende, hwat helpeth hit to hele?°   In the   conceal
Al deth° hit wile from him take.   death

65 "Hwer is Paris and Heleyne,
That weren so bryht and feyre on bleo;°   **on bleo** of feature
Amadas, Tristram, and Ideyne,
Yseude, and alle theo;°   those
Ector with his scharpe meyne,°   **scharpe meyne** fierce retinue
70   And Cesar riche of° worldes feo?°   in   possessions
Heo beoth° i-glyden ut of the reyne°   **Heo beoth** They have   realm
So the schef° is of the cleo.°   sheaf   hill (?)

"Hit is of heom al-so° hit nere.°   **heom al-so** them as if   had never been
Of heom me° haveth wunder i-told,°   people   **wunder i-told** related marvels
75 Nere hit reuthe° for to heren°   **Nere** . . . Were it not pity   hear
Hu hi° were with pyne aquold°   they   **pyne aquold** torment destroyed
And hwat hi tholeden° alyve here.   suffered
Al is heore hot i-turnd to cold.
Thus is thes world of false fere.°   appearance
80 Fol° he is the° on hire° is bold.   A fool   who   it

"Theyh° he were so riche mon   Though
As Henry° ure kyng   Henry III (r. 1216–72)
And al-so veyr° as Absalon,   **al-so veyr** as fair
That nevede° on eorthe non evenyng,°   had not   **non evenyng** any equal
85 Al were sone his prüte agon.°   **prüte agon** pride gone
Hit nere, on° ende, wurth on heryng!°   **nere, on** wouldn't be, in the   **wurth** . . .
     worth a herring
Mayde, if thu wilnest after leofmon,°   **wilnest** . . . wish a lover
Ich teche° thee enne treowe° king.   direct   **enne treowe** to a true

55. He is never found to be faithful

"A, swete,° if thu i-knöwe°   sweetheart   only knew
90 The gode thewes° of thisse childe!°   virtues   squire
He is feyr and bryht of heowe,°   hue
Of glede chere, of mode° mylde,   spirit
Of lufsum lost, of truste treowe,°   **lufsum** ... lovable spirit, true of trust
Freo° of heorte, of wisdom vilde.°   Noble   filled
95 Ne thurhte thee° never rewe,°   **Ne** ... You would need   regret
Myhtestu do thee° in his ylde.°   **Myhtestu** ... If you could put yourself
                                    protection

"He is ricchest mon of londe
So wide so° mon speketh with muth.   **So** ... As far as
Alle heo beoth to° his honde,   **Alle** ... All these lands are in
100 Est and west, north and suth.
Henri king of Engelonde
Of° him he halt° and to hym buhth.°   From   holds as vassal   yields
Mayde, to thee he send° his sonde°   sends   messenger
And wilneth° for to beo thee cuth.°   wishes   **beo** ... be known to you

105 "Ne byt he° with thee lond ne leode,°   **Ne** ... He doesn't demand as dowry
                                              people
Vouh° ne gray, ne rencyan.°   Striped fur   fine cloth
Naveth° he therto none neode;°   Has   **therto** ... no need for that
He is riche and weli° man.   wealthy
If thu him woldest luve beode°   offer
110 And bycumen° his leovemon,°   become   lover
He brouhte° thee to such wede°   would bring   clothing
That naveth king ne kayser° non.   emperor

"Hwat spekestu° of eny bolde°   do you say   building
That wrouhte the wise Salomon
115 Of jaspe,° of saphir, of merede° golde,   jasper   refined
And of mony onother ston?
Hit is feyrure of feole-volde°   **of feole-volde** many times
More than Ich eu telle con.
This bold,° mayde, thee° is bihote°   building   to you   promised
120 If that thu bist° his leovemon.°   will be   lover

"Hit stont° uppon a treowe mote°   stands   **treowe mote** secure eminence
Thar° hit never truke° ne schal,   Where   fail
Ne may no mynur hire underwrote°
Ne never false thene grund-wal.°   **false** ... breach the foundation
125 Tharinne is üich balewes bote,°   **üich** ... each sorrow's cure
Blisse and joye and gleo and gal.°   **gleo** ... mirth and song
This bold,° mayde, is thee bihote°   building   promised
And üych-o° blisse thar wythal.   every

123. Nor can any sapper undermine it

"Ther ne may° no freond fleon other,° | **ne may** can   avoid another
130 Ne non furleosen° his i-ryhte.° | **non furleosen** anyone lose   rights
Ther nys° hate ne wrethth nouther,° | is no   **ne**... or wrath either
Of prüde° ne of onde° of none wihte.° | pride   envy   person
Alle heo schule° wyth engles pleye | **Alle**... They are all destined to
Some and sauhte° in heovene° lyhte. | **Some**... United and reconciled   heaven's
135 Ne beoth heo,° mayde, in gode weye° | **Ne**... Are they not   circumstances
That° wel luveth ure dryhte?° | Who   lord

"Ne may no° mon hine i-seo° | **Ne**... Nor can any   **hine i-seo** see him
Also° he is in his mihte | As
That may withuten blisse beo° | **withuten**... remain joyless
140 Hwanne he i-sihth° ure drihte. | sees
His sihte° is al joye and gleo;° | **His sihte** The sight of him   happiness
He is day wythute nyhte.
Nere he,° mayde, ful seoly° | **Nere he** Would not he be   blessed
That myhte wunye° myd such a knyhte? | dwell

145 "He haveth bitauht° thee o° tresur | granted   a
That is betere than gold other pel° | **other pel** or purple
And bit° thee luke° thine bur° | orders   to close   bower
And wilneth° that thu hit wyte° wel. | wishes   guard
Wyth theoves,° with reveres,° with lechurs | **Wyth theoves** Against thieves   robbers
150 Thu most beo waker and snel.° | **most**... must be watchful and quick
Thu art swetture° thane eny flur | sweeter
Hwile thu witest thene° kastel. | **witest thene** guard the

"Hit is ymston of feor i-boren;° | **ymston**... gemstone brought from afar
Nys° non betere under heovene grunde.° | It is   **heovene grunde** the floor of heaven
155 He° is tofore° alle othre i-coren;° | It (virginity)   before   chosen
He heleth alle luve wunde.° | **luve wunde** the wounds of love
Wel were° alyve i-boren° | would be   born
That° myhte wyten° this ilke stunde, | Anyone who   guard   **ilke stunde** same state
For, habbe thu hine enes forloren,° | **habbe**... once you have lost it
160 Ne byth he° never eft° i-funde. | **Ne**... It will be   again

"This ilke ston that Ich thee nemne° | **thee nemne** name to you
Maydenhod i-cleoped° is. | **Maydenhod i-cleoped** Virginity called
Hit is o derewurthe° gemme. | **o derewurthe** a precious
Of alle othre he berth that pris° | **he**... it wins the prize
165 And bryngeth thee withute wemme° | flaw
Into the blysse of Paradis.
The hwile° thu hyne witest° under thine hemme,° | **The hwile** As long as   guard it   clothing
Thu ert swetture° than eny spis.° | **ert swetture** are sweeter   spice

"Hwat spekstu° of eny stone   do you say
170   That beoth in vertu other in° grace—   **beoth** . . . possesses power or
Of amatiste, of calcydone,°   chalcedony
Of lectorie° and tupace,°   cock-stone   topaz
Of jaspe, of saphir, of sardone,°   sardonyx
Smaragde,° beril, and crisopace?°   Emerald   chrysoprase
175 Among alle othre ymstone°   gemstones
Thes beoth deorre[1] in uyche° place.   every

"Mayde, also° Ich thee tolde,   as
The ymston of thi bur°   bower
He° is betere an hundred-folde   It
180   Than alle theos in heore° culur.   their
He is i-don° in heovene° golde   set   heavenly
And is ful of fyn amur.°   **fyn amur** pure love
Alle that myhte hine wite° scholde,   **myhte** . . . might be able to guard it
He schyneth so bryht in heovene bur.

185 "Hwen thu me dost in thine rede°   **me** . . . consult me
For thee to cheose a leofman,°   lover
Ich wile don as thu me bede°   ask
The beste that Ich fynde con.
Ne doth he,° mayde, on üvele° dede   **Ne** . . . Doesn't he commit   **on üvele** an evil
190   That may cheose of two that on°   **that on** the one
And° he wile withute neode   If
Take thet wurse, the betere let gon?

"This rym, mayde, Ich thee sende
Open and withute sel.°   seal
195 Bidde° Ic that thu hit untrende°   Ask   unroll
And leorny bute bok üych del°
Herof° that thu beo swithe hende,°   Of it   **beo** . . . may be very apt
And tech hit° other maydenes wel.   **tech hit** teach it to
Hwo-so cuthe° hit to than° ende,   **Hwo-so cuthe** Whoever might know   the
200   Hit wolde him stonde müchel stel.°   **stonde** . . . give much aid

"Hwenne thu sittest in longynge,
Drauh thee forth° this ilke wryt.°   **Drauh** . . . Draw you out   **ilke wryt** same composition
Mid swete stephne° thu hit singe,   voice
And do also° hit thee byt.°   as   commands

---

[1] 'These are precious.' Nine of the ten stones mentioned here belong to the group of twelve precious stones enumerated in Rev. xxi. 19–20 (referred to in *The Pearl*, ll. 999 ff.); the other stone, *lectorie* (properly, *alectorie*), according to Bartholomew de Glanville, "exciteth the service of Venus."
196. And learn without book (i.e., by heart) each part

205 To thee he haveth send one° gretynge.   **he** . . . it has sent a

    God almyhti thee beo myd°   **beo myd** be with

    And leve cumen° to his brüdthinge°   **leve cumen** grant you to come   bridal

    Heye° in heovene ther° he sit."°   High   where   sits

    And yeve° him god endynge   give

210 That haveth i-wryten this ilke wryt.°   **ilke wryt** same composition

        Amen.

The Sayings of St. Bernard

(ca. 1275, West Midland or East Midland)

This powerful poem survives in five manuscripts, each of which contains a slightly different version. The Digby Manuscript contains thirty-one stanzas, and the last ten stanzas, which are printed here, were set apart by the scribe under a separate heading.

In the first part of the poem the author warns his listeners against their three foes, the world, the flesh, and the Devil, and he then turns to the familiar question, "Where are those who were before us?" The poem is attributed to St. Bernard of Clairvaux (1090–1153), the great Cistercian leader, but does not correspond to any of his writings except in its spiritual fervor.

The poem is cast in six-line, tail-rhyme stanzas; see Introduction, type 14, page 32.

The best edition of the various versions is still *The Minor Poems of the Vernon MS*, ed. F. J. Furnivall, EETS 117 (London, 1901), 511–22, 757–63. For the Harley manuscript see *Facsimile of British Museum MS. Harley 2253*, ed. N. R. Ker, EETS, 25 (London, 1965), item 74. For bibliography see Wells, ch. 7.30; Brown and Robbins, *Index*, items 2865, 3310.

Ubi sunt qui ante nos fuerunt ?

Were beth they° biforen us weren,   **Were . . .** Where are they who
Houndes ladden,° and hawekes beren,°   led   bore
    And hadden feld and wode?
The riche levedies° in hoere° bour,   ladies   their
5   That wereden gold in hoere tressour,°   coiffures
    With hoere brightte rode,°   complexions

Eten and drounken and maden hem° glad;   themselves
Hoere lif was al with gamen i-lad;°   **gamen i-lad** games spent
    Men keneleden° hem biforen.   knelt
10   They beren hem° wel swithe heye,°   **beren hem** bore themselves   **swithe heye** very high
    And in a twincling of on° eye   an
    Hoere° soules weren forloren.°   Their   lost

Were° is that lawing° and that song,   Where   laughter
That trayling° and that proude yong,°   **That trayling** The trailing clothes   walking
15   Tho° hawekes and tho houndes?   Those

Al that joye is went away;
That wele° is comen te weylaway,°   well-being   **te weylaway** to woe
   To manie harde stoundes.°   trials

Hoere° paradis hy nomen° here,   Their   **hy nomen** they took
20 And now they lien° in helle ifere.°   lie   together
   The füir° hit brennes hevere.°   fire   **brennes hevere** burns ever
   Long is ay,° and long is ho;°   aye   always
   Long is wy,° and long is wo.   alas
    Thennes ne cometh they nevere.

25 Dreghy° here, man, thenne, if thou wilt,   Endure
   A lüitel pine° that me° thee bit.°   torment   people   offer
    Withdrau° thine eyses° ofte.   Draw from   pleasures
   They° thi pine be ounrede,°   Though   extreme
   And° thou thenke on thi mede,°   If   reward
30 Hit sal° thee thinken° softe.   shall   seem

If that fend,° that foule thing,   **that fend** the fiend
Thorou wikke roun,° thorou fals egging,   **wikke roun** wicked spell
   Nethere° thee haveth i-cast,°   Down   cast
   Oup and be god chaunpioun.
35 Stond, ne° fal namore adoun   and
    For a lüytel blast.

Thou tak the rode to° thi staf,   **rode to** cross as
And thenk on him that thereonne yaf°   gave
   His lif that wes so lef.°   precious
40 He hit yaf for thee. Thou yelde° hit him;   repay
   Ayein° his fo that staf thou nim,°   Against   take
    And wrek° him of that thef.°   avenge   thief

Of rightte bileve° thou nim that sheld   **Of...** In true faith
The wiles that° thou best° in that feld.   **The...** While   are
45 Thin hond to strenkthen fonde,°   try
   And kep° thy fo with staves ord,°   oppose   point
   And do that° traytre seien that word.°   **do that** make the   **seien...** surrender
    Biget° that mürie londe.   Gain

Thereinne is day withhouten night,
50 Withouten ende strenkthe and might,
   And wreche° of everich° fo,   vengeance   every
   Mid God himselven eche° lif,   eternal
   And pes and rest withoute strif,
    Wele withouten wo.

55 Mayden Moder, Hevene° Quene,   Heaven's
     Thou might° and const and owest° to bene°   may ought be
       Oure sheld ayein° the fende.°   against fiend
     Help ous sünne for to flen,°   flee
     That we moten° thi sone i-seen°   may see
60   In joye withouten hende.

The Fox and the Wolf

(ca. 1275–1300, Southwestern)

An ancient form of literature, numbering among its early examples the Indian *Panchatantra* and the Greek fables attributed to Aesop, the beast fable is represented in extant Middle English literature before Chaucer's "Nun's Priest's Tale" only by *The Fox and the Wolf*. Nevertheless, the beast fable represents a long and important tradition. Aesop's tales appeared early in Latin collections in the first and fourth centuries and again in a widely popular prose collection of the tenth century. An English translation of the latter is said to have been prepared for Henry I. Perhaps Marie de France was alluding to that lost translation when she declared that her Anglo-Norman *Fables* (ca. 1189) were translated from English.

A number of literary works in this genre appeared on the Continent. A late eighth-century poem by Paulus Diaconus was followed by the efforts of a Cistercian monk, the *Ecbasis Captivi* (ca. 1043–46). Several years later in Flanders a Master Nivardus produced a long Latin poem *Ysengrimus*. In addition to this literary tradition, there sprang up out of oral tradition and international folklore a number of fables concerning Reynard the Fox: the French beast epic *Roman de Renart* (ca. 1175–1250), a German *Reinhart Fuchs* (ca. 1180), by Heinrich Glichezaere, and two Middle Dutch versions (in the thirteenth and fourteenth centuries). The lasting popularity of the tales is demonstrated by the editions in Dutch and English in the later fifteenth century and thereafter, including two editions by Caxton.

The Fox and the Wolf is memorable not only as the earliest humorous beast fable in English but also as the only early example in English of a versified story dealing with Reynard the Fox. Though it corresponds in general to Branch II of the French *Roman de Renart*, no specific source has been positively identified.

Found in the same manuscript as *Dame Sirith*, *The Fox and the Wolf* is composed in four-beat couplets; see Introduction, type 5, page 31. The simplicity and clarity of style fit the subject matter, and even if the poem lacks some of the wit and descriptive powers of its French counterpart and ignores the allegorical potentialities of its theme, it compensates for these weaknesses by its downright humor, as when we are told of the hungry fox:

> Him were levere meten one hen / Then half an oundred wimmen.

Useful editions and commentaries are in G. H. McKnight, *Middle English Humorous Tales in Verse* (Boston, 1913) and J. A. Bennett and G. V. Smithers, *Early Middle English Verse and Prose* (New York, 1968), pp. 65–76, 297–303. For bibliography see Wells, ch. 2.25.

The Fox and the Wolf

A vox gon° out of the wode go,　　　　　　**vox gon** fox did
Afingret° so that him° wes wo.°　　　　　　Hungry　he　woeful
He nes° nevere in none wise°　　　　　　　was　manner
Afingret erour° half so swithe.°　　　　　　before　much
5　He ne hoeld° nouther wey ne strete,°　　kept to　**wey** . . . road nor street
For him° wes loth° men to mete;　　　　　to him　hateful
Him were levere° meten one hen,　　　　　**Him** . . . He would sooner
Then half an oundred° wimmen.　　　　　　hundred
He strok swithe° over al,　　　　　　　　**strok swithe** went quickly
10　So that he ofsei ane° wal.　　　　　　　**ofsei ane** saw a
Withinne the walle wes on° hous,　　　　　a
The vox° wes thider swithe vuous;°　　　　fox　**swithe vuous** very ready
For he thohute° his hounger aquenche,　　intended
Other mid mete, other mid drünche.°
15　Abouten° he biheld wel yerne;°　　　　　About　**biheld** . . . looked very eagerly
Tho eroust° bigon the vox to erne,°　　　　**Tho eroust** Then first　run
Al fort° he come to one° walle.　　　　　　Until　a
And som therof wes afalle,°　　　　　　　fallen down
And wes the wal over al to-broke,°　　　　broken down
20　And on yat° ther wes i-loke.°　　　　　　**on yat** a gate　shut
At the fürmeste brüche° that he fond,　　**fürmeste brüche** first opening
He lep in, and over he wond.°　　　　　　went
Tho° he wes inne, smere° he lou,°　　　　　When　scornfully　laughed
And therof he hadde gome i-nou;°　　　　　**gome i-nou** sport enough
25　For he com in withouten leve
Bothen of haiward° and of reve.°　　　　　**of haiward** from hayward　reeve
　　On° hous ther wes, the dore wes ope,°　A　open
Hennen weren° therinne i-crope,°　　　　　**Hennen weren** Hens had　crept
Five—that maketh anne° flok—　　　　　　a
30　And mid° hem sat on kok.°　　　　　　　with　cock
The kok him wes flowen on hey,°　　　　　high
And two hennen him seten ney.°　　　　　near
　　"Vox,"° quod the kok, "wat dest° thou thare?　Fox　do
Go hom. Crist thee yeve kare!°　　　　　**yeve kare** give sorrow
35　Houre° hennen thou dest ofte shome."°　Our　insult
　　"Be stille, Ich hote, a° Godes nome!"°　**hote, a** command, in　name
Quath the vox. "Sire Chauntecler,
Thou fle° adoun, and com me ner.　　　　fly
I nabbe° don her nout bote° god,　　　　　have not　**her** . . . here anything but
40　I have leten thine hennen blod.
Hy° weren seke° ounder the ribe,　　　　They　sick
That hy ne mightte non lengour libe,°　　**ne** . . . couldn't live any longer
Bote here heddre° were i-take.　　　　　　**Bote** . . . Unless their blood (from veins)
That I do for almes° sake.　　　　　　　charity's

14. Either with food or with drink.

167

45 Ich have hem leten eddre-blod,°	vein blood
And thee, Chauntecler, hit wolde don° god.	do
Thou havest that ilke° ounder the splen;°	same sickness spleen
Thou nestes nevere daies ten,°	
For thine lif-dayes beth° al ago,°	are gone
50 Bote° thou bi mine rede° do.	Unless counsel
I do° thee lete blod ounder the brest,	advise
Other° sone axe° after the prest."	Or else ask
"Go wei," quod the kok; "wo thee bigo!°	befall
Thou havest don oure künne° wo.	kin
55 Go mid than° that thou havest nouthe;°	**mid than** with this now
Acoursed be thou of Godes mouthe.	
For were I adoun,° bi Godes nome,°	down below name
Ich mighte ben siker° of othre shome.°	**ben siker** be sure insult
Ac weste° hit houre° cellerer,	But if knew our
60 That thou were i-comen her,°	**were . . .** had come here
He wolde sone after thee ghonge°	go
Mid° pikes and stones and staves stronge.	With
Alle thine bones he wolde to-breke;	
Then we weren wel awreke."°	avenged
65 He wes stille, ne spak namore,°	**spak namore** spoke no more
Ac° he werth° athürst wel sore.°	But was **wel sore** very sorely
The thürst him dede° more wo	caused
Then hevede rather° his hounger do.°	**hevede rather** had earlier done
Over al he ede and sohute.°	**ede . . .** went and sought
70 On aventure° his wiit° him brohute°	**On aventure** By chance wits brought
To one pütte° wes water inne,	**one pütte** a pit where
That wes i-maked mid° grete ginne.°	with ingenuity
Tuo boketes° ther he founde:	buckets
That other wende° to the grounde,	**That . . .** The one goes
75 That wen me° shulde that on opwinde,°	one **that . . .** the one wind up
That other wolde adoun winde.°	go
He ne hounderstod nout of the ginne;°	trap
He nom° that boket and lep ther-inne,	took
For he hopede i-nou° to drinke.	enough
80 This boket° beginneth to sinke.	bucket
Too late the vox° wes bithout,°	fox concerned
Tho° he wes in the ginne i-brout.°	When brought
I-nou he gon him bithenche,°	**gon . . .** reflected
Ac° hit ne halp mid° none wrenche.°	But helped with trick
85 Adoun he moste,° he wes ther-inne;	must go
I-kaut he wes mid swikele ginne.°	**swikele ginne** treacherous trap
Hit mighte han i-ben wel° his wille	**han . . .** well have been
To lete that boket hongi stille.	

48. You have not lain with a woman for ten days (literally, 'You nest never for ten days')

Wat mid serewe° and mid drede,   sorrow
90 Al his thürst him overhede.°   disappeared
Al thus he com to the grounde,°   bottom
And water i-nou° ther he founde.   enough
Tho° he fond water, yerne° he dronk;   When eagerly
Him thoute° that water there stonk,   **Him thoute** It seemed to him
95 For hit wes toyeines° his wille.   against
   "Wo wörthe,"° quath the vox,° "lust and wille,°   **Wo wörthe** Cursed be fox pleasure
That ne con meth too his mete.°   **ne ...** knows not moderation in food
Yef Ich nevede° too muchel° i-ete,   hadn't much
This ilke shome neddi nouthe,°   **ilke ...** same insult I had not now
100 Nedde lust i-ben of mine mouthe.°
Him is wo° in eche londe,   **Him ...** Woe to him
That is thef mid his honde.
Ich am i-kaut mid swikele ginne,°   **swikele ginne** treacherous trap
Other° soum devel me broute her-inne.   Or
105 I was woned° to ben° wiis,   accustomed being
Ac° nou of° me i-don hit hiis."°   But for is
   The vox° wep, and reuliche° bigan.   fox piteously
Ther com a wolf gon °after than°   walking this
Out of the depe wode blive,°   quickly
110 For he wes afingret swithe.°   **afingret swithe** very hungry
Nothing he ne founde in al the nighte,
Wer-mide° his honger aquenche mightte.   Wherewith
He com to the pütte,° thene vox i-herde.   pit
He him kneu wel by his rerde,°   voice
115 For hit wes his neighebore
And his gossip, of children bore.°
Adoun bi the pütte he sat.
   Quod the wolf: "Wat may ben° that   be
That Ich in the pütte i-here?
120 Hertou Cristine other° mi fere?°   **Hertou ...** Are you Christian or companion
Say° me soth,° ne gabbe° thou me nout,   Tell the truth lie
Wo° haveth thee in the pütte i-brout?"   Who
The vox hine° i-kneu wel for his kün,°   him kin
And tho eroust° kom wiit° to him;   **tho eroust** then first an idea
125 For he thoute, mid somme ginne,°   trick
Himself houp° bringe, thene° wolf ther-inne.   up and the
Quod the vox, "Wo is nou there?
Iche wene° hit is Sigrim that Ich here."   suppose
   "That is soth,"° the wolf sede,   true
130 "Ac° wat art thou, so God thee rede?"°   But help
   "A!" quod the vox, "Ich wille thee telle,

100. Had it not been for the pleasure of my mouth.
116. And his close friend, since they were children.

On alpi° word Ich lie nelle.°   **On alpi** One single   will not
Ich am Reneuard thi frend,
And yif Ich thine come hevede i-wend,°   **thine** . . . your coming had expected
135 Ich hedde° so i-bede° for thee,   had   prayed
That thou sholdest comen to me."
    "Mid thee?" quod the wolf. "War-to?
Wat shulde Ich in the pütte do?"
    Quod the vox, "Thou art ounwiis;°   unwise
140 Her° is the blisse of paradiis.   Here
Her Ich mai evere wel fare
Withouten pine,° withouten kare.°   pain   sorrow
Her is mete,° her is drinke,   food
Her is blisse withouten swinke;°   work
145 Her nis° hounger never mo,°   is   more
Ne non other künnes° wo;   **Ne** . . . Nor other kinds of
Of alle gode her° is i-nou."°   **gode her** good things here   enough
Mid thilke° wordes the wolf lou.°   **Mid thilke** At those   laughed
    "Art thou ded, so God thee rede,°   help
150 Other° of the worlde?" the wolf sede.   Or
Quod the wolf, "Wenne storve° thou,   died
And wat dest° thou there nou?   do
Ne beth nout° thre daies ago   **Ne** . . . It was only
That thou and thi wif also,
155 And thine children, smale and grete,
Alle togedere mid me hete."°   ate
    "That is soth,"° quod the vox.   true
"Gode thonk,° nou hit is thus,   **Gode thonk** Thank God
That Ich am to Criste wend.°   gone
160 Not° hit non of mine frend.   Knows
I nolde,° for al the worldes god,°   wouldn't   goods
Ben° ine the worlde ther° Ich hem fond.   Be   where
Wat° shuld Ich ine the worlde go,   Why
Ther nis bote kare° and wo,   **Ther** . . . There is only sorrow
165 And livie° in fülthe° and in sünne?°   live   filth   sin
Ac her beth° joies fele cünne.°   **her beth** here are   **fele cünne** of many kinds
Her beth bothe shepe and get."°   goats
    The wolf haveth hounger swithe° gret,   very
For he nedde yare° i-ete,   **nedde yare** had not for a long time
170 And tho° he herde speken of mete,°   when   food
He wolde bletheliche° ben thare.   gladly
    "A!" quod the wolf, "gode i-fere,°   companion
Moni god mel° thou havest me binome.°   meal   deprived of
Let me adoun to thee kome,
175 And al Ich wole thee foryeve.°   forgive
    "Ye," quod the vox, "were thou i-srive,°   absolved

And sünnen hevedest al forsake,°   **sünnen** ... had forsaken all sins
And to klene lif i-take,°   turned
Ich wolde so bidde° for thee   pray
180 That thou sholdest comen to me."
    "To wom° shuld Ich," the wolf seide,   whom
"Ben i-knowe° of mine misdede?   **Ben i-knowe** Be confessed
Her nis° nothing alive   is not
That me kouthe° her nou srive.°   could   absolve
185 Thou havest ben ofte min i-fere;°   companion
Woltou nou mi srift° i-here,   confession
And al mi liif I shal thee telle?"
    "Nay," quod the vox, "I nelle."°   won't
    "Neltou,"° quod the wolf, "thin ore?°   Won't you show   mercy
190 Ich am afingret swithe sore.°   **afingret** ... very sorely hungry
Ich wot° tonight Ich wörthe° ded,   know   will be
Bote° thou do me somne reed.°   Unless   **somne reed** some counsel
For Cristes love, be mi prest."
The wolf bey° adoun his brest,   bent
195 And gon° to siken° harde and stronge.   began   sigh
    "Woltou,"° quod the vox, "srift ounderfonge,°   Will you   **srift ounderfonge** undertake confession
Tel thine sünnen on and on,°   **sünnen** ... sins one by one
That ther bileve° never on?"   remain
    "Sone,"° quod the wolf, "wel i-faie.°   At once   **wel i-faie** very gladly
200 Ich habbe ben qued° al mi lif-daie.   evil
Ich habbe widewene kors,°   **widewene kors** widows' curse
Ther-fore Ich fare the wors.
A thousent shep Ich habbe abiten,°   bitten
And mo, yef hy° weren i-writen.   they
205 Ac hit me ofthinketh sore.°   **me** ... I repent sorely
Maister, shall I tellen more?"
    "Ye," quod the vox, "al thou most sügge,°   **most sügge** must say
Other° elles-wer thou most abügge."°   Or   atone
    "Gossip,"° quod the wolf, "foryef° hit me,   Close friend   forgive
210 Ich habbe ofte sehid qued bi° thee.   **sehid** ... said evil about
Men seide that thou on thine live
Misferdest° mid mine wive.   Misbehaved
Ich thee aperseivede° one stounde,°   perceived   moment
And in bedde togedere ou° founde.   you
215 Ich wes ofte ou ful ney,°   near
And in bedde togedere ou sey.°   saw
Ich wende,° al-so othre doth,°   thought   **al-so** ... as others do
That° Ich i-seie° were soth,°   What   saw   true
And ther-fore thou were me loth.°   **me loth** hateful to me
220 Gode gossip,° ne be thou nohut wroth."°   Close friend   **nohut wroth** not angry
    "Wolf," quod the vox him tho,°   then

"Al that thou havest her° bifore i-do,°   here   done
In thohut,° in speche, and in dede,   thought
In eche otheres künnes quede,°   **eche** ... every other kind of evil
225   Ich thee foryeve° at thisse nede."°   forgive   **thisse nede** this hour of need
    "Crist thee foryelde,"° the wolf seide.   reward
"Nou Ich am in clene live,°   **clene live** pure life
Ne recche° Ich of° childe ne of wive.   care   about
Ac sei° me wat I shal do,   tell
230   And ou° Ich may comen thee to."   how
    "Do?" quod the vox. "Ich wille thee lere.°   instruct
I-siist° thou a boket hongi° there?   See   **boket hongi** bucket hanging
Ther is a brüche of hevene° blisse   **brüche** ... opening to heaven's
Lep ther-inne mid i-wisse,°   certainty
235   And thou shalt comen to me sone."°   at once
    Quod the wolf, "That is light° to done."   easy
He lep in, and way sumdel;°   **way sumdel** weighed much
That weste° the vox ful wel.   knew
The wolf gon sinke,° the vox arise.   **gon sinke** began to sink
240   Tho° gon the wolf sore agrise.°   Then   become frightened
Tho° he com amidde° the pütte,°   When   in the middle of   pit
The wolf thene° vox opward mette.   the
    "Gossip,"° quod the wolf, "wat nou?   Close friend
Wat havest thou i-münt?° Weder° wolt thou?"   decided   Whither
245   "Weder Ich wille?"° the vox sede.   wish to go
"Ich wille oup, so God me rede!°   help
And nou go doun with thi meel.°   meal
Thi biyete wörth wel° smal;   **biyete** ... gain will be very
Ac Ich am therof glad and blithe
250   That thou art nomen° in clene live.°   taken   **clene live** pure life
Thi soule-cnül° Ich wille do ringe,   death knell
And masse for thine soule singe."
    The wrecche binethe nothing ne vind°   finds
Bote cold water, and hounger him bind.
255   To colde gistninge° he wes i-bede;°   feast   invited
Vroggen° haveth his dou° i-knede.   Frogs   dough
    The wolf in the pütte° stod,   pit
Afingret° so that he wes wod.°   Hungry   mad
I-nou° he cursede that° thider him broute.   Enough   him who
260   The vox therof lüitle route.°   cared
The püt him wes the house ney°   near
Ther freren woneden swithe sley.°
Tho that° hit com to the time   When
That hoe° shulden arisen ine°   they   within
265   For to süggen° here houssong,°   say   matins

262. Where very shrewd friars dwelled.

O° frere ther wes among,

Of here° slep hem shulde awecche,°   **Of here** Who from their   awake

Wen hoe shulden thidere recche.°   reach

He seide, "Ariseth on and on,°   **on** ... one by one

270 And kometh to houssong heverechon."°   everyone

This ilke° frere heyte° Ailmer;   same   was named

He wes hoere° maister curtiler.°   their   gardener

He wes hofthürst swithe stronge,°   **hofthürst** ... very greatly thirsty

Right amidward° here houssonge.°   in the middle of   matins

275 Alhone° to the pütte° he hede,°   Alone   pit   went

For he wende bete° his nede.   **wende bete** intended to remedy

He com to the pütte, and drou,°   drew up

And the wolf was hevi i-nou.

The frere mid al his maine tey°   **maine tey** might pulled

280 So longe that he thene° wolf i-sey.°   the   saw

For° he sei thene wolf ther sitte,   Since

He gradde,° "The devel is in the pütte."   cried out

To the pütte hy gounnen gon°   **hy** ... they did go

Alle, mid pikes and staves and ston,

285 Ech mon mid that° he hedde.   what

Wo wes him that wepne nedde.°

Hy comen to the pütte, thene° wolf opdrowe.°   the   drew up

Tho hede° the wreche fomen° i-nowe   **Tho hede** Then had   enemies

That weren egre° him to slete°   eager   tear

290 Mid grete houndes, and to bete.°   beat

Wel and wrothe° he wes i-swonge,°   cruelly   beaten

Mid staves and speres he wes i-stounge.°   stung

The vox bicharde° him mid i-wisse,°   tricked   certainty

For he ne fond nones künnes° blisse   **nones künnes** any kind of

295 Ne hof düntes foryevenesse.°   **hof** ... remission of blows

---

286. Woe to him who had not weapons.

Dame Sirith

(ca. 1275–1300, Southwestern)

Nearly 150 *fabliaux* (comic bourgeois tales) appear in French literature between 1150 and 1320. Only one from that period survives in English. The reason is not that the stories of the *fabliaux* were unknown in England, for the existence of a number of ballads based on these ribald stories indicates the contrary. Such ballads as "The Friar in the Well" (Child 276), "The Wife Wrapped in Wether's Skin" (277), and "The Farmer's Curst Wife" (278) were probably of such an origin. The reason that only one such story has survived in written literature is probably best expressed by Chaucer when he apologizes for the greatest of all Middle English *fabliaux*, "The Miller's Tale," as a "cherles tale," and bids his readers:

> . . . therfore, whoso list it nat y-heere,
> Turne over the leef and chose another tale;
> For he shal fynde ynowe, grete and smale,
> Of storial thyng that toucheth gentillesse
> And eek moralitee and hoolynesse.

Certainly Chaucer gave the *fabliau* a place in Middle English literature that it had not held before, but the frequency of complaints about such tales during this period suggests both the moralistic objections to them and their deeply embedded popularity, such as the references to "harlotrie" in *Piers Plowman* (IV, 115; V, 419, below, p. 306) and to "merye tales" in the same work (XIII, 352). After Chaucer a number of *fabliaux* appear, including "The Pardoner and the Tapster," prefixed to *The Tale of Beryn* (p. 504), and *The Freiris of Berwik*, sometimes attributed to Dunbar.

The only extant *fabliau* written in English before Chaucer's time, *Dame Sirith* is composed in lively but irregular tail-rhyme stanzas; see Introduction, type 14, page 32. Portions of the poem are set in couplets, suggesting that the anonymous poet was transforming an earlier source into stanzas. The existence of a fragmentary *Interludium de Clerico et Puella*, dating about fifty years later than *Dame Sirith* and paralleling even verbally the earlier work, further suggests, though by no means conclusively, that the nonextant source of both pieces may have been an early secular dramatic piece.

On the relation of *Dame Sirith* to the interlude, see W. Heuser, "Das Interludium 'De Clerico et Puella,'" *Anglia*, XXX (1907), 306–19. Useful editions and commentaries are in G. H. McKnight, *Middle English Humorous Tales in Verse* (Boston, 1913), J. A. Bennett and G. V. Smithers, *Early Middle English Verse and Prose* (New York, 1968), pp. 77–95, 303–12, and Larry D. Benson and Theodore M. Andersson, *The Literary Context of Chaucer's Fabliaux: Texts and Translations* (Indianapolis, 1971), pp. 372–87. For bibliography see Wells, ch. 2.20.

As I com bi an waie,
Hof on° Ich herde saie,   **Hof on** Of one
   Ful modi° mon and proud.   high-spirited
Wis he wes of lore,
5 And gouthlich° under gore,°   goodly garments
   And clothed in fair sroud.°   dress

To lovien he bigon
On° wedded wimmon;°   A woman
   Therof he hevede° wrong.   did
10 His herte hire° wes alon;°   for her only
   That reste nevede° he non,   had not
   The love wes so strong.

Wel yerne° he him bithoute°   **Wel yerne** Very eagerly **him bithoute**
Hou he hire gete moute°   considered
15 In ani cünnes° wise.   **gete moute** might get
   That befel° on an day,   manner
   The loverd wend° away   **That befel** It happened
   Hon° his marchaundise.°   **loverd wend** lord goes
                                On business

He wente him° to then inne,°   **wente him** went **then inne** the dwelling
20 Ther hoe wonede° inne,   **Ther . . .** Where she dwelled
   That wes riche won;°   **riche won** a splendid dwelling
And com into then halle,
   Ther hoe wes srud° with palle,°   clothed rich cloth
   And thus he bigon:

WILEKIN
25 "God almightten be herinne!"

MARGERI
"Welcome, so Ich ever bide wenne,"°   **bide wenne** feel joy
   Quod this wif.
"His hit° thi wille, com and site,   **His hit** If it is
And wat is thi wille let me wite,°   know
30 Mi leve lif.°   **leve lif** dear love

"Bi houre Loverd, Hevene° King,   **houre . . .** our Lord, heaven's
If I mai don° ani thing   do
   That thee° is lef,°   to you dear
Thou mightt finden me ful fre,°   **ful fre** very generous
35 For bletheli willi° don for thee, **bletheli willi** happily will I
   Withouten gref."°   hesitation

175

WILEKIN

"Dame, God thee foryelde,°
Bote on that° thou me nout bimelde,°
Ne make thee wroth;°
40 Min hernde° willi to thee bede,°
Bote wraththen° thee for ani dede
Were me loth."°

> reward
> **Bote** ... Provided that   **nout bimelde**
> may not betray
> **make** ... become angry
> business   announce
> to anger
> Would be hateful to me

MARGERI

"Nai, i-wis,° Wilekin,
For nothing that ever is min,
45   Thau° thou hit yirne,°
Houncurteis° ne willi° be,
Ne con° I nout on vilté,°
Ne nout I nelle° lerne.

> indeed
> If   yearn for
> Ungracious   **ne willi** I will not
> know   **on vilté** of meanness
> **Ne** ... Naught will I

"Thou mait saien° al thine wille,
50 And I shal herknen° and sitten stille,
That° thou have told.
And if that thou me tellest skil,°
I shal don after° thi wil,
That° be thou bold.°

> **mait saien** can say
> listen to
> What
> **me** ... speak to me right
> **don after** act according to
> Of that   sure

55 "And thau° thou saie me° ani same,°
Ne shal I thee nowight° blame
For thi sawe."°

> if   **saie me** speak to me   shame
> not
> saying

WILEKIN

"Nou Ich have wonne leve,°
Yif that I me shulde greve,°
60   Hit were hounlawe.°

> **wonne leve** gained permission
> grieve
> wrong

"Certes,° dame, thou seist as hende,°
And I shal setten spel on° ende,
And tellen thee al,
Wat Ich wolde° and wi Ich com.
65 Ne con° Ich saien non falsdom,
Ne non I ne shal.°

> Surely   **seist** ... speak courteously
> **setten** ... speak my speech to the
>
> want
> **Ne con** Cannot
> **Ne** ... Nor shall I

"Ich habbe i-loved thee moni yer,
Thau° Ich nabbe° nout ben her
Mi love to schewe.
70 Wile thi loverd° is in toune
Ne mai no mon with thee holden roune°
With no thewe.°

> Though   have
>
> lord
> talk
> good manners

"Yürstendai° Ich herde saie,   Yesterday
As Ich wende° bi the waie,   went
75   Of oure sire.°   **oure sire** your husband
Me° tolde me that he was gon   One
To the feire of Botolfston°   Boston
In Lincolnshire.

"And for° Ich weste° that he wes houte,°   because. knew out
80 Thar-fore Ich am i-gon aboute
To speken with thee.
Him bürth° to liken wel his lif,   **Him bürth** It behooves him
That mightte welde selc° a wif   **welde selc** rule such
In privité.°   privacy

85 "Dame, if hit is thi wille,
Both dernelike° and stille°   secretly quietly
Ich wille thee love."

MARGERI
"That woldi don° for non thing,   **woldi don** would I do
Bi houre Loverd, Hevene° King,   **houre . . .** our Lord, Heaven's
90   That ous° is bove!°   us above

"Ich habbe mi loverd that is mi spouse,
That maiden broute me to house,
Mid menske i-nou.°   **menske i-nou** honor aplenty
He loveth me and Ich him wel;
95 Oure° love is also° trewe as stel,   Our as
Withouten wou.°   wrong

"Thau° he be from hom on his hernde,°   Though business
Ich were ounseli,° if Ich lernede   **were ounseli** would be unhappy
To ben on hore.°   **ben . . .** be a whore
100 That ne shal nevere be,
That I shal don selk falseté,   **selk falseté** such deceit
On bedde ne on flore.°   floor

"Never more his lif-while,
Thau° he were on° hondred mile   Though a
105   Biyende° Rome,   Beyond
For no thing ne shuld I take
Mon on erthe to ben° mi make,°   be mate
Ar° his hom-come."   Before

WILEKIN

"Dame, dame, torn thi mod.°   **torn** ... change your mind
110 Thi curteisi wes ever god,
   And yet shal be.
  For the Loverd° that ous° haveth wrout,° Lord us made
  Amend thi mod, and torn thi thout,°   thought
   And rew on° me."   **rew on** pity

MARGERI

115 "We, we! Holdest° thou me a fol?   Consider
  So Ich ever mote biden Yol,°   **mote** ... must await Yule
   Thou art ounwis.°   unwise
  Mi thout ne shalt thou never wende.° turn
  Mi loverd° is curteis° mon and hende,° lord courteous gracious
120   And mon of pris.°   excellence

  "And Ich am wif bothe god and trewe.
  Trewer womon ne mai no° mon cnowe° **ne** ... cannot any know
   Then Ich am.
  Thilke° time ne shal never bitide°   That come
125 That mon for wouing° ne thoru prüde° wooing **thoru prüde** through pride
   Shal do me scham."

WILEKIN

  "Swete levemon,° merci!   lover
  Same° ne vilani   Shame
   Ne bede° I thee non;   offer
130 Bote derne° love I thee bede,   secret
  As mon that wolde of° love spede° from prosper
   And finde won."°   great store

MARGERI

  "So bide° Ich evere mete other° drinke, expect **mete other** food or
  Her thou lesest° al thi swinke.°   waste toil
135 Thou might gon hom, leve° brother, dear
  For wille Ich thee love ne non other
  Bote mi wedde houssebonde.
  To tellen hit thee ne wille Ich wonde."° hesitate

WILEKIN

  "Certes,° dame, that me forthinketh;° Surely **that** ... I repent of that
140 And wo is° the mon that muchel swinketh,° **wo is** woe to **muchel swinketh** toils
               much
  And at the laste leseth° his sped!° loses success
   To maken menis is him ned.°   **To** ... He needs to make lamentations

Bi me, I saie ful i-wis,
That love the love that I shal mis.°
145 And, dame, have nou godne dai!°   **have** ... good day
And thilke° Loverd, that al welde mai,°   that **welde mai** can rule
Leve° that thi thout° so tourne,°   Allow thought change
That Ich for thee no leng° ne mourne."   longer

Dreri-mod° he wente awai,   Sad-hearted
150 And thoute bothe night and dai
Hire° al for to wende.°   Her change
A frend him radde° for to fare,°   advised go
And leven al his muchele kare,°   **muchele kare** great sorrow
To Dame Sirith the hende.°   courteous

155 Thider he wente him° anon,   **wente him** went
So swithe so° he mightte gon,   **So** ... As quickly as
No mon he ne mette.
Ful he wes of tene° and treie.°   grief sorrow
Mid° wordes mild and eke sleie°   With **eke sleie** also shrewd
160 Faire he hire grette.°   greeted

WILEKIN
"God thee i-blessi, Dame Sirith!
Ich am i-com to speken thee with,
For ful muchele nede.°   **ful** ... very great need
And° Ich mai have help of thee,   If
165 Thou shalt have—that thou shalt se—
Ful riche mede."°   reward

SIRITH
"Welcomen art thou, leve sone.°   **leve sone** dear son
And if Ich mai other cone°   **other cone** or can
In eni wise° for thee do,   manner
170 I shal strengthen me° therto.   **strengthen me** try
For-thi,° leve sone, tel thou me   Therefore
Wat thou woldest I düde° for thee."   did

WILEKIN
"Bote,° leve nelde.° Ful evele I fare;   Help **leve nelde** dear old woman
I lede mi lif with tene° and kare.°   grief sorrow

143–44. Concerning myself, I say it very certainly, I who love the loved one that I shall lose.

175 "With muchel hounsele° Ich lede mi lif,
And that is for on° swete wif°
That heighghte° Margeri.
Ich have i-loved hire moni° dai,
And of hire love hoe seith° me nai.
180 Hider Ich com for-thi.°

muchel hounsele much unhappiness
a woman
is called
many a
hoe seith she says
therefore

"Bote if° hoe wende° hire mod,°
For serewe mon° Ich wakese wod,°
Other miselve quelle.°
Ich hevede° i-thout miself to slö.°
185 For-then radde° a frend me go
To thee mi serewe telle.

Bote if Unless changes mind
serewe mon sorrow must **wakese wod** grow mad
Other . . . Or kill myself
had slay
For-then radde Wherefore advised

"He saide me, withouten faille,
That thou me couthest helpe° and vaile,°
And bringen me of° wo
190 Thoru° thine crafftes° and thine dedes.°
And Ich wile yeve° thee riche mede,°
With that° hit be so."

couthest helpe could assist help
from
Through skills deeds
give reward
With that Provided that

SIRITH
"*Benedicite°* be her-inne!
Her havest thou, sone, mikel senne.°
195 Loverd, for his swete nome,°
Lete thee ther-fore haven no schome!
Thou servest affter Godes grome,°
Wen thou seist on° me silk blame.°
For Ich am old, and sek,° and lame;
200 Seknesse haveth maked me ful° tame.
Blesse thee, blesse thee, leve knave,°
Leste thou mesaventer° have
For this lesing° that is founden°
Oppon me, that am harde i-bounden.°
205 Ich am on° holi wimon;°
On witchecrafft nout I ne con,°
Bote with gode men° almesdede
Ilke° dai mi lif I fede,
And bidde° mi pater-noster and mi crede,
210 That God hem helpe at höre nede°
That helpen me mi lif to lede,
And leve° that hem mote° wel spede.°
His lif and his soule wörthe i-shend°

Blessing
mikel senne great sin
name

anger
seist on tell to **silk blame** such a charge
sick
very
leve knave dear boy
misadventure
deceit found
pressed
a woman
nout . . . I know nothing
men's
Each
pray
höre nede their need

grant may prosper
wörthe i-shend be disgraced

180

That° thee to me this hernde° haveth send.   Who   business
215   And leve me to ben i-wreken°   **ben i-wreken** be avenged
On him this shome me haveth speken."°

WILEKIN
"Leve nelde, bi-lef° al this.   **Leve** ... Dear old woman, stop
Me thinketh° that thou art onwis.°   **Me thinketh** It seems to me   unwise
The mon that me to thee taute°   directed
220   He weste° that thou hous couthest saute.°   knew   **hous** ... could reconcile us
Help, Dame Sirith, if thou maut,°   can
To make me with the sweting saut,°   **sweting saut** darling a reconciliation
And Ich wille geve thee gift ful stark,°   **ful stark** very great
Moni a pound and moni a mark,
225   Warme pilche° and warme shon,°   furs   shoes
With that° mi hernde° be wel don.   **With that** When   business
Of muchel godlec° might thou yelpe,°   **muchel godlec** much goodness   boast
If hit be so that thou me helpe."

[SIRITH]
"Ligh me° nout, Wilekin! Bi thi leute,°   **Ligh me** Lie to me   faithfulness
230   Is hit thin hernest° thou tekest° me?   sincere purpose   show
Lovest thou wel Dame Margeri?"

WILEKIN
"Ye, nelde, witerli.°   **nelde, witerli** old woman, surely
Ich hire love; hit mot° me spille°   must   ruin
Bote° Ich gete hire to mi wille."   Unless

SIRITH
235   "Wat!° God Wilekin, me reweth° thi scathe;°   Oh   **me reweth** I pity   harm
Houre° Loverd sende thee help rathe!°   Our   at once

"Weste Hic° hit mightte ben forholen,°   **Weste Hic** If I knew that   **ben forholen** be concealed
Me wolde thünche° wel folen°   **Me** ... It would seem to me   suited
Thi wille for to füllen.°   fulfill
240   Make me siker° with word ond honde   sure
That thou wolt helen,° and I wile fonde°   conceal   try
If Ich mai hire tellen.

"For al the world ne woldi nout°   **ne** ... I would not
That Ich were to chapitre° i-brout   ecclesiastical court
245   For none selke° werkes.   such

216. On him who has said this shameful thing about me.

Mi jugement were sone i-given
To ben with shome somer-driven°
  With° prestes and with clerkes."   By

WILEKIN

"I-wis, nelde, ne woldi°
250 That thou hevedest vilani°   baseness
  Ne shame for mi goed.°   benefit
  Her° I thee mi trouthe plightte,°   Here   **trouthe plightte** word pledge
  Ich shal helen° bi mi mightte,°   conceal   power
  Bi the holi roed!"°   cross

SIRITH

255 "Welcome, Wilekin, hiderward.
  Her havest° i-maked a foreward°   you have   agreement
  That thee mai ful° wel like.°   very   please
  Thou maight° blesse thilke sith,°   may   **thilke sith** that time
  For thou maight make thee ful blith;°   happy
260 Dar thou namore sike.°   **Dar . . .** You need nevermore sigh

  "To goder hele° ever come thou hider,   **To . . .** For good fortune
  For sone will I gange° thider   go
  And maken hire hounderstande.
  I shal kenne° hire sülke° a lore°   teach   such   lesson
265 That hoe° shal lovien thee mikel° more   she   much
  Then ani mon in londe."

WILEKIN

"Also havi° Godes grith,°   **Also havi** As I have   peace
Wel havest thou said, Dame Sirith,
  And Godes hile° shal ben° thin.   prosperity   be
270 Have her twenti shiling.
This Ich yeve° thee to meding°   give   **to meding** as reward
  To büggen° thee sep and swin."°   buy   **sep . . .** mutton and pork

SIRITH

"So° Ich evere brouke° hous other flet,°   As   may enjoy   **other flet** or floor
Neren° never penes° beter biset°   Were not   pence   employed
  Then thes shulen ben.°   **Then . . .** Than these shall be
  For I shal don° a juperti,°   make   venture
  And a ferli maistri,°   **ferli maistri** wonderful trick
  That thou shalt ful wel sen.

247. To be made to ride shamefully upon an ass
249. Indeed, old woman, I would not wish

"Pepir° nou shalt thou eten;[1]   Pepper
280 This mustart shal ben° thi mete,°   be food
    And gar° thin eien° to renne.°   make eyes run
    I shal make a lesing°   deception
    Of thin heie-renning,°   eye-running
    Ich wot° wel wer and wenne."   know

           WILEKIN
285 "Wat!° nou const° thou no god,   Oh   can do
    Me thinketh that thou art wod.°   crazy
    Yevest thou° the welpe° mustard?"   **Yevest thou** Do you give dog

           SIRITH
    "Be stille, boinard!°   fool
    I shal mit° this ilke gin°   with same trick
290 Gar° hire love to ben° al thin.   Make be
    Ne shal Ich never have reste ne ro,°   quiet
    Til Ich have told hou thou shalt do.
    Abid° me her° til min hom-come."   Wait for here

           WILEKIN
    "Yüs, bi° the somer blome,°   **Yüs, bi** Yes, until **somer blome** summer bloom
295 Hethen nulli ben binomen,°
    Til thou be ayein° comen."   back
    Dame Sirith bigon to go,
    As a wrecche that is wo,°   woeful
    That hoe com hire° to then inne°   **hoe . . .** she came **then inne** the dwelling
300 Ther° this gode wif wes inne.   Where
    Tho hoe° to the dore com,   **Tho hoe** When she
    Swithe reuliche° hoe bigon: **Swithe reuliche** Very pitifully

           SIRITH
    "Loverd," hoe seith, "wo is holde° wives   **wo . . .** woe to old
    That in poverté ledeth ay° lives;   ever
305 Not° no mon so muchel of pine°   Knows not suffering
    As povre wif that falleth in ansine.°   **povre wif** poor woman want
    That mai ilke° mon bi me wite,°   each know
    For mai I nouther gange° ne site.   walk
    Ded woldi ben° ful fain.°   **woldi ben** would I be **ful fain** very gladly
310 Hounger and thürst me haveth nei° slain;   nearly
    Ich ne mai° mine limes on-wold°   can control
    For mikel° hounger and thürst and cold.   great
    War-to° liveth selke° a wrecche!   Why such
    Wi nül° God mi soule fecche?"   **Wi nül** Why will not

---

[1] As line 287 makes clear, this stanza (ll. 279–84) is spoken by Dame Sirith to her dog.
295. Hence I will not be taken away

183

MARGERI

315   "Seli wif,° God thee hounbinde!°   **Seli wif** Good woman unbind
      To-dai wille I thee mete° finde   food
        For love of God.
      Ich have reuthe° of thi wo,   pity
      For evele° i-clothed I se thee go,   poorly
320   And evele i-shoed.

    "Com her-in, Ich wile thee fede."

SIRITH

      "God Almightten do thee mede,°   reward
      And the Loverd that wes on rode i-don,°   **rode i-don** the cross slain
      And faste° fourti daws to non,°   fasted **daws ...** days to the ninth hour
325   And hevene and erthe haveth to welde,°   rule
      As thilke Loverd thee foryelde."°

MARGERI

      "Have her fles° and eke° bred,   **her fles** here meat also
      And make thee glad, hit is mi red.°   counsel
      And have her the coppe° with the drinke."   cup

SIRITH

330   "God do° thee mede° for thi swinke,"°   give reward toil
      Thenne spac° that olde wif°—   spoke woman
      Crist awarie° hire lif—   curse
      "Alas, alas! that ever I live!
      Al the sünne° Ich wolde forgive   sin
335   The mon that smite off min heved!°   head
      Ich wolde mi lif me were bireved!"°   taken from

MARGERI

      "Seli wif,° wat eilleth° thee?"   Good woman ails

[SIRITH]

      "Bote ethe° mai I sori be.   **Bote ethe** Yet easily
      Ich hevede° a douter feir and fre,°   had noble
340   Feirer ne mightte no mon se.
      Hoe° hevede a curteis° hossebonde,   She courteous
      Freour° non mightte no mon fonde.   Nobler
      Mi douter lovede him al too wel;
      For-thi° mak I sori del.°   Therefore **sori del** sorrowful grief
345   Oppon a dai he was out wend,°   gone
      And thar-thoru° wes mi douter shend.°   thereby disgraced

326. May that same Lord reward you.

He hede° on ernde° out of toune;   went   errand
And com a modi clarc° with croune,°   **modi clare** proud clerk   tonsure
To mi douter his love beed,°   offered
350 And hoe nolde nout° folewe his red.°   **nolde nout** would not   counsel
He ne mightte his wille have
For nothing he mightte crave.
Thenne bigon the clerc to wiche,°   use witchcraft
And shop° mi douter til° a biche.°   changed   to   bitch
355 This is mi douter that Ich of speke;
For del° of hire min herte mot° breke.   grief   must
Loke hou hire heien greten,°   **heien greten** eyes cry
On hire cheken the teres meten.
For-thi,° dame, were hit no wonder   Therefore
360 Thau° min herte burste assunder.   If
And wose-ever° is yong houssewif,   whosoever
Hoe loveth ful lüitel hire lif,
And° eni clerc of love hire bede,°   If   offer
Bote° hoe grante and lete him spede."°   Unless   succeed

MARGERI

365 "A! Loverd Crist! Wat mai I thenne do?
This enderdai° com a clarc° me to,   other day   clerk
And bed me love on his manere,
And Ich him nolde nout i-here.°   **nolde** . . . would not hear
Ich trowe° he wolle° me forsape.°   believe   will   transform
370 Hou troustu, nelde,° Ich mowe ascape?"°   **troustu, nelde** do you believe, old woman   **mowe ascape** can escape

SIRITH

"God Almightten be thin help,
That thou be nouther bicche ne welp!
Leve dame, if eni clerc
Bedeth° thee that love werc,°   Offers   work
375 Ich rede° that thou grante his bone°   advise   request
And bicom his lefmon sone.°   **lefmon sone** lover at once
And if that thou so ne dost,
A worse red° thou ounderfost."°   counsel   receive

MARGERI

"Loverd Crist, that me is wo,°   **that** . . . I am sorry for that
380 That the clarc° me hede fro,°   clerk   **hede fro** went from
Ar° he me hevede biwonne.°   Before   **hevede biwonne** had won
Me were levere° then ani fe°   **Me** . . . I would rather   money
That he hevede enes leien° bi me   **enes leien** once lain
And efftsones° bigunne.   again

385 "Evermore, nelde, Ich wille be thin,
    With that° thou feche me Willekin,   **With that** Provided that
      The clarc° of wam° I telle.   clerk   whom
    Giftes will I geve thee
    That thou maight ever the betere be,
390   Bi Godes houne° belle!"   own

SIRITH

"Sothliche,° mi swete dame,   Truly
And if I mai withoute blame,
    Fain° Ich wille fonde.°   Gladly   try
And if Ich mai with him mete
395 Bi eni wei other° bi strete,   or
    Nout ne will I wonde.°   hesitate

"Have god dai, dame. Forth willi° go."   will I

MARGERI

"Allegate° loke that thou do so   At any rate
    As Ich thee bad.°   asked
400 Bote that° thou me Wilekin bringe,   **Bote that** Unless
    Ne mai I never lawe° ne singe   laugh
      Ne be glad."

SIRITH

"I-wis,° dame, if I mai,°   Indeed   can
Ich wille bringen him yet todai,
405   Bi mine mightte."°   power
Hoe wente hire° to hire inne,   **wente hire** went
Ther° hoe founde Wilekinne,   Where
    Bi houre Drightte!°   **houre Drightte** our Lord

SIRITH

"Swete Wilekin, be thou nout dred,°   afraid
410 For of thin hernde° Ich have wel sped.° business   succeeded
Swithe° com forth thider with me,   Quickly
For hoe haveth send affter thee.
I-wis° nou maight thou ben above,   Indeed
For thou havest grantise° of hire love." grant

WILEKIN

415   "God thee foryelde,° leve nelde,   reward
That hevene and erthe haveth to welde!"
This modi° mon bigon to gon   proud
With Sirith to his levemon°   lover

In thilke stounde.°   **thilke stounde** that time
420 Dame Sirith bigon to telle,
And swor bi Godes owene belle,
Hoe hevede° him founde.   She (Sirith) had

SIRITH
"Dame, so have Ich Wilekin sout,°   sought
For nou have Ich him i-brout."

MARGERI
425 "Welcome, Wilekin, swete thing,
Thou art welcomore° then the king."   more welcome

"Wilekin the swete,
Mi love I thee bihete,°   promise
To don al thine wille.
430 Turnd° Ich have mi thout,°   Changed   thought
For I ne wolde nout
That thou thee shuldest spille."°   destroy

WILEKIN
"Dame, so° Ich evere bide noen,°   as   **bide noen** expect the ninth hour
And Ich am redi and i-boen°   prepared
435 To don al that thou saie.
Nelde, *par ma fai!*°   ***par* . . .** by my faith
Thou most gange° awai,   go
Wile° Ich and hoe shulen plaie."   While

SIRITH
"Goddot° so I wille.   God knows
440 And loke that thou mid° hire tille°   with   till
And strek° out hire thes.°   stretch   thighs
God yeve° thee muchel kare°   give   sorrow
Yeif that° thou hire spare   **Yeif that** If
The wile thou here bes.°   are

445 "And wose° is onwis,°   whoever   unwise
And for non pris°   price
Ne con geten his levemon,°   lover
I shal, for mi mede,°   reward
Garen° him to spede,°   Make   succeed
450 For ful wel I con."

The Land of Cokayne

(ca. 1275–1300, Anglo-Irish)

The Land of Cokayne is a forerunner of the Anglo-Irish literature of the nineteenth and twentieth centuries. The poem survives in a unique manuscript, which contains a variety of works in English, French, and Latin, some of which may have been composed by English-speaking settlers in Ireland. Since the manuscript is associated with the Franciscan abbey in Kildare, it has been argued that the poem is a satire aimed by a Franciscan friar specifically against the Cistercian monks in Kildare. More generally, perhaps, the poem is a universal parody of a monk's notion of the "earthly paradise," where he would be relieved of vigils, fasts, and celibacy. Despite this ambiguity of intention and the frivolity of its tone, the stern voice of the preacher is unmistakable.

The word *cokayne* is French, meaning probably "the land of cakes." There are various parallels to this poem: the Old French *Le Fabliau de Coquaigne*, the Anglo-Norman *L'Ordre de Bel Eyse*, and the Irish satire *MacConglinne's Vision*. The Anglo-Irish treatment of the topic, however, is unique in its delightfully racy anticlerical satire and its blend of the frivolous with the didactic.

The meter is rhyming couplets; see Introduction, type 5, page 31.

A useful recent edition of *The Land of Cokayne* is in J. S. Bennett and G. V. Smithers, *Early Middle English Verse and Prose* (New York, 1968), pages 136–44, 336–41. For the manuscript see the facsimile of British Museum MS. Harley 913 (Kildare MS), folio 4r., which contains lines 51–76, reproduced here on page 18. For bibliography see Wells, ch. 4.29; *CBEL*, 1.161.

Fur in see° bi west Spaygne	**Fur** . . . Far over the sea
Is a lond i-hote° Cokaygne;	called
Ther nis° lond under heven riche°	is not **heven riche** heaven's realm
Of wel,° of godnis hit i-liche.°	**Of wel** In well-being **hit i-liche** like it
5 Thogh paradis be miri° and bright,	merry
Cokaygn is of fairir sight.°	appearance
What is ther in paradis	
Bot grasse and flure° and grene ris?°	flowers branches
Thogh ther be joi and gret dute,°	rejoicing
10 Ther nis met bote° frute;	**nis** . . . is no food but
Ther nis halle, bure, no° benche,	**bure, no** bower, nor
Bot watir manis thursto quenche.°	

12. There is only water to quench man's thirst.

188

Beth° ther no men bot two,   Are

Hely° and Enok also.[1]   Elijah

15 Elinglich° may hi° go,   Wretchedly they

Whar ther wonith° men no mo.°   dwell more

   In Cokaigne is met° and drink   food

Withute care, how, and swink.°   **care**... sorrow, trouble, and toil

The met is trie,° the drink is clere°   choice bright

20 To none, russin,° and sopper.   **To**... At noon, afternoon snack

I sigge° for soth, boute were,°   say **soth**... truth, without doubt

Ther nis° lond on erthe is pere;°   is no **is pere** its peer

Under heven nis lond i-wisse°   indeed

Of so mochil° joi and blisse.   much

25 Ther is mani° swete sighte;   many a

Al is dai, nis° ther no nighte.   there is

Ther nis baret nother° strif;   **nis**... is no struggle nor

Nis ther no deth, ac° ever lif;   but

Ther nis lac of met no° cloth;   **met no** food nor

30 Ther nis man no womman wroth;°   angry

Ther nis serpent, wolf, no fox;

Hors no capil,° kowe no ox;   nag

Ther nis° schepe no swine no gote,   is no

No non horwgh, la,° God it wote.°   **horwgh, la** filth, indeed knows

35 Nother harace, nother stode;°   **Nother**... Neither horse breeding, nor stud

The lond is ful of other gode.°   goods

Nis ther flei,° fle, no lowse   fly

In cloth, in toune,° bed, no house.   farmstead

Ther nis dunnir,° slete, no hawle,°   thunder hail

40 No non vile worme° no snawile;°   serpent snail

No non storme, rein, no winde.

Ther nis man no womman blinde,

Ok° al is game,° joi and gle;   But mirth

Wel is him that ther mai be.

45 Ther beth° rivers gret and fine   are

Of oile, melk, honi, and wine;

Watir servith ther to° no thing   for

Bot to sight° and to waiissing.°   looking at washing

Ther is al maner frute;

50 Al is solas° and dedute.°   amusement delight

   Ther is a wel° fair abbei   very

Of white monkes and of grei.

Ther beth bowris° and halles;   **beth bowris** are bowers

Al of pasteiis° beth the walles,   pies

55 Of fleis,° of fisse,° and rich met,°   meat fish food

The likfullist° that man mai et.   most delicious

[1] See 2 Kings 2.11; Gen. 5.24.

189

Fluren° cakes beth the schingles alle   Flour
Of cherche, cloister, boure, and halle.
The pinnes° beth fat podinges,°   pinnacles   sausages
60   Rich met to° princes and kinges.   for
Man mai ther-of et inogh,°   enough
Al with right and noght with wogh.°   sin
Al is commune° to yung and old,   common
To stoute and sterne,° mek and bold.   **stoute ...** proud and fierce
65   Ther is a cloister fair and light,
Brod and lang, of sembli sight.°   **sembli sight** fair appearance
The pilers of that cloister alle
Beth° i-turned of cristale,   Are
With har bas° and capitale   **har bas** their base
70   Of grene jaspe° and rede corale.   jasper
   In the praer° is a tre   meadow
Swithe likful° for to se.   **Swithe likful** Very delightful
The rote is gingevir and galingale,
The siouns beth° al sedwale.°   **siouns beth** shoots are   setwall (zedoary)
75   Trie maces° beth the flure;°   Choice mace   blossom
The rind, canel° of swet odur;   **rind, canel** bark, cinnamon
The frute, gilofre° of gode smakke;°   gillyflower (clove)   flavor
Of cucubes° ther nis no lakke.   cubebs
Ther beth rosis of rede ble°   color
80   And lilie likful° for to se.   delightful
Thai faloweth° never dai no night;   wither
This aght° be a swet sight.   ought to
Ther beth fower willis° in the abbei,   wells
Of triacle and halwei,°   **triacle ...** treacle (medicine) and healing water
85   Of baum and ek peiment,°   **baum ...** balm and also spiced wine
Ever ernend° to right rent°—   running   **right rent** good profit
Of thai stremis al the molde°—
Stonis preciuse and golde.
Ther is saphir and uniune,°   pearl
90   Carbuncle and astriune,°   astrion (star sapphire?)
Smaragde, lugre, and prassiune,°   **Smaragde ...** Emerald, ligure, and chrysoprase
Beril, onix, topasiune,°   topaz
Ametist and crisolite,°   chrysolite
Calcedun and epetite.°   **Calcedun ...** Chalcedony and hepatite
95   Ther beth briddes° mani and fale:°   birds   brownish yellow
Throstil, thruisse,° and nightingale.   **Throstil, thruisse** Throstle, thrush
Chalandre and wodwale,°   **Chalandre ...** Lark and green woodpecker
And other briddes without tale°   count
That stinteth° never bi har° might   stop   their
100   Miri° to sing dai and night.   Merrily

87. From these four wells all the earth thereabout overflows

Yite° I do° yow mo,° to witte: Yet tell more
The gees i-rostid on the spitte
Flees to that abbai, God hit wot,° knows
And gredith:° "Gees, al hote, al hot!" cry out
105 Hi bringeth garlek gret plenté,° quantity
The best i-dight° that man mai se. dressed (stuffed)
The leverokes°—that beth cuth°— larks well known
Lightith adun° to manis° muth, **Lightith adun** Alight down man's
I-dight° in stu° ful swithe° wel, Prepared stew very
110 Pudrid° with gilofre and canel.° Powdered **gilofre** . . . cloves and cinnamon
Nis no spech of no drink,° **of** . . . needed to get a drink
Ak° take inogh° withute swink.° But enough toil
Whan the monkes geeth° to masse, go
Al the fenestres° that beth of glasse windows
115 Turneth in to cristal bright
To yive° monkes more light. give
Whan the masses beth i-seiid
And the bokes up i-leiid,° laid
The cristal turnith into glasse,
120 In state that hit rather wasse.° **rather wasse** earlier was
    The yung monkes ech dai
Aftir met° goth to plai. food
Nis ther hauk no fule° so swifte bird
Bettir fleing bi° the lifte° **fleing bi** flying through sky
125 Than the monkes heigh° of mode° high spirit
With har slevis° and har hode.° **har slevis** their sleeves hood
Whan the abbot seeth ham flee,
That he holt° for moch glee; considers
Ak° natheles al ther amang But
130 He biddith ham light to evesang.° **light** . . . alight for evensong (vespers)
The monkes lightith noght adun,
Ac fürre° fleeth in o randun.° farther **o randun** a rush
Whan the abbot him i-seeth,
That is° monkes fram him fleeth, his
135 He taketh a maidin of the route° company
And turnith up hir white toute° buttocks
And betith the taburs° with is hond, small drums
To make is monkes light° to lond. alight
Whan is monkes that i-seeth,
140 To the maid dun° hi fleeth down
And geth° the wench al abute go
And thakketh° al hir white toute° pat buttocks
And sith° aftir her swinke° then **her swinke** their toil
Wendith meklich hom° to drinke **Wendith** . . . Go meekly home
145 And geth to har collacione,° collation

A wel° fair processione.   very
   An other abbei is ther bi,
For soth,° a gret fair nunnerie,   truth
Up a river of swet milke,
150   Whar is plenté gret° of silk.   **plenté gret** great quantity
Whan the someris° dai is hote,   summer's
The yung nunnes takith a bote
And doth ham° forth in that river,   **doth ham** go
Bothe with oris° and with stere.°   oars   rudder
155   Whan hi° beth für° fram the abbei,   they   far
Hi makith ham° nakid for to plei   themselves
And lepith dune° in to the brimme°   down   stream
And doth ham sleilich° for to swimme.   slyly
The yung monkes, that hi° seeth,   them
160   Hi doth° ham up, and forth hi fleeth   get
And commith to the nunnes anon,
And ech monke him° taketh on°   for himself   one
And snellich berrith° forth har prei   **snellich berrith** quickly bears
To the mochil° grei abbei   great
165   And techith the nunnes an oreisun°   prayer
With jamblevé° up and dun.   raised leg
The monke that wol be stalun° gode   stallion
And kan set aright is hode,°   **is hode** his hood
He schal hab° withoute danger°   have   difficulty
170   Twelve wives eche yere,
Al throgh right and noght throgh grace,
For to do himsilf solace.
And thilk° monke that slepith best   that
And doth is likam° al to rest,   **doth . . .** gives his body
175   Of him is hoppe,° God hit wote,°   hope   knows
To be sone vadir° abbot.   father
   Whose wol° com that lond to,   **Whose wol** Whoever will
Ful grete penance he mot° do: must
Seve° yere in swineis dritte°   Seven   **swineis dritte** swine's dung
180   He mote wade, wol° ye i-witte,°   well   know
Al anon up to the chynne,
So he schal the lond winne.
   Lordinges gode and hend,°   courteous
Mot° ye never of° world wend,°   May   from   go
185   Fort° ye stond to° yure cheance   Unless   **stond to** encounter
And fulfille that penance,
That ye mote that lond i-se°   see
And never more turne awé.°   away
Prey we God, so mote hit be,
190   Amen, pur° Seint Charité.   by

THE EARLY
FOURTEENTH
CENTURY

ROBERT MANNYNG

Handling Sin

(1303–ca. 1317, Northeast Midland)

Robert Mannyng describes himself as belonging to Bourne (Brunne), in Lincolnshire. He was born not later than the year 1283 and studied at Cambridge (ca. 1298–1302). In 1302 he became a canon of the Gilbertine order at Sempringham priory (six miles from Bourne) and in 1303 began the writing of *Handling Sin*. In his prologue written in 1317 or later, which is reprinted below, he tells us that he lived in the priory for fifteen years. The only other definite information we have about him is that he completed his *Story of England* in 1338 at the Gilbertine priory of Sixhills, also in Lincolnshire. Mannyng may also be the author of an adaptation (ca. 1300–25) of the Latin *Meditations on the Life of Christ*, ascribed to St. Bonaventura. In any case, his fame rests secure on his two major poems.

Both are works of considerable size and scope. *Handling Sin* surveys in some twelve thousand lines the entire range of the Ten Commandments, the Seven Deadly Sins, the Sin of Sacrilege, the Seven Sacraments, the Twelve Points of Shrift, and the Eight Joys of Grace. *The Story of England* in some seventeen thousand lines summarizes history from Noah to King Edward I. Both of Mannyng's works are, inevitably, derivative, but Mannyng adapts his sources freely and adds a wealth of anecdotes, observations, and opinions of his own.

The framework of *Handling Sin* is determined by its source, *Le Manuel des Péchés*, an Anglo-Norman poem attributed dubiously to William of Waddington, probably composed around 1260 in Lincolnshire. The tale of the sacrilegious carolers well illustrates the freedom with which Mannyng reworked the cautionary tales contained in his original. He gains immediacy for the miraculous curse of the dancers of Kölbigk by transferring the incident from Saxony to England. From his reading of the *Life of St. Edith of Wilton* (who died in 984) he adds the fascinating sequel concerning the cure of one of the victims. He provides credibility by blandly citing the Bishop of "St. Toulouse" (actually "holy Toul") as his authority. And he softens the theological severity of his *exemplum* by personally sympathizing more with the sacrilegious dancers than with the impatient priest who cursed them.

Mannyng's syntax is often awkward, and his style shows little influence of the rhetorical manuals that he must have studied at Cambridge; but he writes as he probably spoke— colloquially, conversationally, unassumingly. If, as is likely, he was Master of Novices at Sempringham, he naturally thought of himself not as an author seeking literary fame but as a responsible canon teaching young laymen about life. Despite his limitations, Mannyng deserves to be recognized as a worthy predecessor of Gower and Chaucer, the great raconteurs.

The meter is rhyming four-beat couplets; see Introduction, type 5, page 31.

The only convenient edition is Robert of Brunne, *Handlyng Synne*, ed. F. J. Furnivall, EETS 119, 123 (London, 1901–03). For the legend of the dancers, see Kenneth Sisam, *Fourteenth Century Verse and Prose* (Oxford, 1921), pages xxxvi–xxxvii, 204–05. For bibliography, see Wells, ch. 6.2 (and ch. 3.7); *CBEL*, 1.183, 5.122; Legge, 213–14.

Prologue

[Lines 43–88]

For lewde° men Y undyrtoke — unlearned
On° Englyssh tunge to make thys boke, — In
For many ben° of swyche° manere — are such
That talys and rymys wyl blethly° here. — gladly
5   Yn gamys and festys and at the ale
Love men to lestene trotevale° — **lestene trotevale** hear trifles
That may falle ofte to vylanye,° — bawdry
To dedly synne, or other folye.
For swyche° men have Y make this ryme — such
10 That they may weyl dyspende here tyme
And theryn sumwhat for to here
To leve° al swyche foul manere° — desist from   behavior
And for to kunne° knowe therynne — be able to
That they wene° no synne be ynne. — may suppose
15   To alle Crystyn men undir sunne,
And to gode men of Brunne,° — Bourne (Lincolnshire)
And speciali alle be° name — by
The felaushepe of Symprynghame,° — Sempringham
Roberd of Brunne greteth yow
20 In al godenesse that may to prow,° — **to prow** tend to profit
Of Brunnewake° yn Kestevene° — Bourne   Kesteven (Lincolnshire)
Syxe myle besyde Sympryngham evene.
    Y dwelled yn the pryorye
Fyftene yere yn cumpanye.
25 In the tyme of gode Dane Jone° — **Dane Jone** Don John
Of Camelton, that now is gone,
In hys tyme was Y there ten yeres
And knewe and herd of hys maneres;
Sythyn° with Dane Jone of Clyntone — Then
30 Fyve wyntyr wyth hym gan° Y wone.° — did   dwell
Dane Felyp° was mayster that tyme — **Dane Felyp** Don Philip (Master, 1298–1332)
That Y began thys Englyssh ryme.
The yeres of grace fyl than to be
A thousynd and thre hundred and thre.
35   In that tyme turnede Y thys
On° Englyssh tunge out of Frankys° — Into   French
Of a boke as Y fonde° ynne. — found it
Men clepyn° the boke *Handlyng Synne*. — name
In Frenshe, ther° a clerk° hyt sees, — where   scholar
40 He clepyth hyt *Manuel de Pécchés*.
Manuel ys "handlyng with honde."
Pécchés ys "synne," Y undyrstonde.

195

These twey° wurdys that beyn otwynne,°   two   **beyn otwynne** are separated
Do° hem togedyr, ys "handlyng synne"   Put
45 And weyl ys clepyd° for thys skyle,°   named   reason
And, as Y wote,° yow shew Y wyle.   know best

The Sin of Sacrilege

[Lines 8987–9252]
Karolles,° wrastlynges, or somour games,   Round-dance songs
Whosoever hauntheth any swyche° shames   such
Yn cherche other° yn cherche-yerd,   or
Of sacrylage he may be aferd.°   afraid
5 Or° entyrludes or syngynge   Either
Or tabure-bete° or other pypynge.   drumming
Alle swyche thyng forbodyn es°   **forbodyn es** is forbidden
Whyle the prest stondeth at messe.
Alle swyche° to every gode preste ys lothe,°   such   hateful
10 And sunner wyl he make hym wroth°   **hym wroth** himself (the priest) angry
Than he wyl that hath no wyt°   learning
Ne° undyrstondeth nat Holy Wryt.   And
And specyaly at hyghe° tymes   solemn
Karolles° to synge and rede rymys   Round-dance songs
15 Noght yn none° holy stedes°   **Noght . . .** In any   places
That myght dysturble° the prestes bedes,°   disturb   prayers
Or° yyf he were yn orysun°   Either   supplication
Or any outher devocyun,
Sacrylage ys alle hyt tolde,°   counted
20 Thys and many other folde.
But for to leve° yn cherche to daunce,°   desist   **to daunce** from dancing
Y shal yow telle a ful° grete chaunce,°   very   event
And Y trow,° the most° that fel°   believe   greatest part   happened
Ys as soth° as the gospel.   true
25 And fyl° thys chaunce yn thys londe,   happened
Yn Ingland, as Y undyrstonde;
Yn a kynges tyme that hyght Edward°   **hyght Edward** is called Edward (r. 1042–66)
Fyl thys chaunce° that was so hard.   event
Hyt was uppon a Crystemesse nyght
30 That twelve folys a karolle dyght.°   **folys . . .** foolish people set up a round-dance
Yn wodehed, as° hyt were yn cuntek,°   **wodehed, as** madness, as if   strife
They come° to a tounne men calles Colbek.°   came   Kölbigk (Germany)
The cherche of the tounne that they to come
Ys of Seynt Magne,° that suffred martyrdome;   Magnus

35 Of Seynt Bukcestre hyt ys also,
   Seynt Magnes' süster, that they come to.
   Here° names of alle thus fonde° Y wryte,   *Their found*
   And as Y wote,° now shul ye wyte.°   *know know*
   Here lodesman° that made hem glew,°   *leader* **hem glew** *music for them*
40 Thus ys wryte,° he hyghte° Gerlew.   *written was called*
   Twey° maydens were yn here coveyne,°   *Two band*
   Mayden Merswynde and Wybessyne.
   Alle these come thedyr for that enchesone°   **for . . .** *because*
   Of the prestes doghtyr of the tounne.°   **prestes . . .** *town priest's daughter*
45   The prest hyght° Robert, as Y kan ame;°   *was called report*
   Azone hyght hys sone by name;
   Hys doghter that these men wulde have
   Thus ys wryte° that she hyght Ave.   *written*
   Ech oune consented to o° wyl   *one*
50 Who shuld go Ave oute to tyl;°   *entice*
   They graunted° ech one out to sende   *agreed*
   Bothe Wybessyne and Merswynde.
   These wommen yede° and tolled here° oute   *went* **tolled here** *enticed her*
   Wyth hem° to karolle the cherche aboute.   *them*
55 Bevne ordeyned here° karollyng;   **ordeyned here** *directed their*
   Gerlew endyted what they shuld syng.
     Thys ys the karolle that they sunge,
   As telleth the Latyn tunge:

     Equitabat Bevo per silvam frondosam;
60   *Ducebat secum Merswyndam formosam.*
     Quid stamus? Cur non imus?

     By the leved° wode rode Bevolyne;   *leafy*
     Wyth hym he ledde feyre Merswyne.
     Why stonde we? Why go we noght?

65 Thys ys the karolle that Grysly wroght.
   Thys songe sunge they yn the cherche-yerd—
   Of foly were they nothyng aferd°—   **nothyng aferd** *in no way afraid*
   Unto° the matynes were alle done,   *Until*
   And the messe shuld bygynne sone.°   *at once*
70   The preste hym revest° to begynne messe,   **hym revest** *robed himself*
   And they ne left° therfore, neverthelesse,   **ne left** *didn't desist*
   But daunsed furthe as they bygan;
   For alle the messe they ne blan.°   *desisted*
   The preste, that stode at the autere°   *altar*
75 And herde here° noyse and here bere,°   *their clamor*
   Fro the auter down he nam,°   *betook himself*
   And to the cherche porche he cam

And seyd, "On Goddes behalve, Y yow forbede
That ye no lenger do swych° dede,   such
80 But cometh° yn on° feyre manere   come   in
Goddes servyse for to here,°   hear
And doth at° Crystyn mennys lawe.   **doth at** attend to
Karolleth no more, for Crystys awe!
Wurschyppeth hym with alle youre myght
85 That of the Vyrgyne was bore° thys nyght."   born
    For° alle hys byddyng lefte° they noght   Despite   desisted
But daunsed furth as they thoght.°   wished
The prest tharefore was sore agreved.
He preyd God, that° he on belevyd,°   whom   **on belevyd** believed in
90 And for Seynt Magne, that he wulde so werche°— bring it about
Yn whos wurschyp sette was the cherche—
That swych a venjaunce were° on hem° sent,   would be   them
Are° they out of that stede° were went,   Before   place
That they myght ever ryght so wende°   **ryght . . .** continue just so
95 Unto° that tyme twelvemonth ende.   Until
    (Yn the Latyne that Y fonde thore,
He seyth nat "twelvemonth" but "evermore"!)
He cursed hem there al saume°   together
As they karoled on here° gaume.   their
100 As sone as the preste hadde so spoke,
Every hande yn outher° so fast was loke°   other   locked
That no man myght with no wundyr°   **no wundyr** any miracle
That° twelvemonthe parte hem° asundyr.   During that   them
    The preste yede° yn, whan thys was done,   went
105 And commaunded hys sone Azone
That he shulde go swythe° aftyr Ave,   quickly
Oute of that karolle algate° to have.   **karolle algate** round-dance song under all circumstances
But al too late that wurde was seyd,
For on hem alle was the venjaunce leyd.
110 Azone wende° weyl for to spede.°   expected   succeed
Unto the karolle as swythe° he yede;°   quickly as possible   went
Hys systyr by the arme he hente,°   seized
And the arme fro the body wente.
Men wundred alle, that there wore,°   were
115 And merveyle mowe° ye here more,   may
For, sethen° he had the arme yn hande,   after
The body yede furth karoland,°   **yede . . .** went on dancing
And nother° body ne the arme   neither
Bledde never blode, colde ne warme,
120 But was as drye with al the haunche
As of° a stok were ryve° a braunche.   **As of** As if from   torn
    Azone to hys fadyr went

And broght hym a sory present.
"Loke, fadyr," he seyd, "and have hyt here,
125 The arme of thy doghtyr dere
That was myn owne syster Ave
That Y wende° Y myght a save.°   supposed   **myght** ... could have saved
Thy cursyng now sene hyt ys
With venjaunce on thyn owne flessh.
130 Fellyche° thou cursedest and over-sone.°   Maliciously   too quickly
Thou askedest venjaunce. Thou hast thy bone!"°   request
    You thar° nat aske yyf there was wo   need
With the preste and with many mo.°   more
The prest that cursed for that daunce,
135 On some of hys fyl° harde chaunce.   **hys fyl** his kin fell
He toke hys doghtyr° arme forlorn   daughter's
And byryed° hyt on the morn;   buried
And nexte day the arme of Ave
He fonde hyt lyggyng° above the grave.   lying
140 He byryed hyt on anouther° day,   a second
And eft° above the grave hyt lay;   again
The thrydde tyme he byryed hyt,
And eft was hyt kast oute of the pyt.
The prest wulde byrye° hyt no more;   bury
145 He dredde° the venjaunce ferly sore.°   dreaded   **ferly sore** very sorely
Ynto the cherche he bare the arme
For drede and doute° of more harme.   fear
He ordeyned hyt for to be
That every man myght° with ye° hyt se.   could   eye
150   These men that yede° so karolland°   went   carol dancing
Alle that yere hand yn hand,
They never oute of that stede° yede,   place
Ne none myght hem thenne lede.°
There° the cursyng fyrst bygan,   Where
155 Yn that place aboute they ran,
That° never ne felte they no werynes,°   So that   weariness
As many bodyes for goyng dös,°   do
Ne mete° ete ne drank drynke,   **Ne mete** Nor food
Ne slepte onely alepy° wynke.   a single
160 Nyght ne° day they wyst° of none,   or   knew
Whan hyt was come, whan hyt was gone.
Frost ne snogh, hayle ne reyne,
Of colde ne hete felte they no peyne.
Heere ne nayles never grewe,
165 Ne solowed° clothes, ne turned hewe.°   soiled their   complexion
Thundyr ne lyghtnyng dyd hem° no dere;°   them   harm

153. Nor could anyone lead them thence.

Goddes mercy dyd hyt fro hem were;°   shield
But sungge° that songge that the wo wroght: they sang
"Why stonde we, why go we noght?"

170   What man shuld thyr be yn thys lyve
That ne wulde hyt see and thedyr dryve?
The Emperoure Henry° come fro Rome   Henry II (r. 1014–24)
For to see thys harde dome.°   judgment
Whan he hem say,° he wepte sore   saw

175 For the myschefe that he sagh° thore.   saw
He ded come wryghtes° for to make   **ded** ... had carpenters come
Coveryng over hem for tempest sake;
But that° they wroght, hyt was yn veyn,   what
For hyt come to no certeyn,°   **come** ... had no effect

180 For that they sette on oo° day,   one
On the touther° downe hyt lay.   next
Ones, twyys, thryys, thus they wroght,
And alle here° makyng was for noght.   their
Myght no coveryng hyle° hem fro colde   shield

185 Tyl tyme of mercy that Cryst hyt wolde.
    Tyme of grace fyl° thurgh hys myght   happened
At the twelvemonth ende on the Yole° nyght.   Yule
The same oure that the prest hem banned,°   cursed
The same oure atwynne° they woned;°   separated   became

190 That houre that he cursed hem ynne,
That same oure they yede° atwynne;   went
And, as° yn twynkelyng of an ye,°   as if   eye
Ynto the cherche gyn° they flye,°   did   fly
And on the pavement they fyl alle downe

195 As they hade be dede or fal° yn a swone.   fallen
    Thre days styl they lay ech° one,   each
That° none steryd other° flesshe or bone,   So that   **steryd other** stirred either
And at the thre days ende
To-lyfe° God grauntede hem to wende.°   Alive   go

200 They sette hem upp and spak apert°   **spak apert** spoke openly
To the parysshe prest, Syre Robert:
"Thou art ensample and enchesun°   **ensample** ... precedent and cause
Of oure long confusyun.
Thou maker art of oure travayle,

205 That ys to many grete mervayle;
And thy traveyle shalt thou sone° ende,   at once
For to thy long home sone shalt thou wende."°   go
    Alle they ryse° that yche tyde°   rose   **yche tyde** same time
But Ave; she lay dede besyde.

210 Grete sorowe had here° fadyr, here brother;   her
Merveyle and drede had alle outher—

Y trow° no drede of soule dede,°   *suppose*   **soule dede** her soul's death

But with pyne° was broght the body dede.°   *torment*   **broght . . . the body** killed

The fyrst man was the fadyr, the prest,

215 That deyd aftyr the doghtyr nest.°   *next*

Thys yche° arme that was of Ave   *same*

That none myght leye yn grave,

The Emperoure dyd a vessel werche°   *have made*

To do° hyt yn and hange yn the cherche,   *put*

220 That° alle men myght se hyt and knawe   *So that*

And thenk on the chaunce° when men hyt sawe.   *incident*

     These men that hadde go° thus karolland°   *gone*   *carol dancing*

Alle the yere fast hand yn hand,

Thogh that they were than° asunder,   *then*

225 Yyt alle the worlde spake of hem wunder.

That same hoppyng that they fyrst yede,°   *went with*

That daunce yede they thurgh land and lede,°   *nation*

And as° they ne myght fyrst° be unbounde,   *just as*   **ne . . . couldn't at first**

Ne myght they never° come agheyn   **Ne . . .** They could now never

230 Togedyr to oo stede certeyn.°   **oo . . .** one fixed place

     Foure yede to the courte of Rome,

And ever hoppyng aboute they nome.°   *continued*

With sundyr lepys° come they thedyr,   **sundyr lepys** separate leaps

But they come never efte° togedyr.   *again*

235 Here° clothes ne roted,° ne nayles grewe,   *Their*   **ne roted** didn't rot

Ne heere ne wax,° ne solowed hewe,°   *grew*   **solowed hewe** faded their complexion

Ne never hadde they amendement°   *remedy*

That we herde° at any corseynt°   *heard of*   *saint's relic*

But at° the vyrgyne Seynt Edyght.°   **But at** Except from   Edith (d. 984)

240 There was he botened,° Seynt Teodryght.°   *cured*   *Theodoric*

On Oure Lady-Day° yn Lenten tyde,   *March 25*

As he slepte here° toumbe besyde,   *her (Edith's)*

There he hade hys medycyne

At Seynt Edyght, the holy vyrgyne.

245   Brunyng° the bysshope of seynt Tolous°   *Bruno*   **seynt Tolous** holy Toul (France)

Wrote thys tale so merveylous;

Seththe° was hys name of more renoun—   *Later*

Men called hym the Pope Leoun.°   *Leo IX (Pope, 1049–54)*

Thys° at the court of Rome they wyte,°   *This story*   *know*

250 And yn the kronykeles hyt ys wryte°   *written*

Yn many stedys° beyounde the see   *places*

More than ys yn thys cuntré.

Tharfor men seye, and weyl° ys trowed:°   *well*   *believed*

"The nere° the cherche, the fyrther fro God."   *nearer to*

255   So fare° men here by thys tale: *behave*

Some holde hyt but a trotevale;°   *trifle*

Yn other stedys° hyt ys ful dere,°   places   **ful dere** very precious
And for grete merveyle they wyl hyt here.°   hear
A tale hyt ys of feyre shewyng,°   **feyre shewyng** fine significance
260 Ensample° and drede° aghens cursyng.   An example   warning
Thys tale Y tolde yow to make yow aferde°   afraid
Yn cherche to karolle or yn cherche-yerde,
Namely aghens° the prestys wylle.   **Namely aghens** Particularly against
Leveth° whan he byddeth yow be stylle!   Cease

Now Springs the Spray

(ca. 1300, West Midland)

This song belongs to the common heritage of western European lyrics, in Latin, Old French, Provençal, Anglo-Norman, and Middle English. Most of them have survived in undatable manuscripts bereft of the musical settings associated with them. Specifically, it follows the pattern of the *chanson d'aventure*—'song of chance meeting.' The genre eventually sank to the level of nursery rhymes, such as "Where Are You Going, My Pretty Maid?" The brilliance of meter, alliteration, and refrain, however, clearly elevates *Now Springs the Spray* above most examples of the genre, whether early or late. The author of the religious lyric *The Five Joys of Mary* (p. 205, below) may have deliberately imitated the opening line of the first stanza.

The meter is seven-line, tail-rhyme stanzas; see Introduction, type 15, page 32.

The best edition of this lyric is in *English Lyrics of the Thirteenth Century*, ed. Carleton Brown (Oxford, 1932), pages 119–20. For bibliography see Wells, ch. 13.25.

Nou sprinkes the sprai.°	foliage
Al for love Icche am so seek°	sick
That slepen I ne mai.°	*ne mai* cannot

Als° I me rode this endre° dai	As **me** ... rode out the other
O° mi playinge,°	On sport
Seih° I hwar a litel mai°	Saw maiden
Bigan to singge:	
"The clot him clingge!	
Wai es him i louve-longinge	
Sal libben ai."°	

Nou sprinkes the sprai.
Al for love Icche am so seek
That slepen I ne mai.

8–10. May the sod cling to him! Woeful it is for the one who must always live in (unrequited) longing for love.

	Son° Icche herde that mirie note,	As soon as
15	Thider I drogh.°	drew
	I fonde hire° in an herber swot°	her **herber swot** fragrant arbor
	Under a bough	
	With joie inogh.°	enough
	Son° I asked: "Thou mirie mai,°	At once maiden
20	Hwi sinkestou° ai?"	do you sing

Nou sprinkes the sprai.
Al for love Icche am so seek
That slepen I ne mai.

	Than answerde that maiden swote	
25	Midde wordes fewe:	
	"Mi lemman° me haves bihot°	sweetheart **haves bihot** has promised
	Of louve trewe.	
	He chaunges anewe.	
	Yif I mai, it shal him rewe°	**it . . .** he shall rue it
30	Bi this dai."	

Nou sprinkes the sprai.
Al for love Icche am so seek
That slepen I ne mai.

The Five Joys of Mary

(ca. 1330, Southwestern)

The religious lyric *The Five Joys of Mary* and the four love lyrics following (pp. 208–215) are all found in the Harley Miscellany (MS. 2253), which was compiled in Hereford around 1330–39 and includes works of various ages, such as *King Horn* (p. 114, above, ca. 1225) and *The Sayings of St. Bernard* (p. 163, above, ca. 1275), some composed in Middle English, some in Anglo-Norman or French, and some in Latin.

The celebration of the joys of the Virgin was a popular medieval theme. More than a dozen extant Middle English poems deal in one way or another with the topic, and passing references, as in *Sir Gawain and the Green Knight* (p. 376), occur frequently. The Harley *Five Joys* is neither the oldest nor the most extensive of these poems, but it is certainly the most striking because of the compelling way in which it moves from the secular tone of the *chanson d'aventure*, already familiar in *Now Springs the Spray* (p. 203, above), to its devout religious purpose. The joys here celebrated are the Annunciation, the Nativity, the Epiphany (not referred to in the other Middle English treatments), the Resurrection, and the Ascension of Mary; the Assumption, which is handled separately in the other Middle English treatments, is subsumed under the Ascension.

The meter is seven-line, tail-rhyme stanzas; see Introduction, type 19, page 33.

The best edition of the lyric is in George L. Brooks, ed., *The Harley Lyrics: The Middle English Lyrics of MS. Harley 2253*, 2nd ed. (Manchester, 1956), pages 65–66. The manuscript is reproduced in *Facsimile of British Museum MS. Harley 2253*, ed. N. R. Ker, EETS 255 (London, 1965), item 67. For bibliography see Wells, ch. 13.209.

Ase Y me rod this ender° day   **me** ... rode out the other
By grene wode to seche° play,   seek
Mid herte Y thohte al on a may,°   maiden
    Suetest of alle thinge.
5   Lythe,° and Ich ou° telle may   Listen   you
    Al of that swete thinge.

This maiden is suete ant fre° of blod,   noble
  Briht, and feyr, of milde mod.°   spirit
Alle heo mai don us° god   **Alle** ... She may do all of us
10   Thurh hire bysechynge.°   **Thurh** ... Through beseeching her
  Of hire he tok fleysh and blod,
  Jesu Crist, hevene Kynge.

With al mi lif Y love that may.°   maiden
Heo° is mi solas nyht and day,   she

15 My joie, and eke° my beste play,°   also   pleasure
    Ant eke my love-longynge.°   longing for love
Al the betere me° is that day   for me
    That Ich of hire° synge.   her

Of alle thinge Y love hir mest,°   most
20 My dayes blis, my nyhtes rest.
Heo° counseileth and helpeth best   She
    Bothe elde and yynge.°   **elde . . .** old and young
Nou Y may, yef Y wole,°   wish
    The fif joyes mynge.°   enumerate

25 The fürst joie of that wymman:°   woman
When Gabriel from hevene cam
Ant seide God shulde bicome man
    Ant of hire be bore°   born
And bringe up of helle pyn°   **helle pyn** hell's torment
30   Monkyn° that wes forlore.°   Mankind   lost

That other° joie of that may°   second   maiden
Wes o° Cristesmasse day,   on
When God wes bore, on thoro lay,°   **on . . .** a perfect light
    Ant brohte us lyhtnesse.°   illumination
35 The ster° wes seie° byfore day;   star   seen
    This hirdes° bereth wytnesse.   **This hirdes** The shepherds

The thridde joie of that levedy:°   lady
That, men clepeth° the Epyphany,   call
When the kynges come wery
40   To presente hyre° sone   her
With myrre, gold, and encenz,
    That wes mon bicome.°

The furthe joie we telle mawen:°   may
On Ester-morewe,° when hit gon dawen,°   Easter morning   **gon dawen** dawned
45 Hyre sone that wes slawen°   slain
    Aros in fleysh and bon.
More joie ne mai me haven,°   **ne . . .** one cannot have
    Wyf ne mayden non.

42. The son who had become man.

206

The fifte joie of that wymman:°   woman
50   When hire° body to hevene cam,   her
    The soule to the body nam°   united
     Ase hit wes woned to bene.°   **woned** . . . accustomed to be
    Crist, leve° us alle with that wymman   grant
     That joie al for te sene.°   **te sene** to see

55   Preye we alle to oure Levedy°   Lady
    Ant to the sontes° that woneth hire by°   saints   **woneth** . . . dwell with her
    That heo° of us haven merci   they
     Ant that we ne misse
    In this world to ben° holy   be
60   Ant wynne hevene blysse.
       Amen.

Alysoun

(ca. 1330, Southwestern)

Unlike Thomas of Hailes's *Love Rune* (p. 156, above), this courtly *roun* (l. 44) deals with the perennial sufferings of an earthly lover. The meter is seven-line, tail-rhyme stanzas; see Introduction, type 16, page 32.

The best edition is in George L. Brooks, ed., *The Harley Lyrics: The Middle English Lyrics of MS. Harley 2253*, 2nd ed. (Manchester, 1956), page 33. For the manuscript see *Facsimile of British Museum MS. Harley 2253*, ed. N. R. Ker, EETS 255 (London, 1965), item 29. For bibliography see Wells, ch. 13.12.

Bytuene Mersh and Averil°	**Mersh** . . . March and April
Whan spray° biginneth to springe,	foliage
The lütel foul° hath hire° wyl	birds their
On hyre lüd° to synge.	**On** . . . In their language
5 Ich libbe in love-longinge°	longing for love
For semlokest° of alle thynge.	the comeliest
Heo° may me blisse bringe.	She
Ich am in hire baundoun.°	**hire baundoun** her power
An hendy hap Ichabbe y-hent;°	*hendy* . . . gracious fortune I have won
10 *Ichot° from hevene it is me sent.*	I know
From alle wymmen mi love is lent°	turned
And lyht° on Alysoun.	lights
On heu hire her° is fayr ynoh,°	**On** . . . In hue her hair abundantly
Hire browe broune, hire eye blake.	
15 With lossum chere heo° on me loh,°	**lossum** . . . loving look she smiled
With middel smal and wel y-make.	
Bote° heo me wolle to hire take	Unless
For te büen° hire owen make,°	be **owen make** own mate
Longe to lyven Ichulle° forsake	I shall
20 And feye° fallen adoun.	death-fated

Alysoun

An hendy hap Ichabbe y-hent;
Ichot from hevene it is me sent.
From alle wymmen mi love is lent
And lyht on Alysoun.

25   Nihtes when Y wende° and wake,   pace
       Forthi° myn wonges waxeth won,°   Whereby   **wonges...** cheeks grow wan
   Levedi,° al for thine sake   Lady
       Longinge is y-lent me on.°   **y-lent...** imposed on me
       In world nis non so wyter mon°   **nis ...** there is no man so wise
30   That al hire bounté telle con.°   **hire ...** her excellence can count
       Hire swyre° is whittore then the swon,   neck
         And feyrest may° in toune.   **feyrest may** she the fairest maiden

An hendy hap Ichabbe y-hent;
Ichot from hevene it is me sent.
35   *From alle wymmen mi love is lent*
And lyht on Alysoun.

       Ich am for wowyng° al forwake°   loving   weary from sleeplessness
       Wery so° water in wore,°   as   a whirlpool (?)
   Lest eny reve me° my make°   **reve me** rob me of   mate
40   Ychabbe y-yyrned yore.°
       Betere is tholien whyle sore°   **tholien ...** to suffer sorely for a while
       Then mournen evermore.
       Geynest° under gore,°   Loveliest one   clothing
         Herkne to my roun!°   song

45   *An hendy hap Ichabbe y-hent;*
Ichot from hevene it is me sent.
From alle wymmen my love is lent
And lyht on Alysoun.

---

40. Whom I have yearned for long.

Spring

(ca. 1330, Southwestern)

Spring is a fine example of the *reverdie*, the song inspired by the return of spring. The combination of rhyme and alliteration is particularly striking, though sound sometimes overwhelms sense. Line 20 is especially difficult. Perhaps it should read, *Meles meres with hüere makes*, 'Mares murmur with their mates,' but it seems unlikely that the Harley scribe understood what he was writing at this point.

The meter is twelve-line, tail-rhyme stanzas; see Introduction, type 21, page 33.

The best edition of the lyric is in George L. Brooks, ed., *The Harley Lyrics: The Middle English Lyrics of MS. Harley 2253*, 2nd ed. (Manchester, 1956), pages 43–44. For the manuscript see *Facsimile of British Museum MS. Harley 2253*, ed. N. R. Ker, EETS 225 (London, 1965), item 43. For bibliography see Wells, ch. 13.14.

Lenten ys° come with love to toune,°   **Lenten ys** Spring has   men's dwellings
With blosmen,° and with briddes roune,°   blossoms   **briddes roune** birds' songs
    That° al this blisse bryngeth,°   Spring which   brings
Dayes-eyes° in this° dales,   Daisies   the
5 Notes swete of nyhtegales.
    Uch foul° song singeth.   **Uch foul** Each bird a
The threstel-coc him threteth oo.°   **threstel-coc** . . . thrush scolds ever
Away is hüere° wynter woo°   their   sorrow
    When woderove° springeth.   woodruff
10 This° foules singeth ferly fele°   The   **ferly fele** marvelously much
Ant wlyteth° on hüere wynter wele°   look back   state
    That° al the wode ryngeth.   So that

The rose rayleth hire rode;°   **rayleth** . . . puts on her red hue
The leves on the lyhte° wode   gay
15   Waxen° al with wille.°   Grow   a will
The mone mandeth° hire bleo;°   sends out   radiance
The lilie is lossom° to seo,°   lovely   see
    The fenyl,° and the fille.°   fennel   chervil
Wowes this° wilde drakes;   **Wowes this** Woo the
20 Miles mürgeth hüere makes°   **Miles** . . . Creatures (?) delight their mates
    Ase strem that striketh stille.°   **striketh stille** glides silently

Spring

Mody meneth;° so doth mo!°
Ichot° Ych am on° of tho°
For° love that likes ille.°

Mody meneth The passionate lament   **doth mo**
do others
I know   one   those
Because of   **likes ille** ill satisfies

25 The mone mandeth hire° lyht;
So döth the semly° sonne bryht
When briddes° singeth breme.°
Deawes donketh° the dounes;°
Deores° with hüere derne rounes°
30   Domes for te deme;°
Wormes woweth° under cloude;°
Wymmen waxeth wounder° proude,
So° wel hit wol hem seme.°
Yef me° shal wonte° wille of on,°
35 This wünne weole° Y wole forgon°
Ant wyht° in wode° be fleme.°

mandeth hire sends out her
fair
birds   loudly
Deawes donketh Dews soak   hills
Animals   **hüere** ... their secret converse
Domes ... To express their feelings
make love   clod
waxeth wounder grow wondrous
As   **wol** ... will suit them
I   fail to have my   one
wünne weole wealth of joy   abandon
at once   the woods   an exile

211

April

(ca. 1330, Southwestern)

Like *Spring*, this Harley lyric is another fine example of the *reverdie*. The lover complains
(l. 32) that his longing is making him turn, literally, "green," but there is presumably no
intention of comic exaggeration here, for the adjective had a more neutral sense in Middle
English than it does in Modern English.

The meter is eight-line (four long-line), tail-rhyme stanzas; see Introduction, type 11,
pages 31–32.

The best edition of the lyric is in George L. Brooks, ed., *The Harley Lyrics: The Middle
English Lyrics of MS. Harley 2253*, 2nd ed. (Manchester, 1956), page 63. The manuscript is
reproduced in *Facsimile of British Museum MS. Harley 2253*, ed. N. R. Ker, EETS 255 (London,
1965), item 65. For bibliography see Wells, ch. 13.20.

When the nyhtegale singes,		
The wodes waxen° grene.	grow	
Lef ant gras ant blosme springes		
In Averyl,° Y wene.°	April	suppose
5 Ant love is to myn herte gon		
With one° spere so kene,	a	
Nyht ant day my blod hit drynkes;		
Myn herte deth° me tene.°	causes	suffering
Ich have loved al this yer		
10 That° Y may love na more.	So that	
Ich have siked moni syk,°	**siked** ... sighed many a sigh	
Lemmon,° for thin ore.°	Sweetheart	favor
Me nis° love never the ner,°	**Me nis** To me is	nearer
Ant that me reweth° sore.	grieves	
15 Suete lemmon, thench° on me;	think	
Ich have loved thee yore.°	long	
Suete lemmon, Y preye thee		
Of love one° speche.	a	
Whil Y lyve in world so wyde,		
20 Other nülle Y seche.°	**nülle** ... I won't seek	

212

With thy love, my suete leof,°   dear
  My blis thou mihtes eche.°   **mihtes eche** could increase
A suete cös° of thy mouth   kiss
  Mihte be my leche.°   physician

25   Suete lemmon,° Y preye thee   lover
  Of° a love-bene:°   For   love-boon
Yef thou me lovest ase men says,
  Lemmon, as I wene,°   suppose
Ant yef hit thi wille be,
30   Thou loke° that hit be sene.   **Thou loke** Look to it
So müchel° Y thenke upon thee   much
  That al Y waxe grene.°   **waxe grene** grow pale

Bituene Lyncolne ant Lyndeseye,°   Lindsey (Suffolk)
  Norhamptoun ant Lounde,°   London
35   Ne wot° I non so fayr a may°   know   maiden
  As° I go fore y-bounde.°   As the one   in bondage
Suete lemmon,° Y preye thee   sweetheart
  Thou lovie me a stounde.°   while
Y wole mone° my song   direct
40   On wham° that hit ys on ylong.°   **On wham** To whom   **on ylong** due

Love in Paris

(ca. 1330, Southwestern)

The following spirited love lyric from the Harley Miscellany serves as a useful reminder of the multilingual and cosmopolitan culture of the fourteenth century. It is written in perfectly rhymed macaronic stanzas that move effortlessly between Latin and Anglo-Norman and conclude dramatically in English. The reference to the lover's lodging in Paris suggests that he is an English student abroad; and the dialect form *sügge* 'say' (l. 19) may indicate that he belongs to the Southwestern area of England, but all the Harley lyrics are recorded in the same dialect.

The meter is four-line stanzas; see Introduction, type 10, page 31.

The best edition of *Love in Paris* is in George L. Brooks, ed., *The Harley Lyrics: The Middle English Lyrics of MS. Harley 2253*, 2nd ed. (Manchester, 1956), page 55. For the manuscript see *Facsimile of British Museum MS. Harley 2253*, ed. N. R. Ker, EETS 255 (London, 1965), item 55. For bibliography see Wells, ch. 13.24a (s6).

> *Dum ludis floribus velud lacinia,*
> Le dieu d'amour moi tient en tiel *angustia,*
> Merour me tient de duel e de *miseria*
> Si je ne la ay *quam amo super omnia.*
>
> 5   *Eius amor tantum me facit fervere*
> Qe je ne soi *quid possum inde facere.*
> Pur ly covent *hoc seculum relinquere*
> Si je ne pus l'amour de li *perquirere.*
>
> Ele est si bele e gente dame *egregia*
> 10   Cum ele fust *imperatoris filia,*
> De beal semblant e *pulcra continencia;*
> Ele est la flur *in omni regis curia.*
>
> Quant je la vey, je su *in tali gloria*
> Come est la lune *celi inter sidera.*
> 15   Dieu la moi doint *sua misericordia*
> Beyser e fere que *secuntur alia.*
>
> *Scripsi hec carmina in tabulis.*
> Mon ostel est enmi la vile de Paris.
> May Y sügge namore, so wel me is.
> 20   Yef Hi deye for love of hire, duel hit ys!

Love in Paris

[TRANSLATION]

While you sport with the lace-like flowers,
The god of love holds me in such constraint
That he holds me as a mirror of sorrow and misery
If I don't get her whom I love beyond all others.

5   My love for her makes me rage so violently
That I don't know what I can do about it.
For her I shall have to abandon this world
If I can't win her love.

She is an illustrious lady, as beautiful and refined
10   As if she were the emperor's daughter,
Beautiful in appearance and charming in modesty.
She is the flower in the court of any king.

When I see her, I am in the same glory
As the moon in the sky among the stars.
15   God in his mercy bestow her on me
To kiss and to do whatever else follows.

I have written out these verses in my notebook.
My lodging is in Paris town.
I can say no more, so blissful am I.
20   If I die for love of her, a pity it is!

Sir Orfeo

(ca. 1330, East Midland)

The relation of the Middle English lay of Sir Orfeo to the classical myth of the cult hero Orpheus is obscure. For Vergil and for Ovid the connotations of the myth were tragic: the great musician failed in his attempt to regain his beloved Eurydice from the underworld and died of grief (see *Georgics*, IV, and *Metamorphoses*, X–XI). For Boethius the tale served as a warning against the futility of looking backward into hell (see *Consolation of Philosophy*, III, m. 12). But the Middle English minstrel tells a very different version of the tale. Dame Heurodis is abducted by an otherworld lover into a Celtic fairyland, from which Orfeo happily regains her.

The prologue to *Sir Orfeo* claims that the source of the tale is a Breton lay. This origin would explain the Celtic coloration; unfortunately, however, not a single lay composed in the Breton language has survived. Many of the so-called Breton lays composed by Marie de France (ca. 1170–89) and her imitators either in Anglo-Norman or Old French may have been derived from Breton sources; and it is known that an Old French *Lai d'Orphey* (now lost) was in circulation in the twelfth century. Consequently, there is a strong likelihood that Breton minstrels played some part in the shaping of the original poem, which has survived only in this later English redaction.

As a graceful lay celebrating the triumph of marital devotion, *Sir Orfeo* has always been popular; and it is one of those rare works that, like *King Horn* (p. 114), survived in the oral tradition as a ballad (Child, No. 19) down to the nineteenth century.

The version of *Sir Orfeo* printed below is based on the Auchinleck Manuscript (ca. 1330–39), which was apparently compiled in a London bookshop by a group of professional redactors and translators. They were possibly responsible for the bold interpretation of the town of Traciens (l. 47; actually Old French, meaning 'Thracian') as Winchester and of Orfeo as an English king (ll. 25–26) who favors the election of a successor by parliament (l. 216). Lines 1–24 and 33–46 have been supplied from a later manuscript.

The meter is rhyming couplets; see Introduction, type 5, page 31.

The best edition of the lay is *Sir Orfeo*, ed. A. J. Bliss (London, 1954). For the manuscript see facsimile of Auchinleck MS (National Library of Scotland, Advocates 19.2.1), folio 302 r., containing lines 391–478, reproduced on page 20. For bibliography see Severs, ch. 1.86, and John B. Friedman, *Orpheus in the Middle Ages* (Cambridge, Mass., 1970).

We redyn° ofte and fynde y-wryte,°	read written
As clerkes don° us to wyte,°	make know
The layes that ben of harpyng°	**ben** ... are sung with the harp
Ben y-founde° of frely thing.°	composed **frely thing** noble matter

5 Sum ben of wele° and sum of wo,   prosperity
  And sum of joy and merthe also,
  Sum of trechery and sum of gyle,
  And sum of happes° that fallen by whyle,°   events **fallen . . .** happen now and then
  Sum of bourdys° and sum of rybaudry,°   jests   ribaldry
10 And sum ther ben° of the feyré.°   are   fairy
  Of alle thing that men may se,
  Moost to lowe forsothe° they be.   **to . . .** for praise indeed
  In Brytayn this° layes arne y-wrytt,°   **Brytayn this** Brittany these   written
  Fürst y-founde° and forthe y-gete°   composed   **forthe y-gete** brought forth
15 Of aventures that fellen by dayes,°   **fellen . . .** happened long ago
  Wherof Brytouns made her layes.
  When they myght o-wher heryn°   **o-wher heryn** anywhere hear
  Of aventures that ther weryn,
  They toke her harpys° with game,°   **her harpys** their harps   pleasure
20 Maden layes and yaf° it name.   gave
  Of aventures that han befalle,
  Y can sum tell, but nought alle.
    Herken, lordyngys, that ben° trewe,   are
  And Y wol you telle of Syr Orphewe.
25 Orfeo was a ryche king,
  In Ingland an heighe° lording,   noble
  A stalworth° man and hardi bo,°   stalwart   **hardi bo** bold as well
  Large and curteys° he was also.   **Large . . .** Generous and courteous
  His fader was comen of° King Pluto,   from
30 And his moder of King Juno,
  That sum time were as godes y-hold°   considered
  For aventours that thai dede and told.
  Orpheo most of ony thing
  Lovede the gle° of harpyng.   minstrelsy
35 Syker° was every gode harpure   Sure
  Of hym to have moche honour.
  Hymself loved for to harpe,
  And layde ther-on his wittes scharpe.
  He lerned so, ther nothing° was   not at all
40 A better harper in no plas.°   place
  In the world was never man born
  That onus° Orpheo sat byforn,   ever
  And° he myght of his harpyng her,°   If   hear
  He schulde° thinke that he wer   **He schulde** Who would not
45 In one of the joys of paradys,
  Suche joy and melody in his harpyng is.
    This king sojournd in Traciens,
  That was a cité of noble defens.°   fortification
  (For Winchester was cleped tho°   **cleped tho** called then

50 Traciens withouten no.°)   denial
    The king hadde a quen of priis°   excellence
    That was y-cleped Dame Heurodis,
    The fairest levedi° for the nones°   lady   while
    That might gon° on bodi and bones,   walk
55 Ful of love and of godenisse;
    Ac° no man may telle hir fairnise.   But
      Bifel° so in the comessing° of May—   It happened   beginning
    When miri and hot is the day,
    And oway° beth winterschours,°   away   winter showers
60 And everi feld is ful of flours,
    And blosme breme° on everi bough   **blosme breme** fresh blossom
    Overal wexeth° miri anough°—   grows   enough
    This ich° quen, Dame Herodis,   same
    Tok to° maidens of priis°   two   excellence
65 And went in an undrentide°   morning
    To play bi an orchard side,
    To se the floures sprede and spring,
    And to here the foules° sing.   birds
    Thai sett hem° doun al thre   themselves
70 Under a fair ympe-tre,°   orchard tree
    And wel° sone this fair quene   very
    Fel on slepe° opon the grene.   **on slepe** asleep
    The maidens durst hir nought awake,
    Bot let hir ligge° and rest take.   lie
75 So sche slepe til afternone,
    That undertide° was al y-done.°   morning   gone
      Ac° as sone as sche gan awake,°   But   **gan awake** awoke
    Sche crid and lothli bere° gan make.   **crid . . .** cried and a horrible scream
    Sche froted° hir honden and hir fet,   wrung
80 And crached° hir visage;° it bled wete.°   scratched   face   wet
    Hir riche robe hye° al torett°   she   tore
    And was reveyd° out of hir witt.   driven
    The two maidens hir biside
    No durst° with hir no leng° abide,   **No durst** Dared not   longer
85 Bot ourn° to the palays ful right°   ran   straight
    And told bothe squier and knight
    That her quen awede wold,°   **awede wold** was going crazy
    And bad hem go and hir at-hold.°   seize
    Knightes urn and levedis° also,   **urn . . .** ran and ladies
90 Damisels sexti and mo.°   **Damisels . . .** Maidens sixty and more
    In the orchard to the quen hye° come   they
    And her up in her armes nome°   took
    And brought hir to bed atte last
    And held hir there fine° fast.   very

95 Ac° ever she held° in o° cri   But persisted one
    And wold° up and owy.°   wished to go   away
    When Orfeo herd that tiding,
    Never him nas wers for nothing.°
    He come with knightes tene°   ten
100 To chaumber right bifor the quene
    And biheld° and seyd with grete pité: looked
    "O lef liif,° what is° thee,   **lef liif** dear life is wrong with
    That ever yete hast ben so stille,°   quiet
    And now gredest wonder schille?°   **gredest** ... cry wonderfully loud
105 Thi bodi, that was so white y-core,°   excellently
    With thine nailes is al totore!°   torn to pieces
    Alas, thi röde,° that was so red,   face
    Is al wan, as° thou were ded!   as if
    And also thine fingres smale
110 Beth al blodi and al pale!
    Allas! thi lovesum eyghen to°   **lovesum** ... two lovely eyes
    Loketh so° man döth on his fo!   as
    A! Dame, Ich biseche merci!
    Lete ben° al this reweful° cri,   **Lete ben** Stop pitiful
115 And tel me, what thee is° and hou,   is wrong with
    And what thing may thee help now!"
    Tho° lay sche stille atte last   Then
    And gan° to wepe swithe fast°   began **swithe fast** very hard
    And seyd thus the king to:
120 "Allas, mi lord, Sir Orfeo!
    Seththen° we first togider were,   Since
    Ones wroth° never we nere;°   **Ones wroth** Once angry were
    Bot ever Ich have y-loved thee
    As mi liif, and so thou me.
125 Ac° now we mot delen ato;°   But **mot** ... must part
    Do thi best, for Y mot go!"
    "Allas!" quath he, "forlorn Ich am!
    Whider wiltow° go and to wham?   will you
    Whider thou gost, Ichil° with thee,   I will go
130 And whider Y go, thou schalt with me."
    "Nay, nay, sir, that nought nis.°   **nought nis** can't be
    Ichil thee telle al hou it is.
    As Ich lay this undertide°   morning
    And slepe under our orchard side,
135 Ther come to me to° fair knightes   two
    Wele y-armed al to rightes°   **to rightes** properly
    And bad me comen an heighing°   **an heighing** in haste
    And speke with her° lord the king.   their

98. He was never so unhappy over anything.

And Ich answerd at° wordes bold,   with
140 Y durst nought, no y nold.°   **no** . . . nor would I
    "Thai priked oyain, as° thai might drive.°   **priked** . . . spurred again, as fast as   ride
Tho° com her king al so blive°   Then   quickly
With an hundred knightes and mo°   more
And damisels° an hundred also   maidens
145 Al on snowewhite stedes;
As white as milke were her wedes.°   **her wedes** their clothes
Y no seighe° never yete bifore   saw
So fair creatours y-core.°   excellent
The king hadde a croun on hed,
150 It nas° of silver no of gold red,   was not
Ac° it was of a precious ston;   But
As bright as the sonne it schon.
    "And as son as he to me cam,
Wold Ich, nold Ich,° he me nam°   **nold Ich** would I not   took
155 And made me with him ride
Opon a palfray bi his side,
And brought me to his palays,
Wele atird° in ich ways,°   clothed   **ich ways** every way
And schewed me castels and tours,°   towers
160 Rivers, forestes, frith° with flours,   parks
And his riche stedes ichon,°   each one
And seththen° me brought oyain° hom   then   again
Into our owhen° orchard,   own
And said to me thus afterward:
165   'Loke, dame, to-morwe thatow° be   that you
Right here under this ympe-tre,°   orchard tree
And than thou schalt with ous° go   us
And live with ous ever mo.°   more
And yif thou makest ous y-let,°   delayed
170 Whar° thou be, thou wörst y-fet°   Wherever   **wörst y-fet** will be fetched
And totore° thine limes al   torn to pieces
That nothing help thee no schal.
And thei° thou best so totorn,   though
Yete thou wörst with ous y-born.'"°   carried off
175   When King Orfeo herd this cas,°   matter
"O, we!" quath he. "Allas, allas!
Lever me were° to lete° mi liif   **Lever** . . . I would prefer   lose
Than thus to lese the quen mi wiif!"
He asked conseyl at ich° man,   **at ich** of each
180 Ac no man him help no can.
Amorwe° the undertide° is come,   On the next day   morning
And Orfeo hath his armes y-nome,°   taken
And wele ten hundred knightes with him,

	Ich y-armed stout and grim,	
185	And with the quen wenten he	
	Right unto that ympe-tre.°	orchard tree
	Thai made scheltrom° in ich a side°	phalanx **ich . . .** each side
	And sayd thai wold there abide	
	And dye ther everichon°	everyone
190	Er° the quen schuld fram hem gon.°	Before **hem gon** them go
	Ac yete amiddes hem ful right°	**ful right** straightway
	The quen was oway y-twight,°	**oway y-twight** snatched away
	With fairi° forth y-nome,°	magic taken
	Men wist° never wher sche was bicome.°	**Men wist** One knew gone
195	Tho° was ther criing, wepe, and wo!	Then
	The king into his chaumber is go°	gone
	And oft swoned° opon the ston°	fainted stone floor
	And made swiche diol° and swiche mon°	**swiche diol** such sorrow lament
	That neighe° his liif was y-spent.	nearly
200	Ther was non amendement.°	remedy
	He cleped° togider his barouns,	called
	Erls, lordes of renouns,	
	And when thai al y-comen were,	
	"Lordinges," he said, "bifor you here,	
205	Ich ordainy min heighe steward	
	To wite° mi kingdom afterward.	direct
	In mi stede ben° he schal	**stede ben** place be
	To kepe mi londes over al.	
	For now Ichave° mi quen y-lore,°	I have lost
210	The fairest levedi° that ever was bore.°	lady born
	Never eft° Y nil° no woman se.	again will
	Into wildernes Ichil te°	**Ichil te** I will go
	And live ther ever more	
	With wilde bestes in holtes hore.°	**holtes hore** gray woods
215	And when ye understond that Y be spent,°	dead
	Make thou than a parlement	
	And chese° you a newe king.	choose
	Now doth your best with al mi thing."	
	Tho° was ther wepeing in the halle	Then
220	And grete cri among hem° alle.	them
	Unnethe might° old or yong	**Unnethe might** Hardly could
	For wepeing speke a word with tong.	
	Thai kneled adoun al yfere°	together
	And praid him, yif his wille were,	
225	That he no schuld nought fram hem go.	
	"Do way,"° quath he, "it schal be so."	**Do way** Stop
	Al his kingdom he forsoke.	
	Bot° a sclavin° on him he toke,	Only pilgrim's robe

He no hadde kirtel no hode,°   **kirtel** . . . tunic nor hood
230 Schert, ne non other gode.°   goods
Bot his harp he tok algate°   at any rate
And dede him barfot° out atte yate.°   **dede** . . . went barefoot   gate
No man most° with him go.   might
O way! What,° ther was wepe and wo,   Lo
235 When he that hadde ben king with croun
Went so pouerlich° out of town.   poorly
     Thurch wode° and over heth°   **Thurch wode** Through woods   heath
Into the wildernes he geth.°   goes
Nothing he fint° that him° is ays,°   finds   for him   comfort
240 Bot ever he liveth in gret malais.°   discomfort
He that hadde y-werd° the fowe and griis°   worn   **fowe** . . . spotted fur and gray fur
And on bed the purper biis,°   **purper biis** purple linen
Now on hard hethe° he lith;°   heath   lies
With leves and gresse he him writh.°   wraps
245 He that hadde castels and tours,°   towers
River, forest, frith° with flours,   parks
Now, thei° it comenci to snewe and frese,   though
This king mote° make his bed in mese.°   must   moss
He that had y-had knightes of priis°   excellence
250 Bifor him kneland and levedis,°   **kneland** . . . kneeling and ladies
Now seth° he nothing that him liketh,°   sees   pleases
Bot wilde wormes° bi him striketh.°   serpents   glide
He that had y-had plenté
Of mete and drink, of ich deynté,°   **ich deynté** every delicacy
255 Now may he al day digge and wrote,°   root in the soil
Er° he finde his fille of rote.   Before
     In somer he liveth bi wild frut
And berien° bot gode lite.°   berries   **gode lite** little good
In winter may he nothing finde
260 Bot rote, grases, and the rinde.°   bark
Al his bodi was oway dwine°   **oway dwine** dwindled away
For missays,° and al to-chine.°   suffering   scarred
Lord! Who may telle the sore°   trouble
The king sufferd ten yere and more!
265 His here° of his berd blac and rowe°   hair   rough
To his girdel-stede° was growe.   waist
     His harp, wheron was al his gle,°   merriment
He hidde in an holwe tre.
And when the weder was clere and bright,
270 He toke his harp to him wel right°   properly
And harped at his owhen° wille.   own
Into alle the wode the soun gan schille,°   **soun** . . . sound resounded
That alle the wilde bestes that ther beth

For joie abouten him thai teth.°   go
275 And alle the foules° that ther were   birds
    Come and sete on ich a brere°   ich ... each twig
    To here his harping afine,°   to the end
    So miche° melody was therin.   much
    And when he his harping lete° wold,   stop
280 No best bi him abide nold.°   would
    He might se him bisides°   **him bisides** beside him
    Oft in hot undertides°   mornings
    The King o Fairy° with his rout°   **o Fairy** of Fairyland   company
    Com to hunt him al about,
285 With dim cri and bloweing,
    And houndes also with him berking.
    Ac no best thai no nome,°   took
    No never he nist° whider thai bicome.°   knew   went
    And other while he might him° se,   **might him** could
290 As a gret ost,° bi him te°   host   go
    Wele atourned° ten hundred knightes,   equipped
    Ich° y-armed to his rightes,°   Each   **to** ... fittingly
    Of contenaunce stout and fers,°   **stout** ... strong and fierce
    With mani desplaid° baners,   unfurled
295 And ich his swerd y-drawe hold,°
    Ac never he nist° whider thai wold.°   knew   would go
    And other while he seighe° other thing: saw
    Knightes and levedis° com daunceing   ladies
    In queynt° atire gisely,°   elegant   skillfully
300 Queynt pas° and softly.   **Queynt pas** Graceful step
    Tabours and trunpes yede° hem bi   **Tabours** ... Drums and trumpets went
    And al maner menstraci.°   minstrelsy
    And on a day he seighe him biside°   **seighe** ... saw beside him
    Sexti levedis on hors ride,
305 Gentil and jolif° as brid° on ris,°   **Gentil** ... Well bred and gay   bird   a branch
    Nought o° man amonges hem° ther nis.°   one   them   is
    And ich a faucon on hond bere°   bore
    And riden on haukin° bi o° rivere.   **riden** ... rode out hawking   a
    Of game thai founde wel° gode haunt:°   very   plenty
310 Maulardes, hayroun,° and cormeraunt.   **Maulardes, hayroun** Mallards, heron
    The foules of° the water ariseth;   **foules of** birds from
    The faucons hem° wele deviseth;°   them   descry
    Ich faucon his pray slough.°   slew
    That seighe° Orfeo and lough.°   saw   laughed
315 "Parfay,"° quath he, "ther is fair game.   Indeed
    Thider Ichil,° bi Godes name.   I will go
    Ich was y-won swiche° werk to se."   **y-won swiche** accustomed such

295. And could see each knight holding his sword drawn

He aros and thider gan te.°   **gan te** went
To a levedi he was y-come,
320 Biheld, and hath wele undernome,°   recognized
And seth° bi al thing, that it is   sees
His owhen° quen Dam Heurodis.   own
Yern° he biheld hir, and sche him eke,°   Eagerly   also
Ac noither° to other a word no speke.   neither
325 For messais° that sche on him seighe°   discomfort   saw
That had ben so riche and so heighe,°   noble
The teres fel out of her eighe.°   eye
The other levedis this y-seighe
And maked hir oway° to ride;   away
330 Sche most° with him no lenger abide.   might
    "Allas," quath he, "now me is wo!
Whi nil° deth now me slo!°   will not   slay
Allas wreche, that Y no might°   **no might** could not
Dye now after this sight!
335 Allas, too long last° mi liif,   lasts
When Y no dar° nought with mi wiif   dare
No hye° to me o° word speke.   **No hye** Nor she   one
Allas, whi nil° min hert breke!   will not
Parfay,"° quath he, "tide wat bitide,°   Indeed   **tide . . .** happen what may
340 Whider so this° levedis ride,   these
The selve° way Ichil streche.°   same   **Ichil streche** I will go
Of liif no deth me no reche!"°   **me . . .** I care not
    His sclavain° he dede° on al so spac°   pilgrim's robe   put   quickly
And henge his harp opon his bac
345 And had wel gode wil° to gon;°   **wel . . .** very great desire   go
He no spard° noither stub° no ston.   avoided   tree trunk
In at a roche° the levedis rideth,   rock
And he after and nought abideth.°   delays
When he was in the roche y-go
350 Wele thre mile other mo,°   **other mo** or more
He com into a fair cuntray
As bright so° sonne on somers day,   as
Smothe and plain and al grene;
Hille no dale was ther non y-sene.
355 Amidde the lond a castel he sighe,°   saw
Riche and real° and wonder heighe;°   regal   **wonder heighe** wonderfully noble
Al the utmast° wal   outermost
Was clere and schine° as cristal.   bright
    An hundred tours° ther were about   towers
360 Degiselich and bataild° stout.   **Degiselich . . .** Wonderful and battlemented
The butras° com out of the diche,°   buttress   moat
Of rede gold y-arched riche.

The vousour° was avowed° al   vaulting   adorned
Of ich maner divers° aumal.°   **maner divers** different kind of   enamel
365 Within ther wer wide wones°   chambers
Al of precious stones.
The werst piler° on to biholde   **werst piler** worst pillar
Was al of burnist gold.
Al that lond was ever light,
370 For when it schuld be therk° and night,   dark
The riche stones light gonne°   **light gonne** shone
As bright as döth at none° the sonne.   noon
No man may telle no thenche° in thought   think
The riche werk that ther was wrought.
375 Bi al thing him think° that it is   **him think** it seems to him
The proude° court of paradis.   splendid
    In this castel the levedis alight.
He wold° in after yif he might.   would go
Orfeo knokketh atte gate;
380 The porter was redi ther-ate
And asked what he wold have y-do.
    "Parfay,"° quath he, "Icham° a minstrel, lo,   Indeed   I am
To solas thi lord with mi gle,°   minstrelsy
Yif his swete wille be."
385   The porter undede the yate° anon   gate
And lete him into the castel gon.°   go
Than he gan bihold° about al   **gan bihold** beheld
And seighe liggeand° within the wal   lying
Of folk that were thider y-brought
390 And thought dede and nare nought.°
Sum stode withouten hade,°   head
And sum non armes nade;°   had
And sum thurch° the bodi hadde wounde,   through
And sum lay wode,° y-bounde,   crazy
395 And sum armed on hors sete,
And sum astrangled as thai ete,
And sum were in water adreynt,°   drowned
And sum with fire al forschreynt.°   shrivelled
Wives ther lay on child-bedde,
400 Sum ded, and sum awedde.°   gone mad
And wonder fele° ther lay bisides,   **wonder fele** wonderfully many
Right as thai slepe her undertides.
Eche was thus in this warld y-nome,°   taken
With fairi° thider y-come.   **With fairi** By magic
405   Ther he seighe his owhen° wiif,   own
Dame Heurodis his lüf liif,°   **lüf liif** dear life

390. And considered dead but were not.

225

Slepe under an ympe-tre;°   orchard tree
Bi her clothes he knewe that it was he.°   she
And when he hadde bihold this mervails alle,
410 He went into the kinges halle.
Than seighe he ther a semly sight:
A tabernacle° blisseful and bright,   canopy
Ther-in her° maister king sete   **Ther-in her** In which their
And her quen fair and swete.
415 Her crounes, her clothes schine so bright,
That unnethe° bihold he hem might.   hardly
    When he hadde biholden al that thing,
He kneled adoun bifor the king:
"O lord," he seyd, "yif it thi wille were,
420 Mi menstraci° thou schust y-here."   minstrelsy
    The king answerd: "What man artow°   are you
That art hider y-comen now?
Ich no non° that is with me   **Ich** . . . Neither I nor any
No sent never after thee.
425 Seththen that° Ich here regni gan,°   **Seththen that** Since   **regni gan** began to reign
Y no fond so folehardi man
That hider to ous° durst wende,°   us   come
Bot that Ichim wald ofsende."°   **Ichim** . . . I would send for him
"Lord," quath he, "trowe° ful wel,   believe
430 Y nam bot° a pouer menstrel,   **nam bot** am only
And, sir, it is the maner of ous
To seche° mani a lordes hous;   seek
Thei° we nought welcom no be,   Though
Yete we mot proferi° forth our gle."°   **mot proferi** must offer   minstrelsy
435   Bifor the king he sat adoun
And tok his harp so miri of soun°   sound
And tempreth° his harp, as he wele can,   tunes
And blisseful notes he ther gan,°   began
That al that in the palays were
440 Com to him for to here,°   hear
And liggeth° adoun to° his fete;   lie   by
Hem thenketh° his melody so swete.   **Hem thenketh** Seemed to them
The king herkneth° and sitt ful stille;   listens
To here his gle° he hath gode wille.   minstrelsy
445 Gode bourde° he hadde of his gle;   pleasure
The riche quen al-so hadde he.°   she
    When he hadde stint° his harping,   stopped
Than seyd to him the king:
"Menstrel, me liketh° wele thi gle.   pleases
450 Now aske of me what it be,
Largelich Ichil° thee pay.   **Largelich Ichil** Generously I will

Now speke and tow might asay."°   **and . . . if you can try**
　"Sir," he seyd, "Ich biseche thee
Thatow woldest yive° me   give
455 That ich° levedi bright on ble°   same   complexion
That slepeth under the ympe-tre."°   orchard tree
　"Nay," quath the king, "that nought nere!°   **nought nere** would not be fitting
A sori couple of you it were,
For thou art lene, rowe,° and blac,   rough
460 And sche is lovesum° withouten lac.°   lovely   fault
A lothlich° thing it were forthi°   repulsive   therefore
To sen° hir in thi compayni."   see
　"O sir," he seyd, "gentil king,
Yete were it a wele° fouler thing   much
465 To here° a lesing of° thi mouthe.   hear   **lesing of** lie from
So, sir, as ye seyd nouthe,°   just now
What Ich wold aski, have Y schold,°   I should have
And nedes° thou most° thi word hold."°   necessarily   must   keep
　The king seyd, "Seththen° it is so,   Since
470 Take hir bi the hond and go.
Of hir Ichil thatow° be blithe."   **Ichil thatow** I wish that you
　He knelyd adoun and thonked him swithe.°   greatly
His wiif he tok bi the hond
And dede him swithe° out of that lond   **dede . . .** went quickly
475 And went him out of that thede.°   country
Right° as he come the way he yede.°   Just   went
So long he hath the way y-nome,°   taken
To Winchester he is y-come,
That was his owhen° cité;   own
480 Ac no man knewe that it was he.
No forther than the tounes ende
For knoweleche° he no durst wende.°   **For knoweleche** Because of recognition   go
Bot with a begger y-bilt° ful narwe,°   lodged   poorly
Ther he tok his herbarwe°   lodging
485 To° him and to his owhen wiif   For
As a minstrel of pouer liif,
And asked tidings of that lond,
And who the kingdom held in hond.
　The pouer begger in his cot°   cottage
490 Told him everich a grot:°   **everich . . .** every bit
How her quen was stole owy
Ten yer gon with fairy,°   **gon . . .** ago by magic
And hou her king en° exile yede,°   in   went
Bot no man nist° in wiche thede;°   knew   country
495 And hou the steward the lond gan° hold,   did
And other mani thinges him told.

Amorwe, oyain none tide,°   **Amorwe . . .** The next day, toward noontime
He maked his wiif ther abide;
The beggers clothes he borwed° anon,   borrowed
500 And heng his harp his rigge° opon,   back
And went him into that cité,
That men might him bihold and se.
Erls and barouns bold,
Burjays° and levedis him gun° bihold.   Burgesses   did
505 "Lo," thai seyd, "swiche° a man!   such
How long the here° hongeth him opan!   hair
Lo, hou his berd hongeth to his kne!
He is y-clongen also° a tre!"   **y-clongen also** shrivelled like
     And as he yede° in the strete,   went
510 With his steward he gan mete,
And loude he sett on him a crie:
"Sir steward," he seyd, "merci!
Ich am an harpour of hethenisse.°   foreign lands
Help me now in this distresse!"
515   The steward seyd, "Com with me, come!
Of that Ichave° thou schalt have some.   **that Ichave** what I have
Everich° gode harpour is welcom me to   Every
For mi lordes love, Sir Orfeo."
In the castel the steward sat atte mete,°   the meal
520 And many lording was bi him sete.
Ther were trompours and tabourers,°   **trompours . . .** trumpeters and drummers
Harpours fele and crouders.°   **fele . . .** many and fiddlers
Miche melody thai maked alle,
And Orfeo sat stille in the halle
525 And herkneth.° When thai ben° al stille,   listens   are
He toke his harp and tempred schille.°   tuned loudly
The blissefulest notes he harped there
That ever ani man y-herd with ere.°   ear
Ich man liked wele his gle.
530 The steward biheld and gan y-se°   see
And knewe the harp als blive.°   **als blive** at once
     "Menstrel," he sayd, "so mot° thou thrive,°   may   prosper
Where hadestow this harp and hou?
Y pray that thou me telle now."
535   "Lord," quath he, "in uncouthe thede°   **uncouthe thede** strange country
Thurch° a wildernes as Y yede,°   Through   went
Ther Y founde in a dale
With lyouns a man totorn smale,°   **totorn smale** torn to pieces
And wolves him frete° with teth so scharp.   gnawed
540 Bi him Y fond this ich° harp,   same
Wele ten yere it is y-go."

"O," quath the steward, "now me is wo!
That was mi lord, Sir Orfeo.
Allas wreche, what schal Y do,
545 That have swiche° a lord y-lore!°   such   lost
Away° that Ich was y-bore!°   Alas   born
That him was so hard grace y-yarked°   **hard** . . . cruel a fortune ordained
And so vile deth y-marked!"°   appointed
   Adoun he fel aswon° to grounde.   fainting
550 His barouns him toke up in that stounde°   moment
And telleth him hou it geth;°   goes
It nis no bot of° manes deth.   **It** . . . There is no remedy for
King Orfeo knewe wele bi than°   **bi than** from that
His steward was a trewe man,
555 And loved him, as he aught to do,
And stont° up and seyt° thus: "Lo,   stands   says
Steward, herkne° now this thing: listen to
Yif Ich were Orfeo the king,
And hadde y-suffred ful yore°   **ful yore** long ago
560 In wildernisse miche sore,°   **miche sore** great sorrow
And hadde y-won mi quen owy
Out of the lond of fairy,°   magic
And hadde y-brought the levedi hende°   courteous
Right here to the tounes ende,
565 And with a begger her in y-nome,°   **her** . . . provided lodging for her
And were miself hider y-come
Pouerlich to thee, thus stille,
For to asay° thi gode wille,   test
And Ich founde thee thus trewe,
570 Thou no schust° it ever rewe.°   should   regret
Sikerlich° for love or ay°   Surely   fear
Thou schust be king after mi day.
And yif thou of mi deth hadest ben blithe,
Thou schust ben voided also swithe."° **voided** . . . banished at once
575   Tho° al tho° that ther-in sete   Then   those
That it was King Orfeo underyete,°   understood
And the steward him wele knewe.
Over and over the bord° he threwe°   table   knocked
And fel adoun to his fet.
580 So dede everich° lord that ther sete,   **dede everich** did every
And al thai seyd at o° criing: one
"Ye beth our lord, sir, and our king!"
Glad thai were of his live.°   life
To chaumber thai ladde him als blive°   **als blive** at once
585 And bathed him and schaved his berd
And tired° him as a king apert.°   dressed   openly

And seththen° with gret processioun   then
Thai brought the quen into the toun
With al maner menstraci.°   **maner menstraci** kinds of minstrelsy
590 Lord, ther was grete melody!
For joie thai wepe with her eighe,°   eyes
That° hem so sounde° y-comen seighe.   Those that   safe
Now King Orfeo newe coround is
And his quen Dame Heurodis,
595 And lived long afterward,
And seththen° was king the steward.   then
    Harpours in Bretaine° after than°   Brittany   that
Herd hou this mervaile° bigan,   marvel
And made herof a lay of gode likeing°   charm
600 And nempned° it after the king.   named
That lay "Orfeo" is y-hote;°   called
Gode is the lay, swete is the note.
Thus com Sir Orfeo out of his care.°   sorrow
God graunt ous alle wele to fare.

Halidon Hill

(ca. 1333, Northern)

All we know of Laurence Minot is that he composed eleven political poems celebrating the triumphs achieved by King Edward III against the Scots and the French during the period between 1333 and 1352. The poems are written in the Northern English dialect, but that clue merely places the author somewhere in the northeast of England between Yorkshire and the Scottish border.

Halidon Hill is the first of these poems. Edward II had been defeated by the Scots at Bannockburn in 1314 (see Barbour's *Bruce*, p.271, below). Edward III temporarily regained control of the border in 1333 by a victory at Halidon Hill, near Berwick. In commemorating the victory, Minot was still concerned, however, by the possibility that the Scottish merchants might be able to wrest the advantage from England in Bruges and elsewhere in the Low Countries.

The meter of the poem is six-line stanzas; see Introduction, type 12, page 32.

The best edition is in Joseph Hall, ed., *The Poems of Laurence Minot*, rev. ed. (Oxford, 1914), pages 4–6. For a facsimile of the manuscript see Plate 4 and accompanying notes, pages 22–23. For bibliography see Wells, ch. 4.12.

Skottes out of Berwik and of Abirdene,
At the Bannok Burn war ye too kene.°   bold
Thare slogh° ye many sakles, als° it was sene,   slew   **sakles, als** innocent, as
And now has King Edward wroken° it, I wene.°   avenged   trust
5 It es wrokin, I wene; wele wurth° the while!°   **wele wurth** good luck to   event
   War yit with° the Skottes, for thai er° ful of gile.   **War ...** Still beware   are

Whare er ye Skottes of Saint Johnes toune?°   **Saint ...** Perth
The boste of yowre baner es betin all doune.
When ye bosting will bede,° Sir Edward° es boune°   offer   Edward III   ready
10 For to kindel yow care and crak yowre crowne.
   He has crakked yowre croune; wele wurth° the while!°   **wele wurth** good luck to   event
   Schame bityde the Skottes, for thai er° full of gile.   are

Skottes of Striflin° war steren° and stout;   Stirling   stern
Of God ne° of gude men had thai no dout.°   or   fear
15 Now have thai, the pelers, priked° obout,   **pelers, priked** ravagers, raced
   Bot at the last Sir Edward rifild° thaire rout.°   despoiled   band

He has rifild thaire rout; wele wurth° the while!°
Bot ever er° thai, under, bot gaudes° and gile.

Rugh-fute riveling,° now kindels thi care.
20 Bere-bag° with thi boste, thi biging° es bare.
Fals wretche and forsworn, whider wiltou fare?°
Busk thee° unto Brig,° and abide thare.
    Thare, wretche, saltou won, and wery° the while.°
Thi dwelling in Dondé° es done° for thi gile.

25 The Skottes gase° in Burghes° and betes° the stretes.
Al° thise Inglismen harmes he hetes.°
Fast° makes he his mone° to men that he metes,
Bot fone° frendes he findes that his bale betes.°
    Fune° betes his bale; wele wurth° the while!°
30 He uses al threting with gaudes° and gile.

Bot many man thretes and spekes ful ill
That sumtyme war° better to be stane-still.
The Skot in his wordes has wind for to spill,
For, at the last, Edward sall have al his will.
35 He had his will at Berwik; wele wurth° the while!
Skottes broght him the kayes;° bot get° for thaire gile!

wele wurth good luck to   event
are **under** ... underneath,
   nothing but tricks

Rugh-fute riveling Rough-shod
   brogue-wearer
Bag-carrier   dwelling
wiltou fare will you go
Busk thee Hasten   Bruges
saltou ... you shall dwell, and
   curse   event
Dundee   destroyed

go   Bruges   walk
To all   promises
Continually   complaint
few   **bale betes** torment relieve
Few   **wele wurth** good luck to
   event
al ... every kind of threat along
   with tricks

would be

wele wurth good luck to
keys of the town   look out

232

RICHARD ROLLE

The Form of Living

(1349, Northern)

The most famous of the fourteenth-century English mystics was the hermit Richard Rolle (d. 1349), of Hampole in the West Riding of Yorkshire. He wrote *The Form of Living* for the anchoress Margaret Kirkby, of Anderby in the North Riding, near whom he had earlier resided. In this work Rolle achieved a clear and orderly if austere prose style, but the intimate and personal nuances of *The Anchoresses' Rule* (p. 106, above) were beyond or beneath him. Though *The Form of Living* is couched in the form of a letter to an individual anchoress, the brief set of general instructions it provides is suitable for anyone interested in pursuing a mystical experience. Nowhere does Rolle give the sort of personal allusion or specific advice that the unknown author of the earlier work gave his three spiritually minded young ladies. Characteristic of Rolle, however, is his incessant emphasis on the sweetness and joy of the mystical life and on the importance of the *calor* ('warmth'), *canor* ('splendor,' literally, 'song'), and *dulcor* ('sweetness') of divine love.

The selection below consists of the final two chapters. For the most dependable edition see Hope Emily Allen, *The English Writings of Richard Rolle, Hermit of Hampole* (Oxford, 1931). The best study of the man and his work is *Writings Ascribed to Richard Rolle, Hermit of Hampole, and Materials for his Biography*, by the same author (New York, 1927). For bibliography see Wells, ch. 11.5; *CBEL*, 1. 191–94.

Chapter XI

The sevene gyftes of the Haly Gaste that ere° gyfene to   are
men and wymmene that er ordaynede to the joye of
hevene and ledys° theire lyfe in this worlde reghtwysely,   lead
thire° are thay: Wysdome, Undyrstandynge, Counsayle,   these
5 Strenghe, Connynge, Peté, the Drede of God.
    Begynne we at Consaile, for thareof es myster° at the   need
begynnynge of oure werkes, that us myslyke° noghte   may displease
aftyrwarde. With thire sevene gyftes the Haly Gaste teches
sere° mene serely.°   various individually
10   Consaile es doynge awaye of worldes reches and of all
delytes of all thynges that mane may be tagyld° with in   entangled
thoghte or dede, and tharwith° drawynge intill° contem-   thereby into
placyone of Gode.
    Undyrstandynge es to knawe whate es to doo and whate

15 es to lefe,° and that sall° be gyffene, to gyffe it to thaym that   leave alone **that sall** whatever
      shall
has nede, noghte till° other that has na myster.°   to need

Wysedome es forgetynge of erthely thynges and
thynkynge of heven, with discrecyone of° all mens   **discrecyone of** separation
      from
dedys.° In this gyfte schynes° contemplacyone, that es,   deeds shines forth
20 Saynt Austyne° says, a gastely dede° of fleschely affec-   Augustine **gastely dede**
      spiritual act
cyones,° thurghe the joye of a raysede° thoghte.   desires elevated

Strenghe es lastynge to fulfill gude purpose, that it be
noghte lefte for wele° ne for waa.°   happiness woe

Peté es that a man be mylde and gaynesay noghte Haly
25 Writte whene it smyttes his synnys, whethire he undyr-
stand it or noghte; bot in all his myghte purge he the
vilté° of syne in hyme° and other.   vileness himself

Connynge es that makes a man of gude hope, noghte
ruysand hyme of° his reghtewysnes, bot sorowand of his   **ruysand . . .** glorying in
30 synnys, and that man gedyrs erthely gude anely to the
honour of God and prow° to other mene thane hymselfe.   benefit

The Drede of God es that we turne noghte agayne till°   to
oure syne thurghe any ill eggyng.° And than es drede   egging on
perfite° in us and gastely,° when we drede to wrethe° God   perfect spiritual anger
35 in the leste syne that we kane knawe, and flese° it als°   flee as
venyme.

Chapter XII

Twa lyves thar er° that Cristen men lyfes.° Ane es   are live
called actyve lyfe, for it es in mare° bodili warke. Another,   more
contemplatyve lyfe, for it es in mare swetnes gastely.°   spiritually
Actife lyfe es mykel° owteward, and in mare travel° and   much labor
5 in mare peryle for the temptacions that er in the worlde.
Contemplatyfe lyfe es mykel inwarde, and for-thi° it es   therefore
lastandar and sykerar,° restfuller, delitabiler,° luflyer, and   **lastandar . . .** more lasting and
      more secure more delightful
mare medeful.° For it hase joy in Goddes lufe and savowre   rewarding
in the lyf that lastes ay° in this present tyme, if it be right   forever
10 ledde. And that felyng of joy in the lufe of Jesu passes al
other merites in erth. For it es swa° harde to com to for°   so because of
the freelté of oure flesch and the many temptacions that we
er umsett° with, that lettes° us nyght and day. Al other   **er umsett** are surrounded
      hinder
thynges er lyght at° com to, in regarde tharof, for that may   **lyght at** easy to
15 na man deserve, bot anely° it es gifen of Goddes godenes til°   **bot anely** only if to
tham that verrayli gifes tham° to contemplacion and til   themselves
quiete for Cristes luf.

Til men or wymen that takes tham° til actife lyfe, twa
thynges falles.° Ane, for to ordayne thair meyné° in drede
20 and in the lufe of God, and fynd tham thaire necessaries,
and thamself kepe enterely the commandementes of God,
doand til° thar neghbur als° thai wil that thai do til tham.
Another es that thai do at thar power the seven werkes of
mercy, the whilk° es: to fede the hungry; to gyf the
25 thristi a drynk; to cleth the naked; to herbar hym that
hase na howsyng; to viset the seke; to comfort tham that
er° in prysoun; and to grave° dede men. Al that mai,° and
hase cost,° thai may noght be qwyt° with ane or twa of
thir,° bot tham behoves° do tham al, if thai wil have the
30 benyson° on Domesday that Jesu sal til al gyf° that dose
tham. Or els may thai drede the malysoun° that al mon°
have that will noght do tham when thai had godes° to do
tham wyth.

Contemplatife lyf hase twa partyes,° a lower and a heer.
35 The lower party es meditacion of haly wrytyng, that es
Goddes wordes, and in other gude thoghtes and swete that
men hase of the grace of God abowt the lufe of Jesu Criste,
and also in lovyng° of God in psalmes and ympnes° or in
prayers. The hegher party of contemplacion es behaldyng
40 and yernyng of° the thynges of heven, and joy in the Haly
Gaste. That men hase oft, and° if it be swa° that thai be
noght prayand with the mowth, bot anely thynkand of
God and of the fairhede° of aungels and haly sawles.° Than
may I say that contemplacion es a wonderful joy of Goddes
45 luf, the whilk° joy es lovyng of God, that may noght
be talde. And that wonderful lovyng es in the saule, and
for abundance of joy and swettenes it ascendes in til° the
mouth, swa° that the hert and the tonge acordes° in ane,
and body and sawle joyes° in God lyvand.°

50 A man or woman that es ordaynd til contemplatife
lyfe, first God enspires tham to forsake this worlde and
al the vanité and the covayties and the vile luste tharof.
Sythen° he ledes tham by thar ane,° and spekes til thair
hert, and, als the prophete says, he gifes tham at sowke°
55 the swetnes of the begynnyng of lufe, and than he settes
tham in will° to gyf tham haly° to prayers and meditacions
and teres. Sithen, when thai have sufferd many temptacions and foule noyes° of thoghtes that er° ydel and of
vanitées the whilk° wil comber° tham that can noght
60 destroy tham, er° passand away, he gars tham geder° til
tham thair hert, and fest° anely in hym, and opens til the
egh° of thair sawls° the yates° of heven, swa° that the ilk°

---

takes tham devote themselves
are ordained   household

doand til doing to   as

the whilk which

are bury can
hase cost have enough money
  released
these it behooves to
blessing **sal...** shall give to all
curse must
goods

parts

praising hymns

for

even so

fairness souls

the whilk which

to
so agree
sawle joyes soul rejoice
  living

Then **by...** by themselves
at sowke to suck

settes... makes them wish
  wholly

annoyances are
the whilk which encumber
before **gars...** makes them
  gather
fix
eye souls gates so same

egh lokes in til heven; and than the fire of lufe verrali
ligges° in thair hert and byrnes tharin and makes clene of   lies
65 al erthly filth; and sithen forward° thai er° contemplatife   **sithen forward** from then on
men and ravyst° in lufe. For contemplacion es a syght, and   are
thai se in til heven with thar gastly egh.° Bot thou sal witt°   ravished
that na man hase perfite syght of heven whils thai er   **gastly egh** spiritual eye   **sal**
lifand bodili here; bot als° sone als thai dye thai er broght   **witt** shall know
70 before God and sese° hym face til face and egh til egh,   as
and wones° with hym withouten ende. For hym thai soght   see
and hym thai covayted and hym thai lufed in al thar   dwell
myght.

    Loo, Margarete, I have schortly sayde° thee the forme of   told
75 lyvyng and how thou may com til perfection and to lufe
hym that thou hase taken thee til.° If it do thee gude and   **thee til** to you
profit til thee, thank God and pray for me. The grace of
Jesu Criste be with thee and kepe thee. Amen.

THE AGE
OF
CHAUCER

The Parliament of the Three Ages

(ca. 1370, East Midland)

The Parliament (that is, 'Discussion') employs two medieval conventions, the dream frame-work and the debate format, the latter comparable to *The Owl and the Nightingale* (p. 54, above). The closest analogues are to be found in a series of medieval French poems on 'The Three Dead Men and the Three Living Men,' a theme often represented in medieval paintings and illumination.

In *The Parliament*, however, the central issue in Age's argument is the medieval tradition of the Nine Worthies, which seems to have sprung immediately from a French romance on Alexander, *The Vows of the Peacock (Voeux de Paon,* ca. 1312), by Jacques de Longuyon, and ultimately from Celtic sources, probably from the traditional Welsh triads. The Nine Worthies appear in Middle English literature most frequently in the north, the two most notable occurrences being in the alliterative *Morte Arthure* and the present poem. An anony-mous translation of the *Voeux de Paon* was made at a later date into Middle Scots octo-syllabic verse and was entitled *The Avowis of Alexander* (1438). No one version, even the *Voeux,* is clearly identifiable as a source for *The Parliament,* though the author refers to the theme of the peacock with familiarity (p. 252, l. 34). Presumably the author based his own account of the Worthies on a wide acquaintance with romance literature and learned tradition.

Age relates this account of the Worthies as clear evidence of the vanity of all worldly things, and he continues his moral lecture with a brief survey of wise men and famous lovers, all underscoring the theme of *Ubi sunt qui ante nos fuerunt?* ('Where are those who were before us?'), a common medieval motif found in Thomas of Hailes's *Love Rune* (p. 156, above) and *The Sayings of St. Bernard* (p. 163, above), and most memorably expressed at the end of the era by François Villon. The entire *Parliament of the Three Ages* is thus not so much a treatise on the Nine Worthies as it is a moral lesson on the evanescence of everything worldly, showing at least some originality in the author's blending of the separate themes of the Ages, the Worthies, and *Ubi sunt* into an effective didactic piece.

Originality is even more apparent in the description of the setting (p. 239, ll. 1–20), the hunt (pp. 239–41, ll. 21–65), and falconry (pp. 240–41, ll. 40–77)—passages based more on the author's actual experiences and observations than on his erudition. The description of the handling of the slain deer (ll. 66–96) bears comparison with a similar passage in the later *Sir Gawain and the Green Knight* (pp. 419–20, ll. 1323–61) for vivid realism. The passages stand out in what would otherwise be a good but undistinguished representative of the alliterative revival in Northern England. For the meter see Introduction, type 1, page 29.

A useful edition is *The Parlement of the Thre Ages,* ed. I. Gollancz (London, 1915), in which are printed a number of analogues on the Nine Worthies. The best edition and com-mentary are *The Parlement of the Thre Ages,* ed. M. Y. Offord, EETS 246 (London, 1959). For bibliography see Wells, ch. 4.49.

The Parliament of the Three Ages

Prologue

In the monethe of Maye when mirthes bene fele°   **bene fele** are many
And the sesone of somere when softe bene the
    wedres,°   breezes
Als° I went to the wodde° my werdes° to dreghe,°   As   wood   chances   try
Into the schawes° myselfe a schotte me to gete   thickets
5   At ane hert or ane hynde, happen as it myghte,
And as Dryghten° the day drove frome the heven,   the Lord
Als I habade one° a banke be° a bryme° syde,   **habade one** waited on   by   brook's
There° the gryse° was grene, growen with floures—   Where   grass
The primrose, the perwynke, and piliole° the riche—   **perwynke . . .** periwinkle, and pennyroyal
10   The dewe appon daysés donkede° full faire,   spread moisture
Burgons,° and blossoms, and braunches full swete,   Buds
And the mery mystes full myldely gane falle,°   **gane falle** fell
The cukkowe, the cowschote, kene° were thay
    bothen,°   **cowschote, kene** wood-pigeon, lively / both
And the throstills° full throly threpen° in the bankes,   throstles   **throly threpen** eagerly contend at singing
15   And iche foule° in that frythe faynere° than other   **iche foule** each bird   **frythe faynere** wood gladder
That the derke was done and the daye lightenede.
Hertys and hyndes one° hillys thay gowen;°   on   gaze about
The foxe and the filmarte° thay flede to the erthe;   polecat
The hare hurkles° by hawes° and harde thedir
    dryves   crouches   hedges
20   And ferkes° faste to hir fourme° and fatills° hir to   goes   **hir fourme** her nest   readies
    sitt.
Als I stode in that stede,° one° stalkynge I thoghte.   place   on
Bothe my body and my bowe I buskede° with leves   dressed
And turnede towardes a tree and tariede there a
    while.
And als° I lokede to a launde° a littill me besyde,°   as   glade   **me besyde** away from me
25   I seghe ane° hert with ane hede,° ane heghe for the
    nones.°   **seghe ane** saw a   antlered head / **heghe . . .** high one indeed
Alle unburneschede was the beme, full borely the
    mydle,
With iche feetur, as thi fote, forfrayed in the
    greves,°
With auntlers one° aythere syde egheliche° longe.   on   fearfully

---

26–27. All unburnished (with hair rubbed off but not yet the skin) was the main stem of the antlers, very strong was the middle, with each tine, looking like your foot, frayed (with hair rubbed off) against trees in the groves

The ryalls full richely raughten frome the myddes,
30 With surryals full semely appon sydes twayne;
And he assommet and sett of six and of fyve,°
And therto borely° and brode and of body grete,   strong he was
And a coloppe° for a kynge, cache hym who   tasty bit
    myghte.
Bot there sewet° hym a sowre° that servet hym full   followed   buck
    yerne,°   eagerly
35 That woke and warned hym when the wynde
    faylede
That none so sleghe° in his slepe with sleghte°   clever   cunning
    scholde hym dere,°   harm
And went the wayes hym byfore when any wothe
    tyde.°   **wothe tyde** danger happens
My lyame° than full° lightly lete I doun falle,   leash   very
And to the bole° of a birche my berselett° I   trunk   hound
    cowchide.°   made lie down
40 I waitted wiesly° the wynde by waggynge of leves,   **waitted wiesly** watched carefully
Stalkede full stilly, no stikkes to breke,
And crepit° to a crab tre and coverede me ther-   crept
    under.
Then I bende up my bowe and bownede me° to   **bownede me** prepared
    schote,
Tighte° up my tylere and taysede° at the hert,   Set   **tylere** ... crossbow stock and aimed
45 Bot the sowre° that hym sewet° sett up the nese°   buck   followed   nose
And wayttede wittyly° abowte and wyndide° full   **wayttede wittyly** looked carefully   sniffed
    yerne.°   eagerly
Then I moste° stonde als° I stode and stirre no fote   had to   as
    ferrere,°   farther
For, had I myntid° or movede or made any synys,°   aimed   signs
Alle my layke° hade bene loste that I hade longe   sport
    wayttede.°   awaited
50 Bot gnattes gretely me grevede and gnewen° myn   bit
    eghne.°   eyes
And he stotayde and stelkett° and starede full brode,°   **stotayde** ... paused and moved carefully
    full brode very widely
Bot at the laste he loutted° doun and laughte till° his   bent   **laughte till** took up
    mete,°   food
And I hallede to° the hokes° and the hert smote,   **hallede to** pulled back   crossbow catches
And happenyd that I hitt hym byhynde the lefte
    scholdire
55 That the blode braste° owte appon bothe the sydes,   burst

29–31. The royals (second branches of the antlers) extended very splendidly from the middle, with very
fair surroyals (crown antlers) on both sides; and he displayed antlers fully formed and was furnished with
six branches on one antler and with five on the other

And he balkede° and brayed and bruschede° thurgh the greves,°
    stopped   rushed   groves

As° alle had hurlede one ane hepe° that in the holte longede,°
    *As if **hurlede** . . . dashed together in one bunch dwelled*

And sone° the sowre° that hym sewet resorte° to his feris,°
    *at once buck **sewet resorte** followed returned companions*

And thay, forfrayede° of his fare,° to the fellys° thay hyen.°
    frightened behavior moors hurry

60 And I hyede to my hounde and hent hym up° sone
    hent . . . *took him*

And louset° my lyame° and lete hym umbycaste.°
    loosed leash cast about

The breris° and the brakans° were blody byronnen,°
    *briars bracken **blody byronnen** covered with blood*

And he assentis to that sewte° and seches° hym aftire,
    pursuit searches

There° he was crepyde° into a krage and crouschede° to the erthe.
    *Where **was crepyde** had crept **krage** . . . cave and crouched*

65 Dede als° a dore-nayle doun was he fallen.
    as

And I hym hent° by the hede and heryett° hym uttire,°
    took dragged out

Turned his troches and tachede° thaym into the erthe,
    troches . . . *tines and fastened*

Kest° up that keudvart° and kutt of° his tonge,
    Turned rascal off

Brayde° owte his bewells° my berselett° to fede,
    Drew entrails hound

70 And I slitte hym at the assaye° to see how me semyde,°
    breast (where flesh was usually tested) **me semyde** *it seemed to me*

And he was floreschede° full faire of two-fyngere brede.°
    lined with fat breadth

I chese to° the chawylls chefe° to begynn
    chese to *chose at especially* **chawylls chefe** *jowls*

And ritte° doun at a rase° reght to the tayle,
    ripped rush

And than the herbere anone° aftir I makede.
    herbere anone *arber (first stomach) next*

75 I raughte° the righte legge byfore, ritt° it theraftir,
    seized ripped

And so fro legge to legge I lepe° thaym aboute,
    leaped

And the felle° fro the fete fayre I departede°
    skin separated

And flewe° it doun with my fiste faste° to the rigge.°
    flayed right spine

I tighte° owte my trenchore° and toke of° the scholdirs,
    drew knife off

80 Cuttede corbyns° bone and keste it awaye.
    raven's

I slitte hym full sleghely° and slyppede in my fyngere
    full sleghely *very cleverly*

Lesse° the poynte scholde perche° the pawnche or the guttys.
    Lest pierce

I soughte owte my sewet and semblete° it togedire
    sewet . . . *suet and gathered*

And pullede oute the pawnche and putt it in an hole.°
    hole in the ground

85 I grippede owte the guttes and graythede° thaym besyde,
    put

And than the nombles anone name° I thereaftire,   **nombles . . .** entrails next took

Rent up fro the rygge° reghte to the myddis,°   spine   middle

And than the fourches° full fayre I fonge° fro the sydes   haunches   took

And chynede° hym chefely° and choppede of° the nekke,   split along spine   especially   off

90 And the hede and the haulse homelyde° in sondree.   **haulse homelyde** neck cut

The fete of the fourche I feste° thurgh the sydis   fastened

And hevede° alle into ane hole and hidde it with ferne,   heaved

With hethe and with hore° mosse hilde° it about   gray   hid

That no fostere of the fee° scholde fynde it theraftir;   **fostere . . .** forester by inheritance

95 Hid the hornes and the hede in ane hologhe° oke   hollow

That no hunte° scholde it hent° ne have it in sighte.   hunter   take

     I foundede° faste therefro for ferde° to be wryghede°   hastened   fear / discovered

And sett me° oute one a syde to see how it chevede,°   **sett me** seated myself   fared

To wayte° it frome wylde swyne that wyse bene° of nesse.°   guard   are / nose

100 And als° I satte in my sette, the sone was so warme,   as

And I for slepeles was slome and slomerde° a while   **slome . . .** heavy with sleep and slumbered

And there me dremed, in that dowte,° a full dreghe swevynn,°   uncertainty / **dreghe swevynn** long dream

And whate I seghe° in my saule the sothe° I schall telle.   saw   truth

The Three Ages

     I seghe thre thro° men threpden° full yerne°   earnest   who argued   eagerly

And moteden° of myche-whate° and maden thaym full tale.°   spoke   many things / lively in speech

And° ye will, ledys,° me listen ane hande-while,°   If   men   moment

I schall reken° thaire araye redely,° for sothe,°   describe   **araye redely** attire promptly / truth

5 And to yowe neven° thaire names naytly° thereaftire.   name   exactly

     The firste was a ferse freke,° fayrere than thies° othire,   **ferse freke** fierce man   these

A bolde beryn one° a blonke, bownne° for to ryde,   **beryn one** knight on steed,   **blonke, bownne** ready

A hathelle° on ane heghe horse with hauke appon hande.   noble

He was balghe° in the breste and brode in the scholdirs,   deep

10 His axles° and his armes were i-liche° longe, — shoulders   correspondingly
 And in the medill als a mayden menskfully° — gracefully
  schapen.
 Longe legges and large and lele° for to schewe, — fair
 He streghte hym° in his sterapis and stode uprightes. — **streghte hym** stretched
 He ne hade no hode ne no hatte bot his here one,° — **here one** hair only
15 A chaplet one his chefe-lere, chosen for the nones,° — **chefe-lere . . .** head of hair, choice indeed
 Raylede° alle with rede rose, richeste of floures, — Adorned in rows
 With trafoyles and trewloves° of full triede° perles, — **trafoyles . . .** trefoils and love knots   fine
 With a chefe charebocle chosen° in the myddes. — **chefe . . .** fine choice carbuncle
 He was gerede° alle in grene, alle with golde — dressed
  bywevede,° — interwoven
20 Embroddirde alle with besanttes and beralles° full — **besanttes . . .** bezants and beryls
  riche.
 His colere° with calsydoynnes° clustrede full thikke, — collar   chalcedonies
 With many dyamandes full dere dighte° one his — **dere dighte** costly arranged
  sleves.
 The semys with saphirs sett were full many,
 With emeraudes and amatists° appon iche° syde, — **emeraudes . . .** emeralds and amethysts   each
25 With full riche rubyes raylede° by the hemmes. — arrayed
 The price of that perry° were worthe powndes full — jewelry
  many.
 His sadill was of sykamoure that he satt inn,
 His bridell alle of brente° golde with silke brayden° — burnished   plaited
  raynes.
 His cropoure° was of Tartaryne° that traylede to the — crupper   Tartar silk
  erthe,
30 And he throly° was threven° of thritty yere of elde — eagerly   grown up
 And therto yonge and yape,° and Youthe was his — active
  name,
 And the semelyeste segge° that I seghe° ever. — **semelyeste segge** fairest man   saw
   The seconde segge in his sete satte at his ese,
 A renke° alle in rosette° that rowmly° was schapyn, — man   russet clothes   amply
35 In a golyone° of graye girde° in the myddes,° — tunic   belted   middle
 And iche bagge° in his bosome bettir than othere. — **iche bagge** each money bag
 One his golde and his gude° gretly he mousede,° — goods   mused
 His renttes and his reches rekened° he full ofte— — **reches rekened** riches counted
 Of mukkyng,° of marlelyng° and mendynge of — manuring   fertilizing with marl
  howses,
40 Of benes° of his bondemen,° of benefetis many, — extra services   serfs
 Of presanttes of polayle,° of pufilis als,° — poultry   **pufilis als** plots of land also
 Of purches° of ploughe-londes, of parkes full faire, — acquisition
 Of profettis of his pasturs that his purse mendis,° — fill
 Of stiewardes, of storrours, stirkes° to bye,° — **storrours, stirkes** storekeepers, heifers   buy
45 Of clerkes, of countours° his courtes to holde— — legal pleaders

And alle his witt° in this werlde was one° his wele — thought   on
   one.° — **wele one** wealth only
Him semyde,° for to see to,° of sexty yere elde, — **Him semyde** He seemed   **see to** look at
And therfore men in his marche Medill-elde° hym — **marche Medill-elde** district Middle-Age
   callede.
   The thirde was a laythe lede lenyde° one his syde, — **laythe** ... ugly man bent
50 A beryne bownn° alle in blake with bedis in his — **beryne bownn** man dressed
   hande,
Croked and courbede,° encrampeschett for elde.° — bent   **encrampeschett** ... contorted because of old age
Alle disfygured was his face and fadit° his hewe, — faded
His berde and browes were blanchede full whitte,
And the hare one his hede hewede° of the same. — colored
55 He was ballede° and blynde and alle babir-lippede,° — bald   thick-lipped
Totheles and tenefull,° I tell yowe for sothe.° — peevish   truth
And ever he momelide and ment,° and mercy he — **momelide** ... mumbled and moaned
   askede
And cried kenely one Criste and his Crede sayde,° — **Crede sayde** Credo recited
With sawtries° full sere° tymes to sayntes in heven, — psalms   various
60 Envyous and angrye, and Elde° was his name. — Age
I helde° hym be° my hopynge° a hundrethe yeris of — considered   by   belief
   age,
And bot° his cruche and his couche he carede for no — except for
   more.
Now hafe I rekkende° yow theire araye redely° — described to   **araye redely** attire promptly
   the sothe,° — truth
And also namede yow thaire names naytly° there- — exactly
   aftire,
65 And now thaire carpynge° I sall kythe,° knowe it if — talk   make known
   yowe liste.° — it pleases

The Parliament

Now this gome° alle in grene so gayly attyrede, — man
This hathelle one° this heghe horse with hauke one — **hathelle one** noble on
   his fiste,
He was yonge and yape and yernynge° to armes, — **yape** ... lively and eager
And pleynede hym one° paramours and peteuosely — **pleynede** ... lamented about
   syghede.° — **peteuosely syghede** piteously sighed
5 He sett hym° up in his sadill and seyde theis wordes: — **sett hym** seated himself
   "My lady, my leman° that I hafe luffede ever, — sweetheart
My wele° and my wirchip in werlde where thou — happiness
   dwellys,

My playstere° of paramours, my lady with pappis°   balm   breasts
full swete,

Alle my hope and my hele,° myn herte es thyn   well-being
ownn.

10   I byhete° thee a heste, and heghely° I avowe   pledge   **heste** . . . promise, and solemnly

There schall no hode ne no hatt one my hede sitt

Till that I joyntly° with a gesserante justede° hafe   steadily   **gesserante justede** coat of mail
onere°   jousted   with honor

And done dedis for thi love, doghety° in armes."   valiant

    Bot then this gome° alle in graye greved with this   man
wordes

15   And sayde: "Felowe, be my faythe thou fonnes° full   act like a fool
yerne°   eagerly

For alle fantome and foly that thou with faris.°   deal

Where es the londe and the lythe° that thou arte   people
lorde over?

For alle thy ryalle araye,° renttis hase thou none,   attire

Ne for thi pompe and thi pride penyes° bot fewe.   pennies

20   For alle thi golde and thi gude gloes° one thi clothes.   **gude gloes** goods glow

And° thou hafe caughte thi kaple,° thou cares for no   If   horse
fothire.°   wagonload

Bye° the stirkes° with thi stede and stalles thaym°   Buy   heifers   for them
make;

Thi brydell of brent° golde wolde bullokes thee   burnished
gete;

The pryce of thi perrye° wolde purches thee londes;   jewelry

25   And wonne, wy, in thi witt,° for wele-neghe thou   **wonne** . . . keep, man, your wits
spilles."°   ruin yourself

    Than the gome° alle in grene greved full sore   man

And sayd, "Sir, be° my soule, thi consell es feble;   by

Bot° thi golde and thi gude° thou has no god ells,°   Except for   goods   **god ells** other god

For, be the Lorde and the laye° that I leve° inne   faith   believe

30   And by the Gode that me gaffe goste° and soule,   spirit

Me were levere° one this launde lengen° a while,   **Me** . . . I would rather   stay

Stoken° in my stele-wede° on my stede bakke,   Enclosed   steel garment

Harde haspede° in my helme and in my here-   **Harde haspede** Firmly buckled
wedys,°   war dress

With a grym grounden glayfe graythely° in myn   **grym** . . . cruelly sharpened sword ready
honde,

35   And see a kene° knyghte come and cowpe° with   bold   exchange blows
myselven

That I myghte halde that° I hafe highte and heghely°   **halde that** keep what   **highte** . . . promised
avowede   and solemnly

And parfourme my profers° and proven my   promises
strengthes,

245

Than alle the golde and the gude° that thoue gatt ever, — goods

Than alle the londe and the lythe° that thoue arte lorde over; — people

40 And ryde to a revere redily° thereaftir, — **revere redily** river bank promptly

With haukes full hawtayne° that heghe willen flye, — proud

And when the fewlis bene° founden, fawkoneres hyenn° — **fewlis bene** birds are / hurry

To lache° oute thaire lessches and lowsen° thaym sone° — take **lessches . . .** leashes and loose / at once

And keppyn of° thaire caprons° and casten fro honde, — **keppyn of** pull off hoods

45 And than° the hawteste° in haste hyghes° to the towre, — then proudest hurry

With theire bellys so brighte blethely° thay ryngen, — happily

And there they hoven appon heghte° as it were heven° angelles. — **hoven . . .** hover on high / heaven's

"Then the fawkoners full fersely° to floodes° thay hyen,° — eagerly streams / hurry

To the revere° with thaire roddes° to rere° up the fewles, — river bank beating rods rouse

50 Sowssches° thaym full serely° to serven thaire hawkes. — Beat separately

Than tercelettes° full tayttely telys° doun stryken; — male falcons **tayttely telys** swiftly teals

Laners and lanerettis lightten° to thes endes, — **Laners . . .** Female falcons and hawks swoop down

Metyn° with the maulerdes° and many doun striken. — Meet mallards

Fawkons thay founden freely° to lighte,° — **founden freely** hasten quickly swoop down

55 With 'Hoo' and 'Howghe'° to the heron thay hitten hym full ofte, — Huff

Buffetyn hym, betyn hym, and brynges° hym to sege° — bring / seat (defensive position)

And saylen° hym full serely and sesyn° hym there-aftire, — assail **serely . . .** separately and seize

Then fawkoners full fersely founden° tham aftire, — **fersely founden** eagerly hasten

To helpen thaire hawkes thay hyen thaym° full yerne,° — **hyen thaym** hurry / eagerly

60 For° the bitt° of his bill bitterly° he strikes. — Because of sharp edge fiercely

They knelen doun one theire knees and krepyn full lowe,

Wynnen to his° wynges and wrythen° thaym togedire, — **Wynnen** Get at its twist

Brosten° the bones and brekyn thaym in sondire, — Crush

Puttis° owte with a penn° the maryo° one his° glove, — Put feather marrow his (the falconer's

65	And quopes° thaym to the querrye° that quelled hym° to the dethe.	whoops quarry **quelled hym** tormented it (heron)
	He quyrres° thaym and quotes° thaym, quyppeys° full lowde,	quarries calls whips his rod
	Cheres° thaym full chefely ecchekkes° to leve,	Encourages **chefely ecchekkes** especially lesser quarry
	Than henntis° thaym one honde and hodes thaym theraftire,	takes
	Cowples° up theire cowers° thaire caprons° to holde,	Draws leather thongs hoods
70	Lowppes° in thaire lesses° thorowe vertwells° of silvere.	Loops leashes rings
	Than he laches to° his luyre° and lokes to his horse	**laches to** takes up hawk lure
	And lepis upe one the lefte syde als the laghe askes.°	**laghe askes** custom demands
	"Portours° full pristly putten upe° the fowlis°	Bearers **pristly** . . . swiftly make rise from cover birds
	And taryen° for theire tercelettis° that tenyn° thaym full ofte,	wait male falcons annoy
75	For some chosen to the echecheke,° thoghe some chefe° bettire.	lesser quarry achieved
	Spanyells full spedily thay spryngen abowte,	
	Bedagged° for dowkynge° when digges ben enewede;°	Muddied plunging **digges** . . . ducks are driven into water
	And than kayre° to the courte that I come fro,	I return
	With ladys full lovely to lappyn° in myn armes	clasp
80	And clyp° thaym and kysse thaym and comforthe myn hert,	embrace
	And than with damesels dere to daunsen in thaire chambirs,	
	Riche romance to rede, and rekken° the sothe°	tell truth
	Of kempes° and of conquerours, of kynges full noblee,	knights
	How thay wirchipe° and welthe wanne° in thaire lyves;	honor won
85	With renkes° in ryotte° to revelle in haulle,	men merriment
	With coundythes° and carolles and compaynyes sere,°	part-songs various
	And chese° me to the chesse,° that chefe es of gamnes.°	betake chess games
	"And this es life for to lede while I schalle lyfe here,	
	And thou with wandrynge and woo schalte wake for° thi gudes,	**wake for** watch over
90	And be thou dolven° and dede, thi dole° schall be schorte,	buried lamentation
	And he that thou leste luffes° schall layke hym° therewith	**leste luffes** least love **layke hym** amuse himself

And spend that° thou haste longe sparede.° The
    devyll spede° hym ells!"°

what   saved
help   otherwise

Than this renke° alle in rosett rothelede° thies
    wordes.

*man   **rosett rothelede** russett clothes
rattled*

He sayde, "Thryfte and thou have threpid° this
    thirtene wynter.

argued

95 I seghe° wele samples bene sothe° that sayde bene
    ful yore:°

*see   **samples** ... proverbs are true*
***sayde** ... have been said long ago*

'Fole° es that with foles delys.'° Flyte° we no
    lengare."

Fool   deals   Argue

Than this beryn° alle in blake bownnes hym° to
    speke

*man   **bownnes hym** prepared*

And sayde: "Sirres, by my soule, sottes° bene ye
    bothe.

fools

Bot will ye hendely° me herken ane hande-while,°

courteously   moment

100 And I schalle stynte° your stryffe and stillen your
    threpe.°

stop
argument

I sett ensample bi myselfe and sekis° it no forthire.

seek

While I was yonge in my youthe and yape° of my
    dedys,

lively

I was als everrous° in armes as outher° of youreselven

greedy for glory   either

And as styffe° in a stourre° one my stede bake,

firm   battle

105 And as gaye in my gere als any gome ells,°

***gome ells** other man*

And as lelly byluffede° with ladyse and maydens.

***lelly byluffede** faithfully beloved*

My likame° was lovely as lothe° nowe to schewe,

body   loathsome

And as myche wirchip° I wane, i-wis,° as ye
    bothen.

***myche wirchip** much honor   **wane,
i-wis** won, indeed*

And aftir irkede me° with this, and ese was me
    levere°

***irkede me** I became tired*
***me levere** dearer to me*

110 Als man in his medill elde° his makande° wolde
    have.

age   comfort

Than I mukkede and marlede° and made up my
    howses

***mukkede** ... manured and fertilized with
marl*

And purcheste me ploughe-londes and pastures full
    noble,

Gatte gude° and golde full gaynly° to honde.

***Gatte gude** Got goods   readily*

Reches° and renttes were ryfe° to myselven.

Riches   plentiful

115   "Bot elde undiryode° me are° I laste wiste°

*undermined   before   **laste wiste** least
knew*

And alle disfegurede my face and fadide my hewe.

Bothe my browes and my berde blawnchede full
    whitte,

And when he sotted° my syghte, than sowed° myn
    hert,

dulled   grieved

Croked° me, cowrbed° me, encrampeschet° myn
    hondes

Made crooked   bent   twisted

20 That I ne may hefe° tham to my hede ne noghte   *ne ... can't raise*
   helpe myselven
  Ne stale° stonden one my fete bot° I my staffe have.   *firmly   unless*
   "Makes° youre mirrours bi me, men, bi youre   *Make*
   trouthe;
  This schadowe in my schewere schunte° ye no   *schewere schunte mirror avoid*
   while.
  And now es dethe at my dore that I drede moste.
25 I ne wot° wiche daye ne° when ne whate tyme he   *ne wot know not   nor*
   comes,
  Ne whedirwardes° ne whare ne whatte to do aftire;   *whither*
  Bot many modyere° than I, men one this molde,°   *prouder   earth*
  Hafe passed the pase° that I schall passe sone,   *path*
  And I schall neven° yow the names of nyne of the   *name*
   beste,
30 That ever wy° in this werlde wiste° appon erthe,   *man   knew*
  That were conquerours full kene and kiddeste° of   *kene ... bold and most famous*
   other.

The Nine Worthies : Hector

  "The firste was Sir Ector,° and aldeste° of tyme,   *Hector   oldest*
  When Troygens° of Troye were·tried to fighte°   *Trojans   tried ... tested by fighting*
  With Menylawse° the mody° kynge and men out   *Menelaus   proud*
   of Grece
  That° thaire cité assegede and sayled° it full yerne°   *Who   assegede ... besieged and attacked eagerly*
5 For Elayne° his ownn quene that thereinn was   *Helen*
   halden
  That Paresche,° the proude knyghte, paramours°   *That Paresche Whom Paris   passionately*
   lovede.
  Sir Ectore was everous,° als the storye telles,   *eager for glory*
  And, als clerkes in the cronycle cownten the sothe,°   *truth*
  Nowmbron° thaym to nynety and nyne mo° by   *Number   more*
   tale°   *count*
10 Of kynges with crounes he killede with his handes
  And full fele° other folke, als ferly were ellis.°   *many   als ... who were otherwise as wonderful*
   "Then Achilles his adversarye undide with his
   werkes,
  With wyles and no wirchipe° woundede hym to   *honor*
   dethe
  Als he tentid to° a tulke° that he tuke° of were,°   *tentid to took care of   man   took prisoner   war*
15 And he was slayne for that slaughte sleghely°   *slaughte sleghely slaughter cunningly*
   theraftir

With the wyles of a woman as he had wroghte°
byfore.   *done*

Than Menylawse the mody° kynge hade myrthe at   *proud*
his hert

That Ectore,° hys enymy, siche auntoure° hade   *Hector* **siche auntoure** *such mischanc[e]*
fallen,°   *befallen*

And with the Gregeis° of Grece he girde° over the   *Greeks rushed*
walles;

20 The prowde paleys° dide he pulle doun to the erthe   *palace*

That was rialeste° of araye° and rycheste undir the   *most royal adornment*
heven.

And then the Trogens of Troye teneden° full sore   *grieved*

And semblen thaym° full serely, and sadly° thay   **semblen thaym** *assemble* **serely . . .**
foghten;   *order, and stoutly*

Bot the lüre° at the laste lighte° appon Troye,   *defeat fell*

25 For there Sir Priamus the prynce put was to dethe,

And Pantasilia the quene paste° hym byfore.   *died*

Sir Troylus, a trewe knyghte, that tristyly° hade   *faithfully*
foghten,

Neptolemus, a noble knyghte, at nede that wolde
noghte fayle,

Palamedes, a prise° knyghte and preved° in armes,   *excellent proved*

30 Ulixes° and Ercules,° that full everrous° were bothe,   *Ulysses Hercules eager for glory*

And other fele° of that ferde° fared of the same   *many company*

As Dittes and Dares[1] demeden° togedir.   *declared*

---

[1] Dictys Cretensis, reputed author of a pro-Greek diary of the Trojan War. What purported to be a Latin translation (fourth century A.D.) of this nonextant work was popular throughout the Middle Ages. Dares Phrygius, a priest in the *Iliad* (V, 9), was the supposed author of a pro-Trojan work translated into Latin in the fifth century A.D., *De Excidio Trojae*.

Alexander

"Aftir this, Sir Alysaunder alle the worlde
wanne,°   *won*

Bothe the see and the sonde° and the sadde° erthe,   *sand solid*

The iles° of the Oryent to Ercules boundes,°   *islands* **Ercules boundes** *Hercules' pillars*

Ther° Ely and Ennoke[1] ever hafe bene sythen,°   *Where since*

5 And to° the come of Antecriste unclosede° be thay   *until released*
never;

And conquered Calcas° knyghtly theraftire   *Colchis*

---

[1] According to widespread belief, Elias and Enoch were staying in an earthly paradise (*iles of the Oryent*) awaiting the coming of the Antichrist, whom they were to oppose.

Ther jentille Jazon° the Grewe wane° the flese of
    golde.
        Ther . . . Where noble Jason
        Grewe wane Greek won

Then grathede° he hym to Gadres° the gates° full
    righte,°
        prepared to go   Gaza   ways
        straight

And there Sir Gadyfere the gude the Gaderayns°
    assemblet
        people of Gaza

10 And rode oute full ryally to rescowe the praye;°   booty

And than Emenyduse° hym mete and made him
    full tame
        Emenidus

And girdes° Gadyfere to the grounde, gronande°
    full sore,
        strikes   groaning

And there that doughty was dede, and mekill dole
    makede.°

    "Then Alixander the emperour, that athell° kyng noble
    hymselven,

15 Arayed hym° for to ryde with the renkes° that he
    hade:
        Arayed hym attired   men

Ther was the mody Meneduse,° a mane of Artage,°
He was duke of that douth° and a dussypere;°
        mody Meneduse pro‹   Emenidus
        Arcadia
        noble company   one of twelve peers

Sir Filot and Sir Florydase, full ferse men of armes;
Sir Clyton and Sir Caulus, knyghtis full noble;

20 And Sir Garsyene the gaye, a gude man of armes;

And Sir Lyncamoure thaym ledys° with a lighte°
    will.
        leads   cheerful

And than Sir Cassamus thaym kepide,° and the
    kyng prayede
        detained

To fare into Fesome° his frendis to helpe,   Epheson

For one Carrus the kynge was comen owte of Inde

25 And hade Fozome affrayede and Fozayne asegede°

For Dame Fozonase° the faire that he of lufe
    bysoughte.
        Fesonas

The kynge agreed hym to goo and graythed° him
    sone
        prepared

In mendys of Amenyduse° that he hade mysdone.
        mendys . . . amends for Emenidus

Then ferde° he towarde Facron° and by the flode
    abydes,°
        went   Phasis River
        flode abydes water stays

30 And there he tighte° up his tentis and taried there a set
    while.

    "There knyghtis full kenely caughten° theire leve **kenely caughten** eagerly took

To fare into Fozayne° Dame Fozonase° to see   Epheson   Fesonas

And Idores and Edease² alle bydene.°
        together

---

13. And there that valiant one (Gadifer) was dead, and Emenidus made great lamentation.
25. And had frightened Fesonas (Gadifer's daughter) and besieged Epheson
² Idores and Edias, daughters of Antigonus and nieces of Fesonas.

And there Sir Porus and his prynces to the poo
    avowede;[3]
35 Was never speche byfore spoken sped° bettir aftir,   *that succeeded*
For als thay demden° to doo thay deden full even.°   *declared* **deden . . . did exactly**
For there Sir Porus the prynce into the prese
    thrynges°   **prese thrynges** *thick of the fight pushes*
And bare the batelle one bake and abaschede thaym
    swythe.°
And than the bolde Bawderayne bowes° to the kyng   *turns*
40 And brayde° owte the brighte brande° owt of the   *drew*   *sword*
    kynges hande,
And Florydase full freschely foundes° hym aftir   **freschely foundes** *keenly hastens*
And hent° the helme of° his hede and the halse°   *takes*   *off*   *neck*
    crakede.
Then Sir Gadefere the gude[4] gripis his axe
And into the Indyans ofte auntirs hym sone,°   **auntirs . . .** *ventures at once*
45 And thaire stiffe standerte to stikkes he hewes.
And than Sir Cassamus the kene° Carrus releves;   *bold*
When he was fallen appon fote, he fet° hym his   *brought*
    stede,
And aftir that Sir Cassamus Sir Carus he drepitt,°   *killed*
And for that poynte° Sir Porus perset° hym to   *deed*   *pierced*
    dethe.
50 And than the Indyans ofte uttire tham droghen°   **uttire . . .** *betook themselves off*
And fledden faste of the felde, and Alexander suede.°   *pursued them*
    "When thay were skaterede and skayled and
    skyftede in sondere,°   **skayled . . .** *dispersed and split asunder*
Alyxandere, oure athell° kyng, ames hym° to   *noble*   **ames hym** *decides*
    lenge°   *tarry*
And fares into Fozayne, festes° to make,   **Fozayne, festes** *Epheson, celebrations*
55 And weddis wy unto wy° that wilnede° togedire.   **wy . . .** *person to person*   *wished to be*
Sir Porus, the pryce° knyghte moste praysed of   *excellent*
    othere,°   **of othere** *by others*
Fonge Fozonase to fere, and fayne° were thay bothe.   **Fonge . . .** *Took Fesonas as his wife and*
The bolde Bawderayne of Baderose, Sir Cassayle   *glad*
    hymselven
Bele° Edyas, the faire birde, bade° he no nother.   *Beautiful*   **birde, bade** *maiden, asked for*
60 And Sir Betys, the beryne° the beste of his tyme,   *knight*
Idores, his awnn lufe, aughte° he hymselven.   **awnn . . .** *own love, obtained*
Then iche lede° hade the love that he hade longe   **iche lede** *each man*
    yernede.

---

[3] 'Made vows to the peacock.' At a banquet where a roast peacock was the chief dish, Porrus vowed to unhorse Emenidus, while his companion Baudrain (l. 39) vowed to disarm Alexander.
38. And forced the battle line back and confounded them quickly.
[4] Sir Gadifer of Epheson, whose father Gadifer of Larris was slain by Emenidus (ll. 11–13, above).

Sir Alixander, oure emperour, ames hym° to ryde   **ames hym** decides
And bewes° towardes Babyloyne with the beryns   turns
     that were levede°   left
65 Bycause of dame Candace that comforthed hym
     moste.
And that cité he bysegede and assayllede it aftire
While° hym the yatis° were yete, and yolden° the   Until   gates   **yete** ... surrendered, and
     keyes.   given up
And there that pereles prynce was puysonede° to   poisoned
     dede;°   death
Thare he was dede of a drynke—as dole es to here—
70 That the curssede Cassander in a cowpe° hym   cup
     broghte.
He conquered with conqueste kyngdomes twelve
And dalte° thaym to his dussypers° when he the   distributed   twelve peers
     dethe tholede,°   suffered
And thus the worthieste of this werlde wente to his
     ende.

Julius Caesar

"Thane Sir Sezere° hymselven that Julyus was   Caesar
     hatten,°   named
Alle Inglande he aughte° at his awnn° will   obtained   own
When the Bruyte in his booke Bretaygne it callede.°
The trewe toure° of Londone in his tyme he   tower
     makede,
5 And craftely the condithe° he compaste° there-   conduit   contrived
     aftire,
And then he droghe hym° to Dovire and dwellyde   **droghe hym** withdrew
     there a while
And closede° ther a castelle with cornells° full heghe,   fortified   battlements
Warnestorede° it full wiesely,° als witnesses the   Provisioned   wisely
     sothe,
For there es hony° in that holde holden sythen° his   honey   **holde** ... stronghold retained since
     tyme.
10 Than rode he into Romayne and rawnsede° it sone,   **Romayne** ... the Roman realm and
And Cassabalount the kynge conquerede there-   ransomed
     aftire.
Then graythed he hym° into Grece and gete° it   **graythed** ... he prepared to go   conquered
     belyve.°   quickly

3. At a time when the Brut (Lawman's *Brut?*) called it Britain (not England).

The semely cité Alexaunder seside° he theraftire;　　**Alexaunder seside** Alexandria seized
Affrike and Arraby and Egipt the noble,
15　Surry and Sessoyne sessede° he togedir,　　**Surry . . .** Syria and Saxony seized
With alle the iles of the see appon iche a syde.
Thies thre were paynymes full priste and passed°　　**paynymes . . .** greatly esteemed pagans
　　alle othire.　　and surpassed

Joshua

"Of thre Jewes full gentill juggen° we aftir,　　**gentill juggen** noble consider
In the Olde Testament as the storye tellis
In a booke of the Bible that breves° of kynges,　　tells
And renkes° that rede kane *Regum*° it callen.　　men　　Kings
5　The firste was gentill Josue that was a Jewe noble,
Was heryet° for his holynes into heven-riche.°　　carried　　the kingdom of heaven
When Pharaoo had flayede° the folkes of Israelle,　　put to flight
Thay ranne into the Rede° See for radde° of　　Red　　fear
　　hymselven,
And than Josue the Jewe Jhesu° he prayede　　to Jesus
10　That the peple myghte passe unpereschede° that　　unharmed
　　tyme,
And than the see sett up appon sydes twayne
In the manere of a mode° walle that made were　　mud
　　with hondes.
And thay soughten° over the see, sownnde,° alle　　went　　sound
　　togedir,
And Pharaoo full fersely followede thaym aftire.
15　And efte° Josue the Jewe Jhesus he prayede,　　again
And the see sattillede° agayne and sanke thaym　　flowed back
　　thereinn—
A soppe for the Sathanas, unsele° have theire bones!　　**Sathanas, unsele** Satan, misfortune
And aftire Josue the Jewe full gentilly hym bere,°　　**gentilly . . .** nobly bore himself
And conquerede kynges and kyngdomes twelve,
20　And was a conqueroure full kene° and most kyd°　　bold　　renowned
　　in his tyme.

David

"Than David the doughty,° thurghe Drightynes　　valiant one
　　sonde,°　　**Drightynes sonde** the Lord's command
Was caughte° from kepyng of schepe and a kyng　　taken
　　made.

The grete grym Golyas° he to grounde broghte — Goliath
And sloughe° hym with his slynge and with no — slew
   sleghte° ells. — skill
5 The stone thurghe his stele helme stong° into his — pierced
   brayne,
And he was dede of that dynt°—the devyll hafe that — blow
   reche!° — **that reche** him who cares
And than was David full dere to Drightyn° hym- — the Lord
   selven
And was a prophete of pryse° and praysed full ofte. — excellence
Bot yit greved he° his God gretely theraftire, — **yit** . . . he still aggrieved
10 For Urye° his awnn° knyghte in aventure° he — Uriah own peril
   wysede° — sent
There° he was dede at° that dede° as dole° es to here; — Where **dede at** dead by deed grief it
For Bersabee his awnn birde° was alle that bale — lady
   rerede.° — **bale rerede** evil brought about

Judas Maccabeus

"The gentill° Judas Machabee was a Jewe kene° — noble bold
And thereto worthy in were° and wyse of his dedis. — war
Antiochus and Appolyne aythere° he drepide,° — both killed
And Nychanore, another kynge, full naytly° — dexterously
   thereaftir,
5 And was a conquerour kydde° and knawen with — renowned
   the beste.
Thies thre were Jewes full joly° and justers full noble — excellent
That full loughe° have bene layde sythen gane° full — low **sythen gane** since there has passed a
   longe tyme;
Of siche doughety° doers looke what es worthen.° — **siche doughety** such valiant become

King Arthur

"Of the thre Cristen to carpe couthely° thereaftir — **carpe couthely** speak knowledgeably
That were conquerours full kene and kyngdomes
   wonnen,
Areste° was Sir Arthure and eldeste of tyme, — First,
For alle Inglande he aughte° at his awnn° will — held own
5 And was kynge of this kythe° and the crowne hade. — country
His courte was at Carlele° comonly holden — Carlisle
With renkes° full ryalle of his rownnde table — knights
That Merlin with° his maystries° made in his tyme, — by powers

And sett the sege° perilous so semely° one highte,   seat   fairly

10 There° no segge° scholde sitt bot hym scholde   Where   man
    schame tyde°   **schame tyde** disgrace befall

Owthir° dethe withinn the thirde daye demed° to   Or   adjudged
    hymselven,

Bot° Sir Galade° the gude that the gree wanne.°   Except for   Galahad   **gree wanne** Grail won

There was Sir Launcelot de Lake full lusty in armes

And Sir Gawayne the gude that never gome°   man
    harmede,

15 Sir Askanore, Sir Ewayne, Sir Errake fytz Lake,

And Sir Kay the kene and kyd of° his dedis,   **kyd of** renowned for

Sir Percevalle de Galeys that preved° had bene ofte,   tested

Mordrede and Bedwere,° men of mekyll° myghte,   Bedivere   great

And othere fele° of that ferde,° folke of the beste.   many   company

20   "Then Roystone the riche kyng, full rakill° of his   rash
    werkes,

He made a blyot to° his bride of° the berdes of   **blyot to** tunic for   from
    kynges

And aughtilde° Sir Arthures berde one scholde be,   intended

Bot Arthure, oure athell° kynge, another° he   noble   otherwise
    thynkes

And faughte with hym in the felde till he was fey
    worthen.°   **was . . .** became fated to die

25 And than Sir Arthure oure kyng ames hym° to   **ames hym** decides
    ryde;

Uppon Sayn Michaells Mounte mervaylles he
    wroghte,

There° a dragone he dreped° that drede was full   Where   killed
    sore.

And than he sayled over the see into sere° londes   various

Whils alle the beryns° of Bretayne bewede hym to   knights
    fote.°   **Bretayne . . .** Brittany knelt at his feet

30 Gascoyne and Gyane° gatt he thereaftir   Guienne

And conquered kyngdomes and contrees full fele.°   many

  "Then ames he into Inglonde into his awnn
    kythe;°   **awnn kythe** own country

The gates° towardes Glassthenbery° full graythely°   ways   Glastonbury   at once
    he rydes,

And ther Sir Mordrede hym mett by a more syde°   **by . . .** beside a moor

35 And faughte with hym in the felde to° alle were fey   until
    worthen°   **were . . .** became fated to die

Bot° Arthur oure athell° kyng and Wawayne° his   Except   noble   Gawain
    knyghte.

And when the felde was flowen and fey bot°   **flowen ...** fled and fated except for
    thaymselven,
Than Arthure Sir Wawayne athes° by his trouthe   makes swear
That he swiftely his swerde scholde swynge° in the   hurl
    mere,°   sea
40 And whatt selcouthes° he see° the sothe scholde   marvels   might see
    he telle.
And Sir Wawayne swith° to the swerde and   went quickly
    swange° it in the mere,   hurled
And ane hande by the hiltys hastely it grippes
And brawndeschet that brighte swerde and bere it
    awaye.
And Wawayne° wondres of this werke and wendes   Gawain
    bylyve°   **wendes bylyve** goes quickly
45 To his lorde there° he hym lefte and lokes abowte,   where
And he ne wiste° in alle this werlde where he was   knew
    bycomen.°   gone
And then he hyghes hym° in haste and hedis to the   **hyghes hym** hurries
    mere°   sea
And seghe° a bote from the banke and beryns   saw
    thereinn.
Thereinn was Sir Arthure and othire of his ferys°   companions
50 And also Morgn la Faye that myche couthe° of   **myche couthe** knew much
    sleghte,°   cunning
And there ayther segge seghe othir laste,° for sawe   **ayther ...** each man saw the other for
    he hym no more.   the last time

Godfrey of Bouillon

"Sir Godfraye de Bolenn siche° grace of God   such
    hade
That alle Romanye he rode and rawnnsunte it
    sone.°
The Amorelle of Antyoche aftire he drepit°   killed
That was called Corborant, kilwarde° of dedis.   treacherous
5 And aftir he was callede kynge and the crownn hade
Of Jerusalem and of the Jewes gentill° togedir,   noble
And with the wirchipe of this werlde he went to his
    ende.

2. That he rode over the whole Roman realm and put it to ransom at once.

Charlemagne

"Than was Sir Cherlemayne chosen chefe kynge
  of Fraunce,
With his doghty doussypers,° to do als hym   **doghty doussypers** valiant twelve peers
  lykede:°   **als . . .** as he pleased
Sir Rowlande the riche and Duke Raynere of
  Jene,°   Genoa
Olyver and Aubrye and Ogere Deauneys,°   **Ogere Deauneys** Ogier the Dane
5 And Sir Naymes at the nede that never wolde
  fayle,
Turpyn and Terry, two full tryed° lordes,   valiant
And Sir Sampsone hymselfe of the Mounte Ryalle,
Sir Berarde de Moundres, a bold beryn in armes,
And gud Sir Gy de Burgoyne, full gracyous of
  dedis.
10 The katur fitz Emowntez° were kydde° knyghtes   **katur . . .** four sons of Aymon   renowned
  alle,
And other moo° than I may myne° or any man   more   remember
  elles.°   else
  "And then Sir Cherlles° the chefe ches° for to   Charlemagne   chose
  ryde
And paste towardes Polborne° to proven his   Paderborn (Saxony)
  strenghte.
Salamadyne the Sowdane° he sloghe° with his   Sultan   slew
  handis,
15 And that cité he bysegede and saylede° it full ofte   attacked
While° hym his yernynge° was yett° and the yates°   Until   wish   granted   gates
  opynede,
And Witthyne° thaire waryed° kynge wolde nott   Widukind   accursed
  abyde°   stay
Bot soghte° into Sessoyne socoure° hym to gete,   went   **Sessoyne socoure** Saxony help
And Cherlemayne, oure chefe kynge, cheses° into   goes
  the burgh,°   town
20 And dame Nioles anone he name° to hymselven   took
And maried hir to Maundevyle that scho hade
  myche° lovede,   greatly
And spedd hym into hethyn Spayne spedely
  thereaftire
And fittilled hym° by Flagott° faire for to loge.° **fittilled hym** prepared   the Flagot River
  "There Olyver the everous aunterede hymselven°   dwell
                                                      everous . . . eager for glory ventured
25 And faughte with Sir Ferambrace and fonge° hym   took
  one were,°   **one were** in battle
And than they fologhed° hym in a fonte and   baptized
  Florence hym callede.

And than moved he hym to Mawltryple Sir
    Balame to seche,°   seek

And that Emperour at Egremorte aftir he takes

And wolde hafe made Sir Balame a man of oure
    faythe,

30 And garte feche° forthe a founte byfore-with° his   had brought   before
    eghne,°   eyes

And he dispysede it and spitte and spournede it to
    the erthe,

And one° swyftely with a swerde swapped of° his   a man   **swapped of** chopped off
    hede.

And Dame Floripe the faire was cristened there-
    aftire

And kende° thaym to the corownne that Criste had   guided
    one hede

35 And the nayles, anone, nayttly° thereaftire,   properly

When He with passyoun and pyne° was naylede   torture
    one the rode.°   cross

And than those relikes so riche redely he takes,

And at Sayne Denys[1] he thaym dide° and dwellyd   put
    there for ever.

    "And than bod-worde° unto Merchill full boldly   message
    he sendys

40 And bade hym Cristyne bycome and one° Criste   in
    leve°   believe

Or he scholde bette° doun his borowes and brenn°   beat   **borowes . . .** towns and burn
    hym thereinn,

And garte Genyone goo° that erande that grevede   **garte . . .** made Ganelon go on
    thaym alle.

Than rode he to Rowncyvale, that rewed hym°   **rewed hym** he regretted
    aftire,

There° Sir Rowlande, the ryche Duke, refte° was   Where   bereft of
    his lyfe,

45 And Olyver, his awnn fere,° that ay° had bene   comrade   ever
    trewe,

And Sir Turpyn the trewe that full triste° was at   trusty
    nede,

And full fele othir folke, als ferly were elles.°   **als . . .** who were otherwise as wonderful

Then suede° he the Sarazenes seven yere and more,   pursued

And the Sowdane° at Saragose full sothely° he   Sultan   **full sothely** indeed
    fyndis,

50 And there he bett° down the burghe,° and Sir   beat   town
    Merchill he tuke,

---

[1] St. Denis, north of Paris, where Charlemagne rebuilt the church of St. Denis, in which he was later buried.

And that daye he dide hym to the dethe als he had
   wele servede.°   deserved
   "Bot by than his wyes° were wery and woundede   men
   full many,
And he fared into France to fongen° thaire riste°   take   rest
And neghede° towarde Nerbone,° that noyede°   neared   Narbonne   grieved
   thaym full sore,
55 And that cité he asseggede° appone sere halves°   besieged   **sere halves** various sides
While° hym the yates° were yette and yolden°   Until   gates   **yette . . .** surrendered and
   the keyes,   given up
And Emorye° made Emperour even at that tyme,   Aymeri of Narbonne
To kepe it and to holde it to hym and to his ayers.°   heirs
And then thay ferden° into Fraunce to fongen°   went   take
   thaire ese,
60 And at Sayn Denys he dyede, at his dayes tyme.
   "Now hafe I nevened° yow the names of nyne of   named
   the beste
That ever were in this werlde wiste° appon erthe   known
And the doghtyeste° of dedis in thaire dayes tyme,   most valiant
Bot doghetynes,° when dede° comes, ne dare   valiance   death
   noghte habyde.°   **ne . . .** dare not remain

Wise Men

   "Of wyghes° that were wyseste will ye now here,   men
And I schall schortly yow schewe and schutt me°   **schutt me** conclude
   ful sone.
Arestotle he was arste° in Alexander° tyme,   first   Alexander's
And was a fyne philozophire and a fynour° noble,   refiner of metal
5 The° grete Alexander to graythe° and gete golde   For the   prepare
   when hym liste,°   **hym liste** he pleased
And multiplye metalles with mercurye watirs
And with his ewe ardaunt° and arsneke pouders,   **ewe ardaunt** ardent spirit (alcohol)
With salpetir and sal-jeme° and siche° many othire,   crystal salt   such
And menge° his metalles and make fyne silvere,   mix
10 And was a blaunchere° of the best thurgh blaste of   alchemist who whitens metals
   his fyre.
   "Then Virgill, thurgh his vertus,° verrayle he   powers
   maket°   caused
Bodyes of brighte brasse full boldely to speke,
To telle whate betydde° had and whate betyde°   happened   happen
   scholde,

When Dioclesyane was dighte° to be dere°   ordained   noble
　emperour;
15 Of Rome and of Romanye the rygalté° he hade.   sovereignty
　"Than Sir Salomon hymselfe sett hym by hym
　one.°   **hymselfe** . . . sat down by himself
　His Bookes in the Bible bothe bene togedirs;
　That one° of wisdome and of witte wondirfully   **That one** The one (Ecclesiastes)
　teches;
　His sampills° and his sawes bene sett in the tother.°   parables   other (Proverbs)
20 And he was the wyseste in witt that ever wonnede°   dwelled
　in erthe,
　And his techynges will bene trowede° whills the   believed
　werlde standes
　Bothe with° kynges and knyghtis and kaysers°   by   emperors
　therinn.
　　"Merlyn was a mervayllous man and made many
　　thynges,
　And naymely nygromancye nayttede° he ofte   **naymely** . . . especially necromancy
　25 And graythed° Galyan¹ a boure° to gete hyr   practiced
　therin   prepared   bower
　That no wy° scholde hir wielde° ne wynne from   man   possess
　hymselven.
　Theis were the wyseste in the worlde of witt that
　　ever yitt were,
　Bot dethe wondes° for no witt to wende were hym   hesitates
　lykes.°   **wende** . . . go where he pleases

¹ *Galyan* is obscure; see *Nynyve* in Malory; *Niviene* in Old French *Merlin; Vivien* in Tennyson.

Famous Lovers

　"Now of the prowdeste in presse° that   **prowdeste** . . . noblest in battle
　paramoures loveden
　I schalle titly° yow telle and tary° yow no lengere.   quickly   delay
　Amadase and Edoyne,¹ in erthe are thay bothe,
　That in golde and in grene were gaye in thaire
　　tyme.
5 And Sir Sampsone hymselfe, full savage of his dedys,
　And Dalyda° his derelynge,° now dethe has tham   Delilah   darling
　bothe.

¹ Amadas and Idoine, famous hero and heroine of French romance, first mentioned in Middle English in
the *Love Rune* of Thomas of Hailes (p. 158).

Sir Ypomadonn de Poele,[2] full priste° in his armes,　　quick
The faire Fere° de Calabre, now faren° are they　　Proud One　gone
　　bothe.
Generides[3] the gentill,° full joly° in his tyme,　　noble　fair
10　And Clarionas, that was so clere,° are bothe now　　beautiful
　　bot erthe.
Sir Eglamour of Artas, full everous° in armes,　　eager for glory
And Cristabelle the clere maye° es crept in hir grave.　　maid
And Sir Tristrem the trewe, full triste° of hym-　　trusty
　　selven,
And Ysoute, his awnn lufe, in erthe are thay bothe.
15　Whare es now Dame Dido was° qwene of Cartage,　　who was
Dame Candace, the comly, was called quene of
　　Babyloyne?
Penelopie, that was price° and pasten° alle othere　　excellent　surpassed
And Dame Gaynore° the gaye, nowe graven° are　　Guinevere　buried
　　thay bothen,
And othere moo° than I may mene° or any man　　more　tell
　　elles.°　　else
20　"Sythen doughtynes° when dede° comes ne dare　　**Sythen doughtynes** Since valiance
　　noghte habyde,°　　death
　　　　ne... dare not remain
Ne dethe wondes° for no witt to wende where hym　　**Ne...** And death doesn't hesitate
　　lykes,°　　**wende...** go where he pleases
And thereto paramours and pride puttes he full
　　lowe,
Ne there es reches° ne rent may° rawnsone your　　**Ne...** Nor are there riches　which can
　　lyves,
Ne noghte es sekire° to youreselfe in certayne bot　　assured
　　dethe,
25　And he es so uncertayne that sodaynly he comes.
Me thynke° the wele° of this werlde worthes° to　　**Me thynke** It seems to me　wealth
　　noghte.　　turns
Ecclesiastes the clerke declares in his booke
Vanitas vanitatum et omnia vanitas,°
That alle es vayne and vanytés, and vanyté es alle.
30　Forthi amendes° youre mysse° whills ye are men　　**Forthi amendes** Therefore reform　sins
　　here,
Quia in inferno nulla est redempcio,°
For in helle es no helpe, I hete° yow for sothe.°　　promise　**for sothe** indeed

---

[2] Ipomadon of Apulia after numerous adventures married the Duke of Calabria's daughter, known only
as La Fière, The Proud One of Calabria. Three Middle English versions of the Anglo-Norman romance
are extant.
[3] Generides and Clarionas, protagonists of a romance that survives in two late Middle English versions.
28. Vanity of vanities and all is vanity (Eccles. 1:2; 12:8)
31. Because in hell there is no redemption (free paraphrase, Job 7:9)

Als God in his gospelle graythely° yow teches,   fittingly
Ite ostendite vos sacerdotibus,°
35 To schryve yow full schirle° and schewe yow to   completely
    prestis.
Et ecce omnia munda sunt vobis,°
And ye that wronge wroghte° schall worthen° full   did   become
    clene.
    "Thou man in thi medill elde,° have mynde   middle age
    whate I saye.
I am thi sire and thou my sone, the sothe for to telle,
40 And he the sone of thiselfe that sittis one the stede,°   steed
For Elde° es sire of Midill-Elde, and Midill-Elde of   Age
    Youthe.
    "And haves gud daye, for now I go; to grave
    moste me wende;°   **moste** . . . I must go
Dethe dynges° one my dore; I dare no lengare   knocks
    byde."°   remain

Epilogue

When I had lenged and layne a full longe while,
I herde a bogle° one a bonke be blowen full lowde,   bugle
And I wakkened therwith and waytted° me umbe.°   looked   around
Than the sone was sett and syled° full loughe,°   sunk   low
5 And I founded° appon fote and ferkede° towarde   hastened   hurried
    townn.
And in the monethe of Maye thies mirthes° me   delights
    tydde°   befell
Als I schurtted° me in a schelfe° in the schawes°   amused   bank   thickets
    faire,
And belde me° in the birches with bewes° full smale,   **belde me** built myself a blind   boughs
And lugede° me in the leves, that lighte were and   sheltered
    grene.
10 There, dere Drightyne,° this daye dele° us of thi   Lord   give
    blysse,
And Marie that es mylde qwene amende° us of synn.   reform
    Amen. Amen.

---

34. Go show yourselves to the priests (Luke 17:14)
36. And behold all the world is yours (free paraphrase, Luke 17:21)

Morte Arthure

(c. 1360, originally Northwest Midland?)

⤫

The *Alliterative Morte Arthure* is a stirring epic dealing first with Arthur's attempt to win the mastery of the western world by conquering the Emperor of Rome and his tragic overthrow, brought about by the treachery of Mordred. It freely adapts the materials in Wace's Anglo-Norman version of Geoffrey of Monmouth's *History of the Kings of Britain*. A cohesive work written in the alliterative tradition of Lawman's earlier *Brut* (p. 49), the *Morte Arthure* is best known today for a number of brilliant passages—the banquet (ll. 167–230), Arthur's farewell to Guinevere (ll. 695–716), his dream (ll. 756–831), his slaying of the giant (ll. 941–1221), and his final battle with Mordred (ll. 4154–346, printed below). In each of these passages the unknown author displays his mastery not only of the plastic medium of his verse but also of his subject, in his rich profusion of specific details, in his heroic concept of Arthur's grandeur, and in his emphasis on the tragic workings of fate.

The first half of the poem, dealing with Arthur's defeat of the Roman Emperor Lucius, provided the basis for Malory's *The Tale of the Noble King Arthur That Was Emperor Himself* (*Works*, ed. Eugene Vinaver, Oxford, 1959), which appears as Book V in Caxton's version.

The poem is written in conventional alliterative verse; see Introduction, type 1, page 29.

The text of the *Morte Arthure* was edited by E. Brock, EETS 8 (London, 1871), by Mary M. Banks (London, 1900), and by Erich Björkman (London, 1915). A modernization appears in Andrew Boyle, *Morte Arthure*, ed. Lucy A. Paton (London, 1912). For bibliography see Sever, ch. 1.16.

[Lines 4154–346]

Than remys° the riche kynge with rewthe° at his herte, — cries out   pity

Hevys° hys handys one heghte,° and to the hevene lokes: — Raises   on high

"Qwhythene hade Dryghttyne destaynede° at his dere wille — **Qwhythene ...** O that the Lord had destined

That he hade demyd° me todaye to dy for yow alle. — ordained

5 That had I lever° than be lorde alle my lyfe tyme — rather

Off alle that Alexandere aughte qwhilles° he in erthe lengede."° — **aughte qwhilles** owned while / stayed

Sir Ewayne and Sir Errake, thes excellente beryns,° — men

Enters in one° the oste,° and egerly strykes. — **Enters ...** Enter together   host

The ethenys° of Orkkenaye and Irische kynges, — giants

264

10 Thay gobone° of the gretteste with growndene°   strike down   sharpened
     swerdes,
     Hewes one° thas hulkes with theire harde wapyns,   on
     Layed downe thas ledes° with lothely dynttys.°   men   **lothely dynttys** horrible blows
     Schuldirs and scheldys thay schrede° to the hawnches,°   slashed   hips
     And medilles° thourghe mayles° thay merkene in   waists   mail armor
     sondire.°   **merkene . . .** cut asunder
15 Siche° honoure never aughte° none erthely kyng   Such   owned
     At theire endyng daye, bot Arthure hyme selvene.
     So the droughte° of the daye dryede° their hertes,   dryness   made to suffer
     That bothe drynkles they dye. Dole° was the more.   Sorrow
       Now mellys° oure medillewarde,° and mengene°   joins   center   mixes
     togedire.
20 Sir Mordrede the Malebranche with his myche pöple°   **myche pöple** great people
     He had hide hyme behynde within thas holte eynys,°   **thas . . .** that wood's narrow passages
     With halle bataile one hethe, harme° es the more.   **halle . . .** whole army on the heath,
         suffering
     He hade sene the conteke° al clene to the ende,   strife
     How oure chevalrye chevyde be° chaunces of armes.   **chevyde be** prevailed by
25 He wiste° oure folke was forfoughttene° that thare   knew   weary of fighting
     was feye levede.°   **feye levede** fated to be left dead
     To encowntere the kynge he castes hyme sone,°   **castes . . .** determines at once
     Bot the churles chekyne° hade chaungyde his armes.   **churles chekyne** churlish chicken
     He had sothely forsakene° the sawturoure engrelede,[1]   **sothely forsakene** truly abandoned
     And laughte° upe thre lyons alle of whitte silvyre,   taken
30 Passande° in purpre° of perrie fulle° riche,   Surpassing   purple   **perrie fulle**
         precious stones very
     Ffor° the kynge sulde° noghte knawe the cawtelous°   So that   should   cunning
     wriche.
     Because of his cowardys he keste of° his atyre,   off
     Bot the comliche° kyng knewe hym fulle swythe;°   comely   quickly
     Karpis° to Sir Cadors thes kyndly wordez: Speaks
35 "I see the traytoure come yondyr trynande° fulle   proceeding
     yerne;°   eagerly
     Yone° ladde with the lyones es like to hyme selfene.   Yonder
     Hym salle torfere betyde,° may I touche ones,°   **Hym . . .** Harm shall befall him   once
     Ffor alle his tresone and trayne, alls° I am trew lorde.   **trayne, alls** trickery, as
     Today Clarente and Caliburne[2] salle kythe° theme   show
     togedirs
40 Whilke° es kenere of kerfe° or hardare of eghge.   Which sword   cutting
     Ffraiste° sall we fyne stele appone fyne wedis.°   Test   garments
     Itt° was my derlynge daynteuous and fulle° dere   It (the steel sword)   very
     holdene,°   held

[1] The 'engrailed saltire' is Mordred's usual coat of arms, consisting of the saltire, a device similar to the St. Andrew's cross, which is engrailed, or drawn with an edge ornamented with a series of concave indentations.

[2] King Arthur carried Caliburne; Mordred carried Clarente, which he had stolen with Guinevere's help from Arthur's effects.

Kepede fore encorownmentes° of kynges enoynttede.   coronations
One° dayes when I dubbyde dukkes and erlles,   On
45 It was burliche° borne be° the bryghte hiltes.   grandly by
I durste never dere° it in dedis of armes,   injure
Bot ever kepide clene because° of my selvene.   for the sake
Ffor I see Clarent unclede,° that crowne es of swerdes,   unsheathed
My wardrop° of Walyngfordhe I wate° es distroyede.   wardrobe know
50 Wist no wy° of wone° bot Waynor° hir selvene;   Wist ... No man knew dwelling Guinevere
Schö hade the kepynge hir selfe of that kydde° wapyne,   renowned
Off° cofres enclosede that to the crowne lengede,°   Of belonged
With rynges and relikkes and the regale° of Ffraunce,   crown jewels
That was ffowndene one° Sir Ffrolle, whene he was   on
feye levyde."°   feye levyde left dead
55   Than Sir Marrike in malyncoly metys hym sone,°   at once
With a mellyd° mace myghtyly hym strykes.   hammerheaded
The bordoure of his badenett° he bristes in sondire°   steel cap bristes ... bursts asunder
That the schire° rede blode over his brene° rynnys.   bright cuirass (breast armor)
The beryne blenkes° for bale,° and alle his ble°   beryne blenkes man flinches pain
chaunges,   color
60 Bot yitt he byddys° as a bore, and brymly° he strykes.   stands firm bore ... boar, and fiercely
He braydes° owte a brande,° bryghte als° ever ony   draws sword as
sylver,
That was Sir Arthure° awene, and Utere his fadirs,   Arthur's
In the wardrop° of Walyngfordhe was wonte to be   wardrobe
kepede.
Tharewith the derfe° dogge syche° dynttes he rechede,°   stout such gave
65 The tother withdrewe one dreghe° and durste do none   one dreghe aside
other;
Ffor Sir Marrake was mane merrede in elde,°   mane ... man marred by age
And Sir Mordrede was myghty and in his moste
strenghis.
Come none within the compas, knyghte ne none other,
Within the swyng of swerde, that ne he the swete
levyd.°   that ... who left not his life
70   That persayfes° oure prynce, and presses to° faste,   perceives presses to hurries there
Strykes into the stowre° by strenghe of hys handis,   battle
Metis with Sir Mordrede; he melis unfaire:°   melis unfaire speaks harshly
"Turne, traytoure untrewe, thee tydys no bettyre.°   thee ... no better shall befall you
Be° gret Gode, thow salle° dy with dynt of my handys.   By shall
75 Thee schalle rescowe no renke ne reches° in erthe."   renke ... man nor wealth
The kyng with Calaburne knyghtly hym strykes;
The cantelle° of the clere° schelde he kerfes in sondyre°   corner bright in sondyre asunder
Into the schuldyre of the schalke° a schaftmonde large,°   man schaftmonde large a half-foot deep
That the schire° rede blode schwede° on the maylys.°   bright showed mail
80 He° schodirde and schrenkys and schontes° bot lyttille,   He (Mordred) turns aside

Bott schokkes° in scharpely in his schene wedys.°   jumps   **schene wedys** bright garments (armor)

The ffelonne with the ffyne swerde freschely he strykes;

The ffelettes° of the fferere° syde he flassches in sondyre°   fillets   farther   **flassches** . . . rips asunder

Thorowe jopowne and jesserawnte³ of gentille mailes.°   **gentille mailes** noble mail

85   The freke fichede° in the flesche an halfe fotte large.°   **freke fichede** man pierced   deep

That derfe° dynt was his dede,° and dole was the more   stout   **his dede** his (Arthur's) death

That ever that doughtty sulde° dy, bot at Dryghttyns° wylle.   **doughtty sulde** valiant one should   Lord's

     Yitt° with Calyburne his swerde, fulle knyghtly he strykes,   Once more

Kastes ine° his clere° schelde, and coveres him fulle° faire,   **Kastes ine** Draws on   bright   very

90   Swappes of° the swerde hande, als° he by glentes;°   **Swappes of** Strikes off   as   **by glentes** glides by

Ane inche fro the elbowe he ochede° it in sondyre,°   hacked   **in sondyre** asunder

That he° swounnes one° the swarthe° and one swym° fallis—   he (Mordred)   on   sward   faint

Thorowe bracer° of browne stele and the bryghte mayles,°   brassart (arm piece)   mail

That the hilte and the hande appone the hethe ligges.°   lie

95   Thane frescheliche the freke the ffente upe rererys,°

Brochis hym° in with the bronde° to the bryghte hiltys,   **Brochis hym** Stabs him (Mordred)   sword

And he brawles one° the bronde, and bownes° to dye.   **brawles one** sprawls on   prepares

"In faye,"° says the feye° kynge, "sore me forthynkkes   faith   dying

That ever siche° a false theefe so faire an ende haves."   such

100   Qwene° they had ffenyste° this feghte, thane wai the felde wonnene,°   When   finished   won

And the false folke in the felde feye° are bylevede.°   dead   left

Tille° a fforeste they fledde and felle in the grevys,°   Into   groves

And fers feghtande folke folowes theme aftyre,

Howntes° and hewes downe the heythene tykes,°   Hunt   dogs

105   Mourtherys° in the mowntaygnes Sir Mordrede° knyghtes.   Murder   Mordred's

Thare chapyde° never no childe,° cheftayne, ne other,   escaped   man

Bot choppes theme downe in the chace—it chargys° bot littyle.   matters

     Bot whene Sir Arthure anone° Sir Ewayne he fyndys,   next

And Errake the Avenaunt,° and other grett lordes,   Graceful

³ 'Jupon,' a padded tunic, and 'jazeran,' velvet over iron on canvas, the whole ornamented with brass studs.

95. Then briskly the man (Arthur) raises up the flap (*ffente*, covering the slit in Mordred's coat of mail)

110 He kawghte up Sir Cador with care° at his herte,　　sorrow
　　　Sir Clegis, Sir Cleremonde, thes clere° mene of armes,　illustrious
　　　Sir Lothe and Sir Lyonelle, Sir Lawncelott, and Lowes,
　　　Marrake and Meneduke, that myghty ware ever.
　　　With langoure° in the launde° thare he layes theme　sorrow　field
　　　　togedire,
115 Lokede one° theyre lighames,° and with a lowde　on　bodies
　　　　stevene,°　　voice
　　　Alls lede° that liste° noghte lyfe and loste had his　**Alls lede** As a man　desired
　　　　myrthis,
　　　Than he stotays for made,° and alle his strenghe faylez,　**stotays** . . . becomes dizzy from
　　　　　madness
　　　Lokes upe to the lyfte,° and alle his lyre° chaunges.　sky　countenance
　　　Downne he sweys fulle swythe,° and in a swoune　**sweys** . . . sways very quickly
　　　　fallys;
120 Upe he coveris° one kneys° and kryes fulle oftene:　gets　his knees
　　　　"Kyng comly with crowne, in care° am I levyde.°　grief　left
　　　Alle my lordschipe lawe° in lande es layde undyre　low
　　　That has me gyfene gwerdones be° grace of hym　**gwerdones be** rewards by
　　　　selvene,°　**hym selvene** themselves
　　　Mayntenyde my manhede be myghte of theire handes,
125 Made me manly one molde° and mayster in erthe.　earth
　　　In a tenefulle° tyme this torfere was rereryde°　grievous　**torfere** . . . harm arose
　　　That for° a traytoure has tynte° alle my trewe lordys.　because of　lost
　　　Here rystys the riche blude of the Rownde Table,
　　　Rebukkede with a rebawde, and rewthe° es the more.　**rebawde** . . . rascal, and pity
130 I may helples one hethe house by myne one°　**house** . . . dwell by myself
　　　Alls° a wafulle wedowe that wanttes° hir beryne.°　As　lacks　lord
　　　I may werye° and wepe and wrynge myne handys,　curse
　　　Ffor my wytt and my wyrchipe° awaye es for ever.　honor
　　　Off alle lordchips I take leve to myne ende.
135 Here es the Bretones° blode broughte owt of lyfe,　Britons'
　　　And nowe in this journee alle my joy endys."
　　　　Thane relyes° the renkes° of alle the Rownde Table;　rally　men
　　　To the ryalle roy° thay ride tham alle.　king
　　　Than assembles fulle sonne sevene score knyghtes
140 In sighte to thaire soverayne, that was unsownde
　　　　levede.°　**unsownde levede** left unwell
　　　Than knelis the crownede kynge and kryes one
　　　　lowde:°　**one lowde** aloud
　　　　"I thanke thee, Gode, of thy grace, with a gud wylle,
　　　That gafe us vertue and witt to vencows° this beryns°　vanquish　men
　　　And us has grauntede the gree° of theis gret lordes.　ascendancy
145 He sent us never no schame ne schenchipe° in erthe　disgrace
　　　Bot ever yit the overhande of° alle other kynges.　**overhande of** mastery over
　　　We hafe no laysere° now these lordys to seke,　leisure

Ffor yone laythely° ladde me lamede so sore.	**yone laythely** yonder loathsome
Graythe° us to Glaschenbery;° us gaynes° none other;	Take Glastonbury avails
150 Thare we may ryste° us with roo and raunsake° oure wondys.	rest **roo . . .** peace and search
Of this dere day° werke, the Dryghttene° be lovede°	day's Lord praised
That us has destaynede° and demyd to dye in oure awene."°	destined own land
Thane they holde at° his heste hally° at ones	**holde at** fulfill **heste hally** request wholly
And graythes to Glasschenberye the gate° at the gayneste;°	road nearest
155 Entres the Ile of Aveloyne, and Arthure he lyghttes,°	alights
Merkes° to a manere° there, for myghte° he no forthire.	Goes manor could go
A surgyne of Salerne° enserches his wondes.	Salerno
The kyng sees by asaye° that sownde bese° he never,	examination will be
And sone to his sekire° mene he said theis wordes:	trusty
160 "Do calle me a confessour, with Criste in his arms;	
I wille be howselde° in haste, whate happe° so betyddys.°	**be howselde** receive the host **whate happe** whatever fortune befalls
Constantyne my cosyne he salle° the corowne bere,	shall
Alls becommys him of kynde,° yife Criste wille hym thole.°	nature permit
Beryne,° fore my benysone,° thowe berye yone° lordys	Man blessing **berye yone** bury yonder
165 That in baytaille with brondez° are broghte owte of lyfe;	swords
And sythene merke° manly to Mordrede childrene,°	**sythene merke** then go **Mordrede childrene** Mordred's men
That they bee sleghely° slayne and slongene° in watyrs.	cunningly slung
Latt no wykkyde wede° waxe ne wrythe° one this erthe.	**wykkyde wede** evil weed turn
I warne for thy wirchipe, wirke° alls I bydde.	do
170 I foregyffe° alle greffe° for Cristez lufe of hevene.	forgive injury
Yife Waynor° hafe wele wroghte, wele hir betydde."°	Guinevere befall
He saide In manus° with mayne° one molde° whare he ligges,°	**In manus** Into thy hands strength earth lies
And thus passes his speryt, and spekes he no more.	
The baronage of Bretaygne° thane, bechopes, and othire	Britain
175 Graythes theme° to Glaschenbery, with gloppynnande° hertes,	**Graythes theme** Go terror-struck
To bery thare the bolde kynge and brynge to the erthe	
With alle wirchipe and welthe that any wy° scholde.	man
Throly° belles thay rynge and *Requiem* syngys,	Fervently
Dosse° messes and matyns with mournande notes.	Sing
180 Relygeous reveste° in theire riche copes,	dressed
Pontyficalles and prelates in precyouse wedys,°	garments

Dukes and dusszeperis° in theire dule-cotes,°   peers   mourning coats
Cowntasses knelande and claspande theire handes,
Ladys languessande and lowrande° to schewe°—   looking sad   appear
185   Alle was buskede° in blake, birdes° and othire,   **was buskede** were dressed   ladies
That schewede at the sepulture, with sylande° teris.   flowing
Whas never so sorowfulle a syghte seene in theire
     tyme.
Thus endis Kyng Arthure, as auctors alegges,
That was of Ectores blude, the kynge sone of Troye,
190   And of Sir Pryamous,° the prynce, praysede in erthe.   **Sir Pryamous** King Priam's
Ffro thethene° broghte the Bretons° alle his bolde   thence   Britons
     eldyrs
Into Bretaygne° the brode, as the *Bruytte*° tellys.   Britain   Lawman's *Brut*

JOHN BARBOUR

The Bruce

(1375, Northern)

John Barbour was born about 1316, studied at Aberdeen and Oxford and probably also in France, and became an archdeacon of Aberdeen. He received various emoluments from King Robert II, presumably as a reward for his having undertaken the writing of *The Bruce*. He died in Aberdeen in 1395.

The Bruce, which Barbour completed in 1375, is a verse chronicle of more than 13,500 lines in length. It has two main heroes: King Robert the Bruce, who was born in 1274, crowned in 1306, and died in 1329, and his faithful supporter Sir James Douglas (1286–1330), who was called "The Good Douglas" by the Scots and "The Black Douglas" by the English. In a brief prologue Barbour outlines the attempts of King Edward I to control Scotland by his support of the claims of John de Balliol (1249–1315) against Bruce; in the following twenty books he recounts how Bruce decided to win the crown of Scotland, how he led his country to ultimate victory against the English at the battle of Bannockburn (1314), how he died, and how Douglas perished during a vain attempt to carry the heart of Bruce to the Holy Land. Perhaps out of consideration for his royal patron, Robert II (Bruce's grandson), Barbour concludes his work at the year 1332 and thus has no occasion to mention the Battle of Halidon Hill (see p. 231, above) and other subsequent disasters.

Barbour was well qualified for the task he undertook. He was familiar with all the appropriate Biblical, classical, and medieval models, and he had interviewed many informants of the older generation who had personally witnessed the events he described. *The Bruce* is well organized. Centered as it is on Bruce as the defender of liberty and Douglas as the exemplar of loyalty, it possesses a thematic unity seldom found in medieval chronicles. Yet, even if it transcends the chronicle, it is admittedly something less than an epic.

The selections printed below reveal both the strength and the weakness of *The Bruce*. The author's eloquent praise of freedom is related to the central problem of Scottish history. Presumably he remembered the argument of the Scottish Declaration of Independence (composed in Latin at Arbroath in 1320) and was inspired in particular by the noble passage within it, which the anonymous framer had drawn from Sallust:

> So long as a hundred of us are left alive, we will not yield in the slightest way to English domination. We do not fight for glory or wealth or honors; we fight solely for freedom, which no honest man will surrender excepting with his life.

But, not content with the validity of his own adaptation, Barbour spoils the effect by raising a scholarly quibble about the true definition of freedom. He boldly compares his hero, Douglas, to Hector but then gratuitously asserts the superiority of Hector. He recounts Bruce's speech at Bannockburn, presumably using his own imagination, since he was writing sixty-one years after the event, but he provides his hero with a very calm, low-keyed, common-sensical rhetoric. Seldom has a poet been so inhibited by his concern for plain fact. Yet, perhaps because of its very unpretentiousness, *The Bruce* is still cherished as Scotland's national epic. The meter is rhyming couplets; see Introduction, type 5, page 31.

The best edition is *Barbour's Bruce*, ed. W. W. Skeat, STS 31–33 (Edinburgh, 1894). As a dictionary use *DOST*. A good modernization is John Barbour, *The Bruce*, trans. A. A. H. Douglas (Glasgow, 1964). For bibliography see Wells, ch. 3.8; *CBEL*, 1.166–67, 5.118.

The Author's Prologue

[I, 1–36]

	Storyss to rede ar delitabill,°	delightful
	Supposs° that thai be nocht° bot fabill.°	Even supposing nothing fable
	Than suld° storyss that suthfast° wer,	should truthful
	And° thai war said° on gud maner,	If told
5	Have doubill plesance in heryng.	
	The fyrst plesance is the carpyng,°	recital
	And the tothir° the suthfastnes	second
	That schawys° the thing rycht as it wes;	portrays
	And suth° thyngis that ar likand°	true pleasing
10	Tyll° mannys heryng ar plesand.	To
	Tharfor I wald fayne set my will,	
	Giff° my wyt mycht suffice thartill,°	If thereto
	To put in wryt° a suthfast story	writing
	That it lest ay furth° in memory,	**lest** . . . may last evermore
15	Swa° that na lenth of tyme it let°	So impede
	Na ger° it haly° be foryet.°	**Na ger** Nor cause wholly to forgotten
	For aulde storys that men redys°	read
	Representis° to thaim the dedys	Portray
	Of stalwart folk that lyvyt ar°	**lyvyt ar** lived before
20	Rycht as° thai than in presence war.	**Rycht as** Just as if
	And, certis, thai suld weill have pryss°	esteem
	That in thar tyme war wycht° and wyss,	brave
	And led thar lyff in gret travaill,	
	And oft in hard stour off° bataill	**stour off** combat of
25	Wan richt gret price° off chevalry,	renown
	And war voydyt off cowardy,°	**voydyt** . . . free from cowardice
	As wes King Robert off Scotland,	
	That hardy wes off hart and hand,	
	And gud Schyr James off Douglas,	
30	That in his tyme sa° worthy was	so
	That off° hys price° and hys bounté°	for renown excellence
	In fer° landis renownyt wes he.	far
	Off° thaim I thynk this buk to ma.°	Of make
	Now God gyff grace that I may swa°	so
35	Tret° it and bryng it till° endyng	Manage to
	That I say nocht° bot suthfast° thing.	nothing truthful

272

The Scots Under Subjection to Edward I

[I, 219–80]

Alas, that folk that evir wes fre
And in fredome wount° for to be,   accustomed
Throw° thar gret myschance and foly,   Through
War tretyt than sa° wykkytly   so
5   That thar fays° thar jugis° war.   foes   judges
Quhat° wrechitnes may man have mar?°   What   more
    A! Fredome is a noble thing!
Fredome mayss° man to haiff liking;°   causes   pleasure in life
Fredome all solace to man giffis.
10   He levys° at ess° that frely levys.   lives   ease
A noble hart may° haiff nane° ess   can   no
Na ellys nocht° that may him pless   **Na** ... Or anything else
Gyff° fredome failyhe,° for fre liking°   If   fails   choice
Is yharnyt our° all othir thing;   **yharnyt our** yearned for over
15   Na° he that ay° hass levyt° fre   Nor   always   lived
May nocht knaw weill the propyrté,°   peculiar state
The angyr,° na the wrechyt dome°   anguish   fate
That is cowplyt° to foule thyrldome°   coupled   thralldom
Bot gyff° he had assayit it.   **Bot gyff** Unless
20   Than all *per quer*° he suld° it wyt°   *per quer* by heart   should   know
And suld think fredome mar° to pryss°   more   be prized
Than all the gold in warld that is.
    Thus contrar° thingis evirmar°   contrary   always
Discoveryngis° off the tothir° ar;   Revelations   opposite
25   And he that thryll° is has nocht his;°   thrall   his own
All that he hass enbandownyt° is   subjected
Till° hys lord, quhatevir° he be.   To   whatever
Yheyt° has he nocht sa mekill° fre   Yet   **nocht** ... not even so much
As fre liking° to leyve° or do   choice   leave undone
30   That at° hys hart hym drawis to.   which
    Than mayss clerkis° questioun   **mayss clerkis** scholars make
Quhen° thai fall in disputacioun   When
That, gyff° man bad° his thryll owcht° do,   if   ordered   **thryll owcht** thrall something to
And in the samyn° tym come° him to   same   came
35   His wyff and askyt hym hyr det,°   debt
Quhethir° he his lordis neid suld let°   Whether   **neid** ... requirement should ignore
And pay fryst that° he awcht and syne°   **fryst that** first what   **awcht** ... owed and then
Do furth his lordis commandyne,
Or leve onpayit his wyff and do
40   It that commaundyt is him to.
    I leve all the solucioun
Till° thaim that ar off mar° renoun,   To   **off mar** of more

Bot, sen° thai mak sic comperyng°   since **sic comperyng** such comparison
Betwix the dettis off wedding
45   And lordis bidding till his threll,°   thrall
Ye may weile se, thoucht nane° yow tell,   **thoucht nane** though none
How hard a thing that threldome° is,   thralldom
For men may weile se that ar wyss
That wedding is the hardest band°   bond
50   That ony man may tak on hand.
     And thryldome is weill wer° than deid,°   **weill wer** much worse   death
For quhill° a thryll his lyff may leid,   as long as
It merrys° him, body and banys,°   mars   bones
And dede anoyis° him bot anys.°   **dede anoyis** death troubles   once
55   Schortly to say, is nane° can tell   **is nane** there is none who
The halle° condicioun off a threll.   whole
     Thus-gat levyt thai and in sic thrillage,°
Bath pur° and thai off hey parage,°   **Bath pur** Both poor   **off . . .** of high rank
For off the lordis sum thai° slew,   they (the English)
60   And sum thai hangyt, and sum thai drew,
And sum thai put in hard presoune
Forowtyn° causs or enchesoun.°   Without   reason

Sir James Douglas

[I, 360–406]
All men lufyt° him for his bounté,°   loved   excellence
For he wes off full° fayr effer,°   **off full** of very   behavior
Wyss, curtaiss, and deboner.
Larg° and luffand als° wes he   Generous   **luffand als** kind also
5   And our° all thing luffyt lawté.°   above   loyalty
Leawté to luff is gretumly.°
Throuch leawté liffis men rychtwisly.°   **liffis . . .** men live righteously
With a vertu of leawté
A man may yeit sufficyand be
10 And, but° leawté, may nane haiff price°   without   **nane . . .** have no renown
Quhethir° he be wycht° or he be wyss,   Whether   vigorous
For, quhar° it failyeys,° na vertu   where   fails
May be off° price na° off valu   of   nor
To mak a man sa gud° that he   **sa gud** so good
15 May symply gud man callyt be.
He wes in all his dedis lele,°   loyal

57. Thus lived they (the Scots) and in such thralldom
6. Loyalty is greatly to be loved.

For him dedeynyeit nocht° to dele   **him ...** he deigned not
With trechery na with falset.°   falsehood
His hart on hey° honour wes set,   high
20 And hym contenyt° on sic° maner   **hym contenyt** he conducted himself   such
That all him luffyt° that war him ner.   loved
Bot he wes nocht sa° fayr that we   so
Suld° spek gretly off his beauté.   Should
In vysage wes he sumdeill° gray   somewhat
25 And had blak har,° as Ic hard° say;   hair   **Ic hard** I heard
Bot off lymmys he wes weill maid,
With banys° gret and schuldrys braid.°   bones   broad
His body wes weyll maid and lenye,°   lean
As thai that saw hym said to me.
30   Quhen he wes blyth, he wes lufly°   lovable
And meyk and sweyt in cumpany;
Bot quha° in battaill mycht him se,   whoever
All othir contenance had he.
And in spek wlispyt° he sumdeill,°   **spek wlispyt** speech lisped   somewhat
35 Bot that sat° him rycht wondre° weill.   suited   wondrously
   Till° gud Ector of Troy mycht he   To
In mony thingis liknyt° be.   likened
Ector had blak har° as he had,   hair
And stark° lymmys, and rycht weill maid,   strong
40 And wlispyt alswa as° did he,   **wlispyt ...** lisped just as
And wes fullfillyt° of leawté,°   full   loyalty
And wes curtaiss and wyss and wycht.°   vigorous
Bot off manheid and mekill° mycht   **off ...** for manhood and great
Till Ector dar° I nane° comper   dare   none
45 Off all that evir in warld wer.
The quhethyr,° in his tyme sa wrocht° he   **The quhethyr** Nevertheless   **sa wrocht** so wrought
That he suld° gretly lovyt be.   should

Bruce Addresses His Army at Bannockburn

[XII, 210–53]
"Lordyngis, sen° ye will sa,°   since   so
Schapis° tharfor in the mornyng   Prepare
Swa that we be° the sonne-rysing   by
Haf herd mes,° and be buskit° weill,   mass   equipped
5 Ilk° man intill° his awne yscheill,°   Each   in   **awne yscheill** own squadron
Without° the palyownys arayit°   Outside   **palyownys arayit** tents arranged
In battale° with baneris displayit.   battle-order

And luk° yhe na° way brek aray.°   *see to it in no order*
And, as ye luf me, I yow pray
10   That ilk man for his awne honour
Purvay hym° a gud baneour,°   **Purvay hym** *Provide himself* *banner-bearer*
And, quhen° it cummys to the ficht,   *when*
Ilk° man set his hert and mycht   *Each*
To stynt° our fais mekill° pryd.   *quench* **fais mekill** *foes' great*
15   "On horss thai sall arayit° ryd   **sall arayit** *shall in order*
And cum on yow in weill° gret hy.°   *very speed*
Meit thame with speris hardely,°   *bravely*
And wreik° on thame the mekill° ill   *avenge great*
That thai and tharis has° done us till°   **tharis has** *theirs have* **us till** *to us*
20   And ar in will yeit for till° do   **in . . .** *hoping still to*
Gif° thai haf mycht till cum tharto.   *If*
"And, certis, me think° weill that we,   **certis . . .** *certainly, it seems to me*
Forout abasyng,° aucht till be   **Forout abasyng** *Without flinching*
Worthy and of gret vassalage,°   *valor*
25   For we have thre gret avantage.
"The first is that we haf the richt,
And for the richt ilk° man suld ficht.   *each*
"The tothir° is, thai ar cummyn heir,°   *second* **ar . . .** *have come here*
For lypnyng° in thair gret power,   **For lypnyng** *Trusting*
30   To seik° us in our awne° land   *seek own*
And has° broucht her° richt till our hand   *have here*
Richess into° so gret plentée   *in*
That the pouerest of yow sall° be   *shall*
Bath° rych and mychty tharwithall   *Both*
35   Gif that° we wyn, as weill may fall.°   **Gif that** *If* *befall*
"The thrid is that we for our lyvis
And for our childer and our wifis
And for the fredome of our land
Ar strenyeit° in battale for to stand;   *compelled*
40   And thai, for° thair mycht anerly,°   *because of alone*
And for° thai leit° of us lichtly,°   *because think lightly*
And for thai wald° distroy us all,   *would like to*
Mais thame° to ficht. Bot yet ma fall°   **Mais thame** *Force themselves* **ma fall** *it may befall*
That thai sall rew° thar barganyng."°   **sall rew** *shall regret* *undertaking*

WILLIAM LANGLAND

Piers Plowman

(1372–79, Southwestern)

One of the greatest poems of the Middle Ages, *Piers Plowman* is at the same time one of the most complicated. Various clues suggest that the author, William Langland (ca. 1332–ca. 1400) was born at Cleobury Mortimer (Shropshire), was trained as a priest at the Benedictine monastery at Great Malvern (Worcestershire), took minor orders but acquired no benefice, was married, and lived with his wife and daughter at Cornhill, in London, where he secured a meager income by reciting prayers for benefactors.

Langland wrote about religion and human life with the fervor of an Old Testament prophet. In the process of writing he constantly discovered new material to incorporate into his message. Consequently, he revised *Piers Plowman* several times. His first version of *Piers Plowman* (Version A, ca. 1370) ran to 2,567 lines; this was soon followed by an extended second version (Version B, excerpted here, ca. 1377–79) containing 7,242 lines; and this in turn was revised in a slightly longer and considerably different final version (Version C, ca. 1387). It seems unlikely that the poet's restless mind ever considered any of these versions as truly completed works of art.

The poem is complicated by Langland's use of allegory. Like *The Romance of the Rose*, *Piers Plowman* is a dream vision, but though the poem is often personal and even autobiographical, the Poet is not simply to be thought of as Langland. Rather, the Poet is Everyman, baffled and perplexed, and his vision is an apocalyptic revelation of the destiny of mankind; allegorically, Will the Poet is a counterpart of the Human Will searching for his proper direction. The poem, furthermore, is lifted above the level of passive contemplation by the dramatic role of the Poet's mentor, Piers Plowman. Piers first enters into the vision as a simple man who faithfully performs his daily tasks—an exemplar of the laws of the Old Testament dispensation; then he appears as a counterpart of Christ and reveals the nature of charity—the Divine Love unfolded in the new dispensation of the Gospels; and finally he becomes the counterpart of St. Peter—the founder of Holy Church proclaimed in the Acts of the Apostles.

At the narrative level, all of the characters who appear in the Poet's dreams are allegorical. He dreams at first of an assembly of the people, who are visited by their king (Prologue). Lady Holy Church explains that the field where they have gathered is situated between Truth and Falsehood (Canto I); Lady Meed (Graft) is about to marry Falsehood (Canto II) but is tried before the king (Cantos III–IV). The Poet then dreams that Reason preaches to the people and causes the Seven Deadly Sins to repent; the people set out in search of Truth, and Piers Plowman describes the way (Canto V), but he requires that they first turn to work (Canto VI), and he rejects a pardon offered to him by a priest, whereupon the Poet learns that Do-well is better than any pardon (Canto VII).

Here the part usually referred to as "The Vision" concludes, and "The Life of Do-well, Do-better and Do-best" begins. The Poet seeks Do-well and is given counsel by Thought (Canto VIII), Wit (Intelligence) (Canto IX), Study (Canto X), Fortune, Loyalty, Scripture,

Nature, and Reason (Canto XI), Imagination (Canto XII), and Conscience and Patience (Canto XIII). Finally, the Poet learns how the Active Man can be saved from sin (Canto XIV).

Anima (Soul) teaches the Poet about Charity (Canto XV). Piers Plowman shows him the Tree of Charity; the Poet meets Abraham (Faith) (Canto XVI), Moses (Hope), and the Good Samaritan (Charity) (Canto XVII). The Poet dreams of Christ's death and the Harrowing of Hell, awakens on Easter morning, and takes his wife and daughter to mass (Canto XVIII).

In a dream he learns how Christ's life exemplifies Do-well, Do-better, and Do-best and how Piers Plowman as Holy Church serves as Christ's messenger (Canto XIX). Antichrist, however, overturns Truth and besieges Castle Unity, and Conscience must therefore set out on a pilgrimage to find Piers Plowman so that he may destroy the pride of the adversary (Canto XX).

There are many forerunners of Piers Plowman in medieval literature, such as *The Pilgrimage of Human Life, of the Soul, and of Jesus Christ* (ca. 1330–58), by the French Cistercian monk Guillaume de Deguilleville, but none can be said to rival Langland's poem. Despite its complete reliance on allegory, *Piers Plowman* is intensely vivid and realistically concerned with contemporary problems. Despite its heavy freight of dogma, its narrative is more lively than that of many a romance, and it thus escapes the aridity of systematic theological tracts. Its sermons are sympathetic, its satire humane, and its tone arrestingly witty.

Langland was a learned man, his mind saturated with Biblical, liturgical, and patristic lore. Yet the application of his message is inescapably clear. Neither Pope nor friar, king nor plow-man, could have misunderstood the demands that Langland laid on their consciences. He rejoices in paradoxes, as when he perceives that Truth can be fallible (Canto XVIII, l. 142) and that Wisdom cannot of itself secure salvation (Canto X, l. 428), but his paradoxes are arresting rather than mystifying. For, learned though he was, Langland the theologian was never pedantic. If any one passage could provide a motto for his point of view, it would be the comment of Lady Study:

> Theology has tormented me ten score of times.
> The more I muse therein, the mistier it seems.
> And the deeper I divine, the darker it looks to me.
> It is, indeed, no science to subtilize in.
> A most idle thing would Theology be, if there were not Love,
> But since Theology esteems Love best, I love it the better,
> For where Love is leader, Grace never lacks.

> (X, 180–86, modernized)

There are, to be sure, serious obscurities in the poem, such as Piers's rejection of the pardon and the conceptual significance of Do-well, Do-better, and Do-best, but these are rich mysteries, and the Poet consistently presents these aspects of his dreams as revelations whose whole meaning he himself cannot immediately grasp. So too, the ending of the poem, which seems anticlimactically to leave Antichrist in power, effectively expresses the Poet's concern about the state of his corrupt and war-torn world and yet leaves hope in his reader's heart. Indeed, all of these difficult aspects—Piers, Do-well, Do-better, Do-best, and the reign of Antichrist—are distinguishing features of a highly original work of piety that is also a uniquely moving work of art.

The Prologue and Cantos I, V, VII, and parts of XVIII and XIX are printed below.

The meter is alliterative verse; see Introduction, type 1, page 29.

Piers Plowman

The best complete edition is *The Vision of William concerning Piers the Plowman* (Text B), ed. W. W. Skeat, EETS (London, 1869), with Notes and Glossary, EETS 67, 81 (London, 1877, 1885), reprinted along with Versions A and C (Oxford, 1886), 2 vols. A new, definitive edition *Piers Plowman: The A Version*, ed. George Kane (London, 1960), will be followed by similar editions of the texts of B and C. For a modernization see William Langland, *Piers the Ploughman*, trans. J. F. Goodridge (Harmondsworth, 1959). For criticism see *Piers Plowman: Critical Approaches*, ed. S. S. Hussey (London, 1969), and *Style and Symbolism in Piers Plowman: A Modern Critical Anthology*, ed. Robert J. Blanch (Knoxville, 1969). For bibliography see Wells, ch. 4. 51; *CBEL*, 1.197–200, 5.126–28.

Prologue

In a somer seson whan soft was the sonne,
I shope° me in shroudes as° I a shepe° were,
In habite as an heremite unholy° of workes;
Went wyde in this world wondres to here.°
5 Ac° on a May mornynge on Malverne hülles,°
Me byfel a ferly° of fairy, me thoughte.°
I was wery forwandred° and went me to reste
Under a brode banke bi a bornes° side,
And as I lay and lened° and loked in the wateres,
10 I slombred in a slepyng; it sweyved° so merye.
Thanne gan° I to meten° a merveilouse swevene,°
That I was in a wildernesse, wist° I never where.
As I bihelde° into the est an° hiegh to the sonne,
I seigh° a toure° on a toft trielich° y-maked;
15 A depe dale° binethe, a dongeon° there-inne,
With depe dyches and derke, and dredful of sight.
A faire felde ful of folke fonde I there bytwene,
Of alle maner of men, the mene and the riche,
Worchyng and wandryng as the worlde asketh.°
20 Some putten hem° to the plow, pleyed ful selde,°
In settyng and in sowyng swonken° ful harde,
And wonnen that° wastours with glotonye destruyeth.
And some putten hem to prüyde, apparailed° hem there-after,
In contenaunce° of clothyng comen° disgised.
25 In prayers and in penance putten hem manye,
Al for love of owre Lorde lyveden ful streyte,°
In hope for to have heveneriche° blisse,
As ancres° and heremites that holden hem° in here selles°
And coveiten° nought in contré to kairen° aboute

Glosses:
shope dressed; shroudes as rough clothes; as if; shepe shepherd
heremite unholy worldly
here hear
Ac But; hülles hills
ferly marvel; fairy... magic, it seemed; me thoughte to me
wery forwandred weary from wandering
bornes stream's
lened leaned
sweyved flowed
gan began; meten dream; swevene dream
wist knew
bihelde looked; an on
seigh saw; toure tower; toft trielich hill excellently
dale valley; dongeon castle
asketh demands
hem themselves; ful selde very seldom
swonken worked
wonnen that won what
prüyde, apparailed pride, dressed
contenaunce display; comen came
lyveden... lived very strictly
heveneriche heaven's
As ancres Such as anchorites; holden hem stay; here selles their cells
coveiten covet; kairen wander

279

30 For no likerous liflode her lykam° to plese.
    And somme chosen chaffare;° they cheven° the bettere,
As it semeth to owre syght that suche men thryveth;
And somme mürthes° to make as mynstralles conneth,°
And geten gold with here glee, synneles, I leve.°
35 Ac japers and jangelers,° Judas chylderen,
Feynen° hem fantasies and foles hem maketh,°
And han here witte° at wille to worche yif thei sholde.°
    That Poule° precheth of hem,° I nel° nought preve° it here!
Qui turpiloquium loquitur[1] is Luciferes hyne.°
40   Bidders° and beggeres fast about yede°
With her° belies and her bagges of bred ful y-crammed,
Fayteden° for here fode, foughten atte° ale;
In glotonye, God it wote, gon hii° to bedde,
And risen with ribaudye, tho Roberdes° knaves.
45 Slepe and sori sleuthe seweth hem° evre.
    Pilgrymes and palmers plighted° hem togidere
To seke Seynt James° and seyntes in Rome.
Thei went forth in here° wey with many wise tales
And hadden leve to lye al here lyf after.
50 I seigh° somme that seiden thei had y-sought seyntes;
To eche a tale that thei tolde, here tonge was tempred° to lye
More than to sey soth,° it semed bi here speche.
    Heremites on an heep° with hoked staves
Wenten to Walsyngham,[2] and here° wenches after.°
55 Grete lobyes° and longe that loth were to swynke°
Clotheden hem in copis° to ben° knowen fram othere
And shopen hem° heremites, here ese to have.
    I fonde there Freris,° alle the foure ordres,
Preched the peple for profit of hemselven,
60 Glosed° the gospel as hem good lyked,°
For coveitise of copis° construed it as thei wolde.
Many of this maistres° Freris mowe° clothen hem at lykyng,°
For here money and marchandise marchen togideres.°
For sith° Charité hath be chapman and chief° to shryve° lordes,
65 Many ferlis° han fallen in a fewe yeris.
But° Holy Chirche and hii holde° better togideres,

Glosses

likerous . . . sensuous living their body
chaffare;° bargaining — cheven° succeed
mürthes° mirth — conneth,° can
leve° believe
Ac . . . But jesters and clowns
Feynen° Invent — **foles . . .** pose as fools
han . . . have their wits — sholde.° must
That Poule What Paul — hem,° them — nel° will — preve° say
hyne.° servant
Bidders° Beggars — yede° went
her° their
Fayteden° Begged — atte° over
wote . . . knows, they go
ribaudye . . . ribaldry, those vagabond
sleuthe . . . sloth pursue them
plighted° pledged
Seynt James Santiago de Compostela, Spain
here° their
seigh° saw
tempred° tuned
sey soth tell the truth
heep° heap
here° their — after.° with them
lobyes° lubbers — swynke° work
copis° capes — ben° be
shopen hem made themselves
Freris,° Friars
Glosed° Explained — **hem . . .** it well pleased them
coveitise . . . covetousness for clothes
maistres° master — mowe° can
lykyng,° their pleasure
togideres.° since
sith° **be . . .** been merchant and — chief° chiefly — shryve° absolve
ferlis° marvels
But° Unless — **hii holde** they agree

---

[1] 'He who speaks filth.' Possibly reflects Eph. v.4 or Col. iii.8.
[2] Shrine of Our Lady, Walsingham, Norfolk.
63. For their money and their commodity (preaching) prosper mutually.

The moste myschief on molde° is mountyng wel° faste.　　earth　very
　　There preched a Pardonere as° he a prest were,　　as if
　　Broughte forth a bulle° with bishopes seles,　　document
70　And seide that hymself myghte assoilen hem° alle　　**myghte** . . . could absolve them
　　Of falshed of fastyng,° of vowes y-broken.　　**falshed** . . . failure to fast
　　Lewed° men leved° hym wel and lyked his wordes,　　Unlearned　believed
　　Comen up knelyng to kissen his bulles.
　　He bonched° hem with his brevet° and blered here eyes,　　struck　document
75　And raughte° with his ragman° rynges and broches.　　took in　document
　　Thus they geven° here golde, glotones to kepe,°　　give　support
　　And leveth such loseles° that lecherye haunten.　　scoundrels
　　Were the bischop y-blissed° and worth bothe his eres,°　　holy　ears
　　His seel shulde nought be sent to deceyve the peple.
80　Ac° it is naught by° the bischop that the boy° precheth,　　But　against　young pardoner
　　For the parisch prest and the Pardonere parten° the
　　　　silver,　　divide
　　That the poraille° of the parisch sholde° have yif thei
　　　　nere.°　　poor　ought to
　　　　　　　　　　were not there
　　Persones° and parisch prestes pleyned hem° to the
　　　　bischop,　　Parsons　**pleyned hem** complained
　　That here parisshes were pore sith° the pestilence tyme,　　since
85　To have a lycence and a leve at London to dwelle,
　　And syngen there for symonye, for silver is swete.
　　　　Bischopes and bachelers, bothe maistres and doctours—
　　That han cure° under Criste, and crounyng° in tokne°　　**han cure** have charge　tonsure
　　　　　　　　　　token
　　And signe that thei sholden shryven° here paroschienes,°　　absolve　parishioners
90　Prechen, and prey for hem,° and the pore fede—　　them
　　Liggen° in London, in Lenten and elles.°　　Dwell　at other times
　　Some serven the kyng and his silver tellen;°　　count
　　In cheker° and in chancerye chalengen° his dettes　　exchequer　claim
　　Of° wardes and wardmotes, weyves and streyues.°　　From　**wardmotes** . . . ward
　　　　　　　　　　meetings, waifs and estrays
95　And some serven, as servantz, lordes° and ladyes,　　to lords
　　And in stede of stuwardes sytten and demen.°　　judge
　　Here messe° and here matynes, and many of here oures°　　**Here messe** Their mass
　　　　　　　　　　canonical hours
　　Arn don undevoutlych. Drede° is at the laste　　Fear
　　Lest Crist in consistorie acorse ful° manye.　　very
100　　I parceyved of the power that Peter had to kepe,
　　To bynde and to unbynde, as the boke telleth,
　　How he it left with Love, as owre Lorde hight,°　　ordered
　　Amonges foure vertues, the best of alle vertues,
　　That cardinales ben° called, and closyng yatis,°　　are　gates
105　There° Crist is in kyngdome, to close and to shutte,　　Where
　　And to opne it to hem° and hevene blisse shewe.　　them
　　Ac° of the cardinales atte Courte, that caught of° that
　　　　name,　　But　**caught of** took

And power presumed in hem a Pope to make,
To han° that power that Peter hadde, inpugnen° I   have   deny
    nelle;°   will not
110 For in love and letterure° the eleccioun bilongeth;   learning
For-thi° I can, and can naughte, of courte speke more.   Therefore
    Thanne come there a kyng, knyghthod° hym ladde,°   knights led
Might of the comunes° made hym to regne,   common-people
And thanne cam Kynde Wytte,° and clerkes he made,   **Kynde Wytte** Common Sense
115 For to conseille the kyng and the Comune° save.   Commons
    The kyng and knyghthode and clergye bothe°   also
Casten° that the Comune shulde hemself fynde.°   Decided **hemself fynde** provide
                                                       for themselves
The Commune contreved of Kynde Witte craftes°   skills
And, for profit of alle the poeple, plowmen ordeygned
120 To tilie and travaile as trewe lyf asketh.°   demands
The kyng and the Comune and Kynde Witte the
    thridde°   **Comune . . .** Commons and
                                                       Common Sense as the third
Shope° Lawe and Lewté,° eche man to knowe his owne. Arranged Loyalty
    Thanne loked up a lunatik,[3] a lene thing withalle,
And knelyng to the kyng, clergealy° he seyde: seriously
125 "Crist kepe thee, Sire Kyng, and thi kyngriche,°   kingdom
And leve° thee lede° thi londe, so Leuté° thee lovye,°   let rule Loyalty love
And for thi rightful rewlyng be rewarded in hevene!"
    And sithen° in the eyre an° hiegh an angel of hevene   then **eyre an** air on
Lowed° to speke in Latyn—for lewed° men ne coude   Stooped unlearned
130 Jangle° ne jugge that° justifie hem shulde,   Talk about that which
But° suffren and serven—for-thi° seyde the angel: But only therefore
    "*Sum Rex, sum Princeps; neutrum fortasse deinceps.*
O qui jura regis Christi specialia regis,
Hoc quod agas melius, justus es, esto pius!
135 *Nudum jus a te vestiri vult pietate;*
Qualia vis metere talia grana sere.
Si jus nudatur nudo de jure metatur.
Si seritur pietas, de pietate metas!"°
    Thanne greved hym° a Goliardeys,° a glotoun of   **greved hym** was annoyed vagrant
    wordes,
140 And to the angel an° heigh answered after: on
    "*Dum rex a regere dicatur nomen habere,*
Nomen habet sine re nisi studet jura tenere."°

---

[3] Presumably the Poet himself.

132–38. I am king, I am prince, you say; soon perhaps you may be neither. O you who administer the special laws of Christ the King, that you may better do this, as you are just, be merciful. Naked justice should be clothed by you with mercy; sow such grain as you wish to reap. If justice is stripped of mercy, you shall be dealt with by naked justice. If mercy is sown, you shall be dealt with by mercy.

141–42. Since the king is said to have the name of king from the act of ruling, he has the name without anything else unless he is careful to maintain the laws.

And thanne gan° alle the Comune crye in vers of Latin — did
To° the kynges conseille, construe ho-so° wolde: — For; howsoever he

145   *Precepta Regis sunt nobis vincula legis.*°

With that ran there a route° of ratones° at ones, — pack; rats
And smale mys with hem mo° then a thousande, — more
And comen to a conseille for here comune° profit; — common
For a cat of a courte cam whan hym lyked,° — it pleased
150 And overlepe° hem lyghtlich and laughte° hem at his — jumped over; seized
    wille,
And pleyde with hem perilouslych and possed° hem — pushed
    aboute.
"For doute° of dyverse dredes we dar noughte wel — fear
    loke;° — look about
And yif we grucche° of his gamen,° he wil greve° us alle, — complain; games; harm
Cracche° us, or clowe us, and in his cloches holde, — Scratch
155 That us lotheth° the lyf or° he lete us passe. — **us lotheth** we loathe; before; idea
Myghte we with any witte° his wille withstonde, — idea
We myghte be lordes aloft and lyven at owre ese."
A raton° of renon, most renable° of tonge, — rat; ready
Seide for a sovereygne help, to hymselve:° — **help . . .** remedy, in his opinion
160 "I have y-sein segges,"° quod he, "in the cité of London — **y-sein segges** seen men
Beren bighes° ful brighte abouten here nekkes, — collars
And some colers of crafty° werk. Uncoupled° thei — skillful; Unleashed
    wenden
Bothe in wareine° and in waste° where hem leve — warren; open land
    lyketh;° — **leve lyketh** well it pleases
And otherwhile thei aren elles-where as I here telle.
165 Were there a belle on here beigh, bi Jhesu, as me
    thynketh,° — **me thynketh** it seems to me
Men myghte wite° where thei went and awei renne!° — know; run
And right so," quod that ratoun,° "reson me sheweth, — rat
To bügge° a belle of brasse or of brighte sylver, — buy
And knitten° on a colere for owre comune profit, — attach
170 And hangen it upon the cattes hals.° Thanne here we — neck
    mowen° — can
Where° he ritt° or rest or renneth° to playe. — Whether; rides; runs
And yif him list° for to laike,° thenne loke we mowen, — it pleases; play
And peren° in his presence ther while hym plaie liketh,° — appear; **plaie liketh** play pleases
And yif him wrattheth,° be y-war° and his weye — **him wrattheth** he becomes angry; aware
    shonye."° — shun
175 Alle this route° of ratones° to this reson thei assented. — pack; rats
Ac° tho the belle was y-bought and on the beighe° — But; collar
    hanged,

145. The decrees of the king are to us as bonds of law.

There ne was ratoun in alle the route for alle the rewme°   realm
  of Fraunce
That dorst have y-bounden the belle aboute the cattis
  nekke,
Ne hangen it aboute the cattes hals° al Engelonde to   neck
  wynne;
180 And helden hem unhardy° and here conseille feble,   **helden . . . they considered**
  themselves fearful
  And leten° here laboure lost and alle here longe studye.   regarded
    A mous that moche° good couthe,° as me thoughte,°   much   knew   **me thoughte** it
  seemed to me
Stroke° forth sternly and stode biforn hem alle   Moved
And to the route° of ratons reherced° these wordes: pack   **ratons reherced** rats
  pronounced
185 "Though° we cülled° the catte, yüt° sholde ther come   Even if.   killed   yet
  another
To cracchy° us and al owre kynde though we croupe°   scratch   crept
  under benches.
For-thi° I conseille alle the Comune° to lat the catte   Therefore   Commons
  wörthe,°   be
And be we never so bolde the belle hym to shewe;
For I herde my sire seyn, is sevene yere y-passed,
190 There° the catte is a kitoun, the courte is ful elyng.°   Where   **ful elyng** very miserable
That witnisseth Holi Write, who-so° wil it rede: whosoever

Vae terrae ubi puer rex est, etc.[4]

For may no renke° there rest have for° ratones bi nyghte.   man   because of
The while he caccheth conynges,° he coveiteth nought   rabbits
  owre caroyne°   carrion
195 But fet° hym al with venesoun,° defame we hym nevere.   feeds   game
For better is a litel losse than a longe sorwe.°   sorrow
The mase° amonge us alle, though° we mysse° a   **The mase** Confusion   if   lose
  schrewe!°   tyrant
For many mannüs° malt we mys wolde destrüye,   a man's
And also ye route° of ratones rende mennes° clothes,   pack   men's
200 Nere° that cat of that courte that can yow overlepe;   Were it not for
For had ye rattes yowre wille, ye couthe° nought reule°   could   rule
  yowreselve.
I sey° for me," quod the mous, "I se so mykel after,°   speak   **mykel after** much in the
  future
Shal never the cat ne the kitoun bi my conseille be
  greved,°   offended
Ne carpyng° of this coler that costed me nevre.   **Ne carpyng** Nor shall there be talk
205 And though it had coste me catel, biknowen° it I nolde,°   **catel,biknowen** goods, acknowledg
  would not
But suffre as hymself wolde to do as hym liketh,°   it pleases
Coupled° and uncoupled, to cacche what thei mowe.°   Leashed   can
For-thi° üche a wise wighte° I warne: wite° wel his   Therefore   man   guard
  owne."

[4] 'Woe to the land where the king is a child, etc.' Eccles. x.16.

What this meteles bemeneth,° ye men that be merye, **meteles bemeneth** dream means
210 Devine ye, for I ne dar bi dere° God in hevene! dear
    Yit hoved° there an hondreth in houves° of selke, hovered   hoods
    Serjaunts° it semed that serveden atte barre, Law sergeants
    Plededen for penyes° and poundes the lawe, pennies
    And nought for love of owre Lorde unlese° here lippes unloosed
        onis.° once
215 Thow myghtest better mete° the myste on Malverne measure
        hülles° hills
    Than gete a momme of° here mouthe but° money were **momme of** sound from   unless
        shewed.
    Barones and burgeis and bonde-men als° **bonde-men als** peasants also
    I seigh° in this assemblé as ye shul here after. saw
    Baxsteres and brewesteres and bocheres° manye, **Baxsteres . . .** Bakers and brewers
                                                        and butchers
220 Wollewebsteres° and weveres of lynnen, Wool-weavers
    Taillours and tynkeres and tolleres° in marketes, toll-takers
    Masons and mynours° and many other craftes.° miners   skills
    Of alkin libbyng° laboreres lopen° forth somme, **Of . . .** Of all kinds of living   strode
    As dykers and delveres° that doth here dedes ille **dykers . . .** ditch-diggers and diggers
225 And dryven forth the longe day with "*Dieu vous save,*
        Dame Emma!"⁵
    Cokes° and here knaves crieden "Hote pies, hote! Cooks
    Gode gris and gees, gowe dyne,° gowe!" **gris . . .** pigs and geese, come dine
    Taverners until° hem tolde the same;° to   **tolde . . .** spoke similarly
    "White wyn of Oseye° and red wyn of Gascoigne, Alsace
230 Of the Ryne° and of the Rochel,° the roste to defye."° Rhine   Rochelle   digest
    Al this seigh° I slepyng and sevene sythes° more. saw   times

Canto I

    What this montaigne bymeneth° and the merke dale° means   **merke dale** dark valley
    And the felde ful of folke, I shal yow faire schewe.
    A loveli ladi of lere° in lynnen y-clothed face
    Come down fram a castel and called me faire
5   And seide, "Sone, slepestow? Sestow this° poeple, **slepestow . . .** do you sleep? Do you
                                                          see these
    How bisi thei ben° abouten the mase?° are   confusion
    The moste partie° of this poeple that passeth on this **moste partie** greatest part
        erthe,
    Have thei worschip° in this worlde, thei wilne° no **Have . . .** If they have honor   wish
        better; for
    Of other hevene than here holde thei no tale."° account

⁵ 'God save you, Dame Emma.' Probably the refrain of some bawdy popular song.

10	I was aferd of her face, theigh° she faire were,	though
	And seide, "Mercy, Madame, what is this to mene?"°	mean
	"The toure up° the toft,"° quod she, "Treuthe is there-inne,	**toure up** tower on hill
	And wolde that ye wroughte° as his worde techeth;	would do
	For He is Fader of Feith, fourmed° yow alle,	created
15	Bothe with fel° and with face and yaf° yow fyve wittis°	skin gave senses
	For to worschip hym ther-with the while that ye ben° here.	are
	And ther-fore he hyghte° the erthe to help yow üchone°	ordered each one
	Of wollen, of lynnen, of lyflode° at nede,	food
	In mesurable° manere to make yow at ese;°	moderate ease
20	And comaunded of his curteisye in comune° three thinges;	common
	Arne none nedful but tho, and nempne° hem I thinke,°	**tho** . . . those, and name intend
	And rekne° hem bi resoun, reherce° thow hem after.	count **bi** . . . rightly, repeat
	That one is vesture, from chele° thee to save,	chill
	And mete° atte mele for myseise° of thiselve,	food **mele** . . . meal against discomfort
25	And drynke whan thow dryest, ac° do nought out of resoun,	**dryest, ac** thirst, but
	That° thow wörth° the werse whan thow worche shuldest.	Lest be
	"For Loth° in his lifdayes, for likyng of drynke,	Lot
	Dede bi° his doughtres that° the devel lyked;	**Dede bi** Did with what
	Delited hym in drynke, as the devel wolde,°	would wish
30	And lecherye hym laught,° and lay bi hem bothe;	seized
	And al he witt it° wyn, that wikked dede.	**witt it** blamed it on

Inebriamus eum vino, dormiamusque cum eo,
Ut servare possimus de patre nostro semen.[1]

	Thorw wyn and thorw women there was Loth acombred,°	overcome
35	And there gat° in glotonye gerlis° that were cherlis.°	begot sons scoundrels
	For-thi° drede delitable drynke and thow shalt do thee bettere;	Therefore
	Mesure° is medcyne though thow moche yerne.	Moderation
	It is naught al gode to the goste° that the gutte axeth,°	spirit **gutte axeth** belly demands
	Ne liflode° to thi likam° that leef° is to thi soule.	food body dear
40	Leve° not thi likam, for a lyer him techeth,	Believe
	That is the wrecched worlde, wolde thee bitraye.	
	For the Fende° and thi flesch folweth thee togidere;	Fiend
	This and that sueth° thi soule and seith it° in thin herte;	pursue **seith it** speak it (the lie)

[1] 'Let us make him drunk with wine, and let us sleep with him, that we may preserve the seed of our father.' Gen. xix.32.

286

And for° thow sholdest ben y-war,° I wisse° thee the beste." — so that **ben y-war** be aware teach

45 "Madame, mercy," quod I, "me liketh° wel yowre wordes, — please

Ac° the moneye of this molde° that men so faste holdeth, — But earth

Telle me to whom, Madame, that tresore appendeth"° — belongs

"Go to the Gospel," quod she. "That God seide hymselven

Tho° the poeple Hym apposed° with a peny° in the Temple, — When questioned penny

50 Whether thei shulde ther-with worschip° the kyng Sesar. — honor

And God axed° of hem, of whome spake the lettre — asked

And the ymage i-lyke° that there-inne stondeth. — alike

'Cesaris,' thei seide. 'We sen° hym wel üchone.'° — see each one

'*Reddite Cesari*,'° quod God, 'that° *Cesari* bifalleth, — ***Reddite Cesari*** Give to Caesar what

55 *Et que sunt Dei, Deo*,° or elles ye done ille.' — *Et* . . . And what is God's, to God

For rightful reson shulde rewle yow alle,

And Kynde Witte° be wardeyne yowre welthe to kepe, — **Kynde Witte** Common Sense

And tutour° of youre tresore and take° it yow at nede; — guardian bring

For housbonderye° and hii° holden togideres." — thrift they

60 Thanne I frained° hir faire for° Hym that hir made: — asked for the sake of

"That dongeoun in the dale° that dredful is of sighte, — valley

What may it be to mene, madame, I yow biseche?"

"That is the Castel of Care.° Who-so° cometh ther-inne — Sorrow Whosoever

May banne° that he borne was to body or to soule. — curse

65 Ther-inne wonieth° a wighte° that Wronge is y-hote,° — dwells creature called

Fader of Falshed, and founded it hymselve.

Adam and Eve he egged to ille,

Conseilled Cayn to küllen his brother;

Judas he japed° with Juwen° silver, — tricked Jewish

70 And sithen° on an eller° honged hym after. — then elder tree

He is letter° of love and lyeth° hem alle; — hinderer lies to

That° trusten on his tresor bitrayeth he sonnest."° — Those who first

Thanne had I wonder in my witt what womman it were

That such wise wordes of Holy Writ shewed;

75 And asked hir on the hieghe Name, ar heo thennes yeode,° — **ar** . . . before she went thence

What she were, witterli,° that wissed° me so faire. — truly taught

"Holi Cherche I am," quod she; "thow oughtest me to knowe.

I underfonge° thee firste and thee feyth taughte, — received

And broughtest me borwes,° my biddyng to fulfille, — sponsors

80 And to love me lelly° the while thi lyf dureth."°   loyally   endures
    Thanne I courbed° on my knees and cryed hir° of   fell   to her
      grace,
    And preyed hir pitousely prey for my synnes,
    And also kenne° me kyndeli° on Criste to bileve,   teach   properly
    That I mighte worchen° His wille that wroughte° me   do   made
      to man:
85 "Teche° me to no tresore, but telle me this ilke,°   Direct   **this ilke** this very thing
    How I may save my soule, that° seynt art y-holden?"   you who
      "Whan alle tresores aren tried," quod she, "Trewthe
      is the best.
    I do it on° *Deus caritas*,[2] to deme° the sothe.°   **do** … appeal to   judge   truth
    It is as derworth° a drewery° as dere God hymselven.   dear   darling
90 Who-so° is trewe of his tonge and telleth none other,   Whosoever
    And döth the werkis ther-with and wilneth no man ille,
    He is a god bi the Gospel agrounde° and aloft,   on earth
    And y-like to owre Lorde, bi Seynte Lukes wordes.
    The clerkes that knoweth this shulde kenne° it aboute,   make known
95 For Cristene and uncristne clameth° it üchone.°   cry out for   each one
      "Kynges and knightes shulde kepe it bi resoun;°   **bi resoun** rightly
    Riden and rappe° down, in reumes° aboute,   strike   realms
    And taken *trangressores* and tyen hem faste,
    Til Treuthe had y-termyned° her trespas to the ende.°   determined   final result
100 And that is the professioun appertly° that appendeth   plainly
      for° knyghtes,   **appendeth for** pertains to
    And nought to fasten a° Fryday in fyve score wynter,   one
    But holden with him and with hir that wolden al
      Treuthe,°
    And never leve hem for love ne for lacchyng° of   getting
      sylver.
      "For David in his dayes dubbed knightes
105 And did° hem swere on here swerde° to serve trewthe   made   sword
      evere;
    And who-so passed° that poynte° was *apostata*° in the   **who-so passed** whosoever broke
      ordre.   vow   apostate
    But Criste, kingene° kynge, knighted ten,[3]   of kings
    Cherubyn and Seraphin, suche° sevene, and an othre,   of such
    And yaf° hem myghte in His majesté, the muryer hem   gave
      thoughte,°   **hem thoughte** it seemed to them
110 And over his mene meyné° made hem archangeles,   **mene meyné** common household
    Taughte hem bi the Trinitee Treuthe to knowe,

[2] 'God is love.' I John iv.8.
102. But support every man and woman who would wish for entire Truth
[3] Ten orders: Seraphim, Cherubim; Thrones, Dominions, Virtues, Powers, Principalities, Archangels, Angels; and Lucifer's Fallen Angels.

To be buxome° at his biddyng—he bad hem noughte elles.   *obedient*

"Lucifer with legiounes lerned it in hevene,

But, for° he brake buxumnesse,° his blisse gan he tyne,°   *because*   *obedience*   **gan . . . he lost**

115 And fel fro that felawship in a fendes° liknes   *fiend's*

Into a depe derke helle to dwelle there for evre.

And mo° thowsandes with him than man couthe noumbre°   *more*   **couthe noumbre** could count

Lopen° out with Lucifer in lothelich° forme,   *Leaped*   *loathsome*

For thei leveden upon° hym that lyed in this manere: **leveden upon** believed in

120   *Ponam pedem in aquilone, et similis ero altissimo.*[4]

And alle that hoped it mighte be so, none hevene mighte hem holde,

But fellen out in fendes° liknesse nyne dayes togideres,   *fiends'*

Til God of his goodnesse gan stable and stynte,°   **gan . . .** steadied and stopped

And garte° the hevene to stekye° and stonden in quiete.   *made*   *close*

125 "Whan thise wikked went out, wonderwise thei fellen,

Somme in eyre, somme in erthe, and somme in helle depe.

Ac Lucifer lowest lith° of hem alle;   *lies*

For pryde that he pult out,° his peyne hath none ende.   **pult out** put on

And alle that worche with wronge, wenden hii shulle°   **wenden . . .** they must go

130 After her deth-day and dwelle with that shrewe.°   *wretch*

Ac tho° that worche wel, as Holi Writ telleth,   *those*

And enden, as I ere seide, in Treuthe, that is the best,

Mowe be siker° that her soule shal wende to hevene,   **Mowe . . .** Can be sure

Ther° Treuthe is in Trinitee and troneth° hem alle.   *Where*   *enthrones*

135 For-thi I sey as I seide ere, bi sighte of thise textis,

Whan alle tresores arne y-tried, Treuthe is the beste.

Lereth° it this lewde° men, for lettred men it knowen,   *Teach*   **this lewde** to these unlearned

That Treuthe is tresore the triest° on erthe."   *most proven*

"Yet have I no kynde° knowing," quod I. "Yet mote ye kenne° me better   *natural*   *teach*

140 By what craft° in my corps° it comseth° and where."   *skill*   *body*   *originates*

"Thow doted daffe,"° quod she, "dulle arne thi wittes;   **doted daffe** doting dolt

Too litel Latyn thow lernedest, lede,° in thi youthe: *man*

    Heu mihi, quod sterilem duxi vitam juvenilem!°

"It is a kynde knowyng," quod he,° "that kenneth° in thine herte   *she*   *teaches*

---

[4] 'I shall place my foot in the North, and I shall be like to the most high.' See Isaiah xiv.13, 14.

143. Woe is me that I have lived such a barren youth!

145 For to lovye° thi Lorde lever° than thiselve;   *love   dearer*
      No dedly synne to do, dey though thow sholdest.
      This I trowe° be Treuthe. Who° can teche thee better,   *believe   Whoever*
      Loke thow suffre hym to sey,° and sithen lere° it after.   *speak   **sithen lere** then teach*
      For thus witnesseth His worde, worche° thow   *do*
           there-after;°   *accordingly*
150 For Trewthe telleth that Love is triacle° of hevene;   *remedy*
      May no synne be on him sene° that useth that spise,   *seen*
      And alle his werkes he wroughte with Love as him
           liste;°   *it pleased*
      And lered it Moises for the levest° thing and moste like   *dearest*
           to hevene,
      And also the plenté of Pees,° moste precious of vertues.   *Peace*
155 "For hevene myghte noughte holden it, it was so
           hevy of hymself,°   *itself (Love)*
      Tyl it hadde of the erthe yeten his° fylle.   ***yeten his** eaten its*
      And whan it haved of this folde° flesshe and blode taken,   *world*
      Was nevere leef upon lynde° lighter ther-after,   *linden tree*
      And portatyf and persant° as the poynt of a nedle,   ***portatyf** ... easy to carry and piercing*
160 That myghte non armure it lette,° ne none heigh   *stop*
           walles.
      "For-thi is Love leder of the Lordes folke of hevene,
      And a mene,° as the maire° is, bitwene the kyng and the   *mediator   mayor*
           Comune,°   *Commons*
      Right so is Love a ledere and the lawe shapeth;
      Upon man for his mysdedes the merciment° he taxeth.°   *fine   imposes*
165 And, for to knowe it kyndely,° it comseth bi° myght,   *naturally   **comseth bi** originates in*
      And in the herte, there is the hevede° and the heigh   *head*
           welle;°   *fount*
      For in kynde knowynge in herte there a myghte
           bigynneth.
      And that falleth° to the Fader that formed° us alle,   *belongs   created*
      Loked on us with love and lete His Sone deye
170 Mekely for owre mysdedes to amende° us alle;   *redeem*
      And yet wolde° He hem no woo° that wroughte Hym   *wished   evil*
           that peyne,
      But mekelich with mouthe mercy He bisoughte
      To have pité of that poeple that peyned° Hym to deth.   *tortured*
      "Here myghtow° see ensamples in Hymselve one,°   *may you   alone*
175 That He was mightful and meke, and mercy gan
           graunte°   ***gan graunte** granted*
      To hem that hongen Him an° heigh and His herte   *on*
           thirled.°   *pierced*
      "For-thi I rede° yow riche, haveth reuthe° of the   *advise   pity*
           pouere;°   *poor*

Though ye be myghtful to mote,° beth meke in yowre werkes.

For the same mesures that ye mete, amys other elles,°

180 Ye shullen ben° weyen ther-wyth whan ye wende hennes:°

to mote in court

mete ... measure, amiss or otherwise

be

wende hennes go hence

Eadem mensura qua mensi fueritis, remecietur vobis.[5]

For though ye be trewe of yowre tonge and trewliche wynne,°

And as chaste as a childe that in cherche wepeth,

But if° ye loven lelliche and lene° the poure,

185 Such good° as God yow sent, godelich parteth,°

Ye ne have na more meryte in masse ne in houres

Than Malkyn of hire maydenhode that no man desireth.

"For James the gentil° jugged in his bokes

That faith withoute the faite° is righte no thinge worthi

190 And as ded as a dore-tre, but yif° the dedes folwe.

gain

But if Unless   **lelliche** ... loyally and give to

goods   **godelich parteth** generously share

noble

deed

dore-tre ... door bar, unless

Fides sine operibus mortua est, etc.[6]

For-thi chastité withoute charité wörth° cheyned in helle;

It is as lewed° as a laumpe that no lighte is inne.

"Many chapeleynes arne chaste, ac charité is awey;

195 Aren no men avarousere° than hii° whan thei ben avaunced;°

Unkynde to her kyn and to alle Cristene,

Chewen° here charité and chiden° after more.

Such chastité withouten charité wörth° cheyned in helle!

"Many curatoures° kepen hem clene of here bodies,

200 Thei° ben acombred° with coveitise—thei konne nought don° it fram hem,

So harde hath avarice y-hasped° hem togideres.

And that is no treuthe of the Trinité but treccherye of helle,

And lernyng° to lewde° men the latter° for to dele.°

"For-thi this wordes ben° wryten in the Gospel:

205 '*Date et dabitur vobis*, for I dele yow alle.'[7]

And that is the lokke° of love and lateth oute° my grace

To conforte the careful,° acombred with synne.

Love is leche° of lyf, and nexte owre Lorde selve,

And also the graith gate° that göth into hevene.

will be

worthless

more avaricious   they

ben avaunced are advanced

Swallow   cry out

will be

curates

But they   encumbered

take

joined

teaching   unlearned   **the latter** later   give

are

lock   **lateth oute** sets free

sorrowful

physician

graith gate straight way

---

[5] 'And with what measure you have measured out, it shall be measured to you.' Matt. vii.2.

[6] 'Faith without works is dead, etc.' James ii.26.

[7] 'Give and it shall be given to you for I gave you all you have.' Luke vi.38.

210 For-thi I sey as I seide ere by the textis,
Whan alle tresores ben y-tryed, Treuthe is the beste.
Now have I tolde thee what Treuthe is, that no tresore
    is bettere;
I may no lenger lenge° thee with. Now loke° thee owre   stay   guard
    Lorde!"

Canto V

The kyng and his knightes to the kirke° wente   church
To here matynes of the day and the masse after.
Thanne waked I of° my wynkynge° and wo was   from   sleeping
    withalle
That I ne hadde sleped sadder° and y-seighen° more.   more soundly   seen
5 Ac er° I hadde faren° a fourlonge, feyntise° me hente,°   before   gone   faintness   seized
That I ne myghte° ferther a-foot for defaute° of   **ne myghte** couldn't go   lack
    slepynge;
And sat softly adown and seide my Bileve,°   Creed
And so° I babeled on my bedes, thei broughte me   as
    aslepe.
And thanne saw I moche more than I bifore tolde,
10 For I say° the felde ful of folke that I bifore of seyde,°   saw   spoke
And how Resoun gan arrayen hym° alle the reume°   **gan . . .** prepared himself   realm
    to preche,
And with a crosse afor the kynge comsed° thus to   commenced
    techen.
He preved° that thise pestilences[1] were for° pure   showed   because of
    synne,
And the southwest wynde on Saterday at evene[2]
15 Was pertliche° for pure pryde and for no poynt elles.°   clearly   other
Piries° and plomtrees were puffed° to the erthe   Pears   blown
In ensample,° ye segges,° ye shulden do the bettere.   example   men
Beches and brode okes were blowen to the grounde,
Torned upward her tailles in tokenynge of drede
20 That dedly synne at Domesday shal fordon° hem alle.   destroy
Of this matere I myghte mamely ful° longe,   **mamely ful** mumble very
Ac I shal seye as I saw, so me God helpe,
How pertly° afor the poeple Resoun gan° to preche.   clearly   began
He bad Wastoure go worche what he best couthe,°   could
25 And wynnen° his wastyng° with somme manere crafte,°   earn back   money wasted   skill

[1] Pestilence of 1361–62.
[2] Storm of Saturday, January 15, 1362.

And preyed Peronelle° her purfyle° to lete,°
And kepe it in hir cofre° for catel° at hire nede.
Thomme Stowue he taughte to take two staves
And fecche Felice home fro the wyven-pyne.°

30 He warned Watt his wyf was to blame
That hire hed° was worth halve a marke, his hode
    noughte worth a grote,
And bad Bette° kut a bow other tweyne°
And bete Betoun° ther-with but if° she wolde worche.
    And thanne he charged chapmen° to chasten° her
    childeren;

35 Late no wynnynge° hem forweny° whil thei be yonge,
Ne, for no pouste° of pestilence, plese hem noughte out
    of resoun.
    "My syre seyde so to me, and so did my dame,
That the levere° childe, the more lore° bihoveth,
And Salamon seide the same, that Sapience made,°

40   *Qui parcit virge, odit filium.*

The Englich of this Latyn is, who-so° wil it knowe,
'Who-so spareth the sprynge spilleth° his children.'"
    And sithen° he preyed prelatz and prestes togideres,
"That° ye prechen to the peple, preve° it on
    yowreselven,

45 And doth it in dede; it shal drawe yow to good.
If ye lyven as ye leren° us, we shal leve° yow the
    bettere."
    And sithen he radde Religioun° here reule to holde,
"Leste the kynge and his conseille yowre comunes
    appayre,°
And ben° stuwardes of yowre stedes° til ye be ruled
    bettre."

50 And sithen° he conseilled the kynge the Comune°
    to lovye:°
"It is thi tresore, if tresoun ne were, and triacle° at thi
    nede."
And sithen he prayed the Pope have pité on Holi
    Cherche,
And er° he gyve any grace governe firste hymselve.
    "And ye that han lawes to kepe, late° Treuthe be
    yowre covveytise°

55 More than golde or other gyftes, if ye wil God plese.
For who-so contrarieth Treuthe, He telleth in the
    Gospel,

preyed Peronelle begged Lady
   Peacock   furs   let go
chest   goods

ducking stool

headpiece

Bart   **bow . . .** bough or two
Betty   **but if** unless
merchants   chastise

profits   spoil
no pouste any fear of attack

dearer the   instruction
Sapience made wrote Proverbs

whosoever
sprynge spilleth rod spoils
then
What   practice

teach   believe

radde Religioun advised the
   religious orders

comunes appayre provisions
   reduce
be   places

then   Commons
love

remedy

before
let
desire

293

That God knoweth hym noughte, ne no seynte of
    hevene,

    Amen dico vobis, nescio vos.[3]

   And ye that seke Seynte James[4] and seintes of Rome,
60 Seketh seynt Treuthe, for he may save yow alle,
    Qui cum patre et filio. That feire hem bifalle°
That suweth° my sermon." And thus seyde° Resoun.   follow spoke
   Thanne ran Repentance and reherced° his teme,°   declared theme
And gert° Wille to wepe water with his eyen.   made

            Superbia°   Pride
65   Peronelle° Proude-herte platte° hir to the erthe,   Lady Peacock threw
And lay longe ar° she loked, and "Lorde, mercy!"   before
    cryed,
And byhighte° to Hym that us alle made,   promised
She shulde unsowen hir serke° and sette there an heyre°   **unsowen . . .** slit her shift hair
    shirt
To affaiten° hire flesshe that fierce was to synne: tame
70 "Shal nevere heighe herte me hente,° but holde me   seize
    lowe,
And suffre to be myssayde°—and so did I nevere.   abused
But now wil I meke me° and mercy biseche,   **meke me** humble myself
For al this I have hated in myne herte."

            Luxuria°   Lechery
   Thanne Lecchoure seyde "Allas!" and on owre Lady
    he cryed
75 To make mercy for his misdedes bitwene God and his
    soule,
With that he shulde the Saterday sevene yere
    there-after°
Drynke but myd° the doke° and dyne but ones.   **but myd** only water with duck

            Invidia°   Envy
   Envye with hevy herte asked after scrifte,°   confession
And carefullich *mea culpa°* he comsed° to shewe.°   the Confiteor commenced say
80 He was as pale as a pelet,° in the palsye he semed,   stone pellet
And clothed in a caurimaury,° I couthe° it noughte   coarse cloth could
    discreve;
In kirtel and kourteby° and a knyf bi his syde;   **kirtel . . .** jacket and coat
Of a freres frokke° were the forsleves,   **freres frokke** friar's habit

---

[3] 'Amen I say to you, I know you not.' Matt. xxv.12.
[4] James of Compostella.
61. Who with the father and the son (lives and reigns). May good happen to them
76. With provision that he would every Saturday for seven years from that time

And as a leke° hadde y-leye longe in the sonne,   leek which

85 So loked he with lene chekes, lourynge foule.°   **lourynge foule** scowling foully

His body was to-bolle° for wratthe that he bote° his lippes,   swollen bit

And wryngynge he yede° with the fiste; to wreke° hymself he thoughte   went avenge

With werkes or with wordes whan he seighe° his tyme.   saw

Eche a worde that he warpe° was of an addres tonge;   spoke

90 Of chydynge and of chalangynge was his chief lyflode,°   way of life

With bakbitynge and bismer° and beryng of fals witnesse;   slander

This was al his curteisye° where that evere he shewed hym.°   manners himself

"I wolde ben y-shryve,"° quod this schrewe,° "and° I for shame durst;   confessed wretch ' if

I wolde be gladder, bi God, that Gybbe had meschaunce

95 Than thoughe I had this wöke° y-wonne a weye° of Essex chese.   week wey (two to three hundredweights)

"I have a neighbore neyghe° me, I have ennuyed° hym ofte,   near annoyed

And lowen on° hym to lordes to don° hym lese° his silver,   **lowen on** lied about make lose

And made his frendes ben° his foon° thorw my false tonge;   be foes

His grace° and his good happes° greveth me ful° sore.   favor luck very

100 Bitwene many and many I make debate ofte,

That bothe lyf and lyme° is lost thorw my speche.   limb

And whan I mete him in market that I moste hate,

I hailse° hym hendeliche,° as I his frende were;   greet courteously

For he is doughtier° than I, I dar do non other.   stronger

105 Ac hadde I maystrye° and myghte, God wote° my wille!°   mastery knows intention

"And whan I come to the kirke° and sholde knele to the Rode,°   church Cross

And preye for the poeple as the prest techeth,

For pilgrimes and for palmers, for alle the poeple after,°   besides

Thanne I crye on my knees that Cryste yif° hem sorwe°   may give sorrow

110 That baren° awey my bolle° and my broke schete.°   carried bowl **broke schete** torn sheet

Awey fro the auter° thanne turne I my eyghen,°   altar eyes

And biholde how Eleyne hath a newe cote;

I wisshe thanne it were myne and al the webbe° after.   cloth

"And of mennes lesynge° I laughe; that liketh myn herte;   **mennes lesynge** men's losses

115 And for her wynnynge I wepe and waille the° tyme,   all the

And deme° that hii don° ille there° I do wel° worse;   judge   **hii don** they do   where much

Who-so undernymeth° me here-of, I hate hym dedly   takes to task
after.

I wolde that üche a wyght° were my knave,°   **a wyght** man   servant

For who-so hath more than I, that angreth me sore.

120 And thus I lyve lovelees lyke a lüther° dogge,   evil

That al my body bolneth° for bitter° of my galle.   swells   bitterness

    "I myghte noughte° eet, many yeres, as a man   **myghte noughte** could not
oughte,

For envye and yvel wille is yvel to defye.°   digest

May no sugre ne swete thinge asswage my swellynge,

125 Ne no *diapenidion*° dryve it fro myne herte,   sweet medicine

Ne noyther schrifte° ne shame, but ho-so schrape° my   confession   **but . . .** unless someone
mawe?"°   scrapes   stomach

    "Yüs, redili,"° quod Repentaunce, and radde° hym   **Yüs, redili** Yes, indeed   advised
to the beste,

"Sorwe° of synnes is savacioun of soules."   Sorrow

    "I am sori," quod that segge.° "I am but selde other,°   man   **selde other** seldom otherwise

130 And that maketh me thus megre,° for I ne may° me   **thus megre** so thin   **ne may** cannot
venge.

Amonges burgeyses have I be dwellynge at Londoun,

And gert° Bakbitinge be a brocoure° to blame mennes   made   broker
ware.°   **blame . . .** criticize men's wares

Whan he solde and I noughte, thanne was I redy

To lye and to loure° on my neighbore and to lakke° his   scowl   find fault with
chaffare.°   merchandise

135 I wil amende this, yif I may, thorw myghte of God
Almyghty."

Ira°   Anger

Now awaketh Wratthe with two whyte eyen,

And nyvelynge° with the nose, and his nekke hangynge.   snivelling

    "I am Wrath," quod he. "I was sum tyme a frere,°   friar

And the coventes° gardyner for to graffe ympes.°   convent's   **graffe ympes** graft shoots

140 On limitoures and listres lesynges I ymped°

Tyl thei bere leves° of low° speche, lordes to plese,   **bere leves** bore leaves   humble

And sithen° thei blosmed obrode,° in boure° to here   then   out   bower
shriftes.°   **here shriftes** hear confessions

And now is fallen therof a frute that folke han wel
levere°   **han . . .** had much rather

Schewen° her schriftes to hem than shryve° hem to her   Tell   confess
persones.°   parsons

145 And now persones han parceyved that freres parte°   **freres parte** friars share
with hem;

140. On mendicants and preachers I engrafted lies

Thise possessioneres° preche and deprave° freres,   beneficed priests   defame

And freres fyndeth hem in defaute,° as folke bereth   **in defaute** at fault
witnes,

That whan thei preche the poeple in many place aboute,

I, Wrath, walke with hem and wisse° hem of° my   teach   from
bokes.

150   "Thus thei speken of spiritualté, that eyther despiseth
other,

Til thei be bothe beggers and by my spiritualté libben,°   live

Or elles alle riche and riden aboute.

I, Wrath, rest nevere, that I ne moste folwe°   **that** . . . because I must follow

This wykked folke, for suche is my grace.

155   "I have an aunte to nonne° and an abbesse bothe,°   **to nonne** as a nun   too

Hir were levere swowe or swelte° than suffre any peyne.   **Hir** . . . She would rather faint or die

I have be cook in hir kichyne and the covent° served   convent

Many monthes with hem, and with monkes bothe.

I was the Priouresses potagere° and other poure° ladyes,   pottage cook   poor

160 And made hem joutes° of jangelynge° that Dame°   broths   gossip   Mother
Johanne was a bastard,

And Dame° Clarice a knightes doughter, ac a   Sister

kokewolde° was hire syre,   cuckold

And Dame Peronelle° a prestes file.° Priouresse wörth°   Peacock   wench   will be
she nevere,

For she had childe in chirityme,° al owre chapitere it   cherry time
wiste.°   knew

    "Of wykked wordes I, Wrath, here wortes° i-made,   cooked vegetables

165 Til 'Thow lixte'° and 'Thow lixte' lopen° oute at   **Thow lixte** You lie   leaped
ones,

And eyther hitte other under the cheke;

Hadde thei had knyves, bi Cryst, her° eyther had killed   of them
other.

    "Seynt Gregorie was a gode Pope and had a gode
forwit°   forethought

That no priouresse were° prest, for that he ordeigned.   would be

170 Thei had thanne ben *infamis*° the firste day; thei can so   disreputable
yvel hele conseille.°   **yvel** . . . poorly keep a secret

Amonge monkes I might be, ac many tyme I shonye;°   shun them

For there ben many felle frekis° my feres° to aspye,°   **felle frekis** cruel fellows   sort
spy out

Bothe prioure and supprioure° and owre *Pater Abbas*.°   subprior   ***Pater Abbas*** Father
Abbot

And if I telle any tales, thei taken hem° togyderes,   **taken hem** meet

175 And do° me faste Frydayes to bred and to water,   make

And am chalanged° in the chapitelhous as° I a childe   accused   **chapitelhous as** chapter
were,   house as if

And baleised° on the bare ers° and no breche° bitwene.   beaten   buttocks   breeches

For-thi have I no lykyng with tho leodes° to wonye.°   **tho leodes** those men   dwell

I ete there unthende° fisshe and fieble ale drynke;   half-grown

180 Ac other while,° whan wyn cometh, whan I drynke   **other while** sometimes
     wyn at eve,

I have a fluxe of a foule mouthe wel fyve dayes after.

Al the wikkednesse that I wote° bi any of owre   know
     bretheren,

I couth° it in owre cloistre that al owre covent wote it."   make known

   "Now repent thee," quod Repentaunce, "and
     reherce° thow nevre   repeat

185 Conseille° that thow cnowest bi contenaunce° ne bi   Secrets   favor
     righte;

And drynke noughte over delicatly° ne too depe   luxuriously
     noyther,

That thi wille bicause therof to wrath myghte torne.

Esto sobrius,"° he seyde, and assoilled° me after,   ***Esto sobrius*** Be sober   absolved

And bad me wilne to wepe my wikkednesse to amende.

Avaricia

190   And thanne cam Coveytise, can I hym noughte
     descryve,°   describe

So hungriliche and holwe,° Sire Hervy⁵ hym loked.°   hollow   **hym loked** he seemed like

He was bitelbrowed and baberlipped° also,   thick-lipped

With two blered eyghen° as a blynde hagge;   eyes

And as a letheren purs lolled° his chekes;   sagged

195 Wel sydder° than his chyn thei chiveled for elde;°   **Wel sydder** Even lower   **chiveled** ... trembled because of old age

And as a bondman of° his bacoun his berde was   with
     bidraveled.°   slobbered

With an hode on his hed, a lousi hatte above,

And in a tauny tabarde° of twelve wynter age,   short coat

Al totorne and baudy° and ful of lys crepynge.   **totorne** ... torn apart and filthy

200 But if that a lous couthe° have lopen° the bettre,   could   leaped

She sholde noughte have walked on that welche,° so   Welsh cloth
     was it thredebare.

   "I have ben coveytouse," quod this caityve,° "I   wretch
     biknowe° it here.   confess

For some tyme I served Symme atte° Stile,   at the

And was his prentis y-plighte,° his profit to wayte.°   **prentis y-plighte** apprentice pledged   look after

205 First I lerned to lye a leef other tweyne;°   **a** ... for a leaf of the lesson or two

Wikkedlich to weye° was my fürst lessoun.   weigh

To Wy° and to Wynchestre I went to the faire,   Weyhill

With many manere marchandise as my maistre me
     highte;°   ordered

Ne had° the grace of gyle y-go° amonge my ware,   **Ne had** If   had not gone

210 It had be° unsolde this sevene yere, so me God helpe!   **had be** would have been

⁵ A name apparently associated with avarice.

"Thanne drowe° I me amonges draperes, my donet°   went   grammar
    to lerne,
To drawe the lyser° alonge, the lenger it° semed.   selvage   it (the cloth)
Amonges the riche rayes° I rendred° a lessoun,   striped cloths   construed
To broche° hem with a pak-nedle, and plaited hem   pierce
    togyderes,
215 And put hem in a presse and pynned hem ther-inne,
Tyl ten yerdes or twelve hadde tolled° out threttene.   stretched
    "My wyf was a webbe° and wollen cloth made.   weaver
She spak to spynnesteres° to spynnen it oute.   **spak** ... employed spinners
Ac the pounde that she payed by poised a quarteroun
    more°
220 Than myne owne auncere,[6] who-so weyghed treuthe.
    "I boughte hir barly malte; she brewe it to selle.
Peny° ale and podyng° ale she poured togideres   Cheap   good
For laboreres and for low folke; that lay° by hymselve.°   was stored   itself
The best ale lay in my boure° or in my bedchambre,   bower
225 And who-so bummed° therof boughte it ther-after   tasted
A galoun for a grote, God wote,° no lesse;   knows
And yit it cam in cupmel,° this crafte° my wyf used.   cupfuls   trick
Rose the Regratere° was hir righte name;   Retailer
She hath holden hokkerye° al hire lyf-tyme.   huckstering
230   "Ac I swere now, so thee Ik,° that synne wil I lete,°   **so** ... may I prosper   forgo
And nevere wikkedliche weye° ne wikke chaffare°   weight   bargaining
    use,
But wenden° to Walsyngham and my wyf als,°   go   also
And bidde° the Rode° of Bromeholme brynge me oute   pray to   Cross
    of dette."
    "Repentedestow thee° evere," quod Repentance,   **Repentedestow thee** Did you
    "ne restitucioun madest?"   repent
235 "Yüs, ones I was herberwed,"° quod he, "with an hep   lodged
    of chapmen,°   merchants
I roos whan thei were arest° and y-rifled here males."°   at rest   packs
    "That was no restitucioun," quod Repentance, "but
    a robberes thefte!
Thow haddest be better worthy be hanged ther-fore
Than for al that thow hast here shewed."
240 "I wende° ryflynge were restitucioun," quod he, "for   thought
    I lerned nevere rede on° boke,   in
And I can° no Frenche in feith but of° the ferthest ende   know   from
    of Norfolke."
    "Usedestow° evere usurie," quod Repentaunce, "in   Did you use
    alle thi lyf tyme?"

219. But the pound weight that she used to pay them by weighed a quarter more
[6] 'Steelyard.' The Danish steelyard was a pound measure prohibited because of its indefiniteness.

    "Nay, sothly,"° he seyde, "save in my youthe. — truly
    I lerned amonge Lumbardes and Jewes a lessoun,
245 To wey pens° with a peys° and pare the hevyest, — **wey pens** weigh pence   weight
    And lene it for love of the crosse, to legge a wedde and
       lese it;°
    Such dedes I did wryte yif he his day breke.° — **day breke** due day should miss
    I have mo maneres° thorw rerages° than thorw *miseretur* — **mo maneres** more manors   arrears
       et comodat.° — ***miseretur . . .*** have pity and lend
    "I have lent lordes and ladyes my chaffare° — merchandise
250 And ben her brocour° after and boughte it myself. — broker
    Eschaunges and chevesances,° with suche chaffare I dele, — **Eschaunges . . .** Barter and loans
    And lene° folke that lese wol a lyppe at° every noble.° — lend to   **lese . . .** will lose a part of gold   noble
    And with Lumbardes lettres I ladde° golde to Rome — brought
    And toke it by taille° here and tolde° there lasse."° — tally   counted   less
255 "Lentestow° evre lordes for love° of her — Did you lend   desire
       mayntenaunce?"° — support
    "Ye, I have lent lordes loved° me nevere after, — who loved
    And have y-made many a knyghte bothe mercere and
       drapere
    That payed nevere for his prentishode,° noughte a — apprenticeship
       peire gloves."
    "Hastow° pité on pore men that mote° nedes — Have you   must
       borwe?"
260 "I have as moche pité of pore men as pedlere hath of
       cattes,
    That wolde kille hem, yf he cacche hem myghte for
       coveitise of here skynnes."
    "Artow manlyche° amonge thi neighbores of thi — **Artow manlyche** Are you charitable
       mete° and drynke?" — food
    "I am holden," quod he, "as hende° as hounde is in — kind
       kychyne;
    Amonges my neighbores namelich° such a name Ich° — especially   I
       have."
265 "Now, God lene° nevre," quod Repentance, "but° — grant   unless
       thow repent thee rather,° — soon
    Thee grace on this grounde thi good wel to bisette,° — employ
    Ne thine ysue after thee have joye of that thow wynnest,
    Ne thi executours wel bisett the silver that thow hem
       levest;
    And that° was wonne with wronge with wikked men — what
       be despended.° — spent
270 "For were I frere° of that hous there° gode faith and — friar   where
       charité is,

---

246. And lend it for the love of the cross (on the reverse side of the coin), so that the borrower would deposit a pledge (security) and then lose it

I nolde cope° us with thi catel° ne owre kyrke amende,°
Ne have a peny° to my pitaunce of thyne, bi my soule hele,°
For the best boke in owre hous, theighe brent° golde were the leves,
And I wyst wytterly° thow were suche as thow tellest,
275 Or elles that I kouthe° knowe it by any kynnes wise.°

> Servus es alterius, cum fercula pinguia queris;
> Pane tuo pocius vescere, liber eris.°

"Thow art an unkynde° creature. I can thee noughte assoille,°
Til thow make restitucioun and rekne° with hem alle;
280 And sithen that° Resoun rolle° it in the regystre of hevene,
That thow hast made üche man good, I may thee noughte assoille.

> Non dimittitur peccatum, donec restituatur ablatum, etc.[7]

For alle that have of thi good,° have God my trouthe,
Ben holden at the heighe dome° to helpe thee to restitue.
285 And who-so leveth° noughte this be soth,° loke in the Sauter Glose,°
In *Miserere mei Deus*, where° I mene treuthe,

> Ecce enim veritatem dilexisti, etc.[8]

Shal nevere werkman in this worlde thryve wyth that thow wynnest.
Cum sancto sanctus eris[9]—construe me that on Englische!"
290 Thanne wex° that shrewe° in wanhope and walde° have hanged himself,
Ne hadde° Repentaunce the rather reconforted° hym in this manere:
"Have mercye in thi mynde and with thi mouth biseche it,
For Goddes mercye is more than alle hise other werkes;

> Misericordia eius super omnia opera eius, etc.[10]

Glosses: **nolde cope** would not clothe; goods; **kyrke amende** church repair; penny; **soule hele** soul's health; **theighe brent** though burnished; **And...** If I knew surely; could; **kynnes wise** kind of manner; unnatural; absolve; settle; **sithen that** until; enrolls; wealth; judgment; believes; true; Psalter Gloss; **In...** At *Have pity on me, oh God*, whether; fell; wretch; **wanhope...** despair and would; **Ne hadde** If had not; **the...** at once comforted

---

276–77. You are the slave of another when you seek dainty dishes; rather eat bread of your own and you shall be free.
[7] 'A sin is not forgiven until restitution is made, etc.' St. Augustine, *Epistles*, cliii.20.
[8] 'For behold you have desired truth, etc.' Ps. li.6.
[9] 'With the holy you shall be holy.' See Ps. xviii.25, 26.
[10] 'His mercy is above all His other works, etc.' Ps. cxlv.9.

295 And al the wikkednesse in this worlde that man myghte worche or thynke	
Ne is no more to the mercye of God than in the see a glede:°	live coal

Omnis iniquitas quantum ad misericordiam Dei est quasi sintilla in
medio maris.[11]

"For-thi, have mercy in thi mynde; and marchandise, leve it,	
For thow hast no good grounde° to gete thee with a wastel°	justification fine bread
300 But if° it were with° thi tonge or ellis with thi two hondes.	**But if** Unless by
For the good° that thow hast geten bigan al with falsehede,	wealth
And as longe as thow lyvest ther-with, thow yeldest° noughte, but borwest.°	give borrow
And if thow wite° nevere to whiche ne whom to restitue,	know
Bere it to the bisschop and bidde° hym of his grace	ask
305 Bisette° it hymselve as best is for thi soule.	Employ
For he shal answere for thee at the heygh dome.°	judgment
For thee and for many mo,° that man shal yif° a rekenynge,	more give
What he lerned° yow in Lente—leve thow none other—	taught
And what he lent yow of owre Lordes good to lette° yow fro synne."	keep

Gula°   Gluttony

310 Now bigynneth Glotoun for to go to schrifte,°	confession
And kaires hym to-kirke-ward,° his coupe° to schewe.°	**kaires** ... rambles to church sin tell
Ac Beton° the brewestere° bad hym good morwe,°	Betty alewife morning
And axed° of hym with that whiderward he wolde.°	asked would go
"To Holi Cherche," quod he, "for to here° Masse,	hear
315 And sithen I wil be shryven° and synne namore."	confessed
"I have gode ale, gossib,"° quod she. "Glotown, wiltow assaye?"°	neighbor **wiltow assaye** will you try it
"Hastow° aughte in thi purs, any hote spices?"	Do you have
"I have peper and pionés,"° quod she, "and a pounde of garlike,	peony seeds
A ferthyngworth of fenel-seed for fastyng dayes."	
320 Thanne göth Glotoun in and Grete Othes after;	

[11] 'All evil compared to the mercy of God is like a live coal in the middle of the sea.' Attributed to St.
Augustine.

Cesse the souteresse° sat on the benche,	female shoemaker
Watte the warner° and his wyf bothe,°	gamekeeper too
Tymme the tynkere and tweyne° of his prentis,°	two apprentices
Hikke the hakneyman° and Hughe the nedeler,°	liveryman needle-seller
325 Clarice of Cokkes Lane and the clerke of the cherche,	
Dawe the dykere,° and a dozeine other;	ditch-digger
Sire Piers of Pridie and Peronelle of Flaundres,°	
A ribibour,° a ratonere,° a rakyer° of Chepe,°	fiddler rat-catcher scavenger Cheapside
A ropere,° a redyngkyng,° and Rose the dissheres,°	rope-maker groom dish-seller
330 Godfrey of Garlekehithe and Gryfin the Walshe,°	Welshman
And upholderes° an hepe, erly bi the morwe,	old-clothes-sellers
Geven° Glotoun with glad chere° good ale to hansel.°	Gave appearance **to hansel** as a gift
Clement the cobelere cast of his cloke,	
And atte New Faire¹² he nempned° it to selle.	offered
335 Hikke the hakeneyman hitte° his hood after	**hakeneyman hitte** liveryman threw down
And badde Bette° the bochere° ben on his side.	Bart butcher
There were chapmen° y-chose this chaffare° to preise;°	merchants merchandise price
Who-so haveth the hood shuld have amendes of° the cloke.	**amendes of** compensation for
Two risen up in rape and rouned° togideres	**rape** . . . haste and whispered
340 And preised° these penyworthes apart bi hemselve.	appraised
Thei couth° noughte bi her conscience acorden in treuthe,	could
Tyl Robyn the ropere° arose bi the southe,°	rope-maker **bi** . . . for the truth
And nempned hym for a noumpere that no debate nere,°	
For to trye this chaffare° bitwixen hem thre.	**trye** . . . decide this bargain
345 Hikke the hostellere° hadde the cloke	innkeeper
In covenaunte that Clement shulde the cuppe fille	
And have Hikkes hode hostellere° and holde hym y-served.°	**Hikkes** . . . Hick the innkeeper's hood content
And who-so repented rathest° shulde arise after	soonest
And grete Sire Glotoun with a galoun ale.	
350 There was laughyng and louryng° and "Let go the cuppe."	scowling
And seten° so til evensonge° and songen umwhile°	they sat vespers for a while
Tyl Glotoun had y-globbed° a galoun and a jille.°	gulped gill (one-fourth pint)
His guttis gunne° to gothely° as two gredy sowes;	began rumble
His pissed a potel° in a *Pater-noster* while,	pottle (two quarts)
355 And blew his rounde ruwet° at his rigge-bon° ende	horn backbone's
That alle that herde that horne held her nose after	

327. Father Piers of Prie-Dieu and Lady Peacock of Flanders
¹² 'New Fair,' a game of barter. The deputies appointed by the principals Clement and Hick decide the terms of the barter, by which all must abide. Final arbitration rests with the umpire Robyn.
343. And named himself as an umpire so that there might be no quarrel

And wissheden° it had be wexed° with a wispe of firses.°   wished plugged / furze

He myghte neither steppe ne stonde er° he his staffe hadde,   before

And thanne gan° he go, liche a glewmannes° bicche,   began minstrel's

360 Somme tyme aside, and somme tyme arrere,°   to the rear

As who-so leyth lynes° for to lacche foules.°   **leyth lynes** lays snares **lacche foules** catch birds

And whan he drowgh° to the dore, thanne dymmed his eighen;°   drew near / eyes

He stumbled on the thresshewolde and threwe° to the erthe.   tumbled

Clement the cobelere caughte hym bi the myddel

365 For to lyfte hym alofte and leyde him on his knowes.°   knees

Ac Glotoun was a gret cherle° and a grym° in the liftynge,   fellow heavy one

And coughed up a caudel° in Clementis lappe.   mess

Is° non so hungri hounde in Hertford schire   There is

Durst lape of° the levynges, so unlovely thei smaughte.°   **lape of** lap up some of tasted

370   With al the wo of this worlde his wyf and his wenche

Baren hym home to his bedde and broughte hym ther-inne.

And after al this excesse he had an accidie°   fit of sloth

That he slepe Saterday and Sonday til sonne yede° to reste.   went

Thenne waked he of his wynkyng and wiped his eyghen.°   eyes

375 The fyrste worde that he warpe° was "Where is the bolle?"°   uttered / bowl

His wif gan edwite° hym tho° how wikkedlich he lyved,   **gan edwite** rebuked then

And Repentance righte so rebuked hym that tyme:

   "As thow with wordes and werkes hast wroughte yvel in thi lyve,

Shryve thee° and be shamed therof and shewe it with thi mouth."   **Shryve thee** Confess

380   "I, Glotoun," quod the gome,° "gylti me yelde,°   man confess

That I have trespassed with my tonge, I can noughte telle how ofte,

Sworen 'Goddes Soule' and 'So God me help and halidom'°   holy relics

There° no nede ne was nyne hundreth tymes,   Where

And overseye me° at my sopere° and some tyme at nones°   **overseye me** forgotten myself supper noon meal

385 That I, Glotoun, girt° it up er° I hadde gone a myle,   threw before

And y-spilte that° myghte be spared and spended on somme hungrie;   what

Overdelicatly on fastyng dayes drunken and eten bothe,°   *too*

And sat some tyme so longe there that I slepe and ete at ones.

For love of tales in tavernes to drynke the more, I dyned,

390 And hyed° to the mete er none° whan fastyng-dayes were."   *hurried*   **mete . . .** food before midday

   "This shewyng shrifte,"° quod Repentance, "shal be meryte to thee."   **shewyng shrifte** frank confession

   And thanne gan° Glotoun grete° and gret doel to make   *began*   *to cry*

For his lither° lyf that he lyved hadde,   *wicked*

And avowed to fast: "For hunger or for thürst

395 Shal nevere fisshe on the Fryday defien° in my wombe,°   *digest*   *belly*

Tyl Abstinence myn Aunte have yive° me leve;   *given*

And yit have I hated hir al my lyf tyme."

          Accidia°   Sloth

   Thanne come Sleuthe° al bislabered with two slymy eighen,°   Sloth   *eyes*

"I most° sitte," seyde the segge,° "or elles shulde I nappe;   *must*   *man*

400 I may° noughte stonde, ne stoupe, ne withoute a stole° knele.   *can*   *stool*

Were I broughte abedde, but if° my taille-ende it made,°   **but if** unless   *made me*

Sholde no ryngynge do° me ryse ar° I were rype° to dyne."   *make*   *before*   *ready*

He bygan *Benedicite*[13] with a bolke° and his brest knocked,   *belch*

And roxed and rored and rutte° atte laste.   **roxed . . .** stretched and groaned and snored

405 "What! Awake, renke!"° quod Repentance, "and rape° thee to shrifte."   *man*   *hasten*

   "If I shulde deye bi this day, me liste° noughte to loke.°   **me liste** it pleases me   *watch*

I can° noughte perfitly my *Pater-noster* as the prest it syngeth,   *know*

But I can rymes of Robyn Hood and Randolf Erle of Chestre,

Ac neither of owre Lorde ne of owre Lady the leste that evere was made.

410 I have made vowes fourty and foryete° hem on the morne;   *forgotten*

I parfourned° nevre penaunce as the prest me highte,°   *performed*   *ordered*

---

[13] 'Bless me.' Opening of confession formula.

Ne ryghte sori for my synnes yet was I nevere.
And yif I bidde° any bedes,° but if it be in wrath,　　pray rosary beads
That° I telle with my tonge is two myle fro myne herte.　　What
415 I am occupied eche day, haliday and other,
With ydel tales atte ale and otherwhile in cherches;
Goddes peyne and his passioun ful selde thynke I
　　　there-on.
　"I visited nevere fieble men ne fettered folke in
　　　püttes,°　　dungeons
I have levere° here an harlotrie° or a somer game[14] of　　**have levere** would rather　bawdy
souteres,°　　tale　shoemakers
420 Or lesynges° to laughe at and belye° my neighbore,　　lies slander
Than al that evere Marke made, Mathew, John, and
　　　Lucas.
And vigilies and fastyng dayes, alle thise late° I passe,　　let
And ligge° abedde in Lenten and my lemman° in myn　　lie mistress
　　　armes,
Tyl matynes and masse be do,° and thanne go to the　　done
　　　freres;
425 Come I to *Ite, missa est,*° I holde me y-served.°　　***Ite* . . .** Go, the mass is ended finished
I nam° noughte shryven some tyme but if sekenesse it　　am
　　　make,
Nought tweies in two yere, and thanne up gesse° I　　**up gesse** at a guess
　　　schryve me.
　"I have be prest and parsoun passynge thretti wynter,
Yete can I neither solfé° ne synge ne seyntes lyves rede,　　read notes
430 But I can fynde in a felde or in a fourlonge° an hare,　　furrow
Better than in *Beatus vir*[15] or in *Beati omnes*[16]
Construe oon clause wel and kenne° it to my　　teach
　　　parochienes.°　　parishioners
I can holde lovedays and here° a reves rekenynge,°　　**lovedays . . .** settlement days and hear audit accounting
Ac in canoun° ne in the decretales I can noughte rede a　　canon law
　　　lyne.
435 Yif I bigge° and borwe it, but yif it be y-tailled,°　　buy marked on a tally
I foryete° it as yerne,° and yif men me it axe　　forget eagerly
Sixe sithes° or sevene, I forsake° it with othes,　　times deny
And thus tene° I trewe° men ten hundreth tymes.　　injure honest
　"And my servauntz some tyme, her salarye is
　　　bihynde,
440 Reuthe° is to here° the rekenynge° whan we shal rede　　Pity hear accounting
　　　acomptes;
So with wikked wille and wraththe my werkmen I paye.

---

[14] The 'summer game' was a midsummer athletic festival, often conducted indecorously.
[15] 'Blessed is the man.' Ps. i.1.
[16] 'Blessed are all.' Ps. ii.12.

"Yif any man döth me a benfait° or helpeth me at nede,
   good deed

I am unkynde ayein° his curteisye and can noughte understonde it.
   in return for

For I have and have hadde some dele haukes° maneres:
   dele haukes *part of the hunting hawk's*

445 I nam noughte lured with love, but there ligge° aughte under the thombe.
   but . . . *except where lies*

The kyndenesse that myne evene-Cristene kidde° me fernyere,°
   evene-Cristene kidde *fellow Christian showed   formerly*

Sixty sythes° I, Sleuthe,° have foryete° it sith.°
   times Sloth forgotten since

In speche and in sparynge of speche, y-spilte° many a tyme
   I have wasted

Bothe flesche° and fissche and many other vitailles;
   meat

450 Bothe bred and ale, butter, melke, and chese

Forsleuthed° in my servyse til it myghte serve no man.
   Wasted

   "I ran aboute in youthe and yaf° me noughte to lerne,
   gave

And evere sith° have be beggere for my foule sleuthe,°
   since sloth

Heu michi, quod sterilem vitam duxi juvenilem."°

455 "Repentestow thee° naughte?" quod Repentance, and righte with that he° swowned,
   Repentestow thee *Do you repent*
   he (Sloth)

Til *Vigilate°* the veille fette° water at his eyghen,
   Watch **veille fette** *watcher brought*

And flatte° it on his face, and faste on him criede
   dashed

And seide, "Ware thee fram wanhope, wolde° thee bitraye.
   Ware . . . *Beware of despair, which would*

'I am sori for my synnes,' sey so to thiselve,

460 And bete thiselve on the breste and bidde° Hym of grace;
   pray

For is no gült here so grete that His goodnesse nys° more."
   is not

   Thanne sat Sleuthe° up and seyned° hym swithe,°
   Sloth blessed quickly

And made avowe° to-fore God for his foule sleuthe;
   vow

"Shal no Sondaye be this sevene yere, but sykenesse it lette,°
   prevent

465 That I ne shal do° me er day to the dere cherche,
   bring

And heren° matines and masse as° I a monke were.
   hear as if

Shal none ale after mete° holde me thennes,°
   food thence

Tyl I have evensonge herde, I behote° to the Rode.°
   vow Cross

And yete wil I yelde ayein,° if I so moche have,
   yelde ayein *give back*

470 Al that I wikkedly wan sithen° I wytte° hadde.
   since reason

And though my liflode lakke, leten° I nelle,°
   liflode . . . *livelihood be lacking, stop will not*

That eche man ne shal have his ar° I hennes wende:°
   before **hennes wende** *go hence*

And with the residue and the remenaunt, bi the Rode of Chestre,

454. Woe is me that I have lived such a barren youth.

I shal seke Treuthe arst° ar I se Rome!"   first

475   Robert the robbere on *Reddite*[17] lokede,

And for° ther was noughte wher-of,° he wepe swithe°   because **noughte wher-of** no

sore.   wherewithal   very

Ac yet the synful shrewe° seyde to hymselve,   wretch

"Cryst that on Calvarye uppon the crosse deydest,

Tho° Dismas[18] my brother bisoughte yow of grace,   When

480 And haddest mercy on that man for *memento*° sake,   remember me

So rewe° on this robbere that *reddere*° ne have,   pity   to repay

Ne nevere wene° to wynne with crafte that° I owe.   think   **crafte that** skill what

But for thi mykel° mercy mitigacioun I biseche;   great

Ne dampne° me noughte at Domesday for that I did so   condemn

ille."

485   What bifel of this feloun I can noughte faire schewe.

Wel I wote° he wepte faste water with bothe his eyen,   know

And knowleched his gült to Cryst yete eftsones,°   soon after

That *penitencia* his pyke° he shulde polsche° newe,   pikestaff   polish

And lepe with hym over londe al his lyf tyme,

490 For he had leyne° bi Latro,° Luciferes Aunte.   lain   the Robber

And thanne had Repentaunce reuthe and redde° hem   **reuthe...** pity and bade

alle to knele,

"For I shal biseche for al synful owre Saveoure of grace,

To amende us of owre mysdedes and do mercy to us

alle.

"Now God," quod he, "that of thi goodnesse gonne°   did

the worlde make,

495 And of naughte madest aughte and man moste liche to

thiselve,

And sithen suffredest° for to synne, a sikenesse to us alle,   suffered him

And al for the best, as I bileve, what evere the boke

telleth,

O felix culpa! O necessarium peccatum Ade! etc.[19]

For thourgh that synne thi sone sent was to this erthe,

500 And bicam man of a mayde, mankynde to save,

And madest thiself with thi sone and us synful y-liche,°   **synful y-liche** sinful ones alike

*Faciamus hominem ad ymaginem et similitudinem nostram;
Et alibi, qui manet in caritate, in Deo manet, et Deus in eo.*[20]

"And sith° with thi self° sone in owre sute° deydest   then   own   suit of flesh

---

[17] 'Render to all men their dues.' Rom. xiii.7.

[18] Apocryphal name of the penitent thief crucified with Christ.

[19] 'O happy fault: O necessary sin of Adam! etc.' From Holy Saturday canticle *Exsultet*.

[20] 'Let us make man in our image and likeness; and elsewhere: he who dwells in love, dwells in God, and God in him.' Gen. i.26, I John iv.16.

505 On Gode Fryday for mannes sake at ful tyme of the
      daye,
There° thiself ne thi sone no sorwe in deth feledest;   Where
But in owre secte° was the sorwe,° and thi sone it ladde,°   following   sorrow led

    Captivam duxit captivitatem.[21]

The sonne for sorwe therof les° syghte for a tyme   gave up
510 Aboute mydday whan most lighte is° and mele tyme of   there is
      seintes;
Feddest with thi fresche blode owre forfadres in
      derknesse,

    Populus qui ambulabat in tenebris, vidit lucem magnam.[22]

And thorw the lighte that lepe out of thee, Lucifer was
      blent,°   blinded
And blewe° alle thi blissed into the blisse of Paradise.   you heralded
515   "The thrydde daye after thow yedest° in owre sute,°   went   suit of flesh
A synful Marie thee seighe ar° Seynte Marie thi dame,°   before   mother
And al to solace synful,° thow suffredest it so were:°   sinful ones   to be

    Non veni vocare justos, sed peccatores ad penitenciam.[23]

And al that Marke hath y-made, Mathew, Johan, and
      Lucas,
520 Of thyne doughtiest° dedes were don in owre armes.°   most valiant   armor

    Verbum caro factum est, et habitavit in nobis.[24]

And bi so moche, me semeth, the sikerere° we mowe°   more securely   may
Bydde° and biseche if it be thi wille,   Pray
That art owre Fader and owre Brother, be merciable to
      us,
525 And have reuthe° on thise ribaudes° that repente hem   pity   sinners
      here sore,
That evere thei wratthed° thee in this worlde in worde,   angered
      thoughte, or dedes."
  Thanne hent Hope an horne of *Deus, tu conversus*   seized
    vivificabis nos,[25]
And blew it with *Beati quorum remisse sunt iniquitates,*[26]
That alle seyntes in hevene songen at ones:

---

[21] 'He led captivity captive.' Eph. iv.8.
[22] 'The people who walked in darkness have seen a great light.' Isa. ix.2.
[23] 'I came to call not the just, but sinners to penitence.' Matt. ix.13.
[24] 'The word was made flesh and dwelt among us.' John i.14.
[25] 'God, You having turned shall refresh us.' Ps. lxxi.20.
[26] 'Blessed are those whose sins are forgiven.' Ps. xxxii.1.

530   *Homines et jumenta salvabis, quemadmodum multiplicasti*
      misericordiam tuam, Deus, etc.[27]

     A thousand of men tho° thrungen togyderes;   then
     Criede upward to Cryst and to his clene° moder   pure
     To have Grace to go with hem, Treuthe to seke.
       Ac there was wyghte° non so wys the wey thider   man
         couthe,°   knew

535 But blustreden forth as bestes over bankes and hilles,
     Til late was and longe that thei a lede° mette,   man
     Apparailled as a paynym° in pylgrymes wyse.°   Saracen   guise
     He bare a burdoun° y-bounde with a brode liste°   staff   strip of cloth
     In a withewyndes wise° y-wounden aboute.   **withewyndes wise** bindweed's
                                         manner
540 A bolle° and a bagge he bare by his syde;   bowl
     An hundreth° of ampulles° on his hatt seten,°   hundred   phials   were placed
     Signes° of Synay,° and shelles of Galice.°   Emblems   Sinai   Galicia
     And many a cruche° on his cloke and keyes of Rome,   cross
     And the vernicle° bifore, for men shulde knowe   Veronica's veil
545 And se bi his signes whom he soughte hadde.
       This folke frayned° hym firste fro whennes° he come.   asked   whence
       "Fram Synay," he seyde, "and fram owre Lordes
         sepulcre;
     In Bethleem and in Babiloyne I have ben in bothe,
     In Ermonye,° in Alisaundre, in many other places.   Armenia
550 Ye may se bi my signes° that sitten° on myn hatte   emblems   are placed
     That I have walked ful wyde in wete and in drye
     And soughte gode seyntes for my soules helth."
       "Knowestow° oughte a corseint° that men calle   Do you know   holy person
         Treuthe?
     Coudestow° aughte wissen° us the weye where that wy°   Could you   teach   person
         dwelleth?"
555   "Nay, so me God helpe!" seide the gome° thanne,   man
     "I seygh nevere palmere with pike ne with scrippe
     Axen after hym er til° now in this place."   **er til** formerly until
     "Peter!"° quod a plowman and put forth his hed,   By Peter
     "I knowe hym as kyndely° as clerke döth his bokes;   intimately
560 Conscience and Kynde Witte kenned° me to his place,   **Kynde . . .** Common Sense directed
     And deden° me suren° hym sikerly° to serve hym for   made   pledge   surely
         evere,
     Bothe to sowe and to sette° the while I swynke° myghte.   plant   work
     I have ben his folwar al this fifty wyntre;
     Bothe y-sowen his sede and sued° his bestes,   driven
565 Withinne and withouten wayted° his profyt.   looked after
     I dyke° and I delve;° I do that Treuthe hoteth.°   dig ditches   dig   bids

[27] 'You shall save men and beasts, just as you have increased Your mercy, God, etc.' Ps. xxxvi.6, 7.

Some tyme I sowe and some tyme I thresche;

In tailoures crafte° and tynkares crafte what Treuthe can devyse,   *skill*

I weve and I wynde and do what Treuthe hoteth.

570 "For thoughe I seye it myself, I serve hym to paye.°   *his satisfaction*

Ich have my hüire° of hym wel and otherwhiles° more.   *pay sometimes*

He is the prestest° payer that pore men knoweth;   *quickest*

He ne withhalt° non hewe° his hyre that he ne hath it at even.   *withholds laborer*

He is as low° as a lombe and loveliche of speche,   *meek*

575 And yif ye wilneth to wite° where that he dwelleth,   *know*

I shal wisse° yow witterly° the weye to his place."   *teach truly*

  "Ye, leve° Pieres," quod this pilgrymes, and profered hym hüire°   *dear pay*

For to wende with hem to Treuthes dwellyng place.

  "Nay, bi my soules helth," quod Pieres, and gan° for to swere,   *began*

580 "I nolde fange° a ferthynge, for Seynt Thomas shryne!   **nolde fange** *would not take*

Treuthe wolde love me the lasse a longe tyme there-after!

Ac if ye wilneth to wende° wel, this is the weye thider   *go*

That I shal say to yow and sette yow in the sothe.°   *truth*

  "Ye mote° go thourgh Mekenesse, bothe men and wyves,   *must*

585 Tyl ye come into Conscience, that Cryst wite° the sothe,   *may know*

That ye loven owre Lorde God levest° of alle thinges,   *dearest*

And thanne yowre neighbores nexte in non wise apeyre°   **wise apeyre** *manner harm*

Otherwyse than thow woldest he wroughte° to thiselve.   *did*

  "And so boweth° forth bi a broke,° *Beth-buxom°-of-spech,*   *go brook mild*

590 Tyl ye fynden a forth,° *Yowre-fadres-honoureth,*   *ford*

    Honora patrem et matrem,° etc.   **Honora . . .** *Honor father and mother*

Wadeth in that water and wascheth yow wel there,

And ye shul lepe the lightloker° al yowre lyf tyme.   *more lightly*

And so shaltow° se *Swere-noughte-but-if it-be-for-nede-*   *you will*

595 *And-namelich-an-ydel°-the-name-of-God-Almyghti.*   **namelich . . .** *especially-in-vain*

  "Thanne shaltow come by a crofte,° but come thow noughte there-inne;   *enclosure*

That crofte hat° *Coveyte-noughte-mennes-catel-ne-her-wyves-*   *is called*

Ne-none-of-her-servauntes-that-noyen°-hem-myghti.   **that-noyen** *lest-you-injure*

Loke ye breke no bowes° there but if it be yowre owne.   boughs

600 Two stokkes° there stondeth, ac stynte° ye noughte   stocks   stop
       there;
They hatte *Stele-noughte, Ne-Slee°-noughte*; stryke°   Slay   go
       forth by bothe,
And leve hem on thi left halfe° and loke noughte   side
       there-after;
And holde wel thyne haliday heighe° til even.   holy
Thenne shaltow blenche° at a berghe,° *Bere-no-false-*   **shaltow blenche** you will turn
      witnesse.   hill

605 He is frithed° in with floreines° and other fees many;   enclosed   florins
Loke thow plukke no plante there for peril of thi soule.
Thanne shall ye se *Sey-soth°-so-it-be-to-done-*   the truth
In-no-manere-ellis-naughte-for-no-mannes-biddynge.
    "Thanne shaltow come to a courte° as clere as the   mansion court
      sonne;

610 The mote is of Mercy, the manere° aboute,   manor
And alle the wallis ben of Witte° to holden Wille oute;   Wisdom
And kerneled° with Crystendome, man-kynde to save,   crenelated
Boterased° with *Bileve-so-or-thow-beest-noughte-y-saved.*   Buttressed
    "And alle the houses ben hiled,° halles and chambres,   roofed

615 With no lede, but with Love and *Lowe°-speche-as-*   Humble
      bretheren.
The brügge° is of *Bidde°-wel-the-bette°-may-thow-spede;*°   bridge Pray better prosper
Eche piler° is of penaunce, of preyeres to seyntes;   pillar
Of almes deeds ar the hokes that the gates hangen on.
    "Grace hatte° the gateward,° a gode man for sothe,°   is called gatekeeper **for sothe**
      indeed
620 Hys man hatte Amende°-yow, for many man him   Reform
      knoweth.
Telleth hym this tokene, that Treuthe wite° the sothe: may know
'I parfourned° the penaunce the prest me enjoyned   performed
And am ful sori for my synnes, and so I shal evere
Whan I thinke there-on, theighe° I were a pope.'   though
625   "Biddeth° Amende-yow meke him til° his maistre   Ask **meke . . .** to humble himself
      ones,
To wayve° up the wiket that the womman shette   raise
Tho° Adam and Eve eten apples unrosted.   When

      Per Evam cunctis clausa est, et per Mariam Virginem iterum
          patefacta est;°

For he° hath the keye and the cliket° though the Kynge   she latch
      slepe.
630 And if Grace graunte thee to go in this wise,°   manner
Thow shalt see in thiselve Treuthe sitte in thine herte,

628. Through Eve the gate was closed to all, and through Mary the Virgin again it was opened

In a cheyne of charyté, as° thow a childe were,   as if
To suffre Hym and segge° noughte ayein° thi Sires speak against
 wille.
 "Ac bewar thanne of Wraththe, that is a wikked
  shrewe;
635 He hath Envye to Hym that in thine herte sitteth
And pukketh° forth Pruyde to prayse thiselven.   pushes
The boldnesse° of thi bienfetes° maketh thee blynde presumption good deeds
 thanne,
And thanne worstow° dryven oute as dew, and the dore you will be
 closed,
Kayed and cliketed° to kepe thee withouten   **Kayed** ... Locked and latched
640 Happily° an hundreth wyntre ar thow eft° entre. Perhaps again
Thus myght thow lesen° His love, to late° wel by lose think
 thiselve,
And nevere happiliche efte entre but grace thow have.
 "Ac there aren sevene sustren° that serven Treuthe sisters
 evere
And aren porteres of the posternes that to the place
 longeth.°   belong
645 That one hat° Abstenence and Humilité an other, is called
Charité and Chastité ben His chief maydenes,
Pacience and Pees,° moche poeple thei helpeth, Peace
Largenesse° the lady, heo let° in ful manye,   Bounty **heo let** she lets
Heo hath hulpe a thousande oute of the develes
 ponfolde.°   pound
650 "And who° is sibbe° to this sevene, so me God helpe, whoever akin
He is wonderliche° welcome and faire underfongen.° wonderfully received
And but if ye be syb° to summe of thise sevene, akin
It is ful harde bi myne heved,"° quod Peres, "for any of head
 yow alle
To geten ingonge° at any gate there but grace be the entrance
 more."
655 "Now, bi Cryst," quod a cutpurs, "I have no kynne
 there!"
"Ne I," quod an apewarde,° "bi aughte that I monkey-keeper
 knowe!"
"Wite° God," quod a wafrestre,° "wist I° this for Save us wafer-seller **wist I** if I
 sothe,°   knew **for sothe** indeed
Shulde° I nevere ferthere a fote for no freres Should go
 prechynge."
"Yüs," quod Pieres the Plowman, and pukked° hem pushed
 alle to gode,°   **to gode** toward good behavior
660 "Mercy is a maydene there, hath myghte over hem
 alle.

And she is syb° to alle synful and her Sone also.   akin
And thorughe the helpe of hem two—hope thow none
    other—
Thow myghte gete grace there, bi so° thow go   **bi so** provided
    bityme."°   in time
"By Seynt Poule," quod a Pardonere, "peraventure
    I be noughte knowe° there.   known
665 I wil go fecche my box with my brevettes° and a bulle°   documents of indulgence
    with bisshopes lettres!"   document
"By Cryst," quod a comune womman,° "thi   **comune womman** prostitute
    companye wil I folwe,°   follow
Thow shalt sey I am thi süstre." I ne wot° where thei   know
    bicome.°   went

Canto VII

Treuthe herde telle her-of and to Peres he sent,
To taken his teme and tülyen° the erthe,   till
And purchaced° hym a pardoun *a poena et a culpa*[1]   provided
For hym and for his heires for evermore after.
5 And bad hym holde hym at home and eryen° his leyes;° plow   fields
And alle° that halpe hym to erie, to sette,° or to sowe,   to all   plant
Or any other myster° that myghte Pieres availle,°   trade   assist
Pardoun with° Pieres Plowman Treuthe hath   along with
    y-graunted.
Kynges and knyghtes that kepen° Holy Cherche   guard
10 And ryghtfullych in reumes° reulen the peple   realms
Han pardoun thourgh Purgatorie to passe ful lyghtly,
With patriarkes and prophetes in Paradise to be felawes.
Bisshopes y-blessed,° yif thei ben as thei shulden,   consecrated
Legistres° of bothe the lawes,[2] the lewed° there-with to   Advocates   unlearned
    preche,
15 And in as moche as thei mowe, amende° alle synful,°   **mowe, amende** can, correct
Aren peres° with the Apostles (this pardoun Piers   sinful ones
    sheweth),   peers
And at the Day of Dome° atte heigh deyse° to sytte.   Judgment   dais
Marchauntz in the margyne° hadden many yeres,°   margin of the Bull   years of
Ac none *a poena et a culpa*[1] the Pope nolde° hem   indulgence
    graunte,   would not

---

[1] 'From punishment and from guilt.' Indulgences usually removed only punishment.
[2] Both parts of the Ten Commandments: the laws concerning our duty to God and those concerning our duty to our fellow man.

20 For thei holde nought her halidayes as Holi Cherche
        techeth,

And for° thei swere "By her° soule" and "So God   *because   their*
        moste hem helpe"

Ayein° clene conscience her catel° to selle.   *Against   goods*

    Ac under his secret seel Treuthe sent hem a lettre,

That they shulde bügge° boldely that° hem best liked,°   *buy   what   pleased*

25 And sithenes selle it ayein° and save the wynnynge,   *again*

And amende *mesondieux* there-myde and myseyse°   **amende . . .** repair hospitals
        folke helpe,   therewith and unfortunate

And wikked wayes wightlich° hem amende;°   **wikked . . .** bad roads quickly
                                        improve

And do bote° to brügges° that to-broke were,   **do bote** make repairs   bridges

Marien° maydenes or maken hem nonnes;   *Dower*

30 Pore peple and prisounes° fynden hem here fode,°   *prisoners   food*

And sette scoleres to scole or to somme other craftes;

Releve Religioun and renten° hem bettere—   **Releve . . .** Assist religious orders
                                        and endow

"And I shal sende yow, myselve, Seynt Michel myn
        archangel,

That no devel shal yow dere ne fere° yow in yowre   **dere . . .** harm nor frighten
        deyinge,°   *dying*

35 And witen° yow fro wanhope° if ye wil thus worche,°   *guard   despair   do*

And sende yowre sowles in safté° to my seyntes in joye."   *safety*

    Thanne were Marchauntz mery; many wepten for
        joye,

And preyseden Pieres the Plowman that purchaced°   *provided*
        this bulle.°   *document*

Men of lawe lest° pardoun hadde that pleteden° for   *least   pleaded*
        mede,°   *bribe*

40 For the Sauter° saveth hem noughte such as taketh   *Psalter*
        yiftes,°   *gifts*

And namelich of° innocentz that none yvel ne   **namelich of** especially from
        kunneth:°   *know*

        Super innocentem munera non accipies.[3]

Pledoures° shulde peynen hem° to plede for such, and   Pleaders   **peynen hem** trouble
        helpe;   themselves

Prynces and prelates shulde paye for her° travaille: *their (the pleaders')*

45   *A regibus et pryncipibus erit merces eorum.*°

Ac many a justice and juroure wolde for Johan° do   *friend John*
        more

Than *pro Dei pietate,*° leve thow none other!   ***pro . . .*** for devotion to God

---

[3] 'Against the innocent you shall accept no bribes.' See Ps. xv.5.
45. From kings and princes shall be their wages.

Ac he that spendeth his speche and speketh for the
 pore
That is innocent and nedy and no man appeireth,°   harms
50 Conforteth hym in that cas withoute coveytise of
 yiftes,°   gifts
And scheweth° lawe for owre Lordes love as he it hath   explains
 lerned,
Shal no devel at his ded-day deren° hym a myghte°   harm bit
That he ne wörth sauf° and his sowle. The Sauter°   ne ... will not be saved Psalter
 bereth witnesse:

 Domine, quis habitabit in tabernaculo tuo, etc.[4]

55 Ac to bügge° water, ne wynde, ne witte,° ne fyre the   buy intelligence
 fierthe!°—   fourth
Thise foure the Fader of hevene made to this folde° in   earth
 comune.
Thise ben Treuthes tresores, trewe folke to helpe,
That nevere shal wax ne wanye withoute God
 hymselve.
 Whan thei drawen on to deye, and indulgences wolde
 have,
60 Her pardoun is ful petit° at her partyng hennes,°   little hence
That° any mede° of mene° men for her motyng° taketh.   If bribe poor pleading
Ye legistres° and lawyers holdeth this for treuthe,   advocates
That, yif that I lye, Mathew is to blame,
For he bad me make° yow this, and this proverbe me   compose
 tolde,

65 *Quodcumque vultis ut faciant vobis homines, facite eis.*[5]

 Alle lybbyng° laboreres that lyven with° her hondes,   living by
That trewlich taken and trewlich wynnen,
And lyven in love and in lawe for her lowe° hertis,   humble
Haveth the same absolucioun that sent was to Peres.°   Piers
70 Beggeres ne bidderes° ne beth noughte in the bulle,°   spongers document
But if the suggestioun° be soth° that shapeth hem to   reason honest
 begge.
For he that beggeth or bit,° but if he have nede,   asks
He is fals with° the Fende° and defraudeth the nedy,   along with Fiend
And also he bigileth the gyvere ageines his wil.
75 For if he wist° that he were noughte nedy, he wolde   knew
 yive° that another   give
That were more nedy than he so the nediest shuld be
 hulpe.

---

[4] 'Lord, who shall dwell in Thy tabernacle, etc.' Ps. xv.1.
[5] 'Whatever you wish that men should do to you, do to them.' Matt. vii.12.

Catoun kenneth° men thus and the clerke of the stories,[6]   **Catoun kenneth** Cato teaches
Cui des, videto[7] is Catounes techynge,
And in the stories he techeth to bistowe thyn almes:

80   *Sit elemosina tua in manu tua, donec studes cui des.*°

Ac Gregori was a gode man, and bad us gyven alle
That asketh, for His love that us alle leneth:°   gave

*Non eligas cui miserearis, ne forte pretereas illum qui meretur
accipere; quia incertum est pro quo Deo magis placeas.*[8]

For wite ye nevere who is worthi, ac God wote who
      hath nede.
85 In hym that taketh is the treccherye if any tresoun
      wawe;°   goes about
For he that yiveth, yeldeth, and yarketh° hym to reste,   **yiveth...** gives, repays God, and
And he that biddeth,° borweth, and bryngeth hymself   prepares
      in dette.   begs
For beggeres borwen evermo,° and her borghe° is God   evermore   security
      Almyghti
To yelden hem that yiveth hem and yet usure° more: pay interest

90   *Quare non dedisti peccuniam meam ad mensam, ut ego veniens
            cum usuris exegissem illam?*[9]

For-thi biddeth nought, ye beggeres, but if ye have
      gret nede;
For who-so hath to büggen° hym bred, the boke bereth   buy
      witnesse,
He hath ynough that hath bred ynough though he have
      nought elles:

Satis dives est qui non indiget pane.[10]

95 Late° usage be yowre solace of seyntes lyves redynge.   Let
The boke banneth beggarie and blameth hem in this
      manere:

*Junior fui, etenim senui; et non vidi justum derelictum, nec semen
            eius querens panem.*[11]

---

[6] A reference to Peter Comestor (d. 1198), author of *Historia Scholastica*, a miscellaneous collection of narratives from the Bible and other sources.
[7] 'Watch to whom you give.' Breves Sententiae 23, *Distichs*.
80. Let your alms be in your hand until you study to whom you give.
[8] 'Choose not whom you shall pity, nor by chance pass over that one who deserves to receive; because it is uncertain in virtue of whom you are more pleasing to God.' St. Jerome, *Commentary on Eccl.*, xi.6.
[9] 'Why have you not given my money to the bank, so that I, coming, might have required it with interest?' Luke xix.23.
[10] 'He is rich enough who does not lack bread.' St. Jerome, *Epistles*, cxxv.
[11] 'I have been young; now I am old; and I have not seen the just abandoned, nor his seed begging bread.' Ps. xxxvii.25.

For ye live in no love ne no lawe holde;
Many of yow ne wedde nought the wommen that ye
    with delen,
100 But as wilde bestis with wehe wörthen uppe° and   wehe ... a neigh mount
    worchen,
And bryngeth forth barnes° that bastardes men calleth.   children
Or° the bakke or some bone he breketh in his youthe,°   Either   offspring
And sitthe gon faiten° with youre fauntes° for evermore   sitthe ... then go begging
    after.   children
There is moo° mysshape peple amonge thise beggeres   more
105 Than of alle maner men that on this molde° walketh,   earth
And thei that lyve thus here lyf mowe° lothe the tyme   may
That evere he was man wrought whan he shal hennes°   hence
    fare.
Ac olde men and hore,° that helplees ben of   hoary
    strengthe,
And women with childe, that worche ne mowe,°   **ne mowe** cannot
110 Blynde and bede-red° and broken here membres,   bedridden
That taketh this myschief mekelych, as meseles° and   **as meseles** such as lepers
    othere,
Han° as pleyne° pardoun as the plowman hymself.   Have   full
For love of her lowe° hertis owre Lorde hath hem   humble
    graunted
Here penaunce and her purgatorie here on this erthe.
115   "Pieres," quod a prest tho,° "thi pardoun most° I rede,   then   must
For I wil construe eche clause and kenne° it thee on   teach
    Engliche."
And Pieres at his preyere° the pardoun unfoldeth,   request
And I bihynde hem bothe bihelde al the bulle.°   document
Al in two lynes it lay and nought a leef more,
120 And was writen right thus, in witnesse of Treuthe:

    Et qui bona egerunt, ibunt in vitam eternam;
    Qui vero mala, in ignem eternum.[12]

"Peter!"° quod the prest tho.° "I can no pardoun   By Peter   then
    fynde,
But 'Dowel,° and have wel, and God shal have thi   Do-well
    sowle,
125 And do yvel, and have yvel, hope thow non other,
But after thi ded-day the devel shal have thi sowle!' "
And Pieres for pure tene° pulled it atweyne,   vexation

---

[12] 'And those who have done good shall go into eternal life, those who have done evil, into eternal fire.'
Athanasian Creed, from Matt. xxv.46.

And seyde: "*Si ambulavero in medio umbrae mortis,*
Non timebo mala; quoniam tu mecum es.[13]
130 I shal cessen of my sowyng," quod Pieres, "and swynk°   work
    nought so harde,
Ne about my bely joye so bisi be namore!
Of preyers and of penaunce my plow shal ben herafter,
And wepen whan I shulde slepe, though whete° bred   wheat
    me faille.
    "The prophete his payn° ete in penaunce and in   bread
      sorwe;°   sorrow
135 By that° the Sauter° seith, so dede° other manye.   **By that** What Psalter did
That° loveth God lelly,° his lyflode° is ful esy: He who loyally livelihood

    Fuerunt mihi lacrimae meae panes die ac nocte.[14]

And but if Luke lye, he lereth° us bi foules,°   teaches birds
We shulde nought be too bisy aboute the worldes
    blisse.
140 *Ne solliciti sitis*[15] he seyth in the gospel,
And sheweth us bi ensamples us selve to wisse.°   direct
The foules on the felde, who fynt° hem mete° at   finds food
    wynter?
Have thei no gernere° to go to but God fynt hem alle."   barn
    "What!" quod the prest to Perkyn, "Peter, as me
      thinketh,°   **me thinketh** it seems to me
145 Thow art lettred a litel. Who lerned thee on° boke?"   in
    "Abstinence the Abbesse," quod Pieres, "myne
      A B C me taughte,
And Conscience come afterward and kenned me moche
    more."
    "Were thow a prest, Pieres," quod he, "thow
      mighte preche where thow sholdest,
As devynour° in devynyté with *dixit insipiens*[16] to thi   teacher
    teme."°   **to . . . ** as your theme
150   "Lewed lorel!"° quod Pieres. "Litel lokestow° on the   **Lewed lorel** Unlearned fellow do
    Bible,   you look
On Salomones sawes seldon thow biholdest,

    Eice derisores et jurgia cum eis, ne crescant, etc."[17]

The prest and Perkyn apposeden eyther° other,   each
And I thorw here wordes awoke and waited° aboute   looked

[13] 'If I shall walk in the middle of the shadow of death, I shall not fear evil, because You are with me.' Ps. xxiii.4.
[14] 'My tears have been food for me day and night.' Ps. xlii.3.
[15] 'Be not solicitous.' Matt. vi.25, 31.
[16] 'The fool has spoken.' Ps. xiv.1, liii.1.
[17] 'Cast out the scorners and contention with them, so that they may not increase, etc.' Prov. xxii.10.

155 And seigh the sonne in the south sitte° that tyme,   set
    Metelees and monelees° on Malverne hülles,°   Metelees . . . Foodless and moneyless hills
    Musyng on this meteles;° and my waye Ich yede.°   vision went
      Many tyme this meteles hath maked me to studye
    Of that° I seigh slepyng if it so be myghte,   what
160 And also for Peres the Plowman, ful pensyf in herte,
    And which a pardoun Peres hadde, alle the peple to
      conforte,
    And how the prest impugned it with two propre°   distinct
      wordes.
    Ac I have no savoure in songwarie,° for I se it ofte faille.   savoure . . . delight in dream-interpretation
    Catoun and Canonistres° conseilleth us to leve°   Catoun . . . Cato and the Canonists stop
165 To sette sadnesse° in songewarie, for *sompnia ne cures*.[18]   To . . . Putting faith
    Ac for° the boke Bible bereth witnesse   as
    How Danyel devyned the dremes of a kynge
    That was Nabugodonosor nempned of° clerkis,   nempned of named by
    Daniel seyde, "Sire Kynge, thi dremeles° bitokneth   dream
170 That unkouth° knyghtes shul come thi kyngdom to   strange
      cleve;
    Amonges lowere lordes thi londe shal be departed."°   divided
    And as Danyel devyned, in dede it felle° after;   befell
    The kynge lese° his lordship and lower men it hadde.   lost
      And Joseph mette° merveillously how the mone and   dreamed
      the sonne
175 And the ellevene sterres hailsed° hym alle.   greeted
    Thanne Jacob jugged Josephes swevene:°   dream
    "Beau filtz,"° quod his fader, "for defaute° we   Beau filtz Fair son want
      shullen,°   must
    I myself and my sones, seche° thee for nede."   seek
      It bifel as his fader seyde in Pharaoes tyme,
180 That Joseph was justice Egipte to loken;°   look after
    It bifel as his fader tolde; his frendes there hym soughte.
      And al this maketh me on this meteles° to thynke,   vision
    And how the prest preved° no pardoun to Dowel°   proved to Dowel like Do-well
    And demed that Dowel indulgences passed,°   surpassed
185 Biennales, and triennales,° and bisschopes lettres,   Biennales . . . Biennial and triennial masses for the dead
    And how Dowel at the day of dome° is dignelich   judgment
      underfongen,°   dignelich underfongen worthily received
    And passeth al the pardoun of Seynt Petres Cherche.
      Now hath the Pope powere pardoun to graunte the
      peple
    Withouten eny penaunce to passen into hevene.
190 This is owre bileve as lettered men us techeth:

---

[18] 'Pay no heed to dreams.' Cato, *Distichs*, ii.31.

Quodcumque ligaveris super terram, erit ligatum et in celis, etc.[19]

And so I leve lelly° (Lordes forbode ellis!)   *loyally*
That pardoun and penaunce and preyeres don save
Soules that have synned sevene sithes° dedly.   *times*
195 Ac to trust to thise triennales° trewly me thinketh°   *triennial masses for the dead* **me thinketh** *it seems to me*
Is nought so syker° for the soule, certis,° as is Dowel.°   *sure   certainly   Do-well*
   For-thi I rede° yow renkes° that riche ben on this erthe,   *advise   men*
Uppon trust of yowre tresoure triennales to have,
Be ye never the balder° to breke the ten hestes.°   *bolder   commandments*
200 And namelich,° ye maistres,° mayres, and jugges,   *especially   lords*
That han the welthe of this worlde and for wyse men ben holden,°   *considered*
To purchace yow pardoun and the popis bulles,
At the dredeful dome° whan dede shullen° rise,   *judgment   shall*
And comen alle bifor Cryst acountis to yelde,°   *render*
205 How thow laddest thi lyf here and His lawes keptest,
And how thow dedest day bi day, the dome wil reherce.°   *declare*
A poke° ful of pardoun there ne Provinciales lettres,   *sack*
Theigh° ye be founde in the fraterneté of alle the foure ordres,   *Though*
And have indulgences double-folde, but if Dowel° yow helpe,   *Do-well*
210 I sette yowre patentes and yowre pardounz at one pies-hele!°   *pea pod*
   For-thi I conseille alle Cristene to crye God mercy,
And Marie His moder be owre mene° bitwene,   *intermediary*
That God gyve us grace here, ar we gone hennes,°   *hence*
Suche werkes to werche while we ben here
215 That after owre deth-day, Dowel reherce,°   **Dowel reherce** *Do-well may declare*
At the day of dome, we dede° as he highte.°   *did   ordered*

Canto XVIII

[Lines 228–431]
Thanne was there a wighte° with two brode eyen,   *person*
Boke highte° that beupere,° a bolde man of speche.   **Boke highte** *Bible was called*   *reverend father*
"By Godes body," quod this Boke, "I wil bere witnesse,
That tho° this barne° was y-bore° there blased a sterre,   *when   child   born*

[19] 'Whatever you have bound upon earth it shall be bound also in heaven, etc.' Matt. xvi.19.

5 That alle the wyse of this worlde in o witte° acordeden   **o witte** one mind
   That such a barne was borne in Bethleem Citee
   That mannes° soule sholde save and synne destroye.   man's
     "And alle the elementz,"° quod the Boke, "her-of   four elements
      bereth witnesse.
   That He was God that al wroughte, the walkene° firste   welkin
     shewed;
10 Tho° that weren in hevene token *stella comata*°   Those   **token** ... took a comet
   And tendeden° hir as a torche to reverence his birthe.   kindled
   The lyghte folwed° the Lorde into the lowe erthe.   followed
   The water witnessed that He was God, for He went on it.
   Peter the Apostel parceyved his gate,°   going
15 And as He went on the water, wel Hym knewe and
     seyde,

     'Jube me venire ad te super aquas.'[1]

     "And lo! how the sonne gan louke° her lighte in   **gan louke** locked up
      herself
   Whan she seye° Hym suffre that sonne and se made.   saw
   The erthe, for hevynesse that He wolde suffre,
20 Quaked as quykke° thinge and al biquashte° the roche.°   a living   crushed   rock
   Lo! Helle mighte noughte holde,° but opened tho° God   hold together   when
     tholed,°   suffered
   And lete oute Symondes° sons to seen Hym hange on   Simeon's
     Rode.°   Cross
   And now shal Lucifer leve it, thowgh hym loth thinke.°   **hym** ... it disgusts him
   For Gygas the geaunt° with a gynne engyned°   giant   **gynne engyned** engine contrived
25 To breke and to bete doune that° ben ayeines° Jhesus.   those who   against
     "And I, Boke, wil be brent° but Jhesus rise to lyve   burned
   In alle myghtes° of man, and His moder gladye,°   the powers   gladden
   And conforte al His kynne° and out of care° brynge,   kin   sorrow
   And al the Juwen° joye unjoignen and unlouken,°   Jews'   **unjoignen** ... disjoin and undo
30 And, but thei reverencen His Rode° and His resurexioun   Cross
   And bileve on a newe lawe, be lost lyf and soule."
     "Suffre we," seide Treuth. "I here and se bothe
   How a spirit speketh to helle and bit unspere° the yatis,°   **bit unspere** orders them to unbar gates

     Attollite portas, etc."[2]

35 A voice loude in that lighte to Lucifer cryeth,
   "Prynces of this place, unpynneth and unlouketh!
   For here cometh with croune That° kynge is of glorie."   He Who
     Thanne syked° Sathan and seyde to hem alle: sighed
   "Suche a lyghte, ayeines° owre leve, Lazar° it fette;°   against   Lazarus   fetched

---

[1] 'Order me to come to you upon the waters.' Matt. xiv.28.
[2] 'Lift up the gates etc.' Ps. xxiv.9.

40 Care and combraunce° is comen to us alle.   **Care . . .** Sorrow and trouble
    If this Kynge come in, mankynde wil he fecche,
    And lede it ther Hym lyketh, and lyghtlych° me bynde.   easily
    Patriarkes and prophetes han parled° her-of longe   spoken
    That such a lorde and a lyghte shulde lede hem alle
        hennes."°   hence
45 "Lysteneth," quod Lucifer, "for I this Lorde knowe—
    Bothe this Lorde and this Lighte; is longe ago I knewe
        Hym.
    May no deth hym dere,° ne no develes queyntise,°   harm   cunning
    And where He wil, is His waye. Ac war Hym° of the   **war Hym** let Him beware
        periles;
    If He reve° me my righte, He robbeth me by maistrye,°   rob   force
50 For by right and bi resoun, tho renkes° that ben here,   **tho renkes** those men
    Bodye and soule ben myne, bothe gode and ille.
    For Hymself seyde, that Sire is of hevene,
    Yif Adam ete the apple, alle shulde deye,
    And dwelle with us develes. This thretynge° He made,   threat
55 And He that sothenesse° is seyde thise wordes.   truth
    And sitthen° I seised° sevene hundreth wyntre,   since   have been in possession
    I leve° that Lawe nil° naughte lete° Hym the leest."   believe   will   allow
    "That is sothe,"° seyde Sathan, "but I me sore drede,   true
    For thow gete° hem with gyle and His gardyne breke,°   got   broke into
60 And in semblaunce of a serpent sat on the appel-tre,
    And eggedest hem to ete, Eve by hirselve,
    And toldest hir a tale, of tresoun were the wordes;
    And so thow haddest hem oute and hider atte laste.
    It is noughte graythely° geten there° gyle is the rote."°   properly   where   source
65 "For God wil nought be bigiled," quod Gobelyn,
    "ne bijaped.°   tricked
    We have no trewe title to hem, for thorwgh tresoun
        were thei dampned."°   condemned
    "Certes,° I drede me," quod the devel, "leste Treuth   Certainly
        wil hem fecche.
    This thretty° wynter, as I wene,° hath he gone and   thirty   think
        preched;
    I have assailled hym with synne, and some tyme
        y-asked
70 Where° he were God or Goddes sone. He gaf me shorte   Whether
        answere.
    And thus hath he trolled° forth this two and thretty   wandered
        wynter,
    And whan I seighe it was so, slepyng, I went
    To warne Pilates wyf what dones° man was Jhesus.   sort of
    For Juwes hateden Hym, and han done Hym to deth.

75 I wolde have lengthed His lyf, for I leved, yif He
    deyede,
  That His soule wolde suffre no synne in His syghte.
  For the body, whil it on bones yede aboute, was evere
  To save men fram synne yif hemself wolde.
    "And now I se where a soule cometh hiderward
    seyllynge°   sailing
80 With glorie and gret lighte; God it is, I wote wel.
  I rede° we flee," quod he, "faste alle hennes.   advise
  For us were better noughte be than biden° His syghte.   endure
  For thi lesynges,° Lucifer, loste is al owre praye.°   lies   prey
  Firste thorw thee we fellen fro hevene so highe.
85 For° we leved thi lesynges, we loupen° oute alle with Because leaped
    thee;
  And now for thi last lesynge y-lore° we have Adam,   lost
  And al owre lordeship, I leve, a° londe and a water.   on

        Nunc princeps hujus mundi ejicietur foras."[3]

    Efte° the Lighte bad unlouke and Lucifer answered.   Again
90 "What lorde artow?"° quod Lucifer. "*Quis est iste?*"[4]   are you
  "*Rex glorie*"[5] the Lighte sone° seide,   at once
  "And Lorde of myghte and of mayne and al manere
    vertues, *Dominus virtutum.*[6]
  Dukes of this dym place, anon° undo this yates,°   at once gates
  That Cryst may come in, the Kynges Sone of hevene."
95   And with that breth,° helle brake,° with Beliales speech burst
    barres;
  For° any wye or warde° wide opene the yatis.   Before **wye ... man or guard**
  Patriarkes and prophetes, *populus in tenebris,*[7]
  Songen° Seynt Johanes songe, *Ecce Agnus Dei.*[8]   Sang
  Lucyfer loke ne myghte° so Lyghte hym ableynte.° **ne myghte** could not blinded
100 And tho° that owre Lorde loved, into His lighte He those
    laughte,°   took
  And seyde to Sathan, "Lo, here my soule to amendes° ransom
  For alle synneful soules, to save tho that ben worthy.
  Myne thei be and of me; I may the bette° hem clayme. better
  Although resoun recorde° and right of Myself   declare
105 That if thei ete the apple alle shulde deye,
  I bihyghte° hem nought here helle for evere.   promised
  For the dede that thei dede,° thi deceyte it made;   did

[3] 'Now the prince of this world shall be cast out.' John xii.31.
[4] 'Who is that one?' Ps. xxiv.8.
[5] 'King of Glory.' Ibid.
[6] 'Lord of virtues.' Ibid.
[7] 'People in the darkness.' Isa. ix.2; Matt. iv.16.
[8] 'Behold the Lamb of God.' John i.36.

With gyle thow hem gete° agayne al resoun.   gained
For in my paleys,° Paradys, in persone of an addre,   palace
110 Falseliche thow fettest° there thynge that I loved.   took
    "Thus y-lyke a lüsarde° with a lady° visage,   serpent lady's
Thevelich° thow me robbedest. The Olde Law   Thievishly
    graunteth
That gylours be begiled, and that is gode resoun:

Dentem pro dente, et oculum pro oculo.[9]

115 *Ergo,*° soule shal soule quyte,° and synne to synne   Therefore requite
    wende,°   correspond
And al that man hath mysdo, I, man, wyl amende.°   make amends for
Membre for membre bi the Olde Lawe was amendes,°   reparation
And lyf for lyf also; and by that lawe I clayme it:
Adam and al his issue at my wille her-after.
120 And that Deth in hem fordid° my deth shal releve,°   destroyed redeem
And bothe quykke and quyte that queynte was° thorw   **quykke** ... revive and requite what
    synne.   was destroyed
And, that grace gyle destruye, Good Feith it asketh.°
    "So leve° it noughte, Lucifer, ayeine° the lawe I   think against
    fecche hem,
But bi right and by resoun raunceoun° here my lyges:°   ransom subjects

125   *Non veni solvere legem, sed adimplere.*[10]

Thow fettest° myne in my place, ayeines al resoun,   took
Falseliche and felounelich.° Gode Faith me it taughte,   wickedly
To recovre hem thorw raunceoun and bi no resoun
    elles,°   other
So, that with gyle thow gete,° thorw grace it is y-wone.   gained
130 Thow, Lucyfer, in lyknesse of a lüther° addere,   evil
Getest by gyle tho° that God loved;   those
And I, in lyknesse of a leode,° that Lorde am of hevene,   man
Graciousliche thi gyle have quytte. Go gyle ayeine gyle!
And as Adam and alle thorw a tre deyden,
135 Adam and alle thorwe a tree shal torne ayeine° to lyve;   again
And gyle is bigyled and in his gyle fallen:

Et cecidit in foveam quam fecit.[11]

Now bygynneth thi gyle ageyne thee to tourne,
And my grace to growe ay gretter and wyder.

---

[9] 'A tooth for a tooth, and an eye for an eye.' Matt. v.38.
122. And Good Faith (Justice) demands that grace destroy guile.
[10] 'I have not come to destroy the law, but to fulfill it.' Matt. v.17.
[11] 'And he has fallen into the pit that he made.' Ps. vii.15.

140 The bitternesse that thow hast browe, brouke° it   **browe, brouke** brewed, enjoy
    thiselven;
    That° art doctour of deth, drynke that thow madest!   You who
      "For I, that am Lorde of lyf, love is my drynke,
    And for that drynke today, I deyde upon erthe.
    I faughte so, me threstes° yet, for mannes° soule sake.   **me threstes** I thirst   man's
145 May no drynke me moiste, ne my thrüste slake,
    Tyl the vendage° falle in the vale of Josephath,[12]   vintage
    That I drynke righte ripe must *resureccio mortuorum,*[13]
    And thanne shal I come as a kynge crouned with
      angeles
    And han out of helle alle mennes soules.
150 Fendes and fendekynes° bifor me shulle° stande,   **Fendes...** Fiends and little fiends
    And be at my biddynge wheresoevre me lyketh.   will
    And to be merciable to man, thanne my kynde° it   nature
      asketh,
    For we beth bretheren of blode but noughte in
      Baptesme alle.
    Ac alle that beth myne hole° bretheren in blode and in   whole
      Baptesme
155 Shal noughte be dampned° to the deth that is withouten   ·condemned
    ende:

         Tibi soli peccavi, etc.[14]

      "It is nought used in erthe to hangen a feloun
    Ofter than ones, though he were a tretour.
    And yif the Kynge of that kyngedome come in that
      tyme,
160 There the feloun thole° sholde, deth or otherwyse,   suffer
    Lawe wolde,° he yeve° hym lyf if he loked on hym.   would have it   may give
    And I that am Kynge of kynges, shal come such a tyme,
    There dome° to the deth dampneth° al wikked.   sentence   condemns
    And yif lawe wil° I loke on hem, it lithe° in my grace,   decides that   lies
165 Whether thei deye or deye noughte for that thei
    deden° ille.   did
    Be it any thinge aboughte° the boldnesse of her   **any...** in any way atoned
    synnes,
    I may do mercy thorw rightwisnesse° and alle my   righteousness
    wordes trewe.
    And though Holi Writ wil that I be wroke° of hem that   avenged
    deden ille—

---

[12] Scene of the Last Judgment. See Joel iii.2, 12, 13.
[13] 'That I may drink truly ripe new wine of resurrection of the dead.' See Joel iii.18.
[14] 'Against you alone I have sinned, etc.' Ps. li.4.

Nullum malum impunitum, etc.[15]

170 Thei shul be clensed clereliche and wasshen of her
    synnes
    In my prisoun purgatorie til *parce* it hote,°   **parce** ... spare them is commanded
    And my mercy shal be shewed to manye of my
    bretheren.
    For blode° may suffre blode, bothe hungry and a-kale,°   kin cold
    Ac blode may nought se blode blede,° but hym rewe."° bleed   **hym rewe** he grieve for him

175   *Audivi archana verba, quae non licet homini loqui.*[16]

    "Ac my rightwisnesse° and right shal reulen al helle,   righteousness
    And mercy al mankynde bifor me in hevene.
    For I were° an unkynde° Kynge but I my kynde holpe,° would be   unnatural   **kynde**
                                     holpe kin helped
    And namelich° at such a nede ther nedes helpe bihoveth: especially

180   *Non intres in judicium cum servo tuo, domine.*[17]

    Thus bi lawe," quod owre Lorde, "lede I will fro hennes
    Tho° that me loved and leved in my comynge.   Those
    And for thi lesynge° that thow lowe° til Eve,   lie   told
    Thow shalt abye° it bittre"—and bonde hym with atone for
    cheynes.
185   Astaroth and al the route° hidden hem in hernes.°   pack   corners
    They dorste noughte loke on owre Lorde, the boldest
    of hem alle,
    But leten Hym lede forth what Hym lyked and lete° allowed
    what Hym liste.°   **Hym liste** He wished
    Many hundreth of angeles harpeden and songen,

        Culpat caro, purgat caro;
190   *Regnat Deus Dei caro.*[18]

    Thanne piped Pees° of poysye° a note: Peace   poetry

        "Clarior est solito post maxima nebula Phebus,
        Post inimicitias clarior est et amor.°

    After sharpe shoures,"° quod Pees, "moste shene° is the **sharpe shoures** heavy showers
    sonne;   bright
195 Is no weder warmer than after watery cloudes.
    Ne no love levere ne lever frendes,

[15] 'No evil unpunished, etc.' An allusion to Pope Innocent III, *De Contempto Mundi*, Book 3, ch. 15: "He only is a just judge ... who leaves no evil unpunished, no good unrewarded."
[16] 'I have heard secret words, which it is not permitted to man to speak.' II. Cor. xii.4.
[17] 'Enter not into judgment with thy servant, O Lord.' Ps. cxliii.2.
[18] 'The flesh sins, the flesh atones; the Flesh of God reigns as God.' From *Aeterne Rex Altissime*, an Ascension Matins hymn.
192-93. Brighter is the sun after the greatest cloud of Phoebus, after enmities even brighter is love.

Than after werre° and wo, whan Love and Pees° be   war   Peace
    maistres.
Was nevere werre in this worlde ne wykkednesse so
    kene,°   cruel
That ne Love, an hym lüste,° to laughynge ne   **an** . . . if it pleased him
    broughte,°   turned
200 And Pees thorw pacience alle periles stopped."
    "Trewes,"° quod Treuth. "Thow tellest us soth, bi   Truce
    Jhesus!
Clippe° we in covenaunt and üch of us cüsse° other."   Embrace   kiss
    "And lete no peple," quod Pees,° "perceyve that we   Peace
    chydde,
For inpossible is no thyng to Hym that is almyghty."
205 "Thow seist soth," seyde Ryghtwisnesse,° and   Righteousness
    reverentlich hir kyste,
Pees, and Pees here, *per saecula saeculorum.*°   **here** . . . kissed her, world without
    end

Misericordia et veritas obviaverunt sibi, justicia et pax osculatae
sunt.[19]

Treuth tromped tho and songe *Te Deum Laudamus,*°
And thanne luted° Love in a loude note,   played a lute

210 *Ecce quam bonum, et quam jocundum, etc.*[20]

Tyl the daye dawed,° this damaiseles° daunced,   dawned   maidens
That men rongen° to the Resurexioun; and right with   rang bells
    that I waked,
And called Kitte my wyf and Kalote my doughter:
"Ariseth and reverenceth Goddes Resurrexioun,
215 And crepeth to the Crosse on knees, and kisseth it for a
    juwel!
For Goddes blissed body it bar° for owre bote.°   bore   benefit
And it afereth° the Fende, for suche is the myghte,   frightens
May no grysly gost° glyde there it shadweth!"   spirit

Canto XIX

Thus I awaked and wrote what I had dremed,
And dighte° me derely and dede me° to cherche,   dressed   **derely** . . . neatly and went
To here holy° the masse and to be houseled° after.   wholly   **be houseled** receive
In myddes of the masse tho men yede to offrynge,   Communion

[19] 'Mercy and Truth have met each other; Justice and Peace have kissed.' Ps. lxxxv.10.
208. Truth blew a trumpet then and sang *We Praise Thee, God*
[20] 'Behold how good and how pleasant, etc.' Ps. cxxxiii.1.

5 I fel eftsones° aslepe, and sodeynly me mette°   again **me mette** I dreamed
    That Pieres the Plowman was paynted° al blody   stained
    And come in with a crosse bifor the comune peple
    And righte lyke in alle lymes to owre Lorde Jhesu.
    And thanne called I Conscience to kenne me the sothe.
10 "Is this Jhesus the Juster?"° quod I, "that Juwes did to   Jouster (Knight)
        deth?
    Or is it Pieres the Plowman? Who paynted hym so
        rede?"°   red
        Quod Conscience, and kneled tho, "Thise aren
           Pieres armes,
    His coloures and his cote-armure, ac He that cometh so
        blody
    Is Cryst with His crosse, Conqueroure of Crystene."
15 "Why calle ye Hym Cryst?" quod I, "sithenes°   since
        Juwes calle Hym Jhesus?
    Patriarkes and prophetes prophecyed bifore
    That alkyn° creatures shulden knelen and bowen   all kinds of
    Anon° as men nempned° the name of God, Jhesu.   At once named
    Ergo° is no name to° the name of Jhesus,   Therefore like
20 Ne none so nedeful to nempne by nyghte ne by daye.
    For alle derke develles aren adradde° to heren it,   afraid
    And synful aren solaced and saved bi that name.
    And ye callen Hym Cryst, for what cause, telleth me?
    Is Cryst more of myghte, and more worthy name
25 Than Jhesu or Jhesus that al owre joye come of?"
      "Thow knowest wel," quod Conscience, "and° thow   if
        konne° resoun,   understand
    That knyghte, kynge, conqueroure may be o° persone.   one
    To be called a knighte is faire, for men shal knele to
        hym.
    To be called a kynge is fairer, for he may knyghtes
        make;
30 Ac to be conquerour called, that cometh of special
        grace,
    And of hardynesse° of herte, and of hendenesse°   firmness courtesy
        bothe,
    To make lordes of laddes of° londe that he wynneth,   **of . . .** out of lads over
    And fre men foule thralles that folweth nought his
        lawes.
      "The Juwes, that were gentil° men, Jhesu thei   noble
        dispised,
35 Bothe His lore and His lawe; now ar thei lowe cherlis.°   serfs
    As wyde as the worlde is, wonyeth° there none   dwells
    But under tribut and taillage° as tykes° and cherles.   taxation low people

And tho that bicome Crysten by conseille of the
    Baptiste,
Aren frankeleynes,° fre men thorw fullyng° that thei   freemen   baptism
    toke,
40 And gentel° men with Jhesu, for Jhesus was y-fulled,   noble   baptized
And uppon Calvarye on crosse y-crouned Kynge of
    Jewes.
    "It bicometh° to a Kynge to kepe and to defende,   is becoming
And conquerour of conquest, his lawes and his large.°   liberality
And so dide Jhesus the Jewes. He justified and taughte
    hem
45 The lawe of lyf that last shal evere;
And fended fram foule yveles, feveres, and fluxes,
And fro fendes that in hem were, and fals bileve.°   belief
Tho° was He Jhesus of Jewes called, gentel° prophete,   Then   noble
And Kynge of her kyngdome, and croune bar° of   bore
    thornes.
50   "And tho° conquered He on crosse as conquerour   when
    noble,
Myght no deth Hym fordo° ne adown brynge,   destroy
That He ne aros and regned and ravysshed helle.
And tho° was He conquerour called of quikke° and of   then   living
    ded,
For he yaf° Adam and Eve and other mo° blisse   gave   **other mo** others more
55 That longe hadde leyne bifore as Lucyferes cherles.°   serfs
And sith he yaf largely alle his lele lyges°   **lele lyges** loyal liegemen
Places in paradys at her partynge hennes,
He may wel be called Conquerour, and that is Cryst to
    mene.°   mean
    "Ac the cause that He cometh thus, with crosse of
    His passioun,
60 Is to wissen us there-wyth that whan that we ben
    tempted,
Ther-with to fyghte and fenden us fro fallyng into
    synne,
And se bi His sorwe° that who-so loveth joye,   sorrow
To penaunce and to poverté he moste putten
    hymselven,
And moche wo in this worlde willen° and suffren.   desire
65   "Ac to carpe° more of Cryst, and how He come to   speak
    that name,
Faithly forto speke, His firste name was Jhesus.
Tho He was borne in Bethleem as the boke telleth,
And cam to take mankynde,° kynges and aungeles   **take mankynde** take on human
Reverenced Hym faire with richesse of erthe.   nature

70 Angeles out of hevene come knelyng and songe

Gloria in excelsis Deo, etc.[1]

Kynges come after, kneled, and offred
Mirre° and moche golde withouten mercy° askynge,   Myrrh   thanks
Or any kynnes catel,° but knowlechyng Hym   **kynnes catel** kinds of goods
   soevereigne
75 Bothe of sonde,° sonne, and see; and sithenes° thei went   sand (earth)   then
Into her kyngene kyth° by conseille of angeles.   **kyngene kyth** country of kings
And there was that worde fulfilled the which thow of
   speke,

Omnia celestia, terrestria, flectantur in hoc nomine Jhesu.[2]

For alle the angeles of hevene at His bürth kneled,
80 And al the witte° of the worlde was in tho thre kynges.   wisdom
Resoun and Rightwisnesse and Reuth° thei offred;   **Rightwisnesse . . .** Righteousness and Pity
Wherfore and whi,° wyse men that tyme,   **Wherfore . . .** Thus and so
Maistres and lettred men, *Magy*° hem called.   Magi
   "That o° kynge cam with Resoun kevered° under   **That o** The first   symbolized
   sense.°   incense
85 The secounde kynge sitthe sothliche° offred   **sitthe sothliche** then truly
Rightwisnesse under red golde, Resouns felawe.
Golde is likned to Leuté° that last shal evere,   Loyalty
And Resoun to riche golde, to Righte and to Treuthe.
The thridde kynge tho cam, knelyng to Jhesu,
90 And presented Hym with Pitee, apierynge by° myrre;   as
For mirre is mercy to mene° and mylde speche of tonge.   signify
Thre y-liche honest° thinges were offred thus at ones,   **y-liche honest** equally valuable
Thorw thre kynne kynges,° knelynge to Jhesu.   **thre . . .** kings of three races
   "Ac for° alle thise preciouse presentz, owre Lorde   despite
   Prynce Jhesus
95 Was neyther kynge ne conquerour til He gan to wexe°   grow
In the manere of a man, and that by moche sleight,°   skill
As it bicometh a conquerour to konne° many sleightes,   know
And many wyles and witte, that wil ben a leder;
And so did Jhesu in His dayes, who-so had tyme to telle
   it.
100 Sum tyme He suffred and sum tyme He hydde Hym;
And sum tyme He faughte faste, and fleigh otherwhile.°   **faste . . .** hard, and fled sometimes
And some tyme He gaf good° and graunted hele bothe,°   wealth   **hele bothe** healing too
Lyf and lyme, as Hym lyste,° He wrought.   it pleased
As kynde° is of a conquerour, so comsed° Jhesu   nature   commenced
105 Tyle He had alle hem that He fore bledde.°   **fore bledde** bled for

[1] 'Glory to God in the highest, etc.' Luke ii.14.
[2] 'All in heaven and on earth must genuflect at this name, Jesus.' Phil. ii.10.

"In His juvente° this Jhesus, atte Juwen feste,   youth
 Water into wyn tourned, as Holy Writ telleth,
 And there bigan God of His grace to do-wel.
 For wyn is lykned to lawe and lyf of holynesse,
110 And lawe lakked tho,° for men loved nought her **lakked tho** was lacking then
   enemys.
 And Cryst conseilleth thus and commaundeth bothe,° too
 Bothe to lered° and to lewed to lovye owre enemys. learned
 So atte feste firste, as I bifore tolde,
 Bygan God, of His grace and goodnesse, to do-wel.
115 And tho was He cleped° and called nought Holy Cryst, named
   but Jhesu,
 A faunt° fyn, ful of witte, *filius Mariae.*° child ***filius Mariae*** son of Mary
  "For bifor His moder Marie made He that wonder,
 That she fürste and formest° ferme shulde bileve, foremost
 That He thorw grace was gete° and of no gome elles.° begotten **gome elles** other man
120 He wrought that bi no witte,° but thorw worde one, trick
 After the kynde° that He come of, there comsed He nature
   do-wel.
 And whan He was woxen° more in His moder° absence, grown mother's
 He made lame to lepe and yave° lighte to blynde, gave
 And fedde with two fisshes and with fyve loves
125 Sore afyngred° folke mo than fyve thousande. famished
 Thus He conforted carful° and caughte a gretter name, sorrowful
 The whiche was Do-bet° where that He went. Do-better
 For defe thorw His doynges to here, and dombe speke
   He made,
 And alle He heled and halpe that Hym of grace asked.
130 And tho was He called in contré of° the comune peple by
 For the dedes that He did, *fili David, Jhesus!*° ***fili* . . .** Jesus, the son of David
 For David was doughtiest° of dedes in his tyme, mightiest
 The berdes° tho songe:° *Saul interfecit mille, et David* bards sang
  decem milia.[3]
 For-thi the contré there Jhesu cam called Hym *fili*
  David
135 And nempned° Hym of Nazereth, and no man so called
   worthi
 To be kaisere or kynge of the kyngedome of Juda,
 Ne over Juwes justice, as Jhesus was, hem thoughte.° **hem thoughte** it seemed to them
  "Where-of Caiphas hadde envye and other of the
   Jewes,
 And for to done Hym to deth day and nyght thei
   casten.° plotted
140 Külleden° Hym on crosse-wys at Calvarie on Fryday They killed

[3] 'Saul killed thousands and David, tens of thousands.' I Sam. xviii.7.

And sithen buryden His body and beden° that men
    sholde   **bade**
Kepen it fro night-comers with knyghtes y-armed,
For no frendes shulde Hym fecche. For prophetes hem
    tolde
That that blessed body of burieles° shulde rise   **of burieles** from the tomb
145 And gone into Galilé and gladen His Apostles
And His moder Marie—thus men bifore demed.°   declared
The knyghtes that kepten° it biknewe° it hemselven   guarded   confessed
That angeles and archangeles, at° the day spronge,   before
Come knelynge to the corps and songen *Christus*
    resurgens.[4]
150 Verrey° man bifor hem alle and forth with hem He   True
    yede.
    "The Jewes preyed hem pees° and bisoughte the   **hem pees** them (the guards) silence
    knyghtes
Telle the comune° that there cam a compaignye of His   common people
    Aposteles
And bywicched hem as thei woke and awey stolen it.
Ac Marie Magdeleyne mette Hym bi the wey,
155 Goynge toward Galilé, in Godhed° and manhed,   Godhood
And lyves° and lokynge, and she aloude cryde   alive
In eche a compaignye there she cam, *Christus resurgens!*°   ***Christus resurgens*** Christ being
Thus cam it out that Cryst overcam, rekevered, and   raised
    lyved:

    Sic oportet Christum pati, et intrare, etc.[5]

160 For that that° wommen witeth° may noughte wel be   **For ...** For what   know
    conseille!°   secret
    "Peter perceyved al this and pursued after,
Bothe James and Johan, Jhesu for to seke,
Tadde° and ten mo, with Thomas of Ynde.   Thaddeus
And as alle thise wise wyes° weren togideres   men
165 In an hous al bishette° and her dore y-barred,   shut
Cryst cam in—and al closed bothe dore and yates°—   gates
To Peter and to His Aposteles and seyde *Pax vobis!*°   ***Pax vobis*** Peace to you
And toke Thomas by the hande and taughte hym to
    grope
And fele with his fyngres His flesshelich herte.
170 Thomas touched it and with his tonge seyde,

    '*Deus meus et Dominus meus.*[6]

[4] 'Christ being raised.' See Rom. vi.9.
[5] 'Thus it behooved Christ to suffer and rise, etc.' Luke xxiv.46.
[6] 'My God and My Lord.' John xx.28.

Thow art my Lorde, I bileve, God, Lorde Jhesu!
Thow deydest and deth tholedest and deme° shalt us   **tholedest** . . . suffered and judge
   alle,
And now art lyvynge and lokynge and laste shalt evere!'
175   "Crist carped° thanne and curteislich seyde,   spoke
'Thomas, for thow trowest° this, and trewliche bilevest   believe
   it,
Blessed mote° thow be, and be shalt for evere,   may
And blessed mote thei alle be in body and in soule
That nevere shal se me in sighte, as thow doste nouthe,°   now
180   And lellich° bileven al this; I love hem and blesse hem: yet truly

      Beati qui non viderunt, et crediderunt, etc.'[7]

   "And whan this dede was done, Do-best He taughte,
And yaf° Pieres power—and pardoun He graunted   gave
To alle manere man, mercy and foryyfnes°—   forgiveness
185   Hym° myghte men to assoille° of alle manere synnes,   That he   **to assoille** absolve
In covenant that thei come and knowleche° to paye   acknowledge
To Pieres pardon the Plowman,° *redde quod debes.*[8]   **Pieres** . . . Piers the Plowman's
                                               pardon
Thus hath Pieres powere, be° his pardoun payed,   if be
To bynde and to unbynde both here and elleswhere,
190   And assoille men of alle synnes save of dette one.°   **dette one** debt alone
   "Anone° after, an° heigh up into hevene   At once   on
He went and wonyeth° there and wil come atte laste   **went** . . . wends and dwells
And rewarde hym righte wel that *reddit quod debet*°—   **reddit** . . . pays back what he owes
Payeth parfitly° as pure Trewthe wolde.   completely
195   And what persone payeth it nought, punysshen He
    thinketh
And demen° hem at Domes daye, bothe quikke° and   judge   living
    ded;
The gode to the Godhede° and to grete joye,   Godhood
And wikke° to wonye° in wo withouten ende."   wicked   dwell
   Thus Conscience of Crist and of the crosse carped°   spoke
200   And conseilled me to knele ther-to. And thanne come,
    me thoughte,
One *spiritus paraclitus*° to Pieres and to his felawes;   the Paraclete
In lyknesse of a lightnynge he lyghte on hem alle
And made hem konne° and knowe alkyn° langages.   understand   all kinds of
I wondred what that was and wagged° Conscience   nudged
205   And was afered of the lyghte, for in fyres lyknesse
Spiritus paraclitus overspradde hem alle.
   Quod Conscience, and kneled, "This is Crystes
    messager,

---

[7] 'Blessed are they who have not seen and have believed, etc.' John xx.29.
[8] 'Pay back what you owe.' Matt. xviii.28.

And cometh fro the grete God and Grace ys his name.
Knele now," quod Conscience, "and if thow canst synge,

210 Welcome hym and worshipe hym with *Veni,*° *Creator*   Come
    Spiritus."
Thanne songe° I that songe, and so did many hundreth,   sang
And cryden with Conscience, "Help us, God of Grace!"
  And thanne bigan Grace to go with Piers Plowman
And conseilled hym and Conscience the comune° to   common people
  sompne,°   summon

215 "For I wil dele todaye and dyvyde grace
To alkynnes° creatures that han her fyve wittes,°   all kinds of   senses
Tresore to lyve by to her lyves ende,
And wepne° to fyghte with that wil nevre faille.   weapon
For Antecryst and his al the worlde shal greve

220 And acombre° thee, Conscience, but if Cryst thee   overwhelm
  helpe.
And fals prophetes fele,° flatereres and glosers°   many   deceivers
Shullen come and be curatoures over kynges and erlis,
And Pryde shal be Pope, prynce of Holy Cherche,
Coveytyse and Unkyndenesse Cardinales hym to lede.

225 For-thi," quod Grace, "er I go, I wil gyve yow tresore,
And wepne to fighte with whan Antecryst yow
  asailleth."
And gaf eche man a grace to gye° with hymselven,   govern
That Ydelnesse encombre hym nought, Envye ne
  Pryde,

    Divisiones graciarum sunt, etc.[9]

230   Some he yaf Wytte,° with wordes to shewe,   **yaf Wytte** gave Intelligence
Witte to wynne her lyflode° with, as the worlde asketh,   livelihood
As prechoures and prestes and prentyces of lawe,
Thei lelly° to lyve by laboure of tonge,   faithfully
And bi witte to wissen other° as Grace hem wolde   others
  teche.

235 And some he kenned Crafte° and kunnynge of syghte,   **kenned Crafte** taught Trade
With sellyng and büggynge° her bylyf° to wynne,   buying   livelihood
And some he lered to laboure, a lele° lyf and a trewe,   honest
And somme he taughte to tilie,° to dyche° and to   till   dig ditches
  thecche,°   thatch
To wynne with her lyflode° by lore of his techynge.   livelihood

240 And somme to dyvyne and divide, noumbres to kenne;°   know
And some to compas craftily° and coloures to make;   **compas craftily** plan skillfully
And some to se and to saye what shulde bifalle,

[9] 'Diversities of gifts there are, etc.' I Cor. xii.4.

Bothe of wel° and of wo, telle it or° it felle,°   weal   before   happens
As astronomyenes thorw astronomye and philosophres
     wyse.
245 And some to ryde and to recoevre° that unrightfully   recover
     was wonne;
He wissed° hem wynne it ayeyne° thorw wightnesse°   taught   again   quickness
     of handes,
And fecchen it fro fals men, with Folvyles lawes.[10]
    And some he lered to lyve in longynge to ben hennes,
In poverté and in penaunce to preye for alle Crystene.
250 And alle he lered to be lele° and eche a crafte° love   loyal   handicraft
     other,
And forbad hem alle debate° that none were amonge   struggle
     hem.
    "Thowgh some be clenner than somme, ye se wel,"
     quod Grace,
"That he that useth the fairest crafte, to the foulest I
     couth° have put hym.   could
Thinketh° alle," quod Grace, "that grace cometh of my   Remember
     yifte;°   gift
255 Loke that none lakke° other, but loveth alle as   find fault with
     bretheren.
And who that moste maistries can° be myldest of   **who . . .** whoever has the greatest achievements
     berynge,
And crouneth Conscience kynge and maketh Crafte°   Skill
     yowre stuward,
And after° Craftes conseille, clotheth yow and fede.   according to
For I make Pieres the Plowman my procuratour° and   proctor
     my reve,°   steward
260 And regystrere° to receyve *redde quod debes.*°   registrar   **redde . . .** pay back what you owe
My prowor° and my plowman Piers shal ben on erthe,   purveyor
And for to tülye° Treuthe a teme° shal he have."   till   team
    Grace gave Piers a teme, foure gret oxen.
That on° was Luke, a large beste and a lowe-chered,°   **That on** The one   meek-mannered
265 And Marke, and Mathew the thrydde, myghty bestes
     bothe,
And joigned to hem one Johan, most gentil° of alle,   noble
The prys nete° of Piers' plow, passyng° alle other.   **prys nete** chief ox   surpassing
    And Grace gave Pieres of his goodnesse foure stottis,°   bullocks
Al that his oxen eryed,° they to harwe° after.   plowed   harrow
270 On hyghte Austyne,° and Ambrose another,   **On . . .** One was called Augustine
Gregori the grete clerke, and Jerome the gode.
Thise foure, the feithe to teche, folweth° Pieres teme,   follow
And harwed in an handwhile° al Holy Scripture   short time

[10] An uncertain reference, probably signifying something like the modern lynch laws.

Wyth two harwes that thei hadde, an olde and a newe,

275   *Id est, vetus testamentum et novum.*°

And Grace gave greynes,° the cardynales vertues,   seeds
And sewe° hem in mannes soule, and sithen he tolde her   sowed
     names.
Spiritus Prudenciae° the firste seed hyghte,°   ***Spiritus Prudenciae*** Prudence
And who-so eet that, ymagyne he shulde,   is called
280 Ar he did any dede, devyse° wel the ende.   consider
And lerned men a ladel bügge° with a longe stele°   buy   handle
That cast° for to kepe a crokke° to save the fatte aboven.°   plan   **kepe**...watch a pot   on top
    The secounde seed highte *Spiritus Temperanciae.*°   ***Spiritus Temperanciae***
He that ete of that seed hadde suche a kynde,   Temperance
285 Shulde nevere mete ne mochel° drynke make hym to   much
     swelle,
Ne sholde no scorner ne scolde° oute of skyl hym   scold
     brynge,
Ne wynnynge ne welthe of worldeliche ricchesse,
Waste worde of ydelnesse, ne wykked speche meve;°   speak
Shulde no curyous clothe comen on hys rügge,°   back
290 Ne no mete in his mouth that Maister Johan spiced.
    The thridde seed that Pieres sewe was *Spiritus*
     Fortitudinis.°   ***Spiritus Fortitudinis*** Fortitude
And who so eet of that seed hardy was evre
To suffre al that God sent, sykenesse and angres.°   troubles
Myghte no lesynge° ne lyere ne losse of worldely catel°   lie   goods
295 Maken hym for any mournynge that he nas° merye in   was not
     soule,
And bolde, and abydynge bismeres° to suffre,   insults
And playeth al with pacyence *et parce mihi, Domine,*[11]
And covered hym under conseille of Catoun° the wyse: Cato

       Esto forti animo, cum sis dampnatus inique.[12]

300   The fierthe seed that Pieres sewe was *Spiritus*
     Justiciae,°   ***Spiritus Justiciae*** Justice
And he that eet of that seed shulde be evere trewe
With God, and nought agast but of gyle one.°   only
For gyle göth so pryvely° that Good Faith otherwhile°   secretly   sometimes
May noughte ben aspyed for *Spiritus Justiciae.*
305 *Spiritus Justiciae* spareth noughte to spille°   destroy
Hem that ben gulty and for to correcte
The Kynge, yif he falle in gylte or in trespasse.

---

275. That is, the Old and New Testaments.
[11] 'Spare me, O Lord.' Possibly Ps. xvi.1.
[12] 'Be strong in spirit when you are unjustly blamed.' Cato, *Distichs*, ii.14.

For counteth he no kynges wratthe whan he in courte
    sitteth

To demen° as a Domes Man.° Adradde° was he nevre,   judge **Domes Man** Judge

310 Noither of duke ne of deth that he ne dede° the lawe,   **ne dede** administered

For present or for preyere° or any prynces lettres;   petition

He dede equité° to alle, evene forth° his powere.   justice **evene forth** to the extent of

    Thise foure sedes Pieres sewe, and sitthe he did hem
        harwe°   harrow

Wyth olde lawe and newe lawe that Love myghte wexe°   grow

315 Amonge the foure vertues and vices destroye.

For communelich° in contrees kammokes[13] and wedes   commonly

Fouleth the fruite in the felde there thei growe
    togyderes;

And so don vices vertues worthy.

    Quod Piers, "Harweth alle that kunneth Kynde
        Witte bi° conseille of this° doctours,   **kunneth . . .** know Common Sense

320 And tülyeth° after her techynge the cardinale vertues."   with   these

    "Ayeines° thi greynes,"° quod Grace, "bigynneth for   till
        to ripe,   Before   seeds

Ordeigne thee an hous, Piers, to herberwe° in thi   stow
    cornes."

    "By God! Grace," quod Piers, "ye moten° gyve   must
    tymbre

And ordeyne that hous ar ye hennes wende."

325   And Grace gave hym the crosse with the croune of
    thornes

That Cryst upon Calvarye for mankynde on pyned,°   suffered

And of His baptesme and blode that He bledde on
    Rode°   Cross

He made a maner° morter and Mercy it highte.°   kind of   called

And there-with Grace bigan to make a good
    foundement,°   foundation

330 And watteled it and walled it with His peynes° and His   suffering
    passioun,

And of al Holy Writ he made a rofe after,

And called that hous Unité, Holi Cherche on
    Englisshe.

And whan this dede was done, Grace devised

A carte, hyghte Cristendome, to carye Pieres' sheves;

335 And gaf hym caples° to his carte, Contricioun and   horses
    Confessioun,

And made presthode haywarde, the while hymself went

As wyde as the worlde is with Pieres to tülye° Treuthe.   till

---

[13] 'Cammock,' or 'rest harrow,' a low shrub with pink flowers and tough crooked roots that hinder a plow or harrow.

The Pearl

(ca. 1380, West Midland)

The Pearl was written in the northern part of the West Midlands. Other works attributed to the same author because of similarities in dialect and style are *Cleanness, Patience,* and *Sir Gawain and the Green Knight* (p. 376, below). Like *The Romance of the Rose,* with which the author shows acquaintance, the poem is a dream vision. Its seriousness of tone, however, recalls Dante's *Divine Comedy,* and its imagery is largely drawn from the Book of Revelation. Literally, the pearl in the poem is the poet's infant daughter, who died before reaching her second year. Like Dante's Beatrice, she not only reveals to the poet her blissful state in heaven but also corrects his human misunderstanding of the divine plan. Whether the poet, like Dante, intends other allegorical levels of meaning has been widely but inconclusively debated, but the pearl, or *margery,* is also the pearl (*margarita*) of great price that in Matthew xiii.45–46 is an analogue of the Kingdom of Heaven.

Stylistically, *The Pearl* is a remarkable *tour de force.* More than two-thirds of the total number of lines are decorated with the traditional, native-English device of alliteration. At the same time, the poem is composed of carefully wrought stanzas, rhyming ababababbcbc. The stanzas are bound together by an intricate concatenation in groups of five, except for the fifteenth group, which contains six stanzas. Concatenation is maintained by the repetition of a freely varied refrain in the last stanza of each group, by the use of the same c-rhyme (in the tenth and twelfth lines) in all the stanzas comprising a group, and by the repetition, within the first line of each stanza, of some thematic word from the refrain in the preceding stanza. For example, in group II, the last line of each stanza in the group (stanzas vi–x) carries a refrain based on the word *adubbement* ('adornment'); lines 10 and 12 of all five stanzas rhyme together on the syllable *ent*; and the first line of stanza vi echoes the refrain of the last line of stanza v, in group I, by the word *jewel*; the first lines of stanzas vii–x and xi, in group III, echo the refrain of group II with some form of the word *dub.* As a crowning touch, the refrain of the final group in the poem concatenates with the first line of the first stanza, thus fulfilling the self-imposed requirements of the perfect design. The meter type is twelve-line stanzas; see Introduction, type 22, page 33.

The poet also seems to have attempted to reinforce the symmetry of his vision by a numerological connection between his metrical form and his Biblical imagery. The proportions of the Heavenly Jerusalem (as in Revelation xxi) are based on the number twelve; its foundations consist of the twelve precious stones; its gates are twelve *margeries* ('pearls'); and the innocents among whom the pearl has found a place (as in Revelation xiv) number twelve times twelve thousand. Correspondingly, the number of lines in a stanza is twelve; the only break in concatenation (l. 721 lacks the word *right*) occurs immediately after the twelfth group; the total number of lines (because of the supernumerary stanza in group XV) is 1,212. That *The Pearl,* like *Sir Gawain,* contains 101 stanzas may also be part of a symbolic plan, though its purpose is no longer apparent.

Mere style alone, however, will not account for the charm of the poem. Numerology is likely to remain for most readers a hidden ingredient akin to the esoteric patterns of

Gothic architecture—a feature that satisfies the artist but is appreciated only dimly by the observer. More accessible is the poet's personal feeling of grief, his puzzled piety, and the universality of his vision. Like Milton in *Lycidas* or Tennyson in *In Memoriam*, he passionately expresses mankind's eternal questions concerning the deepest mysteries of providence.

The best edition is *Pearl*, ed. E. V. Gordon (Oxford, 1953). Among many modernizations, that in *Medieval English Verse*, trans. Brian Stone (Harmondsworth, 1964), pp. 136–74, is particularly satisfactory. The poem survives, along with *Cleanness*, *Patience*, and *Sir Gawain*, in a single manuscript, of which a facsimile is available in *Facsimile of MS. Cotton Nero A.x*, EETS 162 (London, 1923), folios 39–55. For bibliography see Severs, ch. 2.2. For criticism see John Conley, ed., *The Middle English Pearl: Critical Essays* (Notre Dame, 1970).

I

i

Perle, plesaunte° to prynces paye° — pleasing   pleasure
Too clanly clos° in golde so clere;° — **clanly clos** fairly set   bright
Oute of Oryent, I hardyly saye,
Ne proved I never° her precios pere.° — **Ne** ... I never proved   peer
5 So rounde, so reken° in üche araye,° — fresh   **üche araye** each setting
So smal, so smothe her sydes were,
Where-so-ever I jugged° gemmes gaye,° — judged   fair
I sette hyr sengeley in synglere.° — **sengeley** ... apart as unique
Allas! I leste° hyr in on erbere;° — lost   **on erbere** a garden
10 Thurgh gresse° to grounde hit fro me yot.° — grass   went
I dewyne, fordolked of luf-daungere° — my own
Of that pryvy° perle wythouten spot.

ii

Sythen° in that spote hit fro me sprange, — Since
Ofte haf I wayted, wyschande° that wele,° — wishing for   precious thing
15 That wont was whyle devoyde° my wrange° — **whyle devoyde** formerly to drive away grief
And heven° my happe° and al my hele.° — raise up   happiness   well-being
That dos bot thrych° my hert thrange,° — **bot thrych** only weigh down   heavily
My breste in bale° bot bolne and bele.° — sorrow   **bolne** ... swells and burns
Yet thoght me° never so swete a sange° — **thoght me** there seemed to me   song
20 As stylle stounde° let to me stele; — **stylle stounde** that quiet time
For sothe° ther fleten° to me fele,° — **For sothe** Indeed   flowed   many songs
To thenke hir color° so clad in clot.° — complexion   clay
O moul,° thou marres a myry° juele, — earth   pleasant
My privy perle wythouten spotte.

11. I pine away, grievously wounded by love power

iii

25 That spot of spyses mot° nedes sprede,°   *must be covered*
    Ther° such ryches to rot is runne;   *Where*
    Blomes blayke° and blwe and rede   *yellow*
    Ther schynes ful schyr° agayn the sunne.   *brightly*
    Flor° and fryte may° not be fede°   *Flower* **fryte may** *fruit can* *faded*
30 Ther hit doun drof° in moldes dunne;°   *sank* **moldes dunne** *brown earth*
    For üch gresse mot grow of graynes dede°—
    No whete° were elles to wones wonne.°   *wheat* **wones wonne** *dwellings brought*
    Of goud üche goude is ay° bygonne;   *ever*
    So semly a sede moght fayly° not,   **moght fayly** *could fail*
35 That spryngande spyces up ne sponne°   **up . . .** *would not spring up*
    Of that precios perle wythouten spotte.

iv

    To that spot that I in speche expoun
    I entred in that erber° grene,   *garden*
    In Auguste in a hygh seysoun,°   **hygh seysoun** *festival time*
40 When corne is corven° wyth crokes° kene.   *cut* *sickles*
    On hüyle ther° perle hit trendeled° doun,   **hüyle ther** *the hill where* *rolled*
    Schadowed this wortes ful schyre and schene,°   **this . . .** *these plants very bright and fair*
    Gilofre,° gyngure, and gromylyoun,°   *Gillyflower* *gromwell*
    And pyonys powdered ay° bytwene.   **pyonys . . .** *peonies scattered ever*
45 Yif hit was semly on to sene,°   *look*
    A fayr reflayr° yet fro hit flot.°   *fragrance* *flowed*
    Ther wonys° that worthyly,° I wot and wene,°   *dwells* *precious one* **wot . . .** *know and suppose*
    My precious perle wythouten spot.

v

    Bifore that spot my honde I spenned°   *clasped*
50 For care ful° colde that to me caght.°   **For . . .** *Because of sorrow very* *seized*
    A devely dele° in my hert denned,°   **devely dele** *desolate grief* *lay deep*
    Thagh° resoun sette myselven saght.°   *Though* *at peace*
    I playned° my perle, that ther was spenned,°   *lamented* *confined*
    Wyth fyrce skylles° that faste faght.°   *arguments* **faste faght** *stubbornly fought*
55 Thagh kynde° of Kryst me comfort kenned,°   *nature* *taught*
    My wreched wylle in wo ay wraghte.°   **ay wraghte** *ever suffered*
    I felle upon that floury flaght,°   *turf*
    Suche odour to my hernes° schot.   *brains*
    I slode upon° a slepyng-slaghte°   **slode upon** *slid into* *sudden sleep*
60 On that precios perle wythouten spot.

---

31. For each blade of grass must grow from dead grains

vi

Fro spot my spyryt ther sprang in space.°   **in space** after a while
My body on balke° ther bod° in sweven.°   a mound   stayed   dreams
My goste° is gon in Godes grace   spirit
In aventure ther° mervayles meven.°   where   take place
65   I ne wyste° in this worlde where that hit wace,°   **ne wyste** didn't know   was
Bot I knew me keste° ther klyfes cleven.°   cast   **klyfes cleven** cliffs soared
Towarde a foreste I bere° the face,   turned
Where rych° rokkes wer to dyscreven.°   splendid   be discerned
The lyght of hem° myght no mon leven,°   them   believe
70   The glemande° glory that of hem glent;°   gleaming   glinted
For wern never webbes° that wyghes weven°   fabrics   **wyghes weven** men wove
Of half so dere adubbemente.°   **dere adubbemente** glorious adornment

vii

Dubbed° wern alle tho downes sydes°   Adorned   **tho . . .** those hillsides
Wyth crystal klyffes° so cler of kynde.°   cliffs   nature
75   Holtewodes° bryght aboute hem bydes°   Woods   **hem bydes** them stand
Of bolles° as blwe as ble of Ynde.°   trunks   **blwe . . .** indigo
As bornyst° sylver the lef onslydes,°   burnished   unfolds
That thike con trylle° on üch a tynde.°   **con trylle** quivers   **üch . . .** each branch
When glem of glodes° agayns hem glydes,   bright patches of sky
80   Wyth schymeryng schene ful schrylle° thay   **schymeryng . . .** bright gleam very
     schynde.°   dazzingly   shone
The gravayl that on grounde con grynde°   **con grynde** ground
Wern precious perles of Oryente;
The sunnebemes, bot blo and blynde°   **bot . . .** only dark and dim
In respecte of that adubbement.°   adornment

viii

85   The adubbemente of tho downes dere°   **tho . . .** those glorious hills
Garten° my goste° al greffe foryete.°   Made   spirit   **greffe foryete** grief forget
So frech flavores° of frytes° were   fragrances   fruits
As fode° hit con° me fayre refete.°   food   did   revive
Fowles ther flowen° in fryth in fere,°   flew   **fryth . . .** woods together
90   Of flaumbande hwes,° bothe smale and grete.   **flaumbande hwes** flaming hues
Bot sytole-stryng and gyternere°   **sytole-stryng . . .** citole string and
        cithern-player
Her reken° myrthe moght° not retrete;°   **Her reken** Their ready   could   imitate
For when those bryddes° her wynges bete,   birds
Thay songen° wyth a swete asent.°   sang   harmony
95   So gracios gle couthe° no mon gete   could
As here° and se her adubbement.°   hear   adornment

ix

So al was dubbet on dere asyse°
That fryth ther° Fortwne forth me feres.°
The derthe° therof for to devyse°
100 Nis no wygh° worthy that tonge beres.°
I welke ay° forth in wely wyse;°
No bonk° so byg that did me deres.°
The fyrre° in the fryth, the feirer con ryse°
The playn, the plonttes, the spyse, the peres,°
105 And rawes and randes and rych reveres°—
As fyldor° fyn her bonkes brent.°
I wan° to a water by schore° that scheres.°
Lorde, dere° was hit adubbement!°

dubbet ... adorned in a glorious manner
fryth ther wood where   leads
glory   picture
Nis ... There is no man   has
welke ay walked ever   wely wyse a
   blissful manner
slope   harm
farther   con ryse rose

pears

gold thread   steep
came   bank   courses
glorious   hit adubbement its adornment

x

The dubbemente of tho derworth depe°
110 Wern bonkes bene° of beryl bryght.
Swangeande° swete the water con swepe,°
Wyth a rownande rourde raykande aryght.°
In the fource° ther stonden stones stepe,
As glente° thurgh glas that glowed and glyght,°
115 As stremande sternes,° when strothe-men° slepe,
Staren° in welkyn° in wynter nyght.
For úche a pobbel° in pole° ther pyght°
Was emerad, saffer, other° gemme gente,°
That alle the loghe lemed° of lyght,
120 So dere° was hit adubbement.°

tho ... those splendid depths
fair
Swirling   con swepe swept
rownande ... whispering voice rolling
   straight on
bottom
light   shone
stremande sternes streaming stars
   valley men (mortals)
Shine   sky
úche ... each pebble   stream   set
emerad ... emerald, sapphire, or   noble
loghe lemed pool gleamed
glorious   hit adubbement its adornment

III

xi

The dubbement dere of doun and dales,°
Of wod and water and wlonk° playnes,
Bylde° in me blys, abated my bales,°
Fordidden° my stresse, dystryed° my paynes.
125 Doun after a strem that dryghly hales°
I bowed° in blys, bredful° my braynes.
The fyrre° I folghed° those floty° vales,
The more strenghthe of joye myn herte straynes.°

doun ... hill and valleys
splendid
Aroused   sorrows
Did away with   stresse, dystryed grief,
   destroyed
dryghly hales steadily flows
went   brimful
farther   followed   watery
stirs

105. And hedgerows and borders and splendid river banks

343

As Fortune fares ther as hö fraynes,°   **hö fraynes** she makes trial
130 Whether solace hö sende other° elles sore,°   or   pain
     The wygh° to wham° her wylle hö waynes°   man   whom   grants
     Hyttes° to have ay° more and more.   Chances   ever

xii

     More of wele° was in that wyse°   delight   manner
     Then I cowthe° telle thagh° I tom° hade,   could   though   leisure
135 For ürthely° herte myght not suffyse   earthly
     To the tenthe döle° of tho gladnes glade.°   part   **tho** . . . those joyful joys
     For-thy° I thoght that Paradyse   Therefore
     Was ther over gayn° tho bonkes brade.°   against   **bonkes brade** broad slopes
     I hoped° the water were a devyse°   supposed   division
140 Bytwene myrthes° by meres° made.   delights   pools
     Byyonde the broke, by slente other slade,°   **slente** . . . slope or valley
     I hoped that mote merked wöre.°   **mote** . . . castle would be situated
     Bot the water was depe, I dorst not wade,
     And ever me longed° ay more and more.   **me longed** I longed

xiii

145 More and more and yet wel mare,°   **wel mare** much more
     Me lyste° to se the broke byyonde;   **Me lyste** I wished
     For if hit was fayr ther I con fare,°   **con fare** went
     Wel loveloker° was the fyrre° londe.   lovelier   farther
     Abowte me con I stote° and stare;   **con** . . . I did halt
150 To fynde a forthe° faste con I fonde;°   ford   **con** . . . I tried
     Bot wothes mo, i-wysse,° ther ware,   **wothes** . . . dangers more, indeed
     The fyrre I stalked by the stronde.°   bank
     And ever me thoght° I schulde not wonde°   **me thoght** it seemed to me   flinch
     For wo° ther weles° so wynne wöre.°   **For wo** From danger   delights   **wynne**
                                           wöre joyful were
155 Thenne new note° me com on honde   matter
     That meved my mynde ay more and more.

xiv

     More mervayle con my dom adaunt.°   **con** . . . subdued my reason
     I segh° byyonde that myry mere°   saw   **myry mere** pleasant pool
     A crystal clyffe ful relusaunt;°   **ful relusaunt** very shiny
160 Mony ryal ray con fro hit rere.°   **con** . . . rose from it
     At the fote therof ther sete° a faunt,°   sat   child
     A mayden of menske,° ful debonere.°   grace   gracious
     Blysnande° whyt was hyr bleaunt.°   Gleaming   mantle
     I knew hyr wel, I hade sen hyr ere.

165 As glysnande° golde that man con schere,°   glistening   **man** . . . one cut
    So schon that schene an-under shore.°   **schene** . . . fair one under the hill
    On lenghe° I loked to° hyr there;   **On lenghe** For a long time   at
    The lenger, I knew hyr more and more.

xv

    The more I frayste° hyr fayre face,   scanned
170 Her fygure fyn when I had fonte,°   noticed
    Suche gladande° glory con to me glace°   gladdening   **con** . . . glided to me
    As lyttel° byfore therto was wonte.°   seldom   accustomed
    To calle hyr lyste con me enchace,°   **lyste** . . . longing urged me
    Bot baysment gef° myn hert a brunt.°   **baysment gef** . . . bewilderment gave
                                                          blow
175 I segh° hyr in so strange a place,   saw
    Such a bürre myght° make myn herte blunt.°   **bürre myght** shock could   stunned
    Thenne veres hö° up her fayre frount,°   **veres hö** she lifts   forehead
    Hyr vysayge whyt as playn yvore.°   ivory
    That stonge myn hert, ful stray atcount,°   **ful** . . . very much astounded to distraction
180 And ever the lenger, the more and more.

IV

xvi

    More then me lyste,° my drede aros.   **me lyste** I wished
    I stod ful° stylle and dorste not calle.   very
    Wyth yghen° open and mouth ful clos   eyes
    I stod as hende° as hawk in halle.   quiet
185 I hoped° that gostly° was that porpose;°   supposed   spiritual   significance
    I dred onende° what schulde byfalle,   concerning
    Lest hö° me eschaped° that I ther chos,°   she   eluded   saw
    Er° I at steven° hir moght stalle.°   Before   **at steven** for a meeting   **moght**
                                                            stalle could stop
    That gracios gay° wythouten galle,°   fair one   flaw
190 So smothe, so smal, so seme slyght,°   **seme slyght** becomingly slender
    Ryses up in hir araye ryalle,
    A precios pyece in perles pyght.°   adorned

xvii

    Perles pyghte of ryal prys°   excellence
    There moght mon° by grace haf sene   **moght mon** could one
195 When that° frech as flor-de-lys   that one
    Doun the bonke con boghe bydene.°   **bonke** . . . slope came straightway

Al blysnande° whyt was hir beau biys,° gleaming **beau biys** beautiful mantle
Upon° at sydes, and bounden bene° Open **bounden bene** bordered beautifully
Wyth the myryeste margarys,° at my devyse,° **myryeste margarys** fairest pearls opinion
200 That ever I segh° yet with myn ene;° saw eyes
Wyth lappes° large, I wot° and I wene,° folds know suppose
Dubbed° with double perle and dyghte;° Set adorned
Her cortel of self sute schene,°
Wyth precios perles al umbepyghte.° adorned around

xviii

205 A pyght coroune° yet wer° that gyrle **pyght coroune** adorned crown wore
Of marjorys° and non other ston, pearls
Highe pynakled of cler whyt perle,
Wyth flurted° flowres perfet° upon. figured perfect
To hed° hade hö° non other werle.° **To hed** On her head she attire
210 Her here leke, al hyr umbegon,
Her semblaunt sade for doc other erle,°
Her ble° more blaght° then whalles bon. complexion white
As schorne° golde schyr° her fax° thenne schon, cut bright hair
On schylderes° that leghe unlapped lyghte.° shoulders **leghe** . . . lay unbound lightly
215 Her depe colour yet wonted° non lacked
Of° precios perle in porfyl pyghte.° In comparison to **in** . . . on an embroidered border set

xix

Pyght° was poyned° and üche a° hemme Adorned wristband **üche a** each
At honde, at sydes, at overture,° opening
Wyth whyte perle and non other gemme,
220 And bornyste° whyte was hyr vesture. burnished
Bot a wonder° perle wythouten wemme° wonderful flaw
Inmyddes hyr breste was sette so sure.
A mannes dom moght dryghly demme,° **dom** . . . reason could completely be baffled
Er° mynde moght malte° in hit mesure.° Before comprehend value
225 I hope° no tong moght endure° suppose suffice
No saverly saghe say° of that syght, **No** . . . Any fitting word to say
So was hit clene and cler and pure,
That precios perle ther hit was pyght.° set

xx

Pyght° in perle, that precios pyece Adorned
230 On wyther half° water com doun the schore.° **wyther half** the opposite side bank
No gladder gome hethen° into Grece **gome hethen** man from here
Then I, when hö° on brymme wöre.° she **brymme wöre** bank was

---

203. Her kirtle of the same fair style
210–11. Her hair, encircled all around her, enclosed her face, grave as a duke's or an earl's

Hö was me nerre° then aunte or nece;   nearer
My joy for-thy° was much the more.   therefore
235 Hö profered me speche, that special spece,°   **special spece** excellent person
Enclynande° lowe in wommon lore,°   Bowing   **wommon lore** womanly manner
Caghte of° her coroun of grete tresore   **Caghte of** Took off
And haylsed° me wyth a lote lyghte.°   greeted   **lote lyghte** joyous word
Wel was me° that ever I was bore°   **Wel ... I** was happy   born
240 To sware° that swete° in perles pyghte!°   answer   sweet one   adorned

V

xxi

"O perle," quod I, "in perles pyght,
Art thou my perle that I haf playned,°   mourned
Regretted by myn one on° nyghte?   **myn ...** myself alone at
Much longeyng haf I for thee layned,°   concealed
245 Sythen° into gresse° thou me aglyghte.°   Since   grass   slipped from
Pensyf, payred,° I am forpayned,°   broken   tormented
And thou in a lyf of lykyng lyghte,°   **lykyng lyghte** joy came
In Paradys erde,° of stryf unstrayned.°   land   untroubled
What wyrde° has hyder my juel vayned,°   fate   sent
250 And don° me in thys del° and gret daunger?°   put   sorrow   subjection
Fro we in twynne wern towen and twayned,°
I haf ben a joyles juelere."

xxii

That juel thenne in gemmes gente°   noble
Vered° up her vyse° wyth yghen° graye,   Raised   face   eyes
255 Set on hyr coroun° of perle orient,   crown
And soberly after thenne con hö say:
"Sir, ye haf your tale mysetente,°   misstated
To say your perle is al awaye,°   gone away
That is in cofer so comly clente°   **comly clente** beautifully enclosed
260 As in this gardyn gracios gaye,°   fair
Here-inne to lenge° for ever and play,   stay
Ther mys nee mornyng° com never nere.   **mys ...** loss nor mourning
Her were a forser for thee, in faye,°   noble
If thou were a gentyl° jueler.

---

251. Since we were drawn asunder and parted
263. Here would be a treasure casket for you, in faith

xxiii

265 "Bot, jueler gente,° if thou schal lose   *noble*
     Thy joy for a gemme that thee was lef,°   *dear*
     Me thynk° thee put in a mad porpose,°   **Me thynk** It seems to me   *intention*
     And büsyes thee aboute a raysoun bref;°   **raysoun bref** reason soon gone
     For that° thou lestes° was bot° a rose   *what*   *lost*   *only*
270 That flowred and fayled as kynde° hyt gef.°   *nature*   *gave*
     Now thurgh kynde of the kyste° that hyt con   *casket*
         close°   **con close** encloses
     To a perle of prys hit is put in pref.°
     And thou has called thy wyrde° a thef,   *fate*
     That oght of noght° has mad thee cler.°   **oght . . .** something from nothing   *clearly*
275 Thou blames the bote of° thy meschef;°   **bote of . . .** cure for   *misfortune*
     Thou art no kynde° jueler."   *gentle*

xxiv

     A juel to me then was thys geste,°   *guest*
     And jueles wern hyr gentyl sawes.°   **gentyl sawes** noble words
     "I-wyse,"° quod I, "my blysfol beste,°   *Indeed*   *noblest one*
280 My grete dystresse thou al todrawes.°   *draw away*
     To be excused I make requeste;
     I trawed° my perle don out of dawes.°   *believed*   *days*
     Now haf I fonde hyt, I schal ma feste,°   **ma feste** make rejoicing
     And wony° wyth hyt in schyr wod-schawes,°   *dwell*   **schyr wod-schawes** bright grove
285 And love° my Lorde and al his lawes   *praise*
     That has me broght thys blys ner.
     Now were I at° yow byyonde thise wawes,°   *with*   *waves*
     I were a joyful jueler."

xxv

     "Jueler," sayde that gemme clene,°   *pure*
290 "Why borde° ye men? So madde ye be!   *jest*
     Thre wordes has thou spoken at ene;°   *one time*
     Unavysed, for sothe,° wern alle thre.   **Unavysed . . .** Ill-advised, indeed
     Thou ne woste° in worlde what on dos mene;°   **ne woste** do not know   **on . . .** one mean
     Thy worde byfore thy wytte con fle.°   **con fle** did fly
295 Thou says thou trawes° me in this dene°   *believe*   *valley*
     Bycawse thou may wyth yghen° me se;   *eyes*
     Another° thou says, in thys countré   *Another thing*
     Thyself schal won° wyth me ryght here;   *dwell*
     The thrydde, to passe thys water fre,°   *noble*
300 That may no joyfol jueler.

272. It has proved to be an excellent pearl.

VI

xxvi

"I halde that jueler lyttel to prayse
That leves° wel that° he ses wyth yghe,   believes   what
And much to blame and uncortayse°   discourteous
That leves oure Lorde wolde make a lyghe,°   lie
305 That lelly hyghte° your lyf to rayse,   **lelly hyghte** faithfully promised
Thagh° fortune dyd your flesch to dyghe.°   Though   die
Ye setten Hys wordes ful westernays°   **ful westernays** very contrariwise
That leves nothynk bot° ye hit syghe.°   unless   see
And that is a poynt o sorquydryghe°   **o sorquydryghe** of pride
310 That üche° god mon° may evel byseme,°   to each   man   **evel byseme** ill befit
To leve no tale be true to tryghe°   test
Bot that° hys one skyl° may dem.°   that which   **one skyl** reason alone   judge

xxvii

"Deme now thyself if thou con dayly°   **con dayly** spoke
As man to God wordes schulde heve.°   lift
315 Thou says thou schal won° in this bayly.°   dwell   domain
Me thynk thee bürde° fyrst aske leve,   **Me . . .** It seems to me you ought to
And yet of graunt° thou myghtes fayle.   permission
Thou wylnes° over thys water to weve.°   wish   go
Er moste° thou cever° to other counsayle:°   **Er moste** Before that must   attain   course
320 Thy corse° in clot mot calder keve.°   body   **clot . . .** clay must colder sink
For hit was forgarte° at Paradys greve;°   ruined   grove
Oure yorefader° hit con mysseyeme.°   forefather   **con mysseyeme** neglected
Thurgh drüry° deth bös° üch man dreve,°   cruel   it behooves   to pass
Er° over thys dam° hym Dryghtyn deme."°   Before   stream   **Dryghtyn deme** the Lord may allow

xxviii

325 "Demes thou° me," quod I, "my swete,   **Demes thou** If you condemn
To döl° agayn, thenne I dowyne.°   sorrow   pine away
Now haf I fonte that° I forlete;°   **fonte that** found what   lost
Schal I efte° forgo hit er° ever I fyne?°   again   die
Why schal I hit bothe mysse and mete?°   **mysse . . .** lose and find
330 My precios perle dos me gret pyne.°   sorrow
What serves tresor, bot gares° men grete°   makes   cry
When he hit schal efte° wyth tenes tyne?°   later   **tenes tyne** pains lose
Now rech° I never for to declyne,°   care   fall
Ne how fer of folde° that man° me fleme.°   **fer . . .** far from earth   one   may drive
335 When I am partles° of perle myne,   deprived
Bot durande doel° what may men deme?"°   **durande doel** lasting sorrow   call it

xxix

"Thow demes noght bot° doel-dystresse,"   **demes** ... talk of only
Thenne sayde that wyght.° "Why dos thou so?   person
For dyne of doel of lüres lesse°
340 Ofte mony° mon forgos the mo.°   many a   greater
Thee oghte better thyselven blesse,
And love ay God, in wele and wo,°   **wele** ... prosperity and adversity
For anger gaynes thee not a cresse.°   watercress
Who nedes schal thole,° be not so thro.°   **nedes** ... must suffer   bold
345 For thogh thou daunce as any do,°   doe
Braundysch° and bray thy brathes breme,°   Toss about   **brathes breme** agonies
When thou no fyrre may,° to ne° fro,   fierce
Thou moste abyde that° He schal deme.°   **fyrre may** farther can   or
                                              moste ... must suffer what   judge

xxx

"Deme Dryghtyn,° ever hym adyte,°   **Deme Dryghtyn** Judge the Lord   indict
350 Of° the way a fote ne wyl He wrythe.°   From   **ne** ... He will not swerve
Thy mendes mountes° not a myte,   **mendes mountes** rewards will increase
Thagh° thou for sorwe° be never blythe.°   Though   sorrow   happy
Stynt of thy strot and fyne to flyte,°
And sech Hys blythe° ful swefte and swythe.° **sech** ... seek His mercy   quickly
355 Thy prayer may Hys pyté byte,°   move
That mercy schal hyr craftes kythe.°   **craftes kythe** powers show
Hys comforte may thy langour lythe°   **langour lythe** grief assuage
And thy lüres of lyghtly leme;°   **lüres** ... sorrows gently dispose of
For, marre other madde,° morne and mythe,°   **marre** ... lament or rage   hide feelings
360 Al lys in Hym to dyght and deme."°   **dyght** ... ordain and appoint

VII

xxxi

Thenne demed° I to that damyselle:°   said   maiden
"Ne worthe° no wraththe unto my Lorde,   **Ne worthe** Let there be
If rapely° I rave, spornande in spelle.°   rashly   **spornande** ... stumbling in
My herte was al wyth mysse remorde,°   speech
365 As wallande° water gos out of welle.   **mysse remorde** loss tormented
I do me° ay in hys myserecorde.°   welling
Rebuke me never wyth wordes felle,°   **do me** put myself   mercy
Thagh° I forloyne,° my dere endorde,°   cruel
                                              Though   go astray   adored one

339. For sound of lamentation of lesser sorrows
353. Stop your arguing and cease chiding

Bot kythes° me kyndely your coumforde,°   show   comfort
370 Pytosly thenkande° upon thysse: thinking
Of care° and me ye made acorde°   sorrow   agreement
That er° was grounde of alle my blysse.   **That er** Who before

xxxii

"My blysse, my bale,° ye han ben bothe,   sorrow
Bot much the bygger yet was my mon;°   grief
375 Fro° thou was wroken° fro üch a wothe,°   Since   banished   danger
I wyste° never where my perle was gon.   knew
Now I hit se, now lethes° my lothe.°   abates   woe
And, when we departed,° we wern at on;°   parted   one
God forbede we be now wrothe,
380 We meten so selden° by stok other° ston.   seldom   **stok other** trunk or
Thagh° cortaysly ye carp con,°   Though   **carp con** can speak
I am bot mol° and maneres mysse.°   **bot mol** only dust   lack
Bot Crystes mersy and Mary and Jon,
Thise arn the grounde of alle my blisse.

xxxiii

385 "In blysse I se thee blythely blent,°   set
And I a man al mornyf mate.°   **mornyf mate** mournful and dejected
Ye take theron ful° lyttel tente,°   very   attention
Thagh I hente° ofte harmes hate.°   get   **harmes hate** sorrows burning
Bot now I am here in your presente,°   presence
390 I wolde bysech, wythouten debate,
Ye wolde me say in sobre asente
What lyf ye lede erly and late.
For I am ful fayn° that your astate°   glad   estate
Is worthen to worschyp and wele, i-wysse.°
395 Of alle my joy the hyghe gate°   road
Hit is, and grounde of alle my blysse."

xxxiv

"Now blysse, bürne, mot° thee bytyde,"°   **bürne, mot** man, may   befall
Then sayde that lufsom° of lyth and lere,°   lovely   **lyth . . .** limb and face
"And welcum here to walk and byde,°   stay
400 For now thy speche is to me dere.
Maysterful mod° and hyghe pryde,   **Maysterful mod** Lordly spirit
I hete° thee, arn heterly° hated here.   assure   bitterly
My Lorde ne loves not° for to chyde,   **ne . . .** does not love
For meke arn alle that wones° Hym nere;   dwell

394. Has become one of honor and prosperity, indeed.

405 And when in Hys place thou schal apere,
    Be dep devote in hol° mekenesse.   all
    My Lorde the Lamb loves ay such chere,°   mien
    That is the grounde of alle my blysse.

XXXV

    "A blysful lyf thou says I lede;
410 Thou woldes knaw therof the stage.°   state
    Thow wost° wel when thy perle con schede°   know   **con schede** fell
    I was ful yong and tender of age.
    Bot my Lorde the Lombe thurgh Hys godhede,
    He toke myself to Hys maryage,
415 Corounde° me quene in blysse to brede°   Crowned   flourish
    In lenghe° of dayes that ever schal wage;°   length   endure
    And sesed in° alle Hys herytage°   **sesed in** put in possession of   inheritance
    Hys lef° is. I am holy° Hysse: beloved   wholly
    Hys prese,° Hys prys,° and Hys parage°   worth   excellence   high rank
420 Is rote and grounde of alle my blysse."

VIII

XXXVI

    "Blysful," quod I, "may thys be trewe?
    Dyspleses not if I speke errour.
    Art thou the quene of hevenes blwe,
    That al thys worlde schal do honour?
425 We leven on° Marye that grace of grewe,°   **leven on** believe in   **that...** from whom grace came
    That ber a barne of° vyrgyn flour;   **barne of** child in
    The croune fro hyr who moght remewe°   **moght remewe** could remove
    Bot hö hir passed° in sum favour?   **Bot...** Unless she surpassed her
    Now, for synglerty o° hyr dousour,°   **synglerty o** uniqueness of   sweetness
430 We calle hyr Fenyx of Arraby,
    That, freles, fleghe of° hyr Fasor,°   **freles...** flawless, flew from   Creator
    Lyk to the Quen of cortaysye."

XXXVII

    "Cortayse Quen," thenne sayde that gaye,°   fair one
    Knelande° to grounde, folde° up hyr face,   Kneeling   turned
435 "Makeles° Moder and myryest May,°   Matchless   **myryest May** fairest Maiden
    Blessed bygynner of üch a grace!"

Thenne ros hö up and con restay,°   **con restay** paused
And speke me towarde° in that space:°   **me towarde** to me   time
"Sir, fele° here porchases and fonges pray,°   many   **porchases** . . . seek and get a prize
440 Bot supplantores° none wythinne thys place.   usurpers
That emperise° al hevens has,   empress
And ürthe, and helle, in her bayly;°   rule
Of erytage° yet non wyl hö chace,   **Of erytage** From heritage
For hö is Quen of cortaysye.

xxxviii

445 "The court of the kyndom of God alyve°   living
Has a property in hytself° beyng: its own
Alle that may ther-inne aryve
Of alle the reme° is quen other kyng,   realm
And never other° yet schal depryve,   another
450 Bot üchon fayn° of otheres hafyng,°   **üchon fayn** each one glad   possession
And wolde her corounes wern° worthe tho fyve,°   **her** . . . their crowns might be   **tho fyve**
If possyble were her mendyng.°   five of them
    improvement
Bot my Lady of whom Jesu con spryng,
Hö haldes the empyre over uus ful hyghe;
455 And that dyspleses non of oure gyng,°   company
For hö is Quene of cortaysye.

xxxix

"Of courtaysye, as says Saynt Poule,
Al arn we membres of Jesu Kryst;
As heved° and arme and legg and naule°   head   navel
460 Temen° to hys body ful trew and tryste,°   Are joined   faithfully
Ryght° so is üch a Krysten sawle   Just
A longande lym° to the Mayster of myste.°   **longande lym** limb belonging   mysteries
Thenne loke what hate other any gawle°   bitterness
Is tached other tyghed° thy lymmes bytwyste.°   **tached** . . . attached or tied   between
465 Thy heved° has nauther greme ne gryste,°   head   **greme** . . . anger nor spite
On arme other fynger thagh thou ber byghe.°   **ber byghe** wear a ring
So fare we alle wyth luf and lyste°   joy
To kyng and quene by cortaysye."

xl

"Cortaysé," quod I, "I leve,°   believe
470 And charyté grete, be yow among,
Bot my speche that yow ne greve,°   **yow** . . . may not grieve you
· · · · · · · · · · · · · · · · ·¹

---

¹ Line omitted by scribe.

353

Thyself in heven over hygh thou heve,°   raise
To make thee quen that was so yonge.
475 What more honour moghte he acheve
That hade endured in worlde stronge,°   firmly
And lyved in penaunce hys lyves longe
Wyth bodyly bale° hym blysse to byye?°   harm   buy
What more worschyp° moght he fonge°   honor   get
480 Then corounde° be kyng by cortaysé?   crowned

IX

xli

"That cortaysé is too fre° of dede,°   lavish   deed
Yyf hyt be soth° that thou cones saye.°   true   **cones saye** say
Thou lyfed not two yer in oure thede;°   land
Thou cowthes° never God nauther plese ne pray,   could
485 Ne never nawther° Pater ne Crede;   **Ne ...** Nor ever knew either
And quen mad on the fyrst day!
I may not traw,° so God me spede,   **may ...** cannot believe
That God wolde wrythe° so wrange° away.   turn   wrong
Of countes, damysel, par ma fay,°
490 Wer° fayr in heven to halde asstate,°   It would be   rank
Other elles a lady of lasse aray;°   **lasse aray** lesser position
Bot a quene! Hit is too dere a date."°   end

xlii

"Ther is no date of Hys godnesse,"
Then sayde to me that worthy wyghte,°   person
495 "For al is trawthe that He con dresse,°   **con dresse** established
And He may do nothynk bot ryght.
As Mathew meles° in your messe°   speaks   mass
In sothfol° gospel of God almyght,   truthful
In sample° He can ful graythely gesse,°   parable   **graythely gesse** fittingly devise
500 And lyknes hit to heven lyghte.°   bright
'My regne,'° He says, 'is lyk on hyght°   realm   high
To a lorde that hade a vyne,° I wate.°   vineyard   know
Of tyme of yere the terme was tyght,°   **terme ...** time was come
To labor° vyne was dere° the date.°   cultivate   good   time

489. Of countess, maiden, by my faith

xliii

505 " 'That date of yere wel knawe thys hyne.°
  The lorde ful erly up he ros
  To hyre werkmen to hys vyne,°
  And fyndes ther summe to hys porpos.
  Into acorde thay con declyne°
510 For a pené° on a day, and forth thay gos,
  Wrythen° and worchen and don gret pyne,°
  Kerven and caggen° and man° hit clos.°
  Aboute under° the lorde to marked tos,°
  And ydel men stande° he fyndes ther-ate.
515 " ' "Why stande ye ydel?" he sayde to thos.
  "Ne knawe ye of this day no date?"°

      thys hyne these workers

      vineyard

      con declyne consented
      penny
      Twist toil
      Kerven . . . Cut and bind make secure
      the third hour (9 A.M.) **marked tos**
      market goes
      standing

      end

xliv

  " ' "Er° date of daye hider arn we wonne,"°
  So was al samen her° answar soght.°
  "We haf standen her syn° ros the sunne,
520 And no mon byddes uus do ryght noght."
  " ' "Gos° into my vyne,° dos that° ye conne,"°
  So sayde the lorde, and made hit toght:°
  "What resonabele hyre be naght be runne°
  I yow pay in dede and thoghte."°
525 Thay wente into the vyne and wroghte,°
  And al day the lorde thus yede° his gate,°
  And new men to hys vyne° he broghte
  Welnegh whyl° day was passed date.°

      Before come
      samen her together their given
      standen . . . stood here since

      Go vineyard what can
      an agreement
      hyre . . . wage by night has accumulated
      dede . . . deed and intention (in full)
      worked
      went way
      vineyard
      Welnegh whyl Almost until its end

xlv

  " 'At the date° of day of evensonge
530 On oure° byfore the sonne go doun,
  He segh° ther ydel men ful stronge
  And sade° to hem° wyth sobre soun,°
  " ' "Why stonde ye ydel thise dayes longe?"
  Thay sayden her hyre° was nawhere boun.°
535 "Gos to my vyne, yemen° yonge,
  And wyrkes and dos that at° ye moun."°
  Sone the worlde bycom wel broun;°
  The sunne was doun and hit wex° late
  To take her hyre he mad sumoun;°
540 The day was al apassed date.°

      time
      On oure One hour
      saw
      said them **sobre soun** earnest voice

      her hyre their wage made ready
      vyne, yemen vineyard, yeomen
      dos . . . do what can
      dark
      grew
      mad sumoun gave summons
      its end

X

xlvi

" 'The date° of the daye the lorde con knaw,°   time **con knaw** knew
Called to the reve:° "Lede,° pay the meyny.°   steward Man company
Gyf hem° the hyre° that I hem owe,   them wage
And fyrre,° that non me may repreny,°   further reprove
545 Set hem alle upon a rawe°   row
And gyf üchon inlyche° a peny.   **gyf**...give each one alike
Begyn at the laste that standes lowe,
Tyl to the fyrste that thou atteny."°   reach
And thenne the fyrst bygonne to pleny°   complain
550 And sayden that thay hade travayled° sore: worked
" ' "These bot on oure hem con streny;°   **bot**...only one hour exerted themselves
Uus thynk uus oghe° to take more.   **Uus**...It seems to us we ought

xlvii

" ' "More haf we served, uus thynk so,
That suffred han° the dayes hete,   have
555 Thenn thyse that wroght° not houres two,   worked
And thou dos hem° uus to counterfete."°   **dos hem** make them resemble
Thenne sayde the lorde to on° of tho:°   one those
" ' "Frende, no waning° I wyl thee yete;°   lessening grant
Take that° is thyn owne, and go.   what
560 And I hyred thee for a peny agrete,°   all together
Why bygynnes thou now to threte?°   quarrel
Was not a pené° thy covenaunt thore?°   penny **covenaunt thore** agreement then
Fyrre° then covenaunde° is noght to plete.°   Further agreement plead
Why schalte thou thenne ask more?

xlviii

565 " ' "More, whether lawely is me my gyfte,
To do wyth myn what-so me lykes?°
Other elles thyn yghe° to lyther° is lyfte,°   eye evil turned
For I am goude and non byswykes?"°   **non byswykes** cheat no one
" 'Thus schal I,' quod Kryste, 'hit skyfte:°   ordain
570 The laste schal be the fyrst that strykes,°   goes
And the fyrst the laste, be he never so swyft;
For mony ben° called, thagh fewe be mykes.'°   are friends of Christ
Thus pore men her part° ay pykes,°   **her part** their share get
Thagh thay com late and lyttel wöre;°   **lyttel wöre** humble were
575 And thagh her sweng° wyth lyttel atslykes,°   toil is spent
The merci of God is much the more.

565–66. Moreover, is my act of giving lawful for me, my act of doing with my own whatever I please?

356

xlix

"More haf I of joye and blysse here-inne,
Of ladyschip gret and lyves blom,°   **lyves blom** bloom of life
Then alle the wyghes° in the worlde myght   men
     wynne
580 By the way of ryght to aske dome.°
Whether welnygh° now I con bygynne,   **Whether welnygh** Though almost
In eventyde into the vyne I come,°   came
Fyrst of my hyre° my Lorde con mynne;°   wage   **con mynne** remembered
I was payed anon of al and sum.°   **anon . . .** at once in full
585 Yet other ther werne that toke more tom,°   time
That swange and swat° for long yore,°   **swange . . .** toiled and sweated   past
That yet of hyre nothynk thay nom,°   got
Paraunter° noght schal to-yere° more."   And perhaps   this year

l

Then more I meled° and sayde apert:°   spoke   openly
590 "Me thynk° thy tale° unresounable.   **Me thynk** Seems to me   account
Goddes ryght° is redy and evermore rert,°   justice   exalted
Other Holy Wryt is bot a fable.
In Sauter° is sayd a verce overte°   the Psalter   plain
That spekes a poynt determynable:
595 'Thou quytes üchon° as hys desserte,   **quytes üchon** reward each one
Thou hyghe kyng ay pretermynable.'°   foreordaining
Now he that stod the long day stable,°   firm
And thou to payment com hym byfore,
Thenne the lasse in werke, to take more able,
600 And ever the lenger the lasse, the more."°

XI

li

"Of more and lasse in Godes ryche,"°   kingdom
That gentyl° sayde, "lys no jöparde,°   noble one   **lys . . .** lies no doubt
For ther is üch mon payed inlyche,°   alike
Whether lyttel other much be hys rewarde.
605 For the gentyl Cheventayn° is no chyche,°   Chieftain   niggard
Whether-so-ever he dele nesch° other harde;   soft
He laves° hys gyftes as water of dyche,°   pours   **of dyche** from a ditch
Other gotes° of golf° that never charde.°   streams   a gulf   would cease

580. If they were to ask judgment according to strict justice.
599–600. Then the less work done, the greater the ability to earn; and thus continually, the less work, the more earning.

Hys fraunchyse° is large that ever dard°   freedom has shown fear
610   To° Hym that mas° in synne rescoghe;°   Toward makes rescue
No blysse bes° fro hem reparde,°   is withheld
For the grace of God is gret inoghe.°   enough

lii

"Bot now thou motes,° me for to mate,°   argue confuse
That I my peny haf wrang tan° here;   **wrang tan** wrongly taken
615   Thou says that I that come too late
Am not worthy so gret fere.°   rank
Where wystes° thou ever any bourne abate,°   knew **bourne abate** man lived
Ever so holy in hys prayere,
That he ne forfeted by sumkyn gate°   **sumkyn gate** some kind of way
620   The mede° sumtyme of hevenes clere?°   reward bright
And ay the ofter,° the alder thay were   oftener
Thay laften° ryght and wroghten woghe.°   left **wroghten woghe** did evil
Mercy and grace moste hem° then stere,°   **moste hem** must them guide
For the grace of God is gret innoghe.°   enough

liii

625   "Bot innoghe of grace has innocent.°   the innocent
As sone as thay arn borne, by lyne°   **by lyne** in order
In the water of babtem° thay dyssente;°   baptism descend
Then arne thay broght into the vyne.
Anon° the day, wyth derk endente,°   At once **derk endente** darkness inlaid
630   The myght of deth dos° to enclyne.°   causes sink
That wrogt never wrang er thenne thay wente,°
The gentyle° Lorde thenne payes hys hyne.°   noble **hys hyne** as his workers
Thay dyden° hys heste,° thay wern there-ine;   followed commandment
Why schulde he not her labour alow,°   credit
635   Yys,° and pay hem at the fyrst fyne?°   Indeed **at . . .** at once completely
For the grace of God is gret innoghe.°   enough

liv

"Inoghe is knawen° that mankyn° grete   known mankind
Fyrste was wroght to blysse parfyt;°   perfect
Oure forme fader° hit con forfete°   **forme fader** first father **con forfete** forfeited
640   Thurgh an apple that he upon con byte.
Al wer we dampned° for that mete°   damned food
To dyghe in doel out of delyt,°
And sythen wende° to helle hete,°   **sythen wende** then go **helle hete** hell's heat
Ther-inne to won° wythoute respyt.   dwell

631. Those who never did wrong before they went thence
642. To die in sorrow away from joy

645 Bot theron com a bote as-tyt.°   **bote as-tyt** remedy at once
    Ryche blod ran on rode° so roghe,°   the cross   cruel
    And wynne° water then at that plyt;°   precious   perilous time
    The grace of God wex° gret innoghe.°   grew   enough

lv

    "Innoghe ther wax° out of that welle,   flowed
650 Blod and water of brode wounde.
    The blod uus boght° fro bale° of helle   redeemed   suffering
    And delyvered uus of the deth secounde;
    The water is baptem,° the sothe° to telle,   baptism   truth
    That folghed° the glayve° so grymly° grounde,   followed   spear   cruelly
655 That wasches away the gyltes felle°   **gyltes felle** sins deadly
    That Adam wyth° inne deth uus drounde.   **That . . .** With which Adam
    Now is ther noght° in the worlde rounde   nothing
    Bytwene uus and blysse bot that° he wythdrogh,°   **bot that** except what   removed
    And that° is restored in sely stounde,°   that bliss   **sely stounde** a blessed hour
660 And the grace of God is gret innogh.°   enough

XII

lvi

    "Grace innogh the mon may have
    That synnes thenne new, yif him repente,
    Bot wyth sorw and syt° he mot° hit crave,   **sorw . . .** sorrow and grief   must
    And byde° the payne therto is bent.°   suffer   **therto . . .** which is with it bound
665 Bot resoun, of ryght that con noght rave°   **con . . .** cannot stray
    Saves evermore the innossent.
    Hit is a dom° that never God gave,   judgment
    That ever the gyltles° schulde be schente.°   innocent   discomfited
    The gyltyf may° contryssyoun hente°   **gyltyf may** guilty can   find
670 And be thurgh mercy to grace thryght;°   led
    Bot he to gyle that never glente,°   turned
    That inoscente is saf and ryghte.

lvii

    "Ryght° thus I knaw wel in this cas   Just
    Two men° to save is god by skylle:°   kinds of men   reason
675 The ryghtwys° man schal se hys face,   righteous
    The harmles hathel° schal com hym tylle.°   man   to

The Sauter° hyt sas° thus in a pace:°   Psalter   says   passage
"'Lorde, who schal klymbe Thy hygh hylle,
Other rest wythinne Thy holy place?'
680   Hymself to onsware He is not dylle:°   slow
"'Hondelynges harme that dyt not ille,°
That is of hert bothe clene and lyght,°   pure
Ther schal hys step stable stylle.'°   **stable stylle** stand firm
The innosent is ay saf by ryght.

lviii

685   "The ryghtwys° man also sertayn°   righteous   certainly
Aproche he schal that proper pyle,°   **proper pyle** fair castle
That takes not her lyf in vayne,
Ne glaveres° her nieghbor wyth no gyle.   cheats
Of thys ryghtwys sas° Salamon playn   says
690   How Koyntise° onoure con aquyle.°   Wisdom   **con aquyle** obtained
By wayes ful streght hö con hym strayn,°   guide
And schewed° hym the rengne° of God awhyle,   showed   kingdom
As who° says, 'Lo, yon lovely yle!   one who
Thou may hit wynne if thou be wyghte.'°   brave
695   Bot, hardyly,° wythoute peryle,   surely
The innosent is ay save° by ryghte.   redeemed

lix

"Anende ryghtwys° men yet says a gome,°   **Anende ryghtwys** About righteous   man
David in Sauter, if ever ye segh° hit: saw
"'Lorde, thy servaunt dragh° never to dome,°   bring   judgment
700   For non lyvyande° to thee is justyfyet.'   **non lyvyande** no one living
For-thy° to corte when thou schal com,   Therefore
Ther alle oure causes schal be tryed,
Alegge thee ryght,° thou may be innome°   **Alegge . . .** If you plead privilege for
By thys ilke° spech I have asspyed.°   yourself   refuted
705   Bot He on rode° that blody dyed,   same   observed
Delfully° thurgh hondes thryght,°   the cross
Gyve° thee to passe, when thou arte tryed,   Grievously   pierced
By innocens and not by ryghte.   May He grant

lx

"Ryghtwysly° who con rede,°   Rightly   **con rede** can read
710   He loke° on bok and be awayed°   **He loke** May he look   instructed
How Jesus Hym welke in are-thede,°   **Hym . . .** walked among ancient people
And bürnes° her barnes° unto hym brayde.°   persons   children   brought

---

681. He who with hands harmfully did not perform evil

For happe and hele° that fro Hym yede,°   **happe** . . . good fortune and healing
To touch her chylder° thay fayr Hym prayed.   issued
715 His dessypeles wyth blame let be hem bede°   children
And wyth her resounes ful fele restayed.°   **blame** . . . rebuke bade them cease
Jesus thenne hem swetely sayde: **fele restayed** many restrained
    "'Do way,° let chylder unto me tyght.°
To suche is hevenryche arayed.'°   **Do way** Cease come
720 The innocent is ay saf by ryght.   **hevenryche arayed** heaven's kingdom
        prepared

XIII

lxi

"Jesus con calle to Hym Hys mylde,°   gentle ones
And sayde Hys ryche° no wygh° myght wynne   kingdom man
Bot° he com thyder ryght° as a chylde,   Unless even
Other elles nevermore com ther-inne.
725 Harmles, trewe, and undefylde,
Wythouten mote other mascle° of sulpande°   **mote** . . . stain or spot polluting
    synne,
When such ther cnoken° on the bylde,°   knock dwelling
Tyt° schal hem men the yate unpynne.°   Quickly **yate unpynne** gate unbolt
Ther is the blys that con° not blynne°   can end
730 That the jueler soghte thurgh perré pres,°   **perré pres** gems of value
And solde alle hys goud,° bothe wolen and lynne,° goods linen
To bye hym a perle was mascelles.°   **was mascelles** that was spotless

lxii

"This makelles° perle, that boght is dere,   matchless
The joueler gef° fore alle hys god,   gave
735 Is lyke the reme° of hevenesse clere°—   kingdom bright
So sayde the Fader of folde and flode.°   **folde** . . . earth and water
For hit is wemles,° clene, and clere,   spotless
And endeles rounde, and blythe of mode,°   spirit
And commune° to alle that ryghtwys° were.   common righteous
740 Lo, even inmyddes° my breste hit stode.   in the middle of
My Lorde the Lombe, that schede Hys blode,
He pyght° hit there in token of pes.°   put peace
I rede° thee, forsake the worlde wode°   advise crazy
And porchace thy perle maskelles."°   spotless

lxiii

745 "O maskeles perle in perles pure,
 That beres," quod I, "the perle of prys,°   *excellence*
 Who formed thee thy fayre fygure?
 That° wroght thy wede,° he was ful wys.   *He who   garment*
 Thy beauté com never of nature;
750 Pymalyon° paynted never thy vys,°   *Pygmalion   face*
 Ne Arystotel nawther by hys lettrure°   *learning*
 Of carped° the kynde° these propertés.   **Of carped** *Spoke of   nature of*
 Thy colour passes° the flour-de-lys,   *surpasses*
 Thyn angel-having° so clene cortes.°   *angelic manner* **clene cortes** *purely gracious*
755 Breve° me, bryght, what kyn offys°   *Tell* **kyn offys** *kind of rank*
 Beres the perle so maskelles?"°   *spotless*

lxiv

 "My makeles° Lambe that al may bete,"°   *matchless   amend*
 Quod schö,° "my dere destyné,   *she*
 Me ches to° Hys make,° althagh unmete°   **ches to** *chose as   spouse   unfitting*
760 Sumtyme semed that assemblé.°   *union*
 When I wente fro yor worlde wete,°   *damp*
 He calde me to Hys bonerté:°   *beatitude*
  "'Cum hyder to me, my lemman° swete,   *beloved one*
 For mote° ne spot is non in thee.'   *stain*
765 He gef° me myght and als° bewté;   *gave* **myght...** *power and also*
 In Hys blod He wesch° my wede° on dese,°   *washed   garment   a dais*
 And coronde clene° in vergynté,   **coronde clene** *crowned me pure*
 And pyght me in perles maskelles."°   *spotless*

lxv

 "Why, maskelles bryd° that bryght con flambe,°   *bride* **con flambe** *shines*
770 That reiates° has so ryche and ryf,°   *royal attributes* **ryche...** *splendid and plentiful*
 What kyn° thyng may be that Lambe   *kind of*
 That thee wolde wedde unto Hys wyf?
 Over alle other so hygh thou clambe
 To lede wyth Hym so ladyly° lyf.   *ladylike a*
775 So mony a comly on-uunder cambe°   **comly...** *beautiful one under comb*
 For Kryst han lyved in much stryf;
 And thou con alle tho dere° out dryf   **tho dere** *those dear ones*
 And fro that maryage al other depres,°   *drive away*
 Al-only° thyself so stout and styf,°   *Exclusively* **stout...** *brave and strong*
780 A makeles may and maskelles."°   **makeles...** *matchless and spotless maiden*

XIV

lxvi

"Maskelles," quod that myry° quene,   fair
"Unblemyst I am, wythouten blot,
And that may I wyth mensk menteene.° **mensk menteene** grace maintain
Bot 'makeles quene' thenne sade° I not.   said
785 The Lambes wyves in blysse we bene,° are
A hondred and forty-fowre thowsande flot,° company
As in the Apocalyppes hit is sene.
Sant John hem sygh° al in a knot   saw
On the hyl of Syon,° that semly clot;° Zion hill
790 The apostel hem segh in gostly drem° **gostly drem** spiritual vision
Arayed to the weddyng in that hyl-coppe,° hilltop
The newe cyté o Jerusalem.

lxvii

"Of Jerusalem I in speche spelle.°   tell
If thou wyl knaw what kyn° he be,   kind
795 My Lombe, my Lorde, my dere juelle,
My joy, my blys, my lemman fre,°   **lemman fre** beloved noble
The profete Ysaye of Hym con melle° **con melle** spoke
Pitously° of Hys debonerté:°   Compassionately meekness
"'That gloryous gyltles° that mon con quelle° innocent **mon . . .** was killed
800 Wythouten any sake° of felonye,   charge
As a schep to the slaght ther lad was He;
And, as lombe that clypper° in hande nem;'° shearer took
So closed He Hys mouth fro üch query,
When Jues Hym jugged in Jerusalem.

lxviii

805 "In Jerusalem was my lemman° slayn, beloved one
And rent on rode wyth boyes° bolde. **rode . . .** a cross by wretches
Al oure bales° to bere ful bayn,°   sorrows willing
He toke on Hymself oure cares° colde. sorrows
Wyth boffetes was Hys face flayn°   flayed
810 That was so fayr on to byholde.
For synne, He set° Hymself in vayn° valued **in vayn** at nothing
That never hade non° Hymself to wolde.° any sin own
For uus He lette hym flyghe and folde° **hym . . .** himself be torn and bent
And brede° upon a bostwys bem.°   stretched **bostwys bem** rough beam
815 As meke as lomb that no playnt° tolde, complaint
For uus He swalt° in Jerusalem.   died

lxix

"In Jerusalem, Jordan, and Galalye,
Ther as° baptysed the goude Saynt Jon,
His wordes acorded to° Ysaye.
820 When Jesus con to hym warde° gon,
He sayde of Hym thys professye:
"'Lo, Godes Lombe as trewe as ston,
That dos° away the synnes dryghe°
That alle thys worlde has wroght upon.°
825 Hymself ne wroght never yet non,
Whether° on Hymself He con al clem.'°
Hys generacyoun° who recen con,°
That dyghed for uus in Jerusalem?

Ther as Where
with
to... toward him

takes   heavy
wroght upon practiced

Yet   **con**... claimed them all
ancestry   **recen con** can tell

lxx

"In Jerusalem thus my lemman° swete
830 Twyes for° lombe was taken thare,
By trew recorde of ayther° prophete,
For mode° so meke and al Hys fare.°
The thryde tyme is therto ful mete,°
In Apokalypes¹ wryten ful yare:°
835 Inmydes° the trone, there sayntes sete,°
The apostel John Hym sagh° as bare,°
Lesande° the boke with leves sware°
There seven syngnettes° wern sette in seme;°
And at that syght üche douth con dare°
840 In helle, in erthe, and Jerusalem.

beloved
Twyes for Twice as
each (Isaiah, John)
spirit   demeanor
fitting
clearly
In the middle of   sat
saw   clearly
Opening   square
seals   the border
douth... man feared

XV

lxxi

"Thys Jerusalem Lombe hade never pechche°
Of other huee bot whyt jolyf,°
That mot ne masklle° moght on streche,°
For wolle° whyte so ronk and ryf.°
845 For-thy° üche saule that hade never teche°
Is to that Lombe a worthyly° wyf;
And thagh üch day a store° He feche,°
Among uus commes nouther strot° ne stryf;
Bot üchon enlé° we wolde° were fyf—
850 The mo° the myryer, so God me blesse.
In compayny gret our luf con thryf
In honour more and never the lesse.

a speck
fair
mot... stain nor spot   **on streche** rest o
For wolle Because of wool   **ronk**... ric
and plentiful
Therefore   a stain
worthy
multitude   brings
wrangling
üchon enlé each one singly   wish
more

¹ See Rev. v.6.

lxxii

"Lasse of blysse may non uus bryng
That beren thys perle upon oure bereste,° — breast
855 For thay of mote° couthe never mynge° — dispute; think
Of spotles perles that beren the creste.
Althagh oure corses° in clottes clynge,° — bodies; **clottes clynge** the earth waste away
And ye remen for rauthe° wythouten reste, — **remen** ... cry out in grief
We thurghoutly° haven cnawyng.° — thoroughly; knowledge
860 Of on° dethe, ful oure hope is drest.° — one; drawn up
The Lombe uus glades,° oure care is kest;° — gladdens; driven away
He myrthes uus alle° at üch a mes.° — **myrthes** ... makes us all rejoice; mass
Üchones° blysse is breme° and beste, — **Üchones** Each one's; glorious
And never ones honour yet never the les.

lxxiii

865 "Lest les thou leve° my tale farande,° — believe; **tale farande** enumeration fitting
In Appocalyppece is wryten in wro:° — a passage
"I seghe,'° says John, 'the Loumbe Hym — saw
    stande° — **Hym stande** standing
On the mount of Syon° ful thryven and thro,° — Zion; **thryven** ... mighty and strong
And wyth Hym maydennes an hundrethe
    thowsande,
870 And fowre and forty thowsande mo.° — more
On alle her forhedes wryten I fande° — found
The Lombes nome,° Hys Faderes also. — name
A hue° from heven I herde thoo,° — cry; then
Lyk flodes fele laden runnen on resse,°
875 And as thunder throwes° in torres blo,° — rolls; **torres blo** dark hills
That lote,° I leve,° was never the les. — sound; believe

lxxiv

"'Nautheles,° thagh hit schowted scharpe,° — Nevertheless; **schowted scharpe** sounded strongly
And ledden° loude althagh hit were, — a voice
A note ful newe I herde hem warpe,° — utter
880 To lysten that was ful lufly dere.° — **lufly dere** delightfully pleasant
As harpores harpen in her harpe,
That newe songe thay songen ful cler,
In sounande° notes a gentyl carpe.° — resounding; **gentyl carpe** noble discourse
Ful fayre the modes° thay fonge in fere.° — melodies; **fonge** ... got all together
885 Ryght byfore Godes chayere° — throne
And the fowre bestes that hym obes° — reverençe
And the aldermen° so sadde° of chere,° — elders; serious; countenance
Her songe thay songen never the les.

874. Like the sound of many rivers run together in a rush

lxxv

" 'Nowthelese° non was never so quoynt,°   Nevertheless   skillful
890 For alle the craftes° that ever thay knewe,   skills
     That of that songe myght synge a poynt°   note
     Bot° that meyny° the Lombe that sewe;°   Except   company   follow
     For thay arn boght° fro the ürthe aloynte°   redeemed   far removed
     As newe fryt° to God ful due,   **newe fryt** first fruit
895 And to the gentyl° Lombe hit° arn anjoynt,°   noble   they   united
     As lyk to Hymself of lote and hwe;°   **lote ...** appearance and color
     For never lesyng° ne tale untrewe   lie
     Ne towched her tonge for no dysstresse.
     That moteles meyny° may never remewe°   **moteles meyny** spotless company   part
900 Fro that maskeles mayster, never the les.' "

lxxvi

"Never the les let be my thonc,"°   **be ...** my thanks be
     Quod I, "my perle, thagh I appose.°   question
     I schulde not tempte thy wyt so wlonc,°   noble
     To Krystes chambre that art i-chose.
905 I am bot mokke and mul among,°   **mokke ...** muck and dust mixed
     And thou so ryche° a reken° rose,   splendid   fresh
     And bydes° here by thys blysful bonc°   stay   slope
     Ther lyves lyste° may never lose.°   **lyves lyste** life's joy   fade
     Now, hynde,° that sympelnesse cones enclose,°   gracious one   **cones enclose** enclose
910 I wolde thee aske a thynge expresse,°   plainly
     And thagh I be bustwys° as a blose,°   rough   churl
     Let my bone vayl,° neverthelese.   **bone vayl** prayer avail

XVI

lxxvii

"Neverthelese, cler° I yow bycalle,°   clearly   call on
     If ye con se hyt be to done;°
915 As thou art gloryous wythouten galle,°   spot
     Wythnay° thou never my ruful° bone.   Deny   piteous
     Haf ye no wones° in castel-walle,   dwellings
     Ne maner° ther ye may mete and won?°   manor   dwell
     Thou telles me of Jerusalem the ryche ryalle,°   **ryche ryalle** royal kingdom
920 Ther David dere was dyght° on trone,   set

914. If you can see that it be done

Bot by thyse holtes° hit con not hone,°   woods   **con** . . . can't be situated
Bot in Judee hit is, that noble note.°   structure
As ye ar maskeles under mone,°   **under mone** under the moon (on earth)
Your wones schulde be wythouten mote.°   stain

lxxviii

925 "Thys moteles meyny° thou cones of mele,°   **moteles meyny** spotless company   **cones** . . . spoke of
Of thousandes thryght° so gret a route°—   crowded   company
A gret ceté,° for ye arn fele,°   city   many
Yow byhod° have, wythouten doute.°   **Yow byhod** It behooved you   doubt
So cumly° a pakke of joly° juele   beautiful   fair
930 Wer evel° don, schulde lygh ther-oute;°   ill   **schulde** . . . should they lie outside
And by thyse bonkes° ther I con gele°   slopes   **con gele** linger
I se no bygyng° nawhere aboute.   dwelling
I trowe° alone ye lenge and loute°   suppose   **lenge** . . . linger and walk
To loke on the glory of thys gracious gote.°   stream
935 If thou has other bygynges stoute,
Now tech me to that myry mote."°   **myry mote** fair city

lxxix

"That mote thou menes° in Judy° londe,"   mean   Judea
That specyal spyce° then to me spakk,   **specyal spyce** excellent person
"That is the cyté that the Lombe con fonde
940 To soffer inne sor° for manes° sake,   sorrow   man's
The olde Jerusalem, to understonde;°   **to understonde** that is to say
For there the olde gülte was don° to slake.°   brought   an end
Bot the newe, that lyght° of Godes sonde,°   came down   sending
The apostel in Apocalyppce in theme con take.°   **in theme** . . . adopted as a theme
945 The Lombe ther wythouten spottes blake
Has feryed° thyder Hys fayre flote;°   led   company
And as Hys flok is wythouten flake,°   spot
So is Hys mote° wythouten moote.°   city   stain

lxxx

"Of motes° two to carpe clene°—   cities   **carpe clene** speak exactly
950 And Jerusalem hyght° bothe nawtheles°—   are called   nevertheless
That nys° to yow no more to mene°   is   mean
Bot 'ceté of God' other 'syght° of pes.'°   vision   peace
In that on oure pes was mad° at ene;°   made   once
Wyth payne to suffer the Lombe hit chese.°   chose
955 In that other is noght bot pes to glene°   glean
That ay schal laste wythouten reles.°   cessation

That is the borgh° that we to pres°   city   hurry
Fro that° oure flesch be layd to rote;°   **Fro that** After   rot
Ther glory and blysse schal ever encres
960   To the meyny° that is wythouten mote."°   company   stain

lxxxi

"Moteles may° so meke and mylde,"   **Moteles may** Spotless maiden
Then sayde I to that lufly flor,°   flower
"Bring me to that bygly bylde,°   **bygly bylde** pleasant dwelling
And let me se thy blysful bor."°   bower
965   That schene° sayde: "That God wyl schylde.°   fair one   prevent
Thou may not enter wythinne hys tor,°   tower
Bot of the Lombe I have thee aquylde°   obtained permission
For a syght therof thurgh gret favor.
Utwyth° to se that clene cloystor°   From without   **clene cloystor** pure
                                 enclosure
970   Thou may, bot inwyth° not a fote;   from within
To strech° in the strete thou has no vygour,°   walk   power
Bot° thou wer clene° wythouten mote.   Unless   pure

XVII

lxxxii

"If I this mote° thee schal unhyde,°   city   reveal
Bow° up towarde thys bornes heved,°   Go **bornes heved** stream's head
975   And I anendes° thee on this syde   opposite
Schal sue,° tyl thou to a hil be weved."°   follow   brought
Then wolde I no lenger byde,°   tarry
Bot lurked° by launces° so lufly leved,°   stole   branches **lufly leved** delightfully
                                 leaved
Tyl on a hyl that I asspyed
980   And blusched° on the burghe,° as I forth dreved,° gazed   city   rushed
Byyonde the brok fro me warde keved,°   **fro . . .** which away from me sank
That schyrrer° then sunne wyth schaftes° schon. brighter   rays
In the Apokalypce is the fasoun preved,°   **fasoun preved** fashion shown
As devyses° hit the apostel Jhon.   pictures

lxxxiii

985   As John the apostel hit sygh° wyth syght,   saw
I syghe that cyty of gret renoun,
Jerusalem so newe and ryally dyght,°   **ryally dyght** royally adorned
As° hit was lyght° fro the heven adoun.   As if **was lyght** had come

The borgh° was al of brende° golde bryght — city refined
990 As glemande° glas burnist broun,° — gleaming bright
Wyth gentyl gemmes an-under° pyght — underneath
Wyth banteles° twelve on basyng boun,° — coursings **basyng boun** foundation fixed
The foundementes° twelve of riche tenoun;° — foundations joining
Üch tabelment° was a serlypes° ston; — tier single
995 As derely devyses° this ilk° toun — pictures same
In Apocalyppes the apostel John.

lxxxiv

As John thise stones in writ con nemme,° — **con nemme** named
I knew the name after his tale:
Jasper hyght° the fyrst gemme — is called
1000 That I on the fyrst basse con wale,° — **basse . . .** base perceived
He glente° grene in the lowest hemme;° — **He glente** It glinted course
Saffer° helde the secounde stale;° — Sapphire place
The calsydoyne° thenne wythouten wemme° — chalcedony flaw
In the thryd table con purly pale;° — **table . . .** tier shone pure and pale
1005 The emerade the furthe so grene of scale;° — surface
The sardonyse° the fyfthe ston; — sardonyx
The sexte,° the rybé,° he con hit wale° — sixth ruby **con . . .** noted it
In the Apocalyppce, the apostel John.

lxxxv

Yet joyned° John the crysolyt,° — added chrysolite
1010 The seventhe gemme in fundament;° — the foundation
The aghtthe° the beryl cler and whyt; — eighth
The topasye twynne-hew,° the nente endent;° — **topasye twynne-hew** topaz twin-hued **nente endent** ninth set
The crysopase° the tenthe is tyght;° — chrysoprase fixed
The jacynght,° the enleventhe gent;° — jacinth noble
1015 The twelfthe, the gentyleste in üch a plyt,° — state
The amatyst purpre° wyth ynde blente;° — **amatyst purpre** amethyst purple **ynde blente** indigo mixed
The wal abof the bantels bent° — **bantels bent** coursings set
O jasporye,° as glas that glysnande° schon; — **O jasporye** Of jasper glistening
I knew hit by his devysement° — description
1020 In the Apocalyppes, the apostel John.

lxxxvi

As John devysed yet sagh° I thare — saw
Thise twelve degres wern° brode and stayre;° — which were steep
The cyté stod abof ful sware,° — square
As longe as brode as hyghe ful fayre;° — **ful fayre** exactly

1025 The stretes of golde as glasse al bare,
 The wal of jasper that glent° as glayre;°   *glinted egg-white glaze*
 The wones wythinne enurned° ware   *adorned*
 Wyth alle kynnes perré° that moght repayre.°   **kynnes perré** *kinds of gems come together*
 Thenne helde üch sware° of this manayre°   *square manor*
1030 Twelve forlonge space, er ever hit fon,°   *ceased*
 Of heght,° of brede,° of lenthe to cayre,°   *height breadth extend*
 For meten° hit sygh° the apostel John.   *measured saw*

XVIII

lxxxvii

 As John hym wrytes, yet more I syghe:°   *saw*
 Üch pane° of that place had thre yates;°   *side gates*
1035 So twelve in poursent° I con asspye,   *the encompassing wall*
 The portales pyked° of rych° plates,   *adorned splendid*
 And üch yate of a margyrye,°   *pearl*
 A parfyt perle that never fates.°   *fades*
 Üchon in scrypture a name con plye°   **con plye** *showed forth*
1040 Of Israel barnes,° folewande her dates,   **Israel barnes** *Israel's children*
 That is to say, as her byrth-whates;°   *fortunes of birth*
 The aldest ay fyrst theron was done.
 Such lyght ther lemed° in alle the strates°   *gleamed streets*
 Hem nedde° nawther sunne ne mone.°   **Hem nedde** *They needed moon*

lxxxviii

1045 Of sunne ne mone had thay no nede;
 The self God° was her lombe-lyght,°   **The ...** *God Himself lamplight*
 The Lombe her lantyrne, wythouten drede;°   *doubt*
 Thurgh hym blysned° the borgh° al bryght.   *shone city*
 Thurgh woghe° and won my lokyng yede,°   *wall **lokyng yede** gaze pierced*
1050 For sotyle, cler, noght lette no lyght.°
 The hyghe trone ther moght ye hede°   *behold*
 Wyth alle the apparaylmente umbepyghte,°   **apparaylmente umbepyghte** *adornment set around*
 As John the apostel in termes tyghte;°   **termes tyghte** *exact words set forth*
 The hyghe Godes self° hit set upone.   *Himself*
1055 A rever° of the trone ther ran outryghte,   *river*
 Was bryghter then bothe the sunne and mone.°   *moon*

1050. For being transparent, clear, nothing hindered any light.

lxxxix

Sunne ne mone schon never so swete
As that foysoun flode° out of that flet;°
Swythe° hit swange° thurgh üch a strete°
1060 Wythouten fylthe other galle other glet.°
Kyrk° ther-inne was non yete,°
Chapel, ne temple that ever was set;
The Almyghty was her mynyster mete,°
The Lombe the sakerfyse ther to reget.°
1065 The yates stoken° was never yet,
Bot evermore upen° at üche a lone;°
Ther entres non to take reset°
That beres any spot an-under mone.°

foysoun flode abundant river floor
Swiftly rushed street
galle . . . scum or slime
Church yet

fitting

redeem
yates stoken gates shut
open lane
refuge
an-under mone under the moon (on earth)

xc

The mone may therof acroche° no myghte;
1070 Too spotty hö is, of body too grym,°
And also ther ne is never nyght.
What° schulde the mone ther compas° clym
And to even° wyth that worthly° lyght
That schynes upon the brokes brym?°
1075 The planates arn in too pouer a plyght,°
And the self° sunne ful fer° too dym.
Aboute that water arn tres ful schym,°
That twelve frytes° of lyf con bere ful sone;°
Twelve sythes on° yer thay beren ful frym,°
1080 And renowles° newe in üche a mone.

acquire
ugly

Why circuit
vie glorious
brokes brym river's bank
state

very far
bright
fruits quickly
sythes on times in a richly
renew

xci

An-under mone° so great mervayle°
No fleschly hert ne myght° endeure,
As when I blusched° upon that bayle,°
So ferly° therof was the fasure.°
1085 I stod as stylle as dased quayle
For ferly° of that freuch fygure,°
That felde° I nawther reste ne travayle,°
So was I ravyste° wyth glymme° pure.
For I dar say wyth conciens sure,
1090 Hade bodyly bürne abiden° that bone,°
Thagh alle clerkes hym hade in cure,°
His lyf were loste an-under mone.°

An-under mone under the moon (on earth)
marvel
ne myght could
looked wall (city)
wondrous fashion

wonder **freuch fygure** delicate form
felt labor
ravished radiance

bürne abiden man endured favor
care
an-under mone under the moon (on earth)

XIX

xcii

Ryght° as the maynful° mone con rys | Just mighty
Er thenne° the day-glem dryve° al doun, | **Er thenne** Before goes
1095 So sodanly on a wonder wyse° | **wonder wyse** wonderful manner
I was war° of a prosessyoun. | aware
This noble cité of ryche enpryse° | **ryche enpryse** splendid renown
Was sodanly ful, wythouten sommoun,° | summons
Of such vergynes in the same gyse° | guise
1100 That was my blysful an-under° croun. | under
And coronde wern alle of the same fasoun,° | fashion
Depaynt° in perles and wedes° whyte; | Arrayed garments
In üchones breste was bounden boun° | **bounden boun** fixed firmly
The blysful perle wyth gret delyt.

xciii

1105 Wyth gret delyt thay glod in fere° | **glod . . .** glided in company
On golden gates° that glent° as glasse. | streets glinted
Hundreth thowsandes I wot° ther were, | know
And alle in sute° her livres wasse;° | **in sute** to match **livres wasse** garments were
Tor° to knaw the gladdest chere.° | Hard expression
1110 The Lombe byfore con proudly passe |
Wyth hornes seven of red golde cler;° | bright
As praysed° perles His wedes° wasse. | precious garments
Towarde the throne thay trone a tras.° | **trone . . .** made their way
Thagh thay wern fele, no pres in plyt.° | **pres . . .** crowding in their order
1115 But mylde as maydenes seme at mas |
So drogh° thay forth wyth gret delyt. | went

xciv

Delyt that His come encroched° | **come encroched** coming brought
Too much hit were of for to melle° | **of . . .** to tell of
Thise aldermen,° when He aproched, | elders
1120 Grovelyng to His fete thay felle. |
Legyounes of aungeles togeder voched° | summoned
Ther kesten° ensens of swete smelle. | cast
Then glory and gle was newe abroched;° | uttered
Al songe° to love° that gay° juelle. | sang praise fair
1125 The steven° moght stryke thurgh the ürthe to helle | sound
That the Vertues of heven of° joye endyte.° | for sing out
To love the Lombe His meyny in melle° | midst
I-wysse,° I laght° a gret delyt. | Indeed took

xcv

Delit the Lombe for to devise°	look on
1130 Wyth much mervayle° in mynde went.	wonder
Best was He, blythest, and moste to pryse°	esteem
That ever I herde of speche spent;°	of . . . speech spent on
So worthly° whyt wern wedes° Hys,	gloriously garments
His lokes symple,° Hymself so gent.°	humble noble
1135 Bot a wounde fyl wyde and weete con wyse°	**weete** . . . wet showed
Anende° Hys hert, thurgh hyde torente.°	Over **hyde torente** skin all torn
Of His whyte syde his blod outsprent.°	gushed forth
Alas, thoght I, who did that spyt?°	evil
Ani breste for bale aght haf forbrent°	**bale** . . . sorrow ought to have burned up
1140 Er he therto hade had delyt.	

xcvi

The Lombe° delyt non lyste° to wene.°	Lamb's **non lyste** no one wished doubt
Thagh He were hurt and wounde hade,	
In His sembelaunt° was never sene,	demeanor
So wern His glentes° gloryous glade.	looks
1145 I loked among His meyny schene°	bright
How thay wyth lyf wern laste and lade;°	**laste** . . . filled and laden
Than sagh I ther my lyttel quene	
That I wende° had standen° by me in sclade.°	thought stood a valley
Lorde, much of mirthe was that hö made	
1150 Among her feres° that was so whyt!	companions
That syght me gart° to thenk to wade	made
For luf-longyng in gret delyt.	

XX

xcvii

Delyt me drof in yghe and ere,°	**yghe** . . . eye and ear
My manes° mynde to maddyng malte.°	man's melted
1155 When I segh my frely,° I wolde be there,	fair one
Byyonde the water thagh hö were walte.°	set
I thoght that nothyng myght me dere°	harm
To fetch me bür and take° me halte,	**bür** . . . blow and make
And to start° in the strem schulde non me stere,°	plunge hinder
1160 To swymme the remnaunt,° thagh I ther swalte.°	remainder might die
Bot of that münt° I was bitalt;°	intention shaken
When I schulde° start in the strem astraye,	was about to
Out of that caste° I was bycalt:°	purpose called
Hit was not at my Prynces paye.°	pleasure

xcviii

1165 Hit payed° Hym not that I so flonc°   pleased   flung myself
      Over mervelous meres,° so mad arayde.°   waters   **mad arayde** madly conditioned
      Of raas° thagh I were rasch and ronk,°   rush   overbearing
      Yet rapely° ther-inne I was restayed.°   quickly   restrained
      For, ryght° as I sparred° unto the bonc,   just   rushed
1170 That braththe° out of my drem me brayde.°   violence   roused
      Then wakned I in that erber wlonk;°   **erber wlonk** garden splendid
      My hede upon that hylle was layde
      Ther as° my perle to grounde strayd.   **Ther as** Where
      I raxled,° and fel in gret affray,°   stretched myself   dismay
1175 And, sykyng,° to myself I sayd,   sighing
      "Now al be to that Prynces paye."°   pleasure

xcix

      Me payed° ful ille to be outfleme°   pleased   outcast
      So sodenly of that fayre regioun,
      Fro alle tho syghtes so quyke and queme.°   **quyke** ... lifelike and pleasant
1180 A longeyng hevy me strok in swone,°   a swoon
      And rewfully thenne I con to reme:°   **con** ... cried out
      "O perle," quod I, "of rych° renoun,   splendid
      So was hit me dere that° thou con deme°   **me** ... dear to me what   **con deme** spoke of
      In this veray avysyoun.°   **veray avysyoun** true vision
1185 If hit be veray and soth sermoun°   **veray** ... real and true account
      That thou so stykes° in garlande gay,°   are set   fair
      So wel° is me in thys doel°-doungoun   happy   sorrow
      That thou art to that Prynces paye."°   pleasure

c

      To that Prynces paye hade I ay bente,°   **hade** ... if I had ever bowed
1190 And yerned no more then was me gyven,
      And halden me° ther in trewe entent,°   **halden me** stayed   intention
      As the perle me prayed that was so thryven,°   fair
      As helde,° drawen to Goddes present,°   likely as possible   presence
      To mo° of His mysterys I hade ben dryven.°   more   brought
1195 Bot ay wolde man of happe° more hente°   good fortune   seize
      Then moghte by ryght upon° hem clyven.°   to   belong
      Therfore my joye was sone toriven,°   torn apart
      And I kaste of kythes° that lastes aye.   **kaste** ... cast from regions
      Lorde, mad hit° arn that agayn thee stryven,   they
1200 Other proferen thee oght agayn thy paye.°   pleasure

ci

To pay the Prince other sete saghte°   sete saghte set at peace
Hit is ful ethe° to the god Krystyin;   easy
For I haf founden Hym, bothe day and naghte,°   night
A God, a Lorde, a frende ful fyin.°   noble
1205 Over this hyül° this lote° I laghte,°   hill fortune took
For pyty of my perle enclyin,°   lying prostrate
And sythen° to God I hit bytaghte°   then committed
In Krystes dere blessyng and myn,
That in the forme of bred and wyn
1210 The preste uus schewes üch a daye.
He gef° uus to be His homly hyne°   granted homly hyne household servants
Ande precious perles unto His pay.
Amen. Amen.

Sir Gawain and the Green Knight

(ca. 1390, West Midland)

Sir Gawain is generally attributed to the author of *The Pearl* (see p. 339). Like *The Pearl*, it is a work of considerable finesse. The plot of the romance is derived ultimately from *The Feast of Bricriu*, an Irish heroic legend glorifying Cuchulainn and the magical Curoi; but the wild magic of Celtic legend has been transformed into a courtly Arthurian romance, set within the dramatic framework of the British legendary history that Geoffrey of Monmouth had created in his *History of the Kings of Britain*, which Lawman had already popularized for English audiences (see p. 49). As in many romances, the hero is a paragon of bravery and a master of the art of courtly love. But the author of *Sir Gawain* is a moralist as well as a romancer, and, as in the other writings attributed to him, he is essentially concerned with human behavior and sets greater store on his hero's acquirement of self-knowledge than on knightly self-aggrandizement.

The romance shows the same sense of symmetry that appears in *The Pearl*. The conclusion echoes the opening lines (compare l. 1, Part I, and l. 2255, Part IV). The progress of the hero's adventures is marked by the passing of the four seasons. Gawain's heraldic device, the pentangle, or five-pointed star, has a fivefold signification: the five wits, the five fingers, the five wounds of Christ, the five joys of Mary, and the five virtues. The sequence of the three quarries hunted by the host—the noble deer, the savage bear, and the foul fox—match the decline of Gawain's resolve in his three encounters with the host's wife.

The stanzas are composed in the traditional English alliterative measure, and each is decorated with a final set of five rhyming lines, known as a bob-and-wheel. The bob contains one stress; the following lines of the wheel contain generally three stresses and at least two alliterations; and the rhyme is ababa. (See also Introduction, type 2, p. 30.)

To satisfy alliteration, the poet uses a number of etymologically distinct words for *man*, sometimes without any clear distinction of meaning: *bürn* ('warrior'), *freke* ('knight'), *gome* ('man'), *grome* ('servant'), *hathel* ('leader'), *knight, lede, l(e)ude* ('man'), *lord, mon, prince, renk* ('warrior'), *schalk* ('servant'), *segge* ('man'), *syr(e)* ('sire'), *tulk* ('speaker'), *wyghe* ('person').

Two useful editions of *Sir Gawain and the Green Knight* are ed. J. R. R. Tolkien and E. V. Gordon, rev. Norman Davis (Oxford, 1967) and ed. I. Gollancz, M. Day, and M. S. Serjeantson, EETS 210 (London, 1938). A facsimile of the manuscript will be found in *Facsimile of MS. Cotton Nero A x*, EETS 162 (London, 1923), fols. 91–124. For bibliography see Severs, ch. 1.25. For criticism see *Critical Studies of Sir Gawain and the Green Knight*, ed. Donald R. Howard and Christian Zacher (Notre Dame, 1968).

Part I

i

Sithen° the sege and the assaut was sesed° at Troye,　　After　ceased

The burgh brittened and brent° to brondes and askes,°　　**burgh . . .** city destroyed and burned　ashes

The tulk° that the trammes° of tresoun ther wroght　　man　plots

Was tried for his tricherie, the trewest on erthe.

5　Hit was Ennias° the athel° and his highe kynde°　　Aeneas　splendid　**highe kynde** noble kin

That sithen depreced° provinces, and patrounes° bicome　　**sithen depreced** later conquered　lords

Welneghe° of al the wele° in the west iles.　　Almost　wealth

Fro riche° Romulus to Rome ricchis hym swythe,°　　**Fro riche** When noble　**ricchis . . .** proceeds quickly

With gret bobbaunce° that burghe° he biges upon fyrst°　　pride　city　**biges . . .** builds at first

10　And nevenes° hit his awne nome,° as hit now hat;°　　names　**awne nome** own name　is called

Ticius° to Tuskan, and teldes bigynnes;°　　Ticius goes　**teldes bigynnes** begins to build houses

Langaberde in Lumbardie lyftes up homes;

And fer° over the French flod° Felix Brutus　　far　sea (English Channel)

On many bonkkes ful° brode Bretayn he settes,　　**bonkkes ful** slopes very

15　　wyth wynne;°　　joy

Where werre and wrake° and wonder　　**werre . . .** war and vengeance

Bi sythes has wont° ther-inne,　　**Bi . . .** At times have dwelled

And oft bothe blysse and blunder°　　confusion

Ful skete° has skyfted synne.°　　quickly　**skyfted synne** shifted since

ii

20　Ande when this Bretayn was bigged° bi this bürn rych,°　　built　**bürn rych** noble man

Bolde bredden° ther-inne, baret that lofden,°　　**Bolde bredden** Brave men bred　**baret . . .** who loved strife

In mony turned tyme tene° that wroghten.　　**turned . . .** a time come to pass grief

Mo ferlyes° on this folde han° fallen here oft　　**Mo ferlyes** More marvels　**folde han** land have

Then in any other that I wot,° syn that ilk° tyme.　　know of　same

25　Bot, of alle that here bult,° of Bretaygne kynges　　dwelt

Ay° was Arthur the hendest,° as I haf herde telle.　　Ever　most courteous

For-thi° an aunter in erde° I attle° to schawe,　　Therefore　**aunter . . .** adventure actually　intend

That a selly° in sight summe men hit holden,　　marvel

And an outtrage° aventure of Arthures wonderes.　　extraordinary

30　If ye wyl lysten this laye bot on° littel while,　　**bot on** only a

I schal telle hit as-tit,° as I in toun herde,　　at once

　　with tonge;

377

As hit is stad and stoken°   **stad . . .** placed and written
In stori stif° and stronge,   brave
35 With lel° lettres loken,°   true   linked
In londe so° has ben longe.   as it

iii

This kyng lay at Camylot upon Krystmasse
With mony luflych° lorde, ledes° of the best,   comely   men
Rekenly° of the Rounde Table alle tho rich°   Nobly   **tho rich** those noble
    brether,
40 With rych revel oryght and rechles° merthes.   **oryght . . .** fitting and carefree
Ther tournayed tulkes° by tymes ful° mony,   knights   very
Justed ful jolilé thise gentyle° knightes,   noble
Sythen kayred° to the court, caroles to make.   **Sythen kayred** Then rode
For ther the fest° was i-lyche° ful fiften dayes,   festival   the same
45 With alle the mete° and the mirthe that men   food
    couthe avyse,°   **couthe avyse** knew how to devise
Such glaum° ande gle glorious to here,°   merry sounds   hear
Dere dyn° upon day, daunsyng on nyghtes.   **Dere dyn** Pleasant noise
Al was hap° upon heghe in halles and chambres,   happiness
With lordes and ladies, as levest him thoght.°   **levest . . .** it seemed most delightful to them
50 With alle the wele° of the worlde thay woned°   joy   dwelled
    ther samen,°   together
The most kyd° knyghtes under Krystes selven,°   famous   **Krystes selven** Christ himself
And the lovelokkest° ladies that ever lif haden,   fairest
And he the comlokest° kyng that the court   comeliest
    haldes;°   rules
For al was this fayre folk in her first age,°   **her . . .** their prime
55   on sille,°   the floor
The hapnest° under heven,   most fortunate
Kyng hyghest° mon of wylle;°   noblest   mind
Hit were now gret nye° to neven°   difficulty   name
So hardy a here° on hille.   **hardy . . .** bold a company

iv

60 Wyle New Yer was so yep° that hit was newe   fresh
    cummen
That day doubble on the dece° was the douth°   dais   company
    served.
Fro° the kyng was cummen with knyghtes into   When
    the halle,
The chauntré of° the chapel cheved° to an ende.   **chauntré of** singing from   came
Loude crye was ther kest° of clerkes and other,   cast
65 Nowel nayted° onewe, nevened ful° ofte;   **Nowel nayted** Noel celebrated   **nevened ful** named very

378

And sythen riche° forth runnen to reche
    hondeselle,°
Yeghed yeres° giftes on high, yelde hem° bi
    hond,
Debated busyly aboute tho° giftes.
Ladies laghed ful loude, thogh thay lost haden,
70 And he that wan° was not wrothe, that may ye
    wel trawe.°
Alle this mirthe thay maden to the mete° tyme.
When thay had waschen worthyly,° thay wenten
    to sete,
The best bürne ay° abof, as hit best semed,
Quene Guenore ful gay, graythed° in the myddes,
75 Dressed° on the dere des, dubbed° al aboute,
Smal sendal° bisides, a selure° hir over,
Of tryed Tolouse, of Tars tapites innoghe,°
That were enbrawded and beten° wyth the best
    gemmes
That myght be preved° of prys° wyth penyes° to
    bye,
80   in daye.°
    The comlokest° to discrye°
    Ther glent° with yghen° gray;
    A semloker° that ever he syghe,°
    Soth moght° no mon say.°

sythen riche then nobles
reche hondeselle give New Year's gifts
Yeghed yeres Cried the year's **yelde hem** gave them

those

won

believe
meal
fittingly

bürne ay man ever
Guenore ... Guinevere very fair, set
Placed **dere** ... glorious dais, adorned
Smal sendal Fine silk canopy

enbrawded ... embroidered and set

proved value money

in daye ever
comeliest look on
glanced eyes
comelier one might see
Soth moght Truly could speak of

V

85   Bot Arthure wolde not ete til al were served,
He was so joly of his joyfnes,° and sumwhat
    child-gered;°
His lif liked° hym lyght,° he lovied the lasse°
Auther° too longe lye or too longe sitte,
So bisied° him his yonge blod and his brayn
    wylde.°
90 And also another maner meved° him eke°
That he thurgh nobelay° had nomen:° he wolde
    never ete
Upon such a dere° day er° hym devised° were
Of sum aventurus thyng an uncouthe° tale
Of sum mayn° mervayle that he myght trawe°
95 Of alderes,° of armes, of other aventurus;
Other° sum segg° hym bisoght of sum siker°
    knyght
To joyne wyth hym in justyng, in jöpardé to lay,

youth
boyish
pleased when active less
Either
stirred
restless
maner meved habit moved as well
magnificence undertaken

pleasant before related
strange
great **myght trawe** could believe
princes
Or man trusty

77. Of fine fabric from Toulouse, of many tapestries from Tharsia (Turkestan)

Lede lif for° lyf, leve üchon° other,

As fortune wolde fulsun höm,° the fayrer° to have.

100 This was the kynges countenance° where he in court were,

At üch farand fest° among his fre meny° in halle.

Therfore of face so fere°

He stightles stif in stalle;°

105 Ful yep° in that New Yere,

Much mirthe he mas° with alle.

Lede ... Risk life against **leve üchon** let each

fulsun höm help them fayrer advantage

behavior

farand fest splendid festival **fre meny** noble company

proud

stightles ... stands up fearlessly

bold

makes

vi

Thus ther stondes in stale° the stif kyng hisselven,

Talkkande° bifore the hyghe table of trifles ful hende,°

There gode Gawan was graythed Gwenore° bisyde,

110 And Agravayn à la dure mayn° on that other syde sittes,

Bothe the kynges sister° sunes, and ful siker° knightes.

Bischop Bawdewyn abof bigines the table,

And Ywan, Uryn° son, ette with hymselven.

Thise were dight° on the des, and derworthly° served,

115 And sithen° mony siker segge° at the sidbordes.

Then the first cors come° with crakkyng° of trumpes,°

Wyth mony baner ful bryght that ther-bi henged,

Newe nakryn noyse° with the noble pipes,

Wylde werbles° and wyght-wakned lote,°

120 That mony hert° ful highe hef° at her towches.°

Dayntes dryven° ther-wyth of ful dere metes,°

Foysoun° of the fresche,° and on so fele° disches

That pine° to fynde the place the peple biforne

For to sette the sylveren that sere sewes° halden, on clothe.

125 Iche lede° as he loved° hymselve

Ther laght° withouten lothe;°

Ay° two had disches twelve,

Good ber and bryght wyn bothe.°

in stale up

Talking

ful hende very courteous

graythed Gwenore set Guinevere

à ... of the hard hand

sister's trusty

Urien's

set **des ...** dais, and honorably

then men

came blaring

trumpets

nakryn noyse clamor of kettledrums

warblings **wyght-wakned lote** loud-stirred sound

mony hert many a heart lifted

her towches their tunes

come **dere metes** precious foods

Abundance fresh foods many

it was difficult

sere sewes different stews

Iche lede Each man pleased

took displeasure

Each

too

vii

130 Now wyl I of hör° servise say yow no more, — *their*
    For üch wyghe° may wel wit° no wont that ther — *man   know*
        were.
    Another noyse° ful newe neghed bilive,° — *clamor   **neghed bilive** neared quickly*
    That the lüde° myght haf leve liflode° to cach.° — *man   food   get*
    For unethe° was the noyce not a whyle sesed,° — *hardly   ceased*
135 And the fyrst cource in the court kyndely° served, — *properly*
    Ther hales° in at the halle dor an aghlich mayster,° — *comes   **aghlich mayster** dreadful knight*
    On° the most on the molde on mesure° hyghe; — *One   **molde** ... earth in stature*
    Fro the swyre° to the swange° so sware° and so — *neck   waist   square*
        thik,
    And his lyndes° and his lymes so longe and so — *loins*
        grete,
140 Half etayn in erde° I hope° that he were; — ***etayn** ... giant actually   suppose*
    Bot mon most° I algate mynn° hym to bene,° — *must   **algate mynn** at any rate think   be*
    And that the myriest° in his muckel° that myght — *fairest   size*
        ride;
    For of bak and of brest al were° his bodi sturne,° — *was   strong*
    Both his wombe° and his wast were worthily° — *belly   fittingly*
        smale,
145 And all his fetures folghande° in forme° that he — *following   manner*
        hade,
        ful clene.° — *fair*
    For wonder of his hewe° men hade, — *hue*
    Set in his semblaunt sene;° — ***semblaunt sene** appearance clearly*
    He ferde° as freke were fade,° — *acted   **freke** ... a man who would be hostile*
150 And overal enker° grene. — *very*

viii

    Ande al graythed° in grene this gome° and his — *clothed   man*
        wedes,° — *garments were*
    A strayt° cote ful streght that stek on his sides, — *tight*
    A meré° mantile abof, mensked° withinne — *fair   adorned*
    With pelure pured apert,° the pane° ful clene,° — ***pelure** ... fur trimmed clearly   fur lining fair*
155 With blythe blaunner° ful bryght, and his hod — ***blythe blaunner** gay white fur*
        bothe,° — *too*
    That was laght° fro his lokkes and layde on his — *caught back*
        schulderes;
    Heme, wel-haled° hose of that same grene, — ***Heme, wel-haled** Neat, well-drawn*
    That spenet° on his sparlyr,° and clene spures — *were fastened   calf*
        under

Of bryght golde, upon silk bordes barred° ful ryche, — striped

160 And scholes° under schankes, there° the schalk° rides. — pointed shoes **schankes, there** legs, when man

And alle his vesture verayly was clene verdure,° — **clene verdure** pure green

Bothe the barres of his belt and other blythe° stones — gay

That were richely rayled° in his aray clene° — arranged fair

Aboutte hymself and his sadel, upon silk werkes,° — embroidery

165 That were too tor° for to telle of tryfles° the halve — hard details

That were enbrauded° abof, wyth bryddes and flyghes,° — embroidered **bryddes...** birds and flies

With gay gaudi° of grene, the golde ay inmyddes.° — **gay gaudi** fair color **ay inmyddes** ever in the middle

The pendauntes of his payttrure,° the proude cropure,° — horse trappings cropper

His molaynes° and alle the metail anamayld° was thenne, — bit studs enameled

170 The steropes that he stod on, stayned of the same,

And his arsouns° al after, and his athel skurtes,° — saddlebows **athel skurtes** splendid saddle skirts

That ever glemered and glent° al of grene stones. — glinted

The fole° that he ferkkes° on, fyn° of that ilke,° sertayn;° — horse rides completely same certainly

175 A grene hors gret and thikke,

A stede ful stif to strayne,° — **stif...** hard to restrain

In brawden° brydel quik;° — embroidered lively

To the gome° he was ful gayn.° — man ready

ix

Wel gay° was this gome gered° in grene, — **Wel gay** Very fairly clothed

180 And the here° of his hed, of his hors suete.° — hair **of...** matched that of his horse

Fayre fannand fax umbefoldes° his schulderes; — **fannand...** waving hair hangs about

A much° berd as a busk° over his brest henges, — great bush

That wyth his highlich° here that of° his hed reches, — splendid from

Was evesed° al umbetorne,° abof his elbowes, — clipped around

185 That half his armes ther-under were halched° in the wyse° — enclosed manner

Of a kinges capados° that closes his swyre.° — hood neck

The mane of that mayn° hors, much to hit lyke, — great

Wel cresped and cemmed° wyth knottes ful mony, — **cresped...** curled and combed

Folden in° wyth fildore° aboute the fayre grene, — Entwined gold thread

190 Ay a herle° of the here,° an other of golde; — **Ay...** Ever one strand hair

The tayl and his toppyng twynnen of° a sute,° — **toppyng...** forelock joined in match

And bounden bothe wyth a bande of a bryght grene,

Dubbed° wyth ful dere° stones, as the dok lasted;°   Adorned glorious **dok lasted** tail extended

Sythen thrawen° wyth a thwong,° a thwarle° knot alofte,   twisted thong intricate

195 Ther° mony belles ful bryght of brende° golde rungen.   Where burnished

Such a fole° upon folde, ne freke° that hym rydes,   horse **folde** . . . earth, or man

Was never sene in that sale° wyth syght er° that tyme,   hall before

       with yghe.°   eye

He loked as layt° so lyght,°   lightning bright

200 So sayd al that hym syghe;°   might see

Hit semed as no mon myght°   could

Under his dynttes dryghe.°   **dynttes dryghe** blows survive

X

Whether° hade he no helme, ne hawbergh nauther,°   Yet **helme** . . . helmet, nor coat of mail either

Ne no pysan,° ne no plate that pented° to armes,   breastplate pertained

205 Ne no schafte,° ne no schelde, to schuve° ne to smyte,   spear thrust

Bot in his on° honde he hade a holyn bobbe,°   one **holyn bobbe** holly branch

That is grattest in grene when greves° ar bare,   groves

And an ax in his other, a hoge and unmete,°   **hoge** . . . huge and monstrous

A spetos sparthe,° to expoun° in spelle who-so myght.°   **spetos sparthe** cruel ax describe **spelle** . . . speech whosoever could

210 The hede of an elnyerde° the large lenkthe° hade,   ell (45″ measure) length

The grayn° al of grene stele and of golde hewen,°   spike hammered

The bit burnyst° bryght, with a brod egge,°   **bit burnyst** blade polished edge

As wel schapen to schere° as scharp rasores.   cut

The stele° of a stif staf—the sturne° hit bigrypte°   handle grim one gripped

215 That was wounden wyth yrn° to the wandes° ende,   iron handle's

And al bigraven° with grene, in gracios° werkes;   engraved beautiful

A lace° lapped aboute, that louked° at the hede,   thong fastened

And so after the halme halched° ful ofte,   **halme halched** shaft looped

Wyth tryed° tasseles therto tacched innoghe°   fine **tacched innoghe** fastened many

220 On botouns° of the bryght grene brayden° ful ryche.   **On botouns** To bosses embroidered

This hathel heldes hym° in and the halle entres,   **hathel** . . . knight goes

Drivande° to the heghe dece; dut° he no wothe,°   Coming **dece; dut** dais; feared danger

Haylsed° he never one, bot heghe he over loked.   Greeted

   The fyrst word that he warp,° "Wher is," he sayd,   uttered

225 "The governour of this gyng?° Gladly I wolde   assembly

Se that segg° in syght, and with hymself speke
    raysoun." — man
     To knyghtes he kest his yghe,° — eye
     And reled hym° up and doun, — **reled hym** swaggered
230   He stemmed and con studie° — **stemmed . . .** stopped and looked closely
     Who walt° ther most renoun. — had

xi

Ther was lokyng on lenthe,° the lüde° to beholde, — **lokyng . . .** gazing at length   man
For üch man had mervayle what hit mene myght,° — **mene myght** could mean
That a hathel° and a horse myght such a hewe — knight
    lach,° — **hewe lach** hue take
235 As growe° grene as the gres,° and grener hit semed — to grow grass
Then grene aumayl° on golde glowande° — enamel glowing
    bryghter;
Al studied° that ther stod, and stalked° hym nerre,° — watched moved carefully nearer
Wyth al the wonder of the worlde what he
    worch° schulde. — do
For fele sellyes° had thay sen, bot such never are,° — **fele sellyes** many marvels before
240 For-thi° for fantoum and fayryghe° the folk there — Therefore **fantoum . . .** illusion and magic
    hit demed;
Therfore to answare was arghe mony athel freke,° — **arghe . . .** afraid many a noble man
And al stouned° at his steven, and ston-stil seten — amazed **steven . . .** voice, and sat still as a stone
In a swoghe°-sylence thurgh the sale riche.° — dead **sale riche** splendid hall
As al were slypped upon slepe, so slaked hör lotes°
245   in hyghe;° — haste
     I deme° hit not al for doute,° — judge fear
     Bot sum for cortaysye,
     Bot let hym° that al schulde loute,° — him (Arthur) bow to
     Cast° unto that wyghe.° — Speak man

xii

250   Thenn Arthour, bifore the high dece,° that — dais
    aventure byholdes
And rekenly° hym reverenced, for rad° was he — nobly afraid
    never,
And sayde, "Wyghe, welcum i-wys° to this place. — indeed
The hede of this ostel Arthour I hat;° — am called
Light luflych° adoun and lenge,° I thee praye, — **Light luflych** Alight graciously stay
255 And what-so° thy wylle is, we schal wyt° after." — whatsoever know
     "Nay, as help me," quoth the hathel,° "he that — knight
     on hyghe syttes,
To wone° any whyle in this won,° hit was not — stay dwelling
    myn ernde;° — mission

244. As if all fell asleep, so ceased their cries

384

Bot for the los° of thee, lede,° is lyft up so hyghe,   renown sir
And thy burgh° and thy bürnes° best ar holden,   city men
260 Stifest under stel-gere° on stedes to ryde,   **Stifest . . .** Most fearless in armor
The wyghtest° and the worthyest of the worldes   strongest
    kynde,
Preve° for to play wyth in other pure laykes,°   Valiant **pure laykes** noble sports
And here is kydde° cortaysye, as I haf herd carp,°   shown **herd carp** heard said
And that has wayned° me hider, i-wyis,° at this   brought indeed
    tyme.
265 Ye may be seker° bi this braunch that I bere here,   sure
That I passe as in pes,° and no plyght seche;°   peace **plyght seche** danger seek
For had I founded in fere,° in feghtyng wyse,°   **founded . . .** come in company manner
I have a hauberghe° at home and a helme bothe,°   coat of mail **helme bothe** helmet too
A schelde, and a scharp spere, schinande bryght,
270 Ande other weppenes to welde, I wene wel, als;°   **wene . . .** know well, also
Bot for I wolde no were,° my wedes° ar softer;   fighting clothes
Bot if thou be so bold as alle bürnes° tellen,   men
Thou wyl grant me godly the gomen° that I ask,   sport
    bi ryght."
275 Arthour con onsware,°   **con onsware** answered
    And sayd, "Sir cortays knyght,
    If thou crave batayl bare,°   unarmed
    Here fayles° thou not to fyght."°   lack **to fyght** fighting

xiii

"Nay, frayst° I no fyght, in fayth I thee telle.   seek
280 Hit arn° aboute on this bench bot° berdles chylder;   **Hit arn** There are only
If I were hasped° in armes on a heghe° stede,   buckled noble
Here is no mon me to mach,° for myghtes° so   match **for myghtes** because of your
    wayke.°   powers weak
For-thy° I crave in this court a Crystemas gomen,°   Therefore sport
For hit is Yol° and Newe Yer, and here ar yep°   Yule brave men
    mony;
285 If any so hardy in this hous holdes hymselven,
Be so bolde in his blod, brayn° in hys hede,   mad
That dar stifly° strike a strok for an other,   fearlessly
I schal gif hym of my gyft thys giserne ryche,°   **giserne ryche** noble ax
This ax, that is hevé innogh,° to hondele as hym   **hevé innogh** heavy enough
    lykes,°   it pleases
290 And I schal bide the fyrst bür,° as bare° as I sitte.   blow unarmed
If any freke° be so felle to fonde° that I telle,   man **felle . . .** fierce as to try
Lepe lyghtly me to, and lach° this weppen—   take
I quit-clayme hit for ever; kepe° hit as his   let him keep own
    awen°—
And I schal stonde° hym a strok, stif° on this flet;°   endure fearless floor

295 Elles° thou wyl dight° me the dom° to dele hym another,	Then appoint judgment
barlay,°	none hindering
And yet gif hym respite	
A twelmonyth and a day.	
Now hyghe,° and let se tite,°	hurry **se tite** me see quickly
300 Dar any her-inne oght° say."	anything

xiv

If he hem stowned° upon fyrst, stiller were thanne	amazed
Alle the hered-men° in halle, the hygh° and the loghe;°	retainers noble low
The renk° on his rouncé hym rüched° in his sadel,	man **rouncé...** steed turned himself
And rünischly° his rede yghen° he reled aboute,	fiercely eyes
305 Bende his bresed° browes, blycande° grene,	bristling shining
Wayved his berde for to wayte who-so° wolde ryse.	**wayte who-so** see whosoever
When non wolde kepe° hym with carp,° he coghed ful hyghe,°	engage talk loud
Ande rimed hym° ful richly, and ryght hym° to speke:	**rimed hym** cleared his throat **ryght hym** prepared
"What, is this Arthures hous," quoth the hathel° thenne,	knight
310 "That al the rous rennes of thurgh ryalmes so mony?°	
Where is now your sourquydrye° and your conquestes,	pride
Your gryndel-layk° and your greme° and your grete wordes?	fierceness anger
Now is the revel and the renoun of the Rounde Table	
Overwalt° wyth a worde of on wyghes° speche;	Overturned **on wyghes** one man's
315 For al dares° for drede, withoute dynt° schewed!"	shrink blow
Wyth this he laghes so loude that the lorde greved;	
The blod schot for scham into his schyre° face and lere;°	bright flesh
He wex as wroth as wynde,	
320 So° did alle that ther were.	As
The kyng, as kene bi kynde,°	**kene...** one bold in nature
Then stod that stif° mon nere,°	fearless nearer

---

310. Of whom all the fame runs throughout so many realms?

xv

Ande sayde, "Hathel,° by heven thyn askyng is nys,° — *Knight; foolish*
And as thou foly° has frayst,° fynde thee bihoves;° — *folly sought; fynde . . . it behooves you to find out*
325 I know no gome° that is gast° of thy grete wordes. — *man afraid*
Gif me now thy geserne, upon Godes halve,° — *geserne . . . ax, for God's sake*
And I schal baythen° thy bone° that thou boden habbes."° — *grant boon; boden habbes have asked*
Lyghtly lepes he hym to, and laght at° his honde; — *took*
Then feersly that other freke° upon fote lyghtis. — *man*
330 Now has Arthure his axe, and the halme° grypes, — *shaft*
And sturnely stüres° hit aboute, that stryke wyth hit thoght. — *brandishes*
The stif mon hym bifore stod upon hyght,° — *upon hyght on high*
Herre° then ani in the hous by the hede and more. — *Taller*
Wyth sturne schere° ther he stod; he stroked his berde, — *expression*
335 And wyth a countenaunce dryghe° he drogh° doun his cote, — *unchanging drew*
No more mate° ne dismayd for hys mayn dintes° — *daunted; mayn dintes strong blows*
Then any bürne° upon bench hade broght hym to drynk — *man*
    of wyne.
    Gawan, that sate bi the quene,
340   To the kyng he can enclyne,° — *can enclyne bowed*
    "I beseche now with saghes sene° — *saghes sene words clear*
    This melly mot° be myne. — *melly mot contest may*

xvi

"Wolde ye,° worthilych lorde," quoth Wawan to the kyng, — *Wolde ye If you would*
"Bid me boghe° fro this benche and stonde by yow there, — *go*
345 That I wythoute vylanye moght voyde° this table, — *quit*
And that° my legge° lady lyked not ille, — *if liege*
I wolde com to your counseyl, bifore your cort ryche.
For me think hit not semly—as hit is soth° knawen, — *the truth*
Ther° such an askyng is hevened° so hyghe in your sale,° — *Where raised; hall*
350 Thagh° ye yourself be talenttyf°—to take hit to yourselven — *Though desirous*

Whil mony so bolde yow aboute upon bench
    sytten

That under heven, I hope, non hagherer of wylle,°

Ne better bodyes on bent° ther baret° is rered;°   field strife raised

I am the wakkest,° I wot,° and of wyt feblest,   weakest know

355 And lest lür° of my lyf, who laytes° the sothe,°   **lest lür** least loss seeks truth

Bot, for as much as ye ar myn em,° I am only to   uncle
    prayse;

No bounté bot your blod I in my bodé° knowe;   body

And sythen° this note° is so nys° that noght hit   since business foolish
    yow falles,°   is fitting

And I have frayned° hit at° yow fyrst, foldes° hit   sought from grant
    to me;

360 And if I carp° not comlyly, let alle this cort rych,°   speak decide
    bout° blame."   without

    Ryche° togeder con roun,°   Nobles **con roun** whispered

    And sythen° thay redden° alle same,   then advised

    To ryd° the kyng wyth croun,   relieve

365   And gif Gawan the game.

            xvii

Then comaunded the kyng the knyght for to
    ryse;

And he ful radly° up ros, and rüchched° hym   promptly prepared
    fayre,

Kneled doun bifore the kyng, and caches that
    weppen;

And he luflyly° hit hym laft,° and lyfte up his   graciously gave
    honde,

370 And gef hym Goddes blessyng, and gladly hym
    biddes

That his hert and his honde schulde hardi be
    bothe.

    "Kepe thee,° cosyn," quoth the kyng, "that   **Kepe thee** Take care
    thou on kyrf sette,°   **kyrf sette** cutting apply yourself

And if thou redes° hym right, redly I trowe   deal with

That thou schal byden° the bür° that he schal   survive blow
    bede° after."   offer

375   Gawan gos to the gome,° with giserne° in   man ax
    honde,

And he baldly hym bydes, he bayst° never the   was abashed
    helder.°   more

    Then carppes° to Sir Gawan the knyght in the   speaks
    grene,

352. Than whom there are under heaven, I suppose, none more sound of mind

"Refourme° we oure forwardes, er° we fyrre°   Restate **forwardes, er** agreements,
    passe.   before   farther

Fyrst I ethe° thee, hathel, how that thou hattes,°   entreat   are called

380 That thou me telle trewly, as I tryst° may."   trust

    "In god fayth," quoth the goode knyght,
      "Gawan I hatte,

That bede° thee this buffet, what so bifalles after,   offer

And at this tyme twelmonyth take at° thee   from
    another,

Wyth what weppen so thou wylt, and wyth no
    wygh° elles   man

385   on lyve."°   **on lyve** alive

    That other onswares agayn,

    "Sir Gawan, so mot° I thryve,   may

    As I am ferly fayn°   **ferly fayn** marvelously glad

    This dint° that thou schal dryve.   blow

xviii

390   "Bigog!" quoth the grene knyght, "Sir Gawan,
    me lykes,°   it pleases

That I schal fange at° thy füst° that I haf frayst°   **fange at** receive from   fist   sought
    here;

And thou has redily rehersed, bi resoun ful trewe,

Clanly° al the covenaunt that I the kynge asked,   Wholly

Saf that thou schal siker° me, segge,° bi thi   assure   man
    trawthe,

395 That thou schal seche° me thiself, where-so° thou   seek   **where-so** wherever
    hopes°   suppose

I may be funde upon folde, and foch° thee such   **folde . . .** earth, and fetch
    wages

As thou deles me today bifore this douthe° ryche."   company

    "Where schulde I wale° thee?" quoth Gawan.   seek
      "Where is thy place?

I wot° never where thou wonyes,° bi hym that me   know   dwell
    wroght,

400 Ne I know not thee, knyght, thy cort ne° thi   nor
    name.

Bot teche° me trewly therto, and telle me howe°   direct   what
    thou hattes,°   are called

And I schal ware° alle my wyt to wynne me   spend
    thider,

And that I swere thee for sothe,° and by my seker   truth
    traweth."°   **seker traweth** sure truth

    "That is innogh° in Newe Yer, hit nedes no   enough
    more,"

405 Quoth the gome° in the grene to Gawan the   man
    hende,°   courteous
  "Yif I thee telle trewly when I the tape° have,   blow
  And thou me smothely° has smyten, smartly° I   duly promptly
    thee teche°   shall direct
  Of my hous and my home and myn owen nome.
  Then may thou frayst° my fare, and forwardes°   ask **fare** . . . condition, and covenants
    holde,
410 And if I spende° no speche, thenne spedes° thou   utter succeed
    the better,
  For thou may leng° in thy londe, and layt° no   stay seek
    fyrre,°   farther
      bot slokes;°   **bot slokes** without cease
    Ta° now thy grymme tole° to thee,   Take weapon
    And let se how thou cnokes."°   strike
415   "Gladly, sir, for sothe,"°   truth
    Quoth Gawan; his ax he strokes.°   whets

xix

  The grene knyght upon grounde graythely°   speedily
    hym dresses,°   arranges
  A littel lut° with the hede, the lere° he discoveres;   bowed flesh
  His longe lovelych lokkes he layd over his croun,
420 Let the naked nec to the note° schewe.   blow
  Gawan gripped to his ax, and gederes° hit on   lifts
    hyght,°   high
  The kay° fot on the folde° he before sette,   left earth
  Let hit doun lyghtly lyght° on the naked,°   **lyghtly lyght** swiftly alight bare flesh
  That the scharp° of the schalk schyndered° the   sharp blade **schalk schyndered** man
    bones,   shattered
425 And schrank° thurgh the schyire grece, and scade°   sank **schyire** . . . white flesh, and severed
    hit in twynne,
  That the bit° of the broun stel bot on° the   edge **bot on** bit into
    grounde.
  The fayre hede fro the halce° hit to the erthe   neck
  That fele° hit foyned° wyth her° fete there hit   **That fele** So that many spurned their
    forth roled;
  The blod brayd° fro the body, that blykked° on   spurted shone
    the grene;
430 And nawther faltered ne° fel the freke never the   nor
    helder,°   more
  Bot stythly° he start forth upon styf schonkes,°   firmly **styf schonkes** strong legs
  And rünyschly° he raght° out, there as renkkes°   fiercely reached knights
    stoden,
  Laght° to his lufly hed, and lyft hit up sone,   Took

And sythen boghes° to his blonk;° the brydel he cachches,	**sythen boghes** then goes horse
435 Steppes into stel-bawe° and strydes alofte,	stirrup
And his hede by the here in his honde haldes;	
And as sadly° the segge° hym in his sadel sette	steadily man
As non unhap had hym ayled, thagh° hedles he were,	though
in stedde;°	place
440 He brayde° his bluk° aboute,	twisted body
That ugly bodi that bledde;	
Moni on° of hym had doute,°	**Moni on** Many a one fear
Bi° that his resouns° were redde.°	By the time words declared

XX

For the hede in his honde he haldes up even,°	straight
445 Toward the derrest° on the dece° he dresses the face,	noblest dais
And hit lyfte° up the yghe-lyddes,° and loked ful brode,	lifted eyelids
And meled° thus much with his muthe, as ye may now here.	spoke
"Loke, Gawan, thou be graythe° to go as thou hettes,°	set / promised
And layte° as lelly° til thou me, lüde,° fynde,	seek faithfully man
450 As thou has hette in this halle, herande° thise knyghtes.	hearing
To the grene chapel thou chose,° I charge thee, to fotte°	go / get
Such a dünt° as thou has dalt°—disserved thou habbes°—	blow dealt / **disserved . . .** as you have deserved
To be yederly yolden° on New Yeres morn;	**yederly yolden** quickly given
The Knyght of the Grene Chapel men knowen me mony;	
455 For-thi° me for to fynde if thou fraystes,° fayles thou never.	Therefore seek
Therfore com, other° recreaunt be calde thee behoves."°	or / **be . . .** you must be called
With a rünisch rout° the raynes he tornes,	**rünisch rout** fierce rush
Halled° out at the hal dor, his hed in his hande,	Rushed
That the fyr° of the flynt flaghe° fro fole° hoves.	fire flew the horse's
460 To what kyth° he becom,° knewe non there,	region went
Nevermore then thay wyste° fram whethen° he was wonnen.°	knew whence / come
What thenne?	
The kyng and Gawen thare,	

At that grene° thay laghe and grenne,°	green man	grin
465 Yet breved° was hit ful bare°	made known	plainly
A mervayl among tho° menne.	those	

xxi

Thagh° Arther the hende° kyng at hert hade wonder,	Though	courteous
He let no semblaunt be sene, bot sayde ful hyghe°	nobly	
To the comlych quene, wyth cortays speche,		
470 "Dere dame, today demay° yow never;	be dismayed	
Wel bycommes such craft° upon Cristmasse,	skill	
Laykyng° of enterludes, to laghe and to syng,	Playing	
Among thise kynde° caroles of knyghtes and ladyes.	noble	
Never-the-lece to my mete° I may me wel dres,°	food	turn
475 For I haf sen a selly,° I may not forsake."°	marvel	deny
He glent° upon Sir Gawen, and gaynly° he sayde,	glanced	graciously
"Now sir, heng up thyn ax, that has innogh° hewen."	enough	
And hit was don° abof the dece, on doser° to henge,	put	a tapestry
Ther alle men for mervayl myght° on hit loke,	could	
480 And bi trewe tytel° therof to telle the wonder.	description	
Thenne thay boghed° to a borde,° thise bürnes° togeder,	went	table men
The kyng and the gode knyght, and kene° men hem served	bold	
Of alle dayntyes double, as derrest° myght falle,°	noblest	befall
Wyth alle maner of mete° and mynstralcie bothe;°	food	too
485 Wyth wele walt° thay that day, til worthed° an ende in londe.	**wele walt** joy enjoyed	came
Now thenk wel, Sir Gawan,		
For wothe° that thou ne wonde°	peril	hesitate
This aventure for to frayn,°	seek	
490 That thou has tan on° honde.	**tan on** taken in	

Part II

xxii

This hanselle° has Arthur of aventurus on° fyrst   gift at
In yonge yer, for he yerned yelpyng° to here;   vaunting
Thagh hym° wordes were wane° when thay to   **Thagh hym** Though to him   wanting
   sete wenten,
Now ar thay stoken of° stürne work, staf-ful° her   **stoken of** fully provided with   very full
   hond.
495 Gawan was glad to begynne those gomnes° in   sports
   halle,
Bot thagh the ende be hevy, haf ye no wonder;
For thagh men ben mery in mynde, when thay
   han mayn° drynk,   **han mayn** have strong
A yere yernes° ful yerne,° and yeldes never lyke;°   passes   quickly   the same
The forme° to the fyniment foldes° ful selden.°   beginning   **fyniment foldes** end
      accords   seldom
500 For-thi° this Yol overyede,° and the yere after,   Therefore   **Yol overyede** Yule passed over
And üche sesoun serlepes sued° after other;   **serlepes sued** in turn followed
After Crysten-masse com the crabbed Lentoun,
That fraystes flesch° wyth the fysche and fode   **fraystes flesch** tries meat
   more symple;
Bot thenne the weder of the worlde wyth wynter
   hit threpes,°   struggles
505 Colde clenges° adoun, cloudes up lyften,   shrinks
Schyre schedes° the rayn in schowres ful warme,   **Schyre schedes** Brightly falls
Falles upon fayre flat,° flowres there schewen,   field
Bothe groundes° and the greves,° grene ar her   fields   woods
   wedes,°   **her wedes** their garments
Bryddes busken° to bylde and bremlych° syngen   **Bryddes busken** Birds prepare   loudly
510 For solace of the softe somer that sues° ther-after,   follows
   bi bonk;°   slope
   And blossumes bolne° to blowe,°   swell   bloom
   Bi rawes° rych and ronk,°   hedge rows   luxuriant
   Then notes noble innoghe,°   many
515   Ar herde in wod so wlonk.°   lovely

xxiii

After the sesoun of somer wyth the soft wyndes,
When Zeferus syfles° hymself on sedes and erbes   blows
Welawynne° is the wort° that waxes° ther-oute,   Very joyful   plant   grows
When the donkande° dewe dropes of the leves,   dripping
520 To bide a blysful blusch° of the bryght sunne.   gleam
Bot then hyghes hervest, and hardenes hym° sone,   **hyghes . . .** hastens autumn, and becomes
      severe
Warnes hym° for the wynter to wax ful rype;   it (plant)
He dryves wyth droght the dust for to ryse

	Fro the face of the folde° to flyghe° ful hyghe.	earth fly
525	Wrothe° wynde of the welkyn wrasteles with the sunne,	Fierce
	The leves lancen° fro the lynde and lyghten° on the grounde,	fall **lynde** . . . lime tree and alight
	And al grayes° the gres, that grene was ere;	becomes gray
	Thenne al rypes and rotes° that ros upon fyrst,	**rypes** . . . ripens and rots
	And thus yirnes° the yere in yisterdayes mony,	passes
530	And wynter wyndes° ayayn, as the worlde askes,° no fage.°	returns demands **no fage** in truth
	Til Meghelmas mone°	**Meghelmas mone** Michaelmas (harvest moon
	Was cumen wyth wynter wage;°	challenge
	Then thenkkes Gawan ful sone	
535	Of his anious vyage.°	**anious vyage** wearisome journey

xxiv

	Yet whyl Al-hal-day° with Arther he lenges,°	**whyl Al-hal-day** until All Saints' Day stays
	And he made a fare° on that fest, for the frekes sake,	observance
	With much revel° and ryche° of the Rounde Table;	revelry splendid
	Knyghtes ful cortays and comlych ladies,	
540	Al for luf of that lede in longynge° thay were;	grief
	Bot never-the-lece ne the later° thay nevened bot° merthe;	ne . . . not the less readily **nevened bot** spoke only of
	Mony joyles° for that jentyle japes° ther maden.	joyless ones **jentyle japes** noble one jes
	For aftter mete,° with mournyng he meles° to his eme,°	meal speaks uncle
	And spekes of his passage, and pertly° he sayde,	plainly
545	"Now, lege lorde of my lyf, leve° I yow ask;	leave
	Ye knowe the cost° of this cace; kepe° I no more	terms care
	To telle yow tenes° therof never bot° trifel;	troubles **never bot** but only
	Bot I am boun to° the bür barely to-morne,°	**boun to** ready for **bür** . . . blow without fail tomorrow morning
	To sech the gome of the grene, as God wyl me wysse."°	guide
550	Thenne the best of the burgh boghed° togeder,	**burgh boghed** city went
	Aywan and Errik and other ful mony,	
	Sir Doddinaval de Savage, the duk of Clarence,	
	Launcelot and Lyonel and Lucan the gode,	
	Sir Boos and Sir Bydver, big men bothe,	
555	And mony other menskful,° with Mador de la Port.	dignified ones
	Alle this compayny of court com the kyng nerre,	
	For to counseyl the knyght, with care at her° hert;	**care** . . . sorrow in their
	There was much derve doel driven° in the sale°	**derve** . . . severe sorrow suffered hall

That so worthy as Wawan schulde wende° on that ernde,°
     °go   *°mission*

560 To dryghe° a delful dynt,° and dele no more wyth bronde.°
     °suffer   **delful dynt** *doleful blow*   *°sword*

    The knyght mad ay° god chere,   *°ever*
    And sayde, "What schuld I wonde°   *°fear*
    Of destinés derf and dere?°   **derf . . .** *severe and harsh*

565   What may mon do bot fonde?"°   *°try*

XXV

He dowelles° ther al that day, and dresses on the morn,   *°stays*
Askes erly hys armes, and alle were thay broght;
Fyrst a tulé tapit, tyght° over the flet,°   **tulé . . .** *rich red carpet, spread*   *floor*
And miche was the gyld gere° that glent° ther alofte;   **gyld gere** *gilded armor*   *glinted*

570 The stif° mon steppes theron, and the stel hondeles,   *°strong*
Dubbed° in a dublet of a dere tars,°   *°Adorned*   **dere tars** *glorious silk from Tharsia (Turkestan)*
And sythen° a crafty capados,° closed aloft,   *°then*   **crafty capados** *skillfully-made hood*
That wyth a bryght blaunner° was bounden withinne;   *°white fur*
Thenne set thay the sabatouns° upon the segge° fotes,   *°steel shoes*   *°man's*

575 His leges lapped° in stel with luflych greves,°   *°wrapped*   *°greaves*
With polaynes piched° therto, policed ful clene,°   **polaynes piched** *kneepieces fixed*   **policed . . .** *polished very bright*
Aboute his knes knaged° wyth knotes of golde;   *°riveted*
Queme quyssewes° then, that coyntlych° closed   **Queme quyssewes** *Good thighpieces*   *°cunningly*
His thik, thrawen° thyghes, with thwonges to-tachched;°   *°brawny*   **thwonges to-tachched** *thongs attached*

580 And sythen the brawden bryny° of bryght stel rynges   **brawden bryny** *woven coat of mail*
Umbeweved° that wygh,° upon wlonk° stuffe;   *°Enclosed*   *°man*   *°lovely*
And wel bornyst brace° upon his bothe armes,   **bornyst brace** *burnished armpieces*
With gode cowters and gay,° and gloves of plate,   **cowters . . .** *elbowpieces and fair*
And alle the godlych gere° that hym gayn° schulde that tyde;°   *°armor*   *°benefit*   *°time*

585   Wyth ryche cote-armure,°   *°surcoat*
    His gold spores spend with pryde,°   **spend . . .** *fastened splendidly*
    Gürde° wyth a bront° ful sure   *°Girt*   *°sword*
    With silk sayn umbe° his syde.   **sayn umbe** *girdle around*

XXVI

590 When he was hasped° in armes, his harnays was ryche,   *°buckled*
The lest lachet° over loupe lemed° of golde;   **lest lachet** *smallest clasp*   *shone*

So harnayst as he was, he herknes° his masse,   hears
Offred and honoured at the heghe auter.°   altar
Sythen he comes to the kyng and to his cort-feres,°   court companions
595 Laches lufly° his leve at° lordes and ladyes;   **Laches lufly** Takes graciously   from
And thay hym kyst and conveyed, bikende° hym   **conveyed, bikende** conducted on his way,
    to Kryst.   commending
Bi that was Gryngolet grayth,° and gürde wyth a   set
    sadel
That glemed ful gayly° with mony golde frenges,   brightly
Aywhere naylet° ful newe, for that note ryched;°   **Aywhere naylet** Everywhere nailed
       note ryched occasion enriched
600 The brydel barred° aboute, with bryght golde   striped
    bounden;
The apparayl of the payttrure° and of the proude   neck armor
    skyrtes,
The cropore° and the covertor° acorded wyth the   crupper   cloth cover
    arsounes;°   saddlebows
And al was rayled° on red ryche golde nayles,   arrayed
That al glytered and glent° as glem of the sunne.   glinted
605 Thenne hentes° he the helme,° and hastily hit   takes   helmet
    kysses,
That was stapled stifly, and stoffed withinne;
Hit was hyghe on his hede, hasped° bihynde,   buckled
Wyth a lightly urysoun° over the aventayle,°   **lightly urysoun** light cover   visor
Enbrawden° and bounden wyth the best gemmes   Embroidered
610 On brode sylkyn borde,° and bryddes° on semes°   hem   birds   seams
As papjayes° paynted pernyng bitwene,°   parrots   **pernyng bitwene** preening at
       intervals
Tortors and trulofes, entayled° so thyk   **Tortors . . .** Turtledoves and true-lovers'
       knots, embroidered
As mony bürde ther-aboute° had ben seven   **mony . . .** many a lady engaged on it
    wynter
        in toune;
615 The cercle was more o prys°   **o prys** of excellence
That umbeclypped° hys croun   encircled
Of diamauntes à devys,°   **à devys** perfect
That bothe were bryght and broun.°   shining

          xxvii
Then thay schewed hym the schelde, that was of
    schyr goules,°   **schyr goules** bright gules
620 Wyth the pentangel depaynt° of pure golde   **pentangel depaynt** five-pointed star
    hewes;°   depicted   hues
He braydes° hit by the bauderyk,° aboute the hals   swings   shield strap
    kestes,°   **hals kestes** neck casts
That bisemed° the segge semlyly° fayre.   befitted   becomingly
And why the pentangel apendes° to that prynce   belongs
    noble,

I am intent yow to telle, thof tary° hyt me schulde.　　**thof tary** though delay
625　Hit is a syngne that Salamon set sumwhyle,°　　once upon a time
　　In bytoknyng of trawthe, bi tytle° that hit habbes;　right
　　For hit is a figure that haldes fyve poyntes,
　　And üche lyne umbelappes and loukes° in other,　　**umbelappes . . .** overlaps and locks
　　And aywhere° hit is endeles, and Englych hit　everywhere
　　　callen
630　Overal, as I here,° the endeles knot.　　hear
　　For-thy hit acordes to this knyght and to his cler°　bright
　　　armes,
　　For ay faythful in fyve and sere° fyve sythes,°　　separately　times
　　Gawan was for gode knawen and as golde pured,°　refined
　　Voyded of üche vylany, wyth vertues ennourned°　adorned
635　　in mote;°　　chivalry
　　　For-thy the pentangel° newe　　five-pointed star
　　　He ber in schelde and cote,
　　　As tulk° of tale° most trewe　　man　word
　　　And gentylest° knyght of lote.°　　noblest　aspect

　　　　　xxviii
640　Fyrst he was funden fautles in his fyve wyttes,°　senses
　　And efte° fayled never the freke in his fyve　then
　　　fyngres,
　　And alle his afyaunce° upon folde° was in the fyve　trust　earth
　　　woundes
　　That Cryst kaght° on the croys, as the crede telles;　received
　　And where-so-ever thys mon in melly° was stad,°　battle　placed
645　His thro° thoght was in that, thurgh alle other　earnest
　　　thynges,
　　That alle his fersnes° he fong at° the fyve joyes　power　**fong at** took from
　　That the hende° heven quene had of hir chylde;　noble
　　At this cause the knyght comlyche° hade　fittingly
　　In the more° half of his schelde hir ymage　larger (upper)
　　　depaynted,
650　That when he blusched° therto, his belde° never　looked　courage
　　　payred.°　　failed
　　The fyft fyve that I finde that the frek used
　　Was fraunchyse° and felawschyp forbe° al thyng;　liberality　surpassing
　　His clannes° and his cortaysye croked° were never,　chastity　astray
　　And pité, that passes alle poyntes—thyse pure fyve
655　Were harder happed° on that hathel then on any　fastened
　　　other.
　　Now alle these fyve sythes,° forsothe, were fetled　times
　　　on° this knyght,　　**fetled on** joined in
　　And üchone halched° in other, that non ende hade,　**üchone halched** each one fastened

And fyched° upon fyve poyntes, that fayled never,   fixed

Ne samned° never in no syde, ne sundred°   joined **ne sundred** nor separated
    nouther;

660 Withouten ende at any noke aiwhere° I fynde,   **noke aiwhere** corner anywhere

Where-ever the gomen° bygan or glod° to an   device glided
    ende.

Therfore on his schene° schelde schapen was the   bright
    knot

Ryally wyth red golde upon rede gowles,°   gules

That is the pure pentangel wyth° the peple called,   **pentangel wyth** five-pointed star by

665   with lore.°   learning

    Now graythed° is Gawan gay,   set

    And laght° his launce ryght thore,°   took there

    And gef hem alle goud day,

    He wende° for ever more.   thought

xxix

670   He sperred the sted with the spures, and sprong
    on his way

So stif° that the ston-fyr stroke° out therafter;   hard **ston-fyr stroke** sparks flew

Al that segh° that semly syked° in hert,   saw **semly syked** seemly one sighed

And sayde sothly al same° segges til° other,   together to

Carande° for that comly, "Bi Kryst, hit is scathe°   Anxious a grievous thing

675 That thou, leüde,° schal be lost, that art of lyf   man
    noble!

To fynde hys fere° upon folde, in fayth, is not ethe;°   equal easy

Warloker° to haf wroght° had more wyt° bene,   More warily acted **more wyt** wiser

And haf dyght° yonder dere a duk to have   made
    worthed;°   become

A lowande° leder of ledes° in londe hym wel   shining men
    semes,

680 And so had better haf ben then britned° to noght,   broken

Hadet° wyth an alvisch° mon, for angardes°   Beheaded elfish arrogance's
    pryde.

Who knew ever any kyng such counsel to take,

As knyghtes in cavelaciouns° on Crystmasse   disputes
    gomnes?"°   sport

Wel° much was the warme water that waltered   Very

of° yghen   **waltered of** flowed from

685 When that semly syre soght° fro tho wones°   went **tho wones** the dwelling
    thad° daye;   that

    He made non abode,°   delay

    Bot wyghtly° went hys way;   quickly

    Mony wylsum° way he rode,   **Mony wylsum** Many a wild

690   The bok as I herde say.

xxx

Now rides this renk° thurgh the ryalme of   knight
   Logres,°   Britain
Sir Gawan, on Godes halve, thagh hym no
   gomen thoght;°
Oft leüdles,° alone he lenges° on nyghtes,   companionless   dwells
Ther° he fonde noght hym byfore the fare° that   Where   food
   he lyked.
695   Hade he no fere° bot his fole° bi frythes° and   companion   horse   woods
   dounes,
Ne no gome bot God bi gate° wyth to karp,°   road   speak
Til that he neghed° ful neghe in to the Northe   neared
   Wales;
Alle the iles of Anglesay on lyft half° he haldes,   side
And fares over the fordes by the forlondes,°   lowlands
700   Over at the Holy Hede,[1] til he hade eft bonk°   **hade** ... reached the shore again
In the wyldrenesse of Wyrale;[2] wonde° ther bot   there dwelled
   lyte
That auther God other° gome wyth goud hert   or
   lovied.
And ay he frayned,° as he ferde,° at frekes that he   asked   went
   met,
If thay hade herde any karp° of a knyght grene   talk
705   In any grounde ther-aboute, of the grene chapel;
And al nykked° hym wyth nay, that never in   denied
   her lyve
Thay seghe° never no segge that was of suche   saw
   hewes°   hues
      of grene.
   The knyght tok gates° straunge   roads
710   In mony a bonk unbene;°   **bonk unbene** unpleasant slope
   His cher° ful oft con chaunge,°   mood   **con chaunge** changed
   That chapel er° he myght sene.°   before   see

xxxi

Mony° klyf he overclambe in contrayes   Many a
   straunge;
Fer floten° fro his frendes fremedly° he rydes;   **Fer floten** Far removed   as a stranger
715   At üche warthe other° water ther° the wyghe   **warthe other** shore or   where
   passed,
He fonde a foo° hym byfore, bot ferly° hit were,   foe   marvel

---

692. Sir Gawain, for God's sake, though it seemed no game to him
[1] A promontory in the vicinity of Flint, not Holyhead in Anglesey.
[2] A district in the west midlands of England, between the Dee and Mersey rivers.

And that so foule and so felle° that feght hym   fierce
    byhode.°   behooved
So mony mervayl bi mount° ther the mon   **bi mount** in the mountains
    fyndes,
Hit were too tore° for to telle of the tenthe döle.°   difficult   part
720 Sumwhyle° wyth wormes° he werres,° and wyth   Sometimes   dragons   fights
    wolves als,°   also
Sumwhyle wyth wodwos° that woned° in the   wild men   dwelled
    knarres,°   rocks
Bothe wyth bulles and beres and bores
    otherwhyle,
And etaynes° that hym anelede, of° the heghe   giants   **anelede, of** attacked, from
    felle;°   rocks
Nade he° ben dughty and dryghe,° and Dryghten°   **Nade he** Had he not   **dughty . . .** brave,
    had served,   and enduring   the Lord
725 Douteles he hade ben ded and dreped° ful ofte.   killed
For werre wrathed° hym not so much, that   troubled
    wynter was wors,
When the colde, cler water fro the cloudes
    schadde,
And fres er° hit falle myght to the fale° erthe;   **fres er** froze before   pale
Ner° slayn wyth the slete he sleped in his yrnes°   Nearly   irons
730 Mo° nyghtes then innoghe° in naked rokkes,   More   enough
Ther-as claterande° fro the crest the colde borne°   clattering   stream
    rennes,
And henged° heghe over his hede in hard   hung
    iisseikkles.
Thus in peryl and payne and plytes° ful harde,   straits
Bi contray cayres° this knyght tyl Krystmasse   **Bi . . .** Over the land rides
    even,
735   alone.
    The knyght wel that tyde°   time
    To Mary made his mone,°   complaint
    That hö° hym red° to ryde,   she   might advise where
    And wysse° hym to sum wone.°   guide   dwelling

xxxii

740   Bi a mounte on the morne meryly he rydes
Into a forest ful dep, that ferly° was wylde,   marvelously
Highe hilles on üche a halve, and holtwodes°   woods
    under
Of hore° okes ful hoge° a hundreth togeder.   hoary   huge
The hasel and the hawthorne were harled al
    samen,°   **harled . . .** twisted together
745 With roghe, raged mosse rayled° aywhere,   arrayed

With mony bryddes° unblythe upon bare   birds
    twyges,
That pitosly ther piped for pyne of the colde.
The gome upon Gryngolet glydes hem° under   them (birds)
Thurgh mony misy° and myre, mon al hym one,°   **mony misy** many a quagmire **al . . .** all alone
750 Carande° for his costes,° lest he ne kever° schulde   Worrying devotions arrive
To se the servyse of that Syre, that on that self°   same
    nyght
Of a bürde° was borne, oure baret° to quelle.   maiden grief
    And therfore sykyng° he sayde, "I beseche thee,   sighing
    Lorde,
And Mary, that is myldest° moder so dere,   gentlest
755 Of sum herber ther heghly° I myght here masse   **herber . . .** lodging where devoutly
Ande thy matynes tomorne;° mekely I ask,   tomorrow morning
And ther-to prestly° I pray my *pater* and *ave*   promptly
    and *crede*."
    He rode in his prayere
760   And cryed for his mysdede,
    He sayned hym in sythes sere°   **sayned . . .** crossed himself several times
    And sayde, "Cros-Kryst me spede!"°   help

xxxiii

    Nade° he sayned hymself, segge, bot thrye,°   Had not thrice
Er° he was war° in the wod of a won° in a mote,°   Before aware dwelling moat
765 Abof a launde,° on a lawe, loken° under   plain **lawe, loken** hill, enclosed
    boghes
Of mony borelych bole,° aboute bi the diches,   **borelych bole** burly tree
A castel the comlokest° that ever knyght aghte,°   comeliest owned
Pyched° on a prayere,° a park al aboute,   Set meadow
With a pyked palays, pyned° ful thik,   **pyked . . .** spiked palisade, fastened
770 That umbeteghe° mony tre mo° then two myle.   enclosed more
That holde° on that on° syde the hathel avysed,°   castle one observed
As hit schemered and schon thurgh the schyre°   white
    okes.
Thenne has he hendly of° his helme, and heghly he   **has . . .** he courteously takes off
    thonkes
Jesus and sayn Gilyan,° that gentyle ar bothe,   St. Julian
775 That cortaysly° hade hym kydde° and his cry   courtesy shown
    herkened.
"Now bone hostel,"° quoth the bürne, "I   **bone hostel** good lodging
    beseche yow yette!"°   to grant
Thenne gederes° he to Gryngolet with the gilt   spurs
    heles,
And he ful chauncely° has chosen° to the chef   by chance gone
    gate°   **chef gate** main road

That broght bremly° the bürne to the brygge°   clearly   bridge's
    ende
780   in haste.
    The brygge was breme upbrayde,°   **breme upbrayde** stoutly pulled up
    The yates° wer stoken° faste,   gates   shut
    The walles were wel arayed,°   constructed
    Hit dut° no wyndes blaste.   feared

xxxiv

785   The bürne bode° on bonk,° that on blonk hoved,°   waited the slope **blonk hoved** horse halted
    Of the depe double dich that drof to° the place;   **drof to** enclosed
    The walle wod° in the water wonderly depe,   stood
    Ande eft° a ful huge heght° hit haled upon lofte°   again height **haled . . .** rose aloft
    Of harde hewen ston up to the tables,°   cornices
790   Enbaned° under the abataylment, in the best lawe,°   Buttressed style
    And sythen garytes° ful gaye gered bitwene,°   towers **gered bitwene** built at intervals
    Wyth mony luflych loupe° that louked° ful clene°—   loophole shut neatly
    A better barbican that bürne blusched° upon   looked
      never.
    And innermore he behelde that halle ful hyghe,
795   Towres telded° bytwene, trochet° ful thick,   erected battlemented
    Fayre fylyoles° that fyghed,° and ferlyly° long,   pinnacles fitted marvelously
    With corvon coprounes, craftyly sleghe.°   **corvon . . .** carved tops, skillfully ingenio
    Chalk-whyt chymnees ther ches° he innoghe,°   saw many
    Upon bastel roves° that blenked° ful whyte;   **bastel roves** tower roofs shone
800   So mony pynakle payntet was poudred aywhere°   **poudred aywhere** scattered everywhere
    Among the castel carneles, clambred° so thik,   **carneles, clambred** embrasures, clustered
    That pared° out of papure purely hit semed.   cut
    The fre° freke on the fole° hit fayr innoghe thoght,   noble horse
    If he myght kever° to com the cloyster wythinne,   succeed
805   To herber° in that hostel,° whyl halyday lested,   lodge dwelling
      avinant.°   pleasant
    He calde, and sone ther com
    A porter pure plesaunt;
    On the wal his ernd° he nome°   message took
810   And haylsed° the knyght erraunt.   greeted

xxxv

    "Gode sir," quoth Gawan, "woldes thou go°   go with
      myn ernde
    To the hegh lorde of this hous, herber° to crave?"   lodging
    "Ye, Peter," quoth the porter, "and purely I
      trowee°   believe
    That ye be, wyghe, welcum to won° whyle yow   dwell here
      lykes."

402

815 Then yede° that wyghe ayayn swythe,°	went quickly
And folke frely° hym wyth, to fonge° the knyght.	readily receive
Thay let doun the grete draght and derely° out yeden	**draght** . . . drawbridge and courteously
And kneled doun on her knes upon the colde erthe	
To welcum this ilk° wygh, as worthy höm thoght.°	same **höm thoght** . . . seemed to them
820 Thay yolden° hym the brode yate, yarked° up wyde,	yielded **yate, yarked** gate, opened
And he hem raysed rekenly° and rod over the brygge;	**raysed rekenly** bade rise courteously
Sere° segges hym sesed° by sadel, whel he lyght,°	Several took alighted
And sythen stabeled his stede stif° men innoghe.°	strong many
Knyghtes and swyeres° comen doun thenne	squires
825 For to bryng this bürne wyth blys into halle.	
When he hef° up his helme,° ther highed° innoghe	raised helmet hastened
For to hent° hit at his honde, the hende° to serven;	take noble one
His bronde° and his blasoun bothe° thay token.	sword **blasoun bothe** shield too
Then haylsed° he ful hendly tho hatheles üch one,	greeted
830 And mony proud mon ther presed, that prynce to honour.	
Alle hasped° in his hegh wede,° to halle thay hym wonnen,°	buckled **hegh wede** noble armor brought
Ther fayre fyre upon flet° fersly brenned.°	the hearth burned
Thenne the lorde of the lede loutes° fro his chambre	**lede loutes** people turns
For to mete wyth menske° the mon on the flor.	courtesy
835 He sayde, "Ye are welcum to welde° as yow lykes;	take
That° here is, al is yowre awen,° to have at yowre wylle	That (which) own
and welde."°	control
"Graunt mercy,"° quoth Gawayn,	**Graunt mercy** Many thanks
"Ther Kryst hit yow foryelde."°	reward
840 As frekes that semed fayn°	glad
Ayther other in armes con felde.°	**con felde** embraced

xxxvi

Gawayn glyght° on the gome that godly hym gret,°	looked greeted
And thught hit a bolde bürne that the burgh aghte,°	**burgh aghte** city owned
A hoge hathel for the nones, and of hyghe eldee;°	**for** . . . indeed, and in prime of life
845 Brode, bryght was his berde, and al bever-hewed,	
Sturne, stif on the stryththe° on stalworth schonkes,°	**stif** . . . firm standing legs

Felle° face as the fyre, and fre° of hys speche.   Fierce   noble
And wel hym semed forsothe, as the segge thught,
To lede a lortschyp in lee° of leüdes° ful gode.   lede ... hold a lordship as protector   men
850 The lorde hym charred° to a chambre and chefly°   turned   particularly
    cumaundes
To delyver hym a leüde, hym loghly° to serve.   **hym loghly** him (Gawain) humbly
And there were boun° at his bode° bürnes   ready   command
    innoghe°   many
That broght hym to a bryght boure,° ther   bedroom
    beddyng was noble
Of cortaynes of clene° sylk wyth cler golde   pure
    hemmes,
855 And covertores° ful curious with comlych panes,°   coverlets   panels
Of bryght blaunmer° above, enbrawded bisydes,°   white fur   **enbrawded bisydes** embroidered at the sides
Rüdeles rennande° on ropes, red golde rynges,   **Rüdeles rennande** Curtains running
Tapytes tyght to the woghe, of Tuly and Tars,°
And under fete, on the flet,° of folghande sute.°   floor   **folghande sute** matching sort
860 Ther he was dispoyled,° wyth speches of myerthe,   disrobed
The bürn of his brüny° and of his bryght wedes.°   coat of mail   armor
Ryche robes ful rad renkkes° hym broghten,   **rad renkkes** quickly men
For to charge° and to chaunge and chose of the   put on
    best.
Sone as he on hent, and happed° ther-inne,   **on ...** took one, and enclosed himself
865 That sete on hym semly, wyth saylande° skyrtes;   flowing
The ver° by his visage° verayly hit semed   springtime   appearance
Wel negh° to üche hathel, alle on hewes,   **Wel negh** Very near
Lowande° and lufly, alle his lymmes under.   Brilliant
That a comloker° knyght never Kryst made,   comelier
870   hem thoght.°   **hem thoght** it seemed to them
    Whethen° in worlde he were,   From wherever
    Hit semed as° he moght°   as if   could
    Be prynce withouten pere
    In felde ther felle° men foght.   fierce

xxxvii

875 A cheyer° byfore the chemné,° ther charcole   chair   fireplace
    brenned,
Was graythed° for Sir Gawan graythely° with   ready   speedily
    clothes,°   coverings
Quyssynes° upon queldepoyntes,° that koynt°   Cushions   quilted covers   cunningly
    wer bothe.   made
And thenne a meré° mantyle was on that mon   fair
    cast,
Of a broun bleeaunt, enbrauded° ful ryche,   **bleeaunt, enbrauded** silk, embroidered

858. Tapestries hung on the wall, from Toulouse and Tharsia (Turkestan)

880	And fayre furred wythinne with felles° of the best,	skins
	Alle of ermyn, in erde,° his hode of the same.	**in erde** actually
	And he sete in that settel semlych° ryche,	excellently
	And achaufed hym chefly,° and thenne his cher° mended.	**achaufed** . . . warmed himself quickly mood
884	Sone was telded° up a tabil on trestes° ful fayre,	set trestles
885	Clad wyth a clene clothe that cler whyt schewed,	
	Sanap and salure° and sylverin spones.	**Sanap** . . . Napkin and saltcellar
	The wyghe wesche° at his wylle, and went to his mete.°	washed food
	Segges hym served semly° innoghe	properly
	Wyth sere sewes and sete,° sesounde of the best,	**sere** . . . various stews and fitting
890	Double-felde, as hit falles, and fele kyn fisches,°	**falles** . . . is fitting, and many kinds of fish
	Summe baken in bred, summe brad° on the gledes,°	grilled coals
	Summe sothen,° summe in sewe, savered wyth spyces,	boiled
	And ay sawses so sleghe,° that the segge lyked.	cunningly made
	The freke calde hit a feste° ful frely° and ofte	feast readily
895	Ful hendely,° when alle the hatheles rehayted° hym at ones as hende:°	courteously exhorted courteously
	"This penaunce³ now ye take, And eft° hit schal amende."°	 later improve
	That mon much merthe con make,°	**con make** made
900	For wyn in° his hed that wende.°	to went

xxxviii

	Thenne was spyed and spüred, upon spare wyse°	**spyed** . . . inquired and asked, in a tactful manner
	Bi prevé° poyntes, of that prynce, put to hymselven,	discreet
	That° he beknew° cortaysly, of the court that he were	So that acknowledged
	That athel° Arthure the hende haldes hym one,°	noble **haldes** . . . rules alone
905	That is the ryche, ryal kyng of the Rounde Table;	
	And hit was Wawen hymself that in that won° syttes,	dwelling
	Comen to° that Krystmas, as case° hym then lymped.°	**Comen to** Having arrived chance befell
	When the lorde hade lerned that he the leüde hade,	
	Loude laghed he ther-at, so lef° hit hym thoght;°	pleasant **hym thoght** seemed to him

---

³ Gawain's feast of fish is only penitential fare (*penaunce*) required by the fact that the Vigil of Christmas is a fast day; the real feast will be served on Christmas day.

405

910 And alle the men in that mote° maden much joye   castle
     To apere in his presence prestly that tyme,
     That alle prys and prowes and pured thewes
     Apendes to hys persoun, and praysed is ever;°
     Byfore alle men upon molde° his mensk° is the   earth   courtesy
        most.
915   Ůch segge ful softly sayde to his fere,°   companion
     "Now schal we semlych° se sleghtes° of thewes°   pleasantly   skillful acts   manners
     And the teccheles° termes of talkyng noble.   spotless
     Which spede° is in speche, unspürd° may we lerne,   **Which spede** What success   unasked
     Syn we haf fonged° that fyne fader of nurture.°   received   good breeding
920 God has geven uus his grace godly, forsothe,
     That such a gest as Gawan grauntes uus to have,
     When bürnes blythe of His bürthe schall sitte
        and synge.
       In menyng° of maneres meré°   understanding   fair
925   This bürne now schal uus bryng,
       I hope that° may hym here°   **hope that** suppose that one who   hear
       Schal lerne of luf-talkyng."

           xxxix
       Bi-that° the diner was done, and the dere° up,   When   noble ones
     Hit was negh° at the niyght neghed° the tyme.   almost   drawn near
930 Chaplaynes to the chapeles chosen the gate,°   **chosen . . .** took the way
     Rungen° ful rychely, ryght as thay schulden,   Rang the bells
     To the hersum° evensong of the hyghe tyde.°   devout   festival
     The lorde loutes° therto, and the lady als;°   goes   also
     Into a comly closet coyntly hö° entres.   **closet . . .** pew graciously she
935 Gawan glydes° ful gay and gos theder sone;   hastens
     The lorde laches° hym by the lappe° and ledes   takes   fold of his garment
        hym to sytte,
     And couthly° hym knowes° and calles hym his   familiarly   recognizes
        nome,°   name
     And sayde he was the welcomest wyghe of the
        world.
     And he hym thonkked throly,° and ayther   earnestly
        halched° other,   embraced
940 And seten soberly samen° the servise-whyle.   together
     Thenne lyst° the lady to loke on the knyght;   it pleased
     Thenne com hö° of hir closet° with mony cler   **com hö** she came   pew
        bürdes.°   **cler bürdes** fair maidens
     Hö was the fayrest in felle,° of flesche and of lyre,°   skin   face

911–13. To appear appropriately at that time in the presence of him to whose person belongs all excellence and prowess and refined manners, and who is ever praised

    And of compas° and colour and costes,° of alle   proportion manners
        other,
945 And wener° then Wenore,° as the wyghe thoght.   fairer Guinevere
    He ches° thurgh the chaunsel to cheryche° that   went greet
        hende.°   courteous one
    Another lady[4] hir lad bi the lyft honde,
    That was alder then hö,° an auncian° hit semed,   she aged one
    And heghly honowred with° hatheles aboute.   by the
950 Bot unlyke° on to loke tho° ladyes were,   dissimilar those
    For if the yonge was yep, yölwe° was that other; **yep, yölwe** fresh, yellow
    Riche red on that on rayled aywhere,°   **on rayled . . .** one arrayed everywhere
    Rugh ronkled chekes that other on rolled.°   hung
    Kerchöfes of that on wyth mony cler perles,
955 Hir brest and hir bryght throte, bare displayed,
    Schon schyrer° then snawe that schedes° on   whiter falls
        hilles;
    That other wyth a gorger° was gered° over the   neckerchief clothed
        swyre,°   neck
    Chymbled° over hir blake chyn with mylk-whyte Wrapped
        vayles,
    Hir frount° folden in sylk, enfoubled aywhere,°   forehead **enfoubled aywhere** muffled everywhere
960 Toret and trejeted° with tryfles aboute,°   **Toret . . .** Turreted and adorned
    That° noght was bare of that bürde° bot the blake So that lady
        browes,
    The tweyne° yghen and the nase,° the naked   two nose
        lyppes,
    And those were soure to se and sellyly° blered;   marvelously
    A mensk° lady on molde° mon may hir calle,   dignified earth
965   for° Gode!   before
        Hir body was schort and thik,
        Hir buttokes balgh° and brode;   round
        More lykkerwys on to lyk
        Was that schö hade on lode.°

                xl

970 When Gawayn glyght° on that gay° that   looked fair one
        graciously loked,
    Wyth leve laght° of the lorde he went hem   **leve laght** permission granted
        ayaynes.°   **hem ayaynes** toward them
    The alder he haylses, heldande° ful lowe;   **haylses, heldande** greets, bowing
    The loveloker° he lappes° a lyttel in armes,   lovelier one embraces
    He kysses her comlyly, and knyghtly he meles.°   speaks

---

[4] The first lady is the wife of the lord of the castle; this second is Morgne (Morgan le Fay), as we learn later (Part IV, l. 2446).
968–69. One more sweet to the taste was the one whom she had in her company.

975	Thay kallen° hym of aquoyntaunce, and he hit quyk askes	beg	
	To be her° servaunt sothly, if hemself lyked.°	their	**hemself lyked** it pleased them
	Thay tan° hym bytwene hem,° wyth talkyng hym leden	take	them
	To chambre, to chemné,° and chefly° thay asken	fireplace	particularly
	Spyces, that unsparely° men speded höm° to bryng,	eagerly	**speded höm** hastened
980	And the wynnelych° wyne therwith üche tyme.	joyous	
	The lorde luflych° aloft lepes ful ofte,	graciously	
	Mynned° merthe to be made upon mony sythes,°	Devised	times
	Hent heghly of° his hode, and on a spere henged,	**Hent . . .** Took gaily off	
	And wayned höm° to wynne the worschip° therof	**wayned höm** directed them	honor
985	That most myrthe myght meve° that Crystenmas whyle.	make	
	"And I schal fonde,° bi my fayth, to fylter° wyth the best,	try	contend
	Er me wont° the wede,° with help of my frendes."	**Er . . .** Before I lack	garment
	Thus wyth laghande lotes° the lorde hit tayt° makes,	**laghande lotes** laughing words	merry
	For to glade° Sir Gawayn with gomnes° in halle	gladden	sports
990	that nyght,		
	Til that hit was tyme		
	The lord comaundet lyght.°	lights	
	Sir Gawen his leve con nyme°	**con nyme** took	
	And to his bed hym dight.°	went	

xli

995	On the morne, as üch mon mynes° that tyme	recalls	
	That Dryghten° for oure destyné to deghe° was borne,	the Lord	die
	Wele waxes° in üche a won° in worlde for his sake.	**Wele waxes** Joy grows	dwelling
	So did hit there on that day, thurgh dayntés° mony;	courtesies	
	Both at mes° and at mele, messes° ful quaynt°	lunch **mele, messes** dinner, food cunningly made	
1000	Derf° men upon dece drest° of the best.	Strong	arranged
	The olde, auncian wyf° heghest hö° syttes;	**auncian wyf** aged woman	she
	The lorde lufly her by lent,° as I trowe.°	stayed	believe
	Gawan and the gay bürde° togeder thay seten	maiden	
	Even in-myddes, as the messe metely come;°		
1005	And sythen thurgh al the sale,° as hem° best semed,	hall	to them
	Bi üche grome° at his degré graythely° was served.	person	speedily

1004. Equally in the middle, as the food properly came

Ther was mete, ther was myrthe, ther was much joye,

That for to telle therof hit me tene° were,   trouble

And° to poynte° hit yet I pyned° me paraventure.°   If describe troubled perhaps

1010 Bot yet I wot° that Wawen° and the wale bürde°   know Gawain **wale bürde** fair maiden

Such comfort of her compaynye caghten° togeder   got

Thurgh her dere dalyaunce° of her derne° wordes,   conversation private

Wyth clene,° cortays carp closed° fro fylthe,   pure **carp closed** talk free

That hör° play was passande° üche prynce gomen,°   their surpassing **prynce gomen**

1015   in vayres.°   princely sport truth

    Trumpes and nakerys,°   **Trumpes ...** Trumpets and kettledrums

    Much pypyng ther repayres;°   is present

    Üche mon tented hys,°   **tented hys** attended to his business

    And thay two tented thayres.

xlii

1020 Much dut° was ther dryven° that day, and that other°   mirth made / the next

And the thryd° as thro thronge° in therafter.   third day **thro thronge** equally delightful

The joye of Sayn Jones° day was gentyle to here,   **Sayn Jones** St. John's (December 27)

And was the last of the layk, leüdes° ther thoghten.   **layk, leüdes** entertainment, people

Ther wer gestes° to go, upon the gray morne,   guests

1025 For-thy° wonderly thay woke,° and the wyn dronken,   So stayed awake

Daunsed ful dreghly° wyth dere caroles.   unceasingly

At the last, when hit was late, thay lachen° her leve,   took

Üchon° to wende° on his way that was wyghe strange.°   Each one go **wyghe strange** a stranger

Gawan gef° hym god day, the god mon° hym lachches,°   bade **god mon** host / takes

1030 Ledes hym to his awen° chambre, the chymné° bysyde,   own fireplace

And there he draghes° hym on dryghe,° and derely hym thonkkes   draws **on dryghe** aside

Of the wynne worschip° that he hym wayned° hade,   **wynne worschip** pleasant honor brought

As to honour his hous on that hyghe tyde,°   **hyghe tyde** festival

And enbelyse his burgh° with his bele chere.°   castle **bele chere** good company

1035 "I-wysse,° Sir, whyl I leve, me worthes° the better   Indeed **leve ...** live, I will be

That Gawayn has ben my gest° at Goddes awen fest."°   guest **awen fest** festival

"Grant merci, Sir," quoth Gawayn, "in god fayth hit is yowres,

Al the honour is your awen, the Heghe Kyng
    yow yelde.°   reward
And I am, wyghe,° at your wylle, to worch°   sir   do
    youre hest,°   behest
1040 As I am halden° therto in hyghe and in loghe,°   bound   low
    bi right."
    The lorde fast can hym payne°   **fast** ... earnestly troubled himself
    To holde lenger the knyght.
    To hym answares Gawayn
1045   Bi non way that he myght.°   could hold him longer

xliii

   Then frayned° the freke ful fayre at himselven°   asked   him (Gawain)
What derve° dede had hym dryven, at that dere   brave
    tyme,
So kenly° fro the kynges kourt to kayre° al his   boldly   ride
    one,°   **his one** alone
Er the halidayes holly° were halet° out of toun.   wholly   gone
1050   "For sothe, Sir," quoth the segge, "ye sayn bot°   only
    the trawthe,
A heghe ernde° and a hasty° me hade fro tho   errand   urgent one
    wones,°   **tho wones** the dwelling
For I am sumned myselfe to sech° to a place,   seek
I ne wot° in worlde whederwarde to wende° hit   **ne wot** don't know   go
    to fynde.
I nolde bot if° I hit negh° myght on New Yeres   **nolde** ... would not unless   reach
    morne
1055 For alle the londe inwyth Logres,° so me oure   **inwyth Logres** in England
    Lorde help!
For-thy, Sir, this enquest I require yow here,
That ye me telle with trawthe, if ever ye tale
    herde
Of the grene chapel, where hit on grounde stondes,
And of the knyght that hit kepes, of colour of
    grene.   **stabled** ... established by agreement
1060 Ther was stabled bi statut° a steven° uus bytwene,   tryst
To mete that mon at that mere,° yif I myght last;   appointed place
And of that ilk° New Yere bot neked° now   same   **bot neked** only a little
    wontes,°   it wants
And I wolde loke on that lede,° if God me let   man
    wolde,
Gladloker,° bi Goddes Son, then any god welde!°   More gladly   **god welde** good thing
                                         possess
1065 For-thi, i-wysse,° bi yowre wylle, wende me   indeed
    bihoves.°   **wende** ... it behooves me to go
Naf° I now to busy° bot bare° thre dayes,   Have not   be active   **bot bare** except
                                         barely

And me als fayn to falle feye° as fayly° of myyn   **als . . .** as fain doomed to death   fail
    ernde."

Thenne laghande° quoth the lorde, "Now leng°   laughing   stay
    thee byhoves,

For I schal teche° yow to that terme° bi the tymes   direct   appointed place
    ende.

1070 The grene chapayle upon grounde greve° yow no   let it grieve
    more.

Bot ye schal be in yowre bed, bürne, at thyn ese,

Whyle forth dayes, and ferk° on the fyrst of the   **Whyle . . .** Till late in the day, and go
    yere,

And cum to that merk° at mydmorn, to make   appointed place
    what yow likes
      in spenne.°   **in spenne** there (on that turf)

1075 Dowelles° whyle New Yeres daye,   Remain

And rys and raykes° thenne.   leave

Mon schal yow sette in waye;

Hit is not two myle henne."°   hence

xliv

Thenne was Gawan ful glad, and gomenly° he   happily
    laghed:

1080 "Now I thonk yow thryvandely thurgh° alle   **thryvandely thurgh** heartily beyond
    other thynge;

Now acheved is my chaunce;° I schal at your   adventure
    wylle

Dowelle,° and elles do what ye demen."°   Remain   think fit

Thenne sesed° hym the syre and set hym bysyde,   grasped

Let the ladies be fette,° to lyke hem° the better.   brought   **lyke hem** please them

1085 Ther was seme solace° by himself stille;°   **seme solace** seemly pleasure   **hemself**

The lorde let° for luf lotes° so myry,°   **stille** themselves privately
    uttered   words   fair

As wygh that wolde of his wyte, ne wyst what he
    myght.°

Thenne he carped° to the knyght, criande° loude: spoke   crying

"Ye han demed° to do the dede that I bidde.   **han demed** have determined

1090 Wyl ye halde° this hes° here at thys ones?"°   keep   promise   time

"Ye, Sir, forsothe," sayd the segge trewe,

"Whyl I byde in yowre borghe, be bayn° to   **borghe . . .** castle, I'll be obedient
    yowre hest."°   behest

"For° ye haf travayled," quoth the tulk,°   Since   man

"towen° fro ferre,°   come   far

And sythen waked° me wyth, ye arn not wel   kept vigil
    waryst°   recovered

1095 Nauther of sostnaunce ne of slepe, sothly I knowe.

1087. As someone who was going to go out of his wits and didn't know what he was doing.

411

Ye schal lenge° in your lofte and lyghe° in your ese   stay   **lofte** ... room and lie

To-morn whyle the messe-whyle,° and to mete   **To-morn** ... This morning till mass time
wende,°   go

When ye wyl, wyth my wyf, that wyth yow
schal sitte

And comfort yow with compayny, til I to cort
torne.°   return

1100   Ye lende,°   stay

And I schal erly ryse;

On huntyng wyl I wende."

Gawayn grantes alle thyse,

Hym heldande,° as the hende.°   **Hym heldande** Bowing to him
           courteous one does

xlv

1105   "Yet firre,"° quoth the freke,° "a forwarde° we   further   man   agreement
make:

What-so-ever I wynne in the wod, hit worthes to°   **worthes to** becomes
youres;

And what chek° so ye acheve, chaunge me°   fortune   **chaunge me** exchange with me
ther-forne.

Swete, swap° we so—sware° with trawthe—   **Swete, swap** Good sir, bargain   answer

Whether, leüde,° so lymp lere other° better."   sir   **lymp** ... befall loss or

1110   "Bi God," quoth Gawayn the gode, "I grant
ther-tylle,

And that yow lyst for to layke, lef hit me
thynkes."°

"Who brynges uus this beverage,° this bargayn   drink (to seal the bargain)
is maked."

So sayde the lorde of that lede.° Thay laghed   people
üchone.°   every one

Thay dronken and daylyeden and dalten
untyghtel,°   **daylyeden** ... dallied and dealt
           pleasantries

1115 Thise lordes and ladyes, whyle that hem lyked.°   **hem lyked** pleased them

And sythen with Frenkysch fare and fele° fayre   **Frenkysch** ... French behavior and many
lotes°   words

Thay stoden and stemed and stylly° speken,   **stoden** ... arose and stopped and softly

Kysten ful comlyly, and kaghten° her leve.   took

With mony leüde ful lyght and lemande° torches,   **lyght** ... active and gleaming

1120 Üche bürne to his bed was broght at the laste
ful softe.

To bed yet er thay yede,°   went

Recorded° covenauntes ofte.   They repeated

The olde lorde of that leüde°   people

1125 Cowthe° wel halde layk alofte.°   Could   **halde** ... carry on a game

1111. And that which it pleases you to play, it seems pleasant to me.

412

Sir Gawain and the Green Knight*

Part III

xlvi

Ful erly bifore the day the folk up rysen;
Gestes that go wolde, hör gromes° thay calden,   **hör gromes** their servants
And thay busken up bilyve, blonkkes° to sadel,   **busken** . . . hurry up quickly, horses
Tyffen° her takles, trussen° her males.°   Prepare **takles, trussen** gear, pack bags
1130 Richen hem° the rychest, to ryde alle arayde,   **Richen hem** Dress
Lepen up lightly, lachen° her brydeles,   **lightly, lachen** swiftly, grasp
Üche wyghe on his way ther hym wel lyked.°   pleased
The leve° lorde of the londe was not the last   dear
Arayed for the rydyng, with renkkes° ful mony;   knights
1135 Ete a sop° hastyly, when he hade herde masse;   light meal
With bugle to bent-felde° he buskes bylyve;°   open field **buskes bylyve** hurries quickly
By° that any daylyght lemed° upon erthe,   By the time shone
He with his hatheles on hyghe horsses weren.
Thenne thise cacheres° that couthe, cowpled° hör   hunters **couthe, cowpled** knew how,
    houndes,   leashed
1140 Unclosed the kenel dore and calde hem ther-oute,
Blewe bygly in bugles thre bare mote.°   **bare mote** single notes
Braches° bayed therfore, and breme° noyse maked,   Hounds fierce
And thay chastysed and charred, on chasyng that°   **charred** . . . turned back, astray those
    went,   hounds that
A hundreth of hunteres, as I haf herde telle,
1145   of the best.
    To trystors vewters yod;°   **trystors** . . . stations deerhound-keepers went
    Couples huntes of kest.°   **Couples** . . . Leashes huntsmen cast off
    Ther ros for blastes gode
    Gret rürd° in that forest.   noise

xlvii

1150 At the fyrst quethe° of the quest° quaked the   sound baying
    wylde;°   wild animals
Der drof° in the dale, doted° for drede,   rushed grew mad
Highed° to the hyghe,° bot heterly° thay were   Sped high ground quickly
Restayed with° the stablye,° that stoutly ascryed.°   **Restayed with** Turned by beaters shouted
Thay let the herttes haf the gate,° with the hyghe   **haf** . . . go free
    hedes,
1155 The breme° bukkes also with hör° brode paumes;°   brave their antlers
For the fre° lorde hade defende° in fermysoun   noble forbidden
    tyme°   **fermysoun tyme** closed season
That ther schulde no mon meve to° the male dere.   **ther** . . . anyone should hunt
The hindes were halden in, with "hay!" and
    "war!"
The does dryven with gret dyn to the depe slades.°   valleys

413

1160 Ther myght mon se, as thay slypte, slentyng° of arwes;°

slypte, slentyng were loosed, a rush arrows

At üche wende° under wande wapped° a flone,°

turn wande wapped branches flew arrow

That bigly bote° on the broun,° with ful brode hedes.°

bit brown hides arrowheads

What! thay brayen and bleden, bi bonkkes° thay deghen,°

slopes die

And ay rachches° in a res radly hem folghes,°

hounds res ... rush swiftly follow them

1165 Hunteres wyth hyghe horne hasted hem after,

Wyth such a crakkande° kry as° klyffes haden brusten.°

blaring as if burst

What wylde so atwaped wyghes° that schotten

What ... Whatever animal escaped the men

Was al toraced° and rent at the resayt,°

seized receiving station

Bi° thay were tened° at the hyghe, and taysed° to the wattres.

After worried driven

1170 The ledes° were so lerned° at the loghe trysteres,°

men skilled loghe trysteres low stations

And the grehoundes so grete that geten hem bylyve°

geten ... seized them quickly

And hem tofylched° as fast as frekes myght loke, ther ryght.

pulled down

The lorde, for blys abloy,°

carried away

1175 Ful oft con launce and lyght,°

con ... did gallop and alight

And drof° that day wyth joy

spent

Thus to the derk nyght.

xlviii

Thus laykes° this lorde by lynde-wodes eves,°

plays lynde-wodes eves lime wood's edge

And Gawayn the god mon in gay bed lyges,°

lies

1180 Lurkkes whyl° the daylyght lemed° on the wowes,°

Lurkkes whyl Lies concealed until shone walls

Under covertour ful clere,° cortyned aboute;

fair

And as in slomeryng° he slode, sleghly° he herde

slumbering slode, sleghly glided, warily

A littel dyn° at his dor, and derfly upon;°

sound derfly upon (heard) it quickly open

And he heves up his hed out of the clothes,

1185 A corner of the cortyn he caght up a lyttel,

And waytes° warly thiderwarde, what hit be myght.

looks

Hit was the ladi, loflyest to beholde,

That drogh° the dor after hir ful dernly° and stylle,

drew secretly

And boghed° towarde the bed; and the bürne schamed°

turned was embarrassed

1190 And layde hym doun lystyly and let as° he slepte.

lystyly ... craftily and behaved as if

And hö stepped stilly and stel° to his bedde,

stole

Kest up the cortayn and creped withinne
And set hir ful softly on the bed-syde
And lenged° there selly° longe to loke when he   stayed   very
    wakened.
1195   The lede° lay lurked° a ful longe whyle,   man   hidden
    Compast° in his concience° to what that cace°   Pondered   mind   happening
      myght
Meve other amount, to mervayle hym thoght;°
Bot yet he sayde in hymself, "More semly hit were
To aspye° wyth my spelle in space° what hö   discover   **spelle** ... words soon
    wolde."°   might want
1200 Then he wakenede and wroth° and to-hir-warde   stretched
    torned
And unlouked his yghe-lyddes and let as hym
    wondered,°   **let** ... pretended to be surprised
And sayned hym,° as bi his saghe° the saver° to   **sayned hym** crossed himself   prayer
    worthe,°   safer   become
      with hande.
      Wyth chynne and cheke ful swete,
1205   Bothe whit and red in blande,°   **in blande** together
      Ful lufly con hö lete,°   **lufly** ... graciously she behaved
      Wyth lyppes smal laghande.°   laughing

        xlix
"God moroun, Sir Gawayn," sayde that fayr
    lady,
"Ye are a sleper unslyghe,° that mon° may slyde°   unwary   one   steal
    hider.
1210 Now ar ye tan as-tyt; bot true° uus may schape,°   **tan** ... taken in a moment, unless truce
I schal bynde yow in your bedde, that be ye   be arranged
    trayst."°   sure
Al laghande the lady lanced tho bourdes.°   **lanced** ... uttered those jests
    "God moroun, gay," quoth Gawayn the blythe.°   happy
"Me schal worthe° at your wille, and that me wel   **Me** ... It shall be with me
    lykes;°   pleases
1215 For I yelde me yederly and yeghe° after grace,°   **yederly** ... promptly and cry   mercy
And that is the best, be my dome,° for me   judgment
    byhoves nede."°   **byhoves nede** necessity compells
And thus he bourded° ayayn with mony a blythe   jested
    laghter.
"Bot wolde ye,° lady lovely, then leve me grante   **Bot** ... If you would
And deprece° your prysoun° and pray hym to   release   prisoner
    ryse,
1220 I wolde boghe° of this bed and busk° me better,   go   dress

1197. Result in or mean, as a marvel it seemed to him

I schulde kever° the more comfort to karp° yow   get   speak
    wyth."
   "Nay, for sothe, beau° sir," sayd that swete,   fair
   "Ye schal not rise of your bedde; I rych° yow   intend
    better;
   I schal happe° yow here that other half als,°   wrap   **that . . .** on the other side also
1225 And sythen karp wyth my knyght that I kaght
    have;
   For I wene° wel, i-wysse,° Sir Wowen° ye are,   know   indeed   Gawain
   That alle the worlde worschipes, where-so° ye   **worschipes, where-so** honors, wherever
    ride.
   Your honour, your hendelayk° is hendely praysed   courtesy
   With lordes, wyth ladyes, with alle that lyf bere.
1230 And now ye ar here, i-wysse, and we bot oure
    one.°   **oure one** alone
   My lorde and his ledes ar on lenthe faren,°   **ar . . .** have gone afar
   Other bürnes in her bedde, and my bürdes als,°   **bürdes als** maidens also
   The dor drawen, and dit° with a derf haspe.°   locked   **derf haspe** strong buckle
   And sythen° I have in this hous hym that al lykes,   since
1235 I schal ware° my whyle wel whyl hit lastes,   spend
    with tale.°   speech
     Ye ar welcum to my cors,°   body
     Yowre awen won° to wale;°   will   take
     Me behoves of fyne force°   **fyne force** absolute necessity
1240   Your servaunt be, and schale."°   I shall

l

   "In god fayth," quoth Gawayn, "gayn° hit me   good
    thynkkes,
   Thagh° I be not now he that ye of speken;   Though
   To reche to such reverence as ye reherce° here   relate
   I am wyghe° unworthy, I wot wel myselven.   a person
1245 Bi God, I were glad, and yow god thoght°   **and . . .** if it seemed good to you
   At saghe° other at servyce° that I sette° myght   **At saghe** By word   deed   set myself
   To the pleasaunce° of your prys°—hit were a   pleasure   excellence
    pure joye."
   "In god fayth, Sir Gawayn," quoth the gay lady,
   "The prys and the prowes that pleses al other,
1250 If I hit lakked° other set at lyght, hit were littel   belittled
    daynté.°   courtesy
   Bot hit ar ladyes innoghe that lever wer° nowthe   **that . . .** to whom it might be more
   Haf thee, hende, in hör holde, as I thee habbe   delightful
    here,
   To daly with derely° your daynté wordes,   pleasantly
   Kever° hem comfort and colen° her cares,°   Get   relieve   sorrows

416

1255 Then much of the garysoun° other golde that thay   treasure
        haven.
        Bot I lowe° that ilk° Lorde that the lyfte° haldes,   praise   same   sky
        I haf hit holly° in my honde that al desyres,   wholly
              thurghe grace."
        Schö° made hym so gret chere,°   She   entertainment
1260 That was so fayr of face.
        The knyght with speches skere°   pure
        Answared to üche a cace.°   speech

                           li
        "Madame," quoth the myry° mon, "Mary yow   fair
              yelde,°   reward
        For I haf founden, in god fayth, yowre fraunchis°   liberality
              nobele.
1265 And other° ful much of other folk fongen hör   others
              dedes,°   **fongen** . . . pattern their own actions
        Bot the daynté° that thay delen for my disert   courtesy
              nysen.°   they exaggerate
        Hit is the worschyp° of yourself that noght bot   honor
              wel connes."°   knows how to say
        "Bi Mary," quoth the menskful,° "me thynk hit   honorable lady
              another;°   otherwise
        For were I worth al the wone° of wymmen alyve,   multitude
1270 And al the wele° of the worlde were in my honde,   joy
        And° I schulde chepen° and chose, to cheve° me a   If   bargain   obtain
              lorde,
        For the costes° that I haf knowen upon thee,   manners
              knyght, here,
        Of bewté and debonerté° and blythe semblaunt,°   courtesy   appearance
        And that I haf er herkkened° and halde hit here°   heard of   now
              trewe,
1275 Ther schulde no freke upon folde bifore yow be
              chosen."
        "I-wysse, worthy," quoth the wyghe, "ye haf
              waled° wel better;   taken
        Bot I am proude of the prys° that ye put on me,   esteem
        And soberly, your servaunt, my soverayn I holde
              yow,
        And yowre knyght I becom, and Kryst yow
              foryelde!"°   reward
1280 Thus thay meled° of muchwhat° til mydmorn   spoke   many things
              paste,
        And ay the lady let lyk as° hym loved mych.   **let** . . . behaved as if
        The freke ferde° with defence and feted° ful fayre.   acted   **defence** . . . caution and behaved

"Thagh I were bürde° bryghtest," the bürde in mynde hade,°   maiden   in . . . thought

"The lasse° luf in his lode"°—for lür° that he soght   less   in . . . with him   **for lur** because of

1285   boute hone,°   the disaster   **boute hone** without delay

The dünte° that schulde hym deve,°   blow   stun

And nedes hit most be done.

The lady thenn spek of leve,°   leaving

He graunted hir ful sone.°   at once

lii

1290   Thenne hö gef hym god day, and wyth a glent° laghed,   glance

And as hö stod, hö stonyed° hym wyth ful stor° wordes: astonished   stern

"Now He that spedes° üche spech, this disport yelde° yow!   blesses   **disport yelde** entertainment reward

Bot that ye be Gawan, hit gos in mynde."°   **gos . . .** is debated

"Wherfore?" quoth the freke, and freschly° he askes,   eagerly

1295   Ferde° lest he hade fayled in fourme of his costes.°   Afraid   manners

Bot the bürde° hym blessed, and bi this skyl° sayde: maiden   manner

"So god° as Gawayn gaynly° is halden—   good a man   fittingly

And cortaysye is closed so clene° in hymselven—   fully

Couth° not lyghtly haf lenged° so long wyth a lady   Could   stayed

1300   Bot he had craved a cosse° bi his courtaysye,   kiss

Bi sum towch° of summe tryfle at sum tales° ende."   hint   speech's

Then quoth Wowen,° "I-wysse, worthe° as yow lykes;   Gawain   let it be

I schal kysse at your comaundement, as a knyght falles,°   is fitting for

And fire,° lest he displese yow, so plede hit no more."   further

1305   Hö comes nerre with that, and caches hym in armes,

Loutes° luflych adoun and the leüde kysses.   Bends

Thay comly bykennen° to Kryst ayther° other.   commend   each

Hö dos hir° forth at the dore withouten dyn° more,   **dos hir** goes   sound

And he ryches° hym to ryse and rapes° hym sone,   readies   hastens

1310   Clepes° to his chamberlayn, choses his wede,°   Calls   garments

Boghes forth, when he was boun,° blythely to masse.   ready

And thenne he meved° to his mete° that menskly°   went   meal   duly
     hym keped,°   occupied
And made myry al day til the mone rysed,
     with game.
1315   Was never freke fayrer fonge°   received
     Bitwene two so dyngne° dame,   worthy
     The alder and the yonge;
     Much solace° set thay same.°   delight   together

liii

And ay the lorde of the londe is lent° on his   gone
     gamnes,°   sports
1320 To hunt in holtes° and hethe at hyndes barayne.°   woods   barren
Such a sowme° he ther slowe° bi that the sunne   number   slew
     heldet,°   set
Of dos and of other dere, to deme° were wonder.   tell
Thenne fersly° thay flokked in, folk at the laste,   quickly
And quykly of the quelled° dere a querré° thay   slain   pile
     maked.
1325 The best° boghed therto with bürnes innoghe;°   noblest   many
Gedered the grattest of gres° that ther were,   **grattest . . .** fattest
And didden hem derely° undo as the dede askes.°   neatly   **dede askes** task demands
Serched hem at the asay° summe that ther were,   trial
Two fyngeres° thay fonde of the fowlest° of alle.   fingers thickness   poorest
1330 Sythen thay slyt the slot,° sesed the erber,°   hollow in the breast   first stomach
Schaved° wyth a scharp knyf, and the schyre   Cut it away
     knitten.°   **schyre knitten** tied up the white flesh
Sythen rytte° thay the foure lymmes and rent off   cut
     the hyde;
Then brek thay the balé,° the bales° out token,   belly   bowels
Lystily forlancyng, and lere of the knot.°
1335 Thay gryped to° the gargulun,° and graythely   **gryped to** seized   throat
     departed°   **graythely departed** promptly separated
The wesaunt° fro the wynt-hole, and walt° out   gullet   **wynt-hole . . .** windpipe and flung
     the guttes.
Then scher° thay out the schulderes with her   cut
     scharp knyves,
Haled° hem by a lyttel hole, to have hole° sydes.   Drew   whole
Sithen britned° thay the brest and brayden° hit in   cut   pulled
     twynne.
1340 And eft° at the gargulun bigynes on thenne,   again
Ryves° hit up radly° ryght to the byght,°   Rips   quickly   fork of the legs
Voydes out the avanters,° and verayly therafter   intestines
Alle the rymes° by the rybbes radly thay lance.°   membranes   cut

1334. Skillfully emptying them, and the flesh of the knot of the neck.

So ryde thay off by resoun° bi the rygge° bones,   **ryde . . . they cleared off rightly**   back

1345   Evenden° to the haunche, that henged alle   Down

samen,°   together

And heven hit up al hole° and hewen° hit of   whole   hewed

there;

And that thay neme for° the noumbles° bi nome,°   **neme for** name as   entrails   name

as I trowe,°   believe

bi kynde.°   nature

Bi the byght° al of the thyghes   fork

1350   The lappes° thay lance bihynde;   folds

To hewe hit in two thay hyghes,°   hasten

Bi° the bakbon to unbynde.°   Along   cut open

liv

Bothe the hede and the hals° thay hewen° off   neck   hewed

thenne,

And sythen sunder thay the sydes swyft fro the

chyne,°   backbone

1355   And the corbeles fee° thay kest in a greve.°   **corbeles fee** raven's fee (gristle)   thicket

Thenn thurled° thay ayther° thik side thurgh bi   pierced   each

the rybbe,

And henged thenne ayther bi hoghes° of the   hocks

fourches,°   haunches

Üche freke° for his fee as falles° for to have.   man working   is fitting

Upon a felle° of the fayre best,° fede thay thayr   skin   beast

houndes

1360   Wyth the lyver and the lyghtes,° the lether° of the   lungs   lining

paunches,

And bred bathed in blod blende° ther-amonges.   mixed

Baldely thay blew prys,° bayed thayr rachches;°   **blew prys** sounded the kill   hounds

Sythen fonge° thay her flesche folden° to home,   took   packed

Strakande° ful stoutly mony stif motes.°   Sounding   **stif motes** loud notes

1365   Bi that the daylyght was done, the douthe° was al   company

wonen°   come

Into the comly castel, ther the knyght bides

ful stille,

Wyth blys and bryght fyr bette.°   **fyr bette** fire kindled

The lorde is comen ther-tylle;

1370   When Gawayn wyth hym mette,

Ther was bot wele° at wylle.   joy

lv

Thenne comaunded the lorde in that sale to

samen° alle the meny,°   gather   company

Bothe the ladyes on loghe to lyght° with her bürdes.°   **on** . . . come downstairs / maidens

Bifore alle the folk on the flette,° frekes he beddes°   floor   bids

1375 Verayly his venysoun to fech hym byforne;

And al godly in gomen° Gawayn he called,   sport

Teches hym to° the tayles° of ful tayt° bestes,   **Teches** . . . Shows to him   tally   lively

Schewes hym the schyree grece° schorne upon rybbes.   **schyree grece** white flesh

     "How payes° yow this play? Haf I prys° wonnen?   pleases   praise

1380 Have I thryvandely° thonk thurgh my craft served?"°   heartily / **craft served** skill deserved

     "Ye, i-wysse," quoth that other wyghe. "Here is wayth° fayrest   hunting spoils

That I segh° this seven yere in sesoun of wynter."   saw

     "And al I gif yow, Gawayn," quoth the gome thenne,

"For by acorde of covenaunt ye crave° hit as your awen."   may ask for

1385 "This is soth,"° quoth the segge. "I say yow that ilke;°   true / same

That° I haf worthyly wonnen this wones° wythinne,   That which   dwelling

I-wysse with as god wylle hit worthes to° youres."   **worthes to** becomes

He hasppes° his fayre hals° his armes wythinne,   grasps   neck

And kysses hym as comlyly as he couthe avyse:°   devise

1390 "Tas yow° there my chevicaunce,° I cheved° no more.   **Tas yow** Take   winnings   won

I vowche hit saf fynly,° thagh feler° hit were."   **vowche** . . . would grant it completely / more

     "Hit is god," quoth the god mon.° "Grant mercy° therfore;   **god mon** host / **Grant mercy** Much thanks

Hit may be such, hit is the better, and° ye me breve° wolde   **better, and** better of the two, if / tell

Where ye wan this ilk wele,° bi wytte° of yorselven."   joy   cleverness

1395 "That was not forward,"° quoth he. "Frayst° me no more;   an agreement   Ask

For ye haf tan° that yow tydes; trawe ye° non other   taken   **tydes** . . . is due; be sure

       ye mowe."°   can get

     Thay laghed and made hem blythe

     Wyth lotes° that were to lowe;°   words   praise

1400 To soper thay yede as swythe,°   **as swythe** straightaway

     Wyth dayntés° newe innowe.°   courtesies   many

lvi

And sythen by the chymné° in chamber thay seten.　　*fireplace*

Wyghes the walle° wyn weghed° to hem oft,　　*choice　carried*

And efte° in her bourdyng° thay baythen° in the morn　　*again　jesting　agree*

1405　To fylle the same forwardes that thay byfore maden;

What chaunce so bytydes,° hör chevysaunce° to chaunge,°　　*befalls　winnings　exchange*

What newes° so thay nome,° at naght° when thay metten.　　*new things　took　night*

Thay acorded of the covenauntes byfore the court alle;

The beverage° was broght forth in bourde° at that tyme.　　*drink to seal the bargain　jest*

1410　Thenne thay lovelych leghten° leve at the last,　　*took*

Úche bürne to his bedde busked bylyve.°　　**busked bylyve** *hurried quickly*

Bi that the coke hade crowen and cakled bot thryse,

The lorde was lopen° of his bedde, the leüdes üch one,　　**was lopen** *leaped*

So that the mete and the masse was metely° delyvered;　　*duly*

1415　The douthe dressed° to the wod, er any day sprenged,°　　**douthe dressed** *company repaired*　*broke*

　　to chace.

Hegh° with hunte° and hornes　　*Loudly　huntsman*

Thurgh playnes thay passe in space;°　　*a short while*

Uncoupled,° among tho thornes,　　*Unleashed*

1420　Raches° that ran on race.°　　*Hounds*　**on race** *in haste*

lvii

Sone thay calle of° a quest in a ker° syde,　　*for　marsh*

The hunt rehayted° the houndes that hit fyrst mynged,°　　**hunt rehayted** *huntsman urged*　*noted*

Wylde wordes° hym warp° wyth a wrast° noyce.　　*cries　uttered　loud*

The howndes that hit herde hastid thider swythe,°　　*quickly*

1425　And fellen as fast to the fuyt,° fourty at ones.　　*trail*

Thenne such a glaver ande glam° of gedered rachches°　　**glaver ande glam** *clamor and noise*　*hounds*

Ros that the rocheres° rungen aboute.　　*rocks*

Hunteres hem hardened° with horne and wyth muthe.　　*urged*

Then al in a semblé sweyed° togeder　　**semblé sweyed** *pack rushed*

1430 Bitwene a flosche° in that fryth° and a foo° cragge.	pool wood forbidding
In a knot,° bi a clyffe, at the kerre° syde,	rocky hill marsh
Ther-as° the rogh rocher unrydely° was fallen,	Where ruggedly
Thay ferden° to the fyndyng, and frekes hem after.	**Thay ferden** They (the hounds) went
Thay umbekesten° the knarre° and the knot bothe,	cast about crag
1435 Wyghes, whyl° thay wysten° wel wythinne hem hit were,	until knew
The best° that ther breved° was wyth° the blodhoundes.	beast announced by
Thenne thay beten on the buskes and bede° hym up ryse,	**buskes . . .** bushes and bade
And he unsoundyly out soght segges overthwert.°	
On° the sellokest° swyn swenged° out there.	One of most wonderful rushed
1440 Long sythen fro the sounder° that wight forolde,°	herd **wight forolde** creature grew old
For he was breme° bor alther grattest,°	a fierce **alther grattest** greatest of all
Ful grymme when he gronyed. Thenne greved mony,	
For thre at the fyrst thrast° he thryght° to the erthe,	thrust threw
And sped hym° forth good sped, boute spyt° more.	**sped hym** rushed **good . . .** quickly, without injury
1445 Thise other halowed "Hyghe!" ful hyghe,° and "Hay! Hay!" cryed,	loudly
Haden hornes to mouthe, heterly rechated.°	**heterly rechated** quickly sounded the recall
Mony was the myry mouthe° of men and of houndes	voice
That buskkes° after this bor with bost° and wyth noyse,	hurry outcry
To quelle.°	kill
1450 Ful ofte he bydes° the baye	stands at
And maymes the mute inn melle;°	**mute . . .** pack on all sides
He hurtes of the houndes, and thay	
Ful yomerly° yaule and yelle.	piteously

lviii

Schalkes° to schote at hym schoven to° thenne,	Men **schoven to** pushed forward
1455 Haled° to hym of her arewes,° hitten hym oft.	Loosed arrows
Bot the poyntes payred° at the pyth° that pyght° in his scheldes,°	failed toughness struck flanks
And the barbes of his browen° bite non wolde;	flesh
Thagh the schaven schaft schyndered° in peces,°	splintered pieces
The hede hypped° ayayn, were-so-ever hit hitte.	bounded
1460 Bot when the dyntes° hym dered° of her dryghe° strokes,	blows hurt heavy
Then, braynwod° for bate,° on bürnes he rases,°	frenzied strife rushes

1438. And he dangerously sought out the men athwart his way.

Hurtes hem ful heterly° ther he forth hyghes,° fiercely hastens

And mony arghed° ther-at and on lyte droghen.° grew afraid **on** . . . somewhat drew back

Bot the lorde on a lyght° horce launces° hym after, swift gallops

1465 As bürne bolde upon bent° his bugle he blowes, battlefield

He rechated,° and rode thurgh rones° ful thyk, sounded the recall bushes

Suande° this wylde swyn til the sunne schafted.° Pursuing shone forth

This day wyth this ilk dede° thay dryven on° this task **dryven on** spend in

wyse,° manner

Whyle oure luflych lede lys in his bedde,

1470 Gawayn graythely° at home, in geres° ful ryche properly clothes

of hewe.

 The lady noght foryate,° forgot

 Com to hym to salue;° greet

 Ful erly hö was hym ate

1475 His mode° for to remewe.° mood alter

lix

 Hö commes to the cortyn and at the knyght

 totes.° peeps

Sir Wawen° her welcumed worthy on fyrst, Gawain

And hö hym yeldes ayayn° ful yerne° of hir **yeldes ayayn** replies eagerly

wordes,

Settes hir sofly° by his syde, and swythely° hö gently much

laghes,

1480 And wyth a luflych loke hö layde° hym thyse set forth to

wordes:

"Sir, yif ye be Wawen, wonder me thynkkes,

Wyghe that is so wel wrast° alway to god, disposed

And connes° not of companye° the costes can society

undertake,° **costes undertake** manners understand

And if mon kennes° yow höm to knowe, ye kest° teaches put

höm of your mynde.

1485 Thou has foryeten yederly that° yisterday I taghtte **foryeten** . . . forgotten quickly what

Bi alder truest° token of talk that I cowthe."° **alder truest** truest of all know

 "What is that?" quoth the wyghe. "I-wysse, I

 wot never;

If hit be sothe that ye breve,° the blame is myn declare

awen."

 "Yet I kende° yow of kyssyng," quoth the clere° taught fair one

thenne,

1490 "Where-so countenaunce° is couthe,° quikly to **Where-so countenaunce** Wherever favo[...]

clayme; evident

That bicumes üche a knyght that cortaysy uses."

 "Do way,"° quoth that derf mon, "my dere, **Do way** Cease from

that speche,

424

For that I durst not do, lest I denayed were.
If I were werned,° I were wrang, i-wysse, yif I   refused
   profered."
1495 "Ma fay!"° quoth the meré wyf.° "Ye may not   **Ma fay** My faith   **meré wyf** fair woman
   be werned!
Ye ar stif° innoghe to constrayne wyth strenkthe,   strong
   yif yow lykes,
Yif any were so vilanous that yow devaye°   deny
   wolde."
   "Ye, be God," quoth Gawayn, "good is your
     speche,
Bot threte° is unthryvande,° in thede° ther I lende,°   force unlucky the country live
1500 And üche gift that is geven not with goud wylle.
I am at your comaundement, to kysse when yow
   lykes;
Ye may lach° when yow lyst, and leve° when yow   take leave
   thynkkes,
     in space."°   a short time
   The lady loutes adoun
1505 And comlyly kysses his face.
   Much speche thay ther expoun
   Of druryes greme and grace.°   **druryes** ... love's grief and joy

lx

   "I woled wyt at° yow, wyghe," that worthy   **woled** ... would learn from
     ther sayde,
   "And° yow wrathed° not ther-wyth, what were   If be angry
     the skylle°   reason
1510 That so yong and so yepe° as ye at this tyme,   brisk
So cortayse, so knyghtly, as ye ar knowen oute.°   widely
(And of alle chevalry to chose, the chef thyng
   alosed°   praised
Is the lel layk° of luf, the lettrure° of armes;   **lel layk** faithful game   science
For to telle of this tevelyng° of this trewe   deeds
   knyghtes,
1515 Hit is the tytelet token° and tyxt of her werkkes, **tytelet token** inscribed title
How ledes for her lele° luf hör lyves han auntered,° **her lele** their true have ventured
Endured for her drury dulful stoundes,°   **drury** ... love doleful times
And after venged° with her valour and voyded   avenged themselves
   her care°   sorrow
And broght blysse into boure° with bountees°   bower virtues
   hör awen)
1520 And ye ar knyght comlokest kyd° of your elde,°   **comlokest kyd** comeliest known   age
Your worde and your worschip° walkes aywhere,   honor
And I haf seten by yourself here sere twyes,°   **sere twyes** two separate times

Yet herde I never of your hed° helde no wordes   **of . . .** from you
That ever longed to luf, lasse° no more.   less
1525 And ye, that ar so cortays and coynt° of your   polite
    hetes,°   vows
Oghe to a yonke thynk yern° to schewe   **yonke . . .** young girl eagerly
And teche sum tokenes of treweluf craftes.°   skills
Why! Ar ye lewed,° that alle the los weldes,°   unlearned   **los weldes** renown have
Other elles ye demen° me too dille° your   judge   silly
    dalyaunce° to herken?   conversation
1530   For schame!
    I com hider sengel and sitte
To lerne at° yow sum game;   from
Dos teches° me of your wytte,   **Dos teches** Do teach
Whil my lorde is fro hame."

              lxi

1535 "In goud faythe," quoth Gawayn, "God yow
    foryelde!°   reward
Gret is the gode gle, and gomen° to me huge,   sport
That so worthy as ye wolde wynne° hidere   come
And pyne° yow with so pouer° a mon, as play   trouble   poor
    wyth your knyght
With anyskynnes countenaunce°—hit keveres°   **anyskynnes countenaunce** any kind of
    me ese.   favor   brings
1540 Bot to take the torvayle° to myself to trewluf   travail
    expoun
And towche the temes° of tyxt° and tales of armes   themes   that text
To yow that, I wot wel, weldes° more slyght°   has   skill
Of that art, bi the half, or a hundreth of seche°   such
As I am, other ever schal, in erde ther I leve°—   **in . . .** on earth while I live
1545 Hit were a folé fele-folde,° my fre,° by my   **folé fele-folde** foolishness manifold
    trawthe.°   noble one   word
I wolde yowre wylnyng worche° at my myght,°   **wylnyng worche** will do   power
As I am hyghly bihalden, and evermore wylle
Be servaunt to yourselven, so save me
    Dryghtyn!"°   the Lord
    Thus hym frayned° that fre and fondet° hym   asked   tempted
    ofte,
1550 For to haf wonnen hym to woghe, what-so   **woghe . . .** sin, whatsoever she
    schö° thoght elles.
Bot he defended hym so fayr° that no faut semed,°   graciously   **faut semed** fault appeared
Ne non evel on nawther halve;° nawther thay   side
    wysten°   knew
    bot blysse.
    Thay laghed and layked° longe;   played

1555	At the last schö con hym kysse.°	**con** ... kissed him
	Hir leve fayre con schö fonge,°	**con** ... she took
	And went hir waye, i-wysse.	

lxii

	Then rüthes° hym the renk and ryses to the masse,	bestirs
	And sithen° hör diner was dyght and derely° served.	later **dyght** ... prepared and nobly
1560	The lede with the ladyes layked° alle day,	played
	Bot the lorde over the londes launced° ful ofte,	spurred
	Sues° his uncely° swyn, that swynges° bi the bonkkes	Follows ill-fated rushes
	And bote° the best of his braches° the bakkes in sunder	bit hounds
	Ther he bode in his bay,° tel bawemen hit breken,°	**bode** ... stood at bay overcame
1565	And madee hym, mawgref hed,° for to meve utter,°	**mawgref** ... despite himself **meve utter** move out
	So felle flones° ther flete° when the folk gedered.	**felle flones** many arrows sped
	Bot yet the styffest° to start bi stoundes° he made,	bravest **start** ... flinch at times
	Til at the last he was so mat,° he myght no more renne,	exhausted
	Bot in the hast that he myght, he to a hole wynnes°	goes
1570	Of a rasse,° bi a rokk, ther rennes the boerne.°	bank stream
	He gete the bonk at his bak, bigynes to scrape,°	scrape the ground
	The frothe femed° at his mouth unfayre° bi the wykes,°	foamed horribly corners
	Whettes his whyte tusches.° With hym then irked°	tusks were weary
	Alle the bürnes so bolde that hym by stoden	
1575	To nye° hym on-ferum,° bot neghe° hym non durst	**To nye** Of annoying from afar to approach
	for wothe.°	danger
	He hade hurt so mony byforne	
	That al thought thenne ful lothe°	dangerous
	Be more° wyth his tusches torne	**Be more** To be any more
1580	That breme° was and brayn-wod° bothe.	fierce frenzied

lxiii

	Til the knyght com° hymself, kachande° his blonk,°	came spurring horse
	Sygh° hym byde at the bay, his bürnes bysyde.	Saw
	He lyghtes luflych adoun, leves his corsour,	
	Braydes° out a bryght bront° and bigly forth strydes,	Draws sword

427

1585 Foundes° fast thurgh the forth° ther the felle°   Comes stream fierce one
    bydes.
The wylde was war° of the wyghe with weppen   aware
    in honde,
Hef° hyghly the here,° so hetterly° he fnast,°   Rose bristles fiercely snorted
That fele ferde° for the freke, lest felle° hym the   **fele ferde** many feared befall
    worre.°   worse
The swyn settes hym out on° the segge even,°   **settes** . . . rushes out at straight
1590 That the bürne and the bor were bothe upon
    hepes°   **upon hepes** in heaps
In the wyghtest° of the water. The worre° hade   strongest worst of it
    that other;
For the mon merkkes° hym wel, as thay mette   aims at
    fyrst,
Set sadly° the scharp° in the slot° even,   firmly sharp blade hollow of the breast
Hit hym up to the hült, that the hert schyndered,
1595 And he yarrande° hym yelde,° and yed doun° the   snarling yielded **yed doun** went down
    water   in
       ful tyt.°   quickly
A hundreth houndes hym hent,°   caught
That bremly° con hym bite;   fiercely
Bürnes him broght to bent°   the bank
1600 And dogges to dethe endite.°   **to** . . . put to death

              lxiv
Ther was blawyng of prys° in mony breme°   the kill loud
    horne,
Heghe halowing on highe with hatheles that
    myght.
Brachetes° bayed that best,° as bidden the   Hounds beast
    maysteres,
Of that chargeaunt° chace that were chef huntes.°   difficult huntsmen
1605 Thenne a wyghe that was wys upon° wodcraftes   in
To unlace° this bor lufly bigynnes.   cut up
Fyrst he hewes of his hed and on highe settes,
And sythen° rendes him al roghe° bi the rygge°   then roughly backbone
    after,
Braydes° out the boweles, brennes° höm on glede,°   Pulls broils coals
1610 With bred blent° therwith his braches° rewardes.   **bred blent** bread mixed hounds
Sythen he britnes° out the brawen° in bryght   cuts flesh
    brode scheldes,°   slabs
And has out the hastlettes,° as hightly° bisemes.   entrails fitly
And yet hem halches° al hole the halves togeder,   fastens
And sythen on a stif stange° stoutly hem henges.   pole
1615 Now with this ilk swyn thay swengen° to home.   hurry

The bores hed was borne bifore the bürnes
    selven°   **bürnes selven** very man
That him forferde° in the forthe° thurgh forse of   slew   stream
    his honde
        so stronge.
    Til he segh° Sir Gawayne   saw
1620   In halle hym thoght ful longe,
    He calde, and he com gayn°   **com gayn** came promptly
    His fees ther for to fonge.°   take

lxv

The lorde ful lowde with lote° laghed myry   word
When he seghe Sir Gawayn; with solace° he   delight
    spekes.
1625 The goude ladyes were geten,° and gedered the   brought
    meyny,°   company
He schewes hem the scheldes and schapes° hem   **scheldes . . .** slabs of flesh and gives
    the tale°   tally
Of the largesse° and the lenthe, the lithernes alse,°   size   **lithernes alse** ferocity also
Of the were° of the wylde swyn, in wod° ther he   fight   wood
    fled.
That other knyght ful comly comended his dedes,
1630 And praysed hit as gret prys° that he proved   excellence
    hade;
For suche a brawne° of a best,° the bolde bürne   flesh   beast
    sayde,
Ne such sydes of a swyn segh he never are.°   before
Thenne hondeled thay the hoge hed; the hende
    mon hit praysed,
And let lodly° ther-at, the lorde for to here.°   **let lodly** showed horror   praise
1635 "Now, Gawayn," quoth the god mon, "this
    gomen is your awen
Bi fyn forwarde and faste, faythely° ye knowe,"   **fyn . . .** final agreement and firm, truly
"Hit is sothe," quoth the segge, "and as siker°   surely
    trewe
Alle my get° I schal yow gif agayn,° bi my   booty   in return
    trawthe."°   word
He hent° the hathel aboute the halse° and   took   neck
    hendely hym kysses,
1640 And eftersones° of the same he served hym there.   again
    "Now ar we even," quoth the hathel, "in this
    eventide,
Of alle the covenauntes that we knyt, sythen° I   since
    com hider,
        bi lawe."

The lorde sayde, "Bi Saynt Gile,
1645   Ye ar the best that I knowe.
Ye ben° ryche in a whyle,   will be
Such chaffer and° ye drowe!"°   **chaffer and** trade if   carry on

lxvi

Thenne thay teldet° tables trestes alofte,°   erected **trestes alofte** on trestles
Kesten° clothes upon. Clere° lyght thenne   Put   Bright
1650 Wakned° bi woghes;° waxen torches   Shone   walls
Segges sette, and served in sale° al aboute.   the hall
Much glam° and gle glent° up ther-inne   merry noise   sprang
Aboute the fyre upon flet° and on fele wyse,°   **upon flet** in the hall   ways
At the soper and after, mony athel° songes,   splendid
1655 As coundutes° of Krystmasse and caroles newe,   songs
With alle the manerly merthe that mon may of
telle,
And ever oure luflych knyght the lady bisyde.
Such semblaunt° to that segge semly hö made,   manner
Wyth stille, stollen° countenaunce, that stalworth   **stille, stollen** secret, stealthy
to plese,
1660 That al forwondered° was the wyghe, and wroth   astonished
with hymselven;
Bot he nolde° not for his nurture nurne hir   would
ayaynes,°   **nurne** ... refuse her
Bot dalt with hir al in daynté,° how-se-ever the   courtesy
dede turned
to-wrast.°   amiss
When thay hade played in halle
1665 As longe as hör wylle höm last,
To chambre he° con hym calle,   he (the lord of the castle)
And to the chemné° thay past.°   fireplace   passed

lxvii

Ande ther thay dronken and dalten, and demed°   **dalten** ... spoke, and decided
eft newe°   **eft newe** once again
To norne on° the same note° on Newe Yeres   **norne on** propose   fashion
even;
1670 Bot the knyght craved leve to kayre° on the morn,   go
For hit was negh at° the terme that he to schulde.°   **negh at** near   **to schulde** must go
The lorde hym letted° of that, to lenge° hym   deterred   stay
resteyed,°   bade
And sayde: "As I am trewe segge, I siker° my   assure
trawthe°   word
Thou schal cheve° to the grene chapel, thy   come
charres° to make,   affairs

1675 Leude, on New Yeres lyght,° longe bifore pryme.°	dawn prime (6:00–9:00 A.M.)
For-thy, thow lye in thy loft,° and lach thyn ese,	room
And I schal hunt in this holt and halde° the towches,°	**holt . . .** wood and keep terms
Chaunge° wyth thee chevicaunce,° bi that I charre° hider;	Exchange winnings return
For I haf fraysted° thee twys,° and faythful I fynde thee.	tried twice
1680 Now 'Thrid° tyme, throwe° best,' thenk on the morne;	Third prove
Make we mery whyl we may, and mynne° upon joye,	think
For the lür° may mon lach when-so° mon lykes."	**the lür** sorrow **lach when-so** get whenever
This was graythely° graunted, and Gawayn is lenged.°	speedily **is lenged** stayed
Blithe° broght was hym drynk, and thay to bedde yeden°	Happily went
1685 with light.	
Sir Gawayn lis and slepes	
Ful stille and softe al night,	
The lorde that his craftes° kepes,	affairs
Ful erly he was dight.°	ready

lxviii

1690 After messe° a morsel he and his men token;	mass
Miry° was the mornyng, his mounture° he askes.	Fair mount
Alle the hatheles that on horse schulde helden° hym after	go
Were boun busked° on hör blonkkes,° bifore the halle yates.°	**boun busked** already dressed horses gates
Ferly° fayre was the folde,° for the forst clenged,°	Wondrously ground **forst clenged** frost clung to it
1695 In rede rudede° upon rak° rises the sunne	**rede rudede** redness fiery cloud drift
And ful clere costes° the clowdes of the welkyn.	**clere costes** brightly passes above
Hunteres unhardeled° bi a holt° syde;	unleashed hounds wood
Rocheres roungen bi rys,° for rürde° of her hornes.	**Rocheres . . .** Rocks rang in woods noise
Summe fel in° the fute° ther the fox bade°—	**fel in** hit on track waited
1700 Trayles ofte a traveres°—bi traunt° of her wyles.	**a traveres** crisscross the skill
A kenet° kryes therof, the hunt° on hym calles;	small hound huntsman
His felawes fallen hym to, that fnasted° ful thike,	panted
Runnen forth in a rabel in his ryght fare.°	track
And he fyskes° hem byfore; thay founden hym sone,	rushes
1705 And when thay seghe° hym wyth syght, thay sued° hym fast,	saw followed

431

Wreghande° hym ful weterly° wyth a wroth°
noyse.

And he trantes and tornayees° thurgh mony tene
greve,°

Havilounes and herkenes° bi hegges ful ofte.

At the last bi a littel dich he lepes over a spenné,°

1710 Steles out ful stilly° bi a strothe rande,°

Went haf wylt° of the wode with wyles·fro the
houndes.

Thenne was he went,° er he wyst, to a wale
tryster,°

Ther thre thro° at a thrich thrat° hym at ones,
al graye.

1715   He blenched° ayayn bilyve°

And stifly start onstray.°

With alle the wo on lyve°

To the wod he went away.

lxix

  Thenne was hit list° upon lif to lythen° the
houndes,

1720 When alle the mute° hade hym met, menged°
togeder.

Suche a sorwe° at that syght thay sette on his
hede

As° alle the clamberande° clyffes hade clatered°
on hepes.

Here he was halawed when hatheles hym
metten,

Loude he was yayned° with yarande° speche.

1725 Ther he was threted° and ofte thef called,

And ay the titleres° at his tayl, that tary he ne
myght.

Ofte he was runnen at when he out rayked,°

And ofte reled° in ayayn, so Reniarde was wylé.°

And ye,° he lad hem bi lag-mon,° the lorde and
his meyny,°

1730 On this maner bi the mountes, whyle mid-over-
under°

Whyle the hende knyght at home holsumly
slepes

Withinne the comly cortynes, on the colde
morne.

Bot the lady for luf let° not to slepe,

Ne the purpose to payre,° that pyght° in hir hert,

Reviling	clearly	angry

trantes ... dodges and doubles

tene greve rough thickets

Havilounes ... Doubles back and listens

thorn hedge

quietly   **strothe rande** wood side

Went ... Thought to have escaped

gone

wale tryster choice hunting station

fierce ones   **thrich thrat** rush attacked

drew back   quickly

aside

earth

joy   hear

pack   mingled

imprecation

As if   clustering   clattered down

met   snarling

threatened

hounds

out rayked went for the open

turned   wily

indeed   **bi lag-mon** astray (?)

company

mountes ... hills, until midmorning

allowed herself

fail   was set

1735	Bot ros hir up radly, rayked hir° theder,	**radly** . . . quickly, went
	In a mery mantyle, mete° to the erthe,	extending
	That was furred ful fyne with felles° wel pured.°	pelts trimmed
	No hewes goud° on hir hede, bot the hagher° stones	**hewes goud** precious decorations well-wrought
	Trased° aboute hir tressour° be twenty in clusteres;	Entwined hairnet
1740	Hir thryven° face and hir throte throwen° al naked,	fair exposed
	Hir brest bare bifore, and bihinde eke.°	also
	Hö comes withinne the chambre dore and closes hit hir after,	
	Wayves° up a wyndow and on the wyghe calles,	Throws
	And radly° thus rehayted° hym with hir riche wordes,	quickly rallied
1745	with chere:°	good cheer
	"A! mon, how may thou slepe?	
	This morning is so clere."	
	He was in drowping° depe,	drowsing
	Bot thenne he con hir here.°	**con** . . . heard her

lxx

1750	In dregh° droupyng of dreme draveled° that noble,	heavy muttered
	As mon that was in mournyng of mony thro° thoghtes,	heavy
	How that destiné schulde that day dele hym his wyrde°	fate
	At the grene chapel, when he the gome metes	
	And bihoves° his buffet abide° withoute debate° more;	must suffer defense
1755	Bot when-that comly° he kevered° his wyttes,	fittingly recovered
	Swenges° out of the swevenes and swares° with hast.	He hastens **swevenes** . . . dreams and answers
	The lady luflych com, laghande swete,	
	Felle° over his fayre face, and fetly° hym kyssed.	Bent gracefully
	He welcumes hir worthily with a wale chere.°	**wale chere** fair cheer
1760	He segh hir so glorious and gayly atyred,	
	So fautles of hir fetures and of so fyne hewes,	
	Wight wallande° joye warmed his hert.	**Wight wallande** Ardently welling up
	With smothe smylyng and smolt° thay smeten° into merthe,	gentle fell
	That al was blis and bonchef° that breke hem bitwene,	happiness
1765	and wynne.°	joy

Thay lanced° wordes gode,   **uttered**
Much wele then was ther-inne;
Gret perile bitwene hem stod,
Nif Maré° of hir knyght mynne.°   **Nif Maré** If not Mary   may be mindful

lxxi

1770   For that prynces of pris depresed° hym so   **prynces** ... noble princess importuned
      thikke,°   hard
    Nurned° hym so neghe° the thred,° that nede   Urged   near   limit
      hym bihoved
    Other° lach ther hir luf other lodly° refuse.   Either   **other lodly** or offensively
    He cared° for his cortaysye, lest crathayn° he were,   feared   villain
    And more for his meschef,° yif he schulde make   evil plight
      synne
1775   And be traytor to that tolke° that that telde aght.°   lord   **telde aght** house owned
      "God schylde,"° quoth the schalk.° "That schal   forbid   man
      not befalle!"
    With luf-laghyng° a lyt° he layd hym bysyde°   loving laugh   little   **layd** ... parried
    Alle the speches of specialté° that sprange of her   partiality
      mouthe.
      Quoth that bürde to the bürne: "Blame ye
      disserve,
1780   Yif ye luf not that lyf° that ye lye nexte,   person
    Bifore alle the wyghes in the worlde wounded in
      hert;
    Bot if° ye haf a lemman,° a lever,° that yow lykes   Unless   sweetheart   dearer one
      better,
    And folden° fayth to that fre, festned so harde   plighted
    That yow lausen ne lyst,° and that I leve° nouthe.   wish   believe
1785   And that ye telle me that, now trewly I pray yow.
    For alle the lufes upon lyve, layne° not the sothe   **upon** ... alive, hide
      for gile."°   guile
      The knyght sayde, "Be Sayn Jon,"
      And smethely° con he smyle,   gently
1790   "In fayth I welde right non,°   **welde** ... have none at all
      Ne non wil welde the while."°   **the while** at present

lxxii

      "That is a worde," quoth that wyght,° "that   person
      worst is of alle;
    Bot I am swared forsothe,° that sore° me   **swared forsothe** answered truly   painful
      thinkkes.
    Kysse me now comly, and I schal cach hethen;°   **cach hethen** go hence
1795   I may but mourne upon molde,° as may° that   earth   maiden
      much lovyes."

Sykande° hö sweghe° doun and semly hym   Sighing stooped
    kyssed,
And sithen hö severes° hym fro, and says as hö   parts
    stondes:
"Now, dere, at this departyng, do me this ese,°   comfort
Gif me sumwhat of thy gifte, thi glove if hit were,
1800 That I may mynne° on thee, mon, my mournyng   think
    to lassen."°   lessen
    "Now i-wysse,"° quoth that wyghe, "I wolde I   indeed
    hade here
The levest° thing for thy luf that I in londe   dearest
    welde;°   have
For ye haf deserved, forsothe, sellyly° ofte   very
More rewarde bi resoun° then I reche° myght;   rights offer
1805 Bot to dele° yow for drurye,° that dawed° bot   give **for drurye** a token for love   would
    neked.°   avail little
Hit is not your honour to haf at this tyme
A glove for a garysoun° of Gawaynes giftes;   warrant
And I am here on an erande in erdes uncouthe,°   **erdes uncouthe** lands unknown
And have no men wyth no males° with menskful°   bags valuable
    thinges.
1810 That mislykes° me, ladé,° for your luf at this tyme;   displeases lady
Iche tolke mon° do as he is tan, tas to° non ille   **Iche** ... Each man must **tan** ... placed,
    ne pine."°   take it as **ne pine** nor grief
    "Nay, hende of hyghe honours,"
    Quoth that lufsum under lyne,°   **lufsum** ... lovely linen-clad lady
1815   "Thagh I hade noght of youres,
    Yet schulde ye have of myne."

lxxiii

Hö raght° hym a riche rynk° of red golde   offered ring
    werkes,
Wyth a starande° ston stondande alofte,   shining
That bere° blusschande bemes as the bryght sunne.   cast
1820 Wyt° ye wel, hit was worth wele° ful hoge,°   Know wealth huge
Bot the renk hit renayed,° and redyly he sayde,   refused
"I wil no giftes for gode,° my gay,° at this tyme;   my own fair lady
I haf none yow to norne,° ne noght wyl I take."   offer
Hö bede° hit hym ful bysily,° and he hir bode   offered eagerly
    wernes,°   **bode wernes** offer refuses
1825 And swere swyfte by his sothe° that he hit sese   word
    nolde;°   **sese nolde** would not take
And hö sore° that he forsoke,° and sayde ther-after,   grieved refused
"If ye renay my rynk, too ryche° for hit semes,   costly
Ye wolde not so hyghly halden° be to me,   **hyghly halden** greatly beholden

I schal gif yow my girdel, that gaynes° yow lasse."   profits

1830 Hö laght° a lace lyghtly that leke umbe° hir sydes,   grasped   **leke umbe** was fastened around

Knit° upon hir kyrtel,° under the clere° mantyle;   Knotted   gown   bright

Gered° hit was with grene sylke, and with golde schaped,   Made

Noght bot arounde brayden, beten° with fyngres;   **arounde . . .** embroidered all around, decorated

And that hö bede° to the bürne,° and blythely bisoght,   offered   man

1835 Thagh hit unworthi were, that he hit take wolde.

And he nay that he nolde neghe in no wyse°

Nauther golde ne garysoun,° er God hym grace sende   **Nauther . . .** Either gold or treasure

To acheve to the chaunce° that he hade chosen° there.   adventure   undertaken

"And ther-fore, I pray yow, displese yow noght,

1840 And lettes be° your bisinesse,° for I baythe° hit yow never   **lettes be** cease from   beseeching   will consent

    to graunte.

  I am derely° to yow biholde   deeply

  Bicause of your sembleaunt,°   manner

  And ever in hot and colde

1845   To be your trewe servaunt."

      lxxiv

"Now forsake° ye this silke," sayde the bürde thenne,   refuse

"For hit is symple in hitself, and so hit wel semes?

Lo! So hit is littel, and lasse hit is worthy;°   valuable

Bot who-so° knew the costes° that knit ar ther-inne,   whosoever   qualities

1850 He wolde hit prayse at more prys, paraventure;°   **prys, paraventure** excellence, perhaps

For what gome so is gorde° with this grene lace,   girt

While he hit hade hemely halched° aboute,   **hemely halched** neatly looped

Ther is no hathel° under heven to-hewe° hym that myght;   man   cut down

For he myght not be slayn for slyght° upon erthe."   **for slyght** by any means

1855   Then kest° the knyght, and hit come to his hert,   considered

Hit were a juel for the jöpardé that hym jugged° were,   adjudged

When he acheved to the chapel, his chek° for to fech;°   fortune   get

Myght he haf slypped° to be unslayn, the sleght were noble.   escaped

---

1836. And he said that he would not (literally, 'denied that he would') in any way touch

Thenne he thulged° with hir threpe, and tholed°   was patient   **threpe** . . . argument, and
     hir to speke,   suffered

1860   And hö bere on hym the belt and bede° hit hym   offered
     swythe°—   earnestly

And he granted°—and hym gafe with a goud   agreed
     wylle,

And bisoght hym, for hir sake, discever° hit never,   reveal

Bot to lelly layne° fro hir lorde; the leüde hym   **lelly layne** loyally hide (it)
     acordes°   **hym acordes** agrees

That never wyghe° schulde hit wyt, i-wysse, bot   anyone
     thay twayne,°   two

1865   for noghte.

He thonkked hir oft ful swythe,

Ful thro° with hert and thoght.   heartily

Bi-that, on thrynne sythe°   **thrynne sythe** three times

Hö has kyst the knyght so toght.°   strong

lxxv

1870   Thenne lachches hö hir leve and leves hym
     there,

For more myrthe of that mon moght hö not gete;

When hö was gon, Sir Gawayn geres° hym sone,   dresses

Rises and riches° hym in araye noble,   dresses

Lays up° the luf-lace the lady hym raght,°   **Lays up** Puts away   gave

1875   Hid hit ful holdely,° ther he hit eft fonde.°   carefully   might find

Sythen chevely° to the chapel choses° he the   quickly   takes
     waye,

Prevely° aprochéd to a prest, and prayed hym   Privately
     there

That he wolde lyfte° his lyf and lern hym better   lift up

How his sawle schulde be saved when he schuld
     seye hethen.°   **seye hethen** go hence

1880   There he schrof hym schyrly° and schewed his   fully
     misdedes

Of the more° and the mynne,° and merci beseches,   greater   less

And of absolucioun he on the segge° calles;   priest

And he asoyled° hym surely and sette hym so   absolved
     clene°   pure

As° Domesday schulde haf ben dight° on the   As if   appointed
     morn.

1885   And sythen he mace° hym as mery among the   makes
     fre ladyes,

With comlych° caroles and alle kynnes° joye,   sweet   kinds of

As never he did bot that daye, to the derk nyght,
     with blys.

1890

Üche mon hade daynté° thare — courtesy
Of° hym, and sayde, "I-wysse, — From
Thus myry he was never are,° — before
Syn he com hider, er this."

lxxvi

Now hym lenge° in that lee,° ther luf hym bityde!° — **hym lenge** may he stay   shelter / may befall
Yet is the lorde on the launde,° ledande his gomnes.° — field / sports

1895

He has forfaren° this fox that he folghed° longe. — slain   followed
As he sprent over a spenné,° to spye the schrewe,° — thorn hedge   villain
Ther as° he herd the howndes that hasted° hym swythe,° — **Ther as** Where   pressed / quickly
Renaud com richchande° thurgh a roghe greve,° — running   **roghe greve** rough thicket
And alle the rabel in a res,° ryght at his heles. — rush

1900

The wyghe was war° of the wylde° and warly abides° — aware   creature / waits
And braydes° out the bryght bronde° and at the best castes.° — pulls   sword / thrusts
And he schunt for° the scharp and sculde° haf arered;° — **schunt for** swerved from   would / retreated
A rach rapes° hym to, ryght er he myght,° — **rach rapes** hound rushes   could retreat
And ryght bifore the hors fete thay fel on hym alle

1905

And woried me[5] this wyly° wyth a wroth° noyse. — wily one   angry
The lorde lyghtes bilyve and laches° hym sone, — **lyghtes . . .** alights quickly and seizes
Rased° hym ful radly° out of the rach mouthes, — Snatched   quickly
Haldes heghe over his hede, halowes° faste, — halloes
And ther bayen hym mony brath° houndes; — fierce

1910

Huntes° hyghed hem theder, with hornes ful mony, — Huntsmen
Ay rechatande aryght° til thay the renk seghen; — **rechatande aryght** sounding the recall properly
Bi-that° was comen his compeyny noble, — When
Alle that ever ber bugle blowed at ones,
And alle thise other halowed, that hade no hornes;

1915

Hit was the myriest mute° that ever men herde, — baying
The rich rürd° that ther was raysed for Renaude° saule — noise   Reynard's
      with lote;° — cries
Hör houndes thay ther rewarde,
Her hedes thay fawne and frote,° — **fawne . . .** fondle and stroke

1920

And sythen thay tan° Reynarde — take
And tyrven° off his cote. — strip

[5] Here *me* is the ethic dative of *I* and must be omitted in translation; see also lines 1932, 2014, 2144, and 2459.

lxxvii

And thenne thay helden to° home, for hit was   **helden to** went
    niegh nyght,
Strakande° ful stoutly in hör store° hornes.   Sounding mighty
The lorde is lyght° at the laste at hys lef° home,   **is lyght** alighted dear
1925   Fyndes fire upon flet,° the freke ther byside,   **upon flet** in the hall
Sir Gawayn the gode that glad was withalle;
Among the ladies for luf he ladde° much joye.   had
He were° a bleaunt° of blewe that bradde° to the   wore mantle reached
    erthe;
His surkot semed° hym wel, that softe was   suited
    forred,°   furred
1930   And his hode of that ilke° henged on his schulder;   same material
Blande° al of blaunner° were bothe al aboute.   Decorated white fur
    He metes me this god mon inmyddes the
       flore,
And al with gomen° he hym gret,° and goudly he   sport greeted
    sayde,
"I schal fylle upon fyrst° oure forwardes nouthe,°   **fylle** . . . fulfill first of all **forwardes**
       nouthe agreements now
1935   That we spedly han spoken° ther spared was no   spoken of
    drynk."
Then acoles° he the knyght, and kysses hym   embraces
    thryes
As saverly and sadly as he hem sette couthe.°
    "Bi Kryst," quoth that other knyght, "ye cach
    much sele°   luck
In chevisaunce of° this chaffer,° yif ye hade goud   **chevisaunce of** winning from trade
    chepes."°   bargains
1940   "Ye, of the chepe no charg,"° quoth chefly° that   importance quickly
    other,
"As is pertly° payed the chepes that I aghte."°   plainly owed
    "Mary," quoth that other mon, "myn is
    bihynde,°   lesser
For I haf hunted al this day, and noght haf I geten
Bot this foule fox felle°—the fende° haf the   skin fiend
    godes!°—   goods
1945   And that is ful pore for to pay for suche prys°   excellent
    thinges
As ye haf thryght° me here thro, suche thre cosses°   thrust kisses
    so gode."
       "Inogh," quoth Sir Gawayn,
       "I thonk yow, bi the rode,"°   cross
1950   And how the fox was slayn
       He tolde hym as thay stode.

1937. As pleasantly and firmly as he could place them.

lxxviii

With merthe and mynstralsye, wyth metes at hör
    wylle,
Thay maden as mery as any men moghten—
With laghyng of ladies, with lotes° of bordes,°   words jests
1955 Gawayn and the gode mon so glad were thay
    bothe—
Bot if° the douthe° had doted other° dronken ben   Unless company or
    other.°   else
Bothe the mon and the meyny° maden mony   company
    japes,°   jests
Til the sesoun° was seghen° that thay sever   time come
    moste;°   **sever moste** must part
Bürnes to hör bedde behoved° at the laste.   must go
1960   Thenne loghly° his leve at the lorde fyrst   humbly
Fochches° this fre mon, and fayre he hym   Takes
    thonkkes:
"Of such a selly° sojorne as I haf hade here,   marvelous
Your honour at this hyghe fest, the hyghe kyng
    yow yelde!°   reward
I yef yow me° for on of youres, if yowreself   **yef ...** surrender myself to you
    lykes—
1965 For I mot° nedes, as ye wot, meve to-morne—   must
And° ye me take° sum tolke,° to teche, as ye   If give man
    hyght,°   promised
The gate° to the grene chapel, as God wyl me   way
    suffer
To dele° on New Yeres day the dome° of my   perform doom
    wyrdes."°   fate
    "In god faythe," quoth the god mon, "wyth a
    goud wylle,
1970 Al that ever I yow hyght, halde schal I redé."°   ready
Ther asyngnes he a servaunt to sett hym in the
    waye
And coundue° hym by the downes, that he no   conduct
    drechch° had,   trouble
For to ferk° thurgh the fryth° and fare at the   go wood
    gaynest°   **at ...** most directly
    bi greve.°   thicket
1975   The lorde, Gawayn con thonk,°   **con thonk** thanked
Such worchip° he wolde hym weve;°   honor offer
Then at tho ladyes wlonk°   lovely
The knyght has tan° his leve.   taken

lxxix

With care° and wyth kyssyng he carppes° hem tille,	sorrow	speaks
1980 And fele thryvande° thonkkes he thrat° höm to have,	hearty	urged
And thay yelden° hym ayayn yeply° that ilk;	return	promptly
Thay bikende° hym to Kryst, with ful colde sykynges.°	commended	**colde sykynges** grievous sighs
Sythen fro the meyny° he menskly° departes;	company	courteously
Üche mon that he mette, he made hem a thonke		
1985 For his servyse and his solace° and his sere pyne°	kindness	**sere pyne** individual trouble
That thay wyth busynes had ben aboute hym to serve;		
And üche segge as sore to sever with hym there		
As° thay hade wonde° worthyly with that wlonk° ever.	As if lived lovely one	
Then with ledes° and lyght he was ladde to his chambre	servants	
1990 And blythely broght to his bedde to be at his rest.		
Yif he ne slepe soundyly, say ne dar I,		
For he hade muche on the morn to mynne,° yif he wolde,	think of	
in thoght.		
Let hym lyghe° there stille,	lie	
1995 He has nere that° he soght.	**nere that** nearby what	
And° ye wyl a whyle be stylle,	If	
I schal telle yow how thay wroght.°	did	

Part IV

lxxx

Now neghes° the New Yere, and the nyght passes,	draws near	
The day dryves° to the derk, as Dryghtyn° biddes.	follows the Lord	
2000 Bot wylde wederes° of the worlde wakned ther-oute,°	weather outside	
Clowdes kesten kenly° the colde to the erthe,	**kesten kenly** cast bitterly	
Wyth nyghe innoghe of the northe, the naked to tene.°	punish	

441

The snawe snitered° ful snart,° that snayped° the wylde;° — shivered down bitterly nipped / wild animals

The werbelande° wynde wapped° fro the hyghe — whistling rushed

2005 And drof üche dale ful of dryftes ful grete.

The leüde lystened ful wel, that legh in his bedde,

Thagh he lowkes° his liddes, ful lyttel he slepes; — closes

Bi üch kok that crewe he knewe wel the steven.° — appointed time

Deliverly° he dressed up er the day sprenged, — Quickly

2010 For there was lyght of a laumpe that lemed° in his chambre. — shone

He called to his chamberlayn, that cofly° hym swared,° — promptly / answered

And bede hym bryng hym his brüny° and his blonk sadel.° — mail shirt / **blonk sadel** horse saddle

That other ferkes° hym up and feches hym his wedes° — gets / clothes

And graythes° me Sir Gawayn upon° a grett wyse.° — clothes in **grett wyse** magnificent manner

2015 Fyrst he clad hym in his clothes, the colde for to were;° — ward off

And sythen his other harnays, that holdely° was keped, — faithfully

Bothe his paunce° and his plates, piked° ful clene,° — stomach armor polished bright

The rynges rokked° of the roust° of his riche brüny;° — cleaned rust / mail shirt

And al was fresch as upon° fyrst, and he was fayn° thenne — at glad

2020   to thonk.° — give thanks

    He hade upon° üche pece, — on him

    Wypped° ful wel and wlonk,° — Wiped beautifully

    The gayest into° Grece. — from here to

    The bürne bede bryng his blonk.

lxxxi

2025 Whyle the wlonkest° wedes he warp° on hymselven— — loveliest put

His cote wyth the conysaunce° of the clere werkes° — badge (pentangle) / **clere werkes** fair embroidery

Ennurned° upon velvet, vertuus° stones, — Set potent

Aboute beten° and bounden, enbrauded° semes, — set embroidered

And fayre furred withinne wyth fayre pelures°— — furs

2030 Yet laft° he not the lace,° the ladies gifte; — left belt

That forgat not Gawayn, for gode of hymselven.

Bi° he hade belted the bronde° upon his balghe haunches,° — When sword / **balghe haunches** smooth hips

Thenn dressed he his drurye° double hym aboute. — love token

442

Swythe swethled umbe° his swange° swetely that knyght   **Swythe...** Quickly wrapped around / waist

1035 The gordel of the grene silke that gay wel bisemed

Upon that ryol,° red clothe that ryche° was to schewe.°   regal splendid / look at

Bot wered not this ilk wyghe° for wele° this gordel,   man wealth

For pryde of the pendauntes, thagh polyst thay were,

And thagh the glyterande golde glent° upon endes,   glinted

1040 Bot for to saven hymself, when suffer hym byhoved,

To byde bale° withoute dabate° of bronde° hym to were°   **byde bale** suffer death defense sword / defend

other knyffe.

Bi-that° the bolde mon boun°   Then ready

Wynnes ther-oute° bilyve;   **Wynnes ther-oute** Goes outside

1045 Alle the meyny of renoun

He thonkkes ofte ful ryve.°   much

lxxxii

Thenne was Gryngolet graythe,° that gret was and huge,   made ready

And hade ben sojourned saverly° and in a siker wyse;°   pleasantly / **siker wyse** sure manner

Hym lyst prik° for poynt,° that proude hors thenne.   **lyst prik** it pleases to gallop good / condition

1050 The wyghe wynnes° hym to, and wytes° on his lyre,°   goes looks / coat

And sayde soberly hymself, and by his soth sweres,°   **by...** on his word swears

"Here is a meyny in this mote° that on menske° thenkkes.   castle courtesy

The mon hem maynteines, joy mot° he have!   may

The leve° lady, on lyve° luf hir bityde!°   dear **on lyve** during life befall

1055 Yif thay for charyté cherysen° a gest,°   cherish guest

And halden honour in her honde, the Hathel° hem yelde°   Lord / reward

That haldes the heven upon hyghe, and also yow alle!

And yif I myght lyf° upon londe° lede any whyle,   life earth

I schuld rech yow sum rewarde redyly, if I myght."

1060 Thenn steppes he into stirop and strydes alofte.

443

His schalk schewed° hym his schelde; on schulder he hit laght,   **schalk schewed** servant brought

Gordes to° Gryngolet with his gilt heles,   **Gordes to** Spurs

And he startes° on the ston, stod he no lenger to praunce;   leaps forward

2065   His hathel° on hors was thenne,   master

That bere his spere and launce.

"This kastel to Kryst I kenne,°   commend

He gef hit ay god chaunce!"°   luck

lxxxiii

The brygge was brayde° doun, and the brode yates°   pulled / gates

2070   Unbarred and born open upon bothe halve.

The bürne blessed hym bilyve, and the bredes° passed;   planks

Prayses the porter, bifore° the prynce kneled,   who before

Gef° hym God and goud day, that Gawayn he save;   And who gave

And went on his way with his wyghe° one   servant

2075   That schulde teche hym to tourne to that tene° place   dangerous

Ther the ruful race° he schulde resayve.°   attack   receive

Thay boghen° bi bonkkes ther boghes° ar bare;   went   boughs

Thay clomben bi clyffes ther clenges the colde.

The heven was up halt,° bot ugly ther-under   **heven . . .** clouds were high

2080   Mist muged° on the mor, malt° on the mountes;   drizzled   melted

Üch hille hade a hatte, a myst-hakel° huge.   cloak of mist

Brokes byled and breke bi bonkkes aboute,

Schyre schaterande° on schores,° ther thay doun schouved.°   **Schyre schaterande** Brightly breaking / banks   rushed

Wela wylle° was the way ther thay bi wod schulden,°   **Wela wylle** Very wild / must go

2085   Til hit was sone sesoun° that the sunne ryses that tyde.°   time / time

Thay were on a hille ful hyghe,

The whyte snaw lay bisyde;

The bürne° that rod hym by   man

2090   Bede° his mayster abide.°   Bade   wait

lxxxiv

"For I haf wonnen° yow hider, wyghe, at this tyme,   brought

And now nar° ye not fer° fro that note° place   are   far   noted

That ye han spied and spüryed° so specially after.   **han . . .** have looked for and asked

Bot I schal say yow forsothe, sythen I yow knowe,

2095 And ye ar a lede upon lyve° that I wel lovy,°   **upon lyve** alive   love

Wolde ye worch° bi my wytte,° ye worthed° the   do   advice   would be
      better.

The place that ye prece° to ful perelous is halden;°   hurry   held

Ther wones a wyghe in that waste, the worst upon
      erthe,

For he is stiffe° and sturne, and to strike lovies.   strong

2100 And more he is then any mon upon myddel-erde,°   earth

And his body bigger then the best fowre

That ar in Arthures hous, Hestor, other other.°   **Hestor** ... Hector, or any other

He cheves° that chaunce° at the chapel grene,   brings about   fortune

Ther passes non bi that place so proude in his armes

2105 That he ne dynges° hym to dethe with dynt° of   **ne dynges** doesn't smite   blow
      his honde;

For he is a mon methles,° and mercy non uses,   immoderate

For be hit chorle other chaplayn that bi the chapel
      rydes,

Monk other masseprest other any mon elles,

Hym thynk as queme° hym to quelle as quyk go°   pleasant   **quyk go** alive to go
      hymselven.

2110 For-thy I say thee, as sothe° as ye in sadel sitte,   sure

Com ye there,° ye be kylled, may the knyght rede,°   **Com** ... If you come   manage it

Trawe° ye me that trewely, thagh ye had twenty   Believe
      lyves
           to spende;

He has wonyd here ful yore,°   long

2115 On bent° much baret bende.°   field   **baret bende** strife has led

Ayayn his dyntes sore

Ye may not yow defende."

lxxxv

"For-thy, goude Sir Gawayn, let the gome one,°   alone

And gos away sum other gate,° upon Goddes   way
      halve.°   sake

2120 Cayres° bi sum other kyth,° ther Kryst mot° yow   Ride   land   may
      spede;°   help

And I schal hygh me hom ayayn and hete° yow   promise
      fyrre°   further

That I schal swere bi God and alle his gode
      halghes,°   saints

As help me God and the halydam° and othes   holy relic (on which oaths were sworn)
      innoghe,

That I schal lelly° yow layne and lance° never tale   faithfully   **layne** ... conceal and utter

2125 That ever ye fondet° to fle for freke that I wyst."°   hastened   knew of

"Grant merci," quoth Gawayn, and gruchyng°   reluctantly
  he sayde,
"Wel worth° thee, wyghe, that woldes° my gode;   be   wished
And, that lelly me layne, I leve° wel thou woldes.°   believe   would
Bot helde thou hit never so holde, and° I here   **holde, and** faithfully, if
  passed,
2130 Founded° for ferde° for to fle, in fourme° that thou   Came   fear   manner
  telles,
I were a knyght kowarde; I myght not be
  excused.
Bot I wyl to the chapel, for chaunce that may
  falle,
And talk wyth that ilk tulk the tale° that me lyste,°   account   pleases
Worthe° hit wele other wo, as the wyrde° lykes   Be   fate
2135   hit hafe.
  Thaghe he be a sturn knape°   man
  To stightel, and stad with stave,°
  Ful wel con Dryghtyn schape°   **con** . . . the Lord arranged
  His servauntes for to save."

    lxxxvi
2140 "Mary!" quoth that other mon, "now thou so
  much spelles°   say
That thou wylt thyn awen nye nyme° to   **nye nyme** harm take
  thyselven,
And thee lyst lese thy lyf, thee lette I ne kepe.°
Haf here thi helme° on thy hede, thi spere in thi   helmet
  honde,
And ryde me doun this ilk rake,° bi yon rokke   path
  syde,
2145 Til you be broght to the bothem° of the brem   bottom
  valay.°   **brem valay** wild valley
Thenne loke a littel on the launde,° on thi lyfte   field
  honde,
And thou schal se in that slade° the self° chapel   valley   very
And the borelych° bürne on bent° that hit kepes.   burly   field
Now fares wel on Godes half,° Gawayn the noble.   sake
2150 For alle the golde upon grounde I nolde° go wyth   wouldn't
  thee
Ne bere thee felawschyp thurgh this fryth° on fote   wood
  fyrre."°   farther
Bi-that° the wyghe in the wod wendes° his brydel,   Then   turns
Hit the hors with the heles as harde as he myght,

2137. To master, and armed with a club
2142. If it pleases you to lose your life, I don't care to hinder you.

Lepes hym over the launde and leves the knyght
    there
2155   al one.°   alone
"Bi Goddes self," quoth Gawayn,
"I wyl nauther grete° ne grone;   weep
To Goddes wylle I am ful bayn,°   obedient
And to hym I haf me tone."°   committed

lxxxvii

2160 Thenne gyrdes° he to Gryngolet and gederes°   puts spurs   follows
      the rake,°   path
Schouves° in bi a schore° at a schawe° syde,   Pushes bank wood
Rides thurgh the roghe bonk ryght to the dale.
And thenne he wayted° hym aboute, and wylde   looked
      hit hym thoght,
And seghe no syngne of resette bisydes° nowhere,   **resette bisydes** shelter around
2165 Bot hyghe bonkkes and brent° upon bothe halve,°   steep sides
And rughe knokled knarres° with knorned°   **knokled knarres** rugged crags gnarled
      stones;
The skewes of° the scowtes skayned,° hym thoght.   **skewes of** skies by **scowtes skayned**
                                      rocks touched
Thenne he hoved° and wytthylde his hors at that   halted
      tyde,°   time
And ofte chaunged his cher° the chapel to seche.°   **chaunged**... looked in different
                                        directions seek
2170 He segh non suche in no syde, and selly° hym   **syde**... direction, and marvelous
      thoght,
Save a lyttel on a launde,° a lawe° as hit were,   field mound
A balgh bergh° bi a bonke, the brymme° bysyde,   **balgh bergh** smooth mound   water's edge
Bi a fors° of a flode that ferked° thare;   waterfall ran
The borne blubred° ther-inne as hit boyled hade.   **borne blubred** stream bubbled
2175 The knyght kaches his caple° and com to the lawe,   **kaches**... spurs his horse
Lightes doun lufyly, and at a lynde taches°   **lynde taches** tree ties
The rayne, and his riche, with° a roghe braunche.   **riche, with** noble steed, to
Thenne he boghes to the berghe, aboute hit he
    walkes,
Debatande with hymself what hit be myght.
2180 Hit hade a hole on the ende and on ayther syde,
And overgrowen with gresse in glodes° aywhere,   patches
And al was holgh° inwith—nobot° an olde cave   hollow nothing but
Or a crevisse of an olde cragge; he couthe° hit   could
      noght deme°   tell
         with spelle.°   word
2185 "We!° Lorde," quoth the gentyle knyght.   Alas
"Whether° this be the grene chapelle?   Can
Here myght aboute mydnyght
The Dele° his matynnes telle."°   Devil recite

lxxxviii

"Now i-wysse," quoth Wowayn,° "wysty° is   Gawain desolate
    here;
2190 This oritore is ugly, with erbes overgrowen.
Wel bisemes the wyghe wruxled° in grene   wrapped
Dele° here his devocioun on the Develes wyse;   Perform
Now I fele hit is the Fende,° in my fyve wyttes,°   Fiend senses
That has stoken° me this steven,° to strye° me   fixed tryst destroy
    here.
2195 This is a chapel of meschaunce—that chekke° hit   misfortune
    bytyde!
Hit is the corsedest kyrk° that ever I com° inne."   **corsedest kyrk** most accursed church
    With heghe helme on his hede, his launce in his   came
      honde,
He romes° up to the roffe of tho rogh wones.   makes his way
Thene herde he of that hyghe hil, in a harde
    roche
2200 Biyonde the broke in a bonk, a wonder breme°   fierce
    noyse.
What! hit clatered in the clyff as hit cleve°   break
    schulde,
As one upon a gryndelston° hade grounden a   grindstone
    sythe.
What! hit wharred and whette° as water at a   **wharred** ... whirred and ground
    mulne.°   mill
What! hit rusched and ronge, rawthe° to here.   **ronge, rawthe** rang, terrible
2205 Thenne "Bi Godde," quoth Gawayn, "that
    gere,° as I trowe,°   apparatus believe
Is ryched at the reverence me, renk, to mete
    bi rote!°
    Let God worche; 'We loo,'°   **worche** ... do His will; to say 'Alas'
    Hit helppes me not a mote.°   bit
2210   My lif thagh I forgoo,
    Drede dos me no lote."°

lxxxix

    Thenne the knyght con calle° ful hyghe,°   **con calle** called loudly
"Who stightles° in this sted, me steven° to holde?   rules **sted** ... place, with me tryst
For now is gode Gawayn goande ryght here.
2215 If any wyghe oght wyl, wynne° hider fast,   **oght** ... wishes anything, come
Other now other never, his nedes° to spede."°   business help
    "Abyde," quoth on on the bonke aboven
      over his hede,

2206. Is being readied out of respect to greet me, a knight, in due manner!
2211. No noise will make me fear.

448

"And thou schal haf al in hast that I thee hyght
    ones."°   **hyght ones** promised once
Yet he rusched on that rürde rapely a throwe,°
2220 And wyth° whettyng awharf,° er he wolde lyght;   for   turned aside
And sythen he keveres° bi a cragge and comes of a   goes
    hole,
Whyrlande out of a wro° wyth a felle° weppen,   nook   fierce
A Denes° ax newe dyght,° the dynt with to yelde,°   Danish   sharpened   repay
With a borelych bytte bende° by the halme,°   **borelych** ... huge blade curved   handle
2225 Fyled° in a fylor,° fowre fote large°—   Sharpened   filing bench   wide
Hit was no lasse, bi that lace° that lemed° ful   thong   gleamed
    bryght—
And the gome in the grene gered as fyrst,°   **gered** ... dressed as at first
Bothe the lyre° and the legges, lokkes and berde,   face
Save that fayre° on his fote he foundes° on the   well   goes
    erthe,
2230 Sette the stele° to the stone° and stalked bysyde.   handle   stony ground
When he wan° to the watter, ther he wade nolde!°   came   wouldn't
He hypped° over on hys ax, and orpedly° strydes,   hopped   boldly
Bremly brothe,° on a bent° that brode was aboute,   **Bremly brothe** Fiercely savage   field
    on snawe.
2235   Sir Gawayn the knyght con mete;°   **con mete** greeted
    He ne lutte hym no thyng lowe.°   **ne** ... didn't bow at all low
    That other sayde, "Now, sir swete,
    Of steven° mon may thee trowe."°   agreement   trust

XC

"Gawayn," quoth that grene gome, "God thee
    mot loke!°   **mot loke** may look after
2240 I-wysse, thou art welcom, wyghe, to my place,
And thou has tymed thi travayl° as trewe mon   journey
    schulde;
And thou knowes the covenauntes kest° uus   made
    bytwene:
At this tyme twelmonyth thou toke that° thee   **toke that** took what
    falled,°   befell
And I schulde at this Newe Yere yeply° thee   quickly
    quyte.°   repay
2245 And we ar in this valay° verayly oure one.°   valley   **oure one** alone
Here are no renkes us to rydde, rele° as us likes.   **rydde, rele** part, reel
Haf° thy helme off thy hede, and haf here thy   Take
    pay;
Busk° no more debate° then I thee bede° thenne   Make   defense   offered
When thou wypped° off my hede at a wap° one."   slashed   blow

2219. Yet he kept on making that noise quickly for a while

2250   "Nay, bi God," quoth Gawayn, "that me gost
          lante,°   **gost lante** a spirit gave
   I schal gruch° thee no grue° for grem° that falles;   begrudge   **no grue** not a bit   harm
   Bot styghtel thee upon° on strok, and I schal   **styghtel . . .** limit yourself to
          stonde stylle
   And warp° thee no wernyng° to worch° as thee   give   resistance   do
        lykes,
            nowhare."
2255   He lened with the nek and lutte°   bowed
     And schewed that schyre° al bare   white flesh
     And lette° as he noght dutte;°   acted   feared
     For drede° he wolde not dare.°   fear   shrink

                     xci
   Then the gome in the grene graythed° hym   readied
          swythe,°   quickly
2260   Gederes up hys grymme tole, Gawayn to smyte.
   With alle the bür° in his body he ber hit on lofte,   strength
   Münt° as maghtyly° as marre° hym he wolde;   Aimed   mightily   destroy
   Hade hit° dryven adoun as dregh° as he atled,°   **Hade hit** If it had   fiercely   intended
   Ther hade ben ded of his dynt that° doghty was   he who
          ever.
2265   Bot Gawayn on that giserne glyfte° hym bysyde,   **giserne glyfte** axe glanced
   As hit com glydande adoun on glode° hym to   ground
          schende,°   destroy
   And schranke a lytel with the schulderes for the
          scharp yrne.
     That other schalk° wyth a schunt° the schene°   man   swerve   blade
          wythhaldes,
   And thenne repreved° he the prynce with mony   reproved
          prowde wordes:
2270   "Thou art not Gawayn," quoth the gome,
          "that is so goud halden,
   That never arghed° for no here° by hylle ne be   quailed   army
          vale,
   And now thou fles° for ferde° er thou fele harmes.   flinch   fear
   Such cowardise of that knyght cowthe I never
          here.
   Nawther fyked° I ne flaghe,° freke, when thou   flinched   fled
          myntest,°   aimed
2275   Ne kest° no kavelacion° in kynges hous Arthor.   made   cavilling
   My hede flagh° to my fote, and yet flagh I never;   flew
   And thou, er any harme hent, arghes° in hert;   **hent, arghes** taken, quail
   Wherefore the better bürne me bürde° be called   **me bürde** I ought to
          therfore."

2280	Quoth Gawayn, "I schunt ones,°	**schunt ones** flinched once
	And so wyl I no more.	
	Bot, thagh° *my* hede falle on the stones,	if
	I con not hit restore!	

xcii

	"Bot busk,° bürne, bi thi fayth, and bryng me to the poynt,	hurry
2285	Dele to me my destiné, and do hit out of honde,	
	For I schal stonde thee a strok, and start no more	
	Til thyn ax have me hitte; haf here my trawthe."°	word
	"Haf at thee thenne," quoth that other, and heves hit alofte,	
	And waytes° as wrothely as he wode° were.	looks mad
2290	He myntes° at hym maghtyly,° bot not the mon ryves,°	aims mightily cuts
	Withhelde heterly° his honde er hit hurt myght.	quickly
	Gawayn graythely° hit bydes and glent° with no membre,	properly flinched
	Bot stode stylle as the ston other a stubbe auther°	**other . . .** or else a stump
	That ratheled° is in roché° grounde with rotes a hundreth.	entwined rocky
2295	Then müryly efte con he mele,° the mon in the grene,	**efte . . .** again he spoke
	"So now thou has thi hert holle,° hitte me bihoves.	**hert holle** courage whole
	Halde thee now the hyghe hode° that Arthur thee raght,°	dignity gave
	And kepe° thy kanel° at this kest,° yif hit kever° may."	save neck blow survive
	Gawayn ful gryndelly° with greme° thenne sayde,	fiercely wrath
2300	"Wy, thresch° on, thou thro° mon; thou thretes too longe.	smite fierce
	I hope° that thi hert arghe wyth° thyn awen selven!"	believe **arghe wyth** quails at
	"Forsothe," quoth that other freke, "so felly° thou spekes,	fiercely
	I wyl no lenger on lyte lette° thin ernde° right nowe."	**on . . .** in delay hinder errand
2305	Thenne tas° he hym strythe° to stryke	takes a stance
	And frounses° bothe lyppe and browe.	wrinkles
	No mervayle thagh hym myslyke°	it displeases
	That hoped of no rescowe.	

451

xciii

He lyftes lyghtly his lome and let° hit doun
fayre   *lome ... weapon and lets*

2310 With the barbe° of the bitte° bi the bare nek;   *edge   blade*
Thagh he homered heterly,° hurt hym no more   **homered heterly** *struck fiercely*
Bot snyrt° hym on that on syde, that severed the
hyde.   *nicked*
The scharp schrank° to the flesche thurgh the
schyre° grece,   **scharp schrank** *sharp blade sank*   *white*
That the schene° blod over his schulderes schot
to the erthe.   *bright*

2315 And when the bürne° segh the blode blenk° on
the snawe,   *man (Gawain)   gleam*
He sprit° forth spenne-fote° more then a spere
lenthe,   *sprang   feet together*
Hent heterly° his helme and on his hed cast,°   **Hent heterly** *Seized quickly   put it*
Schot° with his schulderes his fayre schelde under,   *Slung*
Braydes° out a bryght sworde, and bremely he
spekes—   *Pulls*

2320 Never syn that he was bürne borne of his moder,
Was he never in this worlde wyghe half so
blythe—
"Blynne,° bürne, of thy bür; bede° me no mo;   *Cease*   **bür; bede** *violence; offer*
I haf a stroke in this sted° withoute stryf hent,   *place*
And if thow reches° me any mo,° I redyly schal
quyte°   *give   more*   *repay*

2325 And yelde yederly° ayayn, and therto ye tryst,°   *quickly   be sure*
And foo.°   *fiercely*
Bot on° stroke here me falles,   **Bot on** *Only one*
The covenaunt schop° ryght so,   *appointed*
Fetled° in Arthures halles,   *Arranged*

2330 And therfore, hende, now hoo!"°   *stop*

xciv

The hathel heldet hym fro° and on his ax rested,   **heldet ...** *turned*
Sette the schaft upon schore° and to the scharp°
lened,   *ground   sharp blade*
And loked to the leüde that on the launde yede,°   **launde yede** *field went*
How that doghty dredles dervely° ther stondes,   **dredles dervely** *fearless one boldly*

2335 Armed, ful aghles;° in hert hit hym lykes.   *fearless*
Thenn he meles° müryly wyth a much steven,°   *speaks*   **much steven** *big voice*
And wyth a rynkande rürde° he to the renk
sayde,   **rynkande rürde** *ringing noise*
"Bolde bürne, on this bent° be not so gryndel;°   *field   fierce*
No mon here unmanerly thee mysboden habbes,°   **mysboden habbes** *has mistreated*

2340 Ne kyd° bot as covenaunde°at kynges kort   acted   the covenant
     schaped.°   directed
    I hyght° thee a strok, and thou hit has; halde°   promised   consider
     thee wel payed.
    I relece thee of the remnaunt of ryghtes° alle   duties
     other.
    Yif I deliver° had bene, a boffet, paraunter,°   nimble   **boffet, paraunter** blow, perhaps
    I couthe wrotheloker° haf waret,° to thee haf   **couthe wrotheloker** could more harshly
     wroght anger.°   dealt   **wroght anger** done harm
2345 Fyrst I mansed° thee müryly with a mynt one,°   threatened   **mynt one** feint only
    And rove° thee wyth no rof° sore—with ryght I   ripped   gash
     thee profered
    For the forwarde° that we fest° in the fyrst nyght;   agreement   agreed on
    And thou trystyly° the trawthe° and trewly me   faithfully   promise
     haldes:°   keep
    Al the gayne thow me gef,° as god mon schulde.   gave
2350 That other münt° for the morne, mon, I thee   **other münt** second feint
     profered;
    Thou kyssedes my clere° wyf, the cosses me   fair
     raghtes.°   you returned
    For bothe two here I thee bede° bot two bare   offered
     myntes°   feints
       boute scathe.°   **boute scathe** without harm
    Trewe mon trewe° restore,   **Trewe . . .** A true person must honestly
2355 Thenne thar° mon drede no wathe.°   need   danger
    At the thrid,° thou fayled thore,°   third exchange   there
    And therfor that tappe ta° thee.   **tappe ta** blow take

xcv

    "For hit is my wede that thou weres, that ilke
     woven girdel;
    My owen wyf hit thee weved,° I wot wel   gave
     forsothe.
2360 Now know I wel thy cosses° and thy costes° als   kisses   manners
    And the wowyng° of my wyf; I wroght° hit   wooing   arranged
     myselven.
    I sende hir to asay° thee, and sothly me   test
     thynkkes,
    On the fautlest freke° that ever on fote yede.°   **On . . .** One of the most faultless men went
    As perle bi° the white pese° is of prys° more,   compared to   pea   excellence
2365 So is Gawayn, in god fayth, bi other gay knyghtes.
    Bot here yow lakked a lyttel, sir, and lewté° yow   loyalty
     wonted,
    Bot that was for no wylyde° werke, ne wowyng°   guileful   wooing
     nauther,

Bot for° ye lufed your lyf. The lasse° I yow
 blame!"
That other stif mon in study stod a gret whyle,

2370 So agreved for greme,° he gryed° withinne.
Alle the blode of his brest blende° in his face,
That° al he schrank for schome that° the schalk
 talked.
The forme° worde upon folde that the freke
 meled:°
"Corsed worth° cowarddyse and covetyse
 bothe!

2375 In yow is vylany and vyse that vertue disstryes."°
Thenne he kaght° to the knot, and the kest lawses,°
Brayde brothely° the belt to the bürne selven:°
"Lo! ther the falssyng, foule mot° hit falle!°
For care° of thy knokke, cowardyse me taght

2380 To accorde° me with covetyse,° my kynde° to
 forsake,
That is larges and lewté° that longes° to knyghtes.
Now am I fawty° and falce, and ferde° haf ben
 ever
Of trecherye and untrawthe°—bothe bityde
 sorwe°
 and care!

2385 I biknowe° yow, knyght, here stylle,°
Al fawty is my fare.°
Letes me overtake° your wylle,°
And efte° I schal be ware."°

xcvi

Thenn loghe° that other leüde, and luflyly
 sayde:

2390 "I halde hit hardily hole,° the harme that I hade;
Thou art confessed so clene, beknowen° of thy
 mysses,°
And has the penaunce apert° of the poynt of myn
 egge.°
I halde thee polysed° of that plyght and pured° as
 clene°
As thou hades never forfeted sythen° thou was
 fyrst borne.

2395 And I gif thee, sir, the gurdel that is golde-
 hemmed.
For° hit is grene as my goune, Sir Gawayn, ye
 maye

Glosses (right margin):

- because less
- grief trembled
- rushed
- So that while
- first
- spoke
- **Corsed worth** Cursed be
- destroy
- caught **kest lawses** fastening loosens
- **Brayde brothely** Flung fiercely himself
- **falssyng...** betrayer, evil may befall
- fear
- associate covetousness nature
- **larges...** liberality and loyalty belong
- faulty yet afraid
- faithlessness
- **bothe...** may both have sorrow
- confess to privately
- behavior
- gain good will
- afterward careful
- laughed
- **hardily hole** certainly healed
- absolved
- faults
- evident
- sword
- cleaned **plyght...** offense and purified
- pure
- **forfeted sythen** transgressed since
- Since

454

Thenk upon this ilke threpe° ther thou forth contest
thrynges° hasten
Among prynces of prys,° and this a pure token esteem
Of the chaunce° of the grene chapel, at° adventure   among
chevalrous knyghtes.
2400 And ye schal in this Newe Yer ayayn to my
wones,
And we schyn° revel the remnaunt of this ryche shall
fest° festival
ful bene."° pleasantly
Ther lathed° hym fast° the lorde, invited   earnestly
And sayde: "With my wyf, I wene,° suppose
2405 We schal yow wel acorde,° reconcile
That was your enmy kene."° bold

xcvii

"Nay, forsothe," quoth the segge, and sesed hys
helme
And has° hit off hendely and the hathel takes
thonkkes:
"I haf sojorned sadly.° Sele° yow bytyde, enough   Good luck
2410 And He yelde° hit yow yare° that yarkkes° al **He yelde** May he repay   fully   dispenses
menskes.° dignities
And comaundes° me to that cortays,° your commend   courteous one
comlych fere,° wife
Bothe that on and that other, myn honoured
ladyes,
That thus hör knyght wyth hör kest° han trick
koyntly° bigyled. cunningly
Bot hit is no ferly thagh° a fole madde° **ferly thagh** marvel if   **fole madde** fool
act madly
2415 And thurgh wyles of wymmen be wonen° to brought
sorwe;° sorrow
For so was Adam in erde° with one bigyled, **in erde** actually
And Salamon with fele sere,° and Samson **fele sere** many different ones
eftsones°— besides
Dalyda dalt hym hys wyrde!°—and Davyth fate
ther-after
Was blended° with Barsabe, that much bale deluded
tholed.° **bale tholed** woe suffered
2420 Now° these were wrathed wyth° her wyles, hit Since   **wrathed wyth** undone by
were a wynne° huge gain
To luf höm wel and leve° hem not, a° leüde that believe   for a
couthe.° could
For° thes wer forne° the freest, that folghed° Because   of old   **that folghed** whom
alle the sele,° followed   good luck

455

Exellently° of alle thyse other under heven-ryche°   Preeminently   heaven's kingdom
        that mused,°   were bemused
2425 And alle thay were biwyled°   beguiled
      With wymmen that thay used.
      Thagh I be now bigyled,
      Me think me bürde° be excused!   **me bürde** I ought to

xcviii

      "Bot your gordel," quoth Gawayn, "God yow
        foryelde!°   reward
2430 That wyl I welde° wyth good wylle, not for the   wear
        wynne° golde   pleasant
      Ne the saynt° ne the sylk ne the syde   girdle
        pendaundes,°   **syde pendaundes** long pendants
      For wele° ne for worschyp° ne for the wlonk   costliness   worth
        werkkes,°   **wlonk werkkes** lovely workmanship
      Bot in syngne of my surfet.° I schal se hit ofte   fault
      When I ride in renoun, remorde° to myselven   remorsefully recall
2435 The faut and the fayntyse° of the flesche crabbed,°   frailty   perverse
      How tender° hit is to entyse teches° of fylthe;°   liable **entyse teches** attract stains   evil
      And thus when pryde schal me pryk° for prowes   spur
        of armes,
      The loke to this luf-lace schal lethe° my hert.   humble
      Bot on° I wolde yow pray, displeses° yow never: one thing   **pray, displeses** ask, offend
2440 Syn ye be lorde of the yonde° londe ther I haf   yonder
        lent° inne   stayed
      Wyth yow, wyth worschyp—the Wyghe° hit   Lord
        yow yelde
      That uphaldes the heven and on hygh sittes—
      How norne° ye yowre ryght nome? And thenne   call
        no more?"
      "That schal I telle thee trewly," quoth that other
        thenne.
2445 "Bercilak de Hautdesert I hat° in this londe.   am called
      Thurgh myght of Morgne la Faye, that in my
        hous lenges,
      And koyntyse° of clergye,° bi craftes° wel   cunning   magic   skills
        lerned . . .[6]
      The maystrés° of Merlyn, mony hö has taken;°   arts   acquired
      For hö has dalt drury° ful dere° sum tyme   **dalt drury** made love   pleasant
2450 With that conable° klerk, that knowes alle your   excellent
        knyghtes
        at hame.

[6] A line seems to have been lost by the copyist. In substance, it would be, 'It is possible for me to transform myse[lf] into the invulnerable Green Knight.'

Morgne the Goddes,
Therfore hit is hir name;
Weldes non° so hyghe hawtesse°   **Weldes non** No one has   pride
2455 That hö ne con make ful tame.

xcix

"Hö wayned° me upon this wyse° to your   sent   manner
        wynne° halle,   pleasant
For to assay the surquidré,° yif hit soth were   **assay** . . . test your pride
That rennes° of the grete renoun of the Rounde   **That rennes** What is current
        Table.
Hö wayned me this wonder, your wyttes to
        reve,°   take away
2460 For to haf greved Gaynour and gart° hir to   **Gaynour** . . . Guinevere and made
        dyghe°   die
With glopnyng° of that ilke gome that gostlych   horror
        speked
With his hede in his honde bifore the hyghe
        table.
That is hö that is at home, the auncian° lady.   aged
Hö is even thyn aunt, Arthures half-suster,
2465 The duches° doghter of Tyntagelle, that dere°   duchess's   noble
        Uter after
Hade Arthur upon, that athel° is nowthe.[7]   glorious
Therfore I ethe° thee, hathel, to com to thy   ask
        naunt,°   aunt
Make myry in my hous; my meny thee lovies,
And I wol° thee as wel, wyghe, bi my faythe,   wish
2470 As any gome under God, for thy grete trauthe."°   faithfulness
        And he nikked° hym naye, he nolde° bi no   said   would not
        wayes.
Thay acolen° and kyssen and kennen ayther other° embrace **kennen** . . . commend each other
To the Prynce of Paradise, and parten ryght there
        on coolde.°   cold ground
2475 Gawayn on blonk ful bene°   fair
        To the kynges burgh buskes bolde,
        And the knyght in the enker° grene   bright
        Whiderwarde-so-ever he wolde.

---

[7] Morgan had transformed Bercilak into the Green Knight so that he might thus test the pride of the members of the Round Table, take away their senses (*your* in l. 2459 is plural), and terrify Guinevere. The audience would have known from other romances the reason for the sorceress' spite, namely, that Guinevere had expelled her from court because of a love affair. Morgan is Arthur's half-sister (l. 2464) because their mother was the duchess of Tintagel (l. 2465; Morgan's father was the duke of Tintagel; Arthur's father was Uther Pendragon). Morgan is also Gawain's aunt because his mother was another daughter of the duke and duchess of Tintagel.

457

c

	Wylde wayes in the worlde Wowen° now rydes	Gawain
2480	On Gryngolet, that the grace° hade geten of his lyve.	gift
	Ofte he herbered in house and ofte al ther-oute,°	outside
	And mony aventure in vale, and venquyst° ofte	in ... he had en route, and conquered
	That I ne tyght° at this tyme in tale to remene.°	intend recount
	The hurt was hole that he hade hent° in his nek,	received
2485	And the blykkande° belt he bere theraboute,	shining
	A-belef° as a bauderyk,° bounden bi his syde,	Crosswise baldric
	Loken° under his lyfte arme, the lace,° with a knot,	Tied belt
	In tokenyng he was tane° in tech° of a faute;	taken stain
	And thus he commes to the court, knyght al in sounde.°	safety
2490	Ther wakned° wele in that wone when wyst° the grete°	arose learned / great one
	That gode Gawayn was commen; gayn° hit hym thoght.	good
	The kyng kysses the knyght, and the quene alce,°	also
	And sythen mony syker° knyght that soght hym to haylce,°	trusty / greet
	Of his fare that hym frayned;° and ferlyly° he telles,	asked marvelously
2495	Biknowes° alle the costes° of care° that he hade—	Confesses conditions sorrow
	The chaunce° of the chapel, the chere° of the knyght,	adventure behavior
	The luf of the ladi, the lace° at the last.	belt
	The nirt° in the nek he naked hem schewed,	nick
	That he laght° for his unleuté° at the leüdes hondes	got disloyalty
2500	for blame.	
	He tened° when he schulde telle,	grieved
	He groned for gref and grame.°	shame
	The blod in his face con melle°	con melle rushed
	When he hit schulde schewe, for schame.	

ci

2505	"Lo! lorde," quoth the leüde, and the lace hondeled,	
	"This is the bende° of this blame I bere in my nek,	band
	This is the lathe° and the losse that I laght° have	harm received
	Of cowardise and covetyse° that I haf caght thare.	covetousness
	This is the token of untrawthe that I am tan° inne,	taken
2510	And I mot° nedes hit were° wyle I may last;	must wear

For non may hyden his harme bot unhap ne may hit,°

    unhap . . . that misfortune may befall

For ther hit ones° is tachched, twynne° wil hit never."

    once **tachched, twynne** attached, separate

The kyng comfortes the knyght, and alle the court als

Laghen° loude ther-at, and luflyly acorden°

    Laugh agree

2515 That lordes and ladis that longed° to the Table,

    belonged

Üche burne of the brotherhede, a bauderyk° schulde have,

    baldric

A bende a-belef° hym aboute, of a bryght grene,

    bende a-belef band crosswise

And that, for sake of that segge, in suete° to were.°

    following suit wear

For that was acorded the renoun of the Rounde Table,

2520 And he honoured that hit hade, evermore after,

As hit is breved° in the best boke of romaunce.

    written

Thus in Arthurus day this aunter bitidde;°

    aunter bitidde adventure befell

The Brutus bokes therof beres wyttenesse.

Sythen° Brutus, the bolde bürne, boghed° hider fyrst,

    Since came

2525 After the segge° and the asaute was sesed° at Troye, i-wysse,

    siege ceased

Mony aunteres here biforne

Haf fallen suche er this.

Now that bere° the croun of thorne,

    that bere He that bore

2530 He bryng uus to his blysse! AMEN.

JOHN GOWER

The Lover's Confession

(ca. 1393, East Midland)

Little is known definitely about the life of John Gower (ca. 1330–1408). He was reared in Kent, came of a well-connected family, became active in real estate, probably served in the Court of Chancery, and lived in St. Mary Overeys Priory, at Southwark. He was married, apparently for the first time, in 1398. A friend of Chaucer, he was supported in turn by Richard II and Henry IV.

His major work is a loosely articulated trilogy of poems in three languages. In the period between 1374 and 1378 he wrote first an Anglo-Norman poem, *The Mirror of Man* (*Mirour de l'Omme*, or *Speculum Hominis*), which moves from a general exposition of the virtues and vices to a specific condemnation of his sinful contemporaries. By 1381 he had completed the first version of a Latin poem, *The Voice of the Complainant* (*Vox Clamantis*), which deals with the evils that beset the state. By 1390 he had completed the first version of his English poem *The Lover's Confession* (*Confessio Amantis*), which deals with what he calls "the fatuous passions of lovers." All three works are bound together by Gower's search for the "common good" of mankind, which, he felt, men destroy by a selfish regard for their own "singular profit."

Despite the dominance of this basic theme, *The Lover's Confession* progresses discursively. In the Prologue the Poet laments the failure of rulers, the corruption of churchmen, and the lawlessness of the commons. In Book I, like Chaucer in *The Legend of Good Women*, Gower dreams that he meets the God of Love and the Queen of Love. He is smitten by their dart, learns that he is to fail in love, and submits to the queen's priest, Genius, to whom he confesses.

Genius first warns the Lover against the dangers of the assaults of love through the two senses of sight and hearing; then he embarks on a long series of illustrative stories relating to the Seven Deadly Sins. The story dealing with Pride concludes Book I. Envy is the subject of Book II; Wrath, Book III; Sloth, Book IV; Avarice, Book V; and Gluttony, Book VI. Gower digresses in Book VII to summarize the wisdom that Aristotle imparted to Alexander, emphasizing the five points of governing policy—Truth, Largess, Justice, Pity, and Chastity. In Book VIII he deals with some aspects of the seventh Deadly Sin, Lechery.

The Poet ultimately finds himself relieved of the pains of love and resolutely turns to the pursuit of moral virtue and of that divine love confirmed by charity. Returning then to the theme of the Prologue, he concludes the poem with a prayer for the attainment of peace and unity within his troubled land.

The logic of the work will necessarily seem tenuous to a modern reader. The confessor Genius, who is drawn from Jean de Meun's thirteenth-century *Roman de la Rose*, is the priest of nature's propagative principle. Frequently Gower's Genius shows the Poet how the commission of a sin has impeded love and how the exercise of a corresponding virtue may secure love, but he does not share with his Old French predecessor any great concern about the necessity of fecundity, and he evinces no real interest in the Poet's amatory success. Yet, the difference between the two Geniuses is merely a matter of emphasis and poetic enthusiasm. Jean de Meun's Genius admits that the joys of fleshly love, though essential, are

> . . . fables—vain imaginings—
> No stable facts, but fictions that will fade.
> Dances will reach their end, and dancers fail.

The joys of heavenly love, in contrast, are "everlasting joys, sincere and great"; and "all things" in Heaven are "delightful, permanent, and true." And that is Gower's point, too.

Many of the illustrative tales narrated as examples by Genius may seem to be somewhat irrelevant to the substance of the Lover's confession, but ultimately at least, they are for the most part concerned with the role of heavenly love in human affairs, and Gower clearly considered that only heavenly love could secure human salvation.

Chaucer called his friend the "moral Gower," and both poets certainly must have thought of the term *moral* as a compliment. Gower was, admittedly, a lesser poet than his great contemporary, but his works were held in high esteem for two centuries. Sixty-nine manuscripts of *The Lover's Confession*, in whole or part, are still extant; Caxton printed the work in 1483, and Berthelette printed it twice in the sixteenth century; and it was translated into both Spanish and Portuguese during Gower's lifetime. Shakespeare or perhaps a collaborator borrowed the plot of *Pericles* from it and chose Gower as the speaker of his Prologue.

The combination of a clear, simple narrative style and fluent versification joined to enduringly popular stories may in part explain the longevity of *The Lover's Confession*, but Gower also won the instinctive respect of his medieval audience for his moral earnestness. Chaucer, in comparison, characteristically allows comedy or irony to complicate the tone of his narratives. In this respect it is instructive to compare Gower's treatment of Ovid's tale of Ceyx and Halcyon (*Metamorphoses*, xi.266–748) with Chaucer's adaptation of the same source in his *Book of the Duchess*.

The meter is rhyming couplets; see Introduction, type 5, page 31.

The best edition is *The English Works of John Gower*, ed. G. C. Macaulay, EETS 81, 82 (London, 1900, 1901), appearing also in *The Complete Works of John Gower*, ed. Macaulay (Oxford, 1899–1902), vols. 2 and 3. For modernizations see John Gower, *Confessio Amantis: The Lover's Shrift*, trans. Terence Miller (Harmondsworth, 1963); Eric W. Stockton, *The Major Latin Works of John Gower* (Seattle, 1962); and William Burton Wilson, *A Translation of John Gower's Mirour de l'Omme* (University Microfilms 70–18, 159, Ann Arbor, 1970). For criticism see John H. Fisher, *John Gower: Moral Philosopher and Friend of Chaucer* (New York, 1964). For bibliography see Wells, ch. 15.13; *CBEL*, 1.205–08, 5.129–30.

Prologue

[Lines 1–92]

THE POET

Of hem that writen ous tofore,°	before
The bokes dwelle, and we ther-fore	
Ben tawht° of that was writen tho.°	taught then
For-thi,° good is that we also	Therefore

5	In oure tyme among ous hiere	
	Do wryte of newe som matiere	
	Ensampled° of the olde wise,°	Illustrative manner
	So that it myhte in such a wyse,	
	Whan we ben° dede and elleswhere,	are
10	Beleve° to the worldes ere°	Remain hearing ear
	In tyme comende° after this.	coming
	Bot for men sein, and soth° it is,	**sein** . . . say, and true
	That who that al of wisdom writ°	writes
	It dulleth ofte a mannes wit	
15	To him that schal it aldai rede,	
	For thilke° cause, if that ye rede,°	this approve
	I wolde go the middel weie	
	And wryte a bok betwen the tweie,°	two
	Somwhat of lust,° somwhat of lore,	pleasure
20	That of the lasse or of the more	
	Som man mai lyke of that° I wryte.	**of that** some of what
	And for that fewe men endite°	compose
	In oure Englissh, I thenke° make	intend to
	A bok for King Richardes sake,	
25	To whom belongeth my ligeance	
	With al myn hertes obeissance	
	In al that evere a liege man	
	Unto his king may doon° or can.	do
	So ferforth° I me recomande	far
30	To him which al me may comande,	
	Preyende unto the Hihe Regne°	King
	Which causeth every king to regne	
	That his corone° longe stonde.	crown
	I thenke and have it understonde,	
35	As it bifel upon a tyde°	time
	As thing which scholde tho° betyde,	then
	Under the town of Newe Troye,°	**Newe Troye** London
	Which tok of° Brut[1] his ferste joye,	from
	In Temse° whan it was flowende,	Thames
40	As I by bote cam rowende,	
	So as Fortune hir tyme sette,	
	My liege lord parchaunce I mette.	
	And so befel as I cam nyh°	near
	Out of my bot, whan he me syh,°	saw
45	He bad me come into his barge.	
	And whan I was with him at large,	
	Amonges other thinges seid	

[1] Brutus, according to Geoffrey of Monmouth, was a descendant of Aeneas of Troy and founded New Troy (London), in Britain.

He hath this charge upon me leid
And bad me do my besynesse,
50   That to his hihe worthinesse
Som newe thing I scholde boke,°   record
That he himself it mihte loke°   examine
After the forme of my writynge.
And thus upon his comandynge
55   Myn herte is wel° the more glad   very much
To write so as he me bad.
And eek° my fere° is wel the lasse   also fear
That non envye schal compasse
Withoute a resonable wite°   blame
60   To feyne and blame that I write.
A gentil herte his tunge stilleth
That it malice non distilleth
But preyseth that° is to be preised.   what
But he that hath his word unpeysed°   unweighed
65   And handleth onwrong° everything,   wrongly
I pray unto the Hevene King
Fro suche tunges He me schilde,°   shield
And, natheles,° this world is wilde   nevertheless
Of such jangling;° and what° befalle,   evil talk   whatever
70   My kinges heste° schal nought falle°   command   happen
That° I, in hope to deserve   So that
His thonk, ne schal° his wil observe;   **thonk . . .** thanks, may not
And elles were I nought° excused,   **elles . . .** otherwise I would not be
For that thing may nought be refused
75   What that° a king himselve bit.°   **What that** That asks
For-thi,° the symplesse of my wit   Therefore
I thenke if that it myhte avayle
In his service to travaile,
Though I seknesse have upon honde
80   And longe have had, yit wol° I fonde,°   will try
So as I made my beheste,°   promise
To make a bok after his heste°   command
And write in such a maner wise°   **maner wise** kind of manner
Which may be wisdom to the wise
85   And pley° to hem that lust° to pleye.   amusement   wish
But in proverbe I have herd seye
That who that wel his werk begynneth,
The rather° a good ende he wynneth.   sooner
And thus the prologe of my bok
90   After the world that whilom tok,°   **whilom tok** formerly took place
And eek somdel° after the newe,   **eek somdel** also somewhat
I wol begynne for to newe.°   produce

463

Book I

THE POET MEETS VENUS AND GENIUS

    I may noght strecche up to the hevene
Min hand, ne setten al in evene
This world, which ever is in balance;
It stant° noght in my sufficance°   rests ability
5 So grete thinges to compasse.
But I mot° lete it overpasse   must
And treten upon other thinges.
For-thi,° the stile of my writinges   Therefore
Fro this day forth I thenke change,
10 And speke of thing° is noght so strange,   something that
Which every kinde° hath upon honde,   race
And wherupon the world mot° stonde   must
And hath done sithen° it began   since
And schal whil ther is any man,
15 And that is Love, of which I mene
To trete, as after schal be sene.
In which ther can no man him reule,
For Loves lawe is out of reule,
That of too moche or of too lite.°   little
20 Wellnyh° is every man to wyte,°   Nearly blame
And natheles° ther is no man   nevertheless
In al this world so wys that can
Of Love temper the mesure,
Bot as it falleth in aventure.°   **falleth** . . . happens by chance
25 For wit ne° strengthe may noght helpe,   nor
And he which elles° wolde him yelpe°   otherwise **him yelpe** boast
Is rathest° thrown under fote;   soonest
Ther can no wiht° therof do bote.°   man **do bote** remedy
For yet was nevere such covine°   device
30 That couthe° ordeine a medicine   could
To thing which God in lawe of kinde°   nature
Hath set, for ther may no man finde
The rihte salve of such a sor.
It hath and schal ben° evermor   be
35 That Love is maister wher he wile—
Ther can no lif make other skile°—   reasoning
For wher-as evere him list° to sette,°   it pleases settle
Ther is no myht° which him may lette.°   power stop
Bot what schal fallen° ate laste,   happen
40 The sothe° can no wisdom caste,°   truth forecast

Bot as it falleth upon chance;
For if ther evere was balance
Which of Fortune stant° governed,   remains
I may wel lieve° as I am lerned°   believe   taught
45   That Love hath that balance on honde
Which wol no reson understonde.
For Love is blind and may noght se,
For-thi may no certeineté
Be set upon his jugement;
50   Bot as the whiel aboute went,°   turns
He yifth° his graces° undeserved,   gives   favors
And fro that man which hath him served
Ful ofte he takth aweye his fees
As he that pleieth ate dees;°   **ate dees** at dice
55   And ther-upon what schal befalle
He not,° til that the chance falle,°   knows not   happens
Wher° he schal lese° or he schal winne.   Whether   lose
And thus ful° ofte men beginne,   very
That if thei wisten° what it mente   knew
60   Thei wolde change al here entente.°   **here entente** their purpose
      And for to proven it is so
I am miselven on° of tho°   one   those
Which to this scole am underfonge.°   received
For it is siththe go noght longe,°   **siththe . . .** not long ago
65   As for to speke of this matiere
I may you telle, if ye woll hiere,
A wonder hap° which me befell,   **wonder hap** wondrous chance
That was to me bothe hard and fell,°   cruel
Touchende of° Love and his fortune,   **Touchende of** Touching upon
70   The which me liketh° to commune°   it pleases   share
And pleinly for to telle it oute.
To hem° that ben lovers aboute,°   them   **ben . . .** are busily engaged as lovers
Fro point to point I wol declare
And wryten of my woful care,°   sorrow
75   Mi wofull day, my wofull chance,
Than men mowe° take remembrance   may
Of that° thei schall hierafter rede.   what
For in good feith this wolde I rede,°   advise
That every man ensample° take   example
80   Of wisdom which him is betake,°   entrusted
And that he wot of good aprise°   **wot . . .** knows to be worth teaching
To teche it forth, for such emprise°   courage
Is for to preise. And ther-fore I
Woll wryte and schewe al openly
85   How Love and I togeder mette,

Wherof the world ensample fette°   **ensample fette** get example
Mai after this, whan I am go,°   gone
Of thilke unsely, jolif° wo,   **thilke . . .** this unhappy, merry
Whos reule stant° out of the weie,   stands
90   Now glad, and now gladnesse aweie,
And yet it may° noght be withstonde   can
For oght that men may understonde.
   Upon the point that is befalle
Of love, in which that I am falle,°   fallen
95   I thenke° telle my matiere.   intend to
Now herken, who that wol it hiere,
Of my fortune how that it ferde°   fared
This enderday,° as I forth ferde   past day
To walke, as I you telle may.
100   And that was in the monthe of Maii,
Whan every brid° hath chose his make°   bird   mate
And thenkth° his merthes for to make   intends
Of love that he hath achieved.
Bot so was I no thing relieved,
105   For I was further fro my love
Than erthe is fro the hevene above.
And for to speke of eny sped,°   success
So wiste° I me non other red,°   knew   counsel
Bot as it were a man forfare°   worn out
110   Unto the wode I gan° to fare,   began
Noght for to singe with the briddes,°   birds
For whanne I was the wode amiddes
I fond a swote,° grene pleine,   fair
And ther I gan° my wo compleigne,   did
115   Wisshinge and wepinge al myn one,° **myn one** by myself
For other merthes made I none.
   So hard me was that ilke throwe,°   **ilke throwe** same time
That ofte sithes° overthrowe   **ofte sithes** many times
To grounde I was, withoute breth;
120   And evere I wisshide after deth,
Whanne I out of my peine awok,
And caste up many a pitous lok
Unto the hevene, and seide thus:

THE POET
   "O thou Cupide, O thou Venus,
125   Thou god of love, and thou goddesse,
Wher is pité? Wher is meknesse?
Now doth° me pleinly live or dye,   make
For certes° such a maladie   certainly

As I now have and longe have had,
130 It myhte make a wis man mad,
If that it scholde longe endure.
O Venus, Queene of loves cure,°   care
Thou lif, thou lust,° thou mannes hele,°   pleasure health
Behold my cause and my querele
135 And yif° me som part of thi grace,°   give favor
So that I may finde in this place
If thou be gracious or non!"
    And with that word I sawh anon
The Kyng of Love and Queene bothe.
140 Bot he, that kyng, with yhen° wrothe   eyes
His chiere° aweiward fro me caste,   face
And forth he passede ate laste.
Bot natheles, er he forth wente,
A firy dart me thoghte° he hente°   **me thoghte** it seemed to me took
145 And threw it thurgh min herte rote.°   root
In him fond I non other bote,°   remedy
For lenger list° him noght to dwelle.   it pleased
Bot sche, that is the source and welle
Of wel° or wo that schal betide   joy
150 To hem° that loven, at that tide°   them time
Abod; but, for to tellen hiere,
Sche cast on me no goodly chiere.°   countenance
Thus, natheles,° to me sche seide: nevertheless

        VENUS
"What art thou, sone?" And I abreide°   started
155 Riht as a man doth out of slep,
And therof tok sche riht good kep°   heed
And bad me nothing ben adrad;°   **ben adrad** be afraid
Bot for al that I was noght glad,
For I ne sawh° no cause why.   **ne sawh** did not see
160 And eft° sche asketh, what was I?   again

        THE POET
I seide: "A caitif that lith hiere.
What wolde° ye, my ladi diere?   wish
Schal I ben hol° or elles dye?"   **ben hol** be safe

        VENUS
Sche seide: "Tell thi maladie.
165 What is thy sor of which thou pleignest,°   complain
Ne° hyd it noght, for if thou feignest,   Do not
I can do thee no medicine."

THE POET

"Madame, I am a man of thyne
That in thi court have longe served
170 And aske that° I have deserved—   for what
Som wele° after my longe wo."   joy
And sche began to loure tho°   **loure tho** scowl then

VENUS

And seide: "There is manye of you
Faitours,° and so may be that thou   Dissemblers
175 Art riht such on,° and by feintise°   a one feigning
Seist that thou hast me do° service."   done
And natheles° sche wiste° wel   nevertheless knew
My world° stod on an other whiel   fortune
Withouten any faiterie.°   false pretense
180 Bot algate° of my maladie   in any case
Sche bad me telle and seie hir trowthe.

THE POET

"Madame, if ye wolde have rowthe,"°   pity
Quod I, "than wolde I telle you."

VENUS

"Sey forth," quod sche, "and tell me how,
185 Schew me thi seknesse every del."°   part

THE POET

"Madame, that can I do wel,
Be so° my lif ther-to wol laste."   **Be so** Provided
With that, hir lok on me sche caste

VENUS

And seide, "In aunter if° thou live,   **In** ... If it happen that
190 Mi will is ferst that thou be schrive;°   confessed
And, natheles,° how that it is   nevertheless
I wot° miself, bot for al this   know
Unto my prest, which comth anon,
I woll thou telle it on and on,°   **on** ... one by one
195 Bothe all thi thoght and al thi werk.
O Genius, myn oghne° clerk,   own
Come forth and hier this mannes schrifte,"°   confession
Quod Venus tho.° And I uplifte   then
Min hefd° with that, and gan beholde°   head **gan beholde** beheld
200 The selve° prest, which as sche wolde,   same
Was redy there and sette him doun

To hiere my confessioun.
  This worthi prest, this holy man,
To me spekende thus began

GENIUS

205 And seide, "Benedicité.°   Bless you
My sone, of the felicité
Of Love and ek° of all the wo   also
Thou schalt be schrive of bothe two.
What thou er° this for Loves sake   before
210 Hast felt, let nothing be forsake;°   concealed
Tell pleinliche as it is befalle."
    And with that word I gan° doun falle   did
On knees, and with devocioun
And with full gret contricioun

THE POET

215 I seide thanne: "Dominus,
Min holi fader Genius,
So as thou hast experience
Of Love, for whos reverence
Thou schalt me schriven° at this time,   absolve
220 I prai thee let me noght mistime
Mi schrifte,° for I am destourbed   confession
In al myn herte and so contourbed,°   confused
That I ne may° my wittes gete;°   **ne may** cannot recover
So schal I moche thing foryete.°   forget
225 Bot if thou wolt my schrifte oppose°   question
Fro point to point, thanne I suppose
Ther schal no thing be left behinde.
Bot now my wittes ben so blinde,
That I ne can° miselven teche."   **ne can** cannot
230   Tho° he began anon to preche,   Then
And with his wordes debonaire
He seide to me softe and faire:

GENIUS

"Thi schrifte° to oppose° and hiere,   confession question
My sone, I am assigned hiere
235 By Venus the goddesse above,
Whos prest I am, touchende of° love.   **touchende of** touching upon
Bot natheles for certein skile°   reason
I mot algate°—and nedes° wile—   **mot algate** must always necessarily
Noght only make my spekynges
240 Of Love, bot of other thinges,

That touchen to the cause of Vice.
For that belongeth to th'office
Of prest, whos ordre that I bere,
So that I wol nothing forbere
245 That I the vices on and on°   **on**...one by one
Ne schal thee schewen everychon;°   everyone
Wherof thou myht take evidence
To reule with thi conscience.
Bot of conclusion final
250 Conclude I wol in special
For Love, whos servant I am,
And why the cause is that I cam.
So thenke° I to don bothe two: intend
Ferst that° min ordre longeth° to,   what pertains
255 The vices for to telle a rewe;°   **a rewe** in a row
Bot next, above alle other, schewe
Of Love I wol the propretés,°   characteristics
How that thei stonde by degrés
After the disposicioun
260 Of Venus, whos condicioun
I moste folwe,° as I am holde.°   follow bound
For I with Love am al witholde,°   retained
So that the lasse° I am to wyte,°   less blame
Thogh I ne conne° bot a lyte°   know little
265 Of other thinges that ben° wise;   are
I am noght tawht° in such a wise.   taught
For it is noght my comun us°   use (custom)
To speke of vices and vertus,
Bot al of Love and of his lore,
270 For Venus bokes° of no more   books
Me techen, nowther° text ne glose.° neither **ne glose** nor gloss
Bot for als° moche as I suppose   as
It sit° a prest to be wel thewed,°   suits mannered
And schame it is if he be lewed.°   unlearned
275 Of my presthode after the forme
I wol thi schrifte° so enforme,°   confession instruct
That ate leste thou schalt hiere
The vices, and to thi matiere
Of Love I schal hem° so remene°   them apply
280 That thou schalt knowe what thei mene.° mean
For what a man schal axe or sein°   **axe**...ask or say
Touchende of schrifte,° it mot° be plein. **Touchende**...Touching on confession
               must
It nedeth noght to make it queinte,° cunning
For Trowthe hise wordes wol noght peinte.
285 That° I wole axe of thee for-thi,° What therefore

My sone, it schal be so pleinly,
That thou schalt knowe and understonde
The pointz of schrifte° how that thei stonde." confession

Book IV

[Lines 2701–3180]

GENIUS DESCRIBES SOMNOLENCE[1]

"Toward° the slowe progenie   With regard to
Ther is yit on° of compaignie,   one
And he is cleped° Sompnolence,   called
Which doth to Slouthe° his reverence   Sloth
5   As he which is his Chamberlein,
That many an hundrid time hath lein
To slepe whan he scholde wake.
He hath with Love trewes° take,   truce
That wake who-so° wake wile,   **who-so** whosoever
10 If he mai couche° adown his bile,°   lay   bill
He hath al wowed what° him list,°   **al ...** wooed everything that   pleased
That° ofte he goth to bedde unkist   So that
And seith that for no druerie°   lovemaking
He wol noght leve his sluggardie.
15 For thogh no man it wole allowe,
To slepe lever° than to wowe   rather
Is his manere, and thus on nyhtes
Whan that he seth the lusti knyhtes
Revelen wher these wommen are,
20 Awey he skulketh as an hare,
And goth to bedde and leith him softe,
And of his Slouthe° he dremeth ofte,   Sloth
How that he stiketh in the myr,
And how he sitteth by the fyr
25 And claweth on his bare schanckes,
And how he clymbeth up the banckes
And falleth in the slades° depe.   valleys
Bot thanne who-so° toke kepe°   **who-so** whosoever   care
Whanne he is falle in such a drem,
30 Riht as a schip ayein° the strem   against
He routeth° with a slepi noise   snores
And brustleth° as a monkes froise°   rustles   pancake
Whanne it is throwe into the panne.

---

[1] Somnolence here represents one aspect of the deadly sin of Slothfulness in love.

	And otherwhile sieldewhanne°	seldom
35	That he mai dreme a lusti swevene,°	dream
	Him thenkth° as thogh he were in hevene	**Him thenkth** It seems to him
	And as the world were holi° his.	wholly
	And thanne he spekth of that and this	
	And makth his exposicioun	
40	After the disposicioun	
	Of that° he wolde,° and in such wise°	what might wish manner
	He doth to Love all his service;	
	I not° what thonk he schal deserve!	know not
	Bot, sone, if thou wolt Love serve,	
45	I rede° that thou do noght so."	advise

THE POET

	"Ha, goode fader, certes° no.	certainly
	I hadde levere,° by mi trowthe,°	rather word
	Er° I were set on such a slouthe	Before
	And bere such a slepi snoute,	
50	Bothe yhen° of myn hed were oute.	eyes
	For me were betre° fulli die	**me . . .** I would sooner
	Thanne I of such a slugardie	
	Hadde eny name, God me schilde.²	

. . .

71	"For certes,° fader Genius,	certainly
	Yit unto now it hath be thus,	
	At alle time if it befelle	
	So that I mihte come and dwelle	
75	In place ther° my ladi were,	where
	I was noght slow ne slepi there.	
	For thanne I dar wel undertake°	pledge
	That whanne hir list° on nyhtes wake°	**hir list** it pleased her vigil
	In chambre as to carole and daunce,	
80	Me thenkth° I mai me more avaunce	**Me thenkth** it seems to me
	If I mai gon upon hir hond,°	**gon . . .** submit to her
	Thanne if I wonne a kinges lond.	
	For whanne I mai hire° hand beclippe,°	her embrace
	With such gladnesse I daunce and skippe,	
85	Me thenkth I touche noght the flor,	
	The ro,° which renneth on the mor,°	roe moor
	Is thanne noght so lyht as I.	
	So mow° ye witen° wel for-thi,°	may know therefore
	That, for the time, slep I hate.	
90	And whanne it falleth othergate,°	otherwise
	So that hire like° noght to daunce	**hire like** it pleases her

² Lines 2754-70 have been omitted.

Bot on the dees° to caste chaunce,   dice
Or axe° of love som demaunde,   ask
Or elles that hir list° comaunde   **hir list** it pleases her
95 To rede and here of Troilus
Riht as sche wole, or so or thus,
I am al redi to consente.
And if so is, that I mai hente°   take
Somtime among° a good leisir,°   at opportunity
100 So as I dar of mi desir
I telle a part, but whanne I preie,
Anon sche bidt me go my weie
And seith: 'It is ferr in° the nyht.'   **ferr in** far into
And I swere, 'It is even° liht.'   still
105 Bot as it falleth ate° laste   **falleth ate** happens at
Ther mai no worldes joie laste,
So mot° I nedes° fro hire wende°   must necessarily go
And of my wachche make an ende.
And if sche thanne hiede° toke   heed
110 How pitousliche on hire I loke,
Whan that I schal my leve take,
Hire oghte° of mercy for to slake°   **Hire oghte** She ought lessen
Hire daunger,° which seith ever nay.   **Hire daunger** Her resistance
 "Bot he seith often, 'Have good day,'
115 That loth is for to take his leve.
Ther-fore, while I mai beleve,°   remain
I tarie° forth the nyht along.   delay
For it is noght on me along°   **on** ... owing to me
To slep that I so sone go
120 Til that I mot algate° so,   **mot algate** must in any case
And thanne I bidde° 'God hire se,'   pray
And so down knelende on mi kne
I take leve, and if I schal,
I kisse hire and go forth withal.
125 "And otherwhile, if that I dore,°   dare
Er I come fulli to the dore,
I torne ayein° and feigne a thing   again
As thogh I hadde lost a ring
Or somwhat elles, for I wolde
130 Kisse her eftsones,° if I scholde,   again
Bot selden is that I so spede.°   succeed
And whanne I se that I mot nede
Departen, I departe, and thanne
With al my herte I curse and banne°   denounce
135 That ever slep was mad for yhe.°   eye
For, as me thenkth,° I mihte dryhe°   **me thenkth** it seems to me endure

Withoute slep to waken evere
So that I scholde noght dissevere
Fro hire in whom is al my liht.

140   "And thanne I curse also the nyht
With al the will of mi corage°   heart
And seie: 'Awey thou blake ymage,
Which of thi derke, cloudy face
Makst al the worldes lyht deface

145 And causest unto slep a weie,
By which I mot now gone aweie
Out of mi ladi° compaignie.   lady's
O slepi nyht, I thee defie,
And wolde° that thou leye in presse°   wish   **leye** ... lie down below

150 With Proserpine the goddesse
And with Pluto the helle king.
For til I se the daies spring,
I sette slep noght at a risshe.'°
And with that word I sike° and wisshe   sigh

155 And seie: 'Ha, whi ne were it° day?   **whi** ... would it were
For yit my ladi thanne I may
Beholde, thogh I do no more.'**³**

.   .   .

   "Bot slep—I not° wherof it serveth,   know not
Of which no man his thonk° deserveth   thanks

165 To gete him love in eny place,
Bot is an hindrere of his grace°   favor
And makth him ded as for a throwe,°   short time
Riht as a stok° were overthrowe.   log
And so, mi fader, in this wise°   manner

170 The slepi nyhtes I despise
And evere amiddes of mi tale
I thenke upon the nyhtingale,
Which slepeth noght by weie of kinde°   nature
For love, in bokes as I finde.

175 Thus ate° last I go to bedde   at
And yit min herte lith° to wedde   is disposed
With hire wher as I cam fro;
Thogh I depart, he wol noght so.°   do so
Ther is no lock mai schette° him oute,   **mai schette** that can shut

180 Him nedeth noght to gon° aboute,   go
That perce mai the harde wall;
Thus is he with hire overall,

---

153. I consider sleep not worth a rush.
³ Lines 2858–62 have been omitted.

That be hire lief or be hire loth,°
Into hire bedd myn herte goth,

185 And softly takth hire in his arm
And fieleth how that sche is warm,
And wissheth that his body were
To fiele that° he fieleth there.   what
And thus miselven I tormente

190 Til that the dede slep me hente.°   seizes
    "Bot thanne by a thousand score
Wel more than I was tofore°   before
I am tormented in mi slep,
Bot that° I dreme is noght of schep,   what

195 For I ne thenke noght on wulle,
Bot I am drecched° to the fulle   tormented
Of° love that I have to kepe,°   By wait for
That now I lawhe° and now I wepe,   laugh
And now I lese° and now I winne,   lose

200 And now I ende and now beginne.
And otherwhile I dreme and mete°   dream
That I alone with hire mete
And that Danger° is left behinde.   Resistance
And thanne in slep such joie I finde

205 That I ne bede° never awake.   **ne bede** might ask for
    "Bot after, whanne I hiede° take   heed
And schal arise upon the morwe,°   morning
Thanne is al torned into sorwe,°   sorrow
Noght for the cause I schal° arise,   **Noght** . . . Not because I must

210 Bot for I mette° in such a wise,   dreamed
And ate° laste I am bethoght,°   at remembered
That al is vein and helpeth noght,
Bot yit me thenketh° by my wille   **me thenketh** it seems to me
I wold have leie and slepe stille,

215 To meten evere of such a swevene,°   dream
For thanne I hadde a slepi hevene."

              GENIUS
    "Mi sone, and for thou tellest so,
A man mai finde of time ago°   past
That many a swevene° hath be certein,   dream

220 Al be it so that som men sein°   say
That swevenes ben° of no credence.   are
Bot for to schewe in evidence
That thei ful° ofte sothe° thinges   very true
Betoken, I thenke° in my wrytinges   intend

183. That be it (my heart) pleasing to her, or be it hateful to her

225 To telle a tale ther-upon,
Which fell by olde daies gone.
   "This finde I writen in poesie:
Ceix the king of Trocinie
Hadde Alceone to his wif,
230 Which as hire oghne° hertes lif   own
Him loveth. And he hadde also
A brother which was cleped tho°   **cleped tho** called then
Dedalion, and he per cas°   **per cas** by chance
Fro kinde° of man forschape° was   nature transformed
235 Into a goshauk for liknesse.
Wherof the king gret hevynesse°   sorrow
Hath take, and thoghte in his corage° heart
To gon° upon a pelrinage°   go pilgrimage
Into a strange regioun,
240 Wher he hath his devocioun
To don° his sacrifice and preie   make
If that he mihte in eny weie
Toward° the goddes° finde grace   From gods
His brother hele° to pourchace,°   **brother hele** brother's cure procure
245 So that he mihte be reformed
Of that° he hadde be transformed.   what
   "To this pourpos and to this ende
This king is redy for to wende°   go
As he which wolde go by schipe.
250 And for to don him felaschipe,°   **don . . .** give him company
His wif unto the see him broghte
With al hire herte, and him besoghte
That he the time hire wolde sein°   say
Whan that he thoghte come ayein.° **thoghte . . .** expected to return
255 'Withinne,' he seith, 'two monthe day.'
And thus in al the haste he may
He tok his leve and forth he seileth,
Wepende, and sche hirself beweileth,
And torneth hom ther° sche cam fro.   where
260   "Bot whan the monthes were ago°   past
The whiche he set of his comynge,
And that sche herde no tydinge,
Ther was no care° for to seche.°   sorrow seek
Wherof the goddes to beseche
265 Tho° sche began in many wise   Then **many wise** many a manner
And to Juno hire sacrifise
Above alle other most° sche dede,° particularly made
And for hir lord sche hath so bede° prayed
To wite° and knowe how that he ferde° discover fared

270	That Juno the goddesse hire herde	
	Anon, and upon this matiere	
	Sche bad Yris hir Messagere	
	To Slepes hous that sche schal wende°	go
	And bidde him that he make an ende	
275	By swevene,° and schewe al the cas°	vision affair
	Unto this ladi, how it was.	
	"This Yris, fro the hihe stage,°	place
	Which undertake hath the message,	
	Hire reyny cope dede upon,°	**reyny** . . . rain cloak put on
280	The which was wonderli begon,°	worked
	With colours of diverse hewe,	
	An hundred mo° than men it knewe.	more
	The hevene° lich unto a bowe	skies
	Sche bende, and so sche cam down lowe,	
285	The God of Slepe wher that sche fond.°	found
	And that was in a strange lond	
	Which marcheth° upon Chymerie.	borders
	For ther, as seith the poesie,	
	The God of Slep hath mad his hous,	
290	Which of entaille° is merveilous.	sculpture
	"Under an hell° ther is a cave	hill
	Which of the sonne mai noght have,	
	So that no man mai knowe ariht	
	The point betwen the dai and nyht.	
295	Ther is no fyr,° ther is no sparke,	fire
	Ther is no dore which mai charke,°	creak
	Wherof an yhe° scholde unschette,°	eye open
	So that inward ther is no lette.°	hindrance (to sleep)
	And for to speke of that withoute,	
300	Ther stant° no gret tree nyh° aboute,	stands near
	Wheron ther myhte crowe or pie°	magpie
	Alihte for to clepe° or crie.	call
	Ther is no cok to crowe day,	
	Ne beste non° which noise° may	**Ne** . . . Nor any beast disturb
305	The hell,° bot al aboute round	hill
	Ther is growende° upon the ground	growing
	Popi, which berth the sed of slep,	
	With other herbes suche an hep.°	large quantity
	"A stille water for the nones°	time
310	Rennende° upon the smale stones,	Running
	Which hihte of Lethes the rivere,°	
	Under that hell in such manere	
	Ther is, which yifth° gret appetit	gives

311. Which is called the river of Lethe

To slepe. And thus ful of delit

315 Slep hath his hous, and of his couche
Withinne his chambre, if I schal touche,°   treat
Of hebenus° that slepi tree   ebony
The bordes° al aboute be;   boards
And for he scholde slepe softe,

320 Upon a fether bed alofte
He lith° with many a pilwe° of down.   lies   pillow
The chambre is strowed up and down
With swevenes° many thousand fold.   dreams
Thus cam Yris unto this hold,°   stronghold

325 And to the bedd, which is al blak,
Sche goth, and ther with Slep sche spak,
And in the wise° as sche was bede°   manner   ordered
The message of Juno sche dede.°   brought
    "Ful ofte hir wordes sche reherceth,°   repeats

330 Er° sche his slepi eres perceth.   Before
With mochel wo,° bot ate laste   **mochel wo** much suffering
His slombrende yhen° he upcaste   eyes
And seide hir, that it schal be do,°   done
Wherof, among a thousand tho

335 Withinne his hous that slepi were,
In special he ches° out there   chose
Thre, whiche scholden do this dede.
The ferst of hem,° so as I rede,   them
Was Morpheus, the whos nature

340 Is for to take the figure
Of what persone that him liketh,°   pleases
Wherof that he ful° ofte entriketh°   very   ensnares
The lif which slepe schal by nyhte.
And Ithecus that other hihte,°   **that . . .** the other is called

345 Which hath the vois of every soun,
The chiere° and the condicioun   looks
Of every lif, what-so° it is.   **what-so** whatsoever
The thridde, suiende° after this,   **thridde, suiende** third, following
Is Panthasas, which may transforme

350 Of every thing the rihte forme
And change it in an other kinde.
Upon hem thre, so as I finde,
Of swevenes stant al th'apparence,
Which other while is evidence

355 And other while bot a jape.°
    "Bot natheles it is so schape

352–55. From these three, as I find, stems all the form (**apparence**) of dreams, which form at one time is a sign (**evidence**), at another time but a jest.

478

That Morpheus by nyht alone
Appiereth until Alceone
In liknesse of hir housebonde

360 Al naked, ded upon the stronde,°   shore
And how he dreynte° in special   was drowned
These other two° it schewen al.   two (Ithecus and Panthasas)
The tempeste of the blake cloude,
The wode° see, the wyndes loude,   raging

365 Al this sche mette, and sih° him dyen;   **mette** . . . dreamed, and saw
Wherof that sche began to crien
Slepende° abedde ther° sche lay.   Sleeping where
And with that noise of hire affray°   fright
Hir wommen sterten° up aboute,   leaped

370 Whiche of here° ladi were in doute,°   their fear
And axen° hire how that sche ferde.   ask
And sche riht as sche syh° and herde   saw
Hir swevene hath told hem every del.°   part
And thei it halsen° alle wel   explain

375 And sein° it is a token of goode.   say
    "Bot til sche wiste° how that it stoode,   knew
Sche hath no confort in hire herte.
Upon the morwe,° and up sche sterte°   morning leaped
And to the see wher that sche mette°   dreamed

380 The bodi lay, withoute lette°   delay
Sche drowh,° and whan that sche cam nyh,°   approached near
Stark ded, hise armes sprad, sche syh°   saw
Hire lord flietende° upon the wawe.°   floating wave
Wherof hire wittes ben° withdrawe,   are

385 And sche, which tok of deth no kepe,°   heed
Anon forth lepte into the depe
And wolde have cawht him in hire arm.
    "This infortune° of double harm   misfortune
The goddes° fro the hevene above   gods

390 Behield, and for the trowthe° of love   loyalty
Which in this worthi ladi stod,
Thei have upon the salté flod
Hire dreinte° lord and hire also   drowned
Fro deth to lyve torned so

395 That thei ben schapen into briddes°   birds
Swimmende° upon the wawe° amiddes.   Swimming wave
And whan sche sih° hire lord livende   saw
In liknesse of a bridd swimmende,
And sche was of the same sort,

400 So as sche mihte do desport°   **do desport** make merry
Upon the joie which sche hadde,

479

Hire wynges bothe abrod sche spradde,
And him, so as sche mai suffise°   be able
Beclipte and keste° in such a wise°   **Beclipte** ... Embraced and kissed   manner
405 As sche was whilom° wont to do.   formerly
Hire wynges for hire armes two
Sche tok, and for hire lippes softe
Hire harde bile, and so ful° ofte   very
Sche fondeth° in hire briddes° forme   tries   bird's
410 If that sche mihte hirself conforme
To do the plesance° of a wif°   pleasant behavior   woman
As sche did in that other lif.
For thogh sche hadde hir power lore,°   lost
Hir will stod as it was tofore°   before
415 And serveth him so as sche mai.
      "Wherof into° this ilke° day   unto   same
Togeder upon the see thei wone,°   dwell
Wher many a dowhter and a sone
Thei bringen forth of briddes kinde.°   **briddes kinde** birds' nature
420 And for men scholden take in mynde
This Alceoun° the trewe queene,   Halcyon (kingfisher)
Hire briddes yit, as it is seene,
Of Alceoun the name bere.
      "Lo thus, mi sone, it mai thee stere°   move
425 Of swevenes for to take kepe;°   heed
For ofte time a man aslepe
Mai se what after schal betide.
For-thi it helpeth at som tyde°   time
A man to slepe as it belongeth,°   is fitting
430 Bot Slouthe° no lif underfongeth°   Sloth   receives
Which is to Love appourtenant."°   appertaining

THE POET
      "My fader, upon covenant°   agreement
I dar wel make this avow,
Of all mi lif into now
435 Als fer° as I can understonde   **Als fer** As far
Yit tok I nevere slep on honde
Whan it was time for to wake;
For thogh min yhe it wolde take,
Min herte is evere ther ayein.°   again
440 Bot natheles, to speke it plein,
Al this that I have seid you hiere
Of my wakinge, as ye mai hiere,
It toucheth to° mi lady swete,   upon
For otherwise, I you behiete,°   promise

480

445	In straunge place whanne I go	
	Me list° no thing to wake so.	pleases
	For whan the wommen listen° pleie	desire to
	And I hir se noght in the weie	
	Of whom I scholde merthe take,	
450	Me list noght longe for to wake,	
	Bot if° it be for pure schame	**Bot if** Unless
	Of that I wolde eschuie° a name	avoid
	That thei ne scholde have cause non	
	To seie: 'Ha, lo, wher goth such on°	a one
455	That hath forlore° his contenaunce?'	lost
	And thus among I singe and daunce	
	And feigne lust ther as non is.	
	For ofte sithe° I fiele this	**ofte sithe** many times
	Of thoght which in mi herte falleth	
460	Whanne it is nyht, myn hede appalleth,°	grows weak
	And that is for I se hire noght	
	Which is the wakere° of mi thoght.	awakener
	And thus as tymliche as I may	
	Ful° ofte, whanne it is brod day,	Very
465	I take of all these other leve	
	And go my weie, and thei beleve°	remain
	That sen per cas here° loves there.	**That . . .** Who see perhaps their
	"And I go forth as noght ne were°	**noght . . .** though it were nothing
	Unto mi bedd, so that alone	
470	I mai ther ligge,° sighe, and grone,	lie
	And wisshen al the longe nyht,	
	Til that I se the daies lyht.	
	I not° if that be Sompnolence,	know not
	Bot upon youre conscience,	
475	Min holi fader, demeth° ye."	judge

GENIUS

	"My sone, I am wel paid° with thee,	pleased
	Of slep that thou the sluggardie	
	By nyhte in Loves compaignie	
	Eschuied° hast, and do thi peine°	Avoided endeavor
480	So that thi love thar° noght pleine."°	should complain

Book VIII

[Lines 2870–939, 2940–70]

VENUS DISMISSES THE POET

Venus behield me than and lowh,°	laughed
And axeth,° as it were in game,°	asks sport
What love was. And I for schame	
Ne wiste° what I scholde answere,	knew
5 And natheles I gan° to swere	began
That by my trouthe° I knew him noght,	word
So ferr° it was out of mi thoght,	far
Riht as it hadde never be.	

VENUS

"Mi goode sone," tho quod sche,	
10 "Now at this time I lieve° it wel,	believe
So goth the fortune of my whiel.	
For-thi mi conseil is, thou leve."°	leave

THE POET

"Madame," I seide, "by your leve,	
Ye witen° wel, and so wot° I,	know know
15 That I am unbehovely°	unfitting
Your court fro this day forth to serve.	
And for° I may no thonk° deserve,	because thanks
And also for I am refused,	
I preie you to ben° excused.	be
20 And natheles as for the laste,	
Whil that my wittes with me laste,	
Touchende° my confessioun,	Touching
I axe° an absolucioun	ask
Of Genius, er that° I go."	**er that** before
25 The prest anon was redy tho,	

GENIUS

And seide, "Sone, as of thi schrifte,°	confession
Thou hast ful pardoun and foryifte.°	forgiveness
Foryet° it thou, and so wol I."	Forget

THE POET

"Min holi fader, grant mercy,"	
30 Quod I to him, and to the queene	
I fell on knes upon the greene,	
And tok my leve for to wende.°	go

Bot sche, that wolde make an ende
As ther-to which I was most able,
35 A peire of bedes blak as sable
Sche tok and heng my necke aboute.
Upon the gaudes° al withoute   large beads
Was write of gold, *Por reposer.*°   **Por reposer** For resting

VENUS

"Lo," thus sche seide, "John Gower
40 Now thou art ate° laste cast.°   at defeated
This have I for thin ese cast,°   planned
That thou no more of love sieche.°   seek
Bot my will is that thou besieche
And preie hierafter for the pes,°   peace
45 And that thou make a plein° reles   full
To Love, which takth litel hiede°   heed
Of olde men upon the niede,
Whan that the lustes ben° aweie.   **lustes ben** pleasures are
For-thi to thee nys bot o° weie,   **nys** ... is only one
50 In which let Reson be thi guide;
For he may sone himself misguide,
That seth noght the peril tofore.°   before
    "Mi sone, be wel war ther-fore
And kep the sentence of my lore°   teaching
55 And tarie° thou mi court no more,   tarry in
Bot go ther° vertu moral dwelleth,   where
Wher ben thi bokes, as men telleth,
Whiche of long time thou hast write.
For this I do° thee wel to wite,°   make know
60 If thou thin hele° wolt pourchace,   salvation
Thou miht noght make suite° and chace,   pursuit
Wher that the game is nought pernable.°   worth catching
It were a thing unresonable,
A man to be so overseie.°   careless
65 For-thi, tak hede of that I seie.°   say
For in the lawe of my commune°   community
We be noght schape° to commune,°   intended communicate
Thiself and I, nevere after this.
Now have Y seid al that ther is
70 Of love, as for thi final ende.
Adieu, for Y mot° fro thee wende.°   must go
And gret° wel Chaucer whan ye mete,   greet
As mi disciple and mi poete.
For in the floures of his youthe,
75 In sondri wise, as he wel couthe,°   could

Of ditees and of songes glade,
The whiche he for mi sake made,
The lond fulfild is over al.
Wherof to him in special
80 Above alle other I am most holde.°   indebted
For-thi, now in hise daies olde
Thou schalt him telle this message,
That he upon his latere age—
To sette an end of alle his werk,
85 As he which is myn owne clerk—
Do° make his testament of love,   Should
As thou hast do° thi schrifte above,   made
So that mi court it mai recorde."

THE POET
    "Madame, I can me wel acorde,"°   agree
90 Quod I, "to telle as ye me bidde."
And with that word it so betidde,
Out of my sihte al sodeynly,
Enclosed in a sterred sky,
Up to the hevene Venus straghte.°   went
95 And I my rihte weie cawhte°   took
Hom fro the wode, and forth I wente;
Wher as with al myn hole° entente,   whole
Thus with mi bedes upon honde,
For hem that trewe love fonde°   experience
100 I thenke bidde° whil I lyve,   pray
Upon the poynt which I am schryve.°   absolved

The Wyclyfite Bible

(ca. 1395, East Midland)

John Wyclyf (ca. 1320–84) collaborated with his Lollard followers in preparing an English translation of the Bible (completed ca. 1390) for the benefit of laymen unfamiliar with Latin. John Purvey (ca. 1354–ca. 1428), along with others, produced a later, improved version (ca. 1395) of this pioneering work shortly after Wyclyf's death.

The *Prologue for All the Books of the Old Testament*, briefly excerpted here from the later version, contains an extensive discussion not only of the techniques of exegesis but also of the problems of translation.

For the sake of illustrating the prose style of the translation, the Lord's Prayer is also excerpted from the later version.

The best edition is *The Wycliffite Versions of the Holy Bible*, ed. Josiah Forshall and Frederic Madden (Oxford, 1850), 4 vols. For bibliography see *CBEL*, 1.202–05, 5.129; Severs, ch. 3, ch. 4.52.

Prolog for Alle the Bokis of the Oolde Testament

CHAPTER XII

But it is to wite° that Holy Scripture hath   be known
foure understondingis: literal, allegorik, moral,
and anagogik.

The literal understonding techith the thing
5 don in dede,° and literal undirstonding is ground   actual fact
and foundament of thre goostly° undirstond-   spiritual
ingis, in so myche as Austyn in his *Pistle to
Vincent*[1] and othere doctouris seyn° oonly bi the   say that
literal undirstonding a man may argue ayens° an   against
10 adversarie.

Allegorik is a goostly undirstonding that
techith what thing men owen for to° bileeve of   **owen ... ought to**
Crist either° of Hooly Chirche. Moral is a   or
goostly° understonding that techith men what   spiritual
15 vertues thei owen to sue° and what vices thei   strive for
owen to flee. Anagogik is a goostly undir-
stonding that techith men what blisse thei schal
have in Hevene.

[1] St. Augustine, *Letters*, XCIII (A.D. 408).

485

And these foure undirstondingis moun° be
20 taken in this word 'Jerusalem,' for-whi,° to the
literal undirstonding, it signefieth an erthly citée,
as Loundoun either° such another. To allegorie,
it signefieth Hooly Chirche in erthe, that fightith
ayens° synnes and fendis.° To moral undir-
25 stondinge, it signefieth a Cristen soule. To
anagogik it signefieth Hooly Chirche regnynge°
in blisse either in Hevene and tho° that be
therinne.

And these thre goostly° understondingis ben°
30 not autentik:° either of beleeve,° no-but tho
ben° groundid opynly° in the text of Holy
Scripture in oo° place other° other; either° in
opin resoun that may not be distroied;° either
whanne the gospelris° either other apostlis taken
35 allegorie of° the Eelde Testament and con-
feermyn it, as Poul in the *Pistle to Galatians* (in
the fourth *capitulo*°) preveth° that Sara, the free
wiif and principal of Abraham, with Isaac hir
sone signefieth bi allegorie the Newe Testament
40 and the sones of biheeste,° and Agar, the hand-
mayde, with hir sone Ismael signefieth bi
allegorie the Elde Testament and fleschly men
that schulen° not be resseyved° into the eritage
of God with the sones of biheeste that holden the
45 treuthe and freedom of Cristis gospel with
endeles charité.

Also, Holy Scripture hath many figuratif
spechis, and as Austyn seith in the thridde book
of *Cristen Teching*[2] that autouris° of Hooly
50 Scripture usiden moo° figuris (that is, moo
figuratif spechis) than gramariens moun° gesse
that reden° not tho° figuris in Holy Scripture.

[2] St. Augustine, *Christian Doctrine*, III, xxix, 40.

Glosses:
- moun° — can
- for-whi,° — because
- either° — or
- ayens° ... fendis.° — against fiends
- regnynge° — reigning
- tho° — those
- goostly° ... ben° — spiritual are
- autentik:° — authoritative; **of beleeve** for belief
- no-but° — **no-but...** unless they are; opynly° clearly
- oo° ... other° ... either° — one or or
- distroied;° — overturned
- gospelris° — evangelists
- of° — from
- capitulo°) preveth° — chapter proves
- biheeste,° — the new dispensation
- schulen° ... resseyved° — shall received
- autouris° — authors
- usiden moo° — **usiden moo** used more
- moun° — can
- reden° ... tho° — interpret those

The Lord's Prayer

[MATT. vi.9–13]
Oure fadir that art in hevenes, halewid be thi
name. Thi kyngdoom come to. Be thi wille don
in erthe as in hevene. Yyve to us this day oure

breed over othir substaunce, and foryyve to us
5 oure dettis as we foryyven to oure dettouris, and
lede us not into temptacioun, but delyvere us fro
yvel.
      Amen.

A Defense of Translation

(ca. 1382–95, East Midland)

☙

The following passage is excerpted from a Middle English translation, probably by John Purvey, of Wyclyf's Latin tract *De Officio Pastorali*. This passage (Chapter 15), which is inserted by the translator in the middle of Wyclyf's complaint against friars, has no counterpart in the original Latin.

The best edition is *The English Works of Wyclif*, ed. F. D. Matthew, EETS 74 (London, 1880). For bibliography see Severs, ch. 3.50.

Heere the freris° with ther fautours seyn° that   friars   **fautours seyn** abettors say
it is heresye to write thus Goddis lawe in English
and make it knowun to lewid° men. And fourty   unlearned
signes that they bringen for to shewe an heretik
5 ben° not worthy to reherse,° for nought ground-   are   repeat
ith° hem but nygromansye.°   supports   necromancy
    It semyth first that the wit° of Goddis lawe   knowledge
shulde be taught in that tunge that is more
knowun, for this wit is Goddis word. Whanne
10 Crist seith in the Gospel[1] that bothe hevene and
erthe shulen° passe, but his wordis shulen not   shall
passe, he undirstondith° bi his woordis his wit.°   means   **his wit** a knowledge of him
And thus Goddis wit is hooly writ, that may on
no maner be fals.
15   Also, the Hooly Gost yaf° to apostlis wit at   gave
Wit-Sunday[2] for to knowe al maner langagis to
teche the puple Goddis lawe therby, and so God
wolde° that the puple were taught Goddis lawe in   wished
dyverse tungis. But what man on Goddis half°   behalf
20 shulde reverse Goddis ordenaunse and his wille?
    And for this cause Seynt Jerom travelide° and   labored
translatide the Bible fro dyverse tungis into
Lateyn that it myghte be aftir translatid to othere
tungis. And thus Crist and his apostlis taughten

[1] Matt. v.18.
[2] Whitsunday (Pentecost), actually 'White Sunday,' not 'Wit Sunday.'

25 the puple in that tunge that was moost knowun
to the puple. Why shulden not men do now so?
And herfore° autours of the New Law,° that *(therefore; Testament)*
weren apostlis of Jesu Crist, writen° ther gospels *(wrote)*
in dyverse tungis that weren more knowun to the
30 puple.

Also, the worthy reume° of Fraunse, notwith- *(realm)*
stondinge alle lettingis,° hath translatid the Bible *(hindrances)*
and the Gospels with othere trewe sentensis° of *(commentaries)*
doctours° out of Lateyn into Freynsch. Why *(scholars)*
35 shulden not Engliysche men do so? As lordis of
Englond han° the Bible in Freynsch, so it were not *(have)*
ayenus° resoun that they hadden the same *(against)*
sentense° in Engliysch, for thus Goddis lawe *(meaning)*
wolde be betere knowun and more trowid° for *(believed)*
40 onehed° of wit,° and more acord be° bitwixe *(unity; knowledge; would be)*
reumes. *(realms)*

And herfore freris han° taught in Englond the *(**herfore**...therefore friars have)*
Paternoster° in Engliysch tunge, as men seyen,° in *(Lord's Prayer; say)*
the pley° of York and in many othere cuntreys.° *(miracle play; districts)*
45 Sithen° the Paternoster is part of Matheus Gospel, *(Since)*
as clerkis knowen, why may not al be turnyd to
Engliysch trewely, as is this part? Specialy sithen
alle Cristen men, lerid and lewid,° that shulen° be *(**lerid**...learned and unlearned; shall)*
savyd moten algatis sue° Crist and knowe his lore *(**moten**...must anyway follow)*
50 and his lif. But the comyns of Engliyschmen
knowen it best in ther modir tunge, and thus it
were al oon° to lette° siche knowing of the *(**were**...would be the same thing; prevent)*
Gospel and to lette Engliysch men to sue Crist and
come to hevene.

55 Wel Y woot, defaute° may be in untrewe *(**woot, defaute** know, fault)*
translating, as myghten have be° many defautis in *(been)*
turnyng fro Ebrew into Grew,° and fro Grew *(Greek)*
into Lateyn, and from o° langage into another. *(one)*
But lyve men° good lif, and studie many persones *(**lyve men** let men live)*
60 Goddis lawe, and whanne chaungyng of wit° is *(knowledge)*
foundun, amende they° it as resoun wole.° *(**foundun**...found, let them amend; will)*

JOHN DE TREVISA

The Properties of Things

(1398, East Midland)

ᙂ

John de Trevisa (1326–1402) was born in Cornwall, presumably of Cornish-speaking parents. He was a fellow of Exeter College and later of Queen's College, Oxford, and was appointed vicar of Berkeley in Gloucestershire. Under the patronage of Thomas, Lord Berkeley, he completed his two major works, a translation in 1387 of Higden's Latin *Polychronicon* (1327), and a translation in 1398 of the widely used encyclopedia *De Proprietatibus Rerum* (ca. 1250), excerpted here.

The author of the encyclopedia was Bartholomew de Glanville, better known as Bartholomew the Englishman or Bartholomaeus Anglicus, who had joined the Franciscan order in France and had gained renown on the Continent as a scholar. The fundamental purpose of his work was to enumerate the properties of things within the universe, for as the author points out, it is only by an allegorical understanding of the material universe that we can comprehend God's invisible universe. *De Proprietatibus Rerum* became extremely popular and was translated into numerous European languages.

Much of the material is derived from purveyors of "unnatural natural history," such as Isidore of Seville (seventh century) and the authors of bestiaries (see p. 150), lapidaries, and the like. Bartholomew's account of the owl (below) contains none of the rich symbolism implicit in *The Owl and the Nightingale* (p. 54, above), and his enumeration of the properties of the pearl gives no inkling of the allegorical possibilities of the subject as developed by the master poet in *The Pearl* (p. 339, above). Yet Shakespeare, when he wanted a one-volume encyclopedia, is known to have used Batman's version (1582) of Bartholomew, and the work is still curiously interesting because of its characteristically medieval mingling of classical and contemporary beliefs and of learned and popular traditions.

The abridged and somewhat inaccurate printed version of Trevisa published by Wynkyn de Worde (Westminster, 1491) has been used here with some emendations. Another abridgment printed by Berthelet in 1535 has been excerpted in modernized form in *Medieval Lore from Bartholomew Anglicus*, ed. Robert Steele (London, 1893). Trevisa's translation is extant in several manuscripts, but it has never been published in its entirety; two manuscripts are available as microprints: MLA Rotograph 261 (Addit. 27944) and Rotograph 317 (Tollemache), Library of Congress, Washington, D.C. For bibliography see Wells, ch. 10.35 (cf. ch. 3.9); H. S. Bennett, "Science and Information in English Writings of the Fifteenth Century," *Modern Language Review*, 39 (1944), 1–8; Bennett, OHEL, p. 299; CBEL, 1.167, 880, 5.118.

Translator's Prologue

Merveyle not, ye witty° and eloquent reders,
that I, thynne of wytte and voyde of cunnynge,°
have translatid this boke from Latin into our
vulgare langage as a thynge profitable to me and,
5 peraventure, to many other whyche understonde
not Latyne nor have not the knowlege of the
proprytées of thynges, whiche thynges ben
approved° by the bookes of grete and cunnynge
clerkes° and by the experience of moost wytty° and
10 noble phylosophres.

Alle thyse propritées of thynges ben full°
necessary and of grete value to them that wyll, or
be desyrous to, understonde the obscuretées or
derknesse of Holy Scriptures, whiche be yeven° to
15 us under fygures, under parables and semblaunces
or liklihodes° of thynges naturelles and arty-
fycyelles.

Saynt Denys, that grete philosopher and
solempne clerke,° in his boke namyd *Of the Hevenly
20 Ierarchies of Aungelles,*[1] testyfieth and wytnesseth the
same, sayenge in this manere:

"Whatsoever ony man wyll conjecte, feyne,°
ymagyne, suppose, or saye, it is a thynge impos-
syble that the lyghte of the hevenly dyvyne clareté,
25 coverte and closid° in the deyté° or in the godhede,
sholde shyne uppon us yf it were not bi the
dyversitées of holy covertures.° Alls° it is not
possyble that our wytte or entendement° myghte
ascende unto the contemplacyon of the hevenly
30 ierarchyes immaterielles yf our wytte be not ledde
by some materyell thynge as a man is ledde by the
honde, soo by thyse fourmes visibles our wytte may
be led to the consyderacyon of the gretnesse or
magnytude of the moost excellent, bewteuous
35 clareté dyvyne and invysyble."

Reciteth this also the blessyd apposystle Poul in his
Epistles,[2] sayeng that, by thise thynges visybles
whyche ben° made and ben visyble, man may se
and knowe by his inwarde syghte intellectuall the
40 divyne, celestyall, and godly thynges whiche ben
invisibles to this our naturall sighte.

wise
ingenuity

ben approved are attested to
cunnynge clerkes ingenious scholars
wise

very

given

similitudes

solempne clerke distinguished
scholar

conjecte, feyne conjecture, pretend

enclosed   deity

coverings   As
wytte . . . knowledge or understanding

are

[1] Pseudo-Dionysius Areopagiticus, *De Celesti Hierarchia* (ca. A.D. 500), I, 2.
[2] Rom. i.20.

Devowte doctours of theologye or dyvinyté for
this consyderatyon prudently and wysely rede and
use natural philosophye and moral—and poetes in
45 ther ficcions and feyned informacyons—unto this
fyne° or ende so that, by the lyklyhode or simyli- purpose
tude of thynges visible, our wit° or our under- knowledge
stondynge spirytuelly by clere and crafty° utter- compelling
aunce of wordes may be so well ordred and uttred
50 that thyse thynges corporelles maye be cowplid
wyth thynges spyrytuelles, and thyse thynges
visybles may be conjoyned wyth thynges in-
vysybles.

The Owl

BOOK XII, vi

The owle hyghte° *bubo* and hath the name of° is called **name of** name (*bubo*) from
the sowne of her voyce, as Ysydre° sayth, and is a Isidore
wylde byrde, chargyd° wyth fethers. But he° is covered she
alway holde° wyth slouthe,° and is feble to fle,° and held back sloth fly
5 dwellyth by graves by daye and by nyghte and in
chymnés.
    And divynours° tell that they betoken evyl, for soothsayers
they tell that, yf the owle be sette° in a cytée, it settled
sygnyfyeth dystruccion and waste,° as Ysydre° devastation Isidore
10 sayth.
    Arystotle sayth of the owle that the chough° red-beaked crow
fyghtyth with the owle, for he° is feble of syghte at she (the owl)
myddaye and seeth more clerely by nyghte than by
daye. And the owle etyth the choughes egges by
15 nyghte, for the owle is stronger by nyghte than by
daye, and the chough is stronger by daye thanne by
nyghte.
    And other foules fle° abowte the owle by daye **foules fle** birds fly
and pulle hym;° and therfore wyth° the owle **pulle hym** pluck at her by means of
20 foulars take° other byrdes and foules. The fyght- **foulars take** fowlers catch
ynge of thise byrdes, as the fightinge of other
beestes, is not but° for meete other° for dwellynge **not but** only or
places.
    Cryenge of the owle by nyght tokenyth dethe,
25 as divynours conject and deme.° The owle is fedde **divynours . . .** soothsayers conjecture
wyth dyrte and wyth other unclene thynges, and is and judge

492

hatyd of other byrdes, and hauntyth temples by
nyghte to have her fylle of oyle of lampes.

And namely° in fetheres and in becke° she semyth   especially   beak
30 lyke to foules° of pray, but she is all unlyke to   birds
theym in boldnesse and in vertue;° and, whan   power
byrdes and foules assaylleth the owle, she lyeth
upright° and deffendyth herself wyth her becke and   facing up
wyth her fete. And they hounte° and ete myes and   hunt
35 rere-myes° and fle° abowte by nyghte and hyde   bats   fly
theim in chymnés and walles by daye.

The Pearl

BOOK XVI, lxi

Margarita° is chyef of alle whyte precyous stones,   The pearl
as Ysydre° sayth, and hath that name Margarita for°   Isidore   because
it is founde in shelles and in shellefyssh of the see.[1]
It bredyth in flesshe of shellefyssh and is somtyme
5 founde in the brayne of the fysshe and is gendred
of the dewe of heven, the whyche dewe shelfysh
receyve in certayn tymes of the yere.

Of the whyche margarites,° some ben° callyd   pearls   are
uniones[2] and have a covenable° name, for oonly one   appropriate
10 is founde, and never two or moo° togyder.   more

And whyte margarites ben better than yelowe.
And those that ben conceyved of the morowe°   morning
dewe ben made dymme wyth the ayre of the
evyntyde. And some ben° founde kyndly percyd,°   are   **kyndly percyd** pierced by nature
15 and those ben better than other; and some ben
percyd by crafte,° as Plato sayth. And they ben best   craftsmanship
that ben whyte and clere, bryght and rounde.

And they have vertue of comforte, other by°   **vertue**...comforting power, either with
alle the kyndes° therof, as some men meaneth,° or   kinds of pearls   believe
20 for they ben byspronge° wyth certayne kynde; and   associated
it comfortith lymmes and membres, for it clensyth
them of superfluyté of humour,[3] and fastnyth° the   strengthens
lymmes, and helpeth ayenst° the cardiacle passion°   against   **cardiacle passion** heart pain
and ayenst swounynge of hert and ayenst febly-
25 nesse that comyth of flyxe° of medycyn, and   flux

---

[1] This is a fanciful etymology that derives *margarita* from the Latin *mare* 'sea.'
[2] From Latin *unus* 'one.'
[3] Excess of any one of the four humors.

493

helpeth also ayenst rennynge of bloode and ayenst
flyxe of the wombe,° as Plato sayth.   stomach

And, in Plato it is sayd, the margarites ben°   **margarites ben** pearls are
gendryd of dewe. The more dewynge is founde,
30 the more and the gretter they ben. The margarite
is gendryd of the dewe, but it is trowed° that no   believed
margarite growyth passyng of° half a fote.   **passyng of** exceeding

Also, it is sayd there, yf the lyghtnyng or
thondrynge falle whan the margarite sholde° brede   is about to
35 of the dewe that is take,° the shell closyth by   received
sodayn strengthe, and so the gendrynge faylyth and
is caste out.

The beste margarites° come oute of Ynde° and   pearls   India
oute of the Olde Brytayn,° as it is sayd.   **Olde Brytayn** Great Britain

Thomas of Erceldoun

(ca. 1388–1401, Northern)

Thomas of Erceldoun is a peculiarly medieval work. It contains a romance that has fascinated readers from the time of Sir Walter Scott down to the present. For its fourteenth-century audience, however fascinating the narrative, the romance served primarily to fortify the authenticity of the political prophecies embedded in the work. The hero is an actual historical person, Thomas Rymor of Earlston, in Berwickshire, who within his own lifetime (ca. 1210–ca. 1286) had gained a remarkable reputation for his prophetic powers. He became known as Thomas the Rimer, though Rymor may have originally been a mere surname, and prophecies attributed to him circulated orally in Scotland until the ninteenth century.

The poem, inconsistently shifting between first person and third person narration, explains in the first part, or fytte, how Thomas received the gifts of minstrelsy and prophecy by winning the love of an otherworld queen. The second part records the queen's predictions concerning identifiable events in the fourteenth-century struggles between Scotland and England, including Bannockburn (1314; see *The Bruce*, p. 271, above), Halidon Hill (1333; see *Halidon Hill*, p. 231, above), and Otterburn (1388). The third part recounts the queen's ambiguous and vague prophecies of events that do not seem to have occurred in the fourteenth century or, for that matter, at any later period.

Most of the narrative elements in the romance are strikingly similar to counterparts in Celtic legends: the otherworld queen visits this world on a hunt; the hero wins supernatural knowledge from her because of his sexual potency; the queen is capable of changing from beautiful to loathly form; the hero visits the otherworld with the queen despite the power of her husband. The minstrels who transmitted the romance and the scribes who recorded it did not fully understand its primitive background, so the road that leads Thomas to the otherworld is confused with the Christian concept of three alternate roads that lead to heaven (l. 149), purgatory (l. 157), and hell (l. 162). Yet the romance preserves much of the glamor associated with ancient belief. Chaucer may have intended to parody this very poem when he composed *Sir Thopas*, but if so, his parody betrays his affection for his source.

The prophetic elements of the poem are part of a deliberate political technique universally employed in western Europe throughout the Middle Ages. Propagandists would attribute to some ancient and honored seer prophecies concerning events in the immediate past already consummated and then would add appropriate predictions concerning whatever they particularly wished to happen in the immediate future. The scribes clearly understood this utilitarian aspect of *Thomas of Erceldoun*, even though they did not always record the names of people and places correctly. In any case, the literary appeal of the poem has readily outlived its obscure folkloristic origins and its devious political purposes.

The meter is four-line stanzas; see Introduction, type 9, page 31.

James A. H. Murray has edited *The Romance and Prophecies of Thomas of Erceldoun*, EETS 62 (London, 1875) with full introduction and notes. The present selection is based whenever possible on the Thornton Manuscript; it omits a late prologue and includes all of the first fytte, the beginning of the second, and the end of the third (Murray's composite line numbers

25–338, 673–700). See also Child, No. 37; H. M. Flasdieck, *Tom der Reimer: Von keltischen Feen und politischen Propheten* (Breslau, 1934); and Rupert Taylor, *The Political Prophecy in England* (New York, 1911), pp. 62–71. For bibliography see Wells, ch. 4.25; *CBEL*, 1.168, 5.118.

I

Als° I me° wente this endres° daye   As by myself former
Full° faste in mynd makand° my mone°   Very making complaint
In a mery mornynge of Maye
By Huntlé[1] bankkes myselfe allone,
5 I herde the jaye and the throstyll° cokke;   song thrush
The mavys menyde hir of° hir songe;   **mavys . . .** song thrush bemoaned with
The wodewale beryde als° a belle,   **wodewale . . .** wood lark rang like
That alle the wode abowte me ronge.
Allonne in longynge thus als I laye
10 Undyrenethe a semely tree,
Saw I whare a lady gaye°   fair
Cam rydyng over a lovely lee.°   meadow
If I solde° sytt to domesdaye,   should
With my tonge, to wrobbe and wrye,°   **wrobbe . . .** wriggle and twist
15 Certanely that lady gaye,
Never bese scho askryede for° mee.   **bese . . .** would she be described by
Hir palfraye was a dappill graye;
Swylke° one ne saghe° I never none.   Such **ne saghe** saw
Als dose° the sonne on someres daye,   **Als dose** As does
20 That faire lady hirselfe scho schone.
Hir selle° it was of roelle° bone—   saddle rewel
Full semely was that syghte to see—
Stefly° sett with precyous stones   Firmly
And compaste° all with crapotée,°   encircled toadstone
25 Stones of oryente, grete plenté.
Hir hare abowte hir hede it hange.°   hung
Scho° rade over that lovely lee;   She
A° whylle scho blewe, another scho sange.   One
Hir garthes° of nobyll sylke thay were,   girths
30 The bukylls were of berelle stone;
Hir steraps were of crystalle clere
And all with perelle over-by-gone.°   **perelle over-by-gone** pearl covered
Hir payetrelle° was of yral° fyne,   horse's breastplate precious stone
Hir cropoure was of orpharé;°   gold embroidery

[1] Huntley Brae is located near Melrose, below the Eildon Hills, not far from Abbotsford, which overlooks the Tweed.

35 And als clere° golde hir brydill it schone.   **als clere** as bright
One aythir° syde hange bellys three.   **One aythir** On each
Scho° led three grehoundis in a lesshe,°   She   leash
And sevene raches° by hir thay rone.°   hounds ran
Scho bare an horne abowte hir halse°   neck
40 And undir hir belte full° many a flone.°   very   arrow
    Thomas laye and sawe that syghte
Undirnethe ane semly tree.
He sayd, "Yone es° Marye, moste of myghte,   **Yone es** Yonder is
That bare that Childe that dyede for mee.
45 Bot if° I speke with yone lady bryghte,   **Bot if** Unless
I hope° myne herte will bryste in three!   expect
Now sall° I go with all my myghte,   shall
Hir for to mete at Eldoune Tree."[2]
    Thomas rathely° upe he rase,   quickly
50 And he rane over that mountayne hye.
Gyff° it be als° the storye sayes,   If as
He hir mette at Eldone Tree.
He knelyde downe appone his knee
Undirnethe that grenwode spraye°   branch
55 And sayd, "Lufly ladye! rewe one° me,   **rewe one** pity on
Qwene of Hevene, als thou wele maye!"
    Than spake that lady milde of thoghte:
"Thomas, late swylke° wordes be.   such
Qwene of Hevene ne am° I noghte,   **ne am** am
60 For I tuke° never so heghe degré,   took
Bote I ame of ane other countrée.
If I be payrelde° most of prysse,°   appareled   excellence
I ryde aftyre this wylde fee;°   game/
My raches rynnys° at my devyse."°   **raches rynnys** hounds run command
65   "If thou be parelde moste of prysse,
And here rydis thus in thy folye,
Of lufe, lady, als° thou erte wysse,°   as wise
Thou gyffe me leve to lye thee bye."
    Scho° sayde, "Thou mane, that ware folye.   She
70 I praye thee, Thomas, thou late me bee;
For I saye thee full sekirlye,°   surely
That synne will fordoo° all my beauté."   destroy
    "Now, lufly ladye, rewe one° mee,   **rewe one** pity on
And I will ever more with thee dwelle—
75 Here my trouthe I will thee plyghte°—   pledge
Whethir thou will in hevene or helle."
    "Mane of Molde,° thou will me marre,°   Earth   mar
Bot yitt° thou sall hafe all thy will;   yet

---

[2] The Eildon Tree was on the slope of the easternmost of the three Eildon Hills.

And trowe° it wele, thou chevys the werre,°   believe **chevys** . . . come off the worse

80 For alle my beauté will thou spylle."°   destroy

    Downe thane lyghte° that lady bryghte   alighted

Undirnethe that grenewode spraye;°   branch

And als° the storye tellis full° ryghte,   as very

Sevene sythis° by hir he laye.   times

85   Scho sayd, "Mane, thee lykes° thy playe.°   pleases play

Whate byrde° in boure° maye delle° with thee?   maiden bower deal

Thou merrys° me all this longe daye;   mar

I praye thee, Thomas, late me bee!"

    Thomas stode upe in that stede,°   place

90 And he byhelde that lady gaye.°   fair

Hir hare it hange° all over hir hede;   hung

Hir eghne° semede owte that are° were graye;   eyes formerly

And alle the riche clothynge was awaye

That he byfore sawe in that stede;

95 Hir a schanke° blake, hir other graye,   **a schanke** one leg

And all hir body lyke the lede.°   lead

    Thomas laye and sawe that syghte

Undirnethe that grenewod tree.

Than said Thomas, "Allas! Allas!

100 In faythe this es° a dullfull° syghte.   is doleful

How arte thou fadyde thus in the face,

That schane° byfore als the sonne so bryghte!"   shone

    Scho sayd, "Thomas, take leve at° sonne and   of

      mone°   moon

And als° at lefe that grewes on tree.   also

105 This twelmoneth sall° thou with me gone,°   shall go

And medill-erthe° sall thou none see."   earth

    He knelyd downe appone his knee

Undirnethe that grenewod spraye

And sayd, "Lufly lady, rewe° on mee,   pity

110 Mylde qwene of Hevene, als thou beste maye.°   may be

Allas," he sayd, "and wa° es mee!   woe

I trowe° my dedis wyll wirke me care;°   believe sorrow

My saulle, Jhesu, byteche° I thee,°   commit to you

Whedir-some that ever° my banes° sall fare."   **Whedir-some** . . . Wherever bones

115   Scho° ledde hym in at Eldone Hill   She

Undirnethe a derne° lee   secret

Whare it was dirke als mydnyght myrke,°   murk

And ever the water till° his knee.   up to

The montenans° of dayes three   period

120 He herd bot swoghynge° of the flode.   **bot swoghynge** only roaring

At the laste, he sayde, "Full wa° es mee!   **Full wa** Much woe

Almaste I dye, for fawte° of fode."   lack

Scho lede hym intill a faire herbere,°   garden
Whare frwte was growand gret plentée:
125 Pere and appill, bothe ryppe thay were,
    The date, and als° the damasée;°   also   damson plum
    The fygge, and alsso the wyneberye;°   grape
    The nyghtgales byggande° on thair neste.   building
    The papejoyes° faste abowte gane flye,°   parrots **gane flye** flew
130 And throstylls sange° wolde hafe no reste.   **throstylls sange** thrushes' song
    He pressede° to pulle frowyte° with his hande,   hurried **pulle frowyte** pick fruit
    Als mane° for fude that was nere faynt.   a man
    Scho sayd, "Thomas, thou late thame stande,
    Or ells the fende° thee will atteynt.°   fiend   seize
135 If thou it plokk, sothely° to saye,   truly
    Thi saule gose to the fyre of helle.
    It commes never owte or° domesdaye,   before
    Bot ther in payne ay° for to dwelle.   ever
    Thomas, sothely, I thee hyghte,°   bid
140 Come lygge° thyne hede downe on my knee,   lay
    And thou sall se the fayreste syghte
    That ever sawe mane of thi contrée."
    He did in hye° als scho hym badde.   haste
    Appone hir knee his hede he layde,
145 For hir to paye° he was full° glade.   please   very
    And thane that lady to hym sayde:
    "Seese° thou nowe yone° faire waye   Seest   yonder
    That lygges° over yone heghe mountayne?   lies
    Yone es° the waye to hevene for aye,°   is   ever
150 Whene synfull sawles are passede ther payne.
    "Seese thou nowe yone other° waye,   second
    That lygges lawe° bynethe yone rysse?°   low   underbrush
    Yone° es the waye, the sothe° to saye,   Yonder   truth
    Unto the joye of paradyse.
155 "Seese thou yitt yone thirde waye
    That ligges° undir yone grene playne?   lies
    Yone es° the waye, with tene and traye,°   is **tene ...** pain and trouble
    Whare synfull saulis suffiris thaire payne.
    "Bot seese thou nowe yone° ferthe waye   yonder
160 That lygges over yone depe delle?
    Yone es the waye, so waylawaye,°   alas
    Unto the birnande fyre of helle.
    "Seese thou yitt yone faire castelle
    That standis over yone heghe hill?
165 Of towne and towre, it beris the belle;[3]
    In erthe es none lyke it untill.

[3] 'Stands in first place.' The lead animal in a herd usually carried a bell.

Forsothe, Thomas, yone es° myne awenne,°   **yone es** yonder is   own
And the kynges of this countrée.
Bot me ware lever° be hanged and drawene   **me ... ** I would rather
170 Or that° he wyste° thou laye me by.   **Or that** Before   knew
When thou commes to yone castelle gaye,°   fair
I pray thee curtase° mane to bee.   a courteous
And whate-so° any mane to thee saye,   whatsoever
Luke° thou answere none bott mee.   Look
175 My lorde es servede at ylk a mese°   **ylk ... ** each course
With thritty° knyghttis faire and free.   **With thritty** By thirty
I sall saye, syttande at the desse,°   dais
I tuke° thi speche byyonde the see."   captured
    Thomas still als stane he stude,
180 And he byhelde that lady gaye.°   fair
Scho come° agayne als faire and gude   became
And also ryche one° hir palfraye,   **ryche one** splendid on
Hir grewehoundis fillide° with dere° blode,   filled   deer's
Hir raches couplede,° by my faye.°   **raches couplede** hounds leashed   faith
185 Scho blewe hir horne with mayne and mode;°   **mayne ...** might and spirit
Unto the castelle scho tuke the waye.
Into the haulle sothely° scho went.   **haulle sothely** hall truly
Thomas folowed at hir hande.
Than ladyes come, bothe faire and gent,°   noble
190 With curtassye to hir knelande.
Harpe and fethill° bothe thay fande,°   fiddle   found
Getterne,° and alsso the sawtrye,°   Gitterne   psaltery
Lutte and rybybe° bothe gangande,°   rebeck   going
And all manere of mynstralsye.
195   The moste mervelle° that Thomas thoghte   **moste mervelle** greatest marvel
Whene that he stode appone the flore,
For feftty hertis° in were broghte   stags
That were bothe grete and store.°   mighty
Raches° laye lapande in the blode.   Hounds
200 Cokes° come with dryssynge knyfe;   Cooks
Thay brittened° thame als° they were wode.°   cut up   as if   crazy
Revelle amanges thame was full° ryfe.   very
Knyghtis dawnsede by three and three.
There was revelle, gamene,° and playe,   sport
205 Lufly ladyes faire and fre°   noble
That satte and sange one° riche araye.   in
Thomas dwellide in that solace
More thane I yowe saye, pardé,°   indeed
Till one a daye, so hafe I grace,
210 My lufly lady sayde to mee:
    "Do buske° thee, Thomas. Thee buse° agayne,   ready   it behooves to go

500

For thou may here no lengare be.
Hye° thee faste with myghte and mayne.   Hasten
I sall thee brynge till Eldone Tree."
215   Thomas sayde thane with hevy chere,°   **hevy chere** sad countenance
"Lufly lady, nowe late me bee,
For certis,° lady, I hafe bene here   certainly
Noghte bot° the space of dayes three!"   **Noghte bot** Only
    "Forsothe, Thomas, als I thee telle,
220 Thou hase bene here thre yere and more,
Bot langere here thou may noghte dwelle.
The skylle° I sall° thee telle wharefore.   reason   shall
Tomorne° of helle the foulle fende⁴   Tomorrow
Amange this folke will feche his fee;
225 And thou arte mekill° mane and hende;°   a large   courteous
I trowe° full wele he wolde chese° thee.   expect   choose
For alle the golde that ever may bee
Fro hethyne° unto the worldis ende,   hence
Thou bese° never betrayede for° mee.   will be   by
230 Therefore with me I rede° thou wende."°   advise   to go
    Scho broghte hym agayne to Eldone Tree
Undirnethe that grenewode spraye.
In Huntlee bannkes es mery to bee,
Whare fowles synges bothe nyght and daye.
235 "Ferre° owtt in yone° mountane graye,   Far   yonder
Thomas, my fawkone bygges° a neste.   builds
A fawconne es an erlis praye;°   **erlis praye** earl's prey
For-thi° in na place may he reste.   Therefore
Fare wele, Thomas, I wend° my waye,   go
240 For me byhoves° over yon benttis° browne."   it behooves to go   slopes
    Loo here a fytt. More es to saye,
All of Thomas of Erselldowne.

⁴ The fiend of Hell exacts an annual tribute from the otherworld creatures.

II

"Fare wele, Thomas, I wend my waye.
I may no lengare stande with thee."
    "Gyff me a tokynynge, lady gaye,°   fair
That I may saye I spake with thee."
5 "To harpe or carpe, whareso° thou gose,   **carpe, whareso** speak, wherever
Thomas, thou sall hafe the chose sothely."°   **chose sothely** choice truly
    And he saide, "Harpynge kepe° I none,   regard

For tonge es chefe of mynstralsye."
 "If thou will spelle,° or tales telle,   narrate
10 Thomas, thou sall never lesynge lye.°   **lesynge lye** tell a lie
 Whare-ever thou fare, by frythe or felle,°   **frythe ...** field or hill
 I praye thee, speke none evyll of me.
 Fare wele, Thomas, withowttyne gyle,
 I may no lengare dwelle with thee."
15 "Lufly lady, habyde° a while,   wait
 And telle thou me of some ferly!"°   marvel
  "Thomas, herkyne what I thee saye:
 Whene a tree rote es dede,
 The leves fadis thane and wytis° awaye,   die
20 And froyte° it beris nane thane, whyte ne° rede. fruit nor
 Of the Baylliolse blod[1] so sall° it falle: shall
 It sall be lyke a rotyne tree.
 The Comyns and the Barlays alle,
 The Russells and the Fresells free,[2]
25 All sall thay fade and wyte awaye.
 Na ferly° if that froyte than° dye.   **Na ferly** No wonder **froyte than** fruit then
 And mekill bale sall° after spraye,°   **mekill ...** much woe shall spread
 Whare joye and blysse was wonte to bee.
 Fare wele, Thomas, I wende° my waye;   go
30 I may no langer stand with thee."

    .   .   .

[1] 'Baliols' blood,' descendants of John Baliol, rivals of the Bruce family.
[2] Comyns (Cumyns), Barclays, Russells, and Frasers, four families involved in the Baliol-Bruce controversy in the fourteenth century.

III

 Thomas drere° mann was he;   a dreary
 Teares fell over his eyen so graye.
  "Nowe, lovly lady, tell thou me
 If we shall parte for ever and aye."°   ever
5 "Naye," she saide, "Thomas, *par dé*.°   *par dé* indeed
 When thow sitteste° in Erseldown,   are settled
 To Huntlee Bankkis thou take the waye.
 There sall I sekirly° be bowne°   surely ready to go
 And mete thee, Thomas, whene I maye.
10 I sall thee kenne,° whare-ever thou gaa,°   teach go
 To bere the pryce of° curtaysye;   **pryce of** esteem for
 For tunge es wele,° and tunge es waa,°   joy woe

And tunge es chefe of mynstrallsye."
    Sche blewe hir horne on hir palfraye
15 And lefte Thomas undirnethe a tre.
    To Helmesdale° sche tuke the waye,   Helmsdale (Sutherland)
    And thus departede sche and hee.
        Of swilke° an hirdmane° wolde I here°   such   retainer   hear
    That couth° me telle of swilke ferly.°   could   a marvel
20 Jhesu, corounde° with a crowne of brere,°   crowned   briar
    Brynge us to his hevene so hyee.
        Amene, Amene.

THE
FIFTEENTH
CENTURY

The Tale of Beryn

(ca. 1405, East Midland)

ᡣᢁᢃ

The anonymous author of *The Tale of Beryn* calls himself "a son of Thomas's church" (Canterbury Cathedral). His is the first known work after Chaucer's death to attempt a continuation of *The Canterbury Tales*, for which Chaucer had intended to provide further tales told by the pilgrims on the road back from Canterbury. As a resident familiar with Canterbury, he realistically and wittily describes in his prologue (ll. 1–732) the activities of the simpler pilgrims within the town; and then he provides a second tale (ll. 733–4024) for Chaucer's Merchant.

The tale appropriately concerns Beryn, the son of a Roman senator, who himself becomes a merchant and, after trials in Falsetown, marries a duke's daughter. The romance, derived from a French source, is refreshingly bourgeois but, in the halting septenary lines of the English adaptation, is an inadequate competitor for a place among Chaucer's skillfully wrought narratives.

The meter is seven-beat couplets; see Introduction, type 7, page 31.

The best edition is *The Tale of Beryn*, ed. F. J. Furnivall and W. G. Stone, Chaucer Society, 2nd Series, 17, 24 (London, 1876, 1887), reprinted EETS 105 (London, 1909). For the manuscript see Manly-Rickert, I, 387–95 (Northumberland MS. 55 of *The Canterbury Tales*). For bibliography see Hammond, p. 412; *CBEL* 1.254; Bennett, *OHEL*, 17, 70, 317.

[Prologue, lines 130–90]

The knyght and al the feleshipp—and no thing for to ly°—	misrepresent
When they wer all i-loggit,° as skill wold and reson,	lodged
Everich° aftir his degré, to chirch then was seson°	Each time
To passen and to wend,° to maken hir° offringis,	go their
5 Righte° as hir devocioune was, of sylvir broch and ryngis.	According
Then atte chirche dorr the curtesy gan° to ryse,	began
Tyl the knyght, of gentilnes,° that knewe righte wele the guyse,°	nobility manner
Put forth the prelatis, the person, and his fere,°	companions
A monk, that toke the spryngill° with a manly chere,°	sprinkler countenance
10 And did, right as the manner is, moillid° al hir patis,°	wet pates

506

Everich° aftir othir, righte as they wer of states.°   Each   ranks

The ffrere feynyd fetously° the spryngil for to hold   **ffrere ...** friar tried neatly

To spryng oppon the remnaunt, that for his cope he
    nold°   wouldn't

Have lafft that occupacioune in that holy plase,

15 So longid his holy conscience to se the nonnys°   nun's
    fase.

    The knyghte went with his compers° toward the   comrades
      holy shryne,

To do that° they were com fore and aftir for to   what
    dyne.

The pardoner and the miller and othir lewde sotes°   **lewde sotes** unlearned dolts

Sought hem° selffen in the chirch right as lewde   them
    gotes;°   goats

20 Pyrid° fast and pourid highe oppon the glase,°   Peered   stained glass

Countirfeting gentilmen,° the armys for to blase,°   **Countirfeting gentilmen** Imitating
                                   nobles   proclaim

Diskyveryng fast the peyntour, and for the story
    mourned.°   meditated

And a° red it also right° as wolde rammys° horned.   one   **also right** as correctly   rams

    "He berith a balstaff,"[1] quod the toon,° "and els° a   one   besides
      rakis ende."

25 "Thow faillist," quod the miller; "thowe hast nat
    wel thy mynde.

It is a spere, yf thowe canst se, right with a prik
    tofore,°   in front

To bussh° adown his enmy and thurh the sholdir   thrust
    bore."

    "Pese!"° quod the hoost of Southwork, "let   Peace
      stond the wyndow glasid.

Goith up and doith yeur offerynge. Yee semeth half
    amasid.

30 Sith° yee be in company of honest men and good,   Since

Worchith somwhat aftir, and let the kynd of brode°

Pas for a tyme. I hold it for the best,

Ffor who doith after company, may lyve the bet° in   better
    rest."

    Then passid they forth boystly, goglyng° with   **boystly, goglyng** crudely, staring
      hir° hedis,   their

35 Knelid adown tofore the shryne, and hertilich hir
    bedis°   beads

They preyd to Seynt Thomas in such wise° as they   manner
    couth;°   knew how

And sith° the holy relikis ech man with his mowith   then

---

[1] 'Quarterstaff,' here possibly in an illustration of a saint with a staff.
31. Let this go until later (literally 'do somewhat later'), and let the natural disposition

Kissid, as a goodly monke the names told and
    taught;
And sith to othir placis of holynes they raughte°   reached
40 And were in hir devocioun tyl service wer al doon;
And sith they drowgh° to dynerward as it drew to   drew
    noon.
    Then, as manere and custom is, signes° there they   souvenir tokens
    boughte,
Ffor men of contré shulde know whom they hadde
    oughte.°
Ech man set his sylvir in such thing as they likid;
45 And in the meenewhile the miller had i-pikid°   picked
His bosom ful of signys of Cauntirbury brochis,
Huch° the pardoner and he pryvely in hir° pouchis   Which their
They put hem° aftirward, that noon of hem it wist,°   them knew
Save the sompnour seid° somwhat and seyde to   **sompnour seid** summoner saw
    ham,° "List,   them
50 Halff part," quod he, pryvely rownyng on° hir ere.   **rownyng on** whispering in
    "Hussht! Pees!"° quod the miller. "Seist thowe   Peace
    nat the frere,
Howe he lowrith undir his hood with a doggish ey?
Hit shuld be° a pryvy thing that he coude nat aspy;   **shuld be** would have to be
Of every crafft he can° somwhat, Our Lady gyve   knows
    him sorowe!"
55   "Amen," quod the sompnour,° "on eve and eke°   summoner also
    on morowe.°   morning
So cursid a tale he told of me, the devil of hell hym
    spede!²
And me, but yf I pay hym wele and quyte° wele his   repay
    mede,°   reward
Yf it happene homward that ech man tell his tale
As wee did hiderward, thoughe wee shuld set at
    sale°   **set . . .** make use of
60 Al the shrewdnes that I can, I wol hym no thing
    spare,
That I nol° touch his taberd,° somwhat of his   won't cloak
    care."°   sorrow

---

43. So that their countrymen might know from whom they had anything.
² A reference to Chaucer's "Friar's Tale," in *The Canterbury Tales*, directed against the Summoner, who ha[s]
countered the attack in Chaucer's "Summoner's Tale."

THOMAS HOCCLEVE

The Regiment of Princes

(ca. 1412, East Midland)

In the autobiographical introduction to this poem Hoccleve (ca. 1368–ca. 1437) expresses his weariness with the French-English wars and laments the financial insecurity of his annuity, which he finds inadequate as a reward for all his years of service as clerk at the Office of the Privy Seal. He decides to prepare a treatise on the duties of princes, which he will submit to Prince Hal, crowned Henry V in 1413, but he regrets that Chaucer and Gower are no longer alive to inspire him. Freely adapting Jacobus de Cessolis's *Moralized Chess* to this purpose, he advocates dignity, truth, justice, lawfulness, pity, mercy, patience, chastity, magnanimity, generosity (which should guarantee the payment of Hoccleve's annuity), prudence (on which Chaucer has given good advice), and peacefulness (which should lead Henry to marry Catherine of Valois—as he did, in 1420—and to bring peace between England and France).

The literary interest of the poem lies much more in its historical background than in its style. Throughout the work (cf. ll. 1867, 1962, 2078, 4983), Hoccleve praises Chaucer (who had died in 1400), hailing him as a "flower of eloquence" and as his "master dear." He provided at least one manuscript copy of his poem with a miniature of Chaucer, which, it is assumed, was painted from memory by some artist who had known Chaucer.

The meter is seven-line stanzas; see Introduction, type 17, page 32.

The best edition is ed. F. J. Furnivall, EETS 72, (London, 1897). The Harley 4866 folio containing the miniature of Chaucer and the surrounding stanzas is reproduced here in Plate 5, page 24. For bibliography see Bennett, *OHEL*, 123, 148, 150, 285–86; Hartung, ch. 8.2.

[Lines 4978–5019]

The firste fyndere° of oure faire langage	founder
Hath seyde in caas semblable° and othir moo°	similar more
So hyly° wel, that it is my dotage°	very foolishness
Ffor to expresse or touche any of thoo.°	those
5 Alasse! my fadir fro the worlde is goo°—	gone
My worthi maister Chaucer, hym I mene.	
Be thou advoket for hym, Hevenes Quene.	
As thou wel knowest, O Blissid Virgyne,	
With lovyng hert and hye devocioun	
10 In thyne honour he wroot ful° many a lyne.	very
O now thine helpe and thi promocioun,	
To God thi Sone make a mocioun°	proposal

How he thi servaunt was, Mayden Marie,
And lat his love floure and fructifie.

15 Althogh his lyfe be queynt,° the resemblaunce   quenched
Of him hath in me so fressh lyflynesse
That, to putte othir men in remembraunce
Of his persone, I have heere his lyknesse
Do make,° to this ende in sothfastnesse,°   **Do make** Caused to be made   truth
20   That thei that have of him lest° thought and mynde   lost
By this peynture may ageyn him fynde.

The ymages that in the chirche been
Maken folk thenke on God and on his seyntes,
Whan the ymages thei beholden and seen;
25 Wereas unsyte° of hem° causith restreyntes   not seeing   them
Of thoughtes gode. When a thing depeynt° is   painted
Or entailed,° if men take of it heede,   figured
Thoght of the lyknesse it wil in hem brede.°   increase

Yit somme holden oppynyoun and sey
30 That none ymages schuld i-maked° be.   made
Thei erren foule and goon out of the wey;°   **erren . . .** blunder and err
Of trouth have thei scant sensibilité.
Passe over that. Now, Blessid Trinité,
  Uppon my maistres soule, mercy have;
35 Ffor him, Lady, eke° thi mercy I crave.   also

More othir thing wolde I fayne speke and touche
Heere in this booke, but such is my dulnesse—
Ffor that al voyde and empty is my pouche—
That al my lust° is queynt° with hevynesse,°   desire   quenched   grief
40 And hevy spirit commaundith stilnesse.
  And have I° spoke of pees,° I schal be stille.   **have I** when I have   peace
God sende us pees, if that it be his wille.

JOHN LYDGATE

The Siege of Thebes

(ca. 1421, East Midland)

John Lydgate (ca. 1370–ca. 1450) spent most of his life as a Benedictine monk in the wealthy monastery of Bury St. Edmunds, in West Suffolk. With the assistance of the great monastic library there, he wrote numerous lengthy and highly derivative works for a variety of distinguished patrons.

The Siege of Thebes deals with the rivalry between Eteocles and Polyneices, the two sons of Oedipus, over the kingship of Thebes—a classical theme still popular in the Middle Ages. His source was a now lost French prose romance adapted from the Old French poem *Le Roman de Thebes*.

His amusing prologue depicts Daun John Lydgate joining Chaucer's pilgrims at Canterbury just as they set out on the return journey to Southwark. Within this context, his tale provides an appropriate counterpart to Chaucer's "Knight's Tale," and it has been argued in its justification that Lydgate intended his narrative to provide the company with a fitting moral exemplification. As with Chaucer's "Monk's Tale," however, the moral intentions of his pedestrian recital do not suffice to guarantee the enthusiasm of a worldly audience.

The meter is five-beat couplets; see Introduction, type 6, page 31.

The best edition is *The Siege of Thebes*, ed. A. Erdmann and E. Ekwall, Chaucer Society, 2nd Series, 46, and EETS 108, 125 (London, 1911, 1930). The most recent study is Derek A. Pearsall, *John Lydgate* (London, 1970). For the manuscript see Plate 6 and accompanying notes, pages 26–28. For bibliography see *CBEL*, 1.250–52, 5.146; Bennett, *OHEL*, pages 298–93.

[Lines 66–193]

    And this while that the pilgrymes leye
At Canterbury well logged on° and all,   **logged on** lodged one
I not° in soth° what I may it call,   know not   truth
Hap or fortune in conclusioun,°   judgment
5 That me byfil to entren° into toun,   **byfil** . . . it befell that I entered
The holy seynt[1] pleynly to visite
Aftere siknesse, my vowes to aquyte,°   fulfill
In a cope° of blak and not of grene,   cape
On a palfrey slender, long, and lene,
10 With rusty brydel mad nat for the sale,
My man toforn° with a voide male°   in front   **voide male** empty pack
Which° of fortune took myn inne° anon   Who   inn

[1] St. Thomas Becket, of Canterbury.

Wher the pylgrymes were logged everichon.°   **logged everichon** lodged everyone
  The same tyme her° governour, the host,   their
15 Stonding in halle, ful of wynde and bost,
  Lich° to a man wonder° sterne and fers,   Like   wondrously
  Which spak° to me and seide anon, "Daun Pers,°   spoke **Daun Pers** Sir Piers
  Daun Domynyk, Dan Godfrey or Clement,
  Ye be welcom newly into Kent,
20 Thogh youre bridel have neither boos° ne belle.   boss
  Besechinge you that ye wil me telle
  First youre name and of what contré,
  Withoute more, shortely that° ye be   that which
  That loke so pale, al devoyde of blood,
25 Upon youre hede a wonder° thred-bar hood,   wondrously
  Wel araied for to ride late."
    I answerde, "My name was Lydgate,
  Monk of Bery, nygh° fyfty yere of age,   nearly
  Come to this toune to do my pilgrimage
30 As I have hight;° I have therof no shame."   vowed
    "Daun° John," quod he, "wel broke° ye youre name.   Sir uttered
  Thogh ye be soul, beth° right glad and light,   **soul, beth** alone, be
  Preiyng you soupe with us tonyght,
  And ye shal have mad at youre devis°   wish
35 A gret puddyng° or a rounde hagys,°   sausage   haggis
  A Franchemole, a tansey, or a froyse.²
  To ben° a monk, sclender° is youre koyse;°   be slim rump
  Ye han be° seke, I dar myn hede assure,   been
  Or late fed in a feynt pasture.
40 Lift up youre hed; be glad, tak no sorowe,
  And ye shal hom ride with us tomorowe.
    "I seye, whan ye rested han° your fille,   have
  Aftere soper slepe wil do non ille.
  Wrappe wel youre hede with clothes rounde aboute.
45 Strong notty° ale wol make you to route.°   nutty   snore
  Tak a pylow, that ye lye not lowe.
  Yif nede be, spare not to blowe.°   pass wind
  To holde wynde, by myn opynyoun,
  Wil engendre collikes passioun°   suffering
50 And make men to greven° on her roppys°   suffer **her roppys** their guts
  Whan thei han° filled her mawes and her croppys.°   have bellies
  But toward nyght ete some fenel rede,°   **fenel rede** red fennel
  Annys, comyn,° or coriandre sede.   **Annys, comyn** Anise, cumin
  And lik as I power have and myght,

---

² 'Fraunchemole,' a mixture boiled (like haggis) or roasted in a sheep's stomach; 'tansy,' a bitter, aromatic plant much used for stomach ailments and as a vegetable in cooking; 'froise,' a pancake containing chopped meat or fish.

55 I charge yow rise not at mydnyght,
    Thogh it so be the moone shyne cler.
    I wol mysilf be youre orloger°   horologist
    Tomorrow erly whan I se my tyme,
    For we wol forth parcel afore pryme,°
60 A company, pardé,° shal do you good.   indeed
        "What! Look up, Monk, for, by kokkis° blood,   God's
    Thow shalt be mery, who-so that sey nay.°   **who-so** ... no matter who says not
    For tomorowe, anoon as° it is day,   **anoon as** as soon as
    And that it gynne° in the est to dawe,°   begins   dawn
65 Thow shalt be bounde to a newe lawe
    Att goyng oute of Canterbury toune
    And leyn° aside thy professioun.   lay
    Thow shalt not chese° nor thisilf withdrawe   choose
    Yif eny myrth be founden in thy mawe,
70 Lyk° the custom of this compenye.   As is
    For non so proude that dar me denye,
    Knyght nor knave, canon, prest, ne° nonne,   nor
    To telle a tale pleynly as thei konne,
    Whan I assigne and se tyme opportune.
75 And for that we our purpoos wil contune,°   continue
    We wil homward the same custome use,
    And thow shalt not platly° thee excuse.   flatly
    Be now wel war.° Stody wel tonyght.   aware
    But, for al this, be of herte light;
80 Thy wit shal be the sharper and the bet."°   better
        And we anon were to soper sett
    And served wel unto oure plesaunce;°   pleasure
    And sone after, be° good governaunce,   by
    Unto bed goth every maner wight.°   **maner wight** kind of person
85 And towarde morowe, anon as° it was light,   **morowe** ... morning, as soon as
    Every pilgryme bothe bet° and wors,   better
    As bad° oure hoste, toke anon his hors,   ordered
    Whan the sonne roos in the est ful clyere,°   bright
    Fully in purpoos to come to dynere
90 Unto Osspryng° and breke ther our faste.   Ospringe (Kent)
        And whan we weren from Canterbury paste
    Noght the space of a bowe-draught,°   bowshot
    Our hoost in hast hath my bridel rauht°   seized
    And to me seide, as° it were in game,°   as if   jest
95   "Come forth, Daun° John, be° your Cristene name,   Sir   by
    And lat us make some manere° myrth or play.   kind of
    Shet° youre portoos° a twenty develway.   Shut   breviary
    It is no disport° so to patere and seie;   entertainment

59. For we will go forth in a group (literally, 'in part') before prime (6:00 to 9:00 A.M.)

It wol make youre lippes wonder° dreye.   wondrously
100 Tel some tale and make therof a jape,°   jest
For, be° my rouncy,° thow shalt not eskape.   by   horse
But preche not of non holynesse.
Gynne° some tale of myrth or of gladnesse,   Begin
And nodde not with thyn hevy bekke.°   **hevy bekke** sad beak
105 Telle us some thing that draweth to effecte
Only of joye. Make no lenger lette."°   delay
    And whan I saugh it wolde be no bette,°   better
I obeyed unto his biddynge,
So as the lawe me bonde in al thinge,
110 And as I coude,° with a pale cheere,°   **as** ... as best I could   countenance
My tale I gan° anon as ye shal here.°   began   hear
    "Sirs," quod I, "sith° of your curtesye   since
I entred am into your companye
And admitted a tale for to telle
115 By him that hath power to compelle—
I mene our hoste, governour, and guyde
Of yow echon,° ridyng her° beside—   each one   here
Thogh that my wit barayn be and dul,
I wol reherce a story wonderful
120 Touchinge the siege and destruccioun
Of worthy Thebees, the myghty royal toun,
Bylt and begonne of olde antiquité,
Upon the tyme of worthy Josué,
Be dyligence of Kyng Amphioun,
125 Chief cause first of his° fundacioun,   its
For which his fame, which nevere shal away,
In honure floureth yit unto this day,
And in story remembred is and preised."

Christ and His Mother

(ca. 1450, East Midland)

This simple yet subtle lyric is a striking example of the religious use of the genre known as the reverdie, the song inspired by the return of spring (see *Spring*, p. 210, above). Its first and last stanzas are derived ultimately from an earlier religious lyric, "Nu this fules singet hand maket hüre blis" (ca. 1250); but in their total poetic effect its five restrained stanzas outshine the twelve stanzas of its prototype.

The meter is four-line stanzas; see Introduction, type 8, page 31.

The best edition is Carleton Brown, *Religious Lyrics of the Fifteenth Century* (Oxford, 1939), page 119. See also Stephen Manning, "I Syng of a Myden," *PMLA*, 75 (1960), 8–12. The only manuscript is British Museum Sloane 2593, which also contains *St. Stephen and Herod* (p. 516, below) and *Robyn and Gandeleyn* (p. 518, below); it has been published complete in *Songs and Carols from a Manuscript in the British Museum of the Fifteenth Century*, ed. Thomas Wright, Warton Club, 4 (London, 1856). For bibliography see Wells, ch. 13.205.

	I syng of a myden	
	that is makeles.°	matchless/mateless
	Kyng of alle kynges	
	to here° sone sche ches.°	**to here** as her chose
5	He cam also° stylle	as
	ther° his moder was	where
	As dew in Aprylle	
	that fallyt° on the gras;	falls
	He cam also stylle	
10	to his moderes bowr	
	As dew in Aprille	
	that fallyt on the flour;	
	He cam also stylle	
	there his moder lay	
15	As dew in Aprille	
	that fallyt on the spray.	
	Moder and maydyn	
	was never non but sche.	
	Wel may swych° a lady	such
20	Godes moder be.	

St. Stephen and Herod

(ca. 1450, East Midland)

The origin of this ballad, like that of *Judas* (p. 153, above), lies in the ancient apocryphal material that accumulated around the narratives of the New Testament. In another ballad, *The Carnal and the Crane* (Child, No. 55), the same motif of the crowing cock is associated with the Wise Men and Christmas rather than with St. Stephen and the evening before St. Stephen's Day (December 26).

The meter is seven-beat couplets; see Introduction, type 7, page 31.

The best edition is Child, No. 22. Child also provides bibliographical references. The only manuscript is British Museum Sloane 2593, published in *Songs and Carols from a Manuscript in the British Museum of the Fifteenth Century*, ed. Thomas Wright, Warton Club, 4 (London, 1856).

<table>
<tr><td></td><td>Seynt Stevene was a clerk</td><td></td></tr>
<tr><td></td><td>In kyng Herowdes halle</td><td></td></tr>
<tr><td></td><td>And servyd him of bred and cloth</td><td></td></tr>
<tr><td></td><td>As every kyng befalle.°</td><td>it befalls</td></tr>
<tr><td>5</td><td>Stevyn out of kechone cam</td><td></td></tr>
<tr><td></td><td>Wyth boris° hed on honde;</td><td>a boar's</td></tr>
<tr><td></td><td>He saw a sterre was° fayr and bryght</td><td>that was</td></tr>
<tr><td></td><td>Over Bedlem° stonde.</td><td>Bethlehem</td></tr>
<tr><td></td><td>He kyst° adoun the boris hed</td><td>cast</td></tr>
<tr><td>10</td><td>And went into the halle.</td><td></td></tr>
<tr><td></td><td>"I forsak thee, kyng Herowdes,</td><td></td></tr>
<tr><td></td><td>And thi werkes alle.</td><td></td></tr>
<tr><td></td><td>"I forsak thee, kyng Herowdes,</td><td></td></tr>
<tr><td></td><td>And thi werkes alle.</td><td></td></tr>
<tr><td>15</td><td>Ther is a chyld in Bedlem° born</td><td>Bethlehem</td></tr>
<tr><td></td><td>Is° beter than we alle."</td><td>Who is</td></tr>
<tr><td></td><td>"Quat eylyt° thee, Stevene?</td><td>**Quat eylyt** What ails</td></tr>
<tr><td></td><td>Quat is thee befalle?°</td><td>**is** . . . has befallen you</td></tr>
<tr><td></td><td>Lakkyt thee° eyther mete° or drynk</td><td>**Lakkyt thee** Do you lack food</td></tr>
<tr><td>20</td><td>In kyng Herowdes halle?"</td><td></td></tr>
</table>

"Lakkyt me neyther mete ne° drynk   nor
   In kyng Herowdes halle.
Ther is a chyld in Bedlem° born   Bethlehem
   Is beter than we alle."

25 "Quat eylyt° thee, Stevyn?   **Quat eylyt** What ails
   Art thu wod,° or thu gynnyst° to brede?°   crazy begin rave
Lakkyt thee° eyther gold or fe°   **Lakkyt thee** Do you lack property
   Or ony ryche wede?"°   garment

"Lakyt me neyther gold ne fe
30   Ne non ryche wede.
Ther is a chyld in Bedlem° born   Bethlehem
   Xal° helpyn us at our nede."   Who shall

"That is also soth,° Stevyn,   **also soth** as true
   Also soth, i-wys,°   indeed
35 As this capoun° crowe xal   capon
   That lyth here in myn dysh."

That word was not so sone seyd,
   That word in that halle,
The capoun crew "*Cristus natus est*"°   **Cristus** ... Christ is born
40   Among the lordes alle.

"Rysyt° up, myn turmentowres,°   Rise   torturers
   Be to and als be on,°
And ledyt° Stevyn out of this town,   lead
   And stonyt° hym wyth ston."   stone

45 Tokyn he° Stevene   **Tokyn he** They took
   And stonyd hym in the way;
And therfore is his evyn
   On Crystes owyn day.

42. By two and also by one

Robyn and Gandeleyn

(ca. 1450, East Midland)

This is one of the two earliest recorded nonreligious English ballads, the other being *Robin Hood and the Monk* (Child, No. 119). It obviously belongs to a period in which a wide audience was interested in tales of such heroic outlaws as Robin Hood, about whom a whole cycle of ballads developed, and Gamelyn, who is the subject of a romance, *The Tale of Gamelyn* (ca. 1350–70). The resemblance of the name *Robyn* to *Robin Hood* and of *Gandeleyn* to *Gamelyn* is perhaps coincidental, but in its concern for popular justice, the ballad is unmistakably similar to the Robin Hood ballads and the Gamelyn romance. Its terse, impersonal, self-contained, and restrained yet dramatic style is typical of the best ballads that have been recorded in more recent times and presumably also of the innumerable ballads of an earlier age that were never recorded. (According to Piers Plowman in the late fourteenth century, Sloth knew rhymes of Robin Hood better than he knew his paternoster; unfortunately no one at that time bothered to write them down.)

The meter of *Robyn and Gandeleyn* is seven-beat couplets with a repeated refrain; see Introduction, type 7, page 31.

The best edition is Child, No. 115 (cf. No. 117 and No. 119). Child also provides bibliographical material. See also Chambers, *OHEL*, pp. 131–32, 136, 153. The only manuscript is British Museum Sloane 2593, published in *Songs and Carols from a Manuscript in the British Museum of the Fifteenth Century*, ed. Thomas Wright, Warton Club, 4 (London, 1856).

I herde a carpyng° of a clerk	story
Al at yone° wodes ende	that
Of gode Robyn and Gandeleyn;	
Was ther non other thynge.	
5 *Robynn lyth° in grene wode bowndyn.°*	lies bound
Stronge° thevys wern tho chylderin non°	Confirmed **tho . . .** those youths not
But bowmen gode and hende.°	courteous
He° wentyn to wode to getyn hem fleych°	They **hem fleych** themselves meat
If God wold it hem° sende.	to them
10 Al day wentyn tho chylderin too°	two
And fleych fowndyn he non°	none
Til it were ageyn° evyn;	toward
The chylderin wold gon° hom.	**chylderin . . .** youths were about to go

Half an honderid of fat falyf° der   fallow
15   He comyn ayon,°   **comyn ayon** came upon
And alle he° wern fayr and fat inow,°   they (the deer)   enough
  But markyd° was ther non.°   marked   none (of them)
"By dere God," seyde gode Robyn,
  "Hereof we xul° have on."°   shall   one

20 Robyn bent his joly bowe;
  Therin he set a flo.°   arrow
The fattest der of alle
  The herte he clef a to.°   **clef** ... split in two

He hadde not the der i-flawe°   flayed
25   Ne° half out of the hyde,   Nor
There cam a schrewde arwe° out of the west   **schrewde arwe** evil arrow
  That felde Robertes pryde.

Gandeleyn lokyd hym est and west
  Be° every syde.   On
30 "Hoo hat° myn mayster slayin?   **Hoo hat** Who has
  Ho hat don this dede?
Xal I° never out of grene wode go   **Xal I** I shall
  Til I se sydis blede."

Gandeleyn lokyd hym est and lokyd west
35   And sowt° under the sunne.   south
He saw a lytil boy°   churl
  He clepyn° Wrennok of Donne,   **He clepyn** They call

A good bowe in his hond,
  A brod arwe° therine,   arrow
40 And fowre-and-twenti goode arwys
  Trusyd° in a thrumme.°   Placed   holder
"Be war thee,° war thee, Gandeleyn,   **Be** ... Beware
  Herof thu xalt han° summe.   **xalt han** shall have

"Be war thee, war thee, Gandeleyn,
45   Herof thu gyst plenté."°   **gyst plenté** will get plenty
"Ever on° for another," seyde Gandeleyn;   one
  "Mysaunter have he° xal fle!"   **Mysaunter** ... Disaster may he have who

"Qwerat° xal our marke be?"   At what
  Seyde Gandeleyn.
50 "Everyche° at otheris herte,"   Each
  Seyde Wrennok ageyn.°   in reply

"Ho xal yeve° the ferste schote?"   **xal yeve** shall give
    Seyde Gandeleyn.
"And I xul yeve° thee on beforn,"°   give   **on beforn** one at first
55   Seyde Wrennok ageyn.

Wrennok schette a ful° good schote—   very
    And he schet not too hye°—   high
Throw the sanchothis° of his bryk;°   fork (?)   breeches
    It towchyd neyther thye.°   thigh

60 "Now hast thu yovyn° me on beforn,"°   given   **on beforn** one at first
    Al thus to Wrennok seyde he,
"And throw the myght of Our Lady
    A bettere I xal yeve° thee."   **xal yeve** shall give

Gandeleyn bent his goode bowe
65   And set therin a flo.°   arrow
He schet throw his grene certyl;°   short tunic
    His herte he clef on too.°   **clef . . .** split in two

"Now xalt thu never yelpe,° Wrennok,   boast
    At ale ne° at wyn   nor
70 That thu hast slawe° goode Robyn   slain
    And his knave° Gandeleyn.   retainer

"Now xalt thu never yelpe, Wrennok,
    At wyn ne at ale
That thu hast slawe goode Robyn
75   And Gandeleyn his knave."

Robyn lyghth° in grene wode bowndyn.°   lies   bound

The Blacksmiths

(ca. 1450, Northeast Midland)

This indignant satire is directed against the blacksmiths who kept the poet awake at night. Their assaults on his senses inspired a rich vocabulary of invective, the force of which the modern reader may occasionally miss. The poet calls his tormentors "water-burners" (l. 22) because of their practice of plunging the glowing iron in cold water in order to temper it. He calls them "horse-clothiers" (l. 21) perhaps because they prepared stylish armor for horses or perhaps simply because they prepared shoes and harnesses for farmhorses.

The poem is written in conventional alliterative verse; see Introduction, type 1, page 29.

The best edition is Kenneth Sisam, *Fourteenth Century Verse and Prose* (Oxford, 1921), pp. 169–70, 257–58. For bibliography see Wells, ch. 4.41.

	Poem	Glosses
	Swarte, smekyd° smethes, smateryd wyth smoke,	**Swarte, smekyd** Black, smoky
	Dryve me to deth wyth den° of here dyntes.°	din **here dyntes** their blows
	Swech° noys on nyghtes ne herd° men never.	Such **ne herd** heard
	What knavene cry° and clateryng of knockes!	**knavene cry** shouting of workmen
5	The cammede kongons° cryen after col,° col,	**cammede kongons** twisted monsters **after col** for coal
	And blowen here bellewys that° al here brayn brestes.°	so that bursts
	"Huf, puf," seith that on.° "Haf, paf," that other.	**that on** the one
	Thei spyttyn and spraulyn and spellyn° many spelles.	**spraulyn** . . . shamble and recite
	Thei gnauen and gnacchen;° thei gronys° togydere	**gnauen** . . . grind and gnash their teeth **groan**
10	And holdyn hem hote° wyth here° hard hamers.	**holdyn** . . . keep hot their
	Of a bole° hyde ben° here barm-fellys;°	bull are leather aprons
	Here schankes ben schakeled° for the fere-flunderys.°	protectively covered flaming sparks
	Hevy hamerys thei han° that hard ben handled;	have
	Stark° strokes thei stryken on a stelyd stokke.°	Strong **stelyd stokke** steel anvil
15	"Lus, bus, las, das," rowtyn be rowe.°	**rowtyn** . . . they strike in turn
	Swech dolful a dreme°—the devyl it todryve!°	**dolful** . . . a dreary noise confound
	The mayster longith° a lityl and lascheth° a lesse,°	lengthens hammers smaller piece
	Twyneth hem tweyn and towchith a treble.°	
	"Tik, tak, hic, hac, tiket, taket, tyk, tak,	
20	Lus, bus, lus, das." Swych° lyf thei ledyn,°	Such lead
	Alle clothe-merys.° Cryst hem gyve sorwe!°	these horse-clothiers sorrow
	May no man for bren-waterys° on nyght han° hys rest?	water-burners have

18. Twists them in two and reaches a treble note.

THE
SCOTTISH
RENAISSANCE

The Testament of Cresseid

(ca. 1470, Northern)

All that is known with certainty of Robert Henryson (ca. 1425–ca. 1505) is that his literary career flourished in the last three decades of the fifteenth century and that he lived in Dunfermline. He was probably a master at the Benedictine Abbey grammar school there, but was not necessarily a cleric. Nothing is known for certain of his literary career apart from the surviving works identified with him: *Moral Fables, Orpheus and Eurydice, Robene and Makyne, The Testament of Cresseid*, and a number of other shorter pieces. Like many of his contemporaries, including King James I of Scotland, who wrote *The Kingis Quair*, Henryson was an ardent admirer of Chaucer. *The Testament of Cresseid* particularly expresses this admiration, and the poem soon found its way into the early printed editions of Chaucer as a fitting supplement to *Troilus and Criseyde*.

With stern realism but considerable sympathy Henryson relates the pathetic end of Cresseid, a fate that the more tolerant Chaucer would have hesitated to assign her. Written in rhyme royal, the meter of Chaucer's *Troilus* and of *The Kingis Quair*, *The Testament of Cresseid* adds Henryson's own Renaissance scholarship, as seen in the descriptions of the gods (stanzas xxi ff.), to Chaucer's style. The meter is seven-line stanzas; see Introduction, type 17, page 32.

The best recent edition is Robert Henryson, *Testament of Cressid*, ed. Denton Fox (London, 1968). For bibliography see *CBEL*, 1.257–58, 5.147; Bennett, *OHEL*, pages 122, 173–76, 285; Geddie, *BMSP*, pages 166–86.

i

Ane doolie sessoun to ane cairfull dyte°
Suld° correspond and be equivalent.
Richt sa° it wes quhen° I began to wryte
This tragedie, the wedder richt fervent,°
5 Quhen Aries in middis° of the Lent
Schouris° of haill can fra° the north discend,°
That scantlie° fra the cauld I micht defend.°

Should
so when
wedder ... weather being very severe
the middle
Showers **can fra** did from send down
That scantlie So that hardly protect myself

ii

Yit nevertheles within myne oratur°
I stude, quhen° Titan had his bemis° bricht
10 Withdrawin doun and sylit° under cure,°

chapel
stude, quhen stood, when beams
concealed cover

1. A doleful season to a sorrowful poem

And fair Venus, the bewtie of the nicht,
Uprais° and set unto the west full° richt   Rose up   very
Hir goldin face in oppositioun
Of God Phebus direct discending doun.

iii

15 Throw° out the glas hir bemis brast sa° fair   Through   **bemis . . .** beams burst so
That I micht se, on everie syde me by,
The northin wind had purifyit the air
And sched° the mistie cloudis fra° the sky.   scattered   from
The froist freisit,° the blastis bitterly   **froist freisit** frost froze
20 Fra Pole Artick come quhisling° loud and schill,°   whistling   shrill
And causit me remuse aganis° my will.   **remuse aganis** leave against

iv

For I traistit° that Venus, luifis° Quene,   trusted   love's
To quhome sum tyme° I hecht° obedience,   **quhome . . .** whom formerly   promised
My faidit° hart of lufe scho wald° mak grene.   faded   **scho wald** she would
25 And ther-upon with humbill reverence
I thocht° to pray hir hie° Magnificence,   intended   great
Bot for greit cald as than I lattit was°
And in my chalmer° to the fyre can pas.°   chamber   **can pas** passed

v

Thocht° lufe be hait,° yit in ane° man of age   Though   hot   a
30 It kendillis nocht sa° sone as in youtheid°   so   youth
Of quhome° the blude is flowing in ane rage;   whom
And in the auld the curage doif° and deid,   **curage doif** heart dull
Of quhilk the fyre outward is best remeid.
To help be phisike quhair that nature faillit
35 I am expert, for baith I have assaillit.°

vi

I mend the fyre and beikit° me about,   warmed
Than tuik ane° drink my spreitis° to comfort,   a   spirits
And armit me weill fra° the cauld thair-out.   from
To cut the winter nicht and mak it schort,
40 I tuik ane quair°—and left all uther sport—   book
Writtin be° worthie Chaucer glorious   by
Of fair Creisseid and worthie Troylus.

---

27. Except that I was prevented for the time being by the great cold
33–35. For which external heat is the best remedy. In helping through physic when nature's power fails I am expert, for I have known both.

vii

And thair I fand,° efter that Diomeid	found
Ressavit° had that lady bricht of hew,°	Received hue
45 How Troilus neir out of wit abraid°	jumped
And weipit soir° with visage° paill of hew;	sorrowfully face
For quhilk wanhope° his teiris can renew°	**quhilk wanhope** which despair **can renew** flowed
Quhill° Esperus rejoisit° him agane.	Until gladdened
Thus quhyle° in joy he levit,° quhyle in pane.°	for a while lived torment

viii

50 Of hir behest° he had greit comforting,	promise
Traisting° to Troy that scho suld° mak retour,°	Trusting **scho suld** she should return
Quhilk he desyrit maist of eirdly° thing,	earthly
For-quhy° scho was his only paramour.	Because
But quhen° he saw passit baith day and hour	when
55 Of hir ganecome,° than sorrow can oppres°	return **can oppres** oppressed
His wofull hart in cair and hevines.°	**cair . . .** sorrow and grief

ix

Of his distres me neidis nocht reheirs,°	**me . . .** I need not relate
For worthie Chauceir in the samin° buik,	same
In gudelie termis and in joly veirs,°	**joly veirs** pleasant verse
60 Compylit hes° his cairis, quha° will luik.	has whoever
To brek my sleip ane uther quair° I tuik	book
In quhilk° I fand the fatall destenie	which
Of fair Cresseid, that endit wretchitlie.	

x

Quha wait gif° all that Chauceir wrait was trew?	**Quha . . .** Who knows if
65 Nor I wait nocht gif this narratioun	
Be authoreist or fenyeit° of the new	**authoreist . . .** authorized or feigned
Be° sum Poeit, throw° his inventioun,	By through
Maid to report the lamentatioun	
And wofull end of this lustie Creisseid,	
70 And quhat° distres scho thoillit,° and quhat deid.°	what **scho thoillit** she suffered did

xi

Quhen° Diomeid had all his appetyte	When
And mair° fulfillit of this fair ladie,	more
Upon ane uther he set his haill° delyte	whole
And send to hir ane lybell° of repudie°	bill divorce
75 And hir excludit fra° his companie.	from
Than desolait scho° walkit up and doun,	she
And sum men sayis into the court commoun.°	**court commoun** streets

xii

O fair Cresseid, the flour and A per se° **A** . . . matchless one
Of Troy and Grece, how was thow fortunait° destined
80 To change in filth all thy feminitie,
And be with fleschelie lust sa maculait,° **sa maculait** so stained
And go amang the Greikis air and lait,° **air** . . . early and late
Sa giglotlike takand thy foull plesance?°
I have pietie° thow suld fall sic° mischance. pity such

xiii

85 Yit nevertheles quhat° ever men deme° or say, what judge
In scornefull langage, of thy brukkilnes,° frailty
I sall° excuse als far furth° as I may° shall **als** . . . as far can
Thy womanheid, thy wisdome and fairnes,
The quhilk° Fortoun hes° put to sic° distres **The quhilk** Which has such
90 As hir pleisit°—and nathing throw° the gilt pleased **nathing throw** not through
Of thee—throw wickit langage to be spilt.° destroyed

xiv

This fair lady, in this wyse° destitute manner
Of all comfort and consolatioun,
Richt privelie, but° fellowschip, on fute° **Richt** . . . Very secretly, without foot
95 Disgysit,° passit far out of the toun Disguised
Ane myle or twa,° unto ane° mansioun two a
Beildit° full gay, quhair° hir father Calchas Adorned **gay, quhair** fair, where was
Quhilk° than amang the Greikis dwelland was. Who

xv

Quhen° he hir saw, the caus he can inquyre° When **can inquyre** inquired
100 Of hir cumming. Scho° said, siching full soir:° She **siching** . . . sighing very sorrowfully
"Fra° Diomeid had gottin his desyre, When
He wox werie and wald° of me no moir." **wox** . . . grew weary and wished
  Quod Calchas: "Douchter, weip° thow not **Douchter, weip** Daughter, weep
   thair-foir.
Peraventure° all cummis° for the best. Perhaps happens
105 Welcum to me; thow art full deir ane gest."° **deir** . . . dear a guest

xvi

This auld Calchas, efter° the law was tho,° according to **was tho** which was then
Was keiper of the tempill as ane priest
In quhilk° Venus and hir sone Cupido which
War honourit, and his chalmer° was thame neist,° chamber **thame neist** next to them
110 To quhilk Cresseid with baill aneuch° in breist **baill aneuch** sorrow enough
Usit° to pas,° hir prayeris for to say, Used go
Quhill° at the last, upon ane solempne° day, Until feast

83. Like a harlot taking your foul pleasure?

xvii

As custome was, the pepil far and neir,
Befoir the none,° unto the tempill went   noon
115   With sacrifice devoit° in thair maneir.   devout
Bot still Cresseid, hevie° in hir intent,°   sad   mind
Into the kirk wald° not hir self present   **kirk wald** church would
For giving of the pepill ony deming°   suspicion
Of hir expuls fra° Diomeid the King,   from

xviii

120   Bot past° into ane secreit orature°   she went   chapel
Quhair° scho micht weip° hir wofull desteny.   Where   **micht weip** could weep for
Behind hir bak scho cloisit fast the dure
And on hir kneis bair° fell doun in hy.°   **kneis bair** bare knees   haste
Upon Venus and Cupide angerly
125   Scho cryit out, and said on this same wyse,°   manner
"Allace° that ever I maid you sacrifice.   Alas

xix

"Ye gave me anis° ane devine responsaill°   once   response
That I suld° be the flour of luif° in Troy.   should   love
Now I am maid ane unworthie outwaill,°   outcast
130   And all in cair° translatit is my joy.   **in cair** into sorrow
Quha sall° me gyde?° Quha sall me now convoy   **Quha sall** Who shall   guide
Sen° I fra Diomeid and nobill Troylus   Since
Am clene° excludit, as abject° odious.   completely   outcast

xx

"O fals Cupide, is nane to wyte° bot thow   blame
135   And thy mother, of lufe° the blind Goddes.°   love   Goddess
Ye causit me alwayis understand and trow°   believe
The seid of lufe was sawin° in my face,   sown
And ay° grew grene throw° your supplie and   ever   through
     grace.
Bot now allace° that seid with froist° is slane,   alas   frost
140   And I fra luifferis° left and all forlane."°   lovers   forgotten

xxi

Quhen° this was said, doun in ane extasie,   When
Ravischit in spreit, intill° ane dreame scho fell;   **spreit, intill** spirit, into
And be° apperance hard, quhair° scho did ly,   by   **hard, quhair** heard, where
Cupide the King ringand° ane silver bell,   ringing
145   Quhilk° men micht heir fra hevin unto hell,   Which
At quhais° sound befoir Cupide appeiris°   whose   appear
The sevin planetis[1] discending fra thair spheiris,

[1] Seven planets, namely Saturn, Jupiter, Mars, Sun (Phoebus), Venus, Mercury, Moon (Cynthia).

xxii

Quhilk hes power of all thing generabill°   created
To reull and steir° be thair greit influence   **reull** ... rule and steer
150   Wedder° and wind and coursis variabill.   Weather
And first of all Saturne gave his sentence,
Quhilk gave to Cupide litill reverence,
Bot as ane busteous° churl on° his maneir   rough   in
Come crabitlie° with auster° luik and cheir.°   sourly   severe   countenance

xxiii

155   His face fronsit,° his lyre° was lyke the leid.°   wrinkled   complexion   lead
His teith chatterit, and cheverit° with the chin;   shook
His ene° drowpit, how° sonkin in his heid;   eyes   hollow
Out of his nois° the meldrop° fast can rin,°   nose   mucous   **can rin** ran
With lippis bla° and cheikis leine and thin.   livid
160   The iceschoklis° that fra his hair doun hang   icicles
Was wonder° greit, and as ane speir als° lang.   wonderfully   as

xxiv

Atouir° his belt his lyart lokkis° lay   Over   **lyart lokkis** gray locks
Felterit° unfair, ouirfret° with froistis hoir,°   Tangled   decorated   **froistis hoir** white frost
His garmound° and his gyis full gay° of gray;   garment   **gyis** ... very fair attire
165   His widderit weid° fra him the wind out woir.°   **widdereit weid** withered garment   blew
Ane busteous° bow within his hand he boir,°   stout   carried
Under his girdill ane flasche° of felloun flanis°   sheaf   **felloun flanis** deadly arrows
Fedderit° with ice, and heidit° with hailstanis.°   Feathered   headed   hailstones

xxv

Than° Juppiter, richt fair and amiabill,   Then (came)
170   God of the starnis° in the firmament,   stars
And nureis° to all thing generabill,°   nourisher   created
Fra his father Saturne far different,
With burelie° face, and browis bricht and brent,°   strong   **browis** ... brows fair and smooth
Upon his heid ane garland wonder gay°   **wonder gay** wonderfully fair
175   Of flouris fair as it had bene in May.

xxvi

His voice was cleir, as cristall were his ene,°   eyes
As goldin wyre sa glitterand was his hair,
His garmound° and his gyis° full gay of grene,   garment   attire
With goldin listis° gilt on everie gair.°   borders   gore
180   Ane burelie brand° about his middil bair,°   **burelie brand** stout sword   bore
In his richt hand he had ane groundin° speir,   sharpened
Of his Father the wraith° fra us to weir.°   anger   defend

xxvii

Nixt efter him come Mars the God of ire,
Of strife, debait, and all dissensioun,
185 To chide and fecht, als feirs° as ony fyre,　　**fecht** ... fight, as fierce
In hard harnes, hewmound, and habirgeoun,°
And on his hanche° ane roustie fell fachioun;°　　hip **fell fachioun** cruel falchion
And in his hand he had ane roustie sword.
Wrything° his face with mony° angrie word,　　Twisting　many an

xxviii

190 Schaikand° his sword, befoir Cupide he come　　Shaking
With reid visage,° and grislie glowrand ene,°　　face　**glowrand ene** glowering eyes
And at his mouth ane bullar stude° of fome　　**bullar stude** bubble stood
Lyke to ane bair quhetting° his tuskis kene,　　**bair quhetting** boar whetting
Richt tuilyeour-lyke, but° temperance in tene;°　　**tuilyeour-lyke, but** like a bully, without anger
195 Ane horne he blew, with mony bosteous brag,°　　**mony** ... many a rough blast
Quhilk all this warld with weir° hes maid to wag.°　　fear　shiver

xxix

Than° fair Phebus, lanterne and lamp of licht,　　Then came
Of man and beist, baith frute and flourisching,°　　**frute** ... harvest and growth
Tender nureis,° and banischer of nicht,　　nourisher
200 And of the warld causing, be° his moving　　by
And influence, lyfe in all eirdlie° thing,　　earthly
Without comfort of quhome, of force to nocht°
Must all ga° die that in this warld is wrocht.°　　go　made

xxx

As king royall he raid° upon his chair　　rode
205 The quhilk Phaeton gydit sum tyme, upricht.°　　**gydit** ... drove formerly, indeed
The brichtnes of his face quhen it was bair
Nane micht behald for peirsing° of his sicht.　　blinding
This goldin cart with fyrie bemis° bricht　　beams
Four yokkit steidis full° different of hew°　　very　hue
·210 But bait° or tyring throw° the spheiris drew.　　**But bait** Without stopping　through

xxxi

The first was soyr,° with mane als° reid as rois,　　reddish brown　as
Callit Eoye into the Orient.
The secund steid to name hecht° Ethios,　　is called
Quhitlie° and paill, and sum deill ascendent;°　　Whitish　**sum** ... somewhat dominant
215 The thrid Peros, richt hait and richt fervent;°　　**richt hait** ... very hot and very fiery

186. In strong armor, helmet, and coat of mail
202. Without whose comfort, of necessity to nothing

The feird° was blak, callit Phlegoney,[2]　　　　fourth
Quhilk rollis Phebus doun into the sey.°　　　　sea

xxxii

Venus was thair present, that goddes gay,°　　　　fair
Hir sonnis querrell° for to defend, and mak　　　　case
220 Hir awin° complaint, cled in ane nyce° array,　　　　own　odd
The ane half grene, the uther half sabill blak;
Quhyte° hair as gold kemmit and sched° abak,　　　　Fair　**kemmit** . . . combed and parted
Bot in hir face semit° greit variance,　　　　appeared
Quhyles° perfyte treuth, and quhyles inconstance.°　　　　For a while　inconstancy

xxxiii

225 Under° smyling scho was dissimulait,°　　　　When　dissembling
Provocative, with blenkis° amorous,　　　　glances
And suddanely changit and alterait,
Angrie as ony serpent vennemous,
Richt pungitive,° with wordis odious.　　　　stinging
230 Thus variant° scho was, quha list tak keip;°　　　　inconstant　**quha** . . . whoever pleases take
　　　　　　　　　　　　　　　　　　　　　　　　　　heed
With ane eye lauch,° and with the uther weip,　　　　laughs

xxxiv

In taikning° that all fleschelie paramour　　　　tokening
Quhilk Venus hes in reull° and governance,　　　　rule
Is sum tyme sweit, sum tyme bitter and sour,
235 Richt° unstabill, and full of variance,　　　　Very
Mingit° with cairfull° joy and fals plesance,°　　　　Mixed　sorrowful　delight
Now hait,° now cauld, now blyith,° now full of　　　　hot　happy
　　wo,
Now grene as leif, now widderit and ago.°　　　　**widderit** . . . withered and gone

xxxv

With buik in hand than come Mercurius,
240 Richt eloquent, and full of rethorie,°　　　　rhetoric
With polite termis and delicious,°　　　　charming
With pen and ink to report all reddie,
Setting sangis and singand° merilie.　　　　**sangis** . . . songs and singing
His hude° was reid heklit atouir° his croun,　　　　hood　**reid** . . . red fringed around
245 Lyke to ane poeit of the auld fassoun.

xxxvi

Boxis he bair with fyne electuairis,°　　　　electuaries
And sugerit syropis for digestioun,
Spycis belangand° to the pothecairis,　　　　belonging

---

[2] The names of the four horses of the sun are here derived from Ovid, *Metamorphoses*, ii. 153–54: Eous, Aethon, Pyroeis, and Phlegon.

With mony hailsum° sweit confectioun;   **mony hailsum** many a wholesome
250 Doctour in Phisick° cled in ane skarlot goun,   Medicine
And furrit° weill, as sic ane aucht° to be,   furred   ought
Honest and gude, and not ane word culd lie.

xxxvii

Nixt efter him come Lady Cynthia,
The last of all, and swiftest in hir spheir,
255 Of colour blak, buskit° with hornis twa,°   dressed   two
And in the nicht scho listis° best appeir,   is pleased to
Haw° as the leid,° of colour nathing cleir,°   Dull in color   lead   bright
For all hir licht scho borrowis at° hir brother   from
Titan, for of hirself scho hes nane uther.

xxxviii

260 Hir gyse° was gray, and full of spottis blak,   gown
And on hir brest ane churle³ paintit full evin,°   **full evin** very precisely
Beirand° ane bunche of thornis on his bak,   Bearing
Quhilk° for his thift° micht clim na nar° the hevin.   Who   theft   **na nar** no nearer
Thus quhen thay gadderit war, thir° goddes sevin,   **war, thir** were, these
265 Mercurius thay cheisit with ane assent°   **cheisit** . . . chose unanimously
To be foirspeikar° in the Parliament.   spokesman

xxxix

Quha° had been thair, and liken° for to heir   Whoever   minded
His facound° toung, and termis exquisite,   eloquent
Of rethorick the prettick° he micht leir°   practice   learn
270 In breif sermone° ane pregnant sentence wryte.°   discourse   to write
Befoir Cupide veiling° his cap alyte,°   doffing   a little
Speiris° the caus of that vocatioun;°   He asks   summons
And he anone schew° his intentioun.   showed

xl

"Lo!" quod Cupide, "quha° will blaspheme the
name   whoever
275 Of his awin god, outher° in word or deid,   either
To all goddis he dois baith lak° and schame,   **baith lak** both fault
And suld° have bitter panis° to his meid.°   should   torments   reward
I say this by yone° wretchit Cresseid,   **by yone** of yonder
The quhilk throw° me was sum tyme flour° of
lufe,°   through   **sum** . . . formerly flower
    love
280 Me and my mother starklie can reprufe,°   **starklie** . . . severely she reproved

---

³ The Man in the Moon.

xli

"Saying of hir greit infelicitie
I was the caus, and my mother Venus,
Ane blind goddes° hir cald that micht° not se,   *goddess   could*
With sclander and defame° injurious.   **sclander . . .** *slander and defamation*
285 Thus hir leving° unclene and lecherous   **hir leving** *her own living*
Scho wald returne on me and my mother,
To quhome° I schew my grace abone° all uther.   *whom   above*

xlii

"And sen° ye ar all sevin deificait°   *since   deified*
Participant of devyne sapience,
290 This greit injurie done to our hie estait°   *rank*
Me think with pane we suld mak recompence.°
Was never to goddes done sic° violence.   *such*
As weill for yow, as for my self I say,
Thair-foir ga° help to revenge I yow pray."   *go*

xliii

295 Mercurius to Cupide gave answeir
And said: "Schir° King, my counsall is that ye   *Sir*
Refer yow to the hiest planeit heir,
And tak to him the lawest° of degre,   *lowest*
The pane° of Cresseid for to modifie;°   *torment   judge*
300 As God Saturne, with him tak Cynthia."
"I am content," quod he, "to tak thay twa."°   *two*

xliv

Than thus proceidit, Saturne and the Mone,
Quhen thay the mater rypelie° had degest,°   *fully   considered*
For the dispyte° to Cupide scho had done,   *contempt*
305 And to Venus oppin° and manifest,   *clear*
In all hir lyfe with pane° to be opprest,   *torment*
And torment sair° with seiknes incurabill,   *sorrowful*
And to all lovers be abhominabill.

xlv

This duleful sentence Saturne tuik on hand,
310 And passit doun quhair cairfull° Cresseid lay,   **quhair cairfull** *where sorrowful*
And on hir heid he laid ane frostie wand.
Than lawfullie on° this wyse can° he say: **lawfullie on** *by law in*   **wyse can** *manner did*
"Thy greit fairnes and all thy bewtie gay,°   *fair*
Thy wantoun blude, and eik° thy goldin hair,   *also*
315 Heir° I exclude fra thee for evermair.   *Here*

291. It seems to me that with torment we should exact atonement.

xlvi

"I change thy mirth into melancholy,
Quhilk is the mother of all pensivenes;
Thy moisture and thy heit in cald° and dry;   **in cald** into cold
Thyne insolence, thy play and wantones
320 To greit diseis; thy pomp and thy riches
In mortall neid; and greit penuritie
Thow suffer sall,° and as ane beggar die."   shall

xlvii

O cruel Saturne, fraward and angrie!
Hard is thy dome,° and too malitious.   judgment
325 On fair Cresseid quhy° hes thow na mercie,   why
Quhilk° was sa° sweit, gentill, and amorous?   Who so
Withdraw thy sentence and be gracious
As thow was never; sa schawis thow thy deid,°   **schawis**... your deed reveals you
Ane wraikfull° sentence gevin on fair Cresseid.   vengeful

xlviii

330 Than Cynthia, quhen Saturne past away,
Out of hir sait discendit doun belyve,°   quickly
And red ane bill° on Cresseid quhair scho lay,   decree
Contening this sentence diffinityve:
"Fra heit of bodie I thee now depryve,
335 And to thy seiknes sall° be na recure,°   shall   recovery
Bot in dolour thy dayis to indure.

xlix

"Thy cristal ene° minglit with blude I mak;   eyes
Thy voice sa cleir unplesand, hoir, and hace;°   **unplesand**...unpleasing, rough, and
                                                                                      hoarse
Thy lustie lyre° ouirspred with spottis blak;   **lustie lyre** beautiful face
340 And lumpis haw° appeirand in thy face.   livid
Quhair thow cummis, ilk° man sall° fle the place.   each   shall
This° sall thow go begging fra hous to hous,   Thus
With cop° and clapper lyke ane lazarous."°   cup   leprous one

l

This doolie° dreame, this uglye visioun   doleful
345 Brocht to an end, Cresseid fra it awoik.
And all that court and convocatioun
Vanischit away; than rais scho up and tuik
Ane poleist° glas, and hir schaddow culd luik.°   polished   **culd luik** looked at
And quhen scho saw hir face sa deformait,
350 Gif° scho in hart was wa aneuch,° God wait!°   Whether   **wa aneuch** woe enough   know

534

li

Weiping full sair,° "Lo quhat° it is," quod sche,   sorrowfully what
With fraward° langage for to mufe° and steir   perverse move
Our craibit goddis,° and sa is sene on me!   **craibit goddis** irritable gods
My blaspheming now have I bocht full° deir.   **bocht full** paid for very
355 All eirdlie° joy and mirth I set areir.°   earthly **set areir** leave behind
Allace° this day, allace this wofull tyde,°   Alas time
Quhen I began with my goddis for to chyde."

lii

Be° this was said, ane chyld come fra the hall   When
To warne Cresseid the supper was reddy,
360 First knokkit at the dure, and syne culd call:°   **syne . . .** then called
"Madame, your father biddis yow cum in hy.°   haste
He hes mervell° sa lang on grouf° ye ly,   wonder **on grouf** in groveling
And sayis your prayers bene too lang sum deill.°   **too . . .** somewhat too long
The goddis wait° all your intent full weill."   know

liii

365 Quod scho: "Fair chyld, ga° to my father deir,   go
And pray him cum to speik with me anone."°   at once
And sa he did, and said, "Douchter, quhat cheir?"°   **quhat cheir** how are you
"Allace,"° quod scho, "Father, my mirth is gone."   Alas
"How sa?" quod he; and scho can all expone°   **can . . .** set forth everything
370 As I have tauld, the vengeance and the wraik°   punishment
For hir trespas Cupide on hir culd tak.°   **culd tak** took

liv

He luikit on hir uglye lipper° face,   leper
The quhylk befor was quhite° as lillie flour,   white
Wringand his handis, oftymes he said allace°   alas
375 That he had levit° to se that wofull hour,   lived
For he knew weill that thair was na succour
To hir seiknes, and that dowblit° his pane.°   doubled torment
Thus was thair cair aneuch° betwix thame twane.   **cair aneuch** sorrow enough

lv

Quhen thay togidder murnit° had full lang,°   mourned long
380 Quod Cresseid: "Father, I wald° not be kend.°   would known
Thair-foir in secret wyse° ye let me gang°   manner go
Unto yone hospitall at the tounis end.
And thidder sum meit° for cheritie me send   food
To leif° upon, for all mirth in this eird°   live earth
385 Is fra me gane; sic° is my wickit weird."°   such fate

lvi

Than in ane mantill and ane baver° hat,   beaver
With cop° and clapper wonder prively,°   cup **wonder prively** very secretly
He opnit° ane secreit yet,° and out thair at   opened gate
Convoyit hir, that na man suld° espy,   should
390 Unto ane village half ane myle thair-by,
Delyverit hir in at the spittaill° hous,   leper
And daylie sent hir part of his almous.°   sustenance

lvii

Sum knew hir weill, and sum had na knawledge
Of hir becaus scho was sa deformait,
395 With bylis° blak ouirspred in her visage,°   boils face
And hir fair colour faidit and alterait.
Yit thay presumit,° for hir hie regrait°   suspected **hie regrait** great sorrow
And still murning,° scho was of nobill kin;   **still murning** quiet mourning
With better will thair-foir they tuik hir in.

lviii

400 The day passit, and Phebus went to rest;
The cloudis blak ouirquhelmit° all the sky.   overwhelmed
God wait gif° Cresseid was ane sorrowfull gest,°   **wait gif** knows if guest
Seeing that uncouth fair and harbery.°   **uncouth...** unaccustomed fare and lodging
But meit° or drink scho dressit° hir to ly   **But meit** Without food prepared
405 In ane dark corner of the house allone.
And on° this wyse° weiping, scho maid hir mone.°   in manner lamentation

� THE COMPLAINT OF CRESSEID

lix

"O sop of° sorrow, sonkin into cair:°   **sop of** one immersed in sorrow
O cative° Creisseid, for now and ever mair,   wretched
Gane is thy joy and all thy mirth in eird;°   earth
410 Of all blyithnes° now art thou blaiknit bair.°   happiness **blaiknit bair** pale bereft
Thair is na salve may saif° thee of thy sair;°   **may saif** that can cure sorrow
Fell° is thy fortoun, wickit is thy weird.°   Evil fate
Thy blys is baneist,° and thy baill on breird.°   banished **baill...** sorrow overflowing
Under the eirth, God gif° I gravin° wer,   grant buried
415 Quhair° nane of Grece nor yit of Troy micht
heird.°   Where   **micht heird** could hear

lx

"Quhair is thy chalmer° wantounlie besene,°   chamber adorned
With burely° bed and bankouris browderit bene,°   well-made **bankouris...** covers embroidered beautifully
Spycis and wyne to thy collatioun,

    The cowpis° all of gold and silver schene,°   cups   bright
420 The sweit meitis,° servit in plaittis clene,   foods
    With saipheron sals° of ane gude sessoun,°   **saipheron sals** saffron sauce   seasoning
    Thy gay garmentis with mony° gudely goun,   many a
    Thy plesand lawn° pinnit with goldin prene?°   **plesand lawn** pleasing fine cloths   pin
    All is areir,° thy greit royall renoun.   past

lxi

425 "Quhair is thy garding° with thir greissis° gay,   garden   grasses
    And fresche flowris, quhilk the Quene Floray
    Had paintit plesandly in everie pane,°   flowerbed
    Quhair thou was wont full merilye in May,
    To walk and tak the dew be° it was day   when
430 And heir° the merle° and mavis mony ane,°   hear   blackbird   **mony ane** many a one
    With ladyis fair in carrolling to gane,°   go
    And se the royal rinkis° in thair array,   men
    In garmentis gay garnischit on everie grane?°   color

lxii

    "Thy greit triumphand° fame and hie honour,   triumphant
435 Quhair thou was callit of eirdlye wichtis flour,°   **of . . .** flower of earthly creatures
    All is decayit; thy weird° is welterit° so.   fate   reversed
    Thy hie estait° is turnit in darknes dour.°   rank   severe
    This lipper ludge° tak for thy burelie bour,°   **lipper ludge** leper lodging   **burelie bour** goodly bower
    And for thy bed tak now ane bunche of stro;°   straw
440 For waillit° wyne and meitis° thou had tho,°   choice   food which   then
    Tak mowlit° breid, peirrie,° and ceder sour.   mouldy   pear cider
    Bot cop° and clapper, now is all ago.°   **Bot cop** Except for cup   gone

lxiii

    "My cleir voice and courtlie carrolling,
    Quhair I was wont with ladyis for to sing,
445 Is rawk° as ruik,° full hiddeous hoir and hace.°   harsh   rook   **hoir . . .** rough and hoarse
    My plesand port° all utheris precelling,°   bearing   excelling
    Of lustines° I was hald maist conding.°   beauty   excellent
    Now is deformit the figour of my face;
    To luik on it, na leid° now lyking hes.   person
450 Sowpit° in syte,° I say with sair siching,°   Drowned   sorrow   **sair siching** sorrowful sighing
    Ludgeit° amang the lipper leid, 'Allace!'°   Lodged   **lipper . . .** leper people, Alas

lxiv

    "O ladyis fair of Troy and Grece, attend
    My miserie, quhilk nane may comprehend:
    My frivoll° fortoun, my infelicitie;   miserable
455 My greit mischeif quhilk na man can amend.

Be war° in tyme, approchis neir the end;　　　careful
And in your mynd ane mirrour mak of me,
As I am now, peradventure that ye
For all your micht may cum to that same end,
460　Or ellis war, gif ony° war may be.　　　**ellis** . . . else worse, if any

lxv

"Nocht is your fairnes bot ane faiding flour,
Nocht is your famous laud° and hie honour　　　praise
Bot wind inflat° in uther mennis eiris.°　　　blown　ears
Your roising reid° to rotting sall retour.°　　　**roising reid** rosy red　return
465　Exempill mak of me in your memour,
Quhilk of sic° thingis wofull witnes beiris;　　　such
All welth in eird,° away as wind it weiris.°　　　**in eird** on earth　wastes away
Be war° thair-foir; approchis neir the hour.　　　careful
Fortoun is fikkill, quhen scho beginnis and steiris."°　　　rules

lxvi

470　Thus chydand° with hir drerie° destenye,　　　finding fault　sad
Weiping, scho woik° the nicht fra end to end.　　　lay awake
Bot all in vane; hir dule,° hir cairfull cry　　　lament
Micht not remeid,° nor yit hir murning mend.°　　　cure her　**murning mend** mourning
　　　　　　　　　　　　　　　　　　　　　　　relieve
Ane lipper° lady rais and till° hir wend,°　　　leper　**rais** . . . rose and to　went
475　And said: "Quhy spurnis thow° aganis the wall,　　　**Quhy** . . . Why do you hurl yourself
To sla° thy self, and mend nathing at all?　　　slay

lxvii

"Sen° thy weiping dowbillis bot° thy wo,　　　Since　**dowbillis bot** only doubles
I counsall thee mak vertew of ane neid,
To leir° to clap thy clapper to and fro,　　　learn
480　And leir efter° the law of lipper leid."°　　　according to　**lipper leid** leper people
Thair was na buit,° bot furth with thame scho　　　remedy
　　　yeid°　　　went
Fra place to place, quhill° cauld and hounger sair°　　　while　sore
Compellit hir to be ane rank beggair.

lxviii

That samin° tyme, of Troy the garnisoun,°　　　same　warriors
485　Quhilk had to° chiftane worthie Troylus,　　　as
Throw jeopardie of weir° had strikken doun　　　war
Knichtis of Grece in number mervellous.
With greit tryumphe and laude° victorious　　　praise
Agane° to Troy richt° royallie thay raid°　　　Back　very　rode
490　The way quhair Cresseid with the lipper baid.°　　　stayed

lxix

Seeing that companie, thai come; all with ane
    stevin°   **ane stevin** one voice
Thay gaif° ane cry, and schuik coppis gude speid;°   gave   **schuik** . . . shook their cups rapidly
Said: "Worthie Lordis, for Goddis lufe° of hevin,   love
To us lipper, part of° your almous-deid."°   **part of** distribute   charity
495   Than to thair cry nobill Troylus tuik heid,
Having pietie, neir by the place can pas°   **can pas** passed
Quhair Cresseid sat, not witting° quhat scho was.   knowing

lxx

Than upon him scho kest up baith° hir ene,°   **kest** . . . raised both   eyes
And with ane blenk° it come into his thocht   glance
500   That he sumtime hir face befoir had sene.
Bot scho was in sic plye° he knew hir nocht.   state
Yit than hir luik° into his mynd it brocht   appearance
The sweit visage and amorous blenking°   expression
Of fair Cresseid, sumtyme° his awin° darling.   formerly   own

lxxi

505   Na wonder was, suppois in mynd that he°
Tuik° her figure° sa sone, and lo now quhy?°   Recognized   appearance   why
The idole° of ane thing in cace° may be   image   **in cace** by chance
Sa deip imprentit in the fantasy
That it deludis the wittis° outwardly,   senses
510   And sa appeiris in forme and lyke estait,°   condition
Within the mynd as it was figurait.°   pictured

lxxii

Ane spark of lufe° than till° his hart culd spring,°   love   to   **culd spring** sprang
And kendlit all his bodie in ane fyre.
With hait° fevir ane sweit° and trimbling   hot   sweat
515   Him tuik, quhill° he was reddie to expyre.   until
To beir his scheild his breist began to tyre.
Within ane quhyle° he changit mony hew,°   while   **mony hew** many a hue
And nevertheles not ane ane uther knew.°   **not** . . . one knew not the other

lxxiii

For knichtlie pietie and memoriall
520   Of fair Cresseid, ane gyrdill can° he tak,   did
Ane purs of gold, and mony gay jowall,
And in the skirt of Cresseid doun can swak;°   **can swak** threw
Than raid° away, and not ane word he spak,   rode
Pensive in hart, quhill° he come to the toun,   until
525   And for greit cair° oft syis° almaist fell doun.   sorrow   times

505. It was no wonder if he in his own mind

lxxiv

The lipper folk to Cresseid than can draw°   **can draw** drew
To se the equall distributioun
Of the almous,° bot quhen the gold thay saw,   alms
Ilk° ane to uther prevelie can roun,°   Each   **prevelie** . . . secretly whispered
530 And said: "Yone lord hes mair affectioun,
How ever it be, unto yone lazarous,°   leprous one
Than to us all. We knaw be° his almous."   by

lxxv

"Quhat lord is yone," quod scho; "have ye na
     feill,°   knowledge
Hes done to us so greit humanitie?"
535 "Yes," quod a lipper man, "I knaw him weill.
Schir Troylus it is, gentill and fre."°   **gentill** . . . noble and generous
Quhen Cresseid understude that it was he,
Stiffer° than steill° thair stert° ane bitter stound°   Stronger   steel   leapt   pang
Throwout hir hart, and fell doun to the ground.

lxxvi

540 Quhen scho ouircome,° with siching° sair and sad,   came to   sighing
With mony° cairfull cry and cald° "Ochane":   many a   cold
"Now is my breist with stormie stoundis stad,°   beset
Wrappit in° wo, ane wretch full will of wane."°   **Wrappit in** Enveloped by   **will** . . . devoi
     of purpose
Than swounit scho oft or° scho culd refrane,°   before   restrain herself
545 And ever in hir swouning cryit scho thus:
"O fals Cresseid and trew knicht Troylus.

lxxvii

"Thy lufe,° thy lawtie,° and thy gentilnes,   love   faithfulness
I countit small in my prosperitie,
Sa elevait I was in wantones,
550 And clam° upon the fickill quheill° sa hie.   climbed   wheel of fortune
All faith and lufe I promissit to thee
Was in the self° fickill and frivolous: same promise
O fals Cresseid, and trew knicht Troilus.

lxxviii

"For lufe of me thow keipt gude continence,
555 Honest and chaist in conversatioun.
Of all wemen protectour and defence
Thou was, and helpit thair opinioun.°   reputation
My mind in fleschelie foull affectioun
Was inclynit to lustis lecherous:
560 Fy fals Cresseid, O trew knicht Troylus.

lxxix

"Lovers, be war,° and tak gude heid° about   careful heed

Quhome° that ye lufe,° for quhome ye suffer   Whom love

    paine.°   torment

I lat° yow wit,° thair is richt few thair-out   let know

Quhome ye may traist to have trew lufe agane.°   back from

565 Preif° quhen ye will, your labour is in vaine.   Try

Thair-foir, I reid,° ye tak thame as ye find,   advise

For thay ar sad° as widdercok° in wind!   steady weathervane

lxxx

"Becaus I knaw the greit unstabilnes

Brukkill° as glas, into° my self I say,   Frail unto

570 Traisting in uther als° greit unfaithfulnes,   as

Als unconstant, and als untrew of fay:°   faith

Thocht° sum be trew, I wait° richt few ar thay.   Though know

Quha findis treuth,° lat him his lady ruse.°   faithfulness praise

Nane but my self as now I will accuse."

lxxxi

575 Quhen this was said, with paper scho sat doun,

And on this maneir maid hir testament:

"Heir I beteiche° my corps and carioun   bequeath

With° wormis and with taidis° to be rent.   By toads

My cop° and clapper and myne ornament,°   cup jewels

580 And all my gold the lipper folk sall have,

Quhen I am deid, to burie me in grave.

lxxxii

"This royall ring, set with this rubie reid,°   red

Quhilk Troylus in drowrie° to me send,°   **in drowrie** as a love token sent

To him agane I leif it quhen I am deid,

585 To mak my cairfull deid° unto him kend.°   death known

Thus I conclude schortlie and mak ane end;

My spreit° I leif to Diane quhair scho dwellis,   spirit

To walk with hir in waist woddis° and wellis.°   **waist ...** desolate woods springs

lxxxiii

"O Diomeid, thou hes baith° broche and belt,   both

590 Quhilk Troylus gave me in takning°   tokening

Of his trew lufe," and with that word scho swelt.°   died

And sone ane lipper man tuik off the ring,

Syne° buryit hir withouttin tarying;   Then

To Troylus furthwith the ring he bair,

595 And of Cresseid the deith he can declair.°   **can declair** declared

lxxxiv

Quhen he had hard° hir greit infirmitie,   *heard of*
Hir legacie and lamentatioun,
And how scho endit in sic povertie,
He swelt° for wo, and fell doun in ane swoun; *fainted*
600 For greit sorrow his hart to brist° was boun;° *break ready*
Siching° full sadlie, said: "I can no moir,   *Sighing*
Scho was untrew, and wo is me thair-foir."

lxxxv

Sum said he maid ane tomb of merbell gray,
And wrait° hir name and superscriptioun,   *wrote*
605 And laid it on hir grave quhair that scho lay,
In goldin letteris, conteining this ressoun:° *statement*
"Lo, fair ladyis, Cresseid, of Troyis toun,
Sumtyme° countit the flour of womanheid, *Formerly*
Under this stane, lait° lipper, lyis deid." **stane, lait** stone, formerly a

lxxxvi

610 Now worthie wemen, in this ballet° schort *ballad*
Maid for your worschip° and instructioun, *honor*
Of cheritie, I monische° and exhort,   *admonish*
Ming° not your lufe° with fals deceptioun. *Mix love*
Beir in your mynd this schort conclusioun° **schort conclusioun** rapid end
615 Of fair Cresseid, as I have said befoir.
Sen° scho is deid, I speik of hir no moir.   *Since*

WILLIAM DUNBAR

The Dance of the Seven Deadly Sins

(1496 or 1507, Northern)

William Dunbar (ca. 1460–ca. 1521) was born in Scotland, apparently attended St. Andrews University (in Fife), served in the brilliant Scottish court of King James IV, and, evidently late in life, entered the priesthood. In his use of traditional poetic genres, particularly the religious lyric and the satire, he may be said to be one of the last great medieval poets. In his eclectic imitations both of the old alliterative measure and of the intricately rhymed new stanzas of Chaucer, in his experiments with aureate diction, and in his aggressive individualism he is a pioneer of the Renaissance.

Literary personifications of the Seven Deadly Sins were commonplace even before Langland animated them in *Piers Plowman* (p. 277, above), but in *The Dance* Dunbar recreates his own personal vision of them as if he himself had discovered each sin individually, and as a Lowlander, he concludes the poem by directing a characteristically personal satire against his Gaelic-speaking neighbors in the Highlands.

The meter is twelve-line, tail-rhyme stanzas, with two six-line stanzas interspersed; see Introduction, type 21, page 33.

The Poems of William Dunbar, ed. W. M. MacKenzie (Edinburgh, 1932), contains all of the attributed works; *William Dunbar: Poems*, ed. James Kinsley (Oxford, 1958), though only a selection, is very useful. For a dictionary use *DOST*. For the topic of this selection see Morton W. Bloomfield, *The Seven Deadly Sins* (East Lansing, Mich., 1952), pages 236–38. For bibliography see Lewis, *OHEL*; *CBEL*, 1.255–59, 5.147.

Off° Februar the fyiftene° nycht,   Of fifteenth
Full lang° befoir the dayis lycht,   long
I lay intill° a trance;   in
And then I saw baith° hevin and hell.   both
5 Me thocht,° amangis the feyndis fell°   **Me thocht** It seemed to me **feyndis fell** fell fiends
Mahoun gart cry ane° dance   **Mahoun...** Mohammed called out a
Off schrewis° that wer nevir schrevin°   **Off schrewis** Of wretches absolved
Aganis° the feist of Fasternis Evin°   For **Fasternis Evin** Shrove Tuesday
To mak thair observance.
10 He bad gallandis ga graith° a gyis°   **gallandis...** gallants go prepare masquerade
And kast up gamountis° in the skyis   gambols
That last° came out of France.   just

543

"Lat se," quod he, "now quha° begynnis."   who
With that, the fowll Sevin Deidly Synnis
15 Begowth° to leip at anis.°   Begàn   once
And first of all in dance wes Pryd
With hair wyld° bak and bonet on syd,   dressed
Lyk° to mak waistie wanis.°   Likely **waistie wanis** homes
                                                            impoverished
And round abowt him as a quheill°   wheel
20 Hang° all in rumpillis to the heill   Hung
His kethat° for the nanis.°   clothing occasion
Mony prowd trumpour° with him trippit;°   cheater   danced
Throw skaldand° fyre ay° as thay skippit,°   scalding   ever   skipped
Thay gyrnd° with hiddous granis.°   grimaced   groans

25   Heilie° harlottis on hawtane wyis°   Scornful **on . . .** in disdainful manner
Come in with mony sindrie gyis,°   **sindrie gyis** varied style
Bot yit luche° nevir Mahoun.°   laughed   Mohammed
Quhill° preistis come in with bair-schevin nekkis,   When
Than all the feyndis lewche° and maid gekkis,°   laughed   faces
30 Blak Belly and Bawsy Brown.

      Than Yre come in with sturt° and stryfe.   disturbance
His hand wes ay° upoun his knyfe;   ever
He brandeist° lyk a beir.°   menaced   boar
Bostaris, braggaris, and barganeris°   wranglers
35 Eftir him passit into° pairis,   in
All bodin° in feir° of weir,°   ready   equipment   war
In jakkis and stryppis° and bonettis of steill;   **jakkis . . .** padded jackets and bands
Thair leggis wer chenyeit° to the heill.   chainmailed
Frawart° wes thair affeir.°   Aggressive   behavior
40 Sum upoun udir° with brandis beft;°   others   **brandis beft** swords beat
Sum jaggit° uthiris to the heft°   stabbed   hilt
With knyvis that scherp cowd scheir.°   **cowd scheir** could cut

      Nixt in the dance followit Invy,
Fild full of feid° and fellony,   feud
45 Hid° malyce and dispyte.°   Hidden   spite
For pryvie hatrent° that tratour trymlit.°   **pryvie hatrent** secret hatred   trembled
Him followit mony freik dissymlit°   **mony . . .** many a dissembling man
With fenyeit wirdis quhyte,°   **fenyeit . . .** feigned fair words
And flattereris into° menis facis,   to
50 And bakbyttaris in secreit places
To ley° that had delyte,   lie
And rownaris° of fals lesingis.°   whisperers   lies
Allace that courtis of noble kingis
Of thame can nevir be quyte!°   quit

544

Nixt him in dans come Cuvatyce,
Rute of all evill and grund° of vyce,   source
That nevir cowd be content.
Catyvis,° wrechis, and ockeraris,°   Scoundrels   userers
Hud-pykis, hurdaris, and gadderaris°   **Hud-pykis** ... Misers, hoarders, and
60 All with that warlo° went.   gatherers
                                                          deceiver
Out of thair throttis thay schot on udder°   others
Hett° moltin gold, me thocht° a fudder,°   Hot **me thocht** it seemed to me   mass
As fyreflawcht° maist fervent.   **As fyreflawcht** Like lightning
Ay° as thay tomit thame° of schot,   Ever **tomit thame** emptied themselves
65 Feyndis° fild thame new up to the thrott Fiends
With gold of allkin prent.°   **allkin prent** every kind of impression

Syne Sweirnes,° at the secound bidding,   **Syne Sweirnes** Then Sloth
Come lyk a sow out of a midding;°   dung heap
Full slepy wes his grunyie.°   snout
70 Mony sweir, bumbard belly-huddroun,°
Mony slute daw° and slepy duddroun°   **slute daw** a sluttish slattern   sloven
Him servit ay° with sounyie.°   ever   attention
He drew thame furth intill° a chenyie,°   in   chain
And Belliall with a brydill renyie°   rein
75 Evir lascht thame on the lunyie.°   hindquarters
In dance thay war so slaw of° feit,   on their
Thay° gaif thame in the fyre a heit°   They (the fiends)   heating
And maid tham quicker of counyie.°   response (?)

Than Lichery, that lathly cors,°   **lathly cors** loathsome body
80 Come berand° lyk a bagit° hors,   neighing   gelded
And Ydilnes did him leid.
Thair wes with him ane ugly sort°   group
And mony stynkand,° fowll tramort°   **mony stynkand** many a stinking   corpse
That had in syn bene deid.
85 Quhen° thay wer entrit° in the dance,   When   entered
Thay wer full strenge° of countenance   **full strenge** very strange
Lyk turkas birnand reid.°   **turkas** ... tongs glowing red
All° led thay uthir° by the tersis,°   Though   others   penises
Suppois° thay fyllt with thair ersis,°   Which though **with** ... their bottoms
90 It mycht° be na remeid.°   with
                                            It mycht There could   **na remeid** no
                                               remedy

Than the fowll monstir Glutteny
Off wame unsasiable° and gredy   **Off** ... Of belly insatiable
To dance he did him dres.°   **him dres** prepare himself
Him followit mony fowll drunckart°   drunkard
95 With can and collep, cop °and quart,   **collep, cop** flagon, cup
In surffet and exces.

70. Many a slothful, oafish fat hulk

545

Full° mony a waistles wallydrag°   Very   wastrel
With wamis unweildable° did furth wag   **wamis unweildable** bellies unwieldy
In creische° that did incres.   blubber
100 "Drynk!" ay° thay cryit with mony a gaip.°   ever   gasp
The feyndis° gaif thame hait leid° to laip;°   fiends   **hait leid** hot lead   lap up
Thair lovery° wes na° les!   allowance   no

Na menstrallis playit to thame, but° dowt,   without
For glemen thair wer haldin owt°   **haldin owt** kept out
105 Be° day and eik° by nycht,   By   also
Except a menstral that slew a man;
Swa till° his heretage he wan°   **Swa till** So to   won
And entirt° be breif° of richt.°   entered   writ   right

Than cryd Mahoun° for a Heleand padyane;°   Mohammed   **Heleand padyane** Highland pageant
110 Syne° ran a feynd° to feche MakFadyane[1]   Then   fiend
Far northwart in a nuke.
Be° he the correnoch° had done schout,   When   lament
Erschemen° so gadderit him abowt   Ersemen (Highlanders)
In Hell grit rowme° thay tuke.   **grit rowme** great space
115 Thae tarmegantis° with tag and tatter   **Thae tarmegantis** Those savages
Full° lowd in Ersche begowth° to clatter   Very   **Ersche begowth** Erse (Gaelic) began
And rowp° lyk revin and ruke.°   croaked   **revin...** raven and rook
The devill sa devit° wes with thair yell   **sa devit** so dazed
That in the depest pot of hell
120 He smorit° thame with smuke.   smothered

[1] 'MacFadyan,' that is, some typical Highland Scot, or perhaps the traitor MacFadyan, who, according to Henry the Minstrel's *Wallace*, was slain by Wallace.

WILLIAM DUNBAR

On the Resurrection of Christ

(ca. 1500–12, Northern)

As in the previous selection from Dunbar (see p. 543), the topic here is commonplace, but the pealing organ notes of this Ascension Day lyric represent the particular hymnodic genius of Dunbar.

The meter is eight-line stanzas; see Introduction, type 19, page 33.

The Poems of William Dunbar, ed. W. M. MacKenzie (Edinburgh, 1932), contains all the attributed works; *William Dunbar: Poems*, ed. James Kinsley (Oxford, 1958), though only a selection, is very useful. For a dictionary use *DOST*. For bibliography see Lewis, *OHEL*; *CBEL*, 1.258–59, 5.147.

	Done° is a battell on the dragon blak;	Completed
	Our campioun° Christ confountet hes° his force.	champion has
	The yettis° of Hell ar brokin with a crak;	gates
	The signe triumphall ras't° is of the Croce;°	raised Cross
5	The divillis trymmillis° with hiddous voce;°	tremble voice
	The saulis ar borrowit° and to the blis can go;	redeemed
	Christ with his blud our ransonis does indoce.°	ensure
	Surrexit Dominus de sepulchro.°	
	Dungin° is the deidly dragon Lucifer,	Stricken
10	The crewall serpent with the mortall stang,°	sting
	The auld, kene tegir° with his teith on-char,°	**kene tegir** bold tiger ajar
	Quhilk° in await hes lyne° for us so lang,	Who lain
	Thinking to grip us in his clowis strang.°	**clowis strang** strong claws
	The mercifull Lord wald nocht° that it wer so;	**wald nocht** did not wish
15	He maid him for to felye of that fang.°	**felye . . .** miss that grasp
	Surrexit Dominus de sepulchro.	
	He for our saik that sufferit to be slane	
	And lyk a lamb in sacrifice wes dicht°	prepared
	Is lyk a lyone rissin up agane	
20	And as gyane raxit Him on hicht.°	

8. The Lord has risen from the sepulchre.
20. And like a giant has raised Himself on high.

547

Sprungin is Aurora radius° and bright,   radiant
On-loft° is gone the glorius Appollo,   Aloft
The blisfull day depairtit fro the nycht.
Surrexit Dominus de sepulchro.

25   The grit° victour agane is rissin on hicht°   great   high
That, for our querrell,° to the deth was woundit.   cause
The sun that wox° all paill now schynis bricht,   grew
And, dirknes clerit, our faith is now refoundit.°   restored
The knell of mercy fro the hevin is soundit,
30   The Cristin° ar deliverit of thair wo,   Christians
The Jowis and thair errour ar confoundit.
Surrexit Dominus de sepulchro.

The fo is chasit, the battell is done ceis,°   **done ceis** ceased
The presone brokin, the jewellouris fleit and flemit,°   **jewellouris** . . . jailors expelled and routed
35   The weir° is gon, confermit is the peis,   war
The fetteris lowsit,° and the dungeoun temit,°   loosed   emptied
The ransoun maid, the presoneris redemit.
The feild is win, ourcumin° is the fo,   overcome
Dispulit° of the tresur that he yemit.°   Despoiled   guarded
40   *Surrexit Dominus de sepulchro.*

WILLIAM DUNBAR

The Golden Targe

(ca. 1500–12, Northern)

The Golden Targe is an allegorical dream vision heavily indebted to Chaucer. The poet falls asleep on a May morning, is attacked by the forces of Venus, is overcome by Beauty despite the protection of Reason's Golden Shield, is delivered over to Heaviness, and then awakens. Graceful though this highly conventional vision may be, the main point of interest is the modest conclusion excerpted below. Here Dunbar (see p. 543) acknowledges his indebtedness to Chaucer, Gower, and Lydgate as the masters who have inspired him.

The meter is nine-line stanzas; see Introduction, type 20, page 33.

The Poems of William Dunbar, ed. W. M. MacKenzie (Edinburgh, 1932), contains all the attributed works; *William Dunbar: Poems*, ed. James Kinsley (Oxford, 1958), though only a selection, is very useful. For a dictionary use *DOST*. For bibliography see Lewis, *OHEL*; *CBEL*, 1.258–59, 5.147.

[Lines 253–79]

O reverend Chaucere, rose of rethoris° all—   rhetoricians
As in° oure tong ane flour imperiall—   **As in** In
   That raise° in Britane evir, quho redis° richt,   arose   **quho redis** whoever interprets
Thou beris of makaris° the tryumph riall.°   **beris** . . . carry off from poets   royal
5 Thy fresch, anamalit° termes celicall°   enameled   celestial
    This mater coud illumynit° have full° brycht.   illuminated   very
      Was thou noucht of oure Inglisch all the lycht,
    Surmounting eviry tong terrestriall,
      Alls fer° as Mayis morow° dois mydnycht?   **Alls fer** As far   morning

10 O morall Gower and Ludgate laureate,
   Your sugurit lippis and tongis aureate
    Bene° to oure eris cause of grete delyte.   Are
   Your angel mouthis most mellifluate
   Oure rude langage has clere illumynate°   **clere illumynate** brightly illuminated
15   And faire ourgilt° oure speche that imperfyte   overgilded
      Stude or° your goldyn pennis schupe° to wryte.   **Stude or** Stood before   **pennis schupe** pens began
    This ile before° was bare and desolate   **ile before** isle previously
      Off° rethorike or lusty, fresch endyte.°   Of   composition

549

Thou lytill quair,[1] be evir obedient,
20   Humble, subject, and symple of entent
         Before the face of eviry connyng wicht.°   **connyng wicht** competent critic
    I knaw quhat° thou of rethorike hes spent.°   what   **hes spent** have expended
    Off all hir lusty rosis redolent
         Is none into thy gerland sett on hicht.°   high
25   Eschame tharof,° and draw thee° out of sicht.   **Eschame tharof** Be modest therefore
    Rude is thy wede, disteynit,° bare, and rent.   **draw thee** withdraw
         Wele aucht° thou be aferit° of the licht.   **wede, disteynit** garment, stained
                                                          ought   afraid

---

[1] Either the manuscript booklet containing this poem or a volume of the poet's collected works.

LINGUISTIC APPENDICES

The following symbols are used throughout the discussion in Appendices 1, 2, and 3. To clarify the ambiguities of Middle English spelling, diacritical marks have been added to the Middle English examples listed in the center column of Appendix 1 and elsewhere in the linguistic commentary and to the letters *ö* and *ü* printed in the text though these were not used by medieval scribes.

[ ] [:]   Brackets enclose the standard International Phonetic Association Alphabet symbols. Modern approximations of the sounds represented have been provided in Appendix 1. Brackets with no symbol enclosed represent the absence of any sound. A colon after a symbol represents a long sound.

ā ē ī ō ū   represent long vowels contrasting in length of duration with ă ĕ ĭ ŏ ŭ.
ă ĕ ĭ ŏ ŭ   represent short vowels.

ė   represents the final, unstressed *schwa* sound, described under Phoneme 16.

ẹ̄   represents the close *e* sound [e:], described under Phoneme 3.

ē̦ ĕ̦   represent the open *e* sounds [ɛ:] and [ɛ], described under Phonemes 4 and 15.

ȯ   represents the *u* sound of Modern English *pull*, for which Middle English scribes used an *o* in native words such as *son* and *lóvė* (Phoneme 19).

ọ̄   represents the close *o* sound [o:], described under Phoneme 8.

ō̦ ŏ̦   represent the open *o* sounds [ɔ:] and [ɔ], described under Phonemes 9 and 18.

ō̈ ŏ̈   represent the Western Middle English sounds of the mid-position *o* vowels described under the alternate Phonemes 3A and 15A.

ü ü̆   represent the Western Middle English sounds of the mid-position *u* vowels described under the alternate Phonemes 7A and 17A.

551

Appendix 1: The Pronunciation of Middle English

The term *pronunciation* inevitably tends to convey by association the classical fallacy that letters have "values" that we award to them when we pronounce them. Actually, however, letters serve only to indicate what sound groups the writer intends us to utter when we reproduce his words in speech. Speakers of the influential dialect of Middle English in the Southeast Midland area (including London) around 1400, such as Chaucer and Gower, used over forty contrasting sounds, which are listed below as individual phonemes (including, for the sake of clarifying the arbitrary spelling system, some items such as [ks] that are clusters of phonemes).

To represent these sounds, Middle English scribes used the modern alphabet, except that *j* was not usually differentiated from *i*, and *v* was not usually differentiated from *u*, and they employed in addition the Old English letters þ (thorn, for *th*) and ʒ (yogh, used for *gh* and *y* and for some other purposes). Early scribes also used Old English ƿ (wen, for *w*). In the printing of the texts in this anthology, the thorn, yogh, and wen symbols have been replaced by *th*, *gh* or *y* (or other appropriate phonetic representation), and *w* respectively. (See Plates 1–6, pp. 16–28.)

Early Middle English scribes did not always distinguish between *c* and *ch* and between *g* and *y*. In ambiguous cases occurring in the first two selections *c* meaning *ch* has been printed *ċ* (Phoneme 22, below), and *g* meaning *y* has been printed as *ġ* (Phoneme 48). The following list of phonemes, however, does not attempt to list all the phonemes and graphemes of Early Middle English.

Speakers of Western Middle English dialects, such as the author of *The Pearl* (West Midland) and Langland (Southwestern), used four vowels (Phonemes 3A, 7A, 15A, and 17A) as phonetically distinct variants that did not occur in the Southeast Midland area. In our texts, to help the reader recognize and pronounce these vowels, we have specially marked them with umlauts as *ö* and *ü* (without indication of length). There are many other phonetic differences between the various Middle English dialects, but a discussion of them lies beyond the scope of this work.

Middle English scribes did not use a distinct symbol for each distinct sound (the letter *a*, for instance, was used for long Phoneme 1 [ɑ:] *nāmĕ* and for short Phoneme 14 [a] *măn*). Neither did they represent one phoneme consistently by one spelling (Phoneme 3 was spelled indifferently *e* or *ee*, *bẹ̄* or *bẹ̄e* '[to] be'), and usage varied from area to area, even when scribes were representing the same phonetic values (as with *shẹ̄* and *schẹ̄*). Middle English sounds not only varied from dialect to dialect and from social level to social level but also altered during the development of the language. The word 'boat,' for instance, which was spelled *bāt* in Old English and Early Middle English, was pronounced with Phoneme 1 [ɑ:]; in Later Middle English it was spelled *bọ̄ot* and pronounced with Phoneme 9 [ɔ:]; the vowel in Modern English *boat* has shifted to Phoneme 8 [o:].

Middle English phoneme in phonetic spelling (*with modern approximation*)	Middle English spelling(s) with Middle English example	(*Modern English derivative* [*with modern phoneme*])
LONG VOWELS AND DIPHTHONGS		
1. [ɑ:] (f*a*ther)	a (aa) nāmė	(n*a*me [e:])
2. [au] (h*ou*se)	au (aw) cau̅sė	(c*au*se [ɔ:])
3. [e:] (b*a*y)	e (ee) bẹ̄	(b*e* [i:])
3A. [ö:] (Germ. sch*ö*n)	o (eo) bọ̄	(b*e* [i:])
4. [ɛ:] (*e*bb, prolonged)	e (ee) hē̩eth	(h*ea*th [i:])
5. [ɛi] (*e* of *e*bb gliding to *i* of *i*t)	ai (ay), ei (ey) da̅i̅	(d*a*y [e:])
6. [ɛu] (*e* of *e*bb gliding to *u* of p*u*ll)	eu (ew) knē̩w̅	(kn*ew* [ju:]
7. [i:] (f*ea*r)	i (y) fȳr	(f*i*re [ai])
7A. [ü:] (Germ. F*üh*rer)	u (ui) fü̅r	(f*i*re [ai])
8. [o:] (n*o*te)	o (oo) fọ̄dė	(f*oo*d [u:])
9. [ɔ:] (n*au*ght)	o (oo) bō̩ot	(b*oa*t [o:])
10. [ɔi] (b*o*y)	oi (oy) bo̅y̅	(b*o*y [ɔi])
11. [ɔu] (*o* of *o*ft gliding to *u* of p*u*ll)	ou (ow) sō̩w̅lė	(s*ou*l [o:])
12. [u:] (r*u*le)	ou (ow) ho̅u̅s	(h*ou*se [au])
13. [ju:] (c*u*re)	eu (ew), u reu̅lė, cū̅rė	(r*u*le [u:], c*u*re [ju])
SHORT VOWELS		
14. [a] (Germ. M*a*nn)	a mă̆n	(m*a*n [æ])
15. [ɛ] (h*ea*ven)	e hĕ̩venė	(h*ea*ven [ɛ])
15A. [ö] (Germ. *ö*ffnen)	o (eo) hŏ̩venė	(h*ea*ven [ɛ])
16. [ə] (Stell*a*, with un-stressed final)	e nāmĕ̆	(nam*e* [ ])
17. [i] (s*i*n)	i sĭnnė	(s*i*n [ɪ])

Middle English phoneme in phonetic spelling (with modern approximation)	Middle English spelling(s) with Middle English example	(Modern English derivative [with modern phoneme])
17A. [ü] (Germ. Glück)	u *sünnè*	(*sin* [ɪ])
18. [ɔ] (*often*)	o *ǒften*	(*often* [ɔ])
19. [u] (p*u*ll)	o, u *sǒnè*, p*ǔ*llè	(*son* [ʌ], p*u*ll [u])
CONSONANTS		
20. [b] (*boy*)	b *boy*	(*boy* [b])
21. [k] (*c*alm, *k*eep)	c, k *c*almè, *k*epè, *k*nowè	(*c*alm, *k*eep [k], *k*now [ ])
22. [tʃ] (*ch*ild)	ch (cch), ċ *c*ild, *ch*ild, fe*cch*è	(*ch*ild, fet*ch* [tʃ])
23. [d] (*d*eem)	d *d*emè	(*d*eem [d])
24. [f] (*f*eel)	f *f*elè, o*f*	(*f*eel [f], o*f* [v])
25. [g] (*g*ame)	g (gg) *g*amè, do*gg*è, *g*nawè	(*g*ame, do*g* [g], *g*naw [ ])
26. [dʒ] (*g*entle, ju*dg*e)	g (gg), j *g*entil, ju*gg*e	(*g*entle, ju*dg*e [dʒ])
27. [x] (Scot. lo*ch*, Germ. Ba*ch*)	gh ni*gh*t	(ni*gh*t [ ])
28. [h] (*h*ome)	h *h*oom	(*h*ome [h])
29. [ ] (*h*onest)	h *h*onest	(*h*onest [ ])
30. [l] (*l*arge)	l *l*argè	(*l*arge) [l])
31. [m] (*m*ore)	m *m*orè	(*m*ore [m])
32. [n] (*n*ame, sig*n*)	n, gn, *n*amè, sig*n*è	(*n*ame, sig*n* [n])
33. [ŋg] (fi*ng*er)	ng fi*ng*er, thi*ng*	(fi*ng*er [ŋg], thi*ng* [ŋ])
34. [ŋk] (thi*n*k)	nk thi*nk*è	(thi*nk* [ŋk])
35. [p] (*p*age)	p *p*agè	(*p*age [p])
36. [kw] (*qu*een)	qu *qu*enè	(*qu*een [kw])
37. [r] (*r*age)	r *r*agè	(*r*age [r])
38. [s] (*s*ervice)	s, c *s*ervicè, wa*s*	(*s*ervice [s], wa*s* [z])
39. [z] (*z*odiac, cau*s*e)	s, z cau*s*e, *z*odiac	(cau*s*e, *z*odiac [z])

Middle English phoneme in phonetic spelling (with modern approximation)	Middle English spelling(s) with Middle English example	(Modern English derative [with modern phoneme])
40. [ʃ] (*ship*)	sh (sch) *ship*	(*ship* [ʃ])
41. [t] (*teach*)	t *teche*	(*teach* [t])
42. [θ] (*thin*)	th *thynnė, thennė*	(*thin* [θ], *then* [ð])
43. [ð] (*other*)	th *other*	(*other* [ð])
44. [v] (*vice*)	v *vicė*	(*vice* [v])
45. [w] (*was*)	w *was, wrecchė*	(*was* [w], *wretch* [ ])
46. [hw] (*what*, not *watt*)	wh *what, who*	(*what* [hw], *who* [h])
47. [ks] (*six*)	x *six*	(*six* [ks])
48. [j] (*your*)	y, ġ *your, ġaet*	(*your, yet* [j])

Appendix 2: The Middle English Verb

Like their Modern English counterparts, Middle English verbs relied on two different contrast systems to signal differences in tense. Weak verbs added a *d* or *t* to mark the past tense (modern *love*: *loved*), and strong verbs altered the root vowel to mark the past (*ride*: *rode*). The Southeast Midland dialect of Middle English (that of Chaucer and Gower) showed the following typical forms around 1400:

	WEAK				STRONG		
			PRESENT INDICATIVE				
Ī	lóvė	wē	lóvė(n)	Ī	rīdė	wē	rīdė(n)
thou	lóvest	yē	lóvė(n)	thou	rīdest/rītt	yē	rīdė(n)
hē	lóveth	they	lóvė(n)	hē	rīdeth/rītt	they	rīdė(n)
			PRESENT SUBJUNCTIVE				
(if) Ī	lóvė	wē	lóvė(n)	Ī	rīdė	wē	rīdė(n)
thou	lóvė	yē	lóvė(n)	thou	ride	yē	rīdė(n)
hē	lóvė	they	lóvė(n)	hē	ride	they	rīdė(n)
			PAST INDICATIVE				
Ī	lóvedė	wē	lóvedė(n)	Ī	rōd	wē	rīdė(n)
thou	lóvedest	yē	lóvedė(n)	thou	rīde	yē	rīdė(n)
hē	lóvedė	they	lóvedė(n)	hē	rōd	they	rīdė(n)

PAST SUBJUNCTIVE

(if)	Ī̆	lȯvedė̇	wē	lȯvedė̇(n)	Ī̆	rĭdė̇	wē	rĭdė̇(n)
	thou̅	lȯvedė̇	yē	lȯvedė̇(n)	thou̅	rĭdė̇	yē	rĭdė̇(n)
	hē	lȯvedė̇	they̅	lȯvedė̇(n)	hē	rĭdė̇	they̅	rĭdė̇(n)

COMPOUND PAST

Ī havė̇ (y-)lȯved   Ī am (y-)rĭden

Although most of the differences between the verb system of Southeast Midland Middle English and that of the Received Standard of Modern English are self-evident, the following important differences should be noted.

(1) The *thou̅* forms, now archaic, were regularly used in intimate conversation.

(2) The third person singular *hē* present forms, regularly ended in the now archaic *eth*, not *s*, as in Modern English.

(3) All verbs, weak and strong, with roots ending in *d* or *t* could form contracted *thou̅* and *hē* forms in the present indicative: *hē sendeth* or *hē sent* (the past would be *hē sentė̇*).

(4) All plural forms, present and past, of weak and strong verbs ended in *en*, now archaic, and this ending could be contracted to a final unstressed but pronounced *ė̇*.

(5) Contrasting subjunctive forms, now largely archaic, were regularly used with *if* clauses and similar hypothetical expressions (*if hē cȯmė̇*, Modern English, *if he comes*).

(6) In the past indicative of many strong verbs there was a vowel contrast (now eliminated) between the root vowel of the *Ī-hē* forms and the root vowel of the *thou̅-wē-yē-they̅* forms: *Ī rǫd: wē rĭdė̇(n)* (Modern English, *I rode, we rode*); *Ī flē: wē flŭė̇(n)* (modern *flew*); *Ī drănk: wē dronkė̇(n)* (modern *drank*); *Ī stăl: wē stę̄lė̇(n)* (modern *stole*); *Ī ăt: wē ētė̇(n)* (modern *ate*).

(7) In the compound past tense of intransitive verbs, forms of the verb *bē* were used with the past participle instead of, as in Modern English, forms of the verb *have*: thus, *hē is vanished, hē is (y-)rĭden*, instead of *he has vanished, he has ridden*.

IRREGULAR VERBS

The only other frequently occurring irregularities that are likely to seem unfamiliar to the modern reader are the verb *tō bę̄*, which has the forms *wē, yē, they̅ bę̄* or *bę̄en* in addition to the familiar *arė̇(n)*; and the following group of verbs that are peculiar both in form and meaning: *Ī căn, thou̅ cănst, hē căn; wē, yē, they̅ cȯnnė̇(n); Ī cou̅dė̇; wē cou̅dė̇(n)* (conjugated like *lȯvedė̇*) (modern *I can, know how*); *Ī may̅, thou̅ may̅st, hē may̅; wē mǫwė̇(n); Ī mĭghtė̇* (modern *I can, am able*); *Ī mǫot, thou̅ mǫost, hē mǫot; wē mǫote(n); Ī mǫstė̇* (modern *I may, must*); *Ī wǫot, thou̅ wǫost, hē wǫot; wē wĭtė̇(n); Ī wĭstė̇* (modern *I know*).

Appendix 3: Dialect Variations

There was no one Received Literary Dialect of Middle English, and, as a result, manuscripts vary remarkably in recording literary texts. Some authors probably did not even attempt to write their works in a consistent manner that truly represented their own speech, and scribes in recopying texts tended to introduce dialect variations of their own. It is possible, nevertheless, to generalize about broad dialect areas in the fourteenth century, and it is especially useful for the student of literature to recognize the peculiarities of four highly productive areas:

(1) *Southeast Midland* (including London), represented by Gower (*The Lover's Confession*);
(2) *Northern*, represented by Minot (*Halidon Hill*) in Northern England and Barbour (*The Bruce*) in Scotland;
(3) *West Midland*, represented by the author of *The Pearl* and *Sir Gawain and the Green Knight*; and
(4) *Southwestern*, represented by Langland (*Piers Plowman*).

These four dialects, as well as the less productive Southeastern, though individually neither permanent nor homogeneous, differed consistently from one another in numerous ways. In particular they differed in the endings of the third person singular, present indicative, and of the third person plural, present indicative, and in the forms of certain pronouns. Two sentences, *She loves them*, and *They love her*, can be used to display these verbal endings and at the same time to show the variations in the pronouns *she*, *they*, and *them* (*her* was stable). Ignoring a multitude of possible spelling variations and schematizing the geography, the following chart thus presents a reliable guide to characteristic contrasts that occur with high relative frequency:

WEST MIDLAND (*Pearl*)
hō lŏves hĕm
thāy lŭv hĭr

NORTHERN (Barbour)
schō lūfis thāim
thāi lŭv hĭr

SOUTHWESTERN (Langland)
heō lŏveth hĕm
hĭ lŏveth hĭr

SOUTHEAST MIDLAND (Gower)
shē lŏveth hĕm
thēy lŏvė(n) hĭr

Appendix 4: Glossary of Common Words and Phrases

The following words and phrases appear frequently in Middle English in senses unfamiliar to modern readers and are therefore worthy of particular attention.

ac 1. but; 2. and.

again, ayain 1. again; 2. in return, often equivalent to Modern English *re-*, i.e., "yelde ... again" (*Gawain*, 1. 2325), repay; 3. against.

als, also, alswa 1. also; 2. as.

and 1. and; 2. if.

anon (*lit., in one*) at once.

as 1. as; 2. in combinations: *so as*, so; *ther as*, where; *wher as*, where.

ay aye, always.

bi-that 1. *adv.* by that time; 2. *conj.* by the time that.

but 1. but; 2. without.

but if unless.

can, con 1. can; 2. sometimes used like *gan* to form past tense, *i.e., he con ride*, he rode.

eek also.

eft 1. again; 2. then.

er, er that before.

for the nones (*lit., for the once*) indeed.

for-thi therefore.

fro from.

gan (I *ginne*, I *gan*, we *gonnen*) 1. began to; 2. often used to form past tense, *e.g., he gan ride*, he did ride, he rode.

her(e), hir(e) 1. her (see Appendix 3, p. 557); 2. their.

ilk, ilke same.

i-wiss(e) indeed.

lesteth, listeth, lüsteth (it) pleases. The real subject is usually expressed in the dative, *him lesteth*, or in the contracted form, *him lest* (see Introduction, p. 13). The past tense is *him leste*, it pleased him.

liketh 1. *he liketh*, he likes; 2. *him liketh*, it pleases him.

men 1. men; 2. one (*sing.*), which also occurs in the form *man* or *mon*.

mid with.

mo more.

namelich particularly.

natheles nevertheless.

ne 1. not; 2. *ne . . . ne*, neither . . . nor.

o(o), oon one (*o(o)* occurs before consonants, *oon* before vowels).

of "The Kynges son of Rome" is equivalent to modern English "The King of Rome's son."

other 1. other; 2. or; 3. *other . . . other*, either . . . or.

sith, sith that since.

sithen 1. *adv.* then; 2. *conj.* since.

sone soon.

swich such.

swithe   very.

syn, syn that   since.

ther   1. there; 2. where (also *ther as*).

thinketh   1. thinks; 2. *me thinketh*, it seems to me.

tho   1. those; 2. then; 3. when.

wel   1. well; 2. very.

wher   1. where (also *wher as*); 2. whether.

yede   went.

SELECTIVE CRITICAL BIBLIOGRAPHY

BASIC REFERENCES

(referred to in the headnotes by abbreviated titles)

Bennett, *OHEL*
Bennett, H. S. *Chaucer and the Fifteenth Century*. Oxford History of English Literature, vol. 2, pt. 1. Oxford, Eng., 1947. Extensive bibliography.

Brown and Robbins, *Index*
Brown, Carleton, and Rossell Hope Robbins. *The Index of Middle English Verse*. New York, 1943. *Supplement*. Lexington, Ky., 1965. Index by first line of all Middle English poems, listing manuscript and printed sources.

CBEL
Cambridge Bibliography of English Literature, The. Ed. F. W. Bateson. 4 vols. Cambridge, Eng., 1941. *Supplement*. Ed. George Watson. Cambridge, Eng., 1957. References to this work have been given here in those headnotes dealing with those items that have not been treated in Wells or in Severs and Hartung. Indispensable.

Chambers, *OHEL*
Chambers, Sir Edmund K. *English Literature at the Close of the Middle Ages*. Oxford History of English Literature, vol. 2, pt. 2. Oxford, Eng., 1945.

Child
Child, Frances James. *The English and Scottish Popular Ballads*. 10 vols. Boston, 1882–98. Available in various reprints. The ballads included in *Middle English Literature* are referred to by Child's numbers. The one-volume abridgment, edited by Helen C. Sargent and G. L. Kittredge (Cambridge, Boston, 1904), contains at least one version of each of the ballads.

DOST
Dictionary of the Older Scottish Tongue, A. Ed. Sir William A. Craigie. Chicago, 1931–
In progress; necessary for Scottish texts, which are not covered in *Middle English Dictionary*.

EETS
Early English Text Society. Original series. London, 1864–

EETSES
Early English Text Society. Extra Series. London, 1867–

Geddie, *BMSP*
Geddie, William. *A Bibliography of Middle Scots Poets*. Scottish Text Society Publications, 61. Edinburgh, 1912.

Hammond
Hammond, Elizabeth P. *Chaucer: A Bibliographical Manual*. New York, 1908. Contains detailed information about many aspects of fourteenth-century literature.

Hartung
Manual of the Writings in Middle English, 1050–1500, A. Ed. Albert E. Hartung. New Haven, 1972. Continuation in progress of Severs' revision of Wells; referred to by chapter and item numbers. (Volume III consists of Chapters 7–9.)

Legge
Legge, M. Dominica. *Anglo-Norman Literature and Its Background*. Oxford, Eng., 1963.

Lewis, *OHEL*
Lewis, C. S. *English Literature in the Sixteenth Century.* Oxford History of English Literature, Vol. III. Oxford, Eng., 1954.

Manly-Rickert
Manly, John M., and Edith Rickert. *The Text of the Canterbury Tales.* 8 vols. Chicago, 1940. Volume I contains unusually complete descriptions of manuscripts containing the *Canterbury Tales* and often additional works; Volume II, pages 1–45, contains a useful discussion of the establishment of a text.

MED
Middle English Dictionary. Ed. Hans Kurath and Sherman M. Kuhn. Ann Arbor, 1952– In progress. *Plan and Bibliography.* A summary of dates, dialects, and sources of materials abstracted for the *MED.* Ann Arbor, 1954.

Severs
Manual of the Writings in Middle English, 1050–1500, A. Ed. J. Burke Severs. 2 vols. New Haven, 1967, 1970. A revision of Wells' *Manual.* Works included in *Middle English Literature* are referred to by chapter and item numbers. (Volume I consists of Chapter 1, Volume II of Chapters 2–8.) Contains historical and critical commentaries and bibliography on each item.

STS
Scottish Text Society. Publications. Edinburgh, 1884–

Wells
Manual of the Writings in Middle English, 1050–1400, A. Ed. John Edwin Wells. New Haven, 1916. *Supplements, I–IX.* New Haven, 1916–52. Works included in *Middle English Literature* are referred to by chapter and item numbers. Contains historical and critical summaries and an exhaustive bibliography on each item.

BIBLIOGRAPHIES

Ackerman, Robert W. "Middle English Literature to 1400." *The Medieval Literature of Western Europe: A Review of Research.* Ed. John H. Fisher. New York, 1966, pp. 73–123. A useful summary of scholarship from 1930 to 1960; the volume deals with related topics such as Latin, French, and Celtic.

PMLA: Annual International Bibliography. New York, 1957– . Each volume covers the preceding year's scholarship; Middle English literature is treated separately from the Middle English language. Indispensable for keeping abreast of the latest research.

Recent Middle English Scholarship and Criticism. Ed. J. Burke Severs. Pittsburgh, 1971. Suggestive interpretations of new critical trends by D. C. Fowler, D. R. Howard, Lillian H. Hornstein, and Helaine Newstead.

Tucker, Lena L., and R. Benham. *A Bibliography of Fifteenth-Century Literature.* Seattle, 1928. Covers a field not dealt with by Wells, but already largely replaced by *CBEL;* will be completely outdated by Severs and Hartung.

Zesmer, David M., and Stanley B. Greenfield. *Guide to English Literature from Beowulf through Chaucer.* New York, 1961. Greenfield's critical bibliography of Middle English is particularly useful.

LANGUAGE

Baugh, Albert C. *A History of the English Language.* 2nd ed. New York, 1957. Treats not only the linguistic development but also the cultural aspects of English.

Denholm-Young, N. *Handwriting in England and Wales.* Cardiff, Wales, 1954.

Hector, L. C. *The Handwriting of English Documents.* 2nd ed. London, 1966.

Johnson, Charles, and Hilary Jenkinson. *English Court Hand, A.D. 1066 to 1500.* 2 vols. Oxford, Eng. 1915.

Jones, Charles. *An Introduction to Middle English.* New York, 1972. Attempt at a modern structural and generative analysis of sounds, forms, and syntax in Middle English dialects.

Moore, Samuel. *Historical Outlines of English Sounds and Inflections.* Rev. Albert H. Marckwardt. Ann Arbor, 1951; rpt. 1966. Useful systematization of forms.

Mossé, Fernand. *A Handbook of Middle English.* Trans. James A. Walker. Baltimore, 1952. An anthology of brief excerpts with a useful and extensive grammar, particularly helpful on dialects.

Oxford English Dictionary, The. Ed. James A. H. Murray. *Supplement.* 13 vols. Oxford, Eng., 1933. This corrected reissue of *A New English Dictionary (NED)* will remain useful because of its scope even with the completion of the *MED* and the *DOST.*

Parkes, Malcolm B. *English Cursive Book Hands, 1250–1500.* Oxford, Eng., 1969.

Saintsbury, George A. *Historical Manual of English Prosody.* London, 1910; rpt. New York, 1926.
———. *History of English Prosody.* 3 vols. London, 1906–10; rpt. New York, 1961.

Serjeantson, Mary S. *A History of Foreign Words in English.* London, 1935; rpt. New York, 1961.

Stratmann, Francis H. *A Middle English Dictionary.* Rev. Henry Bradley. Oxford, Eng., 1891. Will be necessary until the completion of the *MED.*

Wright, C. E. *English Vernacular Hands from the Twelfth to the Fifteenth Centuries.* Oxford, Eng., 1960.

Wright, Joseph. *An Elementary Middle English Grammar.* 2nd ed. Oxford, Eng., 1928. Still useful.

LITERARY HISTORY

Ackerman, Robert W. *Backgrounds to Medieval English Literature.* New York, 1966. Excellent summary of the relationships between literature and society.

Age of Chaucer, The. Ed. Boris Ford. A Guide to English Literature. Vol. I. Rev. ed. Harmondsworth, Eng., 1963. Contains a number of interpretative essays by various specialists.

Arthurian Literature in the Middle Ages. Ed. R. S. Loomis. Oxford, Eng., 1959. Important collection of essays by experts on Celtic, English, French, and other sources of Middle English literature.

Atkins, J. W. H. *English Literary Criticism: The Medieval Phase.* New York, 1952.

Bronson, Bertrand Harris. *The Traditional Tunes of the Child Ballads with Their Texts.* 4 vols. Princeton, N. J., 1959–72. Should be used in conjunction with Child.

Critical Approaches to Medieval Literature. Ed. Dorothy Bethurum. New York, 1960. Critical methods represented include patristic exegesis and folkloristic methods.

Everett, Dorothy. *Essays on Middle English Literature.* Oxford, Eng., 1955. Important essays by a distinguished critic.

Hibbard, Laura H. *Mediaeval Romance in England.* New York, 1924; rpt. with bibliography added, New York, 1960.

Jackson, W. T. H. *Literature of the Middle Ages.* New York, 1960. A good brief survey of continental medieval literature, touching occasionally on Middle English literature.

Kane, George. *Middle English Literature: A Critical Study of the Romances, the Religious Lyrics, Piers Plowman.* London, 1951

Ker, W. P. *Medieval English Literature.* New York, 1942. Reissue of *English Literature, Medieval,* 1912.

Literary History of England, A. Ed. Albert C. Baugh. New York, 1948. Baugh's section, also published separately along with Kemp Malone's section on Old English, provides an excellent survey of Middle English and Anglo-Norman literature.

Middle English Survey: Critical Essays. Ed. Edward Vasta. Notre Dame, Ind., 1965. Important essays by experts on imagery, *Owl and Nightingale, Gawain, Pearl, Piers Plowman,* Gower, the ballad, and other topics.

Moore, Arthur K. *The Secular Lyric in Middle English.* Lexington, Ky., 1951.

Schlauch, Margaret. *English Medieval Literature and Its Social Foundations.* Warsaw, 1956. Literary criticism with Marxist commentary.

Speirs, John. *Medieval English Poetry: The Non-Chaucerian Tradition.* London, 1957. Opposed to the philological approach.

Valency, Maurice J. *In Praise of Love: An Introduction to the Love Poetry of the Renaissance.* New York, 1958. Wide survey from the Provençal poets to Dante.

Ward, A.W., and A. R. Waller. *The Cambridge History of English Literature.* 15 vols. Cambridge, Eng., 1907–08. Thorough study of Old English and Middle English literature in Volumes I and II.

Wilson, R. M. *Early Middle English Literature.* 3rd ed. London, 1968.

———. *The Lost Literature of Medieval England.* 2nd ed. London, 1970. Examines important though fragmentary evidence of the cultural vitality of the period.

Wimsatt, James I. *Allegory and Mirror: Tradition and Structure in Middle English Literature.* New York, 1970. A compact survey of the allegorical aspects of Middle English literature.

CULTURAL HISTORY

Auerbach, Erich. *Mimesis: The Representation of Reality in Western Literature.* Princeton, N. J., 1953. A profound study of the changes of style, attitude, and philosophy from classical times through later Christian eras.

Bloomfield, Morton W. *The Seven Deadly Sins.* Lansing, Mich., 1952.

Chaucer's World. Ed. Edith Rickert. Chicago, 1948. A fascinating collection of documents illustrating everyday phases of medieval life.

Curry, Walter Clyde. *Chaucer and the Medieval Sciences.* 2nd ed. New York, 1960.

Curtius, Ernst Robert. *European Literature and the Latin Middle Ages.* Trans. W. R. Trask. New York, 1953. Traces survival of the Classical tradition in the rhetorical motifs (*topoi*) of later literature.

Dawson, Christopher H. *Medieval Essays.* London, 1953. Concentrates on religious aspects of medieval culture.

Gilson, Étienne. *History of Christian Philosophy in the Middle Ages.* New York, 1955. The best single book on the medieval scholastic philosophers.

Huizinga, Johann. *The Waning of the Middle Ages.* London and New York, 1924; rpt. Harmondsworth, Eng., 1955. Cultural changes in the late fourteenth and fifteenth centuries.

Katzenellenbogen, Adolf. *Allegories of the Virtues and Vices in Medieval Art.* New York, 1964.

Knowles, David. *The English Mystical Tradition.* London, 1961.

———. *The Monastic Order in England, 943–1216.* 2nd ed. Cambridge, Eng., 1963.

———. *The Religious Orders in England.* 3 vols. Cambridge, Eng., 1948–59. A sequel to *The Monastic Order.*

Lewis, C. S. *The Allegory of Love.* Oxford, Eng., 1936. Highly readable, though in some respects no longer accepted.

———. *The Discarded Image: An Introduction to Medieval and Renaissance Literature.* Cambridge, Eng., 1964. The postclassical origins of the medieval *Weltanschauung.*

Lord, Albert B. *The Singer of Tales.* New York, 1965. An influential study of the role of themes and formulas in oral narrative.

Lubac, Henri de. *Exégèse Médiévale: Les Quatre Sens de l'Écriture.* 2 vols. in 4 parts. Paris, 1959–64. A massive study of the four-part medieval interpretation of the Scriptures.

Meaning of Courtly Love, The. Ed. F. X. Newman. Albany, 1968. Important theoretical papers; brief concluding discussion between participants in conference; useful bibliography.

Mosher, Joseph A. *The Exemplum in the Early Religious and Didactic Literature of England.* New York, 1911.

Owst, Gerald R. *Literature and Pulpit in Medieval England.* 2nd ed. Cambridge, Eng., 1961. A standard work on the relation of popular pulpit styles to literature.

Oxford History of English Art, The. Ed. T. S. R. Boase. Oxford, Eng., 1949– . In progress; relevant volumes are III, T. S. R. Boase, *English Art, 1100–1216;* IV, Peter Brieger, *English Art, 1216–1307;* V, Joan Evans, *English Art, 1307–1461.*

Patch, Howard R. *The Tradition of Boethius.* New York, 1935. On the question of God's providence, Boethius's *Consolation of Philosophy* was probably the most widely read work in the Middle Ages and the Renaissance.

Patterns of Love and Courtesy: Essays in Memory of C. S. Lewis. Ed. John Lawlor. Evanston, Ill., 1966. By various authorities on *Gawain,* Gower Chaucer, Malory, and other topics.

Thompson, Stith. *Motif-Index of Folk-Literature.* Rev. ed. 6 vols. Bloomington, Ind., 1955–58. Provides international parallels for many medieval motifs.

Utley, Francis L. *The Crooked Rib: An Analytical Index to the Argument about Women in English and Scots Literature.* Columbus, Ohio, 1944. An essential key to antifeminist satire.

Works of Geoffrey Chaucer, The. Ed. F. N. Robinson. 2nd ed. Cambridge, Mass., 1957. Though the references are now somewhat outdated, this is still an encyclopedia of Middle English culture.

SOCIAL AND POLITICAL HISTORY

Myers, Alec R. *England in the Late Middle Ages.* Rev. ed. Harmondsworth, Eng., 1956.

Oxford History of England, The. 15 vols. Oxford, Eng., 1934– . Relevant volumes are III, Austin L. Poole, *From Domesday Book to Magna Carta, 1087–1216;* IV, Maurice Powicke, *The Thirteenth Century, 1216–1307;* V, May McKisack, *The Fourteenth Century, 1307–99;* and VI, E. F. Jacob, *The Fifteenth Century.*

Poole, Austin L. *Medieval England.* Rev. ed. 2 vols. Oxford, Eng., 1958. Nineteen encyclopedic essays by various experts on different aspects of medieval English life.

Powicke, Frederick M. *Medieval England, 1066–1485.* London, 1948. An authoritative historical survey.

Stenton, Doris M. *English Society in the Early Middle Ages, 1066–1307.* Harmondsworth, Eng., 1951. A compact and readable history.

BIBLIOGRAPHICAL SUPPLEMENT

BASIC REFERENCES

General

Crosby, Everett U., et al. *Medieval Studies: A Bibliographical Guide*. New York: Garland, 1983.

Strayer, Joseph R., gen. ed. *Dictionary of the Middle Ages*. 12 vols. (and a forthcoming general index). New York: Scribner, 1982–1989.

Middle English

Lewis, Robert E., et al. *Index of Printed Middle English Prose*. New York: Garland, 1985.

Preston, Michael J. *A Concordance to the Middle English Shorter Poem*. 2 vols. Leeds: Maney, 1974.

LITERARY HISTORY

General

Bolton, W. F. *The Middle Ages*. Vol. I of *The New History of Literature*. New York: Bedrick, 1986.

Middle English

Bennett, J. A. W., and Douglas Gray. *Middle English Literature*. Oxford: Clarendon, 1986 (*Oxford History of English Literature*, Vol. I, pt. 2).

Burrow, J. A. *Medieval Writers and Their Works: Middle English Literature and Its Background*. Oxford: Oxford University Press, 1982 (Brief survey).

Special Types and Themes

Ganim, John M. *Style and Consciousness in Middle English Narrative*. Princeton: Princeton University Press, 1983.

Green, Richard F. *Poets and Princepleasers: Literature and the Court in the Middle Ages*. Toronto: Toronto University Press, 1979.

Olson, Glending. *Literature as Recreation in the Later Middle Ages*. Ithaca: Cornell University Press, 1982.

Spearing, A. C. *Medieval Dream Poetry*. Cambridge: Cambridge University Press, 1976.

———. *Readings in Medieval Poetry*. Cambridge: Cambridge University Press, 1987.

Stiller, Nikki. *Eve's Orphans: Mothers and Daughters in Medieval Literature*. Westport, Connecticut: Greenwood, 1979.

Tuve, Rosamund. *Seasons and Months: Studies in a Tradition of Middle English Poetry*. Cambridge: Brewer, 1974.

SOCIAL AND CULTURAL HISTORY

Bornstein, Diane. *Mirror of Courtesy*. Hamden, Connecticut: Shoestring, 1974.

Crane, Susan. *Insular Romance: Politics, Faith, and Culture in Anglo-Norman and Middle English Literature*. Berkeley: University of California Press, 1986.

Fowler, David C. *The Bible in Middle English Literature*. Seattle: University of Washington Press, 1984.

Leonard, Frances M. *Laughter in the Courts of Love: Comedy in Allegory, from Chaucer to Spenser*. Norman, Oklahoma: Pilgrim, 1981.

565

Metlitski, Dorothee. *The Matter of Araby in Medieval England.* New Haven: Yale University Press, 1976.

Patterson, Lee. *Negotiating the Past: The Historical Understanding of Medieval Literature.* Madison: University of Wisconsin Press, 1987 (Anglo-Norman and Middle English).

Vale, Juliet. *Edward III and Chivalry: Chivalric Society and Its Context, 1270–1350.* Woodbridge: Brewer, 1982.

ESSAY COLLECTIONS

Benskin, Michael, and M. L. Samuels, eds. *So Meny People, Longages, and Tongues: Philological Essays in Scots and Mediaeval English Presented to Angus McIntosh.* Edinburgh: Authors, 1981.

Benson, Larry D., ed. *The Learned and the Lewed: Studies in Chaucer and Medieval Literature.* Cambridge: Harvard University Press, 1974.

——, and Siegfried Wenzel, eds. *The Wisdom of Poetry: Essays in Early English Literature in Honor of Morton W. Bloomfield.* Kalamazoo: Western Michigan University Press, 1982.

——, and John Leyerle, eds. *Chivalric Literature.* Kalamazoo, 1980 (Studies in Medieval Culture 14).

Carruthers, Mary J., and Elizabeth D. Kirk, eds. *Acts of Interpretation: The Text in Its Contexts, 700–1600: Essays on Medieval and Renaissance Literature in Honor of E. Talbot Donaldson.* Norman, Oklahoma: Pilgrim, 1982.

Glasscoe, Marion, ed. *The Medieval Mystical Tradition in England.* Cambridge: Brewer, 1984.

Gray, Douglas, and E. G. Stanley, eds. *Middle English Studies Presented to Norman Davis in Honor of His Seventieth Birthday.* Oxford: Clarendon, 1983.

Lawton, David, ed. *Middle English Alliterative Poetry and Its Literary Backgrounds: Seven Essays.* Cambridge: Brewer, 1982.

Pearsall, Derek, ed. *Manuscripts and Readers in Fifteenth-Century England: The Literary Implications of Manuscript Study.* Cambridge: Brewer, 1983.

Stokes, Myra, and T. L. Burton, eds. *Medieval Literature and Antiquities.* Cambridge: Brewer, 1987.

Yeager, Robert F., ed. *Fifteenth-Century Studies: Recent Essays.* Hamden, Connecticut: Archon, 1984.

INDIVIDUAL WORKS

Owl and the Nightingale
  Hume, Kathryn. The Owl and the Nightingale: *The Poem and Its Critics.* Toronto: Toronto University Press, 1974.

King Horn
  Allen, Rosamund, ed. King Horn: *An Edition Based on Cambridge University Library MS Gg 4.27 (2).* New York: Garland, 1984.

Robert Mannyng
  Sullens, Idelle, ed. *Robert Mannyng of Brunne: Handlyng Synne.* Binghamton: SUNY Press, 1983.

The Alliterative Morte Arthure
  Edition
    Hamel, Mary, ed. Morte Arthure: *A Critical Edition.* New York: Garland, 1984.

  Commentary
    Göller, Karl H., ed. The Alliterative Morte Arthure: *A Reassessment of the Poem.* Cambridge: Brewer, 1981.

Piers Plowman
  Bibliography
    Colaianne, A. J. Piers Plowman: *An Annotated Bibliography of Editions and Criticism 1550–1977.* New York: Garland, 1978.

  Editions
    Bennett, J. A. W., ed. Piers Plowman *and Passus I–VII of the B Text as Found in Bodleian MS Laud Misc. 581.* Oxford: Clarendon, 1972.

    Kane, George, and E. Talbot Donaldson, eds. Piers Plowman: *The B Version.* London: Athlone, 1974.

    Pearsall, Derek, ed. Piers Plowman: *An Edition of the C Text.* Berkeley: University of California Press, 1978.

    Schmidt, A. V. C., ed. *The Vision of* Piers Plowman: *A Complete Edition of the B Text.* London: Dent; New York: Dutton, 1978.

  Commentaries
    Aers, David. Piers Plowman *and Christian Allegory.* London: Arnold, 1974.

    Bowers, John M. *The Crisis of Will in* Piers Plowman. Washington, D.C.: Catholic University Press, 1986.

    Carruthers, Mary. *The Search for Truth: A Study of Meaning in* Piers Plowman. Evanston, Illinois: Northwestern University Press, 1973.

    Griffiths, Lavinia. *Personification in* Piers Plowman. Woodbridge: Brewer, 1985.

    Krochalis, Jeanne, and Edward Peters, eds. and trs. *The World of* Piers Plowman. Philadelphia: University of Pennsylvania Press, 1975 (Selections from primary source materials).

The Pearl Poet: Pearl and *Sir Gawain and the Green Knight.*
  Bibliographies
    Andrew, Malcolm. *The Gawain-Poet: An Annotated Bibliography, 1839–1977.* New York: Garland, 1979.

    Blanch, Robert J. Sir Gawain and the Green Knight: *A Reference Guide.* Troy: Whitston, 1983.

  Editions
    Andrew, Malcolm, and Ronald Waldron, eds. *The Poems of the Pearl Manuscript.* Berkeley: University of California Press, 1978.

    Burrow, J. A., ed. Sir Gawain and the Green Knight. New Haven: Yale University Press, 1982.

    Vantuono, William, ed. *The Pearl Poems: An Omnibus Edition.* 2 vols. New York: Garland, 1984 (With translations on facing pages and full critical apparatus).

  Commentaries
    Davenport, W. A. *The Art of the Gawain Poet.* London: Athlone, 1977.

    Elliott, R. W. V. *The Gawain Country.* Leeds: Leeds University Press, 1984 (Landscape in the poem).

    Haines, Victor Y. *The Fortunate Fall of Sir Gawain: The Typology of* Sir Gawain and the Green Knight. Washington, D.C.: University Press of America, 1982 (Sources).

    Shoaf, R. A. *The Poem as Green Girdle: Commercium in* Sir Gawain and the Green Knight. Gainesville: University of Florida Press, 1984.

John Gower, Confessio Amantis
  Bibliography
    Yeager, Robert F. *John Gower Materials: A Bibliography Through 1979.* New York: Garland, 1981.

Edition
Peck, Russell A., ed. *Confessio Amantis*. Toronto: Toronto University Press, 1980 (Medieval Academic Reprints for Teaching 9).

Commentaries
Beidler, Peter G., ed. *John Gower's Literary Transformations in the* Confessio Amantis: *Original Articles and Translations*. Washington, D.C.: University Press of America, 1982.

Gallacher, Patrick J. *Love, the Word, and Mercury: A Reading of John Gower's* Confessio Amantis. Albuquerque: University of New Mexico Press, 1974.

Minnis, Alastair J., ed. *Gower's* Confessio Amantis: *Responses and Reassessments*. Woodbridge: Brewer, 1983.

Peck, Russell A. *Kingship and Common Profit in Gower's* Confessio Amantis. Carbondale: Southern Illinois University Press, 1977.

Thomas of Erceldoune
Nixon, Ingeborg, ed. *Thomas of Erceldoune*. 2 vols. Copenhagen: Akademisk Forlag, 1980–1983 (Publications of the Department of English, University of Copenhagen 9/1–2).

Thomas Hoccleve
Seymour, M. C., ed. *Selections from Hoccleve*. Oxford: Oxford University Press, 1981.

Robert Henryson and *William Dunbar*
Bibliography
Scheps, Walter, and J. Looney. *Middle Scots Poets: A Reference Guide to James I, Robert, Henryson, William Dunbar, and Gavin Douglas*. Boston: Hall, 1986.

Edition
Henryson, Robert. *Poems*, ed. Charles Elliott. 2nd ed. Oxford: Clarendon, 1974.

Commentaries
Kindrick, Robert L. *Robert Henryson*. Boston: Twayne, 1979.

Reiss, Edmund. *William Dunbar*. Boston: Twayne, 1978.

RECORDINGS OF MIDDLE ENGLISH

Bowden, Betsy. *Listeners' Guide to Medieval English*. New York: Garland, 1989 (Lists 95 recordings of Old and Middle English).